Lecture Notes in Computer Science 15409

The series Lecture Notes in Computer Science (LNCS), including its subseries Lecture Notes in Artificial Intelligence (LNAI) and Lecture Notes in Bioinformatics (LNBI), has established itself as a medium for the publication of new developments in computer science and information technology research, teaching, and education.

LNCS enjoys close cooperation with the computer science R & D community, the series counts many renowned academics among its volume editors and paper authors, and collaborates with prestigious societies. Its mission is to serve this international community by providing an invaluable service, mainly focused on the publication of conference and workshop proceedings and postproceedings. LNCS commenced publication in 1973.

José Borbinha · Tiago Prince Sales ·
Miguel Mira Da Silva · Henderik A. Proper ·
Marianne Schnellmann
Editors

Enterprise Design, Operations, and Computing

28th International Conference, EDOC 2024
Vienna, Austria, September 10–13, 2024
Revised Selected Papers

Springer

Editors
José Borbinha
Universidade de Lisboa
Lisbon, Portugal

Tiago Prince Sales
University of Twente
Enschede, The Netherlands

Miguel Mira Da Silva
Universidade de Lisboa
Lisbon, Portugal

Henderik A. Proper
TU Wien
Vienna, Austria

Marianne Schnellmann
TU Wien
Vienna, Austria

ISSN 0302-9743 ISSN 1611-3349 (electronic)
Lecture Notes in Computer Science
ISBN 978-3-031-78337-1 ISBN 978-3-031-78338-8 (eBook)
https://doi.org/10.1007/978-3-031-78338-8

This Springer imprint is published by the registered company Springer Nature Switzerland AG
The registered company address is: Gewerbestrasse 11, 6330 Cham, Switzerland

Preface

EDOC 2024 marked the 28th edition of the International Conference on Enterprise Design, Operations, and Computing, continuing its tradition as a prominent forum for researchers and practitioners in the field of Enterprise Computing. This year's conference took place from September 10–13, 2024, in the beautiful city of Vienna, Austria.

A significant highlight of EDOC 2024 was its co-location with the IEEE Conference on Business Informatics (CBI), bringing together two leading conferences in a shared program (which our local colleagues at the TU Wien branded as "BI Week 2024"). This collaboration enabled extensive interaction between the two communities, fostering enriched scientific discussions and a deeper understanding of the evolving landscape of enterprise systems and business informatics. The joint program featured shared keynotes, technical sessions, and social events, providing participants with a unique opportunity to engage with cross-disciplinary insights in an intellectually stimulating environment.

The EDOC 2024 proceedings include 18 research papers selected from 70 submissions, reflecting a rigorous selection process with an acceptance rate of 25.7%. EDOC had two rounds of submissions: 2 research papers were accepted from 12 submissions after an early call, and 16 from 58 submissions after the second call. Each submission was thoroughly evaluated through a single-blind review process by at least three members of the program committee.

This year's EDOC conference covered a broad range of important topics in enterprise computing. Key areas of focus included Enterprise Architecture, where novel methods for enhancing architectural frameworks and strategies were presented. The field of Business Process Management (BPM) saw advancements in both process mining and monitoring techniques, with a particular emphasis on improving decision-making processes and addressing ethical considerations. Digital Twins were another topic, with papers exploring their integration into enterprise systems to enhance operational resilience and efficiency. In addition, several contributions focused on Sustainability and Resilience, offering design principles and methods for improving sustainable practices within enterprises, aligning business processes with environmental compliance frameworks. The conference also featured research on Artificial Intelligence and Data Analytics, addressing their impact on decision support systems and enterprise innovation.

In contrast, the total of 41 papers presented at the joint EDOC+CBI sessions included an additional 28 research papers from the CBI program plus 14 papers from the joint Forum, thus reflecting an even wider range of topics covered across both conferences.

A novel feature introduced by the CBI community to the EDOC community was the concept of the "Mini Dagstuhl Seminars," which, over two days and across six sessions, provided participants with focused, small-group discussions on cutting-edge topics in enterprise computing and business informatics. These sessions were led by senior members of the EDOC and CBI communities and allowed for in-depth exploration of emerging trends, fostering collaboration and sparking new ideas.

An important moment was the announcement of the Best Paper Award, given to Sylvain Hallé for his outstanding paper "A Tree-Based Definition of Business Process Conformance." This paper was selected from a shortlist of six finalists, three from each of the conferences. The paper stood out for its innovative contribution to the field and was celebrated for advancing the state of research in enterprise computing and business informatics.

Another noteworthy element in this year's conference was a panel discussion on "Revisiting the Business Model of Scientific Publishing,", chaired by Tiago Prince Sales (University of Twente, The Netherlands), where Ulrich Frank (Universität Duisburg-Essen, Germany), Peter Fettke (German Research Center for Artificial Intelligence, Germany), and Erich Neuhold (University of Vienna, Austria) shared their insights and sparked a lively and engaging discussion with the audience.

As in previous years, a separate post-conference volume will be published, featuring papers from the EDOC Forum, along with contributions from workshops and other tracks. This will provide a platform for continued dialogue and exploration of new ideas and perspectives.

We are honored to feature the abstracts of invited talks from two esteemed, joint CBI-EDOC, keynote speakers: Gregor Engels, Paderborn University on *Taking Enterprise Architecture Engineering to the Next Level: Digital Twin-Based Future-Oriented Enterprises*, and Katja Hose, TU Wien, on *Leveraging Knowledge Graphs for Enhanced Business Intelligence: Bridging Data Silos and Unlocking Value.*

We would like to extend our deepest gratitude to the organizing committees of both EDOC and CBI for their tireless efforts in ensuring the success of this joint event. A special thanks goes to the local organizing team at TU Wien, whose dedication made the smooth execution of the conference and the warm atmosphere possible. We are also grateful to our sponsor, the Mayor of Vienna, for their generous support, which contributed significantly to the success of the event.

Finally, our heartfelt thanks go out to the authors, reviewers, and participants. Your invaluable contributions and engagement made EDOC 2024 a memorable and impactful event. We look forward to the ongoing discussions, collaborations, and innovations that will arise from this year's conference.

We hope that you find the proceedings of EDOC 2024 both informative and inspiring.

October 2024

Tiago Prince Sales
José Borbinha
Henderik A. Proper
Miguel Mira Da Silva
Marianne Schnellmann

Organization

General Chairs

Henderik A. Proper	TU Wien, Austria
Miguel Mira da Silva	University of Lisbon, Portugal

Program Committee Chairs

José Borbinha	INESC-ID, IST, Universidade de Lisboa, Portugal
Tiago Prince Sales	University of Twente, The Netherlands

Forum Chairs

Alessandro Gianola	INESC-ID, IST, Universidade de Lisboa, Portugal
Georg Grossmann	University of South Australia, Australia

Workshop Chairs

Monika Kaczmarek-Heß	University of Duisburg-Essen, Germany
Kristina Rosenthal	Niederrhein Univ. of Applied Sciences, Germany
Marek Suchánek	Czech Technical Univ. in Prague, Czech Republic

Tools and Demos Track Chairs

Luiz Olavo Bonino	University of Twente, The Netherlands
Mark Mulder	TEEC2, The Netherlands

Industry and Case Reports Chairs

Pascal Ravesteijn	HU Univ. of Applied Sciences, The Netherlands
Jürgen Jung	Frankfurt University of Applied Sciences, Germany
Andreas Pirkner	Erste Asset Management, Austria

Journal First Chairs

Asif Gill	UT Sydney, Australia
Sérgio Guerreiro	INESC-ID, IST, Universidade de Lisboa, Portugal

Doctoral Consortium Chairs

Oscar Pastor	Universitat Politècnica de València, Spain
Jolita Ralyté	University of Geneva, Switzerland

Proceedings Chair

Marianne Schnellmann	TU Wien, Austria

EasyChair Meta-Chair

Birgit Hofreiter	TU Wien, Austria

Tutorial Chairs

Dominik Bork	TU Wien, Austria
Simon Hacks	Stockholm University, Sweden

Website, Publicity, and Social Media Chairs

Aleksandar Gavric	TU Wien, Austria
Fabrizio Fornari	Università di Camerino, Italy
Ítalo Oliveira	University of Twente, The Netherlands

Local Organization Chairs

Angela Edlinger	TU Wien, Austria
Monika Malinova	.
Mandelburger	TU Wien, Austria

Steering Committee

Alan Wee-Chung Liew	Griffith University, Australia
Colin Atkinson	University of Mannheim, Germany
Dimka Karastoyanova	University of Groningen, The Netherlands
Georg Grossmann	University of South Australia, Australia
Giancarlo Guizzardi	University of Twente, The Netherlands
Henderik A. Proper	TU Wien, Austria
João Paulo A. Almeida	Federal University of Espírito Santo, Brazil
Marten van Sinderen	University of Twente, The Netherlands
Remco Dijkman	Eindhoven University of Technology, The Netherlands
Selmin Nurcan (Chair)	University Paris 1 Panthéon-Sorbonne, France
Sylvain Hallé	Université du Québec à Chicoutimi, Canada
Zoran Milosevic	Deontik, Australia

Program Committee

Alan Wee-Chung Liew	Griffith University, Australia
Alexander Knapp	Universität Augsburg, Germany
Alfred Zimmermann	Reutlingen University, Germany
Amin Beheshti	Macquarie University, Australia
Andrea Marrella	Sapienza University of Rome, Italy
Andreas L. Opdahl	University of Bergen, Norway
Andrew Berry	ResMed Inc, USA
André Vasconcellos	INESC-ID, IST, Universidade de Lisboa, Portugal
Aniruddha Gokhale	Vanderbilt University, USA
Artem Polyvyanyy	University of Melbourne, Australia
Asif Qumer Gill	University of Technology, Sydney, Australia
Axel Korthaus	Swinburne University of Technology, Australia
Barbara Weber	University of St. Gallen, Switzerland
Ben Roelens	Open Universiteit, Belgium & Ghent University, The Netherlands
Benjamin Yen	University of Hong Kon, China
Carlos Azevedo	Federal Institute of Espírito Santo, Brazil
Chiara Di Francescomarino	University of Trento, Italy
Christian Huemer	Vienna University of Technology, Austria
Christian Zirpins	Karlsruhe University of Applied Sciences, Germany
Claudenir M. Fonseca	University of Twente, The Netherlands
Claudio Di Ciccio	Utrecht University, The Netherlands
Colin Atkinson	University of Mannheim, Germany

Cristine Griffo	Eurac Research, Italy
Dimka Karastoyanova	University of Groningen, The Netherlands
Dominik Bork	TU Wien, Austria
Emilio Sulis	University of Turin, Italy
Fadi Mohsen	University of Groningen, The Netherlands
Fatih Turkmen	University of Groningen, The Netherlands
Fethi Rabhi	University of New South Wales, Australia
Flavia Santoro	Universidade Estadual do Rio de Janeiro, Brazil
Florian Matthes	Technical University of Munich, Germany
Frank Leymann	University of Stuttgart, Germany
Frederik Gailly	Ghent University, Belgium
Georg Grossmann	University of South Australia, Australia
Georg Weichhart	Primetals, Austria
Giancarlo Guizzardi	University of Twente, The Netherlands
Giuseppe Di Lucca	University of Sannio, Italy
Guido Governatori	Central Queensland University, Australia
Hans Weigand	Tilburg University, The Netherlands
Hans-Georg Fill	University of Fribourg, Switzerland
Hiroshi Miyazaki	Keio University, Japan
Irene Vanderfeesten	KU Leuven, Belgium
Irina Rychkova	Paris 1 Panthéon-Sorbonne University, France
Ítalo Oliveira	University of Twente, The Netherlands
Jaap Gordijn	Vrije Universiteit Amsterdam, The Netherlands
Jan Øyvind Aagedal	Equatex, Norway
João Moreira	University of Twente, The Netherlands
João Paulo Almeida	Federal University of Espírito Santo, Brazil
John Mylopoulos	University of Ottawa, Canada
Jolita Ralyté	University of Geneva, Switzerland
José Barateiro	Universidade do Algarve, Portugal
José Raúl Romero	University of Córdoba, Spain
Julio César Nardi	Federal Institute of Espírito Santo, Brazil
Julius Köpke	Alpen-Adria-Universität Klagenfurt, Austria
Lam Son Lê	Vietnamese-German University, Vietnam
Ljiljana Brankovic	University of New England, Australia
Lorenzo Rossi	University of Camerino, Italy
Luís Ferreira Pires	University of Twente, The Netherlands
Madhushi Bandara	University of Technology Sydney, Australia
Manfred Reichert	University of Ulm, Germany
Manuel Wimmer	Johannes Kepler University Linz, Austria
Marco Montali	Free University of Bozen-Bolzano, Italy
Maria Teresa Gómez López	University of Seville, Spain
Maria-Eugenia Iacob	University of Twente, The Netherlands

Marten van Sinderen	University of Twente, The Netherlands
Mathias Weske	HPI, University of Potsdam, Germany
Mattia Fumagalli	Free University of Bozen-Bolzano, Italy
Michael Rosemann	Queensland University of Technology, Australia
Michael Schrefl	Johannes Kepler University Linz, Austria
Monique Snoeck	KU Leuven, Belgium
Nicolas Herbaut	Université Paris 1 Panthéon-Sorbonne, France
Oscar Pastor	Universidad Politécnica de Valencia, Spain
Paolo Ceravolo	University of Milan, Italy
Paulo Rupino da Cunha	University of Coimbra, Portugal
Pedro Paulo F. Barcelos	University of Twente, The Netherlands
Peter Bernus	Griffith University, Australia
Peter F. Linington	University of Kent, UK
Peter Fettke	German Research Center for Artificial Intelligence and Saarland University, Germany
Pierluigi Plebani	Politecnico di Milano, Italy
Rainer Schmidt	Munich University of Applied Sciences, Germany
Rajeev Raje	IU Indianapolis, USA
Remco Dijkman	Eindhoven University of Technology, The Netherlands
Renata Guizzardi	University of Twente, The Netherlands
Ronny Seiger	University of St.Gallen, Switzerland
Rüdiger Pryss	University of Würzburg, Germany
Ruth Breu	University of Innsbruck, Austria
Sagar Sunkle	Tata Consultancy Services, India
Said Assar	Institut Mines-Télécom Business School, France
Schahram Dustdar	Vienna University of Technology, Austria
Selmin Nurcan	Université Paris 1 Panthéon - Sorbonne, France
Simon Hacks	Stockholm University, Sweden
Stefan Tai	TU Berlin, Germany
Stefanie Rinderle-Ma	Technical University of Munich, Germany
Sylvain Hallé	Université du Québec à Chicoutimi, Canada
Tiago Prince Sales	University of Twente, The Netherlands
Ulrich Frank	Universität Duisburg-Essen, Germany
Ulrik Franke	RISE Research Institutes of Sweden & KTH Royal Institute of Technology, Sweden
Uwe Zdun	University of Vienna, Austria
Vinay Kulkarni	Tata Consultancy Services Research, India
Wolfgang Maass	Saarland University, Germany
Yigal Hoffner	Shenkar College of Engineering and Design, Israel
Zoran Milosevic	Deontik, Australia

Additional Reviewers

Aleksandar Gavric
Alessandro Gianola
Alessio Galassi
Alexandra Jäger
Alexandra Klymenko
André Augusto
Angelo Casciani
Beate Wais
Bruno Fragoso
Daniel Lehner
Daniel Borcard
Dimuthu Gamage
Divya Neelagiri
Dominik Janssen
Ed Guy
Edoardo Marangone
Eduard Frankford
Fabian Muff
Fabian Stricker
Gabriel Glauber Morais
Janis Stirna
Jeewanie Jayasinghe Arachchige
Jessica Piccioni
José Antonio Peregrina Pérez
Juraj Vladika
Kerstin Andree
Klara Steflova
Laura Waltersdorfer
Leon Bein
Maria C. Borges
Mark Mulder
Maximilian Nebel
Nataliia Klievtsova
Nektarios Machner
Oliver Wardas
Pascal Ravesteyn
Peteris Rudzajs
Philipp Zech
Ralf S. Engelschall
Rebecca Morgan
Samira Khraiwesh
Seyyid Ciftci
Simon Staudinger
Simone Agostinelli
Syed Juned Ali
Thomas Pusztai
Tobias Pfaller
Tri Huynh
Valerio Goretti
Vjatšeslav Antipenko

Keynotes

Taking Enterprise Architecture Engineering to the Next Level: Digital Twin-Based Future-Oriented Enterprises

Gregor Engels

Paderborn University, Germany
gregor.engels@upb.de

Over the past decades, Enterprise Architecture Management has been established as a core means to design and operate enterprises. It has been studied from a variety of perspectives, both academically and industrially. This has led to established concepts of architectural frameworks, model-based development methods, service-oriented system architectures, business process modeling techniques, data and information modeling, and cross-cutting concerns such as security or sustainability. More recently, the concept of a digital twin has been added as a means of monitoring and analyzing ongoing enterprises.

The question is whether the pure integration of all these concepts together with a sophisticated consistency handling will be sufficient to define, realize, and operate the enterprises of the future. Or do we need to rethink all of this? Do we need to develop a much more holistic restructuring and engineering approach?

The keynote will reflect on these questions and propose an engineering approach for managing digital twin-based future-oriented enterprises. The talk is based on joint work with Burkhard Kehrbusch (Kehrbusch Management Consulting).

Leveraging Knowledge Graphs for Enhanced Business Intelligence: Bridging Data Silos and Unlocking Value

Katja Hose

TU Wien, Austria
katja.hose@tuwien.ac.at

In today's data-driven landscape, seamlessly integrating and analyzing data from diverse sources is crucial for maintaining a competitive edge. Yet, many organizations face challenges with fragmented data silos, limiting their ability to extract meaningful insights. Knowledge graphs have emerged as essential tools for bridging these silos, enhancing information sharing, and tapping into the wealth of knowledge available from various sources, including the Web.

This talk will explore the architecture and principles of knowledge graphs, demonstrating how they improve semantic interoperability and enable flexible querying of integrated datasets, while also highlighting recent advancements, including the growing role of artificial intelligence in this domain.

Contents

AI, ML and Agents

BPM and WFM

Business Models, Platforms and Strategic Management

Enterprise and IT Architecture

IT and Software Architecture

Modeling Methods, Data and Component

Process Mining and Monitoring

Sustainability and Resilience

AI, ML and Agents

AI Explainability Methods in Digital Twins: A Model and a Use Case

Tim Kreuzer(✉), Panagiotis Papapetrou, and Jelena Zdravkovic

Stockholm University, 16455 Kista, Sweden
{tim.kreuzer,panagiotis,jelenaz}@dsv.su.se

Abstract. Digital twin systems can benefit from the integration of artificial intelligence (AI) algorithms for providing for example some predictive capabilities or supporting internal decision-making. As AI algorithms are often opaque, it becomes necessary to explain their decisions to a human operator working with the digital twin. In this study, we investigate the integration of explainable AI techniques with digital twins, which we termed XAI-DT system. We define the concept of XAI-DT system and provide a use case in smart buildings, where explainable AI is used to forecast CO_2 concentration. Further, we present a core architectural model for our digital twin, outlining its interaction with the smart building and its internal processing. We evaluate five AI algorithms and compare their explainability for the operator and the entire digital twin model based on standard explainability properties from the literature.

Keywords: Digital Twin · Explainable AI · System Analysis · Forecasting

1 Introduction

A digital twin (DT) is a virtual replica of a physical system, operating in real time on the basis of a bidirectional data stream. The concept has recently gained traction in research [26,31,33], and is increasingly applied in industrial scenarios [4,38], mainly in the domain of manufacturing [34]. A DT mirrors the behavior of its physical counterpart while providing further capabilities benefitting the end-users of the system. This can be achieved by integrating artificial intelligence (AI) methods with a DT, allowing thus performing complex predictive and analysis functions based on the data it processes [17]. For instance, by employing AI algorithms, a DT can forecast the energy demand of a power plant [36] or regulate the heating and ventilation of a smart building using a forecast of temperature and CO_2 concentration [6]. This demonstrates that a digital twin can benefit from AI-based forecasts, which can be made with various machine learning techniques.

Digital twins frequently work in conjunction with human operators [9], who receive feedback from the DT system and can act upon it. When integrating AI with a DT, it is crucial to use explainable AI methods [16], as they can help the

J. Borbinha et al. (Eds.): EDOC 2024, LNCS 15409, pp. 3–20, 2025.
https://doi.org/10.1007/978-3-031-78338-8_1

operator of the system to understand the output of the AI model and the mechanisms that lead to this output. As an example, in the case of a smart building, a facility manager would want to know how a machine learning model came to the conclusion that CO_2 concentration would increase by a certain amount in the next hour. In this scenario, the DT needs to work with explainable AI techniques that are able to both make accurate forecasts and provide explanations for them. As the explainability of an AI algorithm is highly context-specific [2], it depends on the application domain and the problem at hand. With a smart building, for example, an explanation could be based on a cyclic, reoccurring pattern where CO_2 concentration usually increases at 9:00 due to a regular meeting at this time. Explanations can be more complex when more variables are involved: CO_2 concentration might be forecasted to rise due to a measured increase in the number of people in a meeting room, while the ventilation system is scheduled to turn on only an hour later. Explainable AI can help provide such explanations to operators of a digital twin.

Contributions. This paper investigates the problem of integrating explainable AI techniques with digital twins. For this, the addressed research question is: *How can machine learning explainability methods be integrated with digital twins?* More concretely, we formally define the terms *Digital Twin*, *AI-DT system*, and introduce the concept of *XAI-DT system*, combining explainable AI techniques with digital twins. We present a real use case where explainable forecasting methods are used within a DT of a smart building. Moreover, we introduce a core architectural model of a DT for our use case, connecting the proposed definitions with a realistic scenario. Finally, we validate the outlined DT by comparing the performance and explainability of multiple AI methods based on real-world data. We systematically assess explainability based on a set of well-known explainability properties from the literature [23].

2 Background

Artificial intelligence has been employed for a multitude of tasks in digital twins [17] such as optimization, classification, forecasting and outlier (i.e. anomaly) detection; as well as in many domains [27] including manufacturing, medical and transportation. Wang et al. [35] have, for example, introduced a traffic digital twin, replicating drivers, vehicles, and traffic, where AI is used to classify driver types. Li et al. [18] have proposed a system for computing task offloading using reinforcement learning in conjunction with digital twins of unmanned aerial vehicles and mobile terminals. Matulis et al. [22] have used reinforcement learning for movement optimization of a robotic arm, training the arm in a digital twin-based environment.

Explainable AI (XAI) is a field that has recently experienced an increase in interest [25]. Explainability in machine learning can be achieved with *inherently explainable models* that are explainable due to their internal mechanisms without any postprocessing. Alternatively, model-agnostic *post hoc methods* can be used to explain black-box models that are not inherently explainable. Based on the work by Burkart and Huber [5], interpretable models (white-box models) include linear models, decision trees, rule-based models, and Bayesian models. White-box models, however, usually come at a cost of reduced accuracy, flexibility, or usability [29].

In this work, we further follow the definitions of Molnar regarding explainability and the properties of explanations [23]: *Accuracy* shows how well an explanation predicts unseen data, which is only applicable when explanations are used to make predictions. Molnar describes *fidelity* as the property that measures how well an explanation reflects the prediction of the model, which is a key property of any explanation. *Consistency* is defined as the similarity of explanations for different models trained on the same task. *Stability* describes how much explanations of a single model differ for similar data points. Further, *comprehensibility* defines how well humans can understand an explanation. Without a certain degree of comprehensibility, explainable AI techniques are not practical. *Certainty* reflects the ability of an explanation to capture the model's uncertainty regarding its predictions. *Novelty* is connected to certainty; it is high when an explanation can determine that a given data point is novel. The *degree of importance* describes whether an explanation assigns importance to the features of the data. Lastly, *representativeness* characterizes whether an explanation covers a machine learning model as a whole or only an individual prediction.

For the task of time series forecasting, models commonly work on the basis of trend and seasonality and are, therefore, inherently explainable: the trend can be represented with a polynomial of a small degree, while the seasonality is a periodic function. Combining both can reveal the mechanism underlying the model's prediction. This approach is followed in N-BEATS [24] and D-Linear [37], two deep learning architectures for forecasting which decompose their output into trend and seasonality. Recently, transformer architectures have commonly been used for time series forecasting [19,20,39], which are black-box models that are not explainable. Other models, such as ARIMA [3], implement an autoregressive approach, which, despite being statistical in nature, are not inherently interpretable, as they are highly complex. Recent work has also explored the use of large language models for time series forecasting [10]. To explain black-box models' predictions, methods like SHAP [21], have been used in past research [8] to provide post hoc model explanations on a feature importance level. TS-MULE [30] is another method for post hoc explanations, assigning segment-based relevance scores to an input time series. Other explainability methods include counterfactuals [11], which suggest how the inputs should be changed to receive different outputs.

Researchers have investigated the multidisciplinary topic of XAI and digital twins, integrating the concept of explainable AI with a DT. Kapteyn et al. [14,15] have used a decision tree, which is an inherently explainable model, for classification within a DT of an unmanned aerial vehicle. Suhail et al. [32] have presented a platform for a DT of a cyber-physical system, using SHAP to provide explainability. A similar approach was pursued by Kobayashi et al. [16], who employ multiple post hoc approaches, including LIME and SHAP, to provide explainable remaining useful life estimation based on a deep neural network.

3 Explainable AI in Digital Twins

This section describes the integration of explainable AI techniques with digital twins. First, we give formal definitions of a digital twin, an AI-DT system, and an explainable AI-DT system to define the elementary components for the model presented in Fig. 1. Further, we illustrate the definitions with a real-world use case based on the DT of a smart building, employing XAI methods to forecast CO_2 concentration. We provide a pseudo algorithm for the internal processing of the DT and showcase the process with an architectural model. Lastly, we compare multiple AI methods for use within the DT, comparing their performance and explainability on the forecasting task.

3.1 Definitions

Definition 1 (Digital Twin). *Let a **digital twin** D be a tuple, with $D = (I, C, O)$. A digital twin is a virtual replica of a **physical system**, represented by a set of variables P. The physical system is a necessary contextual element for the DT and provides a set of **input streams** I, which are connected to the digital twin, so that $I \subseteq P$. Based on I, D can accurately represent the physical system in its context. The **components** C within the digital twin can be of varied nature and provide internal processing capabilities. With the **output streams** O, the digital twin closes the feedback loop to the physical system, where each output stream is either directly or indirectly related to the physical system.*

To connect Definition 1 to a real-world example, we investigate a digital twin of a smart building, further referred to as D_s, where the smart building is the physical system in the context of the DT, which is represented by the set of variables P_s. The digital twin operates on the basis of sensors installed in the building, measuring time-dependent values such as temperature, CO_2 concentration, or ventilation. We further only consider a CO_2 concentration sensor as the basis for the digital twin. Internally, it processes the data, forecasting changes in CO_2 concentration for the next hour. The DT is connected to the ventilation control system, adapting ventilation based on the results of the internal processing. Further, a dashboard illustrates the current status of the system and the forecast for a human operator.

Definition 2 (Input Stream). *Given a digital twin D, an input stream $i \in I$ is a time-dependent vector of data points i, where $i = <i_1, \ldots, i_t>$. An input stream originates from the physical system in the context of D and is updated in real-time, with the time point t representing the most recent observation. Input streams can have different data types, such as real numbers, images, or text.*

To illustrate Definition 2 in the context of a smart building, the data stemming from an individual CO_2 concentration sensor contribute to an input stream. The sensor takes measurements at regular time intervals, resulting in a temporally ordered sequence of numeric values. When connecting this to a digital twin, the CO_2 concentration sensor acts as the source of the input stream i_C while the digital twin is processing the data.

Definition 3 (Component). *Given a digital twin D, a component $c \in C$ is a function that processes an input x, resulting in an output y, where $c : x \rightarrow y$. The input x of each component is based on a number of input streams and a number of outputs of other components. The output y can be one or more values of multiple data types. Components have distinctive functionality, where each component fulfills a specific role within D.*

To process the previously outlined input stream of CO_2 concentration data, a preprocessing component c_p is introduced. This component takes the input stream i_C as the only input so that $x = \{i_C\}$. Internally, c_p checks the input stream for missing data and imputes them accordingly. If outliers occur within i_C, the preprocessing component records the number of outliers but does not act on them. The output of c_p is the preprocessed input stream, referred to as p, and the number of found outliers k so that $y = \{p, k\}$.

Following the preprocessing component, a forecasting component c_f makes predictions based on the preprocessed input, where $x = \{p\}$. It employs a machine learning algorithm, such as N-BEATS [24], to make a forecast of CO_2 concentration for the next hour, referred to as f. The training phase of the machine learning algorithm is not described here as it is preliminary. With the forecast, the output of the component is defined as follows: $y = \{f\}$.

To visualize the internal activity of c_p, and c_f in the highlighted example, we describe a dashboard component c_d, taking the input $x = \{i_C, f, k\}$. Based on the observed values in i_C and the forecasted CO_2 concentration f, a line chart of past and predicted CO_2 concentrations can be plotted. Additionally, the number of detected outliers k, which is a possible indicator of sensor quality degradation, is indicated in the dashboard. Finally, we define the resulting dashboard, which is the output of this component, as $y = \{d\}$.

Lastly, a rule-based component c_r is introduced for the regulation of the ventilation control system based on the forecasted CO_2 concentration. Its input $x = \{i_C, k, f\}$ is processed, leading to an output $y = \{r\}$ representing the control sequence sent to the ventilation control system.

Definition 4 (Output Stream). *Given a digital twin D, an output stream $o \in O$ is a time-dependent vector of outputs o, where each output is based on I and C. An output stream directly or indirectly affects the physical system P in the context of the digital twin. Similar to input streams, the data type of an output stream can vary depending on the application case.*

With the input stream i_C and the processing within the components c_p, c_f, and c_d, the dashboard d is a resulting output. The dashboard is time-dependent, as it is based on the streamed CO_2 concentration data, which change over time. This output stream o_d connects the digital twin to a human operator who can act on the information presented in the dashboard. o_d is indirectly connected to the physical system P through the operator.

A second output stream o_r directly connects the digital twin to the physical system, streaming the control sequence r, resulting from c_r, to the physical ventilation control system. This closes the feedback loop between D_s and P_s, allowing the twin to influence the smart building based on its internal processing and decision-making.

Finally, given the physical system P_s of a smart building, the outlined digital twin D_s can be described as follows:

$$D_s = (\{i_C\}, \{c_p, c_f, c_d, c_r\}, \{o_d, o_r\}) \tag{1}$$

The digital twin of a smart building outlined in this section employs AI algorithms to forecast CO_2 concentration. This is an example where artificial intelligence is integrated with a digital twin, forming an *AI-DT system*. In the literature [1,12], similar terms to AI-DT system have been used to characterize the concept of integrating AI with a digital twin, however, the term has not been defined in the past, so we give a formal definition here:

Definition 5 (AI-DT system). *We define an* ***AI-DT system*** *as a type of digital twin where artificial intelligence algorithms are integrated with the DT so that* $\exists c \in C$*, where* c *is a component of the digital twin that employs artificial intelligence to compute its outputs.*

Definition 6 (XAI-DT system). *Consider an AI-DT system with an AI component* c*. When* c *is based on inherently explainable AI techniques, we further refer to the AI-DT system as an* ***XAI-DT system****. When* c *is not inherently explainable and a second component* c_x *provides post hoc explanations based on* c*, the AI-DT system can also be considered an* ***XAI-DT system****.*

Expanding upon the smart building use case, D_s can be considered an AI-DT system, as its forecasting component c_f relies on a machine learning algorithm to make CO_2 concentration forecasts. D_s can further be considered an XAI-DT system when using an inherently explainable AI algorithm for the forecasting task. In this case, the output of c_f additionally includes inherent explanations e_i that are displayed by the dashboard component for the human operator. When using an opaque machine learning model that is not explainable, an additional post hoc explainability component needs to be added to make D_s an XAI-DT system. This explainability component c_x takes both the forecast and the machine learning model itself as inputs so that $x = \{f, M\}$ where M represents the machine learning model employed in c_f. Internally, c_x uses a post hoc explainability method such as SHAP, resulting in post hoc explanations e_p, illustrating the forecasting mechanism used to make the forecast so that $y = \{e_p\}$.

3.2 Use Case and Architectural Model

This section presents the overall architectural model of an XAI-DT system, instantiated for our use case in smart buildings. Figure 1 shows the model while using the previously outlined definitions.

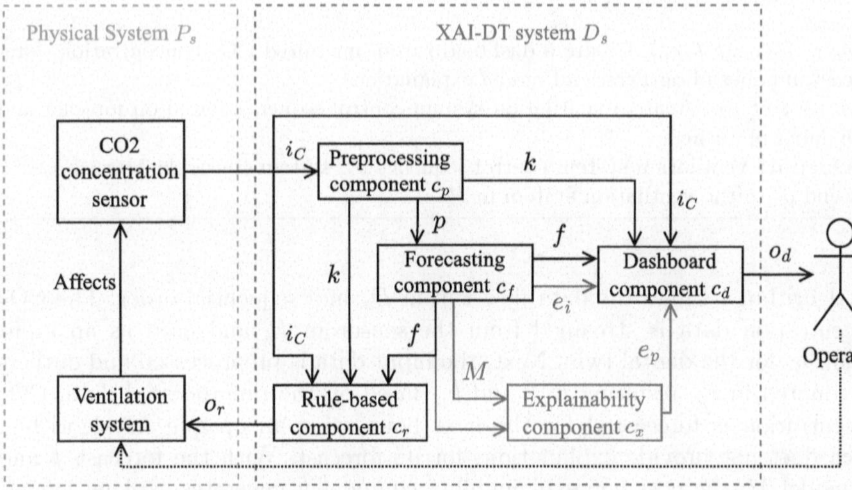

Fig. 1. Architectural model of D_s, representing a digital twin of a smart building P_s. This core model shows two possibilities for the integration of explainable AI: an inherently explainable algorithm providing inherent explanations e_i (pink) and a post hoc explainability component (green) providing post hoc explanations e_p for opaque models. (Color figure online)

The physical system P_s represents the smart building in the context of the DT, containing a CO_2 concentration sensor that is affected by changes in the ventilation system and the environment in the smart building. Measurements from the CO_2 concentration sensor are streamed to the digital twin D_s, resulting in the input stream i_C that is used by the preprocessing, dashboard, and rule-based components. Internally, the components of the digital twin are connected, processing the CO_2 concentration input, making a forecast, and counting outliers, while c_f provides explanations to the dashboard. For opaque machine learning models, the figure also highlights the additional post hoc explainability component c_x (green) that provides explanations for the forecast made by the machine learning model and forwards them to the dashboard. With the explainability component and the forecasting component, D_s is an XAI-DT system. The output of the digital twin consists of two output streams: o_d, which streams a dashboard to the system's Operator, indirectly affecting the smart building, and secondly o_r, which sends a control sequence to the ventilation system, directly influencing P_s.

Algorithm 1. Data flow and processing of D_s with post hoc explainability

Receive i_C from the CO_2 concentration sensor in P_s
Input: CO_2 concentration data stream i_C.
$p, k \leftarrow c_p(i_C)$; Preprocess the CO_2 concentration data and count outliers.
$f, M \leftarrow c_f(p)$; Forecast CO_2 concentration for the next hour with an opaque AI algorithm.
$e_p \leftarrow c_x(f, M)$; Provide post hoc explanations for the AI algorithm and its forecasts.
$o_d \leftarrow c_d(i_C, f, k, e_p)$; Create a dashboard from measured CO_2 concentration, forecast, number of outliers, and model explanations.
$o_r \leftarrow c_r(f, k)$; Create a ventilation system control sequence based on forecast and number of outliers.
Output: Ventilation system control sequence o_r, system status dashboard o_d.
Send o_r to the ventilation system in P_s.

Algorithm 1 shows the data flow within D_s in a sequential order. The CO_2 concentration data is streamed from the sensor in P_s and used as an input stream i_C for the digital twin. Next, the input data is preprocessed and outliers are counted in c_p, resulting in p and k. Based on the preprocessed data, CO_2 concentration is forecasted for the next hour using an opaque AI algorithm, which does not provide explanations for its forecast. With the forecast f and the model M, the post hoc explainability component generates explanations e_p for the forecast, which are used in the dashboard. The dashboard additionally receives the input stream, the forecast, and the number of outliers, which are shown to the operator. Finally, the rule-based component c_r creates a control sequence for the ventilation system based on forecast and the number of outliers, resulting in the output stream o_r. The control sequence is forwarded to the ventilation system in P_s, closing the feedback loop between the digital twin and the physical system in its context.

3.3 Forecasting Methods

We conducted an evaluation of AI methods for the CO_2 concentration forecasting component c_f, comparing their accuracy. This evaluation is relevant to present because it aids in understanding which algorithms are effective for the proposed digital twin, which is an essential quality parameter in addition to explainability being needed for describing the mechanism leading to an output. We evaluate the forecasting algorithms shown in Table 1. Each algorithm providing some form of inherent explainability is additionally categorized as *Explainable*, which is evaluated in more detail in Sect. 3.4. All inherently explainable algorithms are categorized as explainable due to a decomposition-based forecast, which allows for a more fine-grained interpretation of the forecast.

N-BEATS and DEPTS were chosen as they provide decomposition-based explanations, while claiming high performance for the time series forecasting task. The non-stationary transformer was evaluated, as it is a non-explainable, transformer-based method, offering high performance as a black-box model. Lastly, ARIMA was benchmarked to compare a statistical approach with the deep learning methods for time series forecasting.

Table 1. Algorithms evaluated

Algorithm name	Reference	Approach	Explainable
N-BEATS	[24]	Deep Learning	Yes
D-Linear	[37]	Deep Learning	Yes
Non-Stationary Transformer (NST)	[20]	Deep Learning	No
DEPTS	[7]	Deep Learning	Yes
ARIMA	[3]	Statistical	No

We are using historical CO_2 concentration data from a smart building dataset for the evaluation. The data consist of measurements of 106 sensors with a sampling frequency of 5 min that were gathered over a period of 10 days (for the purpose of this study, we have found this timeframe as sufficient.... As the objective of the forecast is predicting CO_2 concentration for the next hour, all evaluated algorithms are trained to forecast the next 12 values. Because explainability is the main focus of this study, we evaluated accuracy to compare the predictive power of different algorithms without the aim of optimizing it. The results of our evaluation of forecasting algorithms on the CO_2 concentration data are shown in Table 2. We compare the performance of the algorithms based on the metrics *mean absolute error* (MAE) and *root mean squared error* (RMSE), as defined in [13], where each metric represents an error, with lower values indicating higher performance. N-BEATS shows the lowest error on both metrics, showing that the algorithm performs best in our CO_2 concentration forecasting scenario. Non-Stationary Transformer and D-Linear show the second-highest performance, while ARIMA and DEPTS have the highest errors.

From the evaluation it has become clear that N-BEATS is the most suitable AI algorithm for the forecasting component in our digital twin of a smart building.

Figure 2 shows a sample of the dashboard d, showing the input stream of CO_2 concentration data i_C as well as the underlying ground truth for the next hour. The figure does not represent the complete dashboard, as it does not display the number of outliers k and the model explanations e_i or e_p. In addition to the input data, the forecasts made by the five evaluated algorithms are shown. As the ground truth would not be available in a production setting with live data, in this case, the dashboard would only show historical data and the forecast of the employed forecasting algorithm. When using a non-explainable algorithm, the forecast trajectory of CO_2 (colored lines) is the only output of the algorithm, as shown in the figure, while no further details are provided on "why" that

Table 2. Evaluation of AI algorithm performance for the CO_2 concentration forecasting task. Best performing algorithm by metric highlighted in bold.

Algorithm	MAE	RMSE
N-BEATS	**30.52**	**66.3**
D-Linear	31.64	70.37
NST	31.11	68.79
ARIMA	35.53	92.59
DEPTS	44.54	84.39

particular forecast has been made. On the contrary an explainable algorithm will provide additional explanations on why the forecasted values follow a particular trajectory. Such explanations can be to link the forecasted values to historical values, patterns, or trends (e.g., upward-going or seasonal) that have occurred in the past and are repeating in the future, such as the ones depicted in Fig. 3.

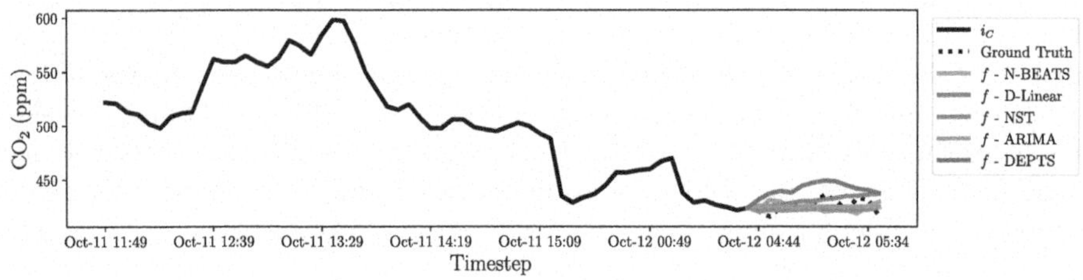

Fig. 2. Sample of the dashboard d showing the input stream i_C, and forecast f made by different machine learning models.

3.4 Explainability of Methods for Operator's Dashboard

In this section, we investigate the explainability of the forecasting methods, which can be either inherent to the AI algorithm or applied post hoc within the DT model. We follow the definitions of Molnar [23] regarding explainability properties, characterizing them as applicable for each method. As the not inherently explainable methods solely provide the numeric values of their output without a rationale behind it, we apply TS-MULE [30], a post hoc explainability method extending LIME [28] for time series data. The post hoc explainability method represents the explainability component c_x for opaque algorithms.

Figure 3 showcases the decomposition of the forecast by N-BEATS into trend and seasonality elements. Trend provides a general direction of the data, showing a long-term increase or decrease in value, while seasonality represents cyclic patterns such as week-weekend cycles. The model's forecast can be obtained by adding the two elements of trend and seasonality. The visualization is based on the decomposition of the prediction as seen in [24]. The forecast is based on a sample from the smart building CO_2 concentration data we use for evaluation in this section. Notably, both elements have a different scale, with the trend having higher absolute values than the seasonality, while the seasonality shows more change over time. This offers a higher degree of comprehensibility for a human operator, different from a non-explainable forecast, where the prediction is solely based on a nonlinear combination of neural network weights and intermediate features. However, comprehensibility is hard to measure, and a qualitative analysis based on human judgment would be necessary to make a conclusive statement on this property. The explanation of N-BEATS is local, representing an individual prediction while not showing the model's certainty or indicating novelty. The fidelity of the explanation is high, as it represents a decomposition, which is equivalent to the actual forecast of the model. However, as the explanation can not be used to predict unseen data, this type of explanation offers low accuracy. During our experiments, it became clear that the stability of N-BEATS is high, as its explanations vary little when perturbing the input.

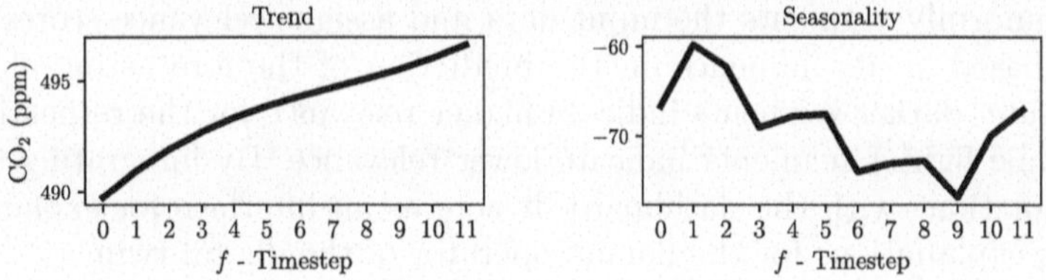

Fig. 3. Inherent explanations e_i provided by N-BEATS, decomposing its forecast into trend and seasonality components.

Another kind of visualization for inherent explanations of the deep learning algorithm DEPTS [7] is shown in Fig. 4, following the approach presented in the original paper. Similar to N-BEATS, DEPTS provides prediction-based explanations based on a periodic element (DEPTS-P) and a local element (DEPTS-L), leading to a low degree of representativeness. Different from the visualization of N-BEATS, the two elements are merged in this graph, sharing the same scale, leading to a different visualization style. DEPTS shows a stable periodicity, indicating that the data do not experience significant cyclic patterns. The local component of DEPTS shows lower absolute values than the periodic component. Overall, the decomposition-based explanation approaches of N-BEATS and DEPTS are similar, basing their forecast on two elements that sum up to the algorithms' forecast. It can be argued that the visualization style of DEPTS' explanations provides a lower degree of comprehensibility than N-BEATS, as both positive and negative values are merged in one figure. Further, similar to N-BEATS, the explanation does not provide certainty or novelty measures, while keeping a high level of fidelity due to the decomposition-based approach. The stability of DEPTS' explanations is high, but it does not present feature importance for the input.

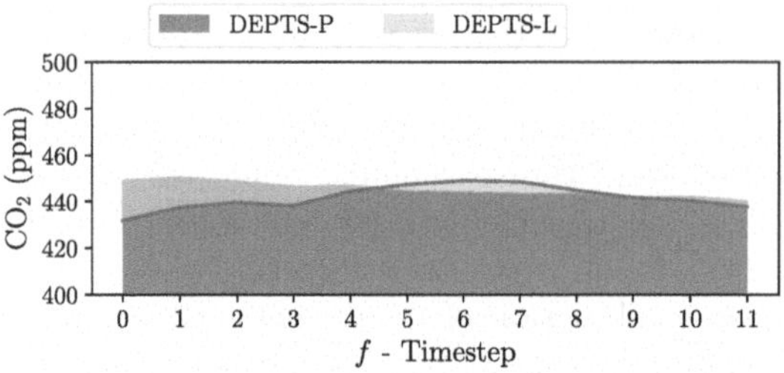

Fig. 4. Inherent explanations e_i provided by DEPTS, decomposing its forecast into periodic (DEPTS-P) and local (DEPTS-L) elements.

We apply the post hoc explainability method TS-MULE [30], which is a generalization of LIME for time series, to the three best-performing forecasting methods D-Linear, N-BEATS, and Non-Stationary Transformer, as seen in Fig. 5. This represents the post hoc explainability component c_x, which generates post hoc explanations e_p based on the forecast and the model used in c_f. TS-MULE uniformly segments the input data and assigns relevance scores to each segment based on its influence on the prediction of the forecasting algorithm. In the figure, darker segments indicate higher relevance for the respective algorithm, while lighter segments indicate lower relevance. By integrating the post hoc explanations with the dashboard, it acts as an interface for explainability, providing explanations for the human operator of the digital twin.

Different from the inherent explanations of N-BEATS and DEPTS, TS-MULE works on an input level, which provides a higher degree of comprehensibility for the operator, as they can judge which past timesteps were critical for the forecasting model, giving a degree of importance for each segment. However, as the relevance is assigned based on input perturbation, the fidelity of the explanations is lower. As the explanations do not provide confidence intervals or other uncertainty measures, TS-MULE does not provide a degree of certainty or novelty regarding the predictions. Similar to N-BEATS and DEPTS, TS-MULE has a low degree of representativeness, as it provides explanations for an individual prediction and does not characterize the forecasting model as a whole. In our experiments, TS-MULE was averaged over 100 runs, as the method has low stability and can provide differing results for the same input.

Both D-Linear (5a) and N-BEATS (5b) have the highest relevance score in the last segment of the input data, showing that the algorithms base their forecasts on the most recent observations. Non-Stationary Transformer (5b) shows the opposite behavior, as it reaches the highest relevance score on the first segment, gradually giving less relevance to further segments, while the last two segments receive the lowest overall relevance. In a production setting, the explanations shown in Fig. 5 are integrated with the dashboard d, which shows both the forecast of the AI algorithm and the explanations, which are applied post hoc by using TS-MULE.

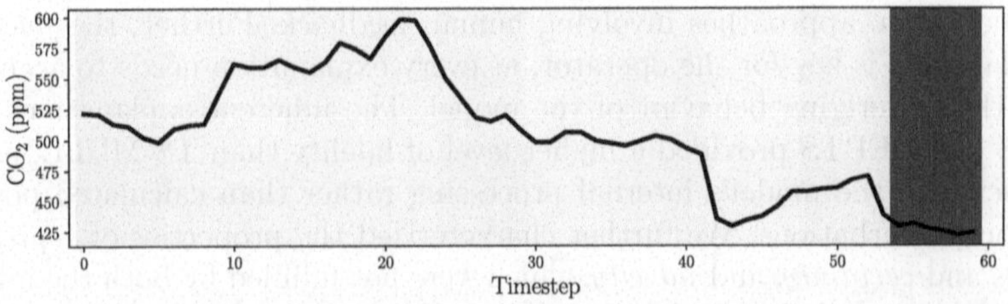

(a) Post hoc explanations e_p of D-Linear with TS-MULE

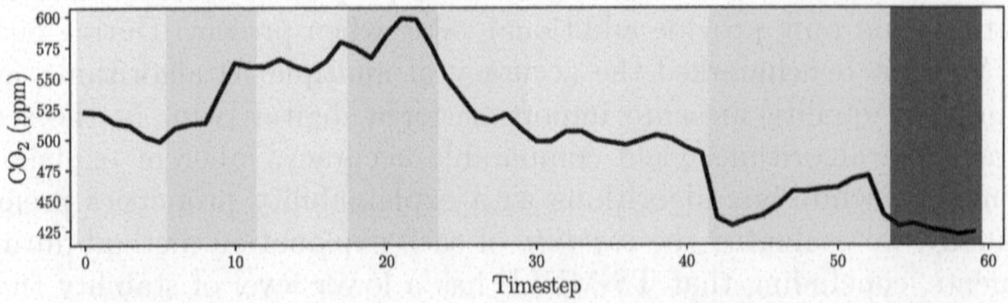

(b) Post hoc explanations e_p of N-BEATS with TS-MULE

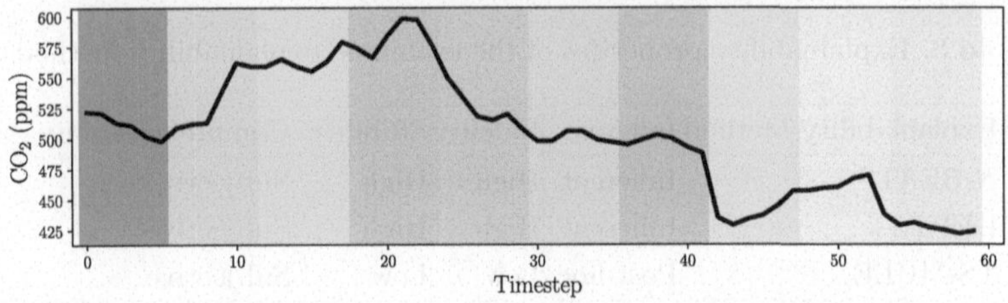

(c) Post hoc explanations e_p of Non-Stationary Transformer with TS-MULE

Fig. 5. Sample of post hoc explanations e_p of the explainability component c_x. The algorithm TS-MULE [30] is used for segment-based relevance, where darker segments indicate higher relevance of the data on the algorithm's prediction.

4 Discussion

Usefulness of Explanations - In the previous section, we introduced an example of a digital twin of a smart building, working solely on the basis of CO_2 concentration data from one type of sensor. The presented explainability methods, both inherent and post hoc, show in different ways how the respective AI algorithms arrived at their projected forecasts. Whether these explanations are useful to an operator depends on the domain and the use case and needs to be evaluated on a case-by-case basis. Table 3 summarizes the explainability properties of the evaluated explainability methods. The usefulness of an explanation is highly dependent on the *comprehensibility* of the explanation, as an incomprehensible explanation does not benefit the operator of the digital twin. As comprehensibility is subjective, a degree of comprehensibility can be estimated with qualitative approaches involving human feedback. Further, the *fidelity* of an explanation is key for the operator, as every explanation needs to accurately reflect the underlying behavior of the model. The inherent explanations of N-BEATS and DEPTS provided a higher level of fidelity than TS-MULE, as they are specific to the model's internal processing rather than calculated post-hoc based on perturbations. We further characterized the properties of *representativeness* and *certainty*, and *novelty*, which were not fulfilled by both the inherent explainability methods of N-BEATS and DEPTS and the post-hoc method TS-MULE. However, it can be argued that these properties are not necessary for explanations and only provide additional value when present. During our evaluation, We first benchmarked the accuracy of multiple AI algorithms, as that is the primary quality measure important for a digital twin. In the scenario where multiple algorithms yield comparable accuracy, inherent explainability is key, making white-box algorithms with explainability properties preferable. Additionally, we evaluated the *stability* of each explanation method during our experiments, concluding that TS-MULE has a lower level of stability than the other methods.

Table 3. Explainability properties of the evaluated explainability methods.*

Explainability Method	Inherent	Fidelity	Stability	Comprehensibility
N-BEATS	Inherent	High	High	Subjective
DEPTS	Inherent	High	High	Subjective
TS-MULE	Post-hoc	Low	Low	Subjective
Explainability Method	**Certainty**	**Novelty**	**Degree of**	**Representativeness**
N-BEATS	Low	Low	Low	Low
DEPTS	Low	Low	Low	Low
TS-MULE	Low	Low	High	Low

* Accuracy and consistency were excluded from the table, as they are not applicable in our case

Architectural Model - The focus of this work is on the definitions and the model of the proposed digital twin for establishing a formal and conceptual basis for integrating explainable AI. Due to this, our evaluation covered the AI component, comparing the accuracy of different algorithms as the essential DT aspect, as well as focusing to the explainability aspect, for investigating and integrating both inherent and post hoc explanations. The introduced rule-based component, representing the feedback loop to the physical system, was not investigated for explainability in this study as it does not work on the basis of AI and therefore also does not have a connection to this quality aspect.

Real-World Setting Complexity - In the study, we limited the use case to the analysis of a single variable (CO_2), to emphasise the core contribution - integration of XAI to the digital twin model. In a real-world setting, a digital twin of a smart building should include additional variables such as temperature, humidity, occupancy, or light intensity. With access to more data, AI algorithms perform better, allowing them to make more accurate forecasts, thereby improving the overall performance of the digital twin. As the complexity of the system increases, the complexity of explanations also increases, requiring the explainability methods to scale with the digital twin. In addition, the digital twin would have more control over the physical system, for example, by adapting the heating system based on occupancy and projected changes in temperature. In this case, an explanation could cover both trends in past temperature and occupancy, providing a more detailed summary of the underlying patterns for the operator.

Generalizability - The architectural model of D_s presented in Sect. 3.2, even specific to our presented use case on CO_2 concentration forecasting in smart buildings, it has been meant for avoiding further details to put forward generalisation. Our proposed component-based notation can be generalized to digital twins of any domain, a similar model can be created for any digital twin D. An architectural model helps visualize the internal flow of information within the DT while also delineating the capabilities of the different components. Still, it is our intention to, in the future study, detail the presented core architecture components by the means of a meta-model.

5 Conclusion and Future Work

In this study, we introduced the concept of explainable AI in digital twins, outlining a use case in smart buildings where an AI algorithm is used to forecast CO_2 concentration. To illustrate our digital twin, we presented an architectural model of the system, showing its interaction with the smart building and a human operator. For the proposed digital twin, we evaluated five AI algorithms, comparing their accuracy in forecasting CO_2 concentration. The deep learning algorithm N-BEATS showed the highest performance in forecasting, indicating that it is the most suitable candidate for our digital twin. We further investigated the explainability of the evaluated AI algorithms, outlining both inherently provided model explanations and post hoc explanations based on TS-MULE.

With the definitions given in this paper, we are planning to further investigate the outlined use case, making use of more sensors and connecting the digital twin to the physical system in real-time. In this more complex scenario, explainability methods must be adapted to the available data showing correlations between variables. To evaluate the practicality of the provided explanations for the DT, we are planning to conduct a qualitative analysis based on operator feedback.

In future work, we are planning to empirically investigate machine learning explainability in digital twins based on a user study. As explainability properties are generally assessed qualitatively and some, such as comprehensibility, can be subjective, a user study could contribute to this line of research.

Acknowledgements. We would like to thank Atrium Ljungberg AB for providing the data for the evaluation conducted in this study.

References

1. Apostolidis, A., Stamoulis, K.P.: An AI-based digital twin case study in the MRO sector. Transp. Res. Procedia **56**, 55–62 (2021)
2. Beaudouin, V., et al.: Flexible and context-specific AI explainability: a multidisciplinary approach. arXiv preprint arXiv:2003.07703 (2020)
3. Box, G.E., Jenkins, G.M., Reinsel, G.C., Ljung, G.M.: Time Series Analysis: Forecasting and Control. Wiley, Hobken (2015)
4. Brenner, B., Hummel, V.: Digital twin as enabler for an innovative digital shopfloor management system in the ESB logistics learning factory at reutlingen-university. Procedia Manuf. **9**, 198–205 (2017)
5. Burkart, N., Huber, M.F.: A survey on the explainability of supervised machine learning. J. Artif. Intell. Res. **70**, 245–317 (2021)
6. Clausen, A., Arendt, K., Johansen, A., Sangogboye, F.C., Kjærgaard, M.B., Veje, C.T., Jørgensen, B.N.: A digital twin framework for improving energy efficiency and occupant comfort in public and commercial buildings. Energy Informatics **4**(2), 1–19 (2021). https://doi.org/10.1186/s42162-021-00153-9
7. Fan, W., et al.: Depts: deep expansion learning for periodic time series forecasting. arXiv preprint arXiv:2203.07681 (2022)
8. Fukas, P., Rebstadt, J., Menzel, L., Thomas, O.: Towards explainable artificial intelligence in financial fraud detection: using Shapley additive explanations to explore feature importance. In: International Conference on Advanced Information Systems Engineering, pp. 109–126. Springer (2022)
9. Gallala, A., Kumar, A.A., Hichri, B., Plapper, P.: Digital twin for human–robot interactions by means of industry 4.0 enabling technologies. Sensors **22**(13), 4950 (2022). https://doi.org/10.3390/s22134950
10. Gruver, N., Finzi, M., Qiu, S., Wilson, A.G.: Large language models are zero-shot time series forecasters. arXiv preprint arXiv:2310.07820 (2023)
11. Guidotti, R.: Counterfactual explanations and how to find them: literature review and benchmarking. Data Min. Knowl. Discov. 1–55 (2022)
12. Huang, Z., Shen, Y., Li, J., Fey, M., Brecher, C.: A survey on AI-driven digital twins in industry 4.0: smart manufacturing and advanced robotics. Sensors **21**(19), 6340 (2021)
13. Hyndman, R.J., Koehler, A.B.: Another look at measures of forecast accuracy. Int. J. Forecast. **22**(4), 679–688 (2006)
14. Kapteyn, M.G., Knezevic, D.J., Willcox, K.: Toward predictive digital twins via component-based reduced-order models and interpretable machine learning. In: AIAA Scitech 2020 Forum, p. 0418 (2020)
15. Kapteyn, M.G., Willcox, K.E.: From physics-based models to predictive digital twins via interpretable machine learning. arXiv preprint arXiv:2004.11356 (2020)
16. Kobayashi, K., Alam, S.B.: Explainable, interpretable, and trustworthy AI for an intelligent digital twin: a case study on remaining useful life. Eng. Appl. Artif. Intell. **129**, 107620 (2024)
17. Kreuzer, T., Papapetrou, P., Zdravkovic, J.: Artificial intelligence in digital twins–a systematic literature review. Data Knowl. Eng. **151**, 102304 (2024). https://doi.org/10.1016/j.datak.2024.102304. https://www.sciencedirect.com/science/article/pii/S0169023X24000284
18. Li, B., Liu, Y., Tan, L., Pan, H., Zhang, Y.: Digital twin assisted task offloading for aerial edge computing and networks. IEEE Trans. Veh. Technol. **71**(10), 10863–10877 (2022)

19. Liu, S., et al.: Pyraformer: low-complexity pyramidal attention for long-range time series modeling and forecasting. In: International Conference on Learning Representations (2021)
20. Liu, Y., Wu, H., Wang, J., Long, M.: Non-stationary transformers: Exploring the stationarity in time series forecasting. Adv. Neural. Inf. Process. Syst. **35**, 9881–9893 (2022)
21. Lundberg, S.M., Lee, S.I.: A unified approach to interpreting model predictions. In: Advances in Neural Information Processing Systems, vol. 30 (2017)
22. Matulis, M., Harvey, C.: A robot arm digital twin utilising reinforcement learning. Comput. Graph. **95**, 106–114 (2021)
23. Molnar, C.: Interpretable machine learning. Lulu. com (2020)
24. Oreshkin, B.N., Carpov, D., Chapados, N., Bengio, Y.: N-beats: neural basis expansion analysis for interpretable time series forecasting. arXiv preprint arXiv:1905.10437 (2019)
25. Patel, S.S.: Explainable machine learning models to analyse maternal health. Data Knowl. Eng. 102198 (2023)
26. Qi, Q.: Enabling technologies and tools for digital twin. J. Manuf. Syst. **58**, 3–21 (2021)
27. Rathore, M.M., Shah, S.A., Shukla, D., Bentafat, E., Bakiras, S.: The role of AI, machine learning, and big data in digital twinning: a systematic literature review, challenges, and opportunities. IEEE Access **9**, 32030–32052 (2021). https://doi.org/10.1109/ACCESS.2021.3060863
28. Ribeiro, M.T., Singh, S., Guestrin, C.: "Why should I trust you?" explaining the predictions of any classifier. In: Proceedings of the 22nd ACM SIGKDD International Conference on Knowledge Discovery and Data Mining, pp. 1135–1144 (2016)
29. Ribeiro, M.T., Singh, S., Guestrin, C.: Model-agnostic interpretability of machine learning. arXiv preprint arXiv:1606.05386 (2016)
30. Schlegel, U., Vo, D.L., Keim, D.A., Seebacher, D.: TS-mule: local interpretable model-agnostic explanations for time series forecast models. In: Joint European Conference on Machine Learning and Knowledge Discovery in Databases, pp. 5–14. Springer (2021)
31. Singh, M., Fuenmayor, E., Hinchy, E.P., Qiao, Y., Murray, N., Devine, D.: Digital twin: origin to future. Appl. Syst. Innov. **4**(2), 36 (2021)
32. Suhail, S., Iqbal, M., Hussain, R., Jurdak, R.: Enigma: an explainable digital twin security solution for cyber-physical systems. Comput. Ind. **151**, 103961 (2023)
33. Tao, F., Xiao, B., Qi, Q., Cheng, J., Ji, P.: Digital twin modeling. J. Manuf. Syst. **64**, 372–389 (2022)
34. Tao, F., Zhang, H., Liu, A., Nee, A.Y.: Digital twin in industry: state-of-the-art. IEEE Trans. Ind. Inf. **15**(4), 2405–2415 (2018)
35. Wang, Z., et al.: Mobility digital twin: concept, architecture, case study, and future challenges. IEEE Internet Things J. **9**(18), 17452–17467 (2022)
36. Xie, X., Parlikad, A.K., Puri, R.S.: A neural ordinary differential equations based approach for demand forecasting within power grid digital twins. In: 2019 IEEE International Conference on Communications, Control, and Computing Technologies for Smart Grids (SmartGridComm), pp. 1–6. IEEE (2019)
37. Zeng, A., Chen, M., Zhang, L., Xu, Q.: Are transformers effective for time series forecasting? In: Proceedings of the AAAI Conference on Artificial Intelligence, vol. 37, pp. 11121–11128 (2023)
38. Zhou, G., Zhang, C., Li, Z., Ding, K., Wang, C.: Knowledge-driven digital twin manufacturing cell towards intelligent manufacturing. Int. J. Prod. Res. **58**(4), 1034–1051 (2020)

39. Zhou, T., Ma, Z., Wen, Q., Wang, X., Sun, L., Jin, R.: Fedformer: frequency enhanced decomposed transformer for long-term series forecasting. In: International Conference on Machine Learning, pp. 27268–27286. PMLR (2022)

Enterprise Design, Operations and Computing with AI Agents: Accountability Using DSL

Zoran Milosevic[1(✉)] and Igor Dejanović[2]

[1] Deontik, Brisbane, Australia
zoran@deontik.com

[2] Faculty of Technical Sciences, University of Novi Sad, Novi Sad, Serbia
igord@uns.ac.rs

Abstract. LLM-powered AI agent systems are bringing new perspectives to enterprise design, operations, and computing (EDOC), particularly in environments where agents can act autonomously and independently, referred to as agentic systems. These capabilities unlock new opportunities for automation, enabling agents to perform intellectually demanding tasks that were previously reserved for humans, while still allowing human oversight of key decisions. However, a critical challenge remains: ensuring clear accountability within these systems across humans and AI Agents, which may involve complex chains of authorization and delegation. As individual agents act independently, pinpointing responsibility becomes increasingly difficult. This paper proposes a novel solution to this problem: a domain-specific language (DSL) based on the ISO ODP Enterprise Language standard, precisely defining the roles and interactions between actors in the enterprise landscape. The DSL is implemented using textX, a contemporary tool-chain which provides rapid prototyping ecosystem. The aim is to provide user-friendly syntax while following the precise semantics of ODP enterprise language.

Keywords: AI Agents · DSL · Policy · Responsible AI · Obligations · ODP

1 Introduction

AI Agents, including Generative Agent systems [22] are transforming the way enterprises function by automating complex tasks and enabling real-time decision-making. By leveraging Large Language Models (LLMs), these systems foster enhanced communication and collaboration between multiple intelligent agents. This collaboration unlocks the potential for novel and efficient solutions to complex enterprise tasks. However, a critical challenge remains: ensuring a clear chain of responsibility within these multi-agent systems. As these systems become more sophisticated, and individual agents exhibit increasing levels of

J. Borbinha et al. (Eds.): EDOC 2024, LNCS 15409, pp. 21–38, 2025.
https://doi.org/10.1007/978-3-031-78338-8_2

agency (acting autonomously within their environment), pinpointing accountability for actions and decisions becomes increasingly complex.

While significant previous research has focused on communication protocols and coordination mechanisms within multi-agent systems prior to their use of LLMs [4,9], ensuring a clear chain of responsibility has received less attention. Existing approaches often rely on centralized control structures or pre-defined rules for task allocation, without considering the intricacies of social environment, such as accountability arising from the organisational or legislative rules. These methods do not provide flexibility in adapting to the dynamic nature of enterprise environments and the growing autonomy of agentic systems.

This paper addresses this critical gap by proposing a novel solution: a domain-specific language (DSL) developed to support enterprise design and operation activities, while placing special attention on the accountability concepts. This DSL can be used to express accountability rules for the enterprise which includes AI agents and multi-agent capabilities, and provide rapid implementation of required monitoring and enforcing capability. This DSL leverages the precise semantics of the ODP Enterprise Language (ODP-EL) standard [10], allowing for a clear and unambiguous definition of roles, responsibilities, and decision-making authority within a multi-agent system. The ODP-EL standard brings credibility but also pragmatic approach to building interoperable distributed systems and by utilizing this DSL, enterprises can design and deploy collaborative AI systems with a well-defined chain of responsibility, fostering trust, transparency, and legal clarity.

Next section provides an overview of related work. This is followed by a brief introduction of multi-agent and agentic AI systems, Sect. 3. Key ODP Enterprise Language concepts are outlined in Sect. 4. The description of our DSL implementation of related ODP-EL concepts is in Sect. 5. Section 6 provides an overview of the integration of DSL tooling with one specific AI agent architecture and discusses some challenges from our implementation. Conclusions and directions for future work are summarized in Sect. 7.

2 Related Work

The problem of designing enterprise structure and behaviour has been subject of many research and industry efforts. Much of the recent research contributions come from various enterprise ontology efforts, the most prominent being a series of proposals from the UFO community, of which UFO-L extension is particularly related to this work [8]. Another example is Open Digital Rights Language (ODRL) [23], which is used to represent permitted and prohibited actions over a certain asset, as well as the obligations required to be met by stakeholders. These ontologies and modelling languages provide an excellent conceptual foundations for expressing key concepts and relationships related to enterprise structure, and have provided insights into our current work.

Further influence comes from our earlier DSL efforts related to Business Contract Language (BCL) [15,17], which was based on the previous version of ODP-EL standard. BCL has similarity with our current DSL efforts, in terms of its focus on developing an implementable language. Current ODP-EL standard however provides more expressive set of concepts which includes a precise framework of expressing delegations and obligations in a way which are more amenable for the distributed system implementations. This, along with the increasing requirements to better modelling of policy frameworks in digital health, where much of our recent industry efforts were involved, motivated us to use the latest version of he ODP-EL as a source of our DSL.

Much of the work above is related to the enterprise objects that model key entities in a system, of which computational agents represent subset of these. The agentic AI solutions are recent development and much focus there was on how to best structure an LLM-based application in terms of the roles undertaking dedicated tasks, with limited current success in supporting planning and collaboration [21]. AI agent architectures are currently concerned with the structure of single AI agents, leaving the communications among agents to the underlying LLM and relevant tools, to support the expression of agent's reflection, planning and collaboration, as demonstrated in the recent work on computational software agents that simulate believable human behavior [22]. Some earlier work has investigated the computational agents in a distributed environment, as for example the Siebog Multi-Agent System [19] where agents can be specified using ALAS DSL [24].

However, the problem of expressing policy constraints over agents actions in distributed systems is currently not addressed and our contribution is to provide architectural positioning of the formalism of deontic and accountability concepts to be integrated with agentic developments, leveraging mature and pragmatic framework from the ODP-EL.

3 Agent AI Systems

3.1 Agent AI Architectures

Agent AI systems have recently emerged as a vehicle of making better use of LLM models in support of specific, AI enabled enterprise tasks. They allow complex tasks to be decomposed into smaller units, i.e. actions, such as in complex activities of writing software or providing financial or health related advice to consumers. Each of these actions can in turn be implemented by a separate, dedicated agent. The actions can include prompting of LLM models in an iterative fashion, invoking tools for specific functions by a single agent, or multiple agents. Some architectures, such as crewAI [20] include mechanisms for delegating actions to other agents who would execute more specific tasks or for farm-out other tasks for resource allocation reasons. A key new quality here is to replace the current's LLM's zero-shot prompt with a sequence of steps undertaken by a single or multiple agents, sometimes referred to as agent workflow, which as experience shows, produces better results than the zero-shot approach. This task decomposition also influences the properties of the agent AI architectures, recently described in terms of the four design patterns [21]:

- Reflection, where a LLM examines its own work to come up with ways to improve it, which may involve creating its own memory stream for this [22].
- Tool Use, where a LLM exploits tools such as web search, code execution, or other functions to help it gather information, take action, or process data.
- Planning, where a LLM creates and executes a multi-step plan, e.g. writing an outline for an essay, then doing online research, then writing a draft.
- Multi-agent collaboration, where multiple AI agents work together, decomposing a complex task and discussing and debating ideas, to come up with better solutions than a single agent would [22].

There are a number of variants of how these patterns can be implemented. In some cases the focus is on their communication and collaboration, with limited autonomy [20,26], while at the other end of spectrum is supporting autonomous decision-making [22]. It should be noted that LLM-based AI agents are not yet designed for distributed environments .

3.2 Policy Constraints Considerations

Ethical, regulatory, and policy considerations are crucial aspects to consider when designing any AI system, including the Agent AI systems. These can be summarised in the context of the following requirements:

Ethical Considerations

- Bias and Fairness: it is essential to ensure AI systems are trained on unbiased data and designed to avoid discriminatory outputs. Techniques like fairness checks and diverse datasets are crucial.
- Transparency and Explainability: this is referred to a need to understand how AI systems reach their decisions; for example, in agentic workflows, this might involve explaining the actions and choices of AI agents, and for generative agents, transparency in content generation is important.
- Human Control and Oversight: While agentic AI and generative agents exhibit agency, it is crucial to maintain human control over their actions and outputs. Clear guidelines and safeguards are necessary.

Regulatory and Policy Constraints

- Data Privacy: The Agent AI systems might involve handling personal data. Regulations like GDPR [5] need to be followed when collecting, storing, and using such data.
- Accountability: Assigning responsibility for the actions of AI systems is crucial, such as identifying who is legally accountable for decisions made by agentic AI systems or the outputs of generative agents.
- Safety and Security: Security measures are essential to prevent malicious actors from manipulating AI systems. Safety measures should ensure that AI agents do not pose a risk to users' physical or psychological well-being.

Enterprise Design and Operations Considerations. Ethical considerations, regulations, and policies should be integrated from the early stages of the design process for agent AI systems, and the experience with the operations of such system can also inform better integration of policy considerations [16].

Our approach to these requirements is to consider well developed semantics from the ODP-EL in a technology neutral way so that it can be integrated with various architecture approaches. While ODP standard has provided many inputs to various distributed systems and architectures [13], less is known about the expressive power of the ODP Enterprise Language [10], its foundation in deontic concepts, and pragmatic translation of these into implementable software artifacts. Our approach is to express these foundational concepts in a programming language independent framework using modern DSL technologies and tooling, such as Xtext [27] and textX [3], as will be discussed in Sect. 5.

3.3 Human and AI Agent Interactions Tracing Accountability

As enterprise applications become more complex, they increasingly involve a mix of human and automated actors, including AI agents, as introduced above. While AI's replacement of human actors may not change the essential behavioural characteristics of the tasks performed, this integration raises critical accountability questions, particularly regarding legal responsibility in human-AI interactions.

Humans can take on two roles in the world of AI [17]. They can be AI creators, designing agents to achieve specific goals and deliver value, as for example developers structuring crewAI application. Alternatively, they can be users who engage existing agents to perform tasks on their behalf, potentially even delegating decision-making authority. Delegation is the first class concept in the principal-agent relationship in economics and law, where one party hires another to act on their behalf. We note that it is also possible for AI agents to delegate their tasks to other AI agents, potentially passing authorisation that was created by their originating principals.

The concepts of authorization, delegation, principal and agent are some of the key accountability modelling concepts defined in the ODP-EL standard [10] and built based on the precise expression of behavioural constraints over actions of objects in the system, and we will use them as a basis for our DSL. We note that the ODP-EL, as other ODP languages, are defined in an abstract way, without commitment to any notation [13], although the ODP family of standards include separate, UML based expression, referred to as UML profile for ODP [2]. Next section provides a summary of some of the key ODP-EL concepts which we use within our DSL.

4 Key ODP Enterprise Language Concepts

4.1 Community

The ODP Enterprise Language (EL) defines the organizational, business and social context in which an IT system is designed, deployed and operated. The main structuring concept here is that of a community, which is a grouping of interested parties to collaborate and satisfy their own and the objective of the community. The objective is defined as a "practical advantage or intended effect, expressed as preferences about future states" [10], emphasising the need to express the objective in measurable terms.

Party is defined as an enterprise object modelling a natural person or any other entity considered to have some of the rights, powers and duties of a natural person [10]. Examples of parties include enterprise objects representing natural persons, legal entities, governments and their parts, and other associations or groups of natural persons. It is important to highlight that parties are responsible for their actions and the actions of their agents.

Therefore, parties, such as IT system providers, service providers and customers, along with the automated systems that support their activities, can participate in a community. Note that the ODP uses the term active enterprise object to model an enterprise object that can be involved in some behaviour. So, community is defined through a community contract, which specifies roles in the community and their expected behaviour to be fulfilled by parties or IT systems (i.e. active enterprise objects), along the constrains on that behaviour. These constraints are typically expressed in terms of rules, such as permissions, prohibitions, obligations and authorisations. There can be also rules that apply across several roles in a community such as the constraints that support separation of duty policies.

A complete enterprise language specification would typically involved several communities, which can be nested or federated (this forming a larger community) and parties can fulfill roles in a number of communities. The use of community pattern supports design re-usability, so that many different parties can participate in the community in one or several instances of communities, instantiated from the community contract (as a template). A community can also evolve, by dynamically adding another role or policy rules.

4.2 Deontic Tokens

The ODP-EL considers obligations, permissions and prohibitions, known as deontic concepts, as fundamental constraints over behaviour of parties. Their semantics is grounded in the deontic logic and normative systems formalism but the standard takes a pragmatic approach to handling these constraints, by applying them to the actions of roles in the community, and thus the object that fulfill them. This is done through bringing the concept of a deontic token which encapsulates these deontic constraints as introduced in [14] and further specified in the standard [10].

The holding of the deontic tokens by active enterprise objects constrains their behaviour. This modelling approach provides a basis for manipulating deontic tokens, for example, passing them between parties to model delegations, and activation or de-activation of policies that apply to the active enterprise objects interactions.

Three types of deontic tokens encapsulate deontic constraints. These are called: burden—representing an obligation, permit—representing permission, and embargo—representing prohibition. In the case of a burden, an active enterprise object holding the burden must attempt to discharge it either directly by performing the specified behaviour or indirectly by engaging some other object to take possession of the burden and perform the specified behaviour. In the case of a permit, an active enterprise object holding the permit is able to perform some specified piece of behaviour, while in the case of an embargo, the object holding the embargo is inhibited from performing the behaviour.

It is to be noted that some actions, referred to as *performative actions*, change the state of the system, such as when one party has authorized another party to do actions on their behalf. In ODP-EL, these actions are referred to as *speech acts*, and they indicate when an action will modify the set of tokens held by the enterprise objects in questions [10,14]. This supports the description of the chain of obligations, permissions or prohibitions across the parties and active enterprise objects, such as AI agents, which we are using in this paper.

Deontic tokens have similarity with the widely used security tokens implementations, such as access tokens in OAuth2.0, and with new OAuth 2.0 Token Exchange specification [12] providing further capabilities for secure exchange of tokens, including support for delegation, as will be discussed in Sect. 6.2.

4.3 Accountability Actions

While deontic constraints are important as a way of implementing constraints over system actions, such as for example in access control, or monitor obligations associated with contracts or compliance regulations, there is further benefit in providing high level of abstraction that are more directly related to the expression of social or organizational responsibility. For that purpose, a family of concepts for expressing responsibility is introduced, called accountability concepts. They support traceability of obligations in the overlapping and interacting communities that form the enterprise, allowing linking the rights and responsibilities of parties to the individual system actions and their consequences [13].

The concept of party is introduced above and it is significant to note that parties can have intentions and are accountable for their actions [10]. Those actions that involve accountability, identified by ODP-EL, are listed next.

Authorization is an action indicating that a particular behaviour shall not be prevented. Unlike a permission, an authorization is an empowerment. The fact that an enterprise object has performed an authorization is expressed by it issuing a required permit and itself undertaking a burden describing its obligation to facilitate the behaviour.

Delegation is the action that assigns something, such as authorization, responsibility or provision of a service to another object. The ODP-EL adopts the language from agency theory to refer to the delegated object as an agent, and to a party that has delegated something (e.g. authorization or provision of service), as a principal. The agent is modelled as an active enterprise object that has been delegated something by, and acts for, a party (e.g. in exercising the authorization, carrying out responsibility). A principal is responsible for the actions of an object acting as an agent. We note that this object can in turn further delegate to another object, if authorised by the principal, thus forming another linked delegation. The first enterprise object in that chain of delegations is the party that is the root of accountability.

Commitment is defined as an action resulting in an obligation by one or more participants in the act to comply with a rule or perform a contract. This effectively means that they will be assigned a burden. Examples include commitments by clinicians to deliver safe, reliable and effective healthcare to patients.

Declaration is defined as an action by which an object makes facts known in its environment and establishes a new state of affairs in its environment. This can, for example, be performed by an AI system (or a party managing it), for example, informing the interested parties about the result of some analysis.

Evaluation is defined as an action that assesses the value of something, which can considered in terms of variables such as importance, preference, usefulness.

Figure 1 shows deontic concepts as primitive constraints over behaviour, and the accountability concepts as an abstraction built on top of deontic concepts.

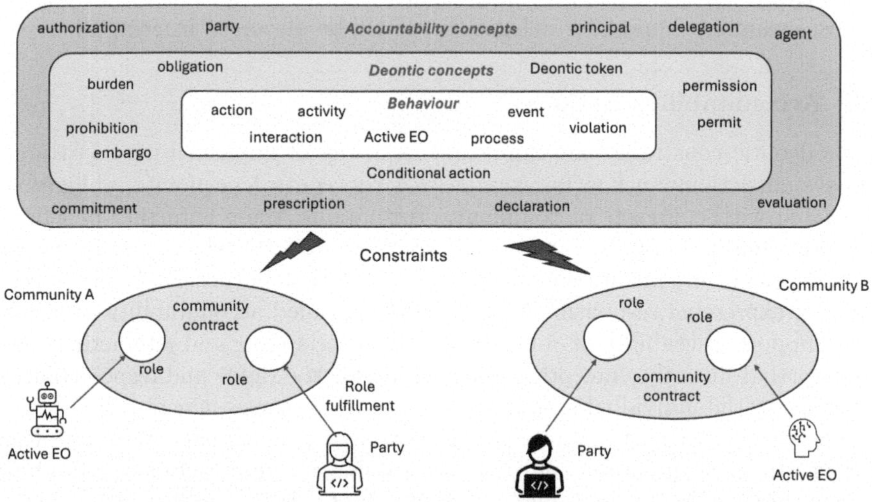

Fig. 1. Accountability and deontic concepts as behavioural constrains.

5 ODP-EL DSL

5.1 Motivations

There are many different type of multi-agent architectures, but common to them is the collaborative aspects of agents and their interactions. The reference architecture based on the ODP community template provides a precise framework for developing guidelines for enterprise design, operations and computing of complex systems which integrate Agent AI components. This is because the ODP community provides the expression of many type of organisational collaborations and interactions, including federations, which can be specified through community contracts. Such contracts also serve as a semantic foundation for a wide range of constraints associated with policies as described in Sect. 3.2.

Further, the expression of roles in community supports the description of an expected abstract behaviour to be fulfilled by entities with compatible behaviour. Initially this can be a human, but at a later stage such a function would be implemented by a system, modelled as an active enterprise object, such as an AI agent (not necessarily a LLM agent). A good example of this is a situation in pathology labs, where the pathology technicians analyse manually the blood test results, but much of that can be delegated to a clinical decision support systems (CDS).

This in turn allows for many different multi-agent proposals to be positioned in relation to the reference architecture. Such a reference architecture, benefits from the semantic precision and pragmatic decisions, developed through proven international standardisation processes, and can thus bring confidence to practitioners, system owners, architects and developers.

In our previous work we have proposed a computable policy framework for supporting privacy consent in healthcare [17], using the concept of consent community. This paper uses that framework as a basis for experimenting with the DSL to support a range of deontic and accountability concepts related to consent. The consent use case was chosen as it often includes many complex security level and (cross-)enterprise level rules which are important when designing and implementing interactions across healthcare providers from different organisational domains, with potential use of third-party services from AI vendors, while supporting policy preferences of consumers.

We begin with introducing general consent community, with the community roles of *Grantor*, the individual whose personal data is being requested, and *Grantee*, the individual or organization requesting access to data. The consent community also includes supporting roles for consent management services, including IT specific roles with no direct accountability (e.g. monitor) and policy specific roles which have accountability (e.g. consent policy maker).

The main action by *Grantee* is to submit data access request to *Grantor*, clearly stating the purpose of accessing data. The main actions by *Grantor* are to review and understand data access request details, decide whether to grant or deny access (i.e. authorization through issuing permits) and revoke (withdraw) access to their data at any time, as needed.

5.2 DSL Tooling

In the development of the DSL presented in this paper we are using textX. textX is a meta-language for building Domain-Specific Languages (DSLs) in Python. From a single language description (grammar), textX builds a parser and a metamodel (a.k.a. abstract syntax) for the language. Building on top of the Python dynamic nature, textX works as an interpreter. Both the parser and the meta-model are built on the fly during run-time. This enables a quick round-trip from the change in the grammar to the working application.

There are two approaches to designing DSLs:

- Meta-model first approach (or Abstract Syntax first). This approach, also known as top-down, starts with the abstract syntax of the language, and the concrete syntax (or syntaxes) is defined later. This route is followed by so-called projectional editing environments where the Abstract Syntax Tree (AST) is manipulated directly by the user through projections that map ASTs to concrete syntaxes presented to the user.
- Concrete Syntax first. This approach, also known as bottom-up, starts with the concrete textual syntax specified by the grammar from which the meta-model is derived. This approach is popularized by the xText tool and is also used in the textX tool which we use in our implementation.

Both approaches have their pros and cons. A good overview of these approaches is given in [25]. We have chosen the second approach as we find it more suited to our development style and background. Also, this approach is directly supported by the textX tool.

5.3 Method

Our approach here is to design a generic consent architecture following the community contract template to specify key roles, such as grantor and grantee, and use this as a starting point for extending and reifying this generic consent for clinical care purpose and for clinical research purposes.

The approach is based on expressing the key ODP-EL concepts described above in terms of language constructs familiar to the domain experts involved in defining policy rules and constraints, see Listing 1. Ideally, this would involve subject matter experts from the legislative domain but also security policy experts, including those defining access control requirements.

In parallel, we developed the language grammar and meta-model using textX tooling. The grammar and meta-model are based on the semantics of the ODP-EL concepts as they were used in our consent use case, making sure that the meta-model is compliant with the ODP-EL while also adopting certain pragmatic decisions from the language designer perspective.

5.4 Results

This section shows parts of our DSL meta-model and fragments of our consent model created using our DSL.

Listing 1 shows a community contract implementing a generic consent, which is required in many different communities. This generic consent contract defines the roles of the grantee (line 6), representing parties who ask for consent, and the grantor (line 11), representing parties who are asked to give consent. Each role owns a set of actions that can be executed by a role filling object, if an associated guard expression is satisfied. The guard expression is a logical expression written inside square brackets.

Listing 1. Generic consent community contract

```
1  community contract genericConsent {
2     objective "Support consumers privacy consent preferences"
3
4     ... <snip>...
5
6     role grantee {
7          action consent_request(data: ConsentRequestData)
8                 emits consent_requested(data: ConsentRequestData)
9     }
10
11    role grantor {
12
13         action review_request(data: ConsentRequestData) [consent_requested(data)]
14                emits consent_reviewed(data: ConsentRequestData)
15
16         authorize give_consent(data: ConsentRequestData)
17             [consent_reviewed(data) && (now - data.subject.birth_date > legal_age)]
18         {
19             permit grant(consent: ConsentRecord) on grantee [this.time + permit_valid]
20
21             burden RespectPrivacy(consent: ConsentRecord) on grantee
22                 triggered by grant_trigger
23                 discharged by [this.time + privacy_valid]
24
25             burden StoreConsentRecord(consent: ConsentRecord) on consentAuthority
26                 discharged by storeConsent(consent: ConsentRecord)
27         }
28
29         declare withdraw_consent (consent: ConsentRecord) {}
30    }
31
32 }
```

When executed, an action can emit an event. For example, the action `consent_request` on line 7 emits an event `consent_requested` carrying `ConsentRequestData`. This event can be used inside a guard condition to allow an action call only if a specific event has occurred previously. On line 13, we see that the grantor can call the action `review_request` only if the `consent_requested` event has occurred.

In the body of an authorization action (lines 18–27), three deontic tokens are created: a permit `grant` given to the grantee and valid for a duration `permit_valid`, defined by the current policy setting; a burden on the grantee to respect privacy; and a burden on the consent authority to store the consent record.

Finally, the action of withdrawing consent is modelled as ODP-EL declaration action, through which the grantor notify parties and their agents in its environment about this decision (line 29).

In order to use this generic consent contract, the DSL has an import facility whose meta-model is shown in Fig. 2. Using the import feature, a community can import generic consent and connect its roles and tokens with the roles and tokens from the generic community contract.

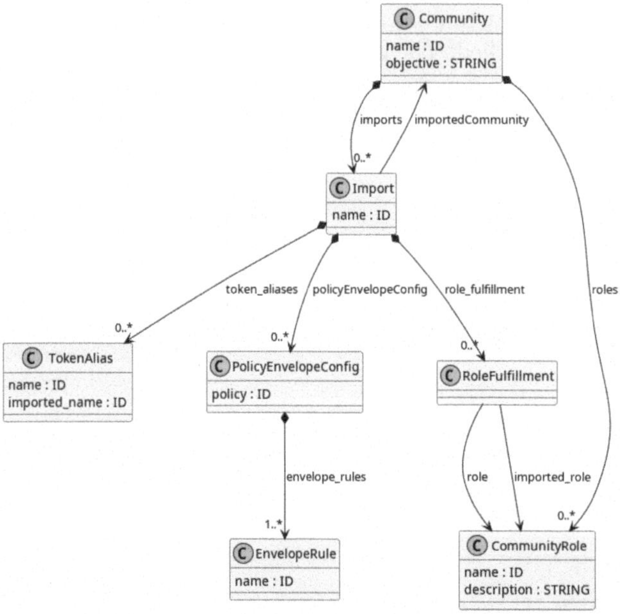

Fig. 2. Language support for community contract imports.

Listing 2. Importing generic consent to a community

```
community HealthCareConsent {
    # Importing and specializing consent authorization for HC community
    # Clinician and Consumer instantiate grantee and grantor respectively.
    # EHR (Electronic Health Record) with patient clinical data is different
    # from consentRecord
    import genericConsent as consumerHealthConsent
          Clinician fulfills grantee                # healthcare provider
          Consumer fulfills grantor                 # healthcare consumer
          AccessEHR as grant                        # alias for grant permit
          grant_trigger.envelope = {
               one of [observation_performed, emergency_arrival]
          }

    ...<snip>...
```

Listing 2 is an example of an import statement that imports `genericConsent` into `HealthCareConsent`, where the role of `Clinician` fulfills the generic role of `grantee`, while the role of `Consumer` fulfills the generic role of `grantor`. Additionally, `AccessEHR` is an alias for the generic permit `grant`. In this community, we model a scenario under which healthcare clinical research is conducted.

It should be noted that our DSL includes the expression of ODP policy concept, as also indicated in this import. ODP policy concept supports the expression of variability of design choices, that can be anticipated at the design stage and changed at a later epoch. The options available are captured through policy envelope rules. Further details of policy concept are available in [10,13].

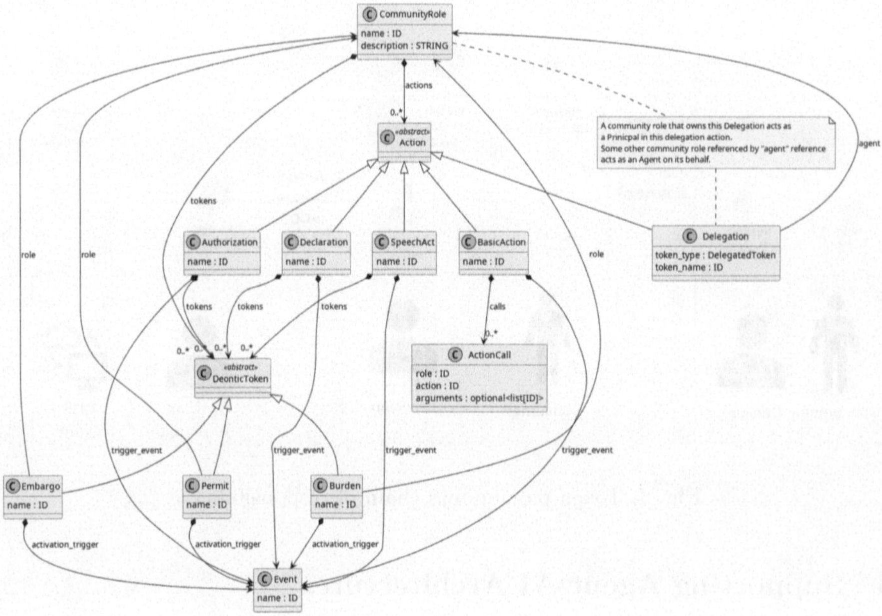

Fig. 3. Accountability and deontic language concepts.

Listing 3. Passing deontic tokens using delegation

```
delegate permit AccessEHR(consentRecord: consumerHealthConsent.ConsentRecord)
  to RecommenderService
      [consentRecord.grantorPreferences.thirdPartySharing]
```

An example of delegation of permit token in a `HealthCareConsent` community is shown in Listing 3. This delegation is specified as a part of `Clinician` role which makes the clinician a `Principal` in the delegation interaction. At the same time, the receiver of the token, a Clinical Decision Support (CDS) system named `RecommenderService`, becomes the agent of the clinician which acts on their behalf while the responsibility of the agent's actions are still on the clinician which initiated the delegation (Fig. 4). The role of the agent is an action-level role, i.e. the role is valid only during the interaction between the clinician and the CDS service.

The principal of the delegation has implicit right to withdraw the permit token at any moment. This principal-agent relation is modelled by the `agent` association between `Delegation` and `CommunitRole` concepts in the meta-model in Fig. 3. The principal is implicitly the owner and initiator of the delegation action, in this case the object fulfilling the `Clinician` community role.

Current version of the grammar/meta-model is available on GitHub under MIT license (https://github.com/igordejanovic/ODP-EL-textX).

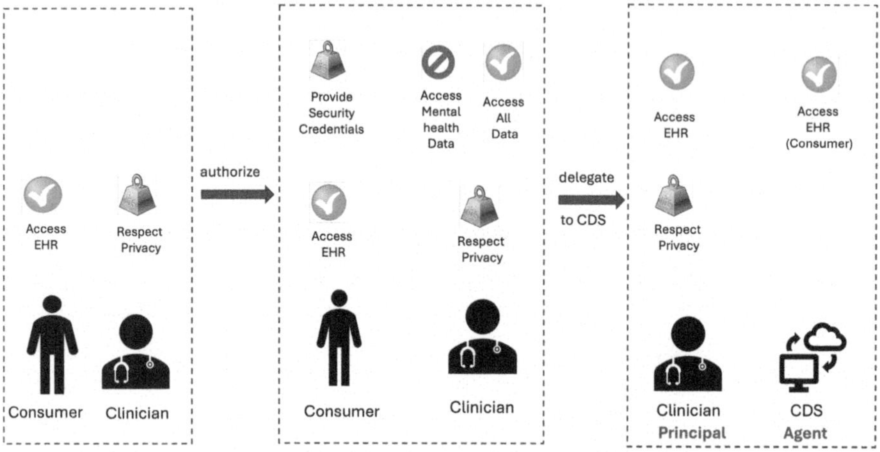

Fig. 4. Token passing and chain of responsibility

6 Supporting Agent AI Architectures

The DSL proposed provides a generic approach to expressing deontic and accountability constraints over the actions of humans and AI agents as special type of active enterprise objects, and supports modelling chains or responsibility.

6.1 Integration Architecture

One way of integrating our DSL with AI Agent architecture is shown in Fig. 5. Our DSL tooling includes a compiler which generates Python code from the DSL specification, which then runs in a Python runtime supporting the management of deontic tokens. This includes the monitoring of token passing and state change as a result of speech acts performative actions.

On the other hand, the LLM based agent architectures bring their own constraints which determine the best integration approach with our DSL tooling. For example, crewAI applications are concerned with structuring LLM applications in terms of AI agents which can collaborate, according to the constraints stated in their configuration definition.

The crewAI Agents are tightly linked to the crewAI runtime and the Python's interpreter, performing their goal-oriented reasoning using LLMs interactions, and actions using configured tools. Computational agents there are not aware of deontic tokens and requirements imposed by our DSL and runtime.

This means that the best integration approach with our DSL is through the use of our runtime created from the DSL to monitor the life-cycle of deontic tokens (Fig. 5). This is our generic approach to support deontic token functionality to other systems, which also requires exposing the deontic tokens management via an API. This is also an approach we adopted in linking with the crewAI system, where our API is accessed by crewAI Agents using a provided tool. This has required adding the tool functionality to crewAI system, to support querying and handling of tokens through our token management API.

Fig. 5. DSL integration with Agent AI architecture: example

6.2 Discussions

Applying a generic DSL for ODP-EL to LLM-based agents presents several challenges. Firstly, their nondeterministic nature (that are dealt by agent architectures through the mechanism of reflection and continual plan updates) would suggest initial adoption of pessimistic enforcement strategy for violation of their accountability actions. It is also possible to support optimistic approaches but these would require sophisticated monitoring mechanisms, which are particularly difficult when monitoring obligations [13]. These mechanisms may rely on human oversight, in a similar way when monitoring behaviour associated with obligations in business contracts [15], or use of AI explainability tools.

The nature of deontic tokens, reflecting their different deontic modalities, requires different mechanisms for their handling in distributed systems. A permit typically benefits its holder, who needs to keep and present it when accessing resources that require possession of the permit. For example, a ticket to a football game is issued to the buyer, who must present the ticket at the stadium entrance. Thus, permit tokens can be distributed to their owners. It is to be noted that permits have broader scope than access tokens developed for granting access to specific resources or APIs in web applications, using OAuth2.0 authorisation protocol, the specific example of which is JSON Web Token (JWT) [11].

On the other hand, burden and embargo tokens are associated with parties that have no incentive to keep or present them. In fact, these parties have an incentive to dispose of these tokens. A good example would be a traffic ticket. Therefore, these tokens must be stored in a central repository where interested parties with the appropriate credentials can verify whether the entities they are interacting with are constrained by any of these tokens.

These general considerations need to be taken into account when integrating with potential future distributed, agent AI architectures.

7 Conclusions and Future Work

This paper proposes a new method for formalising and tracking responsibility in complex enterprise systems involving both humans and AI agents. We achieve this by creating a domain specific language based on ODP-EL concepts. This standard-based language aims to support current and future AI architectures.

Our approach leverages the strengths of ODP-EL while utilizing modern DSL tools for faster development, deployment, and ongoing management of the system. Our emphasis on the precise expression and implementation support for accountability constrains over actions of the parties, and the associated chain of responsibility, is one of the first formal, yet pragmatic frameworks amenable to the contemporary software engineering practices, including user-oriented expressions of their requirements. We demonstrate its effectiveness by applying it to a digital health privacy consent use case.

Our implementation efforts have identified several challenges, arising from the stochastic properties of LLM systems as well as difficulties with monitoring obligations in distributed systems. We will monitor future developments in Agentic systems, and will accordingly update our DSL integration patterns with such architectures.

Our current language supports a set of key ODP-EL concepts, as driven by our digital health consent use case. Our plan is to implement several other concepts such as evaluation and prescription and do a full evaluation with users through several use cases. For example, we are considering applying our DSL to specific industrial applications, including digital twins [18], while leveraging our previous work on the monitoring of obligations in business contracts [15].

We also plan to develop integration of our DSL tooling with specific distributed architecture in health, such as FHIR [6,7]. This can be supported through a Mediator component that would encapsulate the logic for interacting with both the policy engine, which implements our policy language and the FHIR server, which includes a FHIR Consent Resource, similarly to what we used for integration with crewAI. We will also be investigating whether the deontic and accountability concepts can be mapped onto various FHIR Resources and workflow patterns, as a way of enhancing business process modelling with policy constraints, in initiatives such as eRequesting in Australia [1].

Acknowledgements. We would like to express our sincere thanks to Peter Linington for his thought leadership and generous support in shaping the semantics of ODP Enterprise Language, which has also influenced our research.

References

1. HL7 Australia - AU eRequesting Technical Design Group Home - HL7 Australia - FHIR Work Group - Confluence. https://confluence.hl7.org/display/HAFWG/HL7+Australia+-+AU+eRequesting+Technical+Design+Group+Home
2. ISO/IEC IS 19793, Information Technology—Open Distributed Processing—Use of UML for ODP System Specifications (2014). Also published as ITU-T Recommendation X.906

3. Dejanović, I., Dejanović, M., Vidaković, J., Nikolić, S.: Pyflies: a domain-specific language for designing experiments in psychology. Appl. Sci. **11**(17), 27 (2021). https://doi.org/10.3390/app11177823. https://www.mdpi.com/2076-3417/11/17/7823
4. Dorri, A., Kanhere, S.S., Jurdak, R.: Multi-agent systems: a survey. IEEE Access **6**, 28573–28593 (2018). https://doi.org/10.1109/ACCESS.2018.2831228
5. European Parliament, Council of the European Union: General Data Protection Regulation (GDPR) - Legal Text. https://gdpr-info.eu/
6. Fast Healthcare Interoperability Resources V5.0.0 (2023). http://hl7.org/fhir/R5/
7. Fast Healthcare Interoperability Resources: Consent (2023). https://build.fhir.org/consent.html
8. Griffo, C., Almeida, J.P.A., Guizzardi, G., Nardi, J.C.: From an ontology of service contracts to contract modeling in enterprise architecture. In: 2017 IEEE 21st international Enterprise Distributed Object Computing Conference (EDOC), pp. 40–49. IEEE (2017)
9. Hanson, J., Milosevic, Z.: Conversation-oriented protocols for contract negotiations. In: Proceedings of the Seventh IEEE International Enterprise Distributed Object Computing Conference, pp. 40–49 (2003). https://doi.org/10.1109/EDOC.2003.1233836
10. ISO/IEC IS 15414, Information Technology - Open Distributed Processing - Enterprise Language 3rd edn. (2015)
11. Jones, M., Bradley, J., Sakimura, N.: Json web token (JWT). Technical report, Internet Engineering Task Force (IETF) (2015). https://datatracker.ietf.org/doc/html/rfc7519
12. Jones, M.B., Nadalin, A., Campbell, B., Bradley, J., Mortimore, C.: OAuth 2.0 Token Exchange. Request for Comments RFC 8693, Internet Engineering Task Force, p. 27 (2020). https://doi.org/10.17487/RFC8693. https://datatracker.ietf.org/doc/rfc8693
13. Linington, P.F., Milosevic, Z., Tanaka, A., Vallecillo, A.: Building Enterprise Systems with ODP: An Introduction to Open Distributed Processing, 1st edn. Chapman&Hall/CRC Innovations in Software Engineering and Software Development (2011)
14. Linington, P.F., Miyazaki, H., Vallecillo, A.: Obligations and delegation in the ODP enterprise language. In: IEEE 16th International Enterprise Distributed Computing conference (2012)
15. Linington, P., Milosevic, Z., Cole, J., Gibson, S., Kulkarni, S., Neal, S.: A unified behavioural model and a contract language for extended enterprise. Data Knowl. Eng. **51**(1), 5–29 (2004). https://doi.org/10.1016/j.datak.2004.03.005. https://www.sciencedirect.com/science/article/pii/S0169023X0400031X, contact-driven coordination and collaboration in the Internet context
16. Milosevic, Z.: Ethics in digital health: a deontic accountability framework. In: 2019 IEEE 23rd International Enterprise Distributed Object Computing Conference (EDOC), pp. 105–111 (2019). https://doi.org/10.1109/EDOC.2019.00022
17. Milosevic, Z.: Enacting policies in digital health: a case for smart legal contracts and distributed ledgers? Knowl. Eng. Rev. **35**, e6 (2020). https://doi.org/10.1017/S0269888920000089
18. Milosevic, Z., van Schalkwyk, P.: Towards responsible digital twins. In: Sales, T.P., de Kinderen, S., Proper, H.A., Pufahl, L., Karastoyanova, D., van Sinderen, M. (eds.) Enterprise Design, Operations, and Computing. EDOC 2023 Workshops, pp. 123–138. Springer, Cham (2024)

19. Mitrovic, D., Ivanovic, M., Vidakovic, M., Budimac, Z.: Siebog: an enterprise-scale multiagent middleware. Inf. Technol. Control **45**(2), 164–174 (2016)
20. Moura, J.: joaomdmoura/crewAI (2024). https://github.com/joaomdmoura/crewAI, original-date: 2023-10-27T03:26:59Z
21. Ng, A.: Four AI Agent Strategies That Improve GPT-4 and GPT-3.5 Performance (2024). https://www.deeplearning.ai/the-batch/how-agents-can-improve-llm-performance/
22. Park, J.S., O'Brien, J.C., Cai, C.J., Morris, M.R., Liang, P., Bernstein, M.S.: Generative agents: Interactive simulacra of human behavior (2023). https://arxiv.org/abs/2304.03442
23. Recommendation, W.: ODRL information model 2.2 (2018). https://www.w3.org/TR/odrl-model/
24. Sredojević, D., Vidaković, M., Ivanović, M.: Alas: agent-oriented domain-specific language for the development of intelligent distributed non-axiomatic reasoning agents. Enterprise Inf. Syst. **12**(8–9), 1058–1082 (2018)
25. Volter, M.: From programming to modeling-and back again. IEEE Softw. **28**(6), 20–25 (2011)
26. Wu, Q., et al.: AutoGen: enabling next-gen LLM applications via multi-agent conversation. Technical report, MSR-TR-2023-33, Microsoft (2023). https://www.microsoft.com/en-us/research/publication/autogen-enabling-next-gen-llm-applications-via-multi-agent-conversation-framework/
27. Language Engineering for Everyone! (2015). https://eclipse.dev/Xtext/index.html

BPM and WFM

A Tree-Based Definition of Business Process Conformance

Sylvain Hallé(✉)

Laboratoire d'informatique formelle, Université du Québec à Chicoutimi, Saguenay, Canada
shalle@acm.org

Abstract. Conformance checking is a process that typically produces a binary pass/fail verdict. Yet, there exist situations where it is desirable to qualify the extent to which the execution of a process satisfies or violates a given condition. To this end, the paper proposes a relation on event traces that compares the tree resulting from the evaluation of a conformance condition on each of them. This relation neither requires Boolean conditions to be rewritten or adapted, nor expects additional information (such as weights) from the user.

1 Introduction

Conformance checking refers to the task of assessing whether the execution of an information system satisfies a set of conditions stipulating its expected behavior [17]; the process has at times also been labelled as compliance [12,22]. Under different names, this concept can be found in a variety of situations; for instance, it can be used to determine if a business process log follows business rules [3,7, 29,30], to check that the execution of a computer program is exempt from bugs or security policy violations [5], or to verify that a web service is used according to a specified protocol [10,20,33]. To a large extent, even the symbolic pattern matching used by some types of intrusion detection systems can be seen as a form of (anti-) conformance checking [36].

In its simplest form, the result produced by a conformance checking procedure is a Boolean verdict. This all-or-nothing behavior has long been identified as a limitation to the usefulness of such techniques in practice, due to the scarce information provided to a user as to the cause of a violation, its location in the execution of the system, and possibly the severity or impact of this violation on the global operation of the system. Consequently, various approaches have been proposed to complement or replace a true/false verdict with additional elements aimed at facilitating diagnostics: aligning an execution to a process model to identify points of discrepancy [37], identifying subsets of an execution or a property that explain a violation [14,18], or replacing a conformance condition with more general queries on a process log [34].

However, there exist situations where a user may not be interested in locating the source of an error, but rather to assess to what extent a condition has been satisfied or violated. For instance, a process that inverts the expected order of a few operations a few times should be given lower troubleshooting priority than

J. Borbinha et al. (Eds.): EDOC 2024, LNCS 15409, pp. 41–59, 2025.
https://doi.org/10.1007/978-3-031-78338-8_3

another that regularly performs operations out of order. In Sect. 2, we shall see that a few approaches have been put forward to replace a two-valued verdict with a finer-grained scale to which executions of a system can be mapped, and thus ordered; for most of them, that scale is a closed interval of real numbers. However, these techniques require one to explicitly define counters and fine-tune user-defined thresholds, and the numerical result can be likened to a form of "percentage of violation", but its exact semantics is typically difficult to grasp.

After Sect. 3 provides a formal model for expressing conditions on event sequences, Sect. 4 proposes an alternate approach to conformance based on a different premise. Instead of attempting to assign a (seldom meaningful) number to each run of a system, it suggests the use of a relation that simply compares two executions, stating whether one of the two is preferable to the other. It does so by comparing tree structures resulting from the evaluation of a condition written in LTL.

This evaluation procedure has been implemented into a tool that is described in Sect. 5. Experiments show that the proposed relation can efficiently compare executions in logs and on constraints extracted from real-world scenarios. This opens the way to multiple applications and extensions of this principle, which are discussed in Sect. 6.

2 The Need for Finer-Grained Conformance Verdicts

The execution of a system or process can be symbolically represented by a sequence (also called a trace) of data elements representing different operations or actions occurring at different times. A conformance property is a condition on such an execution that is answered with true or false: either the sequence is conforming, or it is not. For example, a statement such as "every received message must be handled with a reply within 24 h" admits only two verdicts, since a message is either dealt with on time or not, even if only by one minute. Such conditions, formulated in this way, do not allow for a "gray area". In this section, we first illustrate situations where a notion of "partial satisfaction" would be appropriate, and then survey the various works that attempted to tackle this problem.

2.1 Motivation

It is important from the outset to clarify what is meant by the notion of "degrees" of satisfaction or violation of a property, which can be confused with other situations. For example, one might think that a condition like "every received message must be replied to within 24 h, with a maximum of one exception" admits multiple degrees of satisfaction. However, this is not the case: it is indeed a property that adds one exception to the rule stated above, but we remain in the Boolean domain—either at least one message is replied to late, or not. There are no more degrees of satisfaction of this condition than in the previous case.

The same applies to Service Level Agreements (SLAs), whose terms are often expressed in the form of a series of levels describing the quality of service promised to a consumer. Thus, one could define Tier 1 of a web hosting service as promising 99.9% uptime, while Tiers 2 and 3 would provide 99% and 90%, respectively. However, what appears to be degrees of satisfaction of a condition is in reality simulated by the overlap of a chain of conditions, each being Boolean in nature (either the service reaches the announced threshold or not) and logically implying the next. What we seek to do is the opposite: state a *single* condition, which at any moment is either true or false, but somehow manage to distinguish multiple degrees of satisfaction or violation.

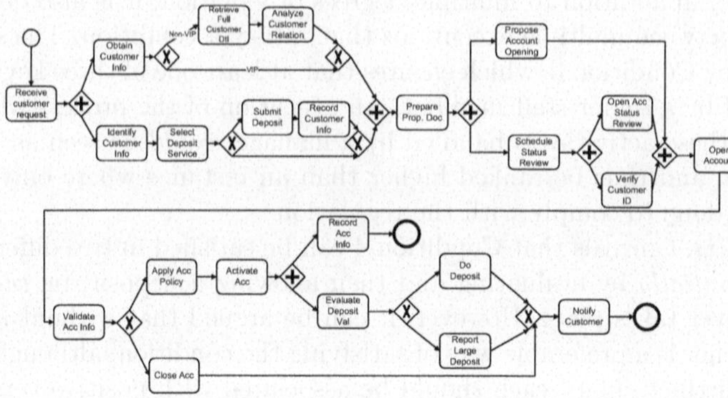

Fig. 1. A BPMN diagram for a banking process; figure reproduced from [2].

As a running example, we consider the business process model taken from [26], illustrated in Fig. 1. It describes the process of creating a new account for a customer and making an initial deposit into it, following the banking regulations imposed by the People's Bank of China. The process has been used in past works on business process conformance (e.g. [2,22]) and is subject to a wide array of potential constraints; however for the purpose of this paper, we shall focus on four such constraints, listed below:

1. No account must be open without first obtaining and verifying customer information.
2. For VIP customers, an account should be open at most one week after the request.
3. A manager must perform either the preparation of the documentation, the opening of the account or the validation of the account.
4. A deposit must be immediately preceded by an evaluation of its amount.

An execution of the process violates Condition 1 either because it is missing the *obtain* action or the *verify* action. However, one could argue that an execution where both of these activities are absent is an even greater violation of the condition. Thus, if evaluating Condition 1 on the former produces the "false" outcome, evaluating it on the latter should produce an even "falser" value. This highlights the need for more than one verdict indicating the violation of a condition.

On its side, Condition 2 is violated when a VIP customer is not given an account in the expected delay. Yet, missing the delay by one hour is probably less detrimental than exceeding it by one week. Here again, multiple levels of violation would allow making such a distinction. Conversely, the condition is satisfied if the account if created on time; however, one could argue that the quicker the account is created, the better; a client getting their account in one day shows a higher quality of service than if their request is being answered at the last possible moment.

Therefore, in addition to multiple degrees of violation, it is also desirable to distinguish between multiple executions that satisfy a condition. The same idea is conveyed by Condition 3, which ensures that at least one of three key activities is conducted by a senior staff member. An execution of the process where more than one of these activities is handled by a manager could be seen as exceeding expectations, and thus be ranked higher than an instance where only the bare minimum is done to comply with the regulation.

Finally, Fig. 1 reveals that Condition 4 can be satisfied in two different ways: either *substantially* by evaluating and then allowing a deposit, or *vacuously* if no deposit ever takes place. However, it can be argued that without additional context, neither is a preferable way of satisfying the condition, although they are essentially distinct. Thus, each should be associated with positive verdicts, but without these verdicts necessarily being comparable. The same can be said, at a higher level, of two non-conformant instances of the process violating a different condition from the list. It would be ill-advised to arbitrarily declare one violation to be worse than another —which highlights the need for uncomparable negative verdicts as well.

2.2 Related Work

Early work has focused on the study of *similarity metrics* between event sequences [13,31]. In this context, two sequences of events are more or less "similar" depending on the amount of edit operations that need to be applied in order to turn one sequence into the other. However, similarity is blind to any notion of correctness with respect to a condition; it is only possible to tell how far apart are two execution sequences. Moreover, events are considered as atomic symbols, so differences in parameters are not taken into account (except for the case of timestamps in [31]).

The degree to which a trace satisfies a specific process description can first be quantified by finding an *alignment*, which can be summarized as a mapping between contiguous events of a trace and contiguous transitions in a process model [37]. Discontinuities in an alignment (e.g. swapping, inserting or deleting an event) indicate a discrepancy between the trace and the model, and such discontinuities can be counted and used as numerical measure of deviation. A similar approach consists of calculating the distance between a target event trace with a set traces used as a reference [27].

On their side, *grey security policies* are conditions on a sequence of events that produce a real value in the unit interval [35]. For example, a condition that states that every file that is open must eventually be closed would assign a score to a trace depending on the number of open files that have not been closed. However, conditions are expressed in an *ad hoc* manner using user-defined counters or other devices providing a numerical outcome, which are specific to each situation. TK-LTL attempts to resolve the issue by providing an extension of Linear Temporal Logic that allows users to write assertions on the number of times a given condition is satisfied [23].

Similarly, fuzzy LTL is an extension of LTL where the truth value of a proposition is replaced by a real number between 0 and 1 [25]. However, non-Boolean verdict is only obtained if the ground terms of an expression take a fractional value; therefore, its measure represents imprecise observations, but not partial satisfaction. Another real-valued semantics of LTL is proposed [4], in which, for example, a temporal operator stating that a condition is always true is relaxed so that it can be false “a few times” without compromising satisfaction. One can also consider the conformance of an execution across multiple dimensions (e.g. time, ordering, cost) and evaluate a user-defined metric on the unit interval on each dimension; those values can then be aggregated to obtain a genral conformance score [24].

When considering properties admitting compensation (such as the case of deontic logic) one can distinguish between executions that are *ideal* (the main condition is fulfilled), *sub-ideal* (the condition is violated, but the stipulated compensation was duly executed) and *non-ideal* (a mandatory compensation was not executed) [28]. The count of possible executions in a business process model belonging to each category can form the basis of a numerical compliance metric, again in $[0, 1]$.

Finally, *informativeness* is a measure that is associated to a trace depending on the number of “non-essential events” it contains, i.e. events that can be removed from a trace without compromising conformance [6]. It was introduced in the context of process mining, in order to quantify the extent to which an execution trace reveals information about optional paths in a process model. However, it presents the downside of only applying to conforming traces, and requires the user to manually assign weights to each event.

2.3 Limitations of Existing Approaches

All these approaches provide a way to quantify, or at the very least, allow some degree of comparison between multiple event traces, and therefore offer a verdict that is arguably more detailed than a simple pass/fail response. That said, they come with several limitations, which we detail below.

With the exception of informativeness, the aforementioned approaches do not distinguish between successful executions. Indeed, a conforming trace has no discontinuity when searching for an alignment with a process model, and logic-based formalisms producing a numerical truth value map all satisfying traces to 1. Yet, we have seen in the examples above that there is value in distinguishing a process that barely conforms with a regulation from another one that largely fulfills expectations. Moreover, many of these approaches consider events as atomic symbols, or otherwise only focus on the order in which the events are observed. This does not allow for measuring deviations from other types of conditions, such as those related to the values of parameters that these events might contain.

In some cases, a condition that was originally expressed as a true/false assertion must be rewritten by the user so that a more detailed verdict can be returned. For example, in the context of TK-LTL, it is indeed possible to relax the condition "every opened file must be closed" to "there are no more than 1% of files that are not closed," but this is only achieved by replacing the original specification with a completely different expression where the count of files and the expected fraction are explicitly mentioned.

More surprisingly, it can also be considered a problem that these approaches associate traces with numerical values, for several reasons. First, calculating this value is generally complex and its precise meaning often eludes intuition. Furthermore, mapping traces to numbers can lead to improper interpretations, such as the fact that an execution obtaining a score of $1/4$ is "half as true" as another with a verdict of $1/2$.

Finally, the last problem lies in the fact that the set of real numbers is subject to a total order, which implies that for any two distinct traces, one of them is always ranked lower than the other —even in situations where this comparison is not appropriate. Consider for example the simple case of the statement $a \wedge b$. According to the semantics of existing works, an execution that satisfies a but not b is equivalent (i.e. is scored identically) to an execution that does the opposite, since both fail for "half" of their arguments. Manually defined weights can give higher precedence to one of the terms, but the eventuality that these two types of failures are simply distinct and incomparable cannot be accounted for.

3 Conditions on Event Sequences

We start by briefly describing the formal foundations of conformance used in this paper. With the exception of evaluation trees (Sect. 3.3), these notions have already been presented and used in past works about conformance, and thus this section should be seen as a quick refresher.

3.1 Event Model

Let P be an arbitrary set of parameter *names*, and V be a set of *values*. An event is modeled as a total function $e : P \to V$, which maps every parameter to a value. We reserve a special symbol # to represent the fact that no value is assigned to a parameter (i.e. that it is absent from an event). Suppose for example that $P = \{\mathsf{a}, \mathsf{b}, \mathsf{c}\}$ is the set of parameter names and their values are natural numbers (i.e. $V = \mathbb{N}$). The fact that an event assigns the value 3 to a and the value 1 to c, leaving b undefined, shall be denoted by $\{\mathsf{a} \mapsto 3, \mathsf{c} \mapsto 1\}$.

We suppose that the execution of a process produces a finite sequence of events $\overline{e} = e_0, \dots, e_k$ called an event *trace*. We denote by $\mathcal{E}^*$ the set of all finite traces of events. Following conventions, the notation $\overline{e}[i]$ will designate the i-th event of $\overline{e}$ (indices starting at 0), $\overline{e}[i..]$ will stand for the suffix of $\overline{e}$ that starts at index i, while $\overline{e}[..i]$ will stand for the prefix of $\overline{e}$ that ends at index i. The length of $\overline{e}$ is noted $|\overline{e}|$, and ϵ designates the unique trace of length 0.

3.2 Linear Temporal Logic

In order to express conditions on what constitute valid traces, we take up an existing logical formalism called Linear Temporal Logic (LTL). A sequence of events $\overline{e}$ is said to satisfy an expression φ, noted $\overline{e} \models \varphi$, if it follows the semantic rules shown in Table 1. In this table, p denotes an arbitrary predicate evaluated on concrete arguments $\pi_1, \ldots, \pi_n$.

Table 1. The formal semantics of LTL with past operators.

$$\overline{e} \models p(\pi_1, \ldots, \pi_n) \Leftrightarrow p(\pi_1, \ldots, \pi_n) \text{ holds in } \overline{e}[0]$$
$$\overline{e} \models \neg\varphi \Leftrightarrow \overline{e} \not\models \varphi$$
$$\overline{e} \models \varphi \wedge \psi \Leftrightarrow \overline{e} \models \varphi \text{ and } \overline{e} \models \psi$$
$$\overline{e} \models \mathbf{X}\,\varphi \Leftrightarrow \overline{e}[1..] \models \varphi$$
$$\overline{e} \models \mathbf{G}\,\varphi \Leftrightarrow \overline{e}[i..] \models \varphi \text{ for every } i \in [0, |\overline{e}| - 1]$$
$$\overline{e} \models \mathbf{Y}\,\varphi \Leftrightarrow \overline{e}[..|\overline{e}| - 2] \models \varphi$$
$$\overline{e} \models \mathbf{H}\,\varphi \Leftrightarrow \overline{e}[..i] \models \varphi \text{ for every } i \in [0, |\overline{e}| - 1]$$

Boolean connectives have their usual meaning. The temporal operator **G** means "globally". For example, the formula $\mathbf{G}\,\varphi$ means that formula φ is true in every suffix of the trace, starting from the current event. The operator **X** means "next"; it is true whenever φ holds in the suffix starting at the next event of the trace. Operators **H** ("historically") and **Y** ("yesterday") are the past duals of **G** and **X**: $\mathbf{H}\,\varphi$ holds for some trace $\overline{e}$ if φ holds in every prefix of $\overline{e}$, while $\mathbf{Y}\,\varphi$ holds if φ holds for the prefix of $\overline{e}$ that omits the last event. The definition of the remaining connectives and operators is obtained through the classical identities.[1] The presence of past-time modalities does not increase the expressiveness of the language, but are sufficient to express the "until" modality using a mix of unary future and past operators, since $\varphi\,\mathbf{U}\,\psi$ can be rewritten as $\mathbf{F}(\psi \wedge \mathbf{H}\,\varphi)$. A specific semantics needs to be specified for these operators in the case of an empty trace; we follow conventional definitions assuming that $\epsilon \models \mathbf{G}\,\varphi$, $\epsilon \not\models \mathbf{X}\,\varphi$, and dually for their past equivalents. This setup it is expressive enough for a wide range of constraints, including temporal patterns for finite-state specifications [11], as well as specification languages whose semantics is grounded in LTL, such as ConDec [32] or DECLARE [1].

We can revisit the conditions of the bank process of Sect. 2.1 and express them as LTL expressions. We assume that each event in the process has attributes respectively representing the name of the activity being executed (a), the status

[1] Namely: $\varphi \vee \psi \equiv \neg(\neg\varphi \wedge \neg\psi)$, $\varphi \rightarrow \psi \equiv \neg\varphi \vee \psi$, $\mathbf{F}\,\varphi \equiv \neg\,\mathbf{G}\,\neg\varphi$, and $\mathbf{O}\,\varphi \equiv \neg\,\mathbf{H}\,\neg\varphi$.

of the client in this process instance (s), the seniority level of the employee performing the activity (ℓ), and the time elapsed since the reception of the original request (τ).

1. $\mathbf{H}\,(\mathsf{a} = \text{“open”} \rightarrow (\mathbf{O}\,(\mathsf{a} = \text{“obtain”}) \wedge \mathbf{O}\,(\mathsf{a} = \text{“verify”})))$
2. $\mathsf{s} = \text{“VIP”} \rightarrow (\mathbf{G}\,(\mathsf{a} = \text{“open”} \rightarrow \tau < 2))$
3. $\mathbf{F}\,(\ell = \text{“manager”} \wedge \mathsf{a} = \text{“prepare”}) \vee \mathbf{F}\,(\ell = \text{“manager”} \wedge \mathsf{a} = \text{“open”}) \vee \mathbf{F}\,(\ell = \text{“manager”} \wedge \mathsf{a} = \text{“validate”})$
4. $\mathbf{H}\,(\mathsf{a} = \text{“deposit”} \rightarrow \mathbf{Y}\,\mathsf{a} = \text{“evaluate”})$

3.3 Evaluation Trees

The recursive evaluation of an LTL expression on a sequence of events induces a tree structure that can be leveraged to compare two executions of a given process or system, which we shall call the *evaluation tree*. In this context, an evaluation tree node can be represented as a vector of the form $t = \langle \ell, [t_1, \dots, t_n] \rangle$, where ℓ is an arbitrary textual label, and the t_i are themselves tree nodes corresponding to the children of t (for a leaf node, the list is simply empty). Given a trace $\overline{e}$ and an LTL expression φ, the evaluation tree of φ on $\overline{e}$, noted $\tau(\varphi, \overline{e})$, is the tree structure resulting from the recursive application of the rules specified in Table 2.

Table 2. Definition of the evaluation tree for an LTL expression evaluated on a trace.

$$\begin{aligned}
\tau(\overline{e}, p(\pi_1, \dots, \pi_n)) &= \langle p, [\pi_1, \dots, \pi_n] \rangle\\
\tau(\overline{e}, \neg\varphi) &= \langle \neg, [\tau(\overline{e}, \varphi)] \rangle\\
\tau(\overline{e}, \varphi_1 \wedge \dots \wedge \varphi_n) &= \langle \wedge, [\tau(\overline{e}, \varphi_1), \dots, \tau(\overline{e}, \varphi_n)] \rangle\\
\tau(\overline{e}, \varphi_1 \vee \dots \wedge \varphi_n) &= \langle \vee, [\tau(\overline{e}, \varphi_1), \dots, \tau(\overline{e}, \varphi_n)] \rangle\\
\tau(\overline{e}, \mathbf{X}\,\varphi) &= \langle \mathbf{X}, [\tau(\overline{e}[1..], \varphi)] \rangle\\
\tau(\overline{e}, \mathbf{G}\,\varphi) &= \langle \mathbf{G}, [\tau(\overline{e}[0..], \varphi), \tau(\overline{e}[1..], \varphi), \dots, \tau(\overline{e}[-1], \varphi)] \rangle\\
\tau(\overline{e}, \mathbf{F}\,\varphi) &= \langle \mathbf{F}, [\tau(\overline{e}[..|\overline{e}| - 2], \varphi), \tau(\overline{e}[1..], \varphi), \dots, \tau(\overline{e}[-1], \varphi)] \rangle\\
\tau(\overline{e}, \mathbf{Y}\,\varphi) &= \langle \mathbf{Y}, [\tau(\overline{e}[1..], \varphi)] \rangle\\
\tau(\overline{e}, \mathbf{H}\,\varphi) &= \langle \mathbf{H}, [\tau(\overline{e}[..|\overline{e}| - 1], \varphi), \tau(\overline{e}[..|\overline{e}| - 2], \varphi), \dots, \tau(\overline{e}[0], \varphi)] \rangle\\
\tau(\overline{e}, \mathbf{O}\,\varphi) &= \langle \mathbf{O}, [\tau(\overline{e}[..|\overline{e}| - 1], \varphi), \tau(\overline{e}[..|\overline{e}| - 2], \varphi), \dots, \tau(\overline{e}[0], \varphi)] \rangle
\end{aligned}$$

The label of each node represents either the predicate, Boolean connective or temporal operator. The children of the nodes correspond to the recursive evaluation of the arguments. For example, in the case of a conjunction $\varphi_1 \wedge \dots \wedge \varphi_n$, children of the "$\wedge$" parent are the evaluation trees resulting from the evaluation of each φ_i. Temporal operators warrant further discussion; the case of a formula of the form $\mathbf{G}\,\varphi$ conveys the general principle followed by the remaining temporal modalities. The top-level node is labeled with $\mathbf{G}$, and the children of this node correspond to the evaluation tree of φ for all non-empty suffixes of the input trace $\overline{e}$.

Nodes can also be associated with a “color” that represents the truth value of the LTL expression they stand for. The root node of $\tau(\overline{e}, \varphi)$ will be colored either green or red, depending on whether $\overline{e} \models \varphi$ or not. Since by construction, the leaf nodes of an evaluation tree are concrete values given as arguments to a predicate, and can be constants of any type, these nodes will be left uncolored.

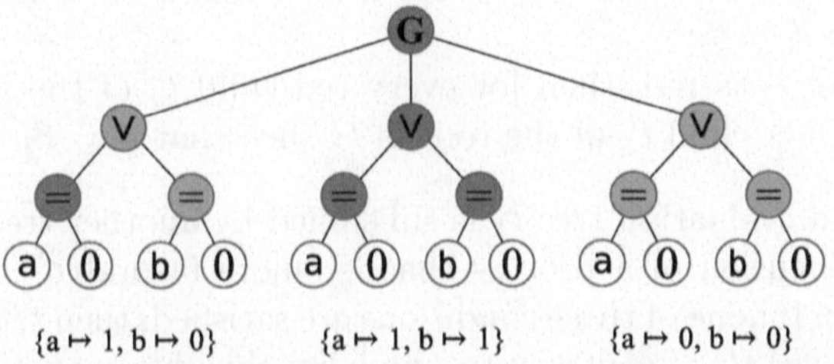

Fig. 2. An example of an evaluation tree. (Color figure online)

Figure 2 shows an example of such a colored evaluation tree, for the expression $\mathbf{G}(\mathsf{a} = 0 \vee \mathsf{b} = 0)$. It is evaluated on a trace $\overline{e}$ of three events, the value of a and b in each of them being shown at the bottom of the figure. As stipulated in Table 2, each suffix of the trace spawns a distinct subtree of the root node labeled “**G**”, where the condition $\mathsf{a} = 0 \vee \mathsf{b} = 0$ is evaluated on the first event of the suffix. The color of each node is assigned according to the satisfaction of the corresponding sub-expression.

4 A Tree-Based Definition of Conformance

As with any other logic-based formalization of valid executions, the semantics of Table 1 only outputs a pass/fail verdict. Based on the observations of the existing multi-valued verdict definitions surveyed in Sect. 2.2, we set on to propose an alternative notion of conformance with respect to a condition that addresses the issues raised in Sect. 2.3.

Since the numerical value that these approaches associate with a trace generally carries little meaning in itself, its only legitimate use lies in the fact that it can be used to compare two traces. Yet, to reach this goal, one can simply establish a *relation* (in the mathematical sense of the term) that allows one to determine, given two traces $\overline{e}$ and $\overline{e}'$, which of the two (if any) comes before the other. Therefore, we propose an alternative notion of conformance that compares the trees resulting from the evaluation of a condition. We shall first formally define this relation, and highlight its key properties through simple examples.

4.1 Definition of a Comparison Relation

In the following, without loss of generality, we assume that an LTL condition φ is expressed in Negated Normal Form (NNF). For two evaluation trees, we then define *subsumption* as follows.

Definition 1. Let $\bar{e}_1$ and $\bar{e}_2$ be two event traces, φ be an LTL formula in NNF, and t_1 and t_2 be the corresponding evaluation trees resulting from the evaluation of φ through τ. We say that t_1 is *subsumed* by t_2, noted $t_1 \sqsubseteq t_2$, if the roots of both trees have the same label, and if the following rules are satisfied:

(a) if the root of t_1 is green, then 1) the root of t_2 is green and 2) for every green child t_1' of the root of t_1, there exists a distinct child t_2' of the root of t_2 such that $t_1' \sqsubseteq t_2'$;
(b) if the root of t_1 is red, then for every red child t_2' of the root of t_2, there exists a distinct child t_1' of the root of t_1 such that $t_1' \sqsubseteq t_2'$.

Intuitively, an evaluation tree t_1 is subsumed by another tree t_2 if the latter represents an execution of a process that is "more favorable" than the former with respect to φ. If none of these conditions are satisfied, then t_1 is not subsumed by t_2; note however that, contrary to numbers, this does not imply the reverse statement (i.e. that t_2 is subsumed by t_1). We shall note $t_1 \sqsubset t_2$ when $t_1 \sqsubseteq t_2$ but $t_2 \not\sqsubseteq t_1$. We also note $t_1 \approx t_2$ when both $t_1 \sqsubseteq t_2$ and $t_2 \sqsubseteq t_1$; this is possible even when $t_1 \neq t_2$. Let us now illustrate the consequences of this definition on a few simple examples.

Boolean Connectives. First, let us consider the property φ defined as $\mathsf{a} = 0 \vee \mathsf{b} = 0$. It imposes a condition on two attributes of the first event of an execution. Figure 3a shows the evaluation tree for two traces made of a single event: the first is such that $\mathsf{a} = 0$ and $\mathsf{b} = 1$, and the second has $\mathsf{a} = 0$ and $\mathsf{b} = 0$. Both of these traces satisfy φ, and thus produce trees with a green root.

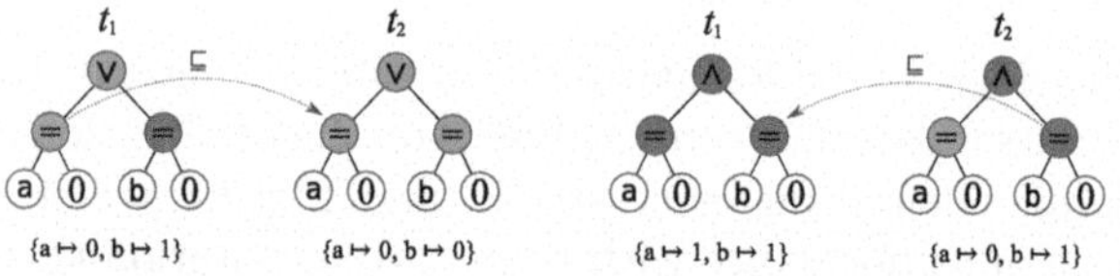

(a) ∨ satisfied (b) ∧ violated

Fig. 3. Two examples of subsumption for the ∧ and ∨ connectives. (Color figure online)

We can apply Definition 1 and conclude that $t_1 \sqsubseteq t_2$. First, condition a.1 is obviously satisfied. For condition a.2, one must exhibit a mapping between the (single) green child t_1' of t_1, and some child t_2' of t_2, such that $t_1' \sqsubseteq t_2'$. The purple arrow shows the only possible mapping. Recursively, one can apply Definition 1 again and observe that t_1' is indeed subsumed by t_2' (the conclusion is direct in this case as the two trees are identical). However, it is not possible to conclude that $t_2 \sqsubseteq t_1$. Since t_2 has two green nodes, by Definition 1, it is impossible to subsume each of its green subtrees by a *distinct* subtree of t. These conclusions match the intuition: φ stipulates that an execution is valid whenever a or b is null in the first event; t represents the case where one of these conditions is fulfilled, while t' represents the case where both are fulfilled. In a way $t \sqsubseteq t'$ illustrates the fact that, while the two executions satisfy the property, the second exceeds the expectations compared to the first.

The reverse argument can be made for two executions that violate a property, as is shown in Fig. 3b. This time, $t_1 \sqsubseteq t_2$ holds because every *red* subtree of t_2 can be associated to a subtree of t_1 that is subsumed by it (purple arrow). By a symmetrical argument, reversing the order of the trees does not satisfy the subsumption relation. The fact that $t_1 \sqsubseteq t_2$, in this case, illustrates the fact that while both executions violate the condition, the first violates it by a larger margin.

Note however that subsumption is not merely a matter of counting how many terms of a connective are satisfied or violated. As an example, consider the trees of Fig. 4, for the property φ defined as $\mathsf{a} = 0 \vee (\mathsf{b} = 0 \wedge \mathsf{c} = 0)$. Although $t_1 \sqsubseteq t_2$ and $t_1 \sqsubseteq t_3$, we have that neither t_2 nor t_3 subsumes the other. The conjunction fails in t_2 because $\mathsf{b} \neq 0$, while it fails in t_3 because $\mathsf{c} \neq 0$; by condition (c) of Definition 1, no subsumption relation exists between these subtrees. This is in line with the observation made previously that violating a property for two distinct "reasons", even though each represents a single failure, should not immediately be deemed equivalent.

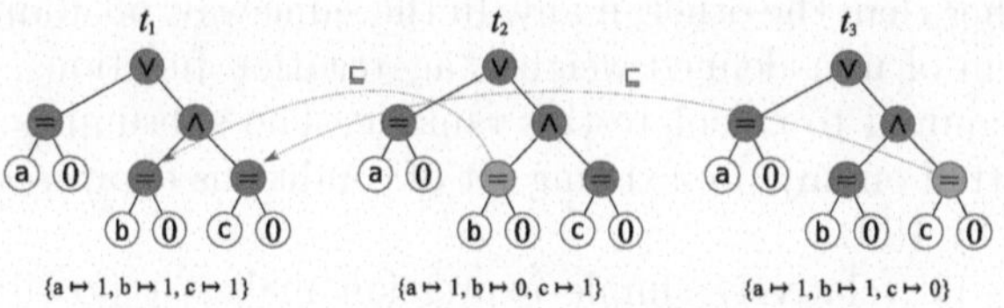

Fig. 4. Three evaluation trees for the property $\mathsf{a} = 0 \vee (\mathsf{b} = 0 \wedge \mathsf{c} = 0)$. (Color figure online)

Temporal Operators. So far, the mapping involved in conditions (a.2) and (b) of Definition 1 has amounted to a direct association between children at matching positions in both trees. However, this is not always the case, as can be seen in the handling of conformance requirements involving temporal operators. Figure 5a shows two evaluation trees for the property $\mathbf{F}(\mathsf{a} = 0)$. The first tree,

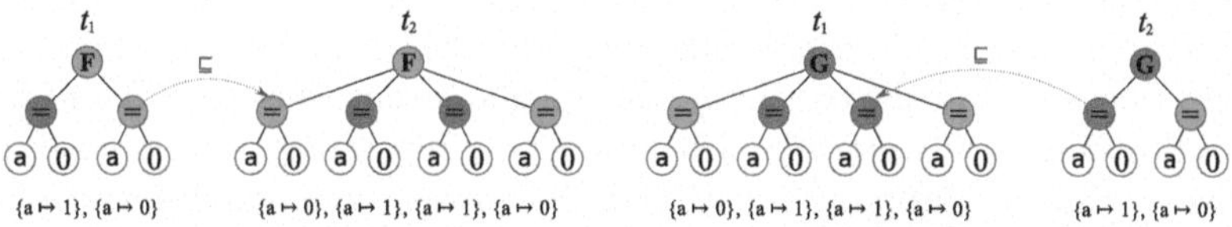

(a) **F** satisfied (b) **G** violated

Fig. 5. Two examples of subsumption for the **F** and **G** temporal modalities. (Color figure online)

t_1, corresponds to a trace of length 2 where $\mathsf{a} = 0$ in the second event, while the second tree, t_2, corresponds to a trace of length 4 where $\mathsf{a} = 0$ in the first and fourth events. One can observe that $t_1 \sqsubseteq t_2$; however, this time the mapping between the second child of t_1 associates it to the first child of t_2.

This example highlights a few characteristics of Definition 1. First, note that the mapping between children of both trees is not unique. Second, the position in the trace where trees are associated is irrelevant –provided that these trees satisfy the subsumption relationship. In other words, two traces that satisfy $\mathsf{a} = 0$ exactly once will be deemed equivalent regardless of the actual index of the event where $\mathsf{a} = 0$. As with Boolean connectives, the dual reasoning can be made on executions that violate a temporal property. Figure 5b shows an example for the condition $\mathbf{G}(\mathsf{a} = 0)$ and the same two traces as before.

4.2 Properties of $\sqsubseteq$

The previous examples have shown that the subsumption relation addresses some of the issues leveled at related works on the topic. First, it works directly on a condition producing a Boolean pass/fail verdict, and does not require it to be somehow rewritten in order to allow a finer-grained verdict. Rather, it extracts additional information from the evaluation of the condition to determine if one trace ranks higher than the other, if any. In the same way, no additional information (in the form of user-defined weights, aggregation functions, external counters, etc.), is required to calculate this ranking. The subsumption relation can thus be retro-fitted on any pre-existing set of conditions expressed in a notation that is covered by LTL.

In addition, its relatively simple expression makes it possible to formally establish properties of the relation. For instance, we can show that this comparison relation is "well-behaved", in the sense that it forms a *preorder* over the set of evaluation trees (the proof is relatively simple and is omitted due to space limitations).

Theorem 1. (Preorder). Let φ be a condition, $\overline{e}_1, \overline{e}_2, \overline{e}_3$ be three traces and t_1, t_2, t_3 be their respective evaluation trees. Then: 1) $t_1 \sqsubseteq t_1$; 2) if $t_1 \sqsubseteq t_2$ and $t_2 \sqsubseteq t_3$, then $t_1 \sqsubseteq t_3$.

Finally, one can remark that in the case of a green root, only *green* children need to be subsumed by some child of the other tree. This entails that, in the case of Fig. 5a, an execution $\overline{e}$ where a is null in 2 out of 4 events will be ranked higher than another $\overline{e}'$ where a is null once out of 2 events. The reasoning behind this behavior is that in the case of t_2, changing an event where $a = 0$ for another value still results in a conforming execution, as a remaining occurrence of $a = 0$ still ensures that the property is satisfied. In contrast, in t_1, conformance hinges on the single occurrence where $a = 0$. There is, therefore, a stronger support for the satisfaction of φ in t_2. Note that this notion is not appropriately conveyed if one were to express conformance through a ratio of true to false terms (which, in that case, would rank $\overline{e}'$ equal to $\overline{e}$).

4.3 Handling Numerical Conditions

The conditions given as examples so far were limited to asserting the equality of certain parameters to constants; the fact that these values were numbers was not considered relevant. However, as seen in Sect. 2, there are scenarios where events can contain numerical values from measurements (timestamps, prices, etc.), and the satisfaction of a constraint may be modulated by the distance from the observed value to a certain reference value.

Although our model based on evaluation trees is entirely discrete and involves no arithmetic calculations, it is still possible, to a certain extent, to model this notion of numerical distance. Consider, for example, the property stating that $\mathsf{a} = 4$. One might wish to view values close to 4, although they represent a violation of the condition, as still preferable to more distant values, as shown at the top of Fig. 6.

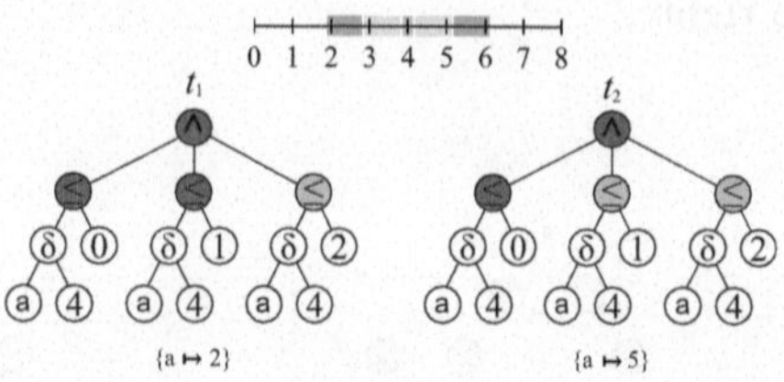

Fig. 6. Subsumption for a condition involving a numerical value. (Color figure online)

It is possible, without changing the definition of subsumption, to achieve such behavior by replacing the original condition with an expression like $\delta(\mathsf{a}, 4) \leq 0 \wedge \delta(\mathsf{a}, 4) \leq 1 \wedge \delta(\mathsf{a}, 4) \leq 2$, where δ is an auxiliary function defined as $\delta(x, y) = |x - y|$. The trees t_1 and t_2 in Fig. 6 show the result of evaluating this condition for two events, the first where $\mathsf{a} = 2$ and the second where $\mathsf{a} = 5$. In the first case, only the last inequality is satisfied, while the last two inequalities are satisfied in the second; as a result, $t_1 \sqsubseteq t_2$.

Note that it is not necessary for the property provided by the user to be directly written in this way. Instead, one could consider that a numerical equality be accompanied by the definition of one or more distance intervals, and that the transformation into a series of inequalities be performed automatically in the background. Also observe that the same "trick" can be used in reverse for satisfaction: one could express the condition that a lies between 2 and 6, and rank traces higher as the value gets close to 4.

4.4 Subsumption for a Set of Traces

The fact that $\sqsubseteq$ is a preorder entails that, given a LTL property φ and set of event traces $E = \{\overline{e}_1, \ldots, \overline{e}_n\}$, one can define the equivalence class of $\overline{e}_i$, noted $[\overline{e}_i]$, as the set $\{\overline{e} \in E : \overline{e} \approx \overline{e}_i\}$. The ordering relation on traces can be lifted to equivalence classes; we have that $[\bar{e}_i] \sqsubseteq [\bar{e}_j]$ if and only if $\bar{e}_i \sqsubseteq \bar{e}_j$. Given a LTL property φ and a set of traces E, it is possible to characterize the structure of E by considering its Hasse diagram [9]. This diagram is defined as a graph whose vertices are the equivalence classes of E, and for every pair of classes $[\bar{e}]$, $[\bar{e}']$, a directed edge from the former to the latter exists whenever $[\bar{e}]$ *covers* $[\bar{e}']$ —that is, $[\bar{e}] \sqsubseteq [\bar{e}']$ and there does not exist a distinct $[\bar{e}'']$ such that $[\bar{e}] \sqsubseteq [\bar{e}''] \sqsubseteq [\bar{e}']$.

As an example, consider the property φ defined as $\mathbf{G}(\mathsf{a} = 0) \vee \mathbf{G}(\mathsf{b} = 0)$ against the set of all traces of length 3 where, in each event, a and b take either the value 0 or 1. This corresponds to a total of 64 distinct traces. Figure 7a shows the Hasse diagram of this set with respect to φ. Each node in the diagram is labeled with the number of distinct traces in the equivalence class it corresponds to. Following convention, the direction of edges is from bottom to top; thus the bottom node labeled "1" corresponds to the single trace where $\mathsf{a} = 0$ and $\mathsf{b} = 0$ in all three events. This trace is directly subsumed by two disjoint set of traces, namely those where a is never null and $\mathsf{b} = 0$ exactly once (to its top left), and the reverse (to its top right).

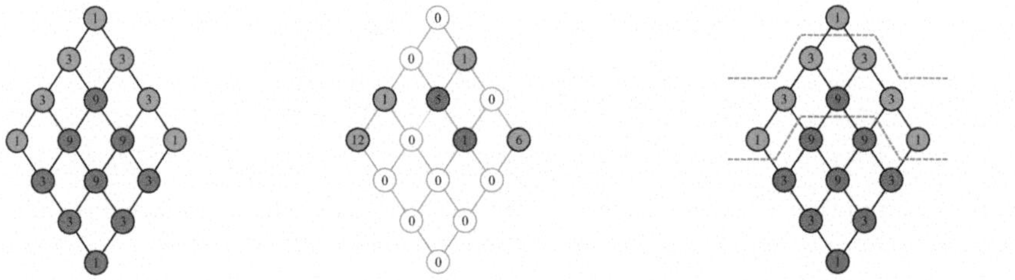

(a) Original (b) Sample log (c) Service Level Agreement

Fig. 7. The Hasse diagram with respect to the property $\mathbf{G}(\mathsf{a} = 0) \vee \mathbf{G}(\mathsf{b} = 0)$. (Color figure online)

The diagram presents a very regular structure, due to the simple and symmetric nature of the underlying condition; more complex formulas induce diagrams with less regularity. One can observe that, due to Definition 1, there exists a clear segregation between conforming (green) and non-conforming (red) traces. In other words, while the subsumption relation admits a form of comparison between execution traces, it never blurs the border between satisfaction and violation.

Figure 7a shows a diagram for a complete set of traces of given length, considering all possible assignments of parameters in all events. In reality, a log of a given process is very unlikely to have this characteristic. Thus, it may be instructive to compute the Hasse diagram of an actual set of logs for a given property, and to compare it to the "abstract" version covering all possible behaviors. Figure 7b shows what such a diagram could look like for a hypothetical log with respect to property φ. Most executions are conforming; however almost all of them do so by satisfying only one of the two temporal conditions: either a is always null but b never is (node labeled "12"), or the reverse (node labeled "6"). Only two traces (the two green nodes "1") satisfy one condition and the other partially. Moreover, the violations observed (red nodes) are still "not too far" from a correct execution: in both cases they have an immediate neighbor that is green.

As one can see, the analysis of this diagram can provide insight in the execution of a process with respect to a conformance condition φ. It allows one to qualitatively assess the degree to which the condition is satisfied or violated by each trace in a log, but also to identify common reasons for a violation —since all traces in the same equivalence class can be seen as sharing similar behavior with respect to φ. Approaches that associate a numerical value to each trace have the result of flattening the whole set on a linear scale that cannot reveal such structures.

5 Evaluating Tree-Based Conformance

The formal definition of conformance introduced in Sect. 4 has been implemented in the form of a stand-alone tool. In this section, we discuss this implementation and present preliminary results of the application of the subsumption relation on sample traces.

The implementation takes the form of a stand-alone Java-based library that is available under an open source license[2]. In addition to the objects it defines and which can be manipulated directly in a Java program, another possible use is as a command-line tool, where one can read traces from local files and compare their evaluation tree with respect to a given LTL conformance property. For example, to compare traces from two XML files against an LTL property contained in text file `phi.ltl`, one would write:

```
$ java -jar tc.jar compare --property phi.ltl file1.xml file2.xml
```

If n trace filenames are provided, the output of the tool is an $n \times n$ matrix, where entry (i, j) is `1` if the trace in file i is subsumed by the trace in file j, and `0` otherwise.

If `compare` is replaced by the action `draw-trees`, an image of the evaluation tree is produced for each of the traces provided, and saved to a local file in the same folder. Finally, the last supported action is `draw-hasse`, which generates the Hasse diagram of the set of traces given as arguments. A command line option allows each evaluation tree to be drawn to a file, with an indication of the node in the Hasse diagram it belongs to.

We proceeded to an experimental evaluation of the performance overhead induced by the evaluation of this relation, for sample LTL conformance properties on sample logs. In addition to the banking example discussed in Sect. 2.1, the scenarios considered are:

[2] https://github.com/liflab/shaded-conformance.

- *Beep Store*: a set of logs from a web service implementing shopping cart manipulations similar to Amazon's ECS [19].
- *CVC Procedure*: operations recorded from multiple instances of a medical procedure, from the Conformance Checking Challenge 2019 [15].

Table 3 summarizes the results for each scenario. For each, the length of the traces considered, the size of the corresponding evaluation trees, and the time required to compare two trees is reported; this time includes the generation of the evaluation trees and the evaluation of the subsumption relation. The T/O (timeout) column indicates the number of tree pairs for which the evaluation of the relation exceeded the predefined timeout of 3 s. In addition, we report on the number of pairs of traces that have been compared, and the number of times the subsumption relation held between two traces.

Table 3. Summary of experimental results.

Scenario	Property	Trace size		Tree size		Pairs	Time (ms)	T/O	Subsumed	Refin.
		Min.	Max.	Min.	Max.					
Beep Store	Search item once	10	100	4	91	1770	2.27	0	802	1712
	Max shopping carts	10	100	8	183	1770	2.96	0	1023	1657
CVC Procedure	Max. duration	26	59	16	66	190	13.2	0	93	140
	Procedure lifecycle	26	59	565	1291	190	106	0	113	73
Bank	Condition 1	13	21	679	1599	45	585	33	13	11
	Condition 2	13	21	16	66	45	53.7	0	45	0
	Condition 3	13	21	277	445	45	133	0	29	39
	Condition 4	13	21	102	150	45	52.2	0	38	15

Interestingly, the last column indicates the number of times the subsumption relation provides more refined information than the simple Boolean evaluation of the condition on each of the two trees t and t' considered. This occurs when both executions either violate or satisfy the conformance condition, but the subsumption relation still manages to distinguish between them (i.e., $t_1 \sqsubset t_2$, or vice versa). We can see that in most cases, the subsumption relation provides added value for a significant proportion of the tree pairs.

6 Conclusion

This paper presented a new relationship that allows the comparison of two execution traces relative to a conformance property, inducing a form of gradation in the level with which a trace respects or violates the said property. Unlike existing approaches that typically associate each trace with a numerical value, we saw that the so-called subsumption relationship relies on the tree structure resulting from the evaluation of a temporal logic formula for a given trace. This relationship can accommodate the comparison of numerical values, and the examples illustrate that the ordering of the traces it produces can be explained intuitively. In this sense, it is an effective and versatile technique for analyzing the level of conformance of a set of traces.

This basic idea opens the way for several applications and extensions. Firstly, the Hasse diagrams produced by a log and discussed in Sect. 4.4 can form the core of a new diagnostic method to identify the reasons why a process meets or violates a requirement. This diagram could also be used in the context of Service Level Agreements (SLA). An SLA could be stated in the form of a Boolean condition, but be equipped with different levels of service corresponding to strata in the Hasse diagram corresponding to the property, as is shown in Fig. 7c.

Finally, although LTL is sufficient to model a large number of conformance constraints, it would be desirable to extend the subsumption relationship itself to more expressive specification languages, such as logics including the possibility of compensation for a violation [16].

References

1. van der Aalst, W.M.P., Pesic, M., Schonenberg, H.: Declarative workflows: balancing between flexibility and support. Comput. Sci. Res. Dev. **23**(2), 99–113 (2009). https://doi.org/10.1007/S00450-009-0057-9
2. Awad, A., Decker, G., Weske, M.: Efficient compliance checking using BPMN-Q and temporal logic. In: Dumas, M., Reichert, M., Shan, M.-C. (eds.) BPM 2008. LNCS, vol. 5240, pp. 326–341. Springer, Heidelberg (2008). https://doi.org/10.1007/978-3-540-85758-7_24
3. Awad, A., Weidlich, M., Weske, M.: Visually specifying compliance rules and explaining their violations for business processes. J. Vis. Lang. Comput. **22**(1), 30–55 (2011)
4. Baresi, L., Pasquale, L.: A temporal semantics for fuzzy linear temporal logic. Technical report. https://www.academia.edu/2935585/A_Temporal_Semantics_for_Fuzzy_Linear_Temporal_Logic
5. Bartocci, E., Falcone, Y., Francalanza, A., Reger, G.: Introduction to runtime verification. In: Bartocci, E., Falcone, Y. (eds.) Lectures on Runtime Verification. LNCS, vol. 10457, pp. 1–33. Springer, Cham (2018). https://doi.org/10.1007/978-3-319-75632-5_1
6. Burattin, A., Guizzardi, G., Maggi, F.M., Montali, M.: Fifty shades of green: how informative is a compliant process trace? In: Giorgini, P., Weber, B. (eds.) CAiSE 2019. LNCS, vol. 11483, pp. 611–626. Springer, Cham (2019). https://doi.org/10.1007/978-3-030-21290-2_38
7. Chesani, F., Mello, P., Montali, M., Riguzzi, F., Sebastianis, M., Storari, S.: Checking compliance of execution traces to business rules. In: BPM Workshops, pp. 134–145 (2008)
8. Claes, J., Poels, G.: Process mining and the ProM framework: an exploratory survey. In: La Rosa, M., Soffer, P. (eds.) BPM 2012. LNBIP, vol. 132, pp. 187–198. Springer, Heidelberg (2013). https://doi.org/10.1007/978-3-642-36285-9_19
9. Davey, B.A., Priestley, H.A.: Introduction to Lattices and Order. Cambridge University Press (2002)
10. Díaz, G., Llana, L.: Contract compliance monitoring of web services. In: Lau, K.-K., Lamersdorf, W., Pimentel, E. (eds.) ESOCC 2013. LNCS, vol. 8135, pp. 119–133. Springer, Heidelberg (2013). https://doi.org/10.1007/978-3-642-40651-5_10

11. Dwyer, M.B., Avrunin, G.S., Corbett, J.C.: Patterns in property specifications for finite-state verification. In: Boehm, B.W., Garlan, D., Kramer, J. (eds.) Proceedings of the 1999 International Conference on Software Engineering, ICSE 1999, Los Angeles, CA, USA, 16–22 May 1999, pp. 411–420. ACM (1999)
12. Fdhila, W., Knuplesch, D., Rinderle-Ma, S., Reichert, M.: Verifying compliance in process choreographies: foundations, algorithms, and implementation. Inf. Syst. **108**, 101983 (2022)
13. Feijs, L.M.G., Goga, N., Mauw, S., Tretmans, J.: Test Selection, Trace Distance and Heuristics, pp. 267–282. Springer, Boston (2002)
14. Francalanza, A., Cini, C.: Computer says no: Verdict explainability for runtime monitors using a local proof system. J. Log. Algebraic Methods Program. **119**, 100636 (2021)
15. de la Fuente, R., Sepúlveda, M., Fuentes, R.: Central veinous catheter, compliance checking challenge 2019 (2019). https://data.4tu.nl/repository/uuid:c923af09-ce93-44c3-ace0-c5508cf103ad
16. Governatori, G.: The regorous approach to process compliance. In: Kolb, J., Weber, B., Hallé, S., Mayer, W., Ghose, A.K., Grossmann, G. (eds.) 19th IEEE International Enterprise Distributed Object Computing Workshop, EDOC Workshops 2015, Adelaide, Australia, 21–25 September 2015, pp. 33–40. IEEE Computer Society (2015). https://doi.org/10.1109/EDOCW.2015.28
17. Groefsema, H., van Beest, N.R.T.P., Governatori, G.: On the use of the conformance and compliance keywords during verification of business processes. In: Ciccio, C.D., Dijkman, R.M., del-Río-Ortega, A., Rinderle-Ma, S. (eds.) Business Process Management Forum - BPM 2022 Forum, Münster, Germany, 11–16 September 2022, Proceedings. Lecture Notes in Business Information Processing, vol. 458, pp. 21–37. Springer, Cham (2022). https://doi.org/10.1007/978-3-031-16171-1_2
18. Hallé, S.: Explainable queries over event logs. In: 24th IEEE International Enterprise Distributed Object Computing Conference, EDOC 2020, Eindhoven, The Netherlands, 5–8 October 2020, pp. 171–180. IEEE (2020)
19. Hallé, S., Villemaire, R.: Constraint-based invocation of stateful web services: the Beep Store (case study). In: Lago, P., Lewis, G.A., Metzger, A., Tosic, V. (eds.) 4th International ICSE Workshop on Principles of Engineering Service-Oriented Systems, PESOS 2012, Zurich, Switzerland, 4 June 2012, pp. 61–62. IEEE (2012)
20. Hallé, S., Villemaire, R.: Runtime enforcement of web service message contracts with data. IEEE Trans. Serv. Comput. **5**(2), 192–206 (2012)
21. Hallé, S.: Event Stream Processing With BeepBeep 3: Log Crunching and Analysis Made Easy. Presses de l'Université du Québec (2018)
22. Hashmi, M., Governatori, G., Lam, H., Wynn, M.T.: Are we done with business process compliance: state of the art and challenges ahead. Knowl. Inf. Syst. **57**(1), 79–133 (2018)
23. Khoury, R., Hallé, S.: Tally keeping-LTL: an LTL semantics for quantitative evaluation of LTL specifications. In: 2018 IEEE International Conference on Information Reuse and Integration, IRI 2018, Salt Lake City, UT, USA, 6–9 July 2018, pp. 495–502. IEEE (2018)
24. Lam, H.-P., Hashmi, M., Kumar, A.: Towards a formal framework for partial compliance of business processes. In: Rodríguez-Doncel, V., Palmirani, M., Araszkiewicz, M., Casanovas, P., Pagallo, U., Sartor, G. (eds.) AICOL/XAILA 2018/2020. LNCS (LNAI), vol. 13048, pp. 90–105. Springer, Cham (2021). https://doi.org/10.1007/978-3-030-89811-3_7

25. Lamine, K.B., Kabanza, F.: History checking of temporal fuzzy logic formulas for monitoring behavior-based mobile robots. In: 12th IEEE International Conference on Tools with Artificial Intelligence (ICTAI 2000), Vancouver, BC, Canada, 13–15 November 2000, pp. 312–319. IEEE Computer Society (2000). https://doi.org/10.1109/TAI.2000.889888
26. Liu, Y., Müller, S., Xu, K.: A static compliance-checking framework for business process models. IBM Syst. J. **46**(2), 335–362 (2007). https://doi.org/10.1147/sj.462.0335
27. Loh, C.S., Sheng, Y.: Maximum similarity index (MSI): a metric to differentiate the performance of novices vs. multiple-experts in serious games. Comput. Hum. Behav. **39**, 322–330 (2014). https://doi.org/10.1016/J.CHB.2014.07.022
28. Lu, R., Sadiq, S.W., Governatori, G.: Measurement of compliance distance in business processes. Inf. Syst. Manag. **25**(4), 344–355 (2008). https://doi.org/10.1080/10580530802384613
29. Ly, L.T., Maggi, F.M., Montali, M., Rinderle-Ma, S., van der Aalst, W.M.P.: Compliance monitoring in business processes: functionalities, application, and tool-support. Inf. Syst. **54**, 209–234 (2015)
30. Maggi, F.M., Montali, M., Westergaard, M., van der Aalst, W.M.P.: Monitoring business constraints with linear temporal logic: an approach based on colored automata. In: Rinderle-Ma, S., Toumani, F., Wolf, K. (eds.) BPM 2011. LNCS, vol. 6896, pp. 132–147. Springer, Heidelberg (2011). https://doi.org/10.1007/978-3-642-23059-2_13
31. Mannila, H., Ronkainen, P.: Similarity of event sequences. In: 4th International Workshop on Temporal Representation and Reasoning, TIME 1997, Daytona Beach, Florida, USA, 10–11 May 1997, pp. 136–139. IEEE Computer Society (1997)
32. Montali, M.: The ConDec Language, pp. 47–75. Springer, Heidelberg (2010)
33. Mulo, E., Zdun, U., Dustdar, S.: Monitoring web service event trails for business compliance. In: IEEE International Conference on Service-Oriented Computing and Applications, SOCA 2009, Taipei, Taiwan, 14–15 December 2009, pp. 1–8. IEEE Computer Society (2009)
34. Polyvyanyy, A., Ouyang, C., Barros, A., van der Aalst, W.M.P.: Process querying: enabling business intelligence through query-based process analytics. Decis. Support Syst. **100**, 41–56 (2017)
35. Ray, D., Ligatti, J.: A theory of gray security policies. In: Pernul, G., Ryan, P.Y.A., Weippl, E. (eds.) ESORICS 2015. LNCS, vol. 9327, pp. 481–499. Springer, Cham (2015). https://doi.org/10.1007/978-3-319-24177-7_24
36. Tidjon, L.N., Frappier, M., Mammar, A.: Intrusion detection systems: a cross-domain overview. IEEE Commun. Surv. Tutorials **21**(4), 3639–3681 (2019)
37. van Zelst, S.J., Bolt, A., Hassani, M., van Dongen, B.F., van der Aalst, W.M.P.: Online conformance checking: relating event streams to process models using prefix-alignments. Int. J. Data Sci. Anal. **8**(3), 269–284 (2019)

Control-Flow Reconstruction Attacks on Business Process Models

Henrik Kirchmann[1](✉), Stephan A. Fahrenkrog-Petersen[1,2], Felix Mannhardt[3], and Matthias Weidlich[1]

[1] Humboldt-Universität zu Berlin, Berlin, Germany
{henrik.kirchmann,stephan.fahrenkrog-petersen,matthias.weidlich}@hu-berlin.de
[2] Weizenbaum Institute for the Networked Society, Berlin, Germany
[3] Eindhoven University of Technology, Eindhoven, The Netherlands
f.mannhardt@tue.nl

Abstract. Process models may be automatically generated from event logs that contain as-is data of a business process. While such models generalize over the control-flow of specific, recorded process executions, they are often also annotated with behavioural statistics, such as execution frequencies. Based thereon, once a model is published, certain insights about the original process executions may be reconstructed, so that an external party may extract confidential information about the business process. This work is the first to empirically investigate such reconstruction attempts based on process models. To this end, we propose different play-out strategies that reconstruct the control-flow from process trees, potentially exploiting frequency annotations. To assess the potential success of such reconstruction attacks on process models, and hence the risks imposed by publishing them, we compare the reconstructed process executions with those of the original log for several real-world datasets.

Keywords: Reconstruction Attacks · Process Analysis · Model Play-out

1 Introduction

Under the umbrella of process mining, event logs that have been recorded by information systems facilitate the analysis of qualitative and quantitative properties of business processes [27]. Event logs support information systems engineering through the discovery of process models [1], which are useful for understanding the flow of the process and, once annotated with performance characteristics, help to identify performance bottlenecks and improvement opportunities.

Discovery algorithms generalize and aggregate the behaviour recorded in an event log. As a consequence, individual process executions are not directly represented, when publishing the model [18], e.g., to an external party for the purpose of process certification, staff training or consulting. However, in practice, process models are not limited to the generalized control-flow of a process. Rather, they also contain summary statistics about the behaviour, most prominently execution frequencies or branching probabilities [3, 4, 10].

J. Borbinha et al. (Eds.): EDOC 2024, LNCS 15409, pp. 60–77, 2025.
https://doi.org/10.1007/978-3-031-78338-8_4

ID	Trace
1	Register (R), IV Liquid (L), Antibio (A), Rel. D (D), Return (U)
2	Register (R), Antibio (A), Antibio (A), Antibio (A), Rel. E (E)
3	Register (R), IV Liquid (L), Rel. B (B), Return (U)

(a)

(b)

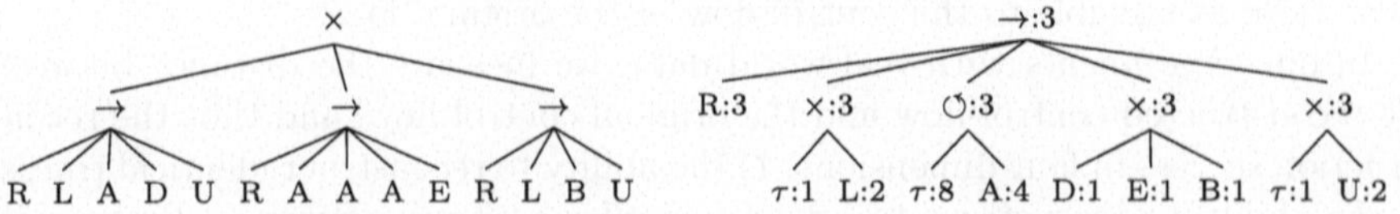

(c) (d)

Fig. 1. (a) A log of patient treatments and three process models for it: (b) a 'flower model' describing any set of traces; (c) a 'trace model' enumerating all traces; (d) a model offering some generalization, potentially annotated with frequencies.

Once a process model is enriched with behavioural statistics, it may be a target of a reconstruction attack. That is, similar to reconstruction attacks in machine learning (ML) [12,14,23], which strive for a characterization of the data used for training the ML model, such an attack aims at deriving insights about the original process executions. Even if the exact reconstruction of the executions is not possible, which would yield severe privacy risks for process stakeholders [28], it is problematic: The combination of the control-flow of a process model with behavioural statistics may facilitate conclusions on confidential information about the underlying business process. For instance, one may reconstruct dependencies between activity executions and behavioural patterns, which reveal internal decision procedures that may be exploited for malicious purposes.

Consider the event log in Fig. 1a, which contains three traces of patient treatments in a hospital. The impact of the generalization adopted in a process model on revealing insights on the original process executions is illustrated by two extreme cases: Fig. 1b shows a 'flower model' that represents any log of traces comprising executions of the respective activities and, hence, does not enable any conclusions. Figure 1c shows a 'trace model', which models a lossless representation of each recorded trace variant, but has no information on their probability or frequency. The model represents an infinite number of possible event logs with different frequencies of those traces. Nonetheless, all possible logs include all steps of all process executions for this procedure in the hospital. A middle ground is offered by the model in Fig. 1d, which enables control-flow reconstruction to some extent. In particular, annotating the model with frequency information reduces number of event logs modeled by this model and reveals certain insights on the treatments: We conclude that (i) antibiotics have been given at least twice to a single patient, (ii) all release types appear to be equally likely, and (iii) there is at least one patient, who returned after receiving intravenous (IV) liquid. These insights are shared across the control-flow of all possible logs that this model represents.

In this paper, we study reconstruction attacks on process models and analyse how the information contained in process models influences one's ability to reconstruct the control-flow of process executions. We formulate reconstruction attacks as play-out strategies that for process models given as process trees will generate new event logs with the goal of incorporating control-flow that should be as close as possible to the control-flow of the original log.

In our experiments with real-world data, we measure the distance between the reconstructed control-flow and the original control-flow, and thus the reconstruction success in four dimensions: 1) the ability to reconstruct identical traces, 2) the ability to reconstruct traces with similar activity sequences, 3) the ability to reconstruct relations between activities and 4) the ability to reconstruct traces of the same length. Our results indicate that frequency-annotated models of structured processes are particularly vulnerable.

Below, we first review related work (Sect. 2), before defining preliminary notions (Sect. 3). We then present our approaches to control-flow reconstruction (Sect. 4), report on our evaluation (Sect. 5), and conclude (Sect. 6).

2 Related Work

Any attempt to reconstruct the original process executions from a process model is related to privacy risks, which received much attention in recent years. However, we notice that existing work on the quantification of privacy risks in process mining [28] and the development of a large number of related privacy-preserving techniques [11,13,21,22] has focused primarily on event logs. As such, there is a reasonable level of understanding of these risks and possible mitigation strategies.

The risks induced by process models discovered from event logs, in turn, have been described only recently in [18]. Here, the authors quantify the re-identification risk in frequency annotated block-structured process models with a two-step approach: First, a play-out strategy is used to reconstruct event logs from the process model. Second, the measures proposed in [20] are used to quantify the re-identification risk in the reconstructed log, to then assess the re-identification risk of the original log caused by the release of the process model. However, this approach is only feasible if there is a strong similarity between the reconstructed logs and the original log. This aspect is not further studied in [18], though, which is a research gap that we close with our work.

Play-out strategies and the comparison of the obtained output with a ground truth are also studied in other process mining settings: Conformance checking [6] relates the behaviour described by a process model with behaviour in an event log. Yet, often we cannot fully trust both our model and the source event log, as indicated in [25]. In our context, missing or extra behaviour in the process model as assumed in conformance checking would further impair the chance of a successful reconstruction attack. As such, we assume the process model to be a good representation of the observed process behaviour, which presents the worst case for any attempt to derive insights on the underlying business process, as it simplifies the reconstruction.

Moreover, in conformance checking, measures for precision quantify how much of the control-flow present in the model does not appear in the log from which the model was discovered. Hence, when a model has high precision, reconstruction might become easier, since the amount of behaviour in the model that is not representing any behaviour of the original event log is smaller.

Both process simulation [5] and stochastic process mining [3] aim to more accurately capture the underlying process observed in process executions. These streams of research investigate how close simulated process executions [7] or the probability distributions in stochastic process model executions [16] are to the actual observations. Unlike our work, however, these approaches do not target the reconstruction of the original log, but on representing the general process behaviour including possible future process executions.

3 Preliminaries

Below, we summarize essential notions for event logs and process trees that are used in the remainder of the paper.

Event Log. Let $\mathcal{A}$ be the universe of activities. A trace $t \in \mathcal{A}^*$, where $\mathcal{A}^*$ is the set of all finite sequences over $\mathcal{A}$, is a sequence of activities. In such a trace, each activity a denotes the recorded event of the execution of a well-defined step in a process. $\mathcal{T} = \mathcal{A}^*$ denotes the universe of traces. A trace $t \in \mathcal{T}$ is represented as $t = \langle a_1, a_2, ..., a_n \rangle$, where $a_1, a_2, ..., a_n \in \mathcal{A}$. With $|t|$ we denote the length of a trace $t \in \mathcal{T}$, i.e., the number of activities in the trace. Denoting with $\mathcal{B}(X)$ the set of all possible multisets over X, let $\mathcal{L} = \mathcal{B}(\mathcal{T})$ be the universe of event logs. An event log $l \in \mathcal{L}$ is a finite multiset of traces.

Process Tree. In this work, we consider process trees as the formal model to capture business processes. A process tree represents a process in a hierarchical (block-structured) way [4,15]. Process trees can be transformed into models of other languages for business processes, such as Petri nets or BPMN models [27]. As such, the ideas outlined in the remainder are not limited to process trees. In general, a process tree denotes a process as a rooted tree. Its leaf nodes represent activities and all other nodes represent operators. Following the aforementioned references, we formally define a process tree as follows:

Definition 1 (Process Tree). *Let $A \in \mathcal{A}$ be a finite set of activities and let $\tau \notin A$ denote the silent activity, which cannot be observed in a trace. A process tree Q, is defined recursively as:*

- *If $a \in A \cup \{\tau\}$, then $Q = a$ is a process tree.*
- *If $n \geq 1$, $Q_1, Q_2, \ldots, Q_n$ are process trees, and $\oplus \in \{\rightarrow, \times, \wedge\}$, then $Q = \oplus(Q_1, Q_2, \ldots, Q_n)$ is a process tree.*
- *If $n \geq 2$, $Q_1, Q_2, \ldots, Q_n$ are process trees, and $\oplus = \circlearrowleft$, then $Q = \oplus(Q_1, Q_2, \ldots, Q_n)$ is a process tree.*

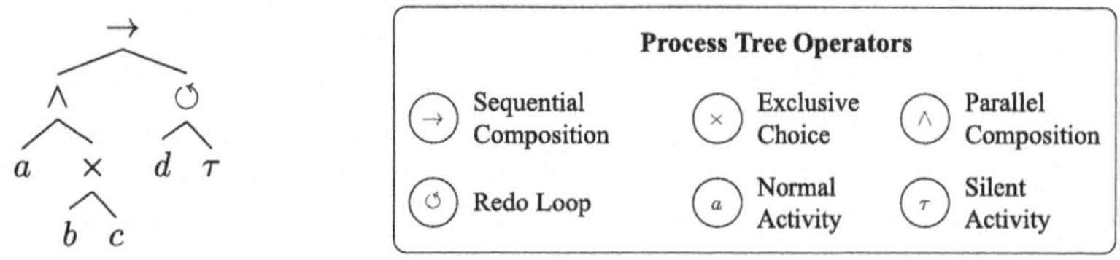

Fig. 2. Visualization of the process tree $Q = \rightarrow (\wedge(a, \times\ (b, c)), \circlearrowleft (d, \tau))$.

A process tree might be annotated with information about probabilities or frequencies of the recorded behaviour. We capture such information by a weight $w \in \mathbb{R}$ that is assigned to a process tree Q, which is denoted by $Q : w$.

Consider Fig. 2, which shows the process tree $Q = \rightarrow (\wedge(a, \times(b, c)), \circlearrowleft (d, \tau))$. The $\rightarrow$ operator refers to the execution of the child nodes in sequential order, i.e., the execution of $\wedge(a, \times(b, c))$ is followed by the execution of $\circlearrowleft (d, \tau)$. The $\wedge$ operator defines the execution of all of its child nodes in any order, while the $\times$ operator specifies an exclusive choice. The $\circlearrowleft$ operator has at least two children, the first being the "do" part of a loop; all other children representing "redo" parts. The "do" part is always executed; execution of the "redo" part is optional and only one of the "redo" parts is executed, before the "do" part is executed again.

To formalize the semantics of process trees, we need the following auxiliary operators for general sequences [27]:

Definition 2 (Auxiliary Operators). *Let $\sigma_1, \sigma_2 \in A^*$ be two sequences over A and let $S_1, S_2, \ldots, S_n \subseteq A^*$. We define two operators as:*

- *Concatenation: $\sigma_1 \cdot \sigma_2 \in A^*$ concatenates two sequences. The concatenation operator can be generalized to sets of sequences by $S_1 \cdot S_2 = \{\sigma_1 \cdot \sigma_2 \mid \sigma_1 \in S_1 \wedge \sigma_2 \in S_2\}$ and $\bigodot_{1 \leq i \leq n} S_i = S_1 \cdot S_2 \cdots S_n$ concatenates an ordered collection of sets of sequences.*
- *Shuffle: $\sigma_1 \diamond \sigma_2 \in A^*$ generates the set of all interleaved sequences. The shuffle operator can be generalized to sets of sequences by $S_1 \diamond S_2 = \{\sigma_1 \diamond \sigma_2 \mid \sigma_1 \in S_1 \wedge \sigma_2 \in S_2\}$ and $\Diamond_{1 \leq i \leq n} S_i = S_1 \cdot S_2 \cdots S_n$ shuffles an ordered collection of sets of sequences.*

Given two sequences $\sigma_1 = \langle a, b \rangle$ and $\sigma_2 = \langle c, d \rangle$, the operators yield $\sigma_1 \cdot \sigma_2 = \langle a, b, c, d \rangle$ as well as $\sigma_1 \diamond \sigma_2 = \{\langle a, b, c, d \rangle, \langle a, c, b, d \rangle, \langle c, a, b, d \rangle, \langle a, c, d, b \rangle, \langle c, a, d, b \rangle, \langle c, d, a, b \rangle\}$. Furthermore, we define the language of a process tree as follows.

Definition 3 (Language of a Process Tree). *Let $Q \in \mathcal{Q}$ be a process tree over a set A. $\mathcal{L}(Q)$ denotes the language of Q, i.e., the set of traces that can be generated. $\mathcal{L}(Q)$ is defined recursively:*

- $\mathcal{L}(Q) = \{\langle a \rangle\}$, *if* $Q = a \in A$,
- $\mathcal{L}(Q) = \{\langle\rangle\}$, *if* $Q = \tau$,
- $\mathcal{L}(Q) = \bigodot_{1 \leq i \leq n} \mathcal{L}(Q_i)$, *if* $Q = \rightarrow (Q_1, Q_2, \ldots, Q_n)$,
- $\mathcal{L}(Q) = \bigcup_{1 \leq i \leq n} \mathcal{L}(Q_i)$, *if* $Q = \times(Q_1, Q_2, \ldots, Q_n)$,

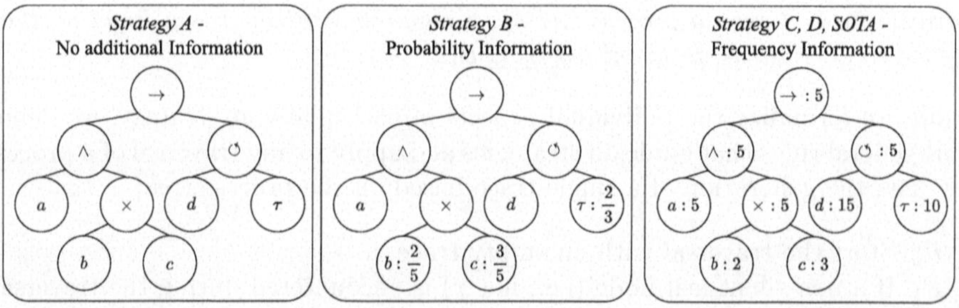

Fig. 3. The three common scenarios how a model discovered from log $L = [\langle a,b,d\rangle, \langle a,c,d\rangle, \langle c,a,d,d,d,d,d\rangle^2, \langle b,a,d,d,d\rangle]$ can be released.

- $\mathcal{L}(Q) = \Diamond_{1\leq i\leq n}\mathcal{L}(Q_i)$, *if* $Q = \wedge(Q_1, Q_2, \ldots, Q_n)$,
- $\mathcal{L}(Q) = \{\sigma_1{\cdot}\sigma_1'{\cdot}\sigma_2{\cdot}\sigma_2'\cdots\sigma_m \in A^* \mid m \geq 1 \wedge \forall\, 1 \leq j \leq m : \sigma_j \in \mathcal{L}(Q_1) \wedge \sigma_j' \in \bigcup_{2\leq i\leq n}\mathcal{L}(Q_i)\}$, *if* $Q = \circlearrowleft(Q_1, Q_2, \ldots, Q_n)$.

Based on the definition above, we see that $\mathcal{L}(\circlearrowleft(Q_1, Q_2, \ldots, Q_n)) = \mathcal{L}(\circlearrowleft(Q_1, \times(Q_2, \ldots, Q_n)))$, i.e., a restriction to a single "redo" child does not lower the expressiveness of the model. As a consequence, without loss of generality, we assume that an $\circlearrowleft$ operator has only one "redo" child in the remainder, to simplify the presentation. Turning to Fig. 2, the language of Q is unbounded due to the loop operator, i.e., $\mathcal{L}(Q) = \{\langle a,b,d\rangle, \langle a,c,d\rangle, \langle b,a,d\rangle, \langle c,a,d\rangle, \langle a,b,d,d\rangle, \langle a,c,d,d\rangle \ldots\}$.

4 Control-Flow Reconstruction

As illustrated in our initial example in Fig. 1, process models may facilitate conclusions on the event log from which the model was discovered. We therefore formulate the respective control-flow reconstruction attacks as five different play-out strategies that, given a process tree, generate a reconstructed event log. We will compare in Sect. 5 the control-flow of the reconstructed log with the control-flow of the original log. The strategies are motivated to reflect the three common ways a process model can be released, see Fig. 3, and how they utilize this information to reconstruct the control-flow. This enables us to analyze the impact different kinds of additional information, as well as different usage of this information, have on the reconstruction success. We first introduce our play-out strategies in Sect. 4.1. Next, in Sect. 4.2, we discuss specific issues related to the handling of loops.

4.1 Play-Out Strategies for Process Trees

In essence, a play-out strategy defines a particular traversal of the process tree according to the control-flow structure defined by it.

Definition 4. *Given a process tree Q, a play-out strategy p is a function that, applied to Q, returns an event log $L_p \subseteq \mathcal{B}(2^{\mathcal{L}(Q)})$.*

Before we formalize the individual aspects of each play-out strategy, we define some general rules that guide all strategies and apply to any traversal of a process tree, i.e., the generation of a single trace based on the process tree:

- R_0 Start the traversal with an empty trace.
- R_1 If a non-silent leaf node (i.e., not τ) is encountered during the traversal, the respective activity is concatenated to the current trace.
- R_2 If a silent leaf node (τ) is encountered during the traversal, the current trace remains unchanged.
- R_3 Once the traversal considered all children of a node Q, it returns to and continues with the parent node. If Q is the root node, the reconstructed trace will be added to the result.

Similarly, we provide some general rules for the play-out of process trees that relate to the operators for sequential composition and parallel composition. $R_\wedge$ does not apply to the *SOTA Strategy* [18].

- $R_\rightarrow$ When $Q = \rightarrow(Q_1, \ldots, Q_n)$ is encountered, the traversal continues with the child nodes $Q_1, \ldots, Q_n$ in the respective order.
- $R_\wedge$ When $Q = \wedge(Q_1, \ldots, Q_n)$ is encountered, all $U_1, \ldots, U_n$ sub-trees are executed until all sub-trees reach a leaf node or Q again, then it is chosen uniformly at random which leaf node is executed. This is repeated until all sub-trees are completely executed and back to Q. Thus, true parallelization of activities is achieved.

Based thereon, we define a first basic play-out strategy that is not based on any additional information on frequencies.

Strategy A. This strategy considers only the semantics of the operators in a process tree. For the exclusive choice operator and the loop operator, the respective control-flow choices are taken uniformly at random:

- $R^A_\times$ When $Q = \times(Q_1, \ldots, Q_n)$ is encountered, traversal continues with one child Q_i, $1 \leq i \leq n$, chosen uniformly at random.
- $R^A_\circlearrowleft$ When $Q = \circlearrowleft(Q_1, Q_2)$ is encountered, traversal continues with the child Q_1. Then, a choice between executing child Q_2 and then child Q_1 or ending the traversal of Q is made. This decision is made with probability $1/2$, until the option to end the traversal of Q is taken.

Strategy B. This strategy interprets the weights assigned to nodes as fixed branching probabilities. These probabilities will be derived from frequencies. For notational purposes, we let the strategy compute these probabilities using the actual frequencies. But the derived fixed probabilities that are computed and used by this strategy correspond to the probabilities a probability-annotated model would have:

$R^B_\times$ When $Q = \times(Q_1 : w_1, \ldots, Q_n : w_n) : w$ is encountered, traversal continues with one child Q_i, $1 \le i \le n$, chosen with probability ${}^{w_i}/_{\sum_{1\le j\le n} w_j}$.

$R^B_\circlearrowleft$ When $Q = \circlearrowleft (Q_1 : w_1, Q_2 : w_2) : w$ is encountered, we follow the approach from $R^A_\circlearrowleft$, but adopt the probability of $1 - {}^{w}/_{w_1}$ for the option to continue with children Q_2 and Q_1, and ${}^{w}/_{w_1}$ for the option to end Q's traversal.

Further strategies leverage the actual frequencies and interpret them in absolute terms. That is, traversal changes the respective counts, which is captured by the following rule that applies to all remaining strategies:

R_4 Upon traversal of a node $Q : w$, the value of w will be decreased by one.

Based thereon, we distinguish two strategies to incorporate the absolute frequencies in the traversal of nodes that model control-flow choices.

Strategy C. This strategy takes control-flow choices related to exclusive choice operators and loop operators, with probabilities that are determined based on the leftover frequencies:

$R^C_\times$ When $Q = \times(Q_1 : w_1, \ldots, Q_n : w_n) : w$ is encountered, traversal continues with one child Q_i, $1 \le i \le n$, chosen with probability ${}^{w_i}/_{\sum_{1\le j\le n} w_j}$. Note that this rule differs from the one of *Strategy B*, since the weights w_i are continuously updated during traversal, as mentioned above.

$R^C_\circlearrowleft$ When $Q = \circlearrowleft (Q_1 : w_1, Q_2 : w_2) : w$ is encountered, traversal first continues with child Q_1. If after this, $w_1 = w_2$ holds, traversal iteratively continues with children Q_2 and Q_1, until $w_1 = 0$. Intuitively, such an approach collects all leftover frequencies with the last trace that is generated. Otherwise, if $w_1 \neq w_2$, we distinguish $w_1 = 0$, in which case traversal of Q ends, and $w_1 > 0$, in which case traversal iteratively continues in the loop as in *Strategy B*, with probability $1 - {}^{w}/_{w_1}$ for the option including the children Q_2 and Q_1, and ${}^{w}/_{w_1}$ for the option to end traversal.

Strategy D with Variance v. This strategy denotes an adaptation of *Strategy C*. While it also takes all control-flow choices with probabilities that are determined based on the leftover frequencies, it includes a normal distribution to decide on the number of loop iterations. As usual, by $\mathcal{N}(\mu, \sigma^2)$, we denote a normal distribution with mean μ and variance σ^2. Then, the strategy replaces the rule of *Strategy C* for the loop operator by the following rule:

$R^D_\circlearrowleft$ When $Q = \circlearrowleft (Q_1 : w_1, Q_2 : w_2) : w$ is encountered, traversal continues the same way as in $R^C_\circlearrowleft$. All rules apply, except for the case when $w_1 \neq w_2$ and $w_1 > 0$. In this case, we will traverse the loop, i.e., children Q_2 and Q_1 a total of $\min(\lfloor |x| \rfloor, w_2)$-times, where x is randomly sampled from the normal distribution, $x \sim \mathcal{N}(\frac{w_2}{w}, v)$. To get a positive integer, we compute $\lfloor |x| \rfloor$. Our experiments have shown that rounding up or concatenating the functions in different order had no measurable impact. We return to the parent node after we traversed the loop $\min(\lfloor |x| \rfloor, w_2)$-times or $w_1 = 0$.

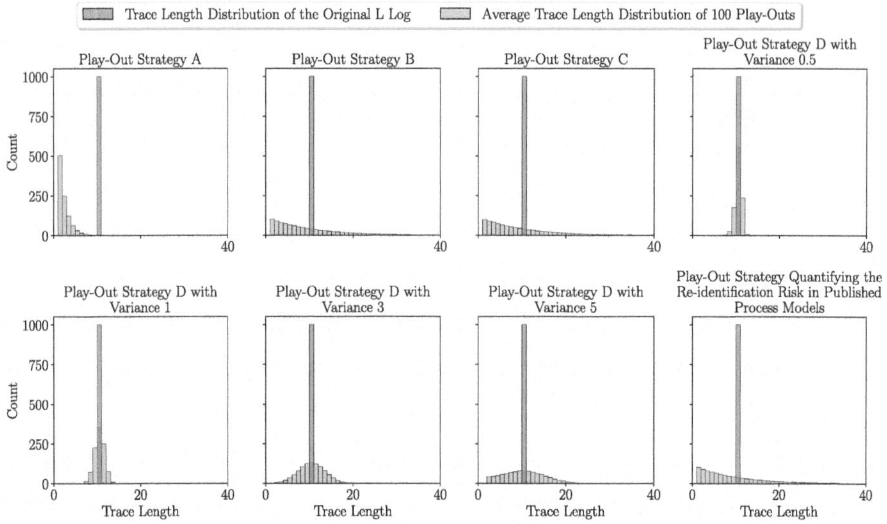

Fig. 4. The distribution of the average trace length when playing out 100 traces using each play-out strategy from $\circlearrowleft$ (a: 10000, τ: 9000): 1000, along with the distribution of the original log $L = [\langle a, a, a, a, a, a, a, a, a, a \rangle^{1000}]$.

State-of-the-Art (SOTA) Strategy. This strategy was introduced in [18]. It traverses a process tree like *Strategy C* but does a sequential play-out for the parallel composition, hence $R_{\wedge}^{SOTA} = R_{\rightarrow}$, and for the exclusive choice operator:

$R_{\times}^{SOTA}$ When $Q = \times(Q_1 : w_1, \ldots, Q_n : w_n) : w$ is encountered, consider the child nodes $Q_1, \ldots, Q_n$ in their respective order. Traversal continues with the first child Q_i with a positive weight, i.e., $w_i > 0$.

4.2 Reconstructing the Number of Loop Iterations

Next, we discuss the motivation for the approach presented in *Strategy D* that determines the number of loop iterations upfront, instead of relying solely on branching probabilities.

As an illustrative example, consider the process tree $\circlearrowleft$ (a: 10000, τ: 9000): 1000 discovered from event log $L = [\langle a, a, a, a, a, a, a, a, a, a \rangle^{1000}]$. Figure 4 shows the trace length distribution of L and the normalized trace length distribution of 100 play-outs, each containing 1000 traces for each play-out strategy. The majority of traces produced by all strategies except *Strategy D* are much shorter than the traces of log L. The reason is that these play-out strategies, and modelling techniques such as [24] or partly [4], capture the execution of the "redo" child of a loop operator with some probability p. Suppose p is fixed, like in *Strategy A* and *B*. In that case, each iteration is a Bernoulli trial with the number of iterations being a geometric variable [4]. Because in *Strategy C* and the *SOTA*

Strategy, the probability changes at each loop iteration, the sequence of iterations is not a sequence of Bernoulli trials. Nonetheless, our experiments show that the resulting distributions of iterations are actually close to a geometric distribution.

To reconstruct traces with consistently more loop iterations, one must decide on the number of loop iterations upfront. When playing out a process tree $Q = \circlearrowleft (Q_1 : w_1, Q_2 : w_2) : w$, we know that the traces of the original log, took in w $\circlearrowleft$-executions, on average $^{w_2}/_{w}$ loop repetitions. In our example, traces took, on average, $^{9000}/_{1000} = 9$ loop repetitions. *Strategy D* uses this information to set the mean of the normal distribution to $^{w_2}/_{w}$, each time we execute the $\circlearrowleft$ node. Here, the choice of a normal distribution is motivated by the fact that, in each process execution, multiple choices on (re)entering the loop are taken. Once these choices can be assumed to be independent and identically distributed (i.i.d.), the observational error is expected to tend to a normal distribution. Even in the absence of knowledge on the variance parameter v of the distribution, we expect it to provide a suitable representation of the number of loop iterations per process execution.

Compared to *Strategy D* the other strategies will perform worse when number of loop iterations is distributed such that the values are large and the variance is low. *Strategy D* performs worse when the number of loop iterations is distributed with large variance and the values are not centered around the chosen mean.

5 Experimental Evaluation

In this section, we evaluate how well our proposed play-out strategies can reconstruct the control-flow of logs from their discovered models. We present our experimental setup in Sect. 5.1, and discuss evaluation measures in Sect. 5.2. Then, we describe our results in Sect. 5.3 and discuss them in Sect. 5.4.

5.1 Experimental Setup

Experimental Pipeline. We use the inductive miner without noise filtering to discover the process trees. The lack of noise filtering results in a perfect fitting process model, a necessary condition to be able to fully reconstruct the log from the model. In our setting, it is impossible to reconstruct control-flow information about the event log that is not present in the model. To determine the frequency of nodes, we replay each trace of the original event log on the process tree. Each time we visit a node, we increase its weight by one. For each strategy, we do 100 play-outs of each process tree to obtain the evaluation logs. For *Strategy A* and *Strategy B*, we fix the number of traces generated to the number of traces in the original log. Hence, our results for these strategies are an upper bound for the reconstruction risks, since usually the number of traces is not known to the adversary, when the model is not annotated with absolute frequencies.

Dataset. We evaluate the play-out strategies using four real-world event logs: the BPIC 2015 Municipalities log [9], the BPIC 2017 log [8], the BPIC 2013

Closed Problems log [26], and the Sepsis log [19]. In Table 1 we show certain characteristics of the logs. The logs range from unstructured (BPIC 2015) to structured (BPIC 2013) and also differ drastically in the number of their activities. In addition to different levels of structuredness, we also considered different trace lengths, since longer traces are potentially harder to reconstruct. The logs differ from having relatively short (BPIC 2013) to very long traces (BPIC 2015).

Implementation. Our implementation is available on GitHub[1]. We used the inductive miner and earth mover's distance of PM4Py [2]. The runtime of our implemented play-out strategies is fast. On a machine with an AMD Ryzen 5600G a play-out of the BPIC 2013 log is generated in under one second and in 30 s one play-out for the BPIC 2017 log.

Table 1. Descriptive statistics of the event logs.

Event Log	# of Traces	# of Variants	# of Variants / # of Traces	Trace Length			# of Activities
				Min.	Avg.	Max.	
BPIC 2017	31509	15930	0.505	10	38.1	180	27
BPIC 2015 Municipalities	1199	1170	0.975	2	43.5	101	399
BPIC 2013 Closed Problems	1487	183	0.123	1	4.4	35	5
Sepsis Cases	1050	846	0.805	3	14.4	185	17

5.2 Evaluation Measures

Trace Length Distribution. We look into the trace length distribution to investigate the impact of how different play-out strategies handle the $\circlearrowleft$ operator. We plot the normalized distributions of each play-out strategy and the distribution of the original log as histograms for the BPIC 2017 log. The plots for the other event logs can be found in our appendix[2]. We calculate the similarity of the distributions using the normalized histogram intersection for all logs:

Definition 5. (Normalized histogram intersection (NHI) size). *Let I and M be histograms, each containing n bins, and let I_j respectively M_j denote the number of elements in bin j of I respectively of M. The normalized histogram intersection size is defined to be*

$$NHI(I, M) = \frac{\sum_{j=1}^{n} \min(I_j, M_j)}{\sum_{j=1}^{n} M_j}.$$

[1] https://github.com/henrikkirchmann/Control-Flow-Reconstruction.

[2] https://github.com/henrikkirchmann/Control-Flow-Reconstruction/tree/main/Appendix.

Earth Mover's Distance (EMD). We compare the reconstructed logs with the original log through the earth mover's distance (EMD) introduced in [17]. The EMD measures the distance, by the Levenshtein distance function, between the trace variant distributions of the event logs. Through the EMD, we can measure the difference between the logs in terms of their control-flow of each trace. This allows us to see if the play-out strategies produce logs that have similar control-flow to the original log, without the need for traces to be the same.

Normalized Multiset Intersection (NMI) Size. The multiset intersection size between two event logs represents the count of traces from the original log that are completely and successfully reconstructed. The normalized multiset intersection size, denoted by $NMI(L_1, L_2)$, is defined as the sum of the minimum occurrences of each trace σ in both multi sets L_1 and L_2 divided by $|L_1|$. For example, given the event logs $L_1 = [\langle a, b\rangle^2, \langle a, b, c\rangle^2]$ and $L_2 = [\langle a, b\rangle^3, \langle a, b, b\rangle]$, we have $NMI(L_1, L_2) = {}^2/_4$. Through this metric, we can determine if the play-out strategies create traces that are exactly the same as the traces of the original log.

Reconstructed Eventually Follows Relations. To check how many dependencies between activities we can reconstruct, we compare the eventually follows relations of the reconstructed logs to the original log. An eventually follows relation between two activities a and b, can be one of three types: (i) The relation between a and b is of type *always follows* when in all traces of the log activity b will occur eventually after a; (ii) *sometimes follows* when in some but not all traces of the log b will occur eventually after a; (iii) *never follows* when in no trace of the log b will eventually occur after a. To quantify the differences between the predicted eventually follows relations of our play-out strategies and the ones of the original log, we calculate the F_1-Scores, as the harmonic mean of precision and recall.

5.3 Results

Trace Length Distribution. Table 2 shows the NHI size with higher values, meaning better reconstruction of the trace length distribution. We can observe NHI values above 0.7 for 3 out of 4 of the event logs, with the exception being the BPIC 2015 log. Therefore, we can conclude that it is generally possible to mimic the trace length distribution and to rediscover general control-flow properties.

Considering the results in more detail, the success of the reconstruction might depend highly on the handling of loops. This aspect can be seen by the difference between the different settings for *Strategy D*. For BPIC 2015 the worst setting (*Strategy D with Variance 0.5*) reached a NHI of 0.19, while the best setting (*Strategy D with Variance 5*) led to a NHI value of 0.44. In Fig. 5, we can see that, compared to the other strategies, *Strategy D with Variance 0.5-3* creates considerably fewer traces of length below 20.

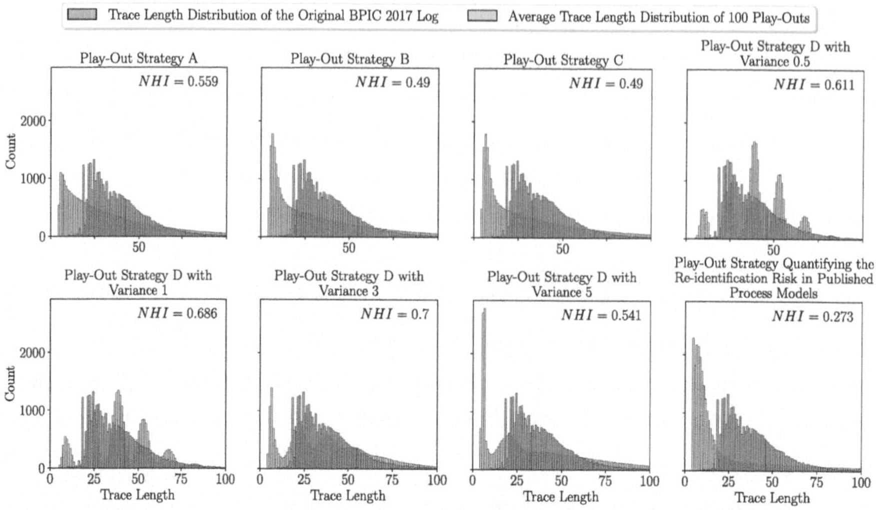

Fig. 5. The trace length distributions for the BPIC 2017 log.

Earth Mover's Distance. Table 2 shows the EMD. Smaller values, correspond to higher similarity between the control-flow of the play-outs and the original log. Unfortunately, computing the EMD for the BPIC 2017 log was not feasible. We can observe that for the BPIC 2013 log, it is possible to generate logs that can be very close to the original event log. However, the BPIC 2015 log shows that this might not be possible for all logs. We can observe that the difference between the logs is significantly larger than between the strategies. This lets us conclude that specifics of the process itself determine the chance of success for the adversary. *Strategy A* that has no additional information about the control-flow performs the worst but is followed by the *SOTA Strategy*, despite having knowledge about the absolute frequencies. The other Strategies reconstruct the control-flow of the original log with similar success in terms of the EMD.

Normalised Multiset Intersection Size. For all logs except the BPIC 2013 log, the NMI Size was below 0.01. The values for the BPIC 2013 log are shown in Table 2. This strongly suggests that the adversary might often not be able to generate the specific traces of the original log. However, for the BPIC 2013 log, we can see that *Strategy A* performs worse than the strategies with knowledge about frequencies. The results indicate again that knowledge about relative or absolute frequencies in process models can significantly increase the reconstruction success. Also, differences between the different settings of *Strategy D* can be significant.

Reconstructed Eventually Follows Relations. Table 3 shows the F_1-Scores of the reconstructed eventually follows relations. Regarding the reconstruction of always follows (AF) relations, all strategies perform similar, except for *A*, which performed the worst, and the *SOTA Strategy*, which is the second worst. Notably,

Table 2. NHI size, EMD and NMI size of 100 play-out logs and the original log. Higher NHI/NMI values and lower EMD values denote higher reconstruction success, the values that indicate the highest reconstruction success are bold.

	BPIC17		BPIC13			BPIC15		Sepsis		Average	
Strategy	NHI	EMD	NHI	EMD	NMI	NHI	EMD	NHI	EMD	NHI	EMD
A	0.55	-	0.66	0.35	0.19	0.17	0.93	0.50	0.74	0.47	0.67
B	0.49	-	0.83	**0.10**	**0.59**	0.43	0.87	**0.70**	0.52	0.61	0.50
C	0.49	-	0.83	0.11	**0.59**	0.43	0.87	**0.70**	0.51	0.61	0.50
D Var. ½	0.61	-	0.60	0.22	0.37	0.19	**0.86**	0.54	0.51	0.48	0.53
D Var. 1	0.68	-	0.66	0.18	0.44	0.22	**0.86**	0.61	**0.50**	0.54	0.51
D Var. 3	**0.70**	-	**0.88**	**0.10**	**0.59**	0.38	0.87	0.61	0.51	**0.64**	**0.49**
D Var. 5	0.54	-	0.76	0.17	0.51	**0.44**	0.87	0.51	0.53	0.56	0.52
SOTA [18]	0.27	-	0.83	0.14	0.52	0.38	0.92	0.69	0.62	0.54	0.56
Avg. for Log	0.54	-	0.75	0.17	0.47	0.33	0.88	0.60	0.55	0.55	0.53

the F_1-Scores of *SOTA* are by far the lowest in 3 out of 4 evaluated logs. For the sometimes follows (SF) relations, the *SOTA Strategy* again performs the worst, despite having access to absolute frequency information, that is not available to strategies *A* and *B*. Strategy *B* outperforms *D*, despite having only knowledge of branching probabilities and the number of traces to generate. In the case of never follows (NF) relations, the performance of all strategies, except for *A*, which performed the worst, is again very similar.

Overall, we observe a significant level of variance in the F_1-Scores, reaching from cases where no reconstruction is possible to values as high as 0.89. While it is expected that the highest values are obtained for the never follows (NF) relations, since they relate to behaviour that shall not be generated according to the process model, we also observe relatively high F_1-Scores for the always follows (AF) relations. Those can be interpreted as invariants on the presence of activity executions, and hence, are particular interesting from a reconstruction point of view. With F_1-Scores around 0.6, we conclude that a good share of these relations are reconstructed successfully.

5.4 Discussion

Comparison of Play-Out Strategies. Overall, *Strategy A* performed the worst of all play-out strategies. This is expected, since *Strategy A* lacks information about probabilities or frequencies in the process model. We conclude that it is indeed harder or even impossible to successfully reconstruct much of the control-flow of the original log the un-annotated process model was discovered from.

The play-outs from *Strategy B* and *Strategy C* were almost similar in our evaluated statistics. Knowledge of each node's left-over frequency did not help

Table 3. Average F_1-scores of 100 play-outs for the reconstructed always (AF), sometimes (SF) and never follows (NF) relations. Higher values denote higher reconstruction success, the highest values are bold.

	BPIC17			BPIC13			BPIC15			Sepsis			Average		
Strat.	AF	SF	NF	AF	SF	NF	AF	SF	NF	AF	SF	NF	AF	SF	NF
A	0.40	0.38	0.39	0.69	0.63	0.00	0.03	0.16	0.81	0.23	0.46	0.02	0.34	0.41	0.30
B	0.52	0.54	0.47	**0.75**	**0.80**	0.87	0.20	0.48	0.71	0.52	0.60	0.33	0.51	**0.61**	0.60
C	0.55	**0.55**	0.47	**0.75**	0.79	0.85	0.20	**0.49**	0.76	0.49	0.60	0.32	0.50	**0.61**	0.60
D ½	**0.64**	0.54	0.46	0.64	0.52	0.87	0.22	0.48	0.80	**0.59**	**0.61**	0.36	**0.52**	0.54	**0.62**
D 1	**0.64**	0.52	0.46	0.63	0.50	**0.89**	**0.23**	0.47	0.79	0.57	0.60	0.35	**0.52**	0.52	**0.62**
D 3	0.61	0.43	0.45	0.61	0.43	0.86	**0.23**	0.44	0.77	**0.59**	0.60	0.30	0.51	0.48	0.60
D 5	0.62	0.43	0.46	0.61	0.43	0.86	**0.23**	0.43	0.76	0.56	0.57	0.25	0.51	0.47	0.58
SOTA	0.16	0.30	**0.57**	0.71	0.71	0.41	0.01	0.06	**0.86**	0.14	0.34	**0.53**	0.44	0.35	0.59
Avg.	0.51	0.46	0.47	0.67	0.60	0.70	0.17	0.36	0.78	0.46	0.55	0.31	0.48	0.50	0.56

Strategy C to make better reconstruction decisions than *Strategy B*, when *Strategy B* knows how many traces to generate. This indicates that when a log with branching probabilities and the number of how many traces the original log contains are released, the model will reveal nearly the same amount of control-flow information as it would have done when released with absolute frequencies.

Strategy D with Variance v was unable to consistently outperform *Strategy C* or *Strategy B*. In our experiments, we could observe that setting the variance value between 1 and 3 led to good results. A limitation of this strategy is that an attacker does not know what variance to pick. When we sample from the normal distribution with a large variance, like in *Strategy D with Variance* 5 we generate traces that took numerous loop iterations. The longest trace we generated with *Strategy D with Variance* 5 for the BPIC 2017 log was 863 activities long. Those long traces consume much of the frequency weights, thus forcing the other reconstructed traces to be shorter.

The *State-of-the-Art Strategy* [18] performed worse than *Strategy B* despite knowing the left-over frequencies of each node. This indicates that we should not execute $\times$ and $\wedge$ nodes sequentially if we want to reconstruct the control-flow from the original log. We saw for example that this results in many false positive always follows relations and hence low F_1-scores.

Assessment of Reconstruction Risk. In our experiments, we observed that we were able to reconstruct control-flow properties (trace length distribution). Additionally, we were also able to generate logs with a small distance to the original log for one process and a reasonable distance for another. However, we were only able to reconstruct concrete cases from one log. Finally, we illustrated that information on the eventually follows relations of the underlying process may be reconstructed to a significant extent, revealing co-occurrences of activity executions and their mutual exclusiveness.

However, we acknowledge that, in practice, an attacker also always faces uncertainty about the reconstructed information, i.e., if a reconstructed trace was actually part of the original log. This, in general, hinders the operationalization of the insights obtained through a reconstruction attack. This leads to the following assessment in terms of the reconstruction risk of process models: In general, it is possible to retrieve traces from process models. However, this is not possible for all process models. Therefore, reconstruction risks of process models need to be considered and taken seriously, but their risk should not be overstated. Instead, it should be considered that while process models might not lead to the reconstruction of complete traces, even partially reconstructed information might be exploitable for an adversary.

6 Conclusion

To mitigate confidentially risks, one may resort to publishing a process model instead of an event log for operational analysis. In this paper, we argued that such an approach also potentially incurs risks, since some information about the original process executions may be reconstructed from the released process model. We studied this risk and formulated reconstruction attacks as play-out strategies for models given as process trees. We conclude from our experiments that the reconstruction risk for process trees modelled by the inductive miner from complex real-world event logs is very low. However, there is a considerable reconstruction risk for more structured event logs. The annotation of process trees with frequency information increases the reconstruction risk considerably. Compared to the state of the art, our approaches can consistently provide better results, even with less background knowledge.

In future work, we plan to shift our focus from the quantity of information that can be reconstructed to a more nuanced analysis. This will involve examining the specific types of information that can be reconstructed and the associated uncertainties from an attacker's point of view. Our goal is to develop algorithms capable of answering questions such as: given a process model, which traces can be reconstructed that occurred with absolute certainty in the original log.

Acknowledgements. This work was supported by the German Federal Ministry of Education and Research (BMBF), grant number 16DII133 (Weizenbaum-Institute).

References

1. Augusto, A., et al.: Automated discovery of process models from event logs: review and benchmark. IEEE TKDE **31**(4), 686–705 (2019)
2. Berti, A., van Zelst, S.J., Schuster, D.: Pm4py: a process mining library for python. Softw. Impacts **17**, 100556 (2023). https://doi.org/10.1016/J.SIMPA.2023.100556
3. Burke, A., Leemans, S.J., Wynn, M.T.: Stochastic process discovery by weight estimation. In: ICPM Workshops, pp. 260–272. Springer, Cham (2020)
4. Burke, A., Leemans, S.J., Wynn, M.T.: Discovering stochastic process models by reduction and abstraction. In: Petri Nets, pp. 312–336. Springer, Cham (2021)

5. Camargo, M., Dumas, M., González, O.: Automated discovery of business process simulation models from event logs. DSS **134**, 113284 (2020)
6. Carmona, J., van Dongen, B.F., Solti, A., Weidlich, M.: Conformance Checking - Relating Processes and Models. Springer (2018). https://doi.org/10.1007/978-3-319-99414-7
7. Chapela-Campa, D., Benchekroun, I., Baron, O., Dumas, M., Krass, D., Senderovich, A.: Can I trust my simulation model? measuring the quality of business process simulation models, vol. 14159, pp. 20–37 (2023). https://doi.org/10.1007/978-3-031-41620-0_2
8. van Dongen, B.: BPI challenge 2017. 4tu. Centre for Research Data, Dataset (2017)
9. van Dongen, B.F.: BPI challenge 2015. In: 11th International Workshop on Business Process Intelligence (BPI 2015) (2015)
10. Elkoumy, G., Pankova, A., Dumas, M.: Privacy-preserving directly-follows graphs: balancing risk and utility in process mining. arXiv preprint arXiv:2012.01119 (2020)
11. Fahrenkrog-Petersen, S.A., Kabierski, M., van der Aa, H., Weidlich, M.: Semantics-aware mechanisms for control-flow anonymization in process mining. Inf. Syst. 102169 (2023)
12. Hidano, S., Murakami, T., Katsumata, S., Kiyomoto, S., Hanaoka, G.: Model inversion attacks for online prediction systems: without knowledge of non-sensitive attributes. IEICE Trans. Inf. Syst. **101-D**(11), 2665–2676 (2018). https://doi.org/10.1587/TRANSINF.2017ICP0013
13. Hildebrant, R., Fahrenkrog-Petersen, S.A., Weidlich, M., Ren, S.: PMDG: privacy for multi-perspective process mining through data generalization. In: CAiSE. Lecture Notes in Computer Science, vol. 13901, pp. 506–521. Springer, Cham (2023)
14. Hilprecht, B., Härterich, M., Bernau, D.: Monte Carlo and reconstruction membership inference attacks against generative models. Proc. Priv. Enhancing Technol. **2019**(4), 232–249 (2019). https://doi.org/10.2478/POPETS-2019-0067
15. Leemans, S.J.J., Fahland, D., van der Aalst, W.M.P.: Discovering block-structured process models from event logs - a constructive approach. In: Colom, J.M., Desel, J. (eds.) Petri Nets. LNCS, vol. 7927, pp. 311–329. Springer, Cham (2013)
16. Leemans, S.J.J., Polyvyanyy, A.: Stochastic-aware precision and recall measures for conformance checking in process mining. Inf. Syst. **115**, 102197 (2023)
17. Leemans, S.J., Syring, A.F., van der Aalst, W.M.: Earth movers' stochastic conformance checking. In: BPM Forum, pp. 127–143. Springer, Cham (2019)
18. Maatouk, K., Mannhardt, F.: Quantifying the re-identification risk in published process models. In: ICPM Workshops, pp. 382–394. Springer, Cham (2021)
19. Mannhardt, F.: Sepsis cases-event log, 4tu. ResearchData. Dataset (2016). https://doi.org/10.4121/uuid:915d2bfb-7e84-49ad-a286-dc35f063a460
20. Rafiei, M., van der Aalst, W.M.P.: Towards quantifying privacy in process mining. In: ICPM Workshops. LNBIP, vol. 406, pp. 385–397. Springer, Cham (2020)
21. Rafiei, M., van der Aalst, W.M.P.: Group-based privacy preservation techniques for process mining. Data Knowl. Eng. **134**, 101908 (2021)
22. Rafiei, M., Wangelik, F., Pourbafrani, M., van der Aalst, W.M.P.: Travag: differentially private trace variant generation using GANs. In: RCIS. LNBIP, vol. 476, pp. 415–431. Springer, Cham (2023)
23. Rigaki, M., García, S.: A survey of privacy attacks in machine learning. ACM Comput. Surv. **56**(4), 101:1–101:34 (2024). https://doi.org/10.1145/3624010
24. Rogge-Solti, A., van der Aalst, W.M., Weske, M.: Discovering stochastic petri nets with arbitrary delay distributions from event logs. In: BPM Workshops, pp. 15–27. Springer, Cham (2014)

25. Rogge-Solti, A., Senderovich, A., Weidlich, M., Mendling, J., Gal, A.: In log and model we trust? A generalized conformance checking framework. In: BPM. LNCS, vol. 9850, pp. 179–196. Springer, Cham (2016)
26. Steeman, W.: BPI challenge 2013, closed problems (2013). https://doi.org/10.4121/uuid:c2c3b154-ab26-4b31-a0e8-8f2350ddac11
27. Van Der Aalst, W.: Process Mining: Data Science in Action, vol. 2. Springer, Cham (2016)
28. Nuñez von Voigt, S., et al.: Quantifying the re-identification risk of event logs for process mining: empirical evaluation paper. In: CAiSE, pp. 252–267. Springer, Cham (2020)

Business Models, Platforms and Strategic Management

Value Assessment of Consumer Electronics with Digital Product Passports: A Case Study of Lifetime Extension Assessment of Disposed Washing Machines

Frank Stiksma[1(✉)], Marten van Sinderen[2], and João Luiz Rebelo Moreira[2]

[1] Saxion University of Applied Sciences, P.O. Box 70000, 7500 KB Enschede, The Netherlands
f.k.s.stiksma@saxion.nl

[2] University of Twente, P.O. Box 217, 7500 AE Enschede, The Netherlands

Abstract. The rapid increase in e-waste poses significant environmental challenges. Most disposed Electrical and Electronic Equipment (EEE) products, including computers, mobile phones, and household appliances, are currently recycled for materials rather than reused, due to perceived low residual value. This approach conflicts with circular economy goals, which emphasize extending products' lifetime. Many disposed EEE items are "end-of-use" rather than "end-of-life," indicating potential for reuse after refurbishment or repair. However, effective lifetime extension is hampered by inadequate data sharing and complex data systems within the EEE sector. This research addresses the data sharing problem, which is essential for circular strategies and improving EEE lifetime extension. Digital transformation, particularly through the Digital Product Passport (DPP), can facilitate comprehensive product life cycle management, supporting sustainable practices. We propose an EEE ecosystem modelling approach to compare traditional and circular business models through e3-value models, focusing on washing machines. We investigated the applicability of DPPs to aid decision-making for lifetime extension at collection points.

Keywords: Circular Ecosystem · Lifetime Extension · Digital Product Passport · E-Waste · Electrical and Electronic Equipment

1 Introduction

The waste flow from disposed Electrical and Electronic Equipment (EEE), or e-waste, is one of the fastest growing waste streams[1]. EEE refers to products such as heaters and coolers, computers, screens and monitors, mobile phones, lamps, white goods, and household appliances. According to the Global E-waste Monitor 2024 [1], the amount of e-waste worldwide was 62 billion kilograms in 2022 and is expected to increase to 82 billion kilograms by 2030. Most disposed EEE products are treated as e-waste with

[1] https://environment.ec.europa.eu/topics/waste-and-recycling/waste-electrical-and-electronic-equipment-weee_en.

J. Borbinha et al. (Eds.): EDOC 2024, LNCS 15409, pp. 81–98, 2025.
https://doi.org/10.1007/978-3-031-78338-8_5

little residual technical and economic value to justify reuse. Materials recycling is the preferred strategy for handling the e-waste stream.

Product lifetime extension of EEE is a critical lever to diminish e-waste and utilize the residual value of disposed EEE. However, the current focus on materials recycling is at odds with the ambition of governments to work towards a circular economy promoting product lifetime extension [2]. A critical factor that complicates lifetime extension is that disposed EEE devices are currently treated as "end-of-life" products. Such products are considered as obsolete [3]. In many cases, however, it is questionable whether a disposed EEE product is functionally and technically obsolete [4]. Consumers tend to stop using a product if they can afford a new product with better performance, more functionality, or higher visual attractiveness. The disposed product in these cases is often "end-of-use" rather than "end-of-life", and lifetime extension could initiate a new use cycle with another user until the product reaches the next end-of-use (or ultimately, end-of-life).

Lifetime extension implies a decision that the residual value of a product justifies another use cycle, possibly after necessary refurbishment or repair. However, obtaining the necessary data for easy and objective decision-making is hampered by characteristics of the EEE sector, including lack of data sharing across supply chains and complex data systems [5]. The goal of this paper is to address the problem of data sharing for circular strategies in the EEE sector and especially for improving lifetime extension of EEE.

A business barrier for data sharing is the lack of business incentives for making data available. Due to the absence of an EEE ecosystem perspective that provides insights in new circular business models based on collaboration, individual EEE businesses are reticent when it comes to making investments regarding data sharing that make such collaboration possible. Collaboration between different actors in an ecosystem is necessary to develop a joint circular value proposition [6–8]. Therefore, we propose in this paper an EEE ecosystem modelling approach to represent and compare traditional and circular strategy business models based on collaboration between various actors. We focus on washing machines as a specific EEE sector in which the lifetime extension of goods is important, yet currently at best only partially successful. We aim to address some of the issues behind the slow progress in this sector, especially the current lack of residual value recognition of disposed goods by collection agents (i.e., organizations that offer e-waste collection services at some physical locations).

Next to the business barrier, technical barriers exist with respect to data sharing in the EEE sector. Not only are data systems within and across EEE supply chains incompatible [5], there is also no clear roadmap on deciding which data to share, how to share the data, and how to use the data for circular strategies including lifetime extension. Digitalization and digital transformation are important enablers of making better and more efficient use of (digital) data, but these developments do not necessarily lower the technical barriers. One application enabled by digital transformation, namely the digital product passport (DPP), might help to develop a focus on choosing, sharing and using data in the EEE sector. A DPP collects and makes available product data throughout the product's entire life cycle, which can facilitate sustainable product life cycle management in a circular value chain [9]. In this paper, we investigate the applicability of a DPP for the EEE sector. Again, we focus on washing machines as a specific EEE sector and we look at the use of DPP data to support decision-making for lifetime extension of washing machines at collection agents. As a source of inspiration and to acquire a baseline for required data, we also study the current practice of lifetime extension of washing machines. Furthermore, we suggest to use an ecosystem perspective, e.g., as supported by our EEE ecosystem modelling approach, as a starting point to identify required data for desired collaboration in a selected business model. Based on this, we propose information categories to include in the DPP and a decision process blueprint that could be implemented at collection agents.

Figure 1 shows the overall approach that we followed for the research reported in this paper. It also shows how this is related to the structure of the paper: Sect. 2 provides background on the economic and technical topics related to the e-waste problem; Sect. 3 discusses an ecosystem perspective on the washing machines sector that allows analysis of the current value chain and projecting circular alternatives; Sect. 4 presents results of field studies on lifetime extension of washing machines in current practices; Sect. 5 proposes a digital transformation based on a digital product passport for washing machines and decision support at collection points; Sect. 6 relates the results to an ecosystem of the future, while identifying the need for a suitable infrastructure to support data sharing; and Sect. 7 presents our concluding remarks.

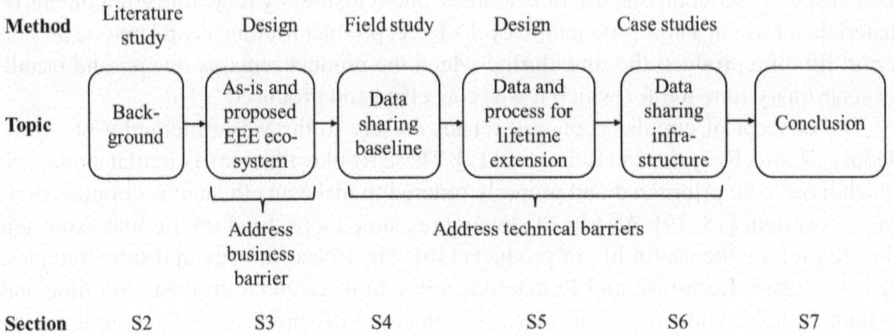

Fig. 1. Overall research approach

2 Background

2.1 Circular Ecosystems

Long-term collaborative relations with partners in a network and transparency of information across supply chains greatly facilitate the implementation of a circular economy in the EEE sector [5]. Nonetheless, a circular economy requires an ecosystem innovation based on circular principles that address circular strategies [7]. Collaboration between different actors in such a circular ecosystem is necessary to develop a joint circular value proposition from a product life cycle perspective that integrates lifetime extension.

A circular ecosystem is "a co-evolving, dynamic and potentially self-organizing configuration, in which actors integrate resources and co-create circular value flows in interaction with each other." [10] A circular ecosystem aligns the multilateral dependencies and complementarities among actors in a value network in order to maximize a collective value proposition where the whole acts as one unit [6, 11]. Thus, ecosystem actors achieve joint circular strategies and goals because their activities are jointly coordinated; they act interdependently and carry them out together [7].

Digital technologies and data play a crucial role in circular ecosystems [8]. They are enablers of data integration and sharing, which in turn support informed decision-making and value creation [10]. Orchestration and governance mechanisms can be used to structure the data sharing, collaboration, and value sharing amongst circular ecosystem actors. The vitality and innovation of circular ecosystems does not only depend on technology enablers and business motivation, but are also affected by factors such as initial context of the ecosystem, legislation, environmental pressures, trust among ecosystem actors, and product properties [12].

2.2 Circularity and Lifetime Extension

Circularity can be realized by slowing, narrowing, and closing resource loops [13–15]. 'Slowing' is achieved by designing long-life products and by product lifetime extension, 'narrowing' by reducing the use of resources, and 'closing' by recycling components or materials for use in a new product life cycle. Here, product lifetime is understood as "the useful life of a product; the time during which the product remains integer and usable for its primary function for which it was conceived and produced" [16].

The concept of circular economy relates closely to the waste hierarchy of '4Rs': Reduce, Reuse, Recycle, and Recovery [17]. These Rs play the role of circular strategies, which have to be prioritized and properly ordered to make an efficacious circular economy ecosystem [18, 19]. As part of slowing resource loops, product lifetime extension aims to prolong the useful life of products [16]. The Reuse strategy and sub-strategies, such as Repair, Refurbish and Remanufacture, aim to extend a product's lifetime and its parts [20]. Maximizing lifetime by designing long-life products and encouraging the reuse of products, parts, and materials ensures that the economic and environmental value of EEE products is preserved for as long as possible and prevents unnecessary value destruction. The product lifetime and the extension of EEE depends on various product-related, use-related, service-related and circumstantial factors. These factors need to be considered when defining lifetime extension assessment criteria. For example, the lifetime of washing machines depends on factors such as mechanical stress, abrasion, performed maintenance activities, new technologies, aesthetics, energy efficiency, and environmental conditions [21, 22]. EEE's repairability also affects lifetime extension. Repairability is the ability and ease with which a product can be repaired during its life cycle [23]. The corresponding repairability score is determined by information provision, product design for repair (e.g., modular and standardized design, ease of disassembly), and supportive services (e.g., spare part supply) [24].

An environmental impact assessment should be carried out to assess the possible extension of the lifespan of energy-using EEE products [25]. For washing machines, water and energy efficiency determine environmental impact highly [26]. Therefore, a life cycle analysis is required, assessing the environmental impact of EEE on quantified CO2 emissions for the whole life cycle [27–29]. Another consideration is that Internet of

Things technologies are a driver for circular innovation of the washing machine industry ecosystem [30, 31].

2.3 Digital Product Passport

The EU Green Deal Action plan sees digitization of product information throughout the entire product life cycle as an enabler towards a circular economy [32]. A DPP contains unique product identifiers allowing data storage, retrieval, and sharing by various value chain actors throughout the product life cycle [33]. Consequently, DPPs can support sustainable product life cycle management and value retention in a circular value chain [34, 35]. DPP is a promising instrument to gather and share product data for decision-making [36, 37] and addressing currently existing information asymmetries [34, 38, 39].

A common definition of DPP is "a product-specific data set, which can be electronically accessed through a data carrier to electronically register, process and share product-related information amongst supply chain businesses, authorities, and consumers" [40]. The information in the passport relates to the product's environmental sustainability and is, therefore, relevant for resource-efficient, sustainable, and circular production and consumption systems [41, 42]. DPPs support end-of-use circular strategies [40]. The reuse of products can be determined more accurately because the data in a DPP will objectify the residual value of the products. Repair and maintenance can be better predicted and programmed over time. Detailed technical, repairability, product, usage, and spare parts information contribute favorably to lifetime extension services provided by repairers and maintenance service providers [33].

Recently, several DPP initiatives were introduced for specific product categories [35], such as electric vehicle batteries [9], textile products [43], and construction products [44]. However, many DPP initiatives emphasize an individual stakeholder in a value chain or an industry instead of assuming an integral ecosystem perspective that involves all stakeholders [35]. The fragmentation of the desired data across multiple value chain actors and data sources hinders DPP creation and handling [37]. Therefore, the DPP orchestration should be positioned in a Digital Product Passport Ecosystem that enables different DPP applications for different stakeholders in value networks [45, 46]. Such a DPP ecosystem requires an underlying digital infrastructure and standardized data governance requirements that enable data sharing among stakeholders in the ecosystem [47].

3 Electrical and Electronic Equipment Ecosystem

Several actors can be identified in the current EEE ecosystem. Forward supply actors such as manufacturers and retailers strive for operational efficiency, technical product innovation, and profit maximization by selling new EEE. Consumers mainly strive for low prices. After usage, they want to dispose their EEE efficiently. Consequently, EEE lifetime extension is not a key driver of these actors, resulting in a large flow of low-quality EEE. Affected by the extended producer responsibility, manufacturers and retailers delegate reverse supply chain activities to Waste Electrical and Electronic

Equipment (WEEE) management centers. As part of the reverse supply chain, collection agents and WEEE management take care of reverse logistics and the collection, sorting, dissembling, and administration of discarded EEE. Subsequently, recycling companies focus on materials recycling. A fixed fee based on the weight of collected EEE favors materials recycling. On a minor scale, repair facilities realize reuse of disposed EEE. We developed a current and envisioned EEE ecosystem specialized for washing machines using the e3-value modeling language. *e3-value* is a language to build and analyze value networks [48]. An e3-value model represents a value network in which actors exchange value objects, resulting in a perceived benefit for each actor. The set of value transfers in a value network results in a collective value proposition that meets customer needs.

Figure 2 presents the e3-value model of a value network corresponding to the current washing machine market. In short, the e3-value graphical notation used in the models presented here includes: actor (square), value activity (rounded square), value exchange (connector), value interface (two opposite arrows within an ellipse), customer need (circle with dot) and boundary element (circle with 'x'). Figure 2a) shows how a customer need motivates a collection of value exchanges to satisfy the need. The financial and product-related value exchanges encourage consumers, retailers, manufacturers, materials and component suppliers to participate in the value network.

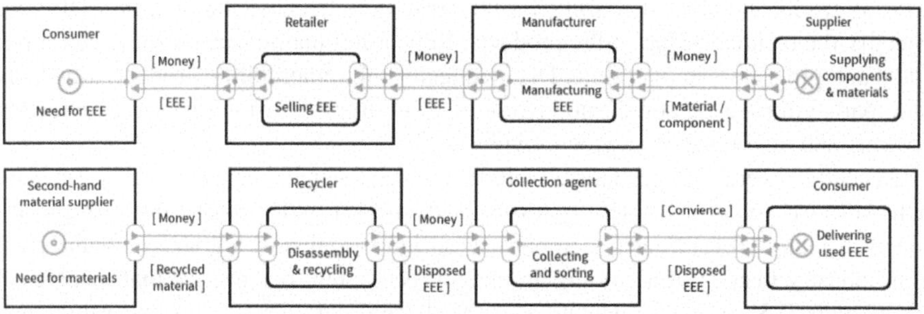

Fig. 2. Value network of current EEE ecosystem: **a)** Satisfying the need of a consumer of having a functioning washing machine; and **b)** satisfying the need of a second-hand material supplier to have second-hand (components and materials of) washing machines that can be offered for sale.

Figure 2b) shows that a customer need of a material supplier for second-hand materials motivates financial and material value exchanges among second-hand material suppliers, recyclers, collection agents, and consumers. Our model shows the value network of the current washing machines market as two separated parts, emphasizing that second-hand material suppliers generally purchase materials that are not reused in washing machines but applied for other recycling purposes. The value network clarifies that the value exchanges between actors are only economically attractive to them when selling new EEE or recycling materials. Value exchanges based on product lifetime extension are not economically attractive to them. A collective circular value proposition aiming to extend the lifetime of EEE is hampered by several factors, most importantly the lack of EEE ecosystem orchestration, poor capabilities to identify EEE's residual technical and economic value, and inadequate digital data sharing.

Lifetime extension of discarded EEE is a collective task of the actors in the ecosystem. To tackle the abovementioned issues, we propose an e3-value model of a future EEE ecosystem that favors more lifetime extension of disposed washing machines (see Fig. 3). We choose the perspective of a collection agent who has a critical role in identifying the residual value of collected EEE and harvesting spare parts suitable for reuse. Information sharing is critical to keeping products and materials in the product life cycle as long as possible [49]. Therefore, we introduce a DPP manager who is responsible for the creation and handling of DPPs.

Furthermore, the value network is modeled based on the assumption that all actors involved make their data available to the DPP and collectively contribute to a circular value proposition that favors EEE lifetime extension. The data in the DPPs support the collection agent in assessing collected washing machines. The content of the DPP and a related data-driven process diagram are described in Sect. 5. We also introduce the business roles of repairer and spare parts supplier in our model to enable the lifetime extension of washing machines. The logistics of EEE and materials have no direct added value for our circular task and have, therefore, been ignored. We omitted materials recycling in our model since we wanted to focus on lifetime extension to enable reuse of EEE.

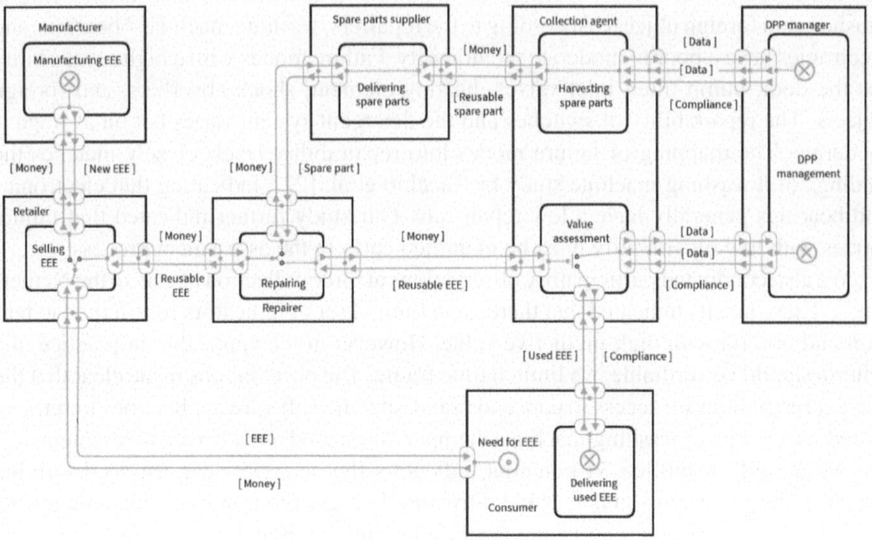

Fig. 3. Proposed future e3-value model

The customer need for a new or second-hand washing machine triggers the value network. In our model, we assume that manufacturers still produce new washing machines but that retailers, influenced by growing second-hand markets, sell second-hand washing machines in addition to new ones. The demand for second-hand washing machines requires a value network in which the value activities and the mutual value transfers between consumers, retailers, repairers, spare parts suppliers, collection agents, and disposing consumers are economically attractive. Another possibility is that compliance directs actors to perform a value transaction, such as sharing data in DPPs. The model shows that a DPP manager who takes care of DPP management supports the circular value activities of a collection agent. A cloud provider can execute the DPP manager's role. Furthermore, in our value model, harvested parts are identified and registered by recording associated data in the DPP. Although these data are valuable for spare parts providers and repairers when repairing collected washing machines, it falls outside the scope of our value model.

4 Field Studies

The repairability of a washing machine largely determines the extent to which lifetime extension is possible [24, 50]. The repairability in turn is strongly affected by diagnosis time, ease of disassembly, repairability time, and repair expertise [51]. We conducted semi-structured interviews with four professional repairers to gain further insight into factors that are decisive in practice for assessing whether lifetime extension is possible. Repairers indicated that most failure modes in non-functioning washing machines can be traced back to electronics, bearings, door, pump, pump filter, shock absorbers, carbon brushes, and foreign objects. According to the repairers, washing machines' bearings and electronics have a poor to moderate repairability. Failure modes with a high repairability are the door, pump filter, inlet valves, heating element, shock absorbers, and foreign objects. The repairability of switches and the detergent system varies but on average is moderate. The mapping of failure modes into repairability levels closely matches the findings of a washing machine study by Tecchio et al. [22], indicating that electronics and bearings generally have a low repair rate. Our study further indicated that failure modes with low repairability must be identified early in the assessment process.

We also conducted participatory observations at three collection agents in the Netherlands. These agents indicated that there are a limited set of indicators for lifetime extension and criteria with high predictive value. However, to be applicable in practice, the criteria should be verifiable in a limited time frame. The observations made clear that the current restrictions on access to data and brand-specific software applications to retrieve stored usage data in washing machines hamper automated, data-driven assessment.

We initially identified 34 potential indicators that assessors can use to determine whether lifetime extension is feasible. Structured observations at two collection agents clarified that experts assess washing machines mainly on brand, visual condition, completeness, quality of bearings, age, and product type. Usage information is normally not directly available, but it can be indirectly derived from visual inspections of washing machines. The lack of cross-brand standardization of product labels hindered the understandability of product-specific information, such as product year and model number. Therefore, information on product labels was usually rejected as input for cross-brand lifetime assessment. Potentially useful information for assessment, such as initial catalog price and year of construction, were also rejected as indicators because data was not always available. Observations revealed that the experts' valuation of indicators was affected by the availability of repair facilities and the harvesting of spare parts for reuse in repairable washing machines. Furthermore, assessing lifetime extension of washing machines depends highly on the expert's tacit knowledge, which hampered objective identification of useful indicators and criteria.

Based on these findings, a simplified set of ten indicators for washing machines' lifetime extension was determined and validated in subsequent structured observations at collection agents: washing machine type, brand, condition of bearings, dents, rust, housing completeness, control panel completeness, soap tray completeness, door completeness, and door construction quality. Some indicators are proxies for other relevant information which is not accessible or available. For example, according to the interviewed experts at collection agents, the brand is a proxy for a washing machine's product and material quality, repairability, energy and water consumption, and expected market demand.

The indicators were operationalized in procedures for establishing their data values. A distinction was made between primary and proxy indicators. Primary indicators directly refer to aspects of a washing machine relevant for objectively assessing lifetime extension. Proxy indicators indirectly refer to such aspects and often have a subjective component. Suggestions have been made for possible information sources to verify criteria in terms of these indicators. Acceptance standards were linked to the selected indicators and criteria in coordination with collection agents and professional repairers. For example, a practical criterion for accepting the lifetime extension of a washing machine was that the washing machine has a German brand and has functioning bearings.

The study provided valuable insights on lifetime extension in current practice, including the lack of access to data related to relevant information for lifetime extension, the use of less desirable proxy indicators for this reason, and the coarse-grained data values that could be obtained for selected indicators. We believe that DPPs can alleviate if not eliminate some of these disadvantages.

5 Digital Product Passport and Decision Support

We conceptualized a DPP[2] for washing machines to support decision-making across the EEE ecosystem during the product life cycle. For this purpose, four use cases have been developed for EEE manufacturers, retailers, collection agents, and repairers to explore the practical relevance and content of the DPP. Due to the focus of this study on lifetime extension assessment, in this paper, we only present the use case of a collection agent. This use case was created based on ecosystem analysis (see Sect. 3) and a semi-structured interview with a collection agent. Central to the use case is the business role change of collection agents from distribution and sorting centers to value assessment centers, where the pursuit of high-quality reuse options for collected washing machines is pivotal. As noted in Sect. 3, this requires collection agents to be able to recognize and quantify the residual value of washing machines and their spare parts. Such a circular role for collection agents is only possible if they have sufficient information and data.

[2] The documentation of the DPP information categories, generic lifetime extension assessment process, and the DPP application are openly available in: https://github.com/jonimoreira/dpp/tree/main/Stiksma_2024_Disposed_washing_machines.

DPPs support collection agents to perform the residual value assessment. Product information, technical information, product health, historical usage and repair information, and information about expected ecological impact of lifetime extension are, among other things, necessary to arrive at an informed decision regarding lifetime extension.

In line with the conceptualization of the digital battery passport [9], our DPP consists of four information categories: (1) Washing machine product, (2) Value chain actors, (3) Status, diagnostics, and performance, and (4) Sustainability and circularity properties. Each information category is further structured into subcategories and finally into properties for which concrete data values can be provided (similar to the indicators for lifetime extension identified in Sect. 4).

When assessing returned washing machines, it is first essential to gain insight into the product characteristics as the foundation of the assessment process. Therefore, the first information category provides decision-makers with information on product identification, product support information, and product properties. The product identification of a washing machine 'refers to, among others, the brand, the product type or model, the Global Trade Item Number, and the serial number. Identification of collected EEE enables value chain actors to access product data, such as product specifications and spare part numbers. The product support information refers to the documents that provide insight into the product features of a washing machine and support the technical repair process, such as failure diagnostics codes and product manuals. Product characteristics include specifications (e.g., washing machine type and load capacity) and performance. The performance category quantifies various performance indicators, such as energy and water consumption, noise level, and washing results.

The second information category "Value chain actors" provides transparency into ecosystem actors who have interacted with a device at any point during the product life cycle of a washing machine, e.g., during manufacture, sale, use, disposal, collection, or repair. The information on ecosystem actors covers general actor information, log data, and chain of custody. The general actor information contributes to the identification of involved value chain actors, their role in the value chain, their status, and their location. Log data refers to the collection and storage of data during the product life cycle of a washing machine. Such historical records provide actors insight into the data, status, and activities carried out by different value chain actors during a washing machine's life cycle. This might include the production date, repairs, upgrades, error messages, transport movements, and the location of the collection point where a washing machine has been discarded. Information concerning the chain of custody clarifies the actor's responsibilities, e.g., regarding the physical washing machine itself and its sustainability and circularity performance [9]. This information explains which value chain actor has been responsible for a washing machine product or part during a defined period.

The third information category "Status, diagnostics, and performance", is relevant for determining whether a washing machine can still be used for a potential second life phase after its disposal. This information category responds directly to the need for product and usage information to objectify whether lifetime extension is feasible or not, based on technical parameters. Information on the washing machine's health, such as its physical condition, failure diagnostics, usage history, and residual lifetime is crucial. Information about maintenance history provides insight into the maintenance and repair activities that have taken place during a washing machine's product life cycle. The washing machine's performance may decrease during a life cycle. Information in the DPP therefore provides insight into the current performance of a washing machine, including its residual lifetime and energy and water consumption.

The fourth information category "Sustainability and circularity" is becoming relevant for actors in circular ecosystems. Actors are increasingly requested to objectify their sustainable and circular performance. Life cycle analysis methods and calculations play a significant role in the quantification of this information [52]. Information about sustainability-related properties in the conceptualized DPP provides insight into a product's environmental and social impact [9]. This environmental impact information relates to categories of impact, performance indicators, indicator calculation methods, inventory data, and impact assessment methods. The social impact can theoretically be operationalized in information related to working condition properties. The information on circularity-related properties relates to circularity performance and the product design-related properties of washing machines. Circularity performance can be operationalized in a similar way to information about sustainability properties. The underlying information refers to resource efficiency, materials used, increase in durability, and the useful lifetime of washing machines [9]. Circular performance assessments and provision for underlying information play a central role in this [53]. The information on the product design of washing machines provides insight into the applied circular product design strategy and the reparability of a product.

Based on the DPP conceptualization, we designed a generic assessment process where DPP data support the lifetime extension assessment process. The following assumptions directed the design of the assessment process:

i. Digital Product Passports for EEE are implemented in 2030 [54].
ii. Discarded washing machines are, to a large extent, still collected and assessed by collection agents.
iii. By 2030, a large part of collected washing machines will incorporate digital technologies such as Internet-of-Things, allowing insight into historical usage data and allocation of washing machines' generated data to the cloud.
iv. All data in the DPP are assumed to be available and accessible by collection agents.
v. The information systems in the EEE ecosystem are highly automated. Information sharing across EEE ecosystem actors is commonplace.
vi. When designing the process diagram, it was assumed that the intake of washing machines and their lifetime extension assessment at a collection point take place as a one-off assessment.
vii. Despite future digitalization initiatives in the EEE ecosystem, lifetime extension assessment also requires manual visual inspections, e.g., to assess the inside quality of a washing machine, to confirm previous data-driven diagnoses, and to identify root causes.
viii. Parallel to a data-driven assessment of washing machines, we assume that a decision support system (DSS) is available to check the data properties values in the DPP against acceptance standards. Due to the explorative character of the assessment process, the standards have not been defined yet and specification of the type and architecture of DSS fall outside our study's scope.

The assessment process tests in six steps whether the DPP data values associated with a washing machine pass the criteria for lifetime extension of that washing machine, i.e. meet the acceptance standards applied by the DSS (see Fig. 4). In step 1, a collected washing machine arrives at a collection point and is registered. By scanning a machine-readable optical label, the washing machine's identification data are extracted from the DPP. In step 2, the lifetime extension assessment of the washing machine starts. At the product level, a washing machine is assessed for generic factors. These generic factors relate to product characteristics, technical performance, market demand, and ecological impact. The assessment is based on the information in the DPP, whereupon relevant property values are compared to the standards in the DSS. If a washing machine does not meet these standards, it is not eligible for lifetime extension. In the case of acceptable values, the washing machine is diagnosed in step 3. This diagnosis focuses on the washing machine's status and health. During the diagnosis, the washing machine is assessed for physical condition, technical condition, product usage status, and maintenance and repair history. If the relevant property values in the DPP are acceptable, a washing machine is visually inspected in step 4, such as completeness, rust, dents, and usage marks. This process step can be partially automated, for example, using photograph analysis. However, we assume, an internal inspection of the washing machine still requires a technical employee's involvement. In step 5, a final diagnosis of the washing machine is performed based on the assessment results in steps 3 and 4. The current status of the washing machine, as recorded in the DPP, is used in a 'diagnosis-recipe' approach by the DSS to determine which possible repair activities must take place to extend the washing machine's lifetime. Based on the estimated repair activities, the economic, technical, and ecological feasibility of extending the lifetime is tested in step 6. If this data-driven assessment meets the standards set in the DSS, the assessed washing machine qualifies for a lifetime extension. The feasibility test results in this process step are recorded in the DPP. If a washing machine is not eligible for lifetime extension, the DSS suggests whether parts or materials can be harvested from the washing machine.

The assessment process described above suggests that the DSS can make the lifetime extension assessment of a washing machine based on applying criteria or standards to data (values) representing the history, status and context of the washing machine, all of which are extracted from a DPP, and on a visual inspection. However, sometimes data from the DPP is not enough. For example, to test economic feasibility, often additional digital instruments and calculation methods are required for this purpose. We don't consider such instruments and methods further, since they are not addressed by a DPP and therefore outside the scope of this paper".

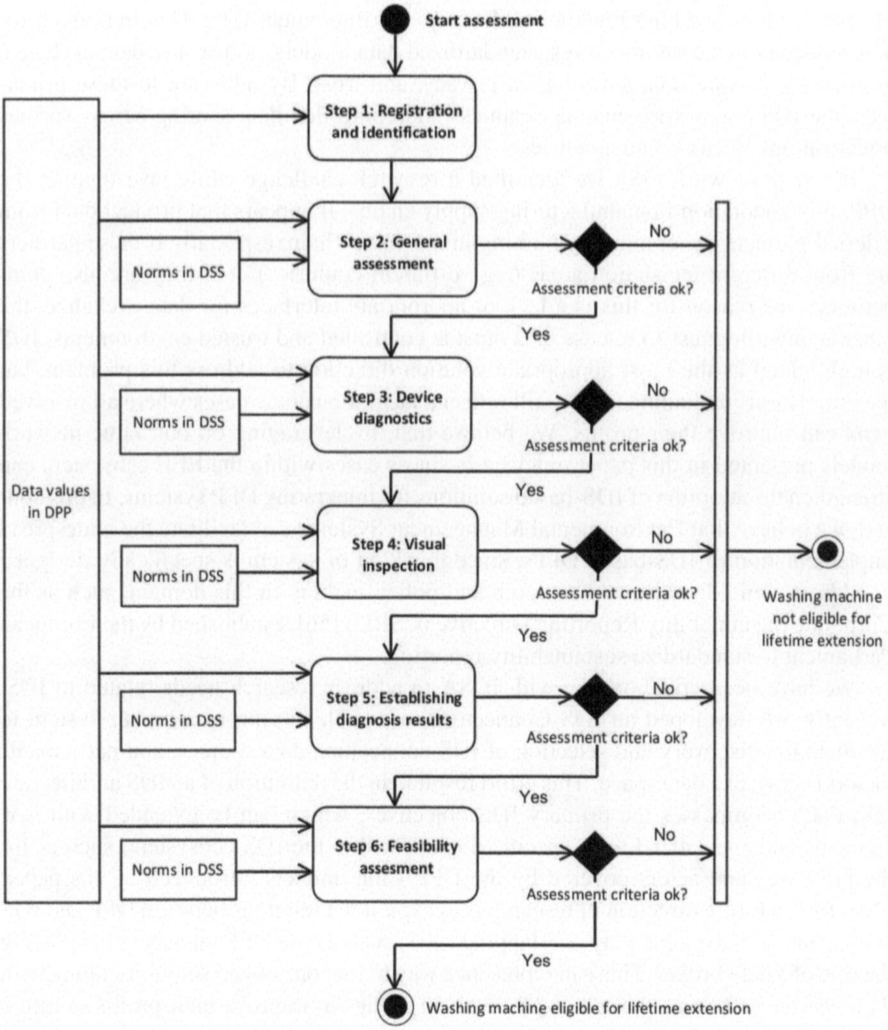

Fig. 4. Proposed lifetime extension assessment process

6 Discussion

In previous sections, we discussed how DPPs for washing machines support the lifetime extension assessment performed by collection agents. This role of DPPs to share necessary data for decision-making in circular EEE practices should be harnessed by a reliable infrastructure that can address the concerns of data providers, enhance the trust of consumers, and facilitate compliance with regulatory standards. A notable ongoing initiative is the International Data Space (IDS), led by the International Data Spaces Association (IDSA). IDS aims to create a secure and trustworthy data ecosystem for data sharing and collaboration with emphasis on data sovereignty. The IDSA is a global network of organizations working together to develop and implement IDS. This initiative promotes decentralized architectures, standardized data models, and secure data exchange protocols to ensure data sovereignty, privacy, and trust. By adhering to these principles, the IDS framework enables seamless and controlled data sharing across various organizations, sectors, and countries.

In our prior work [55], we identified a research challenge while investigating the DPP implementation in manufacturing supply chains. It appears that product data from external partners are commonly missing in the value chain, especially if these partners are from different legislation areas (e.g., different countries) or if they are also competitors. One reason for this is a lack of appropriate interfaces for data exchange, the other is unwillingness to release data outside controlled and trusted environments. IDS is highlighted as the most appropriate solution direction to address this problem, but the criticism from manufacturers still reflect a lack of business cases where all involved parts can improve their profits. We believe that, by leveraging on our value network models presented in this paper, relevant business cases within the EEE ecosystem can strengthen the adoption of IDS-based solutions for integrating DPP systems. In this context, we believe that Environmental Management Systems can facilitate the widespread implementation of IDS-based DPPs, since this kind of system is specifically designed to address some directives on research and policy-making in this domain, such as the Corporate Sustainability Reporting Directive (CSRD) [56], established by the European Parliament to standardize sustainability reporting.

We have been collaborating with IDSA to address research needs related to IDS. Recently, we developed an IDS Connector Store [57], serving as a broker system to facilitate the discovery and selection of IDS connectors, data sources, and participants (actors) active in a data space. This effort resulted in the definition of an IDS architecture [58] that encompasses the primary IDS objectives, which can be extended with new elements and specialized for a specific domain within the IDS ecosystem, such as for the processes and actors covered by the DPP value models introduced in this paper. Therefore, a future direction of research is to exploit the relations between DPP and IDS actors, and how they can play overlapping roles, such as the DPP manager also playing the role of a data broker. This can represent a way to find optimized solutions, along with their service offerings, that allow all involved parties to improve their profits in future value exchange practices of manufacturing supply chains.

7 Conclusion

This paper addressed the current problem that data sharing in the EEE ecosystem is not common place, and that the lack of data sharing is an obstacle for facilitating lifetime extension of disposed EEE products after end-of-use. We discussed how the DPP concept can enable data sharing across EEE ecosystem actors. Specifically, this paper explored how future DPPs have the potential to support collection agents to perform lifetime extension assessment for washing machines. We conceptualized the DPP and proposed a generic data-driven assessment process that includes DPP data. Our study demonstrated that a lifetime extension assessment of collected EEE requires a systemic-holistic perspective [59]. The necessary data for conducting such assessments within a

DPP must be generated and utilized across the entire product life cycle. This requires the coordination of data sharing between actors within a circular ecosystem and the establishment of shared standards among participants, which underpin the data sharing in a future international data space. Our contributions address several issues but are insufficient to overcome the described problem in full. For instance, though the role of a DPP and DSS has been explored in a generic data-driven assessment process, a practical demonstration is required. Moreover, digital technologies in washing machines enable continuous monitoring, but it is not practical nor feasible to stream all data in real-time to a DPP. Instead, selected information should be sent to the DPP in order to update dynamic properties at a rate that makes sense. How this should be done remains a topic for future research. However, how additional dynamic properties should be defined in the DPP for washing machines remains a topic for future research. Furthermore, our results are based on an analysis of one specific sector, the washing machine market. Our assumption that the data in the DPP for washing machines are accessible and available for collection agents depends on its adoption by the EEE sector and final legislation and regulations to reinforce this. Such adoption depends on the economic attractiveness of the value transactions between EEE ecosystem actors. For this purpose, future research also focuses on quantifying the proposed future e3-value model in various market scenarios to test the sensitivity of the value network to different market conditions. Nevertheless, we believe that our contributions and results can inspire extensions and generalizations beyond the mentioned issues and specific sector of washing machines.

References

1. Baldé, C.P., et al.: The global E-waste monitor 2024. In: International Telecommunication Union (ITU) and United Nations Institute for Training and Research (UNITAR): Geneva/Bonn (2024)
2. European Commission, Circular economy action plan - for a cleaner and more competitive Europe. European Commission: Brussels (2019)
3. Mellal, M.A.: Obsolescence–a review of the literature. Technol. Soc. **63**, 101347 (2020)
4. Ylä-Mella, J., Keiski, R.L., Pongrácz, E.: End-of-use vs. end-of-life: when do consumer electronics become waste? Resources **11**(2), 18 (2022)
5. Rizos, V., Bryhn, J.: Implementation of circular economy approaches in the electrical and electronic equipment (EEE) sector: barriers, enablers and policy insights. J. Clean. Prod. **338**, 130617 (2022)
6. Bertassini, A.C., et al.: Circular business ecosystem innovation: a guide for mapping stakeholders, capturing values, and finding new opportunities. Sustain. Prod. Consum. **27**, 436–448 (2021)
7. Konietzko, J., Bocken, N., Hultink, E.J.: Circular ecosystem innovation: an initial set of principles. J. Clean. Prod. **253**, 119942 (2020)
8. Voulgaridis, K., et al.: IoT and digital circular economy: principles, applications, and challenges. Comput. Netw. 109456 (2022)
9. Berger, K., Schöggl, J.-P., Baumgartner, R.J.: Digital battery passports to enable circular and sustainable value chains: conceptualization and use cases. J. Clean. Prod. **353**, 131492 (2022)
10. Trevisan, A.H., et al.: Unlocking the circular ecosystem concept: evolution, current research, and future directions. Sustain. Prod. Consum. **29**, 286–298 (2022)
11. Pietrulla, F.: Circular ecosystems: a review. Clean. Circular Bioecon. **3**, 100031 (2022)

12. Barquete, S., et al.: Exploring the dynamic of a circular ecosystem: a case study about drivers and barriers. Sustainability **14**(13), 7875 (2022)
13. Bocken, N.M., et al.: Product design and business model strategies for a circular economy. J. Ind. Prod. Eng. **33**(5), 308–320 (2016)
14. Geissdoerfer, M., et al.: The circular economy–a new sustainability paradigm? J. Clean. Prod. **143**, 757–768 (2017)
15. Stahel, W.R.: The circular economy. Nature **531**(7595), 435–438 (2016)
16. Ertz, M., et al.: Made to break? A taxonomy of business models on product lifetime extension. J. Clean. Prod. **234**, 867–880 (2019)
17. Pires, A., Martinho, G.: Waste hierarchy index for circular economy in waste management. Waste Manag. **95**, 298–305 (2019)
18. Alcalde-Calonge, A., Sáez-Martínez, F.J., Ruiz-Palomino, P.: Evolution of research on circular economy and related trends and topics. A thirteen-year review. Ecol. Inform. 101716 (2022)
19. Kirchherr, J., Reike, D., Hekkert, M.: Conceptualizing the circular economy: an analysis of 114 definitions. Resour. Conserv. Recycl. **127**, 221–232 (2017)
20. Potting, J., et al.: Circular economy: measuring innovation in the product chain. Planbureau voor de Leefomgeving (2544) (2017)
21. Prakash, S., et al.: Influence of the service life of products in terms of their environmental impact: establishing an information base and developing strategies against "obsolescence" Umweltbundesamt (2020)
22. Tecchio, P., Ardente, F., Mathieux, F.: Understanding lifetimes and failure modes of defective washing machines and dishwashers. J. Clean. Prod. **215**, 1112–1122 (2019)
23. Flipsen, B., Bakker, C., van Bohemen, G.: Developing a reparability indicator for electronic products. In: 2016 Electronics Goes Green 2016+(EGG). IEEE (2016)
24. Bracquene, E., et al.: Analysis of evaluation systems for product repairability: a case study for washing machines. J. Clean. Prod. **281**, 125122 (2021)
25. Bovea, M.D., et al., Variables that affect the environmental performance of small electrical and electronic equipment. Methodology and case study. J. Clean. Prod. **203**, 1067–1084 (2018)
26. Pakula, C., Stamminger, R.: Energy and water savings potential in automatic laundry washing processes. Energ. Effi. **8**, 205–222 (2015)
27. Okumura, S.: Reuse-efficiency model for evaluating circularity of end-of-life products. Comput. Ind. Eng. **171**, 108232 (2022)
28. Omer, A.M.: Energy use and environmental impacts: a general review. J. Renew. Sustain. Energy **1**(5), 053101 (2009)
29. Park, P.-J., Lee, K.-M., Wimmer, W.: Development of an environmental assessment method for consumer electronics by combining top-down and bottom-up approaches (11 pp). Int. J. Life Cycle Assess. **11**, 254–264 (2006)
30. Bressanelli, G., Perona, M., Saccani, N.: Reshaping the washing machine industry through circular economy and product-service system business models. Procedia CIRP **64**, 43–48 (2017)
31. Saarikko, T., Westergren, U.H., Blomquist, T.: The Internet of Things: are you ready for what's coming? Bus. Horiz. **60**(5), 667–676 (2017)
32. European Commission, Proposal for a regulation of the European parliament and of the council establishing a carbon border adjustment mechanism. E. Commission, Editor. Brussels (2021)
33. Saari, L., et al.: Digital product passport promotes sustainable manufacturing: whitepaper (2022)
34. Berg, H., et al.: Overcoming information asymmetry in the plastics value chain with digital product passports: how decentralised identifiers and verifiable credentials can enable a circular economy for plastics. Wuppertal Institut für Klima, Umwelt, Energie (2022)
35. Jansen, M., et al.: Current approaches to the digital product passport for a circular economy: an overview of projects and initiatives (2022)

36. van Capelleveen, G., et al.: The anatomy of a passport for the circular economy: a conceptual definition, vision and structured literature review. Resour. Conserv. Recycl. Adv. **17**, 200131 (2023)
37. Jensen, S.F., et al.: Digital product passports for a circular economy: data needs for product life cycle decision-making. Sustain. Prod. Consum. **37**, 242–255 (2023)
38. Ducuing, C., Reich, R.H.: Data governance: digital product passports as a case study. Competition Regul. Netw. Ind. **24**(1), 3–23 (2023)
39. Plociennik, C., et al.: Towards a digital lifecycle passport for the circular economy. Procedia CIRP **105**, 122–127 (2022)
40. Götz, T., et al.: Digital product passport: the ticket to achieving a climate neutral and circular European economy? (2022)
41. Adisorn, T., Tholen, L., Götz, T.: Towards a digital product passport fit for contributing to a circular economy. Energies **14**(8), 2289 (2021)
42. Walden, J., Steinbrecher, A., Marinkovic, M.: Digital product passports as enabler of the circular economy. Chem. Ing. Tec. **93**(11), 1717–1727 (2021)
43. Ospital, P., et al.: A digital product passport to support product transparancy and circularity. In: Global Fashion Conference 2022 (2022)
44. Ruismäki, W.: Digital product passports for construction products. In: Chemical, Biochemical and Materials Engineering. Aalto University, Aalto (2023)
45. King, M.R., Timms, P.D., Mountney, S.: A proposed universal definition of a Digital Product Passport Ecosystem (DPPE): worldviews, discrete capabilities, stakeholder requirements and concerns. J. Clean. Prod. **384**, 135538 (2023)
46. Langley, D.J., et al.: Orchestrating a smart circular economy: guiding principles for digital product passports. J. Bus. Res. **169**, 114259 (2023)
47. Jansen, M., et al.: Stop guessing in the dark: identified requirements for digital product passport systems. Systems **11**(3), 123 (2023)
48. Gordijn, J.: E-business value modelling using the e3-value ontology. In: Value Creation from e-Business Models, pp. 98–127. Elsevier (2004)
49. Jäger-Roschko, M., Petersen, M.: Advancing the circular economy through information sharing: a systematic literature review. J. Clean. Prod. **369**, 133210 (2022)
50. Bracquené, E., et al.: Repairability criteria for energy related products. Study in the BeNeLux Context to Evaluate the Options to Extend the Product Life Time Final Report (2018)
51. Cordella, M., Alfieri, F., Sanfelix, F.J.V.: Analysis and development of a scoring system for repair and upgrade of products. Publications Office of the European Union, Luxembourg (2019)
52. Alejandre, C., Akizu-Gardoki, O., Lizundia, E.: Optimum operational lifespan of household appliances considering manufacturing and use stage improvements via life cycle assessment. Sustain. Prod. Consum. **32**, 52–65 (2022)
53. Sassanelli, C., et al.: Circular economy performance assessment methods: a systematic literature review. J. Clean. Prod. **229**, 440–453 (2019)
54. European Commission, Communication from the commission to the European parliament, the council, the economic and social committee and the committee of the regions (2011)
55. Wiesner, M., et al.: A reference architecture for digital product passports at batch level to support manufacturing supply chains. In: International Conference on Research Challenges in Information Science. Springer (2024)
56. Poulle, J.-B., et al.: Corporate sustainability reporting directive. In: EU Banking and Financial Regulation, pp. 648–653. Edward Elgar Publishing (2024)
57. Firdausy, D.R., et al.: A data connector store for international data spaces. In: International Conference on Cooperative Information Systems. Springer (2022)

58. Firdausy, D.R., et al.: Towards a reference enterprise architecture to enforce digital sovereignty in international data spaces. In: 2022 IEEE 24th Conference on Business Informatics (CBI). IEEE (2022)
59. Bressanelli, G., et al.: Circular Economy in the WEEE industry: a systematic literature review and a research agenda. Sustain. Prod. Consum. **23**, 174–188 (2020)

Enterprise and IT Architecture

How to Measure the Speed of Enterprise IT? – An Enterprise Architecture-Based Case Study in a Very Large Enterprise

Oleg Kanin(✉) and Paul Drews

Institute of Information Systems, Leuphana University Lüneburg, Lüneburg, Germany
oleg.kanin@stud.leuphana.de, paul.drews@leuphana.de

Abstract. In most enterprises, the speed at which information technology (IT) is delivered becomes increasingly important. Lately, many enterprises strive to increase the speed of IT delivery, e.g. through the establishment of a bimodal or fast IT. However, research and practice lack a grounded understanding of how this speed can be defined or measured. This paper advances the understanding of how to measure the speed of enterprise IT while also considering the interdependence with IT quality, resources, costs and business value of IT. We categorize the speed of enterprise IT according to the phases plan, build and run. In our case study, we identified 10 activities to estimate and measure speed of enterprise IT in a very large enterprise based on expert interviews. We describe how the speed of enterprise can be measured in practice and identify factors that can speed up or slow down IT delivery. The findings identify options for increasing the speed through adapting the IT delivery in digital transformation (DT) projects as well though enterprise architecture management (EAM).

Keywords: Speed of Enterprise IT · Enterprise Architecture (EA) · Digital Transformation · IT Delivery · Fast IT · Bimodal IT

1 Introduction

Technological and strategic decisions force organizations to change their value creation paths as part of their DT [1]. Changing these paths requires to acquire the needed expertise, to introduce new technological solutions and to improve business and IT processes for addressing the new or changed requirements and challenges. While DT encompasses significant changes in the technological domain, it also requires quickness and flexibility within the organization in order to recognize changes in requirements and to react to changes of customer and market demand in time. Organizations need to be agile in order to react to them promptly by further developing existing or innovating new products and services [2]. Research uncovered that enterprises that use DT to innovate business models and develop new IT products or services often create new business units as fully agile structures [3].

For enabling this agility, the management of a company must redesign the IT organization in order to be able to implement changes quickly and flexibly while ensuring

J. Borbinha et al. (Eds.): EDOC 2024, LNCS 15409, pp. 101–118, 2025.
https://doi.org/10.1007/978-3-031-78338-8_6

stability and effective provision of IT at the same time [2]. As a reaction to this challenge, many companies see the need of establishing a new "digital IT" (or "fast IT") unit or of shifting responsibility for IT systems to the business units to foster decentralized decision making. These changes should allow the business to be better informed, more flexible, and faster in adapting its IT as well as its IT-enabled services and products to market opportunities and customer needs [5]. Therefore, the introduction of agile practices and structures is required not only in IT, but also in the business units in order to increase the flexibility and speed of the entire organization [3].

Customer value becomes the focus of strategic and operational planning and development, both of business and IT [2]. As a result, strategies and plans are increasingly aligned with customer value [2]. In addition, more and more organizations are aligning their corporate structures along the value streams of their customers by adapting internal services, processes, and the underlying IT landscape. [2]. As digital products and services are inextricably linked to the underlying IT infrastructure, organizational agility depends on the agility of IT and the IT function [2]. However, IT departments are often neither structurally nor procedurally prepared to fulfill this new role [4].

To accelerate business and IT within the enterprise, the operational level is empowered to increasingly make (semi-) autonomous decisions, both business- and technology-related [2]. If companies establish a fast or bimodal IT as a part of their DT, they need to align this new IT with the existing IT and with the business. [5]. If they fail to react faster than their competitors, they risk losing their competitive advantage [5]. As technology change accelerates and new digital solutions emerge, many companies feel the pressure to perform a DT and to increase the speed of IT delivery [5].

A high degree of diversity in the goals and requirements of DT in projects and in the design of IT architectures and services influences business architecture and business IT alignment in multiple ways [6]. As EAM promises to support the alignment between IT and the business, it is required to purposefully accompany DT projects [7]. Additionally, EA aims to provide organizations with various benefits like improving organizational agility [8]. An increased organizational agility is an essential capability for organizations and a necessity to be able to respond and adapt to the rapidly changing environment [8]. Therefore, many organizations seek to leverage their EAM function to increase agility [9]. Previous studies [8, 9] based on the dynamic capabilities view explain how EAM investments lead to increased agility and how agility is promoted by strategic alignment. In this context, the EAM function holds a central role for supporting digital transformation in cross-functional issues for delivery teams and services [6].

Hence, our study addresses the following research question: *How do large enterprises measure the speed of enterprise IT by considering an EA perspective?*

This article is structured as follows. The following section summarizes the related research. The third section explains the research approach including the data gathering and data analysis. The fourth section presents the results of our study. The final sections of this article comprise a discussion and a conclusion.

2 Related Research

The following sections describe the theoretical foundations of DT and enterprise IT, the role of fast IT and EA in supporting DT projects, and existing approaches for measuring the speed of enterprise IT.

2.1 Theoretical Foundations of DT and Enterprise IT

The understanding of DT in this study in grounded on Wessel et al.'s study [10], which distinguishes between digital and IT-driven transformation. DT leverages digital technologies to (re)define an organization's value proposition, while IT-driven organizational transformation (ITOT) adopts digital technologies to support the value proposition [10]. DT is about creating a new organizational identity, while IT-driven organizational transformation is about improving an existing organizational identity [10].

In a conceptual sense, DT and ITOT can be divided into two types: First, into transformation activities for DT, where digital technology (re)defines the value proposition, and for ITOT, where digital technology supports the existing value proposition [10]. The result of DT is the emergence of a new organizational identity, while the result of ITOT is the emergence of a strengthened organizational identity [10].

Most of the digital technologies are not inherently revolutionary, but rather develop their innovative power through greater efficiency, significantly improved connectivity, and widespread adoption and use [4]. Legner et al. [11] describe the change in digitization in waves: The first the wave of technologies aims at the automation of work processes, the second wave focuses on the Internet as a global communication infrastructure, and finally the third wave is created by converging technologies with increasing computing power, storage capacity, and communication bandwidth.

The trend towards digitalization has increased the importance of IT due to its inherent focus on technology and increased the expectations towards IT functions in companies, making business activities not only more efficient but also inconceivable without IT [12]. Flexible and rapid adaptation of information systems is therefore of great importance in the digital age [12]. Based on experience with the development of corporate IT, it is not surprising that IT departments are often not optimally prepared for the challenges of DT [12].

To face the challenges of digitalization, the IT function needs to continuously transform and reorganize itself and adopt new forms of collaboration and integration with the business [12]. In this context, concepts such as cross-functional digital teams, IT innovation management and bimodal EAM can be seen as precursors of the 'new IT function', which is transforming IT from a service provider to a consultant, enabler and innovator [12]. The increasing importance of the IT function in DT raises questions about its effectiveness but also about how its speed can be measured.

2.2 Fast IT and EA as Support for DT Projects

Due to the fact that IT plays an important role in enabling the perceptiveness and responsiveness of organizations, IT is a key agility-enabling (or restricting) factor [15].

IT functions still primarily follow the business by having the main task of providing IT services with a high level of stability and compliance and effectively managing increasingly complex IT infrastructures [2]. In many organizations, the IT function is still focused on efficiency and the provision of reliable, scalable and secure IT services [13]. Therefore, a new balance is needed between providing and maintaining (new) digital services [4], optimizing existing IT-enabled products, services and business models for customer needs, and securing the underlying IT architecture for optimal service delivery by the IT function [2].

This means that organizations must (1) decide on a desired form of the IT function and its integration into the overall organizational design, and (2) continuously assess the status quo and desired goal [2]. As a result, many companies have started to scale agile values and methods in their software and product development [2]. However, as the transformational journey towards agility affects the corporate way of how to do business at its core, agility involves (re)evaluating the organization as a whole – business and IT strategies, business models as well as organizational and IT structures, IT architectures, and methods [2]. Therefore, it is important to find ways to deal with change, speed and flexibility with their strategies and business models, organizational structures and business processes as well as IT infrastructure and IT architecture [2]. With bimodal IT functions, existing processes that encompass traditional and agile IT must also be reconsidered and changed, as otherwise there is a risk that traditional and agile IT will hinder each other [14].

Both IT and EA are seen as important factors in supporting DT projects regarding cost and technology decisions. For this reason, it makes sense to examine the role of IT not only in terms of cost savings, but also as an enabler of speed in supporting DT projects.

2.3 Measuring the Speed of Enterprise IT

To understand how enterprise IT speed is defined and how it can be measured, we conducted a systematic literature review (SLR) [16]. The review revealed, among other things, that there is no common understanding of speed of enterprise IT and of how it can be measured. The literature mentions several heterogeneous influences on the speed of enterprise IT, but its conceptualization is still weak [16]. However, from a practical point of view, measuring the speed of IT delivery in DT projects can bring several benefits in managing the various activities and measures [16]. We also identified the potential direct or indirect impact of these activities on enterprise IT and its speed. The results of the SLR showed that this research topic is largely unexplored and that a better understanding could support the collaboration and expectation management between the IT and business functions [16].

3 Research Approach

The following sections describe the research method, the data gathering process and the data analysis.

3.1 Research Method

To answer the research question, we conducted an explanatory, interpretive case study in a very large enterprise [17]. In the case study, we empirically investigated the phenomenon of "speed of enterprise IT" by exploring the details of this concept in practice. The selected very large enterprise is a prime candidate for such a study as it runs many DT projects and initiatives and also has a decade-long established EAM function. The company has a few hundred thousand employees, is technology-oriented, has well-established IT processes and widely uses standardized EA frameworks and agile methods in IT projects. The focus of the study is to understand the definition of the speed of enterprise IT and to investigate the measurement of the speed of enterprise's IT to support IT delivery.

3.2 Data Gathering: Qualitative Expert Interviews

We conducted 10 expert interviews with staff in different positions and working areas to develop a better understanding of the meaning of "speed of enterprise IT" and the challenges of measuring speed of enterprise IT. The qualitative expert interviews were developed, planned and conducted based on Kaiser's [19] data collection method. The interview guidelines were developed for experts in the fields of EA, DT projects as well as strategy. The interview guidelines were written as scripts for semi-structured interviews [18].

We created the interview guidelines for the experts in the work areas of EA, DT projects and strategy and adapted the questions according to the roles. The interview guideline for people working in EA, DT projects and strategy included qualitative questions on the speed of EA review of DT projects, the response to EA changes, the correct or incorrect IT delivery of DT projects, the evolution of the speed of enterprise IT, the role of IT complexity on the speed of enterprise IT, the speed of IT architecture in relation to IT platforms, the measures to increase or decrease the speed of enterprise IT, the interactions between the speed of enterprise IT and IT architecture, and the resources and their influence on the speed of enterprise IT, ways to increase or decrease the speed of enterprise IT, interactions between the speed of enterprise IT and IT architecture, resources and their influence on the speed of enterprise IT, practical ways to objectively or subjectively measure the speed of enterprise IT, and the estimation of the speed of enterprise IT by business units. We have supplemented the guidelines for DT projects and strategy with questions on the degree of automation of project management and the strategic relevance of speed in the implementation of DT projects. As planned, the interviews lasted an average of 60 min, some of them ten or fifteen minutes longer than planned, with 12 questions for the EA business unit experts and 14 questions for the project level experts and the EAM experts.

Experts were selected for voluntary interviews on the basis of their position, status, knowledge and experience. Other criteria for selecting experts were knowledge of relevant functions, ability to provide accurate information and availability for interview [19]. The expert interviews were conducted in accordance with the principles of protection of personal data, informed consent, anonymity, integrity and objectivity. The interviews were conducted continuously during the fourth quarter of 2023. The interviews were fully transcribed and analyzed with the help of MaxQDA. For further analysis, directly identifying features such as interviewee names were replaced with function and position descriptions. For pseudonymization, respondents were assigned consecutive alphanumerical codes.

We selected the candidates for the interviews on the basis of working areas such as EA, DT project or strategy. To obtain relevant information and gain access to the functional knowledge of the experts, we also selected candidates with experience in one of the three areas of work DT projects, EA and strategy. Around 50% of the respondents deal with EA in their respective DT projects and business areas, a further 40% of the business experts work in the area of DT projects, and the remaining 10% of respondents are EAM managers. The interviewed experts have different positions and functions with regard to DT projects and EA. The experience of the interviewed experts related to project management and EA equates to several years of professional activity in their enterprise. Table 1 lists the experts' positions by alphanumeric code.

Table 1. Positions of the experts in the enterprise.

Expert	Position	Working area
E1	Enterprise and technical architect	EA
E2	Enterprise and technical architect	EA
E3	EA consultant	EA
E4	Enterprise and technical architect	EA
E5	Enterprise and technical architect	EA
E6	Project manager	DT project
E7	Project manager	DT project
E8	Product owner	DT project
E9	Product owner	DT project
E10	Enterprise architect	EAM

The experts working in the areas of project-related functional architecture, project management and EAM have shown particular interest in the findings of this case study, which relates to defining and measuring of speed in enterprises IT in order to measure their performance, improve the quality and timeliness of IT delivery and avoid time loss.

3.3 Data Analysis: Qualitative Content Analysis of the Expert Interviews

The general and basic information on IT processes in EA, IT delivery in DT projects and the company's EAM strategy, as well as the central EA tool, were taken from expert interviews. Relevant information was derived from the expert interviews according to qualitative content analysis to Mayring [20]. From this amount of relevant information, findings and results were developed in the form of core statements and classified according to their significance for the importance of IT in the company. The core statements were compiled and categorized according to the areas of DT projects, EA, business and IT processes, degree of IT automation and strategy, as well as according to the measurement activities. The further subdivision of the core statements was based on the model of an IT organization in a company. In the core statements, we observed various activities in the conception and organization of IT. The observed activities were classified deductively as plan, build and run.

In a systematic process, we analyzed the key statements according to the information from the interviews in terms of source, area, description, reason, possible solution and evaluation. We further analyzed this information to measure the speed of enterprise IT. We categorized the information into activities, areas, factors that slow down or speed up IT, what to measure and how to measure, for measurement within the enterprise. In addition, the selected key statements were discussed with and verified by the EAM expert.

The identified key messages present new challenges or new questions that are relevant for measuring of speed in enterprise IT and IT delivery in the enterprise, and which activities can influence the speed of enterprise IT. The findings also show that the speed of enterprise IT is related to the context of quality, resources and cost, as well as to the business value of IT.

4 Results

We present the key findings from our case study in the form of a concept of the speed of enterprise IT, which will enable DT projects, IT department and the EAM function to work with a joint understanding for measuring the speed of enterprise and improving IT delivery.

Definition: Based on the findings of our study we propose that measuring the speed of enterprise IT cannot be done objectively but only subjectively. The speed can only be measured subjectively for two reasons: Firstly, different people may arrive at different measurements based on their experiences and expectations, and secondly, the measurement is subjective because subjectively defined plan values are used as a benchmark for evaluating the IT as 'fast' or 'slow'. In certain contexts, the speed of enterprise IT can also be determined in relation to external reference values (benchmarks). If the realization of compliance requirements is not achieved by a certain deadline, it can be concluded that the IT was 'too slow' compared to this reference value. Where appropriate, the business strategy can also quantify certain targets as benchmarks in terms of lost business value, which can also have an impact on future IT value.

The measurement of the speed of enterprise IT is based on the subjective estimation by various stakeholders by judging on the difference between the expected delivery time in relation to reference values such as planned, target, expected and actual delivery time. This measurement can be grounded on one or more interactions with the IT deliveries in plan, build and run. We consider the speed of enterprise IT in the context of factors such as the quality of IT, resource utilization, the cost of IT delivery and the potential benefits of enterprise IT. Speed must therefore be measured in relation to the available resources (high speed might require additional resources), the quality (high speed might lead to low quality) and the business value of IT (high speed might be required to realize business value).

The experts suggested measuring speed based on various data and information that can stem from different IT tools or other enterprise IT sources. In particular, data and values from IT or EA tools, process indicators, data-driven project documentation, customer reviews and survey tools are used as a source for objectively measuring the speed of enterprise IT. But the objective measurement of the speed of enterprise IT from these potential objective metrics is limited because the potential measures of experts are based on subjective benchmarks and subjective plan values. While one could measure that a project meets the expected delivery time of one year and is being perceived as "fast enough" by one person, another person could have the expectation that this project could be done within six months resulting in an evaluation as being "too slow". Another reason for the limited objectivity is that there is no uniform definition of the speed of enterprise IT (neither in the literature nor in the investigated company). Therefore, the subjective interpretation of the measurements is more important to people than the objective measurements.

For this reason, we divide the measurement of the speed of enterprise IT into two parts. One part is the subjective measurement of the speed of enterprise IT, and the second part consists of the sources of objective measures related to the speed of enterprise IT. Figure 1 shows a visual representation of the definition.

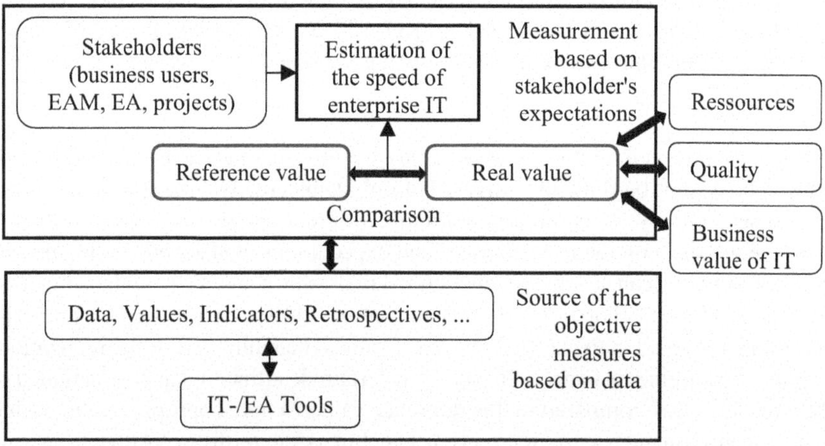

Fig. 1. The visual definition of the approach to measuring the speed of enterprise IT.

Based on interviews with experts, we have developed a definition for the speed of enterprise IT focusing on the project perspective: In general, we understand the speed of enterprise IT as the workload of a project divided by time. By the specific project-related speed of enterprise IT, we mean the correct deployment and delivery of IT according to defined time schedules based on planned resources while adhering to the target EA and otherwise constant conditions. Figure 2 shows the general definition of the speed of enterprise IT.

$$\text{Speed of enterprise IT (general)} = \frac{\text{Workload of project}}{\text{Time}}$$

Fig. 2. The definition of the speed of enterprise IT in general.

Regardless of the distinction between traditional and agile projects, all DT projects go through the following three modes: they are planned, they built solutions and they run systems and services. We refer to these modes as plan, build and run [21]. For plan, build and run, the speed of enterprise IT means something different. In general, speed of enterprise IT in plan mode is measured by the time it takes to plan a project or an IT product. In build mode, speed of enterprise IT is measured by the time it takes to develop, implement or improve IT. In run mode, speed of enterprise IT is measured by how fast the IT service processes (e.g. incident management, time-to-recovery, etc.) work. In a product-oriented organization, development and IT operations (DevOps) teams are formed to perform these tasks. Since all tasks in DevOps teams, especially in build and run mode, are performed by one team, the separation between plan, build and run IT should be understood as functional and not organizational.

Although it is not possible to measure speed of enterprise IT objectively, it is possible to measure the speed of enterprise IT subjectively in a regulatory and indicative way. For this approach, we were able to use the key findings to identify the potential activities that directly or indirectly affect the speed of enterprise IT. We extracted the measurement objects from the results as well as the reference and real values as indicators with corresponding sources to measure or estimate the speed of enterprise IT. In addition, we identified delay factors or speed-up factors for speed of enterprise IT. Figure 3 provides an overview of the approach to measure the speed of enterprise IT related to of the activities used to measure enterprise IT speed and in terms of the delay and speed-up factors.

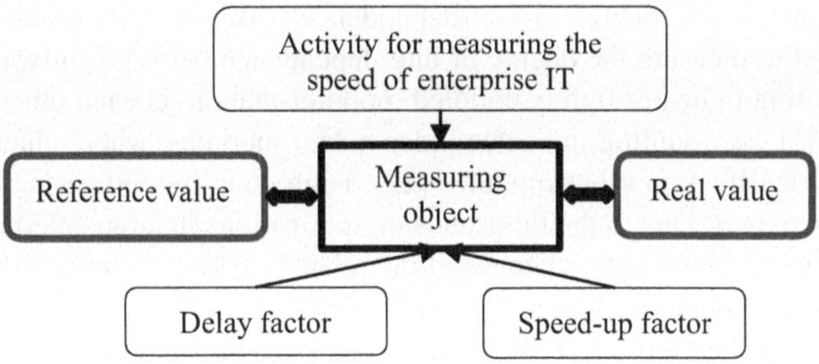

Fig. 3. Overview of the approach to measure the speed of enterprise IT.

We have identified the following 10 key activities for measuring the speed of enterprise IT (see Table 2). The activities are categorized according to the respective modes and working areas.

Table 2. Measuring activities by working area and mode.

No	Working area	Activity	Mode
1	EA	Measure speed of enterprise IT through measuring IT complexity	Run
2	EA	Measure speed of enterprise IT through processing of the EA review	Plan
3	EA	Measure speed of enterprise IT through the specification and quality of requirements	Plan
4	EA	Measure time required to implement an IT requirement	Build
5	DT project	Measure speed of enterprise IT as a function of waiting times	Plan
6	DT project	Measure speed of enterprise IT based on the realization of IT delivery in projects	Build
7	DT project	Measure speed of enterprise IT based on speed on databases and technical resource consumption	Build
8	DT project	Measure speed of enterprise IT based on the quality of IT delivery	Build
9	Strategy	Measure speed of enterprise IT based on the complexity of strategy implementation of IT guidelines and architecture principles	Plan
10	Strategy	Measure delayed IT deliveries	Build

The activity **(1) measure speed of enterprise IT through measuring IT complexity** in run mode can be used to evaluate synchronous or asynchronous communication as a measure of coupling between systems and/or applications. The experts mentioned that the coupling of synchronous or asynchronous communication is an important reference value that is often seen as a response to functional requirements that lead to more or less coupling. The experts also explained that the speed of enterprise IT is negatively impaired by a highly complex application landscape.

Coupling refers to the degree of interdependence between software modules [22]. Coupling is used to measure the degree of interdependence between software modules [22]. High coupling indicates tightly coupled modules that affect each other as a result of changes [22]. Low coupling indicates independent modules, where changes in one module have little effect on other modules [22]. High coupling indicates higher complexity, says the expert. Due to the thousands of applications in large enterprises, a low degree of coupling enables faster changes of the related systems as fewer other systems are affected by the change.

Experts say that the focus of IT has traditionally been on applications. Applications support specific business functions. The applications are usually ordered by a department or are created indirectly and are usually delivered as departmental monoliths to support the department's employees in many roles. To support multiple business processes, multiple applications from different departments need to be integrated. The employees involved in the business process operate certain of the applications involved on a role-specific basis via the user interfaces of these applications.

When the IT support for a business process is changed, at least one application in such an IT landscape must be changed. In the case of the departmental monolith, this means that a function or part of the user interface must be changed, but the technical dependencies of many other parts of the application must also be taken into account. This makes the change more difficult than if the application only contained parts that belong to the context of the change. Due to the size of the monolith and the dependencies, several teams usually must work closely together. This requires additional communication and coordination across team boundaries.

As reference values, the experts mentioned the number of interfaces between systems or applications, e.g. master data, personnel planning, bookings, complaints. These interfaces can be read out as real values both visually in system context diagrams in MS Visio, Enterprise Architect, draw.io tools and in text form in asset management tools. Other reference values are IT infrastructures that are to be designed as IT commodities and modular IT as a measure of elastic and faster IT with few redundancies. Factors such as rigid and non-modular IT, limited coupling and slow response to new business requirements delay IT responsiveness and contribute to IT complexity. Better control of IT complexity can be achieved through speed up factors, such as improving communication coupling, creating flexible IT in the sense of modularizing IT, providing the technical basis of the EA architecture as a scalable capability, developing small-scale IT infrastructures into IT commodities through EAM, using of automated IT, production-oriented IT, flexible EA as well as creating smaller IT.

To **(2) measure the speed of enterprise IT through processing of the EA review** in plan mode, the measurement objects such as the duration of the EA review in days, the quality assurance of the projects reviewed by EA, the duration of the inventory, the duration of the creation of the target EA and the gap analyses can be applied. The following reference values are used for assessing the speed: date of project receipt until the date of project approval, difference number of EA reviewed projects and rejected project proposal, date of contract approval to date of contract conclusion. The real values for this can be obtained from MS Project or the central EA tool. Factors such as the lack of automatic information capture for EA reviews, significantly increased IT security requirements, increasing demand for more EA support for analysis, manual data input and output in the central EA tool, no automatic review of EA principles and guard rails in EA reviews in projects delay the processing and speed of EA reviews. To improve the speed of the EA review, the experts mentioned speed up potential such as prioritizing the review of only critical requirements of the DT project to quickly deliver the first review results from the review, automatic creation of EA documentation using EA tools as well as the use of automatic EA templates for EA reviews in projects.

(3) Measuring the speed of enterprise IT through the specification and quality of requirements in plan mode is based on the understanding of IT requirements by developers, business engineers, EA architects and business experts. The error rate for incorrect requirements, the number of unclear requirements, the avoidance of time lost due to clarifications, the reduction in the number of changes such as change or new requests, the avoidance of IT false developments and additional costs were mentioned from experts as reference values. Corresponding real values from tools such as MS Project, JIRA and Enterprise Architect are used for comparison. The creation of specifications by customers as non-IT specialists rather than IT developers and the lack of functional requirements engineering from the outset, delay the creation of requirements and degrade their quality, as implementation project specialists often do not understand the customer's requirements properly. A lack of standardization of requirement documentation also leads to case-by-case reviews and delays in project work. In order to improve the specification and quality of requirements, and to avoid additional time needed for clarification, the experts mentioned speed up factors such as creating requirements specifications with the help of the project's IT specialists, performing early specification of requirements, using standard solutions, specifying requirements using checklists, creating a back-end system to manage interactions between all partners in order to respond quickly to new requirements.

How long does it take until the requirement is in production? How much testing is required? Is test automation (TA) available as a basic requirement? These questions can be answered by **(4) measuring the time required to implement the IT requirement** in build mode. The experts suggested to take the following values as reference values in build mode: time of response to new requirements, means date of receipt of requirement until start of implementation, time span between date of processing and date of actual solution, scope and type of testing, frequency of delivery cycle, time to market. According to the interviews there are numerous real values in tools like MS Project, JIRA and ALM Explorer. Lack of test automation (TA), rigid delivery cycles, low delivery frequency, lack of transparency in the implementation of architecture and IT security requirements at department and IT service level, unclear requirements even in agile projects at the beginning of the project and a lack of standard solutions for requirements significantly delay the implementation of IT requirements. Experts call for more responsibility to be given to project managers or product owners to optimize release management. In addition, they recommend a flexible delivery cycle with a net release time of 2 weeks compared to a gross release time of 4 weeks. Two IT deliveries per day is a benchmark for flexible delivery. TA must be included in all deliveries and the TA should always be extensible.

Activity **(5) measure speed of enterprise IT as a function of waiting times** in plan mode is designed to answer questions such as: How long do approvals for personnel, funding and IT take? How long does it take for the introduction of new technologies to be approved? Waiting times and additional costs were named by experts as key reference values that need to be measured and reduced. Experts claim that the time in days for approval by the works council committee and the estimate of costs and lost benefits for the customer in MS Project can be used as real values for these reference values. Additionally, the experts cited long approval procedures for the introduction of new IT in the project as a delaying factor. By shifting approval decisions to DT projects and shortening long procedures, approvals for the introduction of new technologies, for personnel deployment and for financial decisions need to be accelerated, according to the experts.

Enterprises can **(6) measure speed of enterprise IT based on the realization of IT delivery in projects.** The realization rate of requirements and the delivered stories in agile IT projects compared to project costs, resources and quality can be measured in build mode. The experts suggest using the period from project start to project end, the resource consumption such as personnel costs in days and the costs per month or the number of completed stories per sprint as reference values. The experts can access collecting the real values for this from JIRA, MS Project and retrospectives with customers. The main delay factors for delayed IT development mentioned by the experts are a lack of customer retrospectives and target/actual comparisons, long planning and review processes, too few resources, especially IT staff, lack of skills/competences, too much manual work in reviewing extensive approval bases and security requirements and no possibility of automatic review, lack of EA review of projects and delays in clarification. In addition, the highly complex management structure delays decisions and project meetings can be too complex. At the end of the project, top management can cause unexpected changes in IT delivery. The factors recommended by experts to speed up IT delivery are to conduct weekly or monthly retrospectives with the customer during IT delivery and at the end of the project. It is important to implement shorter cycles, work closely with the customer, create a minimum viable product, use an agile mindset for product testing with customers and bring the DevOps team into the tasks earlier. The interviewees recommend to transfer decision rights to the side with more knowledge and increase the power of the project manager and the DevOps team.

The activity **(7) measuring the speed of enterprise IT based on speed of databases and technical resource consumption** in build mode can compare resources in terms of costs and quantities between providers (hyperscalers like AWS, Azure, IBM Cloud) as measurement objects, according to the expert. As reference values, the experts suggest analyzing the information in the AWS and Azure accounts (quantity, licenses, etc.) and checking the invoices for product consumption on a monthly basis. To compare reference values with real values, invoices should be evaluated as real values for the product in order to check consumption and comparison and find favorable providers. Inefficient use of service resources and unused licenses and costs hinder and delay the use of technical resources in projects. Experts suggested increasing the transparency of the use and efficiency of hyperscalers databases, accelerating IT services, predicting the costs of software development and enabling the use of faster databases. The expert explained that technical resource consumption is of great importance when measuring the speed of enterprise IT, as the use of faster databases means that required data or relevant information can be searched for and found more easily and quickly, or customers' IT requirements can be met more quickly thanks to faster IT services.

Using the activity **(8) measure speed of enterprise IT based on the quality of IT delivery** in build mode, objects such as software components, modularization, time consumption, costs, functionality can be measured. Experts suggest to consider the extent of modularization of software components, time spent on software development, costs and functionality as reference values. As real comparative values for this, delivered software should be recorded and time and money contracts with the business units should be checked. As the main causes of delayed IT deliveries, the experts cite software monoliths, long and extensive projects, too few EA reviews of DT projects and customers' rough ideas and specifications regarding requirements. The experts suggest that the delivery of high quality IT can be improved by making software solutions more modular, by not delivering software monoliths and by organizing projects in smaller and shorter time frames. A balance should also be struck between time and quality.

The activity **(9) measure speed of enterprise IT based on the complexity of strategy implementation of IT guidelines and architecture principles** in plan mode can be used to answer the following questions. How complex is the strategy? How long will it take to implement the strategy? How self-interested is the mindset of the business units? The number of planned activities, the implementation period and the mindset of the business units should be used as reference values. The real values for this can be collected with the central EA tool and the use of survey tools. The experts named the following as the main delaying factors: uncertain process for the functioning of the architectural principles, reworking of the EAM strategy, long agreement on the implementation of the strategy due to business units interests. In addition, local ways of thinking about the use of resources, budgets and personnel make strategy implementation more difficult. According to the experts, speed up factors such as executing the strategy more effectively, analyzing whether the strategy is being implemented too slowly or the activities are inappropriate, deriving the connection between activities and target achievement, aligning the strategy for IT technologically with the future and defining a strategic EA target for the next few years help to master the complexity of strategy implementation.

The activity **(10) measure delayed IT deliveries** in build mode is used to measure the loss of benefit due to a delayed IT delivery. Business value is selected as the measure object. The impact on the operational benefit of business units due to delayed IT deliveries can be applied as a reference value. Real values from the central EA tool, MS Project, retrospective with customers can be taken to compare the impact on the operational benefit. The delay factors are a lack of contract transparency and lost benefits due to delayed IT deliveries. By creating more transparency in contracts, delayed IT deliveries can be reduced, according to the experts.

5 Discussion

The results presented in our case study focus on the development of a concept for measuring the speed of enterprise IT. This approach can help to increase the speed of enterprise IT, reduce time to market and strategically leverage the impact of IT in the enterprise.

In this case study we have identified and described 10 specific activities used in the case company to measure and evaluate the speed of enterprise IT. This article describes the measurement objects, the reference and real values as well as the delay and speed up factors for each activity based on the experts' responses. We also highlighted the role of different IT and EA tools for supporting these activities. These tools are specific to the 10 described activities and contain matching data, values or information, which are considered in the activities. With these 10 specific activities we advance research on measuring the speed of enterprise IT by providing a set of empirically grounded activities.

For example, if a change shortens the average time for an architecture review for DT projects while maintaining quality or deliberately accepting minor compromises in quality this change can increase the speed of enterprise IT in the plan mode. An increase in the speed of enterprise IT could also be achieved through additional staff or fewer review tasks. In the case of fewer review tasks, the quality of the EA review might be reduced. If a project is delayed because the IT infrastructure takes a long time to deploy, this causes a negative impact on the speed of enterprise IT and IT delivery is slowed down. If measures are taken to eliminate the causes, IT can be delivered more quickly.

The main goal of this case study was to determine how the speed of enterprise IT is being measured in practice. With regard to this question, our study provides five major insights: (1) The speed of enterprise IT cannot be measured objectively, but only subjectively. (2) In certain contexts, the speed of enterprise IT can be determined in relation (relatively) to external benchmarks (like meeting a deadline for fulfilling a legal requirement). (3) The speed of enterprise IT must always be considered in the context of resource consumption, cost, quality and the future business value of IT. (4) In general, high speed is considered desirable and worthwhile as long as it is not achieved at the expense of quality or excessive resource consumption. (5) Achieving a high speed of the enterprise IT is not an end in itself. It helps to maintain and improve the enterprise's competitive position, to differentiate itself from the competition, to meet internal and external customer expectations early, and to meet regulatory requirements on time.

EAM plays a significant role in enterprises for connecting IT with the business and for achieving the best possible implementation of the business strategy. This has been evident in many organizations for several years [23]. By virtue of its role, EAM is obliged to support DT projects in these tasks. With regard to EA/EAM, our study provides the following results: (1) The extensive planning and monitoring of DT projects by EAM can be time-consuming and may slow down project progress. However, proactive and strategic architectural planning can accelerate future projects by identifying and implementing necessary architectural measures early on. (2) Architectural approaches such as microservices can help to increase the speed of enterprise IT by enabling (sub-) components to be developed, tested and deployed as independently as possible. (3) The high cost and duration of EA reviews of project proposals can be reduced by prioritizing the review of only the critical requirements of the DT project and using automated EA templates to quickly deliver the initial review results. New EA approaches can increase the speed of enterprise IT by enabling the development of (sub-)components or small IT deliveries of SW.

For DT, the implications of our study are fourfold: (1) In DT projects, a great deal of emphasis is often placed on speed in the conception and prototyping phase, which is at the expense of architectural conformity, stability, security, etc. (2) Delays occur when these are to be integrated into the regular IT infrastructure and scaled. (3) DT projects often have to be subject to fewer restrictions in the conception and prototyping phase which helps to be fast. (4) Continuous monitoring of DT projects by the EAM fosters the convergence between project activities and architectural requirements.

For strategy, we see two major implications: (1) The successful implementation of a strategy requires that the organization's IT department is able to deliver IT products and services quickly, in high quality and with low resource input. (2) As major changes to the IT architecture or the IT department may be required, these changes must be included in the strategy to ensure that they are sufficiently targeted and supported with the necessary resources.

6 Conclusion

This study contributes to research by improving the understanding of the estimation and measurement of speed of the enterprise IT and IT delivery in projects.

The findings were empirically investigated and based on a single case study in a large enterprise, using data from qualitative expert interviews. This paper provides results in the form of a structured approach to activities for measuring the speed of enterprise IT, identifies factors that increase or decrease the speed of enterprise IT, and outlines strategies for advancing IT in terms of quality, resources and costs, business value of IT and management of IT complexity. In this study, we found that the speed of enterprise IT can be made measurable based on objective measures. However, within the organization, the subjective interpretation and evaluation of these measures were more important than the objective values which were measured.

Our findings highlight the relevance of a subjective understanding of the speed of enterprise IT. While it is possible to objectively measure time and resources used for a project as well as if the intended scope and features are delivered, the results can still be interpreted as "(too) slow", "as expected" or "fast" based on subjective plans or benchmark values. In our data, we could see a heterogeneous understanding of the speed of enterprise IT. Different people are involved in different activities and evaluate the speed of enterprise IT based on these activities.

The main findings of the case study can be described as follows: (1) **Subjective measurement:** IT speed is evaluated based on individual perceptions and experiences. (2) **Benchmark comparison:** IT speed can be measured against industry standards and external benchmarks. (3) **Comprehensive metrics:** IT speed should be measured in terms of resource consumption, cost, quality and the future value of IT investments. (4) **Balanced speed:** Delivering at high speed is beneficial as long as the required quality is ensured and an excessive consumption of resources avoided. (5) **Competitive edge:** A high speed of the enterprise IT is critical to remaining competitive, meeting customer expectations and ensuring regulatory compliance.

While our findings are based on a single case study, we assume that similar measures of the speed of enterprise IT can be found in other large enterprises. However, due to its methodological limitations, our study does not claim to be applicable to all large companies. Subsequent case studies may show that other organizations can identify similar or different activities for measuring speed of IT in enterprises. In the future, further case studies on this research question could be conducted in other large enterprises as well as in small in medium-sized companies.

References

1. Vial, G.: Understanding digital transformation: A review and a research agenda. J. Strateg. Inf. Syst. **28**(2), 118–144 (2019). https://doi.org/10.1016/j.jsis.2019.01.003
2. Horlach, B.: Shaping the IT Function for the Digital Age – Re-Designing and Re-Conceptualizing IT Governance Decision Areas and Business IT Alignment for Organizational Agility. Hamburg, Germany (2021)
3. Gerster, D., Dremel, C., Brenner, W., Kelker, P.: How enterprises adopt agile structures: a multiple-case study. In: Proceedings of the 52nd Hawaii International Conference on System Sciences (HICSS), pp. 4958–4964 (2019). https://hdl.handle.net/10125/59933

4. Urbach, N., et al.: The impact of digitalization on the IT department. Bus. Inf. Syst. Eng. **61**(1), 123–131 (2019)
5. Horlach, B., Drews, P., Schirmer, I.: Bimodal IT: business-IT alignment in the age of digital transformation. In: Proceedings of MKWI 2016, pp. 1417–1425 (2016)
6. Drews, P., Schirmer, B., Horlach, B., Tekaat, C.: Bimodal enterprise architecture management. the emergence of a new EAM function for a BizDevOps-based fast IT. In: 2017 IEEE 21st International Enterprise Distributed Object Computing Conference Workshop, pp. 57–59 (2017)
7. Robertson, E., Peko, G., Sundaram, D.: Enterprise architecture maturity: a crucial link in business and IT alignment. In: PACIS 2018 Proceedings, VOL. 308, pp. 1–15 (2018). https://aisel.aisnet.org/pacis2018/308
8. Pattij, M., Van de Wetering, R., Kusters, R. J.: From enterprise architecture management to organizational agility: the mediating role of IT capabilities. In: 32nd Bled Econference Humanizing Technology for a Sustainable Society, Juni 16–19, 2019, Bled, Slovenija, pp. 561–576 (2019). https://doi.org/10.18690/978-961-286-280-0.30
9. Pattij, M., Van de Wetering, R., Kusters, R.J.: Improving agility through enterprise architecture management: the mediating role of aligning business and IT. In: Proceedings of AMCIS 2020, pp. 1–8 (2020)
10. Wessel, L., Baiyere, A., Ologeanu-Taddei, R., Cha, J., Blegind-Jensen, T.: Unpacking the difference between digital transformation and it-enabled organizational transformation. J. Assoc. Inf. Syst. **22**(1), 102–119 (2021). https://aisel.aisnet.org/jais/vol22/iss1/6
11. Legner, C., et al.: Digitalization: opportunity and challenge for the business and information systems engineering community. Bus. Inf. Syst. Eng. **59**(4), 301–308 (2017). https://doi.org/10.1007/s12599-017-0484-2
12. Urbach, N., Drews, P., Ross, J.: Digital business transformation and the changing role of the IT function. MIS Q. Exec. **16**(2), 2–4 (2017)
13. Haffke, I., Kalgovas, B., Benlian, A.: Options for transforming the IT function using bimodal IT. MIS Q. Exec **16**(2), 102–116 (2017). https://aisel.aisnet.org/misqe/vol16/iss2/2
14. Jöhnk, J., Oesterle, S., Winkler, T.J., Nørbjerg, J., Urbach, N.: Juggling the paradoxes-governance mechanisms in bimodal IT organizations. In: Proceedings of the 27th European Conference on Information Systems (ECIS), Stockholm & Uppsala (2019). https://aisel.aisnet.org/ecis2019_rp/93
15. Horlach, B., Drechsler, A., Schirmer, I., Drews, P.: Everyone's going to be an architect. In: Proceedings of the 53rd Annual Hawaii International Conference on System Sciences, HICSS (2020), pp. 6197–6205
16. Kanin, O., Drews, P.: Measuring the speed of information technology in enterprises a systematic literature review. In: Proceedings of PACIS 2024 (2024). https://aisel.aisnet.org/pacis2024/track09_digittrans/track09_digittrans/8
17. Yin, R.K.: Case Study Research and Applications: Design and Methods. Sage Publications Inc., Thousand Oaks (2018)
18. Myers, M., Newman, M.: The qualitative interview in IS research: examining the craft. Inf. Organ. **17**(1), 2–26 (2007)
19. Kaiser, R.: Qualitative Experteninterviews - Konzeptionelle Grundlagen und praktische Durchführung. Springer Wiesbaden (2014)
20. Mayring, P.: Qualitative content analysis. Theoretical foundation, basic procedures and software solution. In: Social Science Open Access Repository SSOAR, pp. 39–43. (2014). http://nbn-resolving.de/urn:nbn:de:0168-ssoar-395173
21. Agarwal, H., Bommadevara, N., Weinberg, A.: Using a plan-build-run organizational model to drive IT infrastructure objectives. McKinsey&Company, pp. 3–4. (2013). https://www.mckinsey.com.br

22. https://www.geeksforgeeks.org/software-engineering-coupling-and-cohesion/. Accessed 25 June 2025
23. Schwarzer, B.: Einführung in das Enterprise Architecture Management. Books on Demand, Norderstedt (2009)

Towards Role Mappings in Hybrid Cloud Environments: A Systematic Literature Review

Maximilian Niedermeier(✉) and Holger Wittges

Technical University of Munich, Boltzmannstr. 3, 85748 Garching, Germany
{max.niedermeier,holger.wittges}@tum.de

Abstract. In current IT landscapes, there is a trend towards deploying multiple services each incorporating its own identity management system. When implementing role-based access control (RBAC), each system might utilize different roles adjusted to its own domain. We consider inter-domain role mapping as a solution to this problem. In contrast to most of the existing work, we focus on synchronizing multiple access control systems used by a single organization. Therefore, we first introduce a framework as well as requirements for the successful implementation of role mappings from one central, organizational domain to various target domains. Next, we conduct a systematic literature review and show the current state-of-the-art in inter-domain role mapping. Finally, we compare the contents of the analyzed literature with our requirements to find open issues for effectively managing RBAC in hybrid cloud environments.

Keywords: Inter-Domain · Role Mapping · Interoperability · RBAC · Access Control · Hybrid Cloud · SaaS · Systematic Literature Review

1 Introduction

Role-based access control (RBAC) is one of the most popular models for access management. For example, RBAC is the preferred choice for managing the security of electronic health record systems [1]. Today, organizations tend to not just use a single software, but a hybrid landscape consisting of multiple services. For example, current research in the field of ERP system design deals with the question of how to successfully integrate on-premise infrastructure and software-as-a-service (SaaS) products [2]. Such implementations correspond to the definition of hybrid clouds which can, for example, consist of a private cloud hosted on-premise and several public or community cloud-based extensions [3]. As interoperability is a requirement for identity management systems [4], hybrid cloud deployments require companies to synchronize the roles of various independent RBAC units.

If, on the other hand, an organization views their access control systems independently of each other, there is a risk that it will lose track of its user authorizations. The IRBAC 2000 model [5] aims to bring interoperability to

J. Borbinha et al. (Eds.): EDOC 2024, LNCS 15409, pp. 119–139, 2025.
https://doi.org/10.1007/978-3-031-78338-8_7

RBAC by adding inter-domain role mappings. Such mappings connect roles of different domains and thereby specify which permissions a user of a certain role has in each other domain. There are many research papers expanding the IRBAC 2000 model by deep-diving into various aspects of inter-domain role mapping. However, conducting role mappings is not trivial: Security officers always need to keep in mind that unwise mappings could result in the violation of security guidelines. To the best of our knowledge, an overview of existing work is missing. This hampers researchers to quickly find open issues or answers to cross-literature questions. Also, an overview would allow security officers to conduct role mappings according to state-of-the-art guidelines.

In this work, we are interested in the question whether role mapping is suited for hybrid cloud architectures consisting of several distributed domains that all belong to the same organization. Therefore, we conduct a literature review on the topic of role mapping and aim to answer the following two research questions:

RQ1: What is the current state-of-the-art in inter-domain role mapping research?

RQ2: What are open challenges in inter-domain role mapping research, especially in regards to hybrid clouds consisting of several stand-alone domains?

Whereas our literature review directly answers *RQ1*, we propose a more complex method for answering *RQ2*: First, we propose a hybrid cloud role mapping framework which is based on the IRBAC 2000 model. In contrast to the original model, our framework maps roles between domains that all belong to the same organization. Also, our mappings are unidirectional and connect central, organizational roles with domain-specific roles. Next, we introduce several requirements which an organization needs to consider when mapping roles in such a setting. Finally, we compare these requirements to the results of our literature review and thereby find open challenges which current research does not address.

The following paper contents are structured as follows: Sect. 2 presents background knowledge necessary to fully understand our research contribution. In Sect. 3, we propose our hybrid cloud role mapping framework and the corresponding implementation requirements. Section 4 explains the methodology of our scientific literature review. Afterwards, Sect. 5 shows the outcome of our literature review as it summarizes the different concepts found. In Sect. 6, we answer our research questions as previously explained, mention the limitations of our contribution and show a future research agenda. Finally, we conclude our findings and summarize our research in Sect. 7.

2 Background

In this section, we consolidate fundamental concepts required for understanding the following contents of this research paper. Subsection 2.1 summarizes key features of RBAC, an access control model that utilizes roles for granting permissions to users. Afterwards, Subsect. 2.2 presents the IRBAC 2000 model which introduces role-to-role mappings between different domains. Finally, Subsect. 2.3 explains hybrid hierarchies and the inter-domain role mapping (IDRM) problem.

2.1 Role-Based Access Control (RBAC)

Ferraiolo et al. [6] propose a NIST standard for *Role-Based Access Control* (RBAC). In our summary, we do not address every single element of their RBAC model, but rather explain the concepts which are generally used in inter-domain role mapping research; the core RBAC concepts are depicted in Fig. 1.

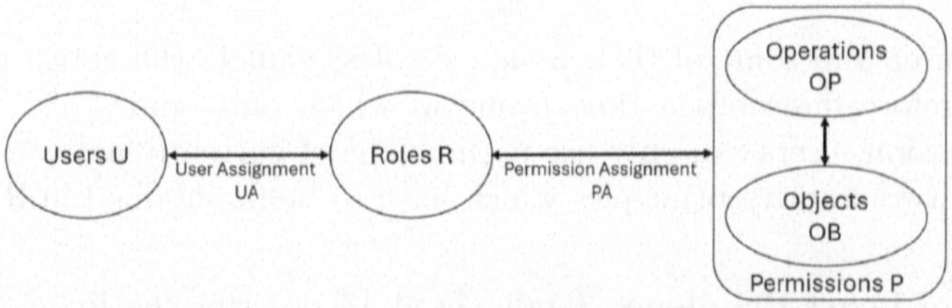

Fig. 1. The interaction between users, roles and permissions in RBAC.

- Users U are human persons, for example employees or guests, who need access to at least one object.
- Roles R are the key concept of RBAC. In a simplified example, a company could use their job positions as roles.
- Objects OB are use-case dependent, access-restricted resources. For example, an object could be a text file, an executable program or a database table.
- Operations OP are executed by users on objects. For example, reading or writing to a text file (object) are operations.
- Permissions $P = 2^{(OB \times OP)}$ are a set of all possible authorization subset combinations including the empty set and the full set. The Cartesian product $OB \times OP$ includes all combinations of object and operation elements.
- The user assignment $UA \subseteq U \times R$ is a many-to-many relation between users and roles. This means, that a user can be assigned to multiple roles and a role could be granted to different users.
- The permission assignment $PA \subseteq P \times R$ is a many-to-many relation between roles and permissions. This means, that a role could be assigned to multiple permission elements and a permission could be granted to different roles.

The authors define general role hierarchies H as partial orders on the role set R, thus $H \subseteq R \times R$. If $(x, y) \in H$ (also written as $x > y$), then the role x is an ancestor of y and inherits all permissions granted to the successor role y. Figure 2 shows a small example in which $R = \{$Administrator, Consultant, Developer$\}$ and $H = \{($Administrator, Consultant$)$, $($Administrator, Developer$)\}$. This hierarchy follows, that users of the ancestor role *Administrator* have all permissions assigned to the successor roles *Consultant* and *Developer*.

Core RBAC also includes sessions S, which allow RBAC systems to distinguish between assigned and activated roles. More precisely, a session is a mapping

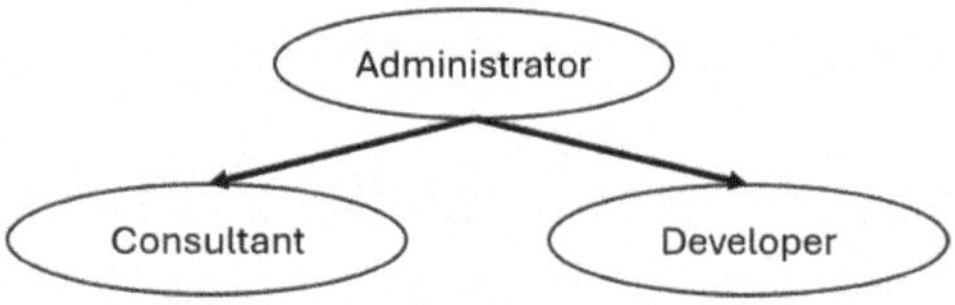

Fig. 2. A simple example of a general role hierarchy.

between a user and some of their assigned roles, namely the active roles. Each session therefore describes a time frame in which only some roles are active. During a session, users can only use permissions of currently active roles. Next, we propose two security principles which have to be maintained in RBAC.

Principle of Least Privilege. Sandhu et al. [7] describe the *Principle of Least Privilege* as an administrative security approach which grants users only those rights which they actually need to perform their job, and no more. In regards to RBAC, assigning this minimized set of permissions works by defining a proper user and permission assignment.

Separation of Duty. Simon and Zurko [8] define *Separation of Duty* (SoD) as a security approach tackling fraud by requiring multiple people for the completion of certain tasks. The authors differ between two variants: *Static Separation of Duty* prevents a user from being a member of conflicting roles. *Dynamic Separation of Duty* allows users being assigned conflicting roles if certain conditions are met. For example, users may not activate conflicting roles in the same session.

2.2 IRBAC 2000 Model

Kapadia et al. [5] propose the *IRBAC 2000* model and extend RBAC by adding a role mapping framework for collaborative environments. To be more precise, the authors consider two different administrative domains D_0 and D_1, each having their own role set R_0, R_1 and hierarchy H_0, H_1. The organizations now decide to work together and give users of domain D_1 access to domain D_0. Therefore, let us assume any roles $x \in R_0$ and $y \in R_1$. In the following, we represent these role set assignments as x_{R_0} or respectively y_{R_1}. An association $y_{R_1} \mapsto x_{R_0}$ implies, that there is a role translation and users of role y_{R_1} in domain D_1 are now considered as of role x_{R_0} in domain D_0. Figure 3 shows an example.

In this setting, the company of domain D_1 sends human resources to a project in domain D_0. The administrator of domain D_0 conducts a role mapping (shown as dashed arrows) from H_1 to H_0. If a translation is marked with *NT*, it is non-transitive. Otherwise, role mappings are transitive. If our exemplary role mapping $y_{R_1} \mapsto x_{R_0}$ is transitive, it follows that $\forall z \in R_1$, if $z_{R_1} > y_{R_1}$ then $z_{R_1} > x_{R_0}$. This means, that all ancestors z_{R_1} of role y_{R_1} inherit its role translations and are implicitly mapped to the role x_{R_0} of domain D_0. For non-transitive role mappings, this property does not hold.

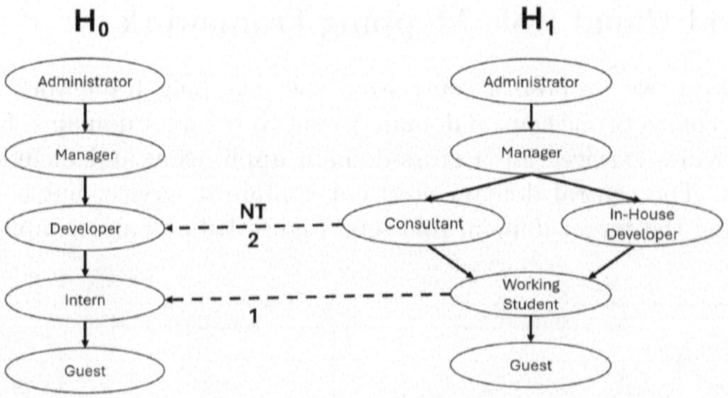

Fig. 3. A simple role mapping example between two hierarchies H_0 and H_1.

Figure 3 includes a transitive role mapping $WorkingStudent_{R_1} \mapsto Intern_{R_0}$. Thus, all users of domain D_1 which are not only a $Guest_{R_1}$, have at least the same rights as an $Intern_{R_0}$ in domain D_0. There is also a non-transitive role translation $Consultant_{R_1} \mapsto_{NT} Developer_{R_0}$. Thus, all $Consultant_{R_1}$ users of domain D_1 have the same access rights as a $Developer_{R_0}$ in domain D_0. However, users of role $Manager_{R_1}$ or $Administrator_{R_1}$ in domain D_1 are still considered an $Intern_{R_0}$ in domain D_0.

2.3 Role Mapping in Hybrid Hierarchies

The *Generalized Temporal Role-Based Access Control* (GTRBAC) model extends RBAC by putting emphasis on temporal constraints for role activations [9]. In [10], Joshi et al. distinguish between three types of role hierarchies which are suitable for working with the GTRBAC model. For simplicity, we only introduce the unrestricted version of each hierarchy. In an *I-hierarchy*, the *permission-inheritance* known from the previously introduced general role hierarchy holds. Therefore, users who activate an ancestor role can also use the permissions actually assigned to successor nodes. An *A-hierarchy* relies on *activation-inheritance*, which means that users who can currently activate a certain ancestor role can also activate the corresponding successor roles. Finally, in an *IA-hierarchy*, both of the previously explained concepts apply.

Du and Joshi [11] define a *hybrid hierarchy* as a role hierarchy whose relation set can contain any relation that belongs to one of the three hierarchy types just introduced. They show that in a hybrid hierarchy, the complexity of finding the minimum role set that fulfills the permissions requested by a user is NP-complete. This issue is referred to as the *Inter-Domain Role Mapping* (IDRM) *problem*. The IDRM problem aims to fulfill the principle of least privilege for role mappings based on collaborative permission requests in hybrid hierarchies.

3 Hybrid Cloud Role Mapping Framework

In this section, we propose a centralized role mapping framework for hybrid clouds that connects one central domain to multiple target domains. Each target domain provides services for a cross-domain application and includes an own RBAC unit. The central domain does not contain a service, but is crucial for synchronizing the target domain role sets. Figure 4 shows an exemplary model.

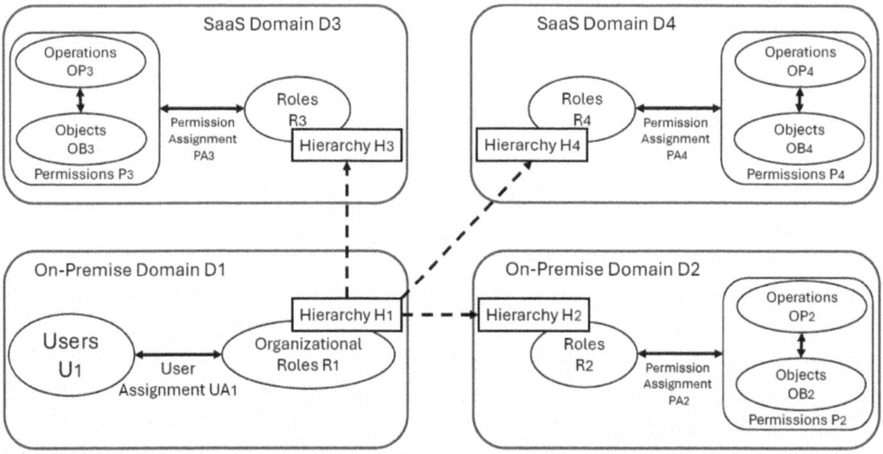

Fig. 4. Our centralized role mapping framework for hybrid cloud infrastructures in a simplified setting which consists of one central domain and three target domains.

As all domains belong to the same organization, there is only a single set of users U_1 stored in a central user database. These users require different permissions P_2, P_3 and P_4 in the target domains D_2, D_3 and D_4. In theory, it would be possible to consider all target domains independently of each other and only work with three user assignments UA_2, UA_3 and UA_4. However, this method could result in a security hazard as the overall access control structure would be difficult to trace, especially when there are more than three domains.

In our example, domain D_1 includes the central user database and thus we refer to it as the central domain. Therein, the user assignment UA_1 directly maps the users U_1 to organizational roles R_1. Since it is important to have full control over the user database, D_1 is an on-premise domain. Just as in the IRBAC 2000 model, role mappings (shown as dashed arrows) between the role hierarchies determine which technical roles in R_2, R_3 or R_4 are assigned to the users U_1. In contrast to the original model, our framework only allows unidirectional mappings from H_1 to the other hierarchies H_2, H_3 and H_4. Thereby, we intend to simplify the user management and bring interoperability to the distributed access control systems. After all, the mappings unify the technical roles of all target domains based on which organizational role(s) the users are assigned to.

Depending on the organization design, different role sets and role hierarchies may be more or less similar, which makes the creation of role mappings more or less difficult. Cloud services could have a similar role structure to on-premise services if the company only uses them as replicas. For example, cloud backups can be used for disaster recovery [12]. However, different domains often complement each other and therefore deploy different services, each with its own role structure. Based on our framework, we present six requirements for successfully conducting role mappings in a hybrid cloud consisting of heterogeneous domains.

- **REQ1:** Liu and Huang [13] mention that role mapping is limited to a coarse-grained user-role assignment as it only allows exact mappings between roles of different domains. The authors state that in a more realistic scenario, organizations could prefer to only map some users of a certain role to another role. Similarly, we state that organizations might also prefer to only map parts of the permissions assigned to a role. Both issues correlate to the principle of least privilege and thus follow that *non-requested permissions granted by role mappings should be minimized.*
- **REQ2:** Role mappings between different domains may generate conflicts in the access control structure. In [5], Kapadia et al. already mention some security issues as well as possible resolutions. However, the authors do not mention how to guarantee separation of duty. We require that there are *no role mappings that allow a user to activate conflicting roles at the same time.*
- **REQ3:** Due to the increased complexity and workload faced when integrating various, rapidly changing cloud-based identity management systems, generating role mappings should be *automated as much as possible.*
- **REQ4:** Li et al. [14] state that changing the role of a user might lead to unauthorized access and could even have cascading effects. In our case, modifying a user assignment may have major consequences for their assigned permissions in all other domains as the mappings for the new role directly apply. Thus, it is important that security officers can *effectively monitor* role mappings as well as their impact.
- **REQ5:** Usually, each target domain is managed by an own designated administrator who is specialized in the respective domain topic. Thus, establishing role mappings from the central domain to each other domain involves both the target domain administrators and the security officers who create the mappings. As a result, mapping roles is a highly collaborative task which needs to be *easily understandable* for each actor taking part.
- **REQ6:** Our role mapping framework synchronizes role-based access control across different domains. However, there is a need for assuring that *only trusted domains participate in this process.* In the worst case, a foreign domain that belongs neither to the own organization nor to a known collaborating company would be able to map their roles to the local infrastructure.

4 Research Methodology

Our goal is not only to find the current state-of-the-art in inter-domain role mapping, but also to examine the emerging challenges in hybrid cloud environments.

Therefore, we compare the requirements introduced in Sect. 3 against results from a concept-centric literature review according to Webster and Watson [15].

In April 2024, we began to search for suitable articles by systematically querying the *Scopus* database. Thereby, we only included work having the exact term *role mapping* written in the paper abstract. Also, we limited our search by only including journal articles and conference papers. In this process, we could generate 124 hits. Similarly, we queried the *ACM Digital Library*, the *AIS eLibrary* and the *IEEE Xplore* database. When analyzing the results of searching the *ACM Digital Library* and *IEEE Xplore*, we found that the hits were a subset of our *Scopus* search results. Querying the *AIS eLibrary* resulted in two new hits.

Besides *Scopus*, the *Web of Science Core Collection* is another world-leading source for academic work [16]. Thus, in August 2024, we also queried this database and found 65 hits. When comparing the results to our *Scopus* hits, we noticed that the search in the *Web of Science Core Collection* resulted in four new hits.

In total, we could generate 130 unique hits. We first read the abstract of each paper and if we afterwards still had doubts whether the article is relevant for our research, we continued to look into the paper contents. As for inclusion criteria, we classified a hit as relevant if it contributes to **expanding** the research field of inter-domain role mapping presented in our background Sect. 2. Also, the article had to be **available** to us in any online library. After analyzing all hits, we found 44 relevant sources. Finally, we also performed a backward and forward search, which resulted in four more relevant publications. This means, that we include a total of 48 papers in our review. Table 1 provides an overview of the scientific literature search we just proposed in this section.

Table 1. An overview of our scientific literature search to the topic of inter-domain role mapping between April and August 2024.

Database	Limited to	Search String	Hits	Relevant
ACM Digital Library	RESEARCH-ARTICLE, ARTICLE	Abstract:("role mapping")	2	2
AIS eLibrary	Journal, Conference, Series	abstract:"role mapping"	2	0
IEEE Xplore	Journals, Conferences	("Abstract":"role mapping")	32	19
Scopus	Article, Conference Paper	ABS("role mapping")	124	43
Web of Science Core Collection	Article, Proceeding Paper	"role mapping" (Abstract)	65	26
Sum (Unique)			**130**	**44**
Backward & Forward Search				4
In Total				**48**

5 Results

When scanning the documents in more detail, we assign each article at least one concept and thereby group publications topic-wise. In the following subsections, we further explain each concept and focus on mentioning the respective contributions of each article. Table 2 shows our concept matrix with columns ordered according to the concept sizes. Overall, we can find six different topics.

Table 2. Concept matrix resulting from our systematic literature review.

Authors	Article	Concept					
		Conflict Resolution	Principle of Least Privilege	Trust Management	Implementation Project	Cloud Computing	Automation
Abdelfattah et al.	[17]		•			•	
Abdelfattah et al.	[18]		•			•	
Chen and Crampton	[19]		•				
Chen and Crampton	[20]	•	•				
Chen et al.	[21]	•					
Chen et al.	[22]			•			
Deng et al.	[23]	•					
Deng et al.	[24]	•		•			
Diao et al.	[25]						•
Du et al.	[26]	•					
Fan et al.	[27]			•			
Fan et al.	[28]	•			•		
Geethakumari et al.	[29]			•	•		
Ghosh et al.	[30]		•				
Guo et al.	[31]			•			
Hu et al.	[32]	•	•				
Hu et al.	[33]	•					
Hu et al.	[34]	•		•			
Huang et al.	[35]		•			•	
Huang et al.	[36]	•					
Kamath et al.	[37]	•			•		•
Kun et al.	[38]			•			
Li et al.	[39]	•		•			
Li et al.	[40]	•		•	•	•	
Li et al.	[41]						•
Lv et al.	[42]	•		•			
Pan et al.	[43]	•	•		•		
Shafiq et al.	[44]	•	•				
Shehab et al.	[45]	•		•			
Solanki et al.	[46]					•	
Sun et al.	[47]			•			
Tang et al.	[48]	•	•				
Tang et al.	[49]	•					
Unal and Caglayan	[50]				•		
Wang et al.	[51]			•			
Wang et al.	[52]	•					
Wang et al.	[53]	•					
Wang et al.	[54]	•	•				
Xia	[55]	•	•				
Xiang et al.	[56]	•	•				
Yang et al.	[57]	•			•		•
Yu et al.	[58]	•					
Zhang and Joshi	[59]	•	•				
Zhang and Joshi	[60]		•				
Zhang and Li	[61]			•	•	•	
Zhang et al.	[62]		•				
Zhang et al.	[63]						•
Zuo et al.	[64]	•			•		

5.1 Conflict Resolution

The largest subset of role mapping research is concerned with the algorithmic resolution of associated conflicts. There are particularly many articles resolving separation of duty conflicts. We find research about both assuring static SoD [23,24,26,32–34,49,52,54,55,64] and dynamic SoD [43–45,48,59]. In terms of static SoD, some authors directly mention to work with constraints for *Static Mutually Exclusive Roles* (SMER) [23,24,26,32–34,49,64]. In [33] and [34], the authors also discuss the possibility to adjust the RBAC policies of the target domain in order to enable interoperation. Determining whether a static SoD problem can be solved is NP-complete [20].

When it comes to dynamic SoD, Zhang and Joshi [59] propose and solve the *User Authorization Query* (UAQ) problem which describes the issue of finding sufficient roles which can be activated during one session. Solving the UAQ problem is NP-hard [20]. Research also suggests to conduct role mappings based on *activation-inheritance* when connecting conflicting roles in a hybrid hierarchy [43]. This also applies to the case where two users are not allowed to activate the same role at the same time [48]. Shehab et al. [45] examine multi-domain access paths based on role mappings in order to resolve constraints for *Dynamic Mutually Exclusive Roles*. It may happen, that the joint use of two role mappings leads to a SoD conflict. Shafiq et al. [44] show how to formulate integer programs that efficiently decide which mapping should be removed.

Besides examining separation of duty conflicts, focus also lies on resolving cyclic inheritance [21,36,39,40,42–45,52–54,56,58]. This issue describes a situation in which cyclic role mappings across different domains map a successor role to a higher-ranking ancestor role from the same domain. As a result, users which are actually assigned to the successor role can now also use the rights assigned to the ancestor role. Lastly, some contributions [28,37,44,57] resolve semantic conflicts when creating a global access control policy based on role mappings. For example, different local policies may differ in naming conventions.

5.2 Principle of Least Privilege

Our results show that examining the principle of least privilege is another large subset of role mapping research. For example, we find solution approaches based on rules [54], also allowing direct permission assignments [32], creating new roles [17,18] or splitting existing roles [43,44,48,62]. Latter technique maps foreign roles to new subsets of local roles which are created based on the requested permissions. In [48], the authors also utilize request-splitting and thereby create subsets of permission requests. This approach is helpful if not all requested permissions can be acquired in the target domain.

Huang et al. [35] use a greedy approach for mining a minimal role set in a role mapping scenario. We find various articles proposing greedy algorithm(s) for solving the IDRM problem [19,30,55,56,59]. In [19], the authors state that their solution approach is based on an *availability* point of view which aims to find a minimal role set being assigned the requested permissions but only a minimized set of additional permissions. In contrast, the *safety* perspective is about finding a minimal role set granting the maximal set of requested permissions, but no other permissions. Similarly, Zhang and Joshi [59] also differ between an *availability* and a *least privilege*-based approach. Latter option is similar to the *safety* perspective introduced in [19]. In terms of computational complexity, the IDRM-availability problem is NP-hard, but the IDRM-safety problem is in P [20].

Ghosh et al. [30] solve the IDRM-availability problem and use various evaluations metrics for showing that their approach outperforms [11] and [19]. In [55] and [56], the authors improve the greedy algorithm introduced in [11]. In [60], Zhang and Joshi introduce the role-based domain discovery problem which is about finding domains that contain all resources correlating to a set of requested permissions. For fulfilling the principle of least privilege, the authors use one of the greedy algorithms presented in [59].

5.3 Trust Management

Before mapping roles from foreign domains to the local infrastructure, companies have to define trust relationships with the requesting organizations. After all, no untrusted users shall access the own systems. In relation to this topic, we find that most articles suggest [51] or use [22,27,31,38,40] a *Public Key Infrastructure* (PKI) for their authentication framework. In [22], the authors show research about role mappings in different circles of trust. Each cycle deploys its own PKI, which already connects different identity providers. When defining a trust relationship between identity providers of different trust cycles, these exit points require certificates of both PKIs associated with the two trust domains. Other articles do not directly mention PKIs, but also utilize private and public keys for secure communication between domains [39,45,47].

In [39] and [40], there is a central server connecting collaborating domains. When conducting role mappings, participating domains are never linked directly but the mappings always pass through a virtual role hierarchy. In [29] and [42], a central server is used for defining a global ranking system of domain-specific roles. In contrast, we also find research focusing on a distributed approach: Zhang and Li [61] only deploy a client-side and a target-side authentication module.

Some articles look at the topic of trust from a perspective other than authentication. Deng et al. [24] consider the migration of SMER constraints between collaborating domains. The authors state that the domain migrating a constraint needs to trust the other domains to understand and not manipulate the transferred constraint. In the architecture provided by Hu et al. [34], each domain implements a monitor module for evaluating the risk of an incoming request.

5.4 Implementation Project

Some research articles present practical projects that implement inter-domain role mappings. For example, Sun et al. [47] use a blockchain to make role mapping rules readable for the public. Some authors [28,29,40,43,57,61] mention to use XACML for defining access control policies. SAML is used to define role memberships [40] or general authentication mechanisms [57,61]. Both technologies are markup languages based on XML. Zuo et al. [64] use XML to define role mappings between domains. The authors structure their XML document as follows: Each domain contains its roles as sub-elements and, in turn, each role contains the roles to which it is mapped as sub-elements. Kamath et al. [37] use X-RBAC [65], which is a XML-based language for defining RBAC policies in multi-domain settings. Unal and Caglayan [50] introduce an own XML-based language for inter-domain access control including role mappings.

Besides the technologies used, we consider two projects to be especially useful for security officers who need to define role mappings: Fan et al. [28] develop a tool that automatically detects conflicts which are based on role mappings. The tool also summarizes the conflicts in corresponding analysis reports. Pan et al. [43] present a tool for visualizing multi-domain RBAC policies and illustrate in-between role mappings by connecting roles from different domains.

5.5 Cloud Computing

Due to our research question, we are especially interested in how role mapping is applied in cloud environments. We find that most research assumes different organizations which collaborate by sharing a cloud service [17,18,30,46]. Some articles [17,18,46] directly mention the multi-tenancy of cloud products and focus on role mappings between the tenants. In [46], Solanki et al. introduce a super tenant which holds a mediaton role for the final mapping specifications. Ghosh et al. [30] assume that the provider domain conducts all role mappings based on the requests of the remote domains. In [40], the authors mention that there is a trend towards building a central, virtual server for connecting private and public cloud resources.

Even if not directly mentioning cloud computing, we also assign articles that focus on web services to this topic [35,61]. In our understanding, web services are an equivalent to SaaS products. In [35], Huang et al. consider a composite web service which is similar to our hybrid cloud model consisting of multiple domains. Just like our considerations in Sect. 3, the authors mention that there are two options when granting employees access to a new domain: Either the organization creates additional users for all employees in each new domain (this correlates to extending the user assignments) or a single sign-on mechanism based on role mappings is implemented.

5.6 Automation

Zhang et al. [63] propose an algorithm for calculating the semantic similarity between two roles in a single role hierarchy. Therefore, the authors consider both the distance between the roles and their similarity in terms of assigned permissions. Similar to this approach, Diao et al. [25] and Li et al. [41] introduce inter-domain role mapping recommendations based on semantic similarities. This means that the latter two publications focus on the similarity of roles in different hierarchies. As for recommendation criteria, both articles use the following factors:

- **Similarity of concept sets:** The concept set of a role consists of various properties such as for example its name, its permissions and its description. When comparing concept sets between two roles, not only the actual terms but also WordNet-based synonyms are taken into consideration.
- **Similarity based on role hierarchy:** The position of a role within a hierarchy and its relationships to the other roles are also important factors to

consider. To give a simple example, two roles from different domains may be very similar if both only have successors but no ancestors.

Other research aims to automate role mappings based on attributes [37,57]. In [37], roles are considered more similar if the respectively assigned users share similar attributes. The authors also consider the synonyms of the attributes. Yang et al. [57] first translate attributes to numerical values and thus also prevent the issue that different domains may have assigned unequal terms to their roles.

6 Discussion

In this section, we interpret our results from Sect. 5. First, Subsect. 6.1 shows a state-of-the-art in inter-domain role mapping research as we map the requirements from Sect. 3 to the concepts shown in Table 2. If we cannot map each requirement to an existing concept, we discover open issues that have not yet been addressed in scientific publications. In Subsect. 6.2, we briefly mention the limitations of our research contribution. Finally, in Subsect. 6.3, we conclude our discussion by showing our concrete future research directions.

6.1 Main Findings

Our literature review shows that existing work is very theoretical in its approach. Most research (see Subsects. 5.1 and 5.2) aims to find algorithmic solutions for separation of duty conflicts or for the fulfillment of the principle of least privilege. We map both concepts to our requirements **REQ1** and **REQ2**. However, we have further remarks for applying the principle of least privilege: First, the original IDRM problem aims to find sufficient roles for a single user request. As to our understanding, however, it is possible to apply shown solutions for role-to-role mappings if entire user groups (sharing a common role) require certain permissions in another domain. Secondly, in contrast to approaches such as role splitting, solutions to the IDRM problem never create new roles and therefore prevent a role explosion. However, each variant of the IDRM problem also has disadvantages: Solving the IDRM-availability problem can lead to a solution which grants users additional, non-requested permissions and thus does not fully comply with the principle of least privilege. When solving the IDRM-safety problem, users may not be provided with every permissions needed. The bottom line is that security officers have to decide on a particular course of action, but would maybe prefer a trade-off between fulfilling the principle of least privilege and not generating a role explosion while still granting all permissions as requested.

Next, Subsect. 5.3 shows how to set up a role mapping environment that only allows trusted domains to join a collaboration. We map this concept to our requirement **REQ6** which corresponds to this topic. Existing sources focus on PKIs but in [34], the authors also mention to evaluate the risks of foreign requests. We believe that such approaches are important because role mappings could contain errors. False mappings would allow users to exploit roles which they actually should not be assigned to. In order to prevent such issues, we recommend to investigate fraud detection mechanisms in inter-domain role mapping.

REQ3 states that role mappings should be automated as far as possible. We map this requirement to the corresponding concept that describes current automation approaches. As Subsect. 5.6 shows, these are based on semantic similarity or attribute mappings. Both methods are not based on permission requests and are therefore difficult to reconcile with the principle of least privilege. However, we suggest to investigate a specific use case: Organizations may rent various cloud infrastructure platforms and thus use several, predefined roles provided by different cloud vendors. We wonder if roles predefined by different cloud vendors are similar and, if so, whether those can be mapped semantically.

REQ4 emphasizes the importance of efficiently monitoring role mappings. In found literature, there is only one approach which visualizes inter-domain role mappings [43]. We see this project as a first step in the right direction, but could not find an article which focuses on monitoring large role mapping architectures, whose impact may be difficult for humans to track. Thus, we do not consider this requirement to be met. Subsection 5.4 summarizes used technology stacks behind practical projects which implement role mappings. Researchers in the fields of security or software architecture can use this knowledge and build monitoring solutions which reduce the risk of losing track of complex mapping structures.

REQ5 states that conducting role mappings is a collaborative task and should therefore be easy to understand for everyone involved. However, we cannot find guidelines that explain how to proceed in a realistic setting. As said, most of the found sources are theory-based. Thus, current research cannot fulfill this requirement. Subsection 5.5 summarizes existing publications dealing with role mappings in cloud environments. However, current research does not focus on practical cloud computing examples in enterprise structures. Rather, cloud computing serves as a more modern example for role mapping algorithms due to its multi-tenancy capabilities. We suggest to extend this research domain by showing how to implement role mappings in a corporate cloud setting.

6.2 Limitations

First of all, it is important to mention that this article only considers RBAC. As already mentioned in the introduction, the reason for this is that RBAC is a popular choice for access control. Also, many systems support its implementation. However, there are also other access control models, such as *Attribute-Based Access Control* (ABAC) [66]. In contrast to RBAC, ABAC does not use roles but attributes and policies to decide on authorization requests. In complex environments with multiple domains, the use of ABAC would therefore prevent security officers from having to manage a large number of roles.

Secondly, our literature review only includes role mapping research. When creating inter-domain role mappings based on permission requests, role mapping research assumes that both collaborating domains already contain role sets. Even if the role sets in target domains can be manipulated by splitting roles or adding new roles, the question remains as to how an organization should restructure their unified access control systems or build a solution from the ground up.

6.3 Future Research Agenda

Given the users U, the permissions P and the permissions each user requires, the basic *Role Mining Problem* (RMP) aims to find roles R, user assignments UA and permission assignments PA while minimizing the number of roles and matching the requested permissions with the permissions obtained by assigning the proposed roles [67]. For example, mining roles can be based on clustering [68], an **unsupervised machine learning** technique. In [67], the authors not only present the basic RMP, but also several of its variants, such as the *Minimal Noise Role Mining Problem* (MinNoise RMP), which fixes the number of roles while minimizing the difference between required permissions and actually assigned permissions. The number of roles can therefore be considered as an input parameter which influences how well the output correlates to the principle of least privilege. Referring to our findings in Subsect. 6.1, role mining thus allows security officers to find trade-offs between only assigning required permissions and generating a reasonable number of roles. Also, now referring to the limitations outlined in Subsect. 6.2, role mining outputs the entire role set and its assignments to users and permissions. Role mining therefore suits the (re-)organization of role structures from the bottom up.

We are interested in examining how the RMP can be applied to a multi-domain environment. In particular, we aim to find a solution for the framework we presented in Sect. 3. Therefore, we propose a bottom-up approach which first mines the technical roles of the target domains and then creates the organizational roles. The procedure below describes this algorithm in more detail:

1. For all target domains D_2, D_3 and D_4, find out which permissions in P_2, P_3 and P_4 each user in U_1 requires (or does not require anymore).
2. Decide on a value for an input parameter that determines whether the subsequent mining processes focus more on fulfilling the principle of least privilege or on generating a reasonable number of roles.
3. For all target domains D_2, D_3 and D_4, solve some variant of the RMP.
4. For the central domain D_1, apply an algorithm which mines the organizational roles R_1 and the user assignment UA_1. This algorithm must take into account that UA_2, UA_3 and UA_4 can be replaced by adding role mappings between the hierarchy H_1 and the target domain hierarchies H_2, H_3 and H_4.
5. If not satisfied with the outcome, go back to step 2 and re-run the algorithm with a changed input parameter.

After reviewing existing literature on the topic of role mining, we will further develop the proposed algorithm and test whether it is suited for realistic settings.

7 Conclusion

In this paper, we show two major research contributions: First, we define a hybrid cloud framework for inter-domain role mappings. In contrast to most of the existing literature, we assume role mappings between different domains that all belong to the same organization. We highlight several requirements which an organization should consider when implementing role mappings in such a distributed environment. Secondly, we conduct a systematic literature review and present the current state-of-the-art in the field of inter-domain role mapping. Our results show that existing research is mainly concerned with algorithmic solutions and less with practical examples in the field of cloud computing.

Finally, we combine our two contributions by mapping the requirements for our framework to the different concepts we found in existing literature. In doing so, we reveal various open challenges which future researchers can address to further improve the feasibility of a hybrid cloud role mapping framework. For example, current role mapping research lacks a direct comparison between fulfilling the principle of least privilege and generating a reasonable number of roles. We consider role mining as a suitable solution for filling this research gap. Thus, our next step is to further develop a multi-domain role mining algorithm.

Acknowledgments. This work is part of a research project funded by SAP SE to investigate *Very Large Business Applications* (VLBA). Also, we would especially like to thank Stefanie Rinderle-Ma for her constructive feedback on this research project. Finally, we would like to thank the anonymous reviewers for their valuable comments on this submission.

Disclosure of Interests. The authors have no competing interests to declare that are relevant to the content of this article.

References

1. Fernández-Alemán, J.L., Señor, I.C., Lozoya, P.Á.O., Toval, A.: Security and privacy in electronic health records: a systematic literature review. J. Biomed. Inform. **46**(3), 541–562 (2013). https://doi.org/10.1016/j.jbi.2012.12.003
2. Niranga, M., Wickramarachchi, R.: A model for on-premises ERP system and cloud ERP integration. In: Proceedings of the International Conference on Industrial Engineering and Operations Management, pp. 1381–1392. IEOM Society International, Dubai (2020)
3. Mell, P.M., Grance, T.: The NIST definition of cloud computing. NIST Spec. Publ. **800**(145), 1–3 (2011). https://doi.org/10.6028/NIST.SP.800-145
4. Pöhn, D., Hommel, W.: An overview of limitations and approaches in identity management. In: Proceedings of the 15th International Conference on Availability, Reliability and Security, pp. 1–10. ACM, Virtual Event Ireland (2020). https://doi.org/10.1145/3407023.3407026
5. Kapadia, A., Al-Muhtadi, J., Campbell, R. H., Mickunas, D.: IRBAC 2000: secure interoperability using dynamic role translation. In: 1st International Conference on Internet Computing, pp. 231–238. Las Vegas (2000)
6. Ferraiolo, D.F., Sandhu, R., Gavrila, S., Kuhn, D.R., Chandramouli, R.: Proposed NIST standard for role-based access control. ACM Trans. Inf. Syst. Secur. **4**(3), 224–274 (2001). https://doi.org/10.1145/501978.501980

7. Sandhu, R., Ferraiolo, D., Kuhn, R.: The NIST model for role-based access control: towards a unified standard. In: Proceedings of the Fifth ACM Workshop on Role-Based Access Control, pp. 47–63. ACM, Berlin (2000). https://doi.org/10.1145/344287.344301
8. Simon, R.T., Zurko, M.E.: Separation of duty in role-based environments. In: Proceedings 10th Computer Security Foundations Workshop, pp. 183–194. IEEE, Rockport (1997). https://doi.org/10.1109/CSFW.1997.596811
9. Joshi, J.B., Bertino, E., Latif, U., Ghafoor, A.: A generalized temporal role-based access control model. IEEE Trans. Knowl. Data Eng. **17**(1), 4–23 (2005). https://doi.org/10.1109/TKDE.2005.1
10. Joshi, JB., Bertino, E., Ghafoor, A.: Temporal hierarchies and inheritance semantics for GTRBAC. In: Proceedings of the Seventh ACM Symposium on Access Control Models and Technologies, pp. 74–83. ACM, Monterey (2002). https://doi.org/10.1145/507711.507724
11. Du, S., Joshi, J. B.: Supporting authorization query and inter-domain role mapping in presence of hybrid role hierarchy. In: Proceedings of the Eleventh ACM Symposium on Access Control Models and Technologies, pp. 228–236. ACM, Lake Tahoe (2006). https://doi.org/10.1145/1133058.1133090
12. Abualkishik, A.Z., Alwan, A.A., Gulzar, Y.: Disaster recovery in cloud computing systems: an overview. Int. J. Adv. Comput. Sci. Appl. **11**(9), 702–710 (2020). https://doi.org/10.14569/IJACSA.2020.0110984
13. Liu, S., Huang, H.: Role-based access control for distributed cooperation environment. In: 2009 International Conference on Computational Intelligence and Security, pp. 455–459. IEEE, Beijing (2009). https://doi.org/10.1109/CIS.2009.206
14. Li, W., Wan, H., Ren, X., Li, S.: A refined RBAC model for cloud computing. In: 2012 IEEE/ACIS 11th International Conference on Computer and Information Science, pp. 43–48. IEEE, Shanghai (2012). https://doi.org/10.1109/ICIS.2012.13
15. Webster, J., Watson, R.T.: Analyzing the past to prepare for the future: writing a literature review. MIS Q. **26**(2), 13–23 (2002)
16. Zhu, J., Liu, W.: A tale of two databases: the use of web of science and scopus in academic papers. Scientometrics **123**(1), 321–335 (2020). https://doi.org/10.1007/s11192-020-03387-8
17. Abdelfattah, D., Hassan, H.A., Omara, F.A.: A novel role-mapping algorithm for enhancing highly collaborative access control system. Distrib. Parallel Databases **40**(2), 521–558 (2022). https://doi.org/10.1007/s10619-022-07407-9
18. Abdelfattah, D., Hassan, H.A., Omara, F.A.: Enhancing highly-collaborative access control system using a new role-mapping algorithm. Int. J. Electr. Comput. Eng. **12**(3), 2765–2782 (2022). https://doi.org/10.11591/ijece.v12i3.pp2765-2782
19. Chen, L., Crampton, J.: Inter-domain role mapping and least privilege. In: Proceedings of the 12th ACM Symposium on Access Control Models and Technologies, pp. 157–162. ACM, Sophia Antipolis (2007). https://doi.org/10.1145/1266840.1266866
20. Chen, L., Crampton, J.: Set covering problems in role-based access control. In: Backes, M., Ning, P. (eds.) ESORICS 2009. LNCS, vol. 5789, pp. 689–704. Springer, Heidelberg (2009). https://doi.org/10.1007/978-3-642-04444-1_42
21. Chen, X., Wu, D., Lin, J., Zhu, M.: A security violation detection method for RBAC based interoperation. In: 2006 International Conference on Computational Intelligence and Security, pp. 1491-1496. IEEE, Guangzhou (2006). https://doi.org/10.1109/ICCIAS.2006.295308
22. Chen, J., Wu, G., Ji, Z.: Secure interoperation of identity managements among different circles of trust. Comput. Stan. Interfaces **33**(6), 533–540 (2011). https://doi.org/10.1016/j.csi.2011.02.008

23. Deng, L., He, Y., Xu, Z.: Enforcing separation of duty in ad hoc collaboration. In: 2008 The 9th International Conference for Young Computer Scientists, pp. 1545–1552. IEEE, Hunan (2008). https://doi.org/10.1109/ICYCS.2008.131
24. Deng, L., Xu, Z., He, Y.: Trust-based constraint-secure interoperation for dynamic mediator-free collaboration. J. Comput. **4**(9), 862–872 (2009)
25. Diao, L., Wang, H., Alsarra, S., Yen, I.L., Bastani, F.: A smart role mapping recommendation system. In: 2019 IEEE 43rd Annual Computer Software and Applications Conference, pp. 135–140. IEEE, Milwaukee (2019). https://doi.org/10.1109/COMPSAC.2019.10196
26. Du, J., Chen, C., Zhu, J., Li, X.: Research on association securities in cross-domain interoperation model in pervasive computing. In: 2008 Third International Conference on Pervasive Computing and Applications, pp. 953–958. IEEE, Alexandria (2008). https://doi.org/10.1109/ICPCA.2008.4783748
27. Fan, H., Xian, Z., Guanglin, X.: Distributed role-based access control for coaliagion application. Geo-spatial Inf. Sci. **8**(2), 138–143 (2005). https://doi.org/10.1007/BF02826854
28. Fan, B., Liang, X., Luo, Y., Bo, Y., Xia, C.: Conflict detection model of access control policy in collaborative environment. In: 2011 International Conference on Computational and Information Sciences, pp. 377–381. IEEE, Chengdu (2011). https://doi.org/10.1109/ICCIS.2011.112
29. Geethakumari, G., Negi, A., Sastry, V.N.: A cross-domain role mapping and authorization framework for RBAC in grid systems. Int. J. Comput. Appl. **6**(1), 1–12 (2009)
30. Ghosh, N., Chatterjee, D., Ghosh, S.K.: An efficient heuristic-based role mapping framework for secure and fair collaboration in SaaS cloud. In: 2014 International Conference on Cloud and Autonomic Computing, pp. 227–236. IEEE, London (2014). https://doi.org/10.1109/ICCAC.2014.19
31. Guo, X., Chen, C., Du, J., Li, X.: Design of a cross-domain privilege management prototype system. In: 2008 9th International Conference on Computer-Aided Industrial Design and Conceptual Design, pp. 1091–1095. IEEE, Kunming (2008). https://doi.org/10.1109/CAIDCD.2008.4730752
32. Hu, J., Li, R., Lu, Z.: Establishing RBAC-based secure interoperability in decentralized multi-domain environments. In: Nam, K.-H., Rhee, G. (eds.) ICISC 2007. LNCS, vol. 4817, pp. 49–63. Springer, Heidelberg (2007). https://doi.org/10.1007/978-3-540-76788-6_5
33. Hu, J., Li, R., Lu, Z.: On role mappings for RBAC-based secure interoperation. In: 2009 Third International Conference on Network and System Security, pp. 270–277. IEEE, Gold Coast (2009). https://doi.org/10.1109/NSS.2009.76
34. Hu, J., Li, R., Lu, Z., Lu, J., Ma, X.: RAR: A role-and-risk based flexible framework for secure collaboration. Futur. Gener. Comput. Syst. **27**(5), 574–586 (2011). https://doi.org/10.1016/j.future.2010.09.008
35. Huang, C., Sun, J.L., Wang, X.Y., Si, Y.J.: Minimal role mining method for Web service composition. J. Zhejiang Univ.-SCI. C (Comput. Electron.) **11**(5), 328–339 (2010). https://doi.org/10.1631/jzus.C0910186
36. Huang, C., Sun, J., Wang, X., Wu, D.: Inconsistency resolution method for RBAC based interoperation. IEICE Trans. Inf. Syst. **93**(5), 1070–1079 (2010). https://doi.org/10.1587/transinf.E93.D.1070
37. Kamath, A., Liscano, R., El-Saddik, A.: User-credential based role mapping in multi-domain environment. In: Proceedings of the 2006 International Conference on Privacy, Security and Trust: Bridge the Gap Between PST Technologies and

Business Services, Article No.: 62. ACM, Markham (2006). https://doi.org/10.1145/1501434.1501507
38. Kun, H., Jing, Y., Xiaoming, D., Lu, W.: Distributed access control model over multi-trust domain. In: 2012 International Conference on Computer Science and Electronics Engineering, pp. 595–598. IEEE, Hangzhou (2012). https://doi.org/10.1109/ICCSEE.2012.34
39. Li, J., Huai, J., Hu, C.: PEACE-VO: a secure policy-enabled collaboration framework for virtual organizations. In: 2007 26th IEEE International Symposium on Reliable Distributed Systems, pp. 199-208. IEEE, Beijing (2007). https://doi.org/10.1109/SRDS.2007.12
40. Li, J., Huai, J., Hu, C., Zhu, Y.: A secure collaboration service for dynamic virtual organizations. Inf. Sci. **180**(17), 3086–3107 (2010). https://doi.org/10.1016/j.ins.2010.05.014
41. Li, F., Wang, H., Diao, L., Yen, I.L., Bastani, F.: Toward semi-automated role mapping for IoT systems in smart cities. In: 2019 IEEE International Smart Cities Conference (ISC2), pp. 205–211. IEEE, Casablanca (2019). https://doi.org/10.1109/ISC246665.2019.9071758
42. Lv, B., Zhang, D., Mao, R., Yang, H.: A multi-level cross-domain access control model based on role mapping. In: 2016 4th International Conference on Mechanical Materials and Manufacturing Engineering, pp. 230–235. Atlantis Press, Wuhan (2016). https://doi.org/10.2991/mmme-16.2016.53
43. Pan, L., Liu, N., Zi, X.: Visualization framework for inter-domain access control policy integration. China Commun. **10**(3), 67–75 (2013). https://doi.org/10.1109/CC.2013.6488831
44. Shafiq, B., Joshi, J.B., Bertino, E., Ghafoor, A.: Secure interoperation in a multidomain environment employing RBAC policies. IEEE Trans. Knowl. Data Eng. **17**(11), 1557–1577 (2005). https://doi.org/10.1109/TKDE.2005.185
45. Shehab, M., Bertino, E., Ghafoor, A.: SERAT : SEcure role mApping technique for decentralized secure interoperability. In: Proceedings of the Tenth ACM Symposium on Access control Models and Technologies, pp. 159–167. ACM, Stockholm (2005). https://doi.org/10.1145/1063979.1064007
46. Solanki, N., Zhu, W., Yen, I.L., Bastani, F., Rezvani, E.: Multi-tenant access and information flow control for saas. In: 2016 IEEE International Conference on Web Services (ICWS), pp. 99–106. IEEE, San Francisco (2016). https://doi.org/10.1109/ICWS.2016.21
47. Sun, S., Chen, S., Du, R.: Trusted and efficient cross-domain access control system based on blockchain. Sci. Program. **2020**(1), 8832568 (2020). https://doi.org/10.1155/2020/8832568
48. Tang, Z., Li, R., Lu, Z.: A request-driven role mapping for secure interoperation in multi-domain environment. In: 2007 IFIP International Conference on Network and Parallel Computing Workshops (NPC 2007), pp. 83–90. IEEE, Dalian (2007). https://doi.org/10.1109/NPC.2007.33
49. Tang, G.Y., Wang, H.F., Cui, L.J.: Research of role-mapping associate conflict detection methods. Appl. Mech. Mater. **380**, 2699–2702 (2013). https://doi.org/10.4028/www.scientific.net/AMM.380-384.2699
50. Unal, D., Caglayan, M.U.: XFPM-RBAC: XML based specification language for security policies in multi-domain mobile networks. Secur. Commun. Netw. **6**(12), 1420–1444 (2013). https://doi.org/10.1002/sec.411
51. Wang, J., Zhang, H., Zhang, B.: Research on safe privilege management model in trusted-domains. In: 2008 International Symposium on Knowledge Acquisition

and Modeling, pp. 350–355. IEEE, Wuhan (2008). https://doi.org/10.1109/KAM.2008.101

52. Wang, X., Gu, T., Guo, Y., Zheng, Y., Zong, J.: An efficient algorithm of role mapping across security domains in data-sharing environments. In: 2008 The Ninth International Conference on Web-Age Information Management, pp. 606–611. IEEE, Zhangjiajie (2008). https://doi.org/10.1109/WAIM.2008.73
53. Wang, X., Sun, J., Yang, X., Huang, C., Wu, D.: Security violation detection for RBAC based interoperation in distributed environment. IEICE Trans. Inf. Syst. **91**(5), 1447–1456 (2008). https://doi.org/10.1093/ietisy/e91-d.5.1447
54. Wang, X., Gu, T., Guo, Y., Zheng, Y., Zong, J., Gong, B.: An algorithm for role mapping across multi-domains employing RBAC. Chin. J. Electron. **18**(1), 37–41 (2009)
55. Xia, X.: An equivalent access based approach for building collaboration model between distinct access control models. In: De Decker, B., Dittmann, J., Kraetzer, C., Vielhauer, C. (eds.) CMS 2013. LNCS, vol. 8099, pp. 185–194. Springer, Heidelberg (2013). https://doi.org/10.1007/978-3-642-40779-6_16
56. Xiang, H., Xia, X., Hu, H., Wang, S., Sang, J., Ye, C.: Approaches to access control policy comparison and the inter-domain role mapping problem. Inf. Technol. Control **45**(3), 278–288 (2016). https://doi.org/10.5755/j01.itc.45.3.13187
57. Yang, Z., Yang, L., Luo, X., Ma, L., Kou, B.S., Zhang, K.: Model of domain based RBAC and supporting technologies. J. Comput. **8**(5), 1220–1229 (2013)
58. Yu, G., Li, Z., Li, R., Mudar, S.: Centralized role-based access control for federated multi-domain environments. Wuhan Univ. J. Nat. Sci. **11**(6), 1688–1692 (2006). https://doi.org/10.1007/BF02831851
59. Zhang, Y., Joshi, J.B.: UAQ: a framework for user authorization query processing in RBAC extended with hybrid hierarchy and constraints. In: Proceedings of the 13th ACM Symposium on Access Control Models and Technologies, pp. 83–92. ACM, Estes Park (2008). https://doi.org/10.1145/1377836.1377850
60. Zhang, Y., Joshi, J.B.: Role-based domain discovery in decentralized secure interoperations. In: 2010 International Symposium on Collaborative Technologies and Systems, pp. 84–93. IEEE, Chicago (2010). https://doi.org/10.1109/CTS.2010.5478522
61. Zhang, W., Li, Y.: Federation access control model based on web-service. In: 2010 International Conference on E-Business and E-Government, pp. 38–41. IEEE, Guangzhou (2010). https://doi.org/10.1109/ICEE.2010.17
62. Zhang, S., Kong, X., Wang, B.: Study on role-spliting and its ontology-based evaluation methods during role mapping of inter-domain. In: 2008 International Conference on Computer Science and Software Engineering, pp. 642–645. IEEE, Wuhan (2008). https://doi.org/10.1109/CSSE.2008.1401
63. Zhang, S., Chen, J., Wang, B.: The research of semantic similarity algorithm consideration of multi-factor ontology-based in access control. In: 2010 International Conference on Computer Application and System Modeling (ICCASM 2010), pp. V3-538–V3-542. IEEE, Taiyuan (2010). https://doi.org/10.1109/ICCASM.2010.5620685
64. Zuo, C., Li, R., Han, H., Lu, Z.: Security assurance for dynamic role mapping in a multi-domain environment. In: 2007 International Conference on Computational Intelligence and Security (CIS 2007), pp. 735–739. IEEE, Harbin (2007). https://doi.org/10.1109/CIS.2007.134
65. Joshi, J.B., Bhatti, R., Bertino, E., Ghafoor, A.: Access-control language for multidomain environments. IEEE Internet Comput. **8**(6), 40–50 (2004). https://doi.org/10.1109/MIC.2004.53

66. Hu, V.C., et al.: Guide to attribute based access control (ABAC) definition and considerations. NIST Spec. Publ. **800**(162), 1–37 (2013). https://doi.org/10.6028/NIST.SP.800-162
67. Vaidya, J., Atluri, V., Guo, Q.: The role mining problem: finding a minimal descriptive set of roles. In: Proceedings of the 12th ACM Symposium on Access control Models and Technologies, pp. 175–184. ACM, Sophia Antipolis (2007). https://doi.org/10.1145/1266840.1266870
68. Vaidya, J., Atluri, V., Warner, J.: RoleMiner: mining roles using subset enumeration. In: ACM Conference on Computer and Communications Security, pp. 144–153. ACM, Alexandria (2006). https://doi.org/10.1145/1180405.1180424

A Longitudinal View on the Perceived Contribution of Enterprise Architecture in The Netherlands

Henk Plessius[1](✉), Marlies van Steenbergen[2], Pascal Ravesteijn[2], and Johan Versendaal[2]

[1] Eduples, Amersfoort, The Netherlands
henk@eduples.nl
[2] University of Applied Sciences Utrecht, Utrecht, The Netherlands
{marlies.vansteenbergen,pascal.ravesteijn, johan.versendaal}@hu.nl

Abstract. Since the rise of Enterprise Architecture (EA) in the first decade of this century, three surveys about the perceived contribution of EA have been conducted in the Netherlands. This paper compares these three surveys mutually and with the international literature about EA benefits. Developments in the perceived contribution of EA over time are analyzed using a set of 31 categories where benefits of EA can be expected, called the EA benefit areas. We found a set of 12 EA benefit areas (which we have called the core EA benefit areas) that are mentioned in most of the literature about EA benefits and score (relatively) high in all three surveys. We also found a notable increase in the perceived contribution of EA in the second and third surveys compared to the first, indicating that generally EA is assessed as a useful discipline nowadays. The analysis further shows that over time, the focus of EA has extended from an internal orientation to include the environment of the organization. From the observed evolution in EA benefit areas, we conclude that the areas where a contribution of EA to the organization is perceived are not static but have increased over time. Based on recent developments in and around EA, we have extrapolated where changes in the perception of the contribution of EA may be expected in the future. The results of this research may support architects in optimizing the value they contribute to their organization.

Keywords: Enterprise Architecture · Enterprise Architecture Value · Enterprise Architecture Value Survey · Longitudinal Research

1 Introduction

In the literature, many benefits of Enterprise Architecture (EA) can be found, but most of these claims are not supported by empirical evidence [1–4]. To illustrate: Shanks et al. [2] found in 2018 only 12 publications with empirical evidence about EA benefits, among them 8 surveys, and in 2021 Ahleman et al. [4] counted 13 surveys about EA benefits, EA practices, and EA success factors. To obtain more empirical evidence about EA value,

J. Borbinha et al. (Eds.): EDOC 2024, LNCS 15409, pp. 140–159, 2025.
https://doi.org/10.1007/978-3-031-78338-8_8

we conducted a survey in the spring of 2021 into the perceived contribution of EA in the Netherlands. Including this survey, since 2010 three surveys tailored to the perceived contribution of EA in the Netherlands have been conducted: in 2010 by Foorthuis et al. [5], in 2014 by Plessius et al. [6, 7], and, as already mentioned above, in 2021 by Plessius et al. [8]. These three surveys divide the discussion about the contribution of EA in timeframes. In this paper, we look at changes visible across these timeframes, both in the international literature about EA value and in the outcomes of the three surveys. A challenge in comparing these three surveys is that no commonly accepted classification of EA benefits exists [1, 9–11] and as a result, the constructs used in the three surveys are different. To overcome this problem, we used the classification from [8] and defined a mapping procedure to represent the benefits of the other two surveys in this classification.

This research contributes by providing insight into the changes in the areas where a contribution of EA to organizations is perceived and in which direction these changes may continue in the future. The research question addressed is: *How has the perception of the contribution of EA in the Netherlands evolved over time*? In a practical sense, this research highlights the areas where the expectations about the contribution of EA are greatest and supports architects in choosing which areas to focus on to create maximum impact.

The paper is structured as follows. In the next section, we discuss the background of the classification used, followed in Sect. 3 with the research approach chosen, including the mapping procedure. In Sect. 4, the results of the comparison can be found, which are analyzed in more detail in Sect. 5. In Sect. 6 we look at the areas where in the future EA contributions may be expected. Section 7 closes the paper with a discussion of the results and the conclusions.

2 Background

2.1 The Three Surveys

In the first survey [5], 18 questions were asked about EA benefits, divided into questions about EA benefits for the organization as a whole and EA benefits for projects. The outcomes were mainly positive, but a distinct difference was found between EA creators (for example enterprise architects) and EA users (for example project members and line managers) where the first group scored higher than the second group. They also found that compliance of projects with EA is a crucial factor in organizational performance.

In the second survey [6, 7], a difference was made between creators, implementers (for example solution architects and project managers) and users of EA. The questions were tailored to each of the three groups, and the survey questions were categorized in the four perspectives of the balanced scorecard [12]: Financial, Customer, Internal processes and Learning and Growth. The outcomes showed a notable increase in the perceived contribution of EA compared to the previous survey and were again mainly positive, except for questions in the Customer perspective where hardly any benefits of EA were perceived (in the first survey [5], no questions about this perspective were asked).

In the third survey [8], the same three respondent groups as in the second one [6, 7] were discerned. To categorize the survey questions a subdivision of the four perspectives of the balanced scorecard was used. The outcomes are comparable to those in the second survey [6, 7], but most questions from the Customer perspective scored higher, indicating, according to the authors, a shift towards a more 'outside-looking-in' attitude of the architects [8].

We expected that differences in questions and outcomes of the three surveys could (at least partly) be explained by changes in the perception of EA as expressed by Lapalme [13] in his three schools of thought: Enterprise IT architecting, Enterprise integrating, and Enterprise ecological adaptation:

1. *Enterprise IT architecting:* the scope is the IT/IS within the organization and the main goal of EA is aligning the IT/IS of an organization with the enterprise strategy. "*EA is the glue between enterprise and IT*".
2. *Enterprise integrating:* takes a holistic view on the enterprise and is concerned with all aspects of the enterprise, including the IT/IS. "*EA is the link between strategy and execution*".
3. *Enterprise ecological adaptation:* considers the organization in its environment and as a consequence, puts adaptation and organizational learning central. "*EA is the means for organizational innovation and sustainability*".

2.2 The EA Benefit Areas

For a benefit to be credited as a contribution of EA, it is important that this benefit can (at least partly) be attributed to the activities of the EA function and is relevant, which in previous research [14] we have defined as contributing to the goals of the organization. These two properties are used in [14] to define a classification of EA benefits: by organizational goal and by activity of the EA function: "*an EA benefit is the positive contribution from (one or more) EA activities towards the desired state of affairs for an organization as stated by some goal of that organization (based on the definitions given by Renkema and Berghout* [15]*)*".

In a Delphi study [16], with the help of 13 Dutch EA experts, a set of 31 categories were discerned that together cover the organizational goals where a contribution of EA may be expected: the *EA benefit areas.* In Table 1 these areas are summarized by keyword and categorized in the four perspectives of the balanced scorecard [12], the starting point for this classification. The full description of the EA benefit areas can be found in the Appendix of this paper. For example, the keyword 'Costs' stands for the benefits of EA concerned with goals related to the reduction in expenses made by the organization.

This classification was used in the most recent survey of Plessius et al. [8]. In the questions of this survey the EA benefit areas 'Costs' and 'Revenues' were combined and the areas 'Procurement' and 'Technology (non-IT)' were left out as no EA benefits were found in the papers consulted by the authors [8]. With these adaptations, the classification is used as a 'common denominator' to compare the three surveys mentioned in the Introduction.

Table 1. The EA benefit areas: goal areas where a contribution of EA may be expected [16]

Balanced scorecard perspectives			
Financial and accountability	Customer and partnerships	Internal processes	Learning and growth
Costs Revenues Investments Compliance Governance Risk management Societal responsibility	(Customer) experience (Customer) relationships Product position Market strategy Ecosystem	Logistics Procurement Business (production) processes Marketing and sales Service delivery Data management Information mgt Technology (non-IT) General management Quality management HRM Innovation	Competences Culture Communication and knowledge mgt Alignment Agility Technology research Evaluation and re-use

3 Research Approach

The three surveys mentioned in the previous sections were conducted from October 2009 to May 2010 [5], December 2013 to January 2014 [6, 7], and April 2021 to May 2021 [8]. These surveys define three timeframes:

1. Up to 2010, including the survey of Foorthuis et al. [5].
2. From 2010 until 2014, including the survey of Plessius et al. [6, 7].
3. From 2014 until 2021, including the survey of Plessius et al. [8].

To be able to compare the three surveys, they must be (made) comparable. This encompasses the background characteristics of the respondents and the questions asked in the surveys. In all three surveys, a 5-point Likert scale was used but the questions about the contribution of EA turned out to be quite different in the three surveys. To make the questions and outcomes comparable we used the classification from Table 1. These EA benefit areas were already used in the third survey [8] but for the other two surveys [5] and [6, 7], a mapping was defined. As far as we know, no fixed method exists for such mappings and we had to devise our way of working. As such a mapping is many to many, meaning that a survey question may map on more EA benefit areas and several survey questions may map on the same EA benefit area, two decisions had to be made:

1. A 'cut-off' limit. If a survey question maps marginally on some EA benefit area, what is the limit beyond which this mapping can be neglected?
2. An arithmetic. How to weight the various mappings on the same EA benefit area?

To reduce the subjective nature of these decisions, we had the mappings done twice, once by one of the authors of this paper and once by one of the creators of the original survey. To decide whether the mapping of a survey question on an EA benefit area can be neglected, we used the following criteria:

1. Do the survey question and the definition of the EA benefit area (see Appendix) cover some *common ground*?
2. Is the mapping *necessary* or *desirable* in the context of the question?

If both experts answer the questions posed above with 'yes', the mapping is included, but if a question is answered with 'no' by both experts, it is not included. If the experts disagree or have reasonable doubt about an answer, a decision is made in mutual agreement.

An example from the survey by Foorthuis et al. [5] is the question: *EA turns out to be a good instrument to integrate, standardize, and/or deduplicate related processes and systems.* It is not a priori clear which processes are included in the survey question. After a discussion, it was decided that the question is related mainly to the definitions of the EA benefit areas 'information management', 'data management', 'and 'business processes', and it seems at least desirable to include these EA benefit areas. While there is some overlap with processes in EA benefit areas such as 'logistics' and 'marketing and sales', these mappings were found neither necessary nor desirable, to avoid giving this question too much weight in those areas.

Ideally, the weighting of various questions on the same EA benefit area should balance the contribution of these questions to that EA benefit area. However, we found no way to balance the various contributions, so we decided after consulting the authors of the original surveys, to weight all mappings on the same EA benefit area equally and average the scores given. Both the mapping procedure and the weighting method chosen are debatable so the numbers derived in this way are an indication and should not be interpreted as absolute. However, as the mapping and the weighting of all questions are done in the same way, the numbers derived can be used for ranking.

As the questions in the surveys are based on benefits found in the literature, we decided to compare the surveys with the literature referenced in the corresponding study. Second, to highlight possible changes over time, we decided to use only papers published in that timeframe. In the third place, to make the scoring uniform, we wanted to use the same number of papers in each timeframe. In the last study [8] there were only five papers that met these restrictions, so we selected, based on our earlier research into the literature about EA value [8, 14, 16], the same number of papers from the first two studies ([5] and [6, 7]). The benefits mentioned in the papers were mapped in the EA benefit areas in the same way as the mapping of the questions in the surveys. But while in the surveys a valuation is given to the benefits, in the papers they are only listed. While some contributions were mentioned in only one paper consulted, others were mentioned in several, and sometimes all, papers. To qualitatively reflect the degree of agreement between the various papers, we used the following rating: if an EA benefit area is mentioned in one of the papers, it is scored with a ' +'. If it is mentioned in two or three papers, we rate the area with a '++' and if it is found in four or five papers, we rate that area with a '+++'. By this rating a ' +' corresponds with: 'has been mentioned', a '++' with: 'has been mentioned several times', and'+++' with 'is mentioned in (almost) all papers'.

4 Results

4.1 Background of the Respondents

In Table 2, we have listed the number of respondents in the three surveys, together with the calculated error margin for a confidence level of 95%. The error margins in the first two surveys are comparable, but the error margin in the last survey is greater, due to a (much) smaller sample size.

Table 2. Survey size and calculated margin of error

	2010 survey [5]	2014 survey [6, 7]	2021 survey [8]
Number of respondents	293	287	105
Margin of error (in percentage points) *	6%pt	6%pt	10%pt

*) Confidence level 95%

In Table 3 the economic sectors of the respondents are listed.

Table 3. Distribution over economic sector

The organization I work for can be classified in the following economic sector:	2010 survey [5]	2014 survey [6, 7]	2021 survey [8]
No answer	0%	0%	0%
Agriculture, fishing, forestry and mining	1%	2%	0%
Industry and construction	6%	3%	13%
Energy, water and waste processing	5%	5%	4%
Education and research	2%	6%	7%
Health and community work	3%	5%	11%
Government (including Defense)	31%	24%	28%
Financial and insurance services	30%	35%	14%
Information, communication & recreation	12%	6%	7%
Trade, transport and other services	10%	13%	15%

In the first two surveys, we see comparable numbers while in the third survey, the percentage of respondents in the industry sector is higher and the percentage in the financial and insurance sector is much lower. In [8] this is explained by the fact that the sector'Financial and insurance services' has diminished considerably in the Netherlands in the last decade. However, considering the error margins (Table 2), the differences could also be explained by the uncertainty in the outcomes.

As a final reference point, we looked at the reported organizational size in the three surveys. As Table 4 shows, the percentage of organizations with less than 2000 employees has increased over time, which in [8] is explained by the fact that EA has become more generally implemented since 2010, even in smaller organizations (of which there are more than larger companies). Again, different explanations are possible here.

Table 4. Organizational size

Number of employees	2010 survey [5]	2014 survey [6, 7]	2021 survey [8]
<2000	28%	38%	50%
2000–5000	27%	23%	22%
>= 5000	44%	38%	29%

We conclude that because all three surveys are considered representative [5–8] and differences in the background of the respondents can be explained, they are mutually comparable. However, it should be taken into account that the third one, due to the lower number of respondents, has a greater error margin.

4.2 First Timeframe: Up to 2010

The results of all timeframes can be found in Table 5 where empty cells mean that no references to that EA benefit area were found in the literature consulted or that there are no survey questions that could be mapped into that EA benefit area.

For the first timeframe, we collected EA benefits from the papers by Morganwalp and Sage [17], Ross et al. [18], Niemi [9], Kappelman et al. [19] and Slot et al. [20] and mapped these on the EA benefit areas as discussed in Sect. 3. From these papers, we learned that EA benefits in this timeframe are mainly found in the Financial and Accountability perspective, in the EA benefit areas concerning business processes, IT and management of the Internal processes' perspective, and in the EA benefit areas 'alignment', 'agility', and 'communication and knowledge management' from the Learning and Growth perspective. Areas related to the environment of the own organization are hardly mentioned as a source for EA benefits which is most obvious in the Customer and Partnerships perspective. This is in line with the objectives of EA practice in that timeframe: flexibility, adaptability, and reliability [21] or alignment, agility, interoperability, and standardization [22]. It is also consistent with the Enterprise IT architecting and Enterprise integrating schools of Lapalme [13] in which EA is focused on internal business and IT processes, not on the interaction with the outside world. In the survey that ends this timeframe [5], for each EA benefit area we added the percentages of respondents who scored high in that area (scores 4 and 5 on the 5-point Likert scale).

Table 5 lists these high scores, together with the middle scores (a 3 on the 5-point Likert scale). The high and middle scores together indicate the percentage of respondents who find there is at least some contribution of EA visible in that EA benefit area. The survey follows the papers selected for this period and no questions were asked concerning the customer or the market. It follows that no conclusions can be drawn about the perceived importance of these areas.

In the high-scores column, the relatively low scores in the EA benefit areas ‘costs and revenues’, ‘ecosystem’, ‘culture’, and ‘agility’ stand out. The low importance given to ‘costs and revenues’ may be explained by the fact that in this timeframe, EA is a relatively new discipline and has in most organizations not yet produced tangible results. The low evaluations of ‘ecosystem’, ‘culture’, and ‘agility’ are in line with the focus of EA in this timeframe [13]: internally oriented and mainly concerned with aligning business and IT. The other EA benefit areas are evaluated as average (mid scores) to important or very important (high scores), supporting the attention of EA to ‘internal affairs’ in this timeframe, but no scores stand out particularly.

Table 5. Importance of the EA benefit areas in the literature consulted and in the surveys

Ma *BSC perspective*	Timeframe 1			Timeframe 2			Timeframe 3		
Goal area	Lit	% h	% m	Lit	% h	% m	Lit	% h	% m
Financial and accountability									
Costs and revenues	+++	13.4	49.4	+++	37.6	36.5	+++	51.5	24.6
Investments	++			+++			++	59.6	24.2
Compliance	+++	55.6	31.0	+++	51.9	38.7	++	83.0	11.4
Governance	+++	52.7	31.3	+++	72.3	23.6	+++	57.5	24.0
Risk management	+++	51.1	43.1	++	46.8	22.4	++	63.9	27.8
Societal responsibility				+				40.0	30.0
Customer and partnerships									
(Customer) experience				++	32.1	59.3	++	61.6	19.3
(Customer) relationships	+			++	53.6	34.6	++	56.9	23.6
Product position	++			++	42.9	53.7	++	23.8	23.0
Market strategy	+			++				50.1	13.7
Ecosystem	+	28.2	55.9	++	69.2	27.3	+++	59.2	17.5
Internal processes									
Logistics	+			+			+	49.7	23.9
Business processes	+++	55.6	31.0	+++	50.3	45.9	++	65.7	21.9
Marketing and sales				++			+	32.3	33.7
Service delivery							++	48.8	27.0
Data management	+++	55.6	31.0	++	68.0	29.9	++	68.4	17.1
Information management	+++	55.6	31.0	+++	61.5	35.6	+++	64.3	21.6
General management	+++	56.2	24.4	+++	52.8	40.7	+++	52.0	28.3
Quality management	+++	38.7	44.4	+++	51.4	39.9	+++	57.4	22.7
HRM	++			++	42.9	43.9	+++	55.3	33.2
Innovation	++			++	55.5	36.9	+++	50.9	28.7

(continued)

Table 5. (*continued*)

Ma *BSC perspective*	Timeframe 1			Timeframe 2			Timeframe 3		
Goal area	Lit	% h	% m	Lit	% h	% m	Lit	% h	% m
Learning and growth									
Competences	++			+++	67.6	31.9	+++	60.9	19.3
Culture	+	28.5	46.4	+++	62.2	34.5	++	64.5	15.3
Alignment	+++	57.4	30.8	+++	75.4	22.0	+++	65.1	23.8
Agility	+++	25.3	50.2	+++	57.1	33.1	+++	60.1	24.3
Technology research							+	35.1	40.1
Communication and KM	+++	46.2	40.1	+++	42.9	33.1	+++	53.6	28.9
Evaluation and re-use	++			+++	38.2	60.0	++	33.6	29.9

Lit: the relative importance of the EA benefit area in the papers selected for that timeframe
% h: the percentage of respondents who considered the contribution of EA as (very) important (4 or 5)
% m: the percentage of respondents who considered the contribution of EA as average (3)
Empty cells: no references found in the literature selected/ no question asked in the survey

4.3 Second Timeframe: From 2010 Until 2014

For the second timeframe, we collected EA benefits from the papers of Boucharas et al. [10], Tamm et al. [23], van der Raadt [24], Lange et al. [25], and Wan et al. [26]. In these papers we discern, compared to the first timeframe, an increasing agreement that EA benefits can be found in areas related to the outside world. The increasing interest to include the outside world in the EA is evident in the Customer and Partnerships perspective (see Table 5). It seems that EA has started to look 'outside in', possibly influenced by the interest in customer journeys [27] which connect the outside world with internal business processes and IT, areas that were already recognized as EA benefit areas. Also, in the Learning and Growth perspective, EA benefits are mentioned more often than in the preceding timeframe, marking a beginning transition towards the Enterprise ecological adaptation school of Lapalme [13].

The increased attention to the outside world is reflected in the survey of Plessius et al. [6, 7] that ends this timeframe and in which most EA benefit areas in the Customer and partnerships perspective are present (albeit with a relatively low percentage of respondents who score the contribution of EA to the customer experience as high).

Noteworthy is the still low importance given to the EA benefit area 'costs and revenues'. While the area is deemed more important than in the previous survey, it is only in the third timeframe that EA seems to pay out. On the other hand, very high evaluations are given to the EA benefit areas 'governance' and 'alignment'. The scores in the high-scores column of most areas in the Learning and Growth perspective are among the highest given in this timeframe, which is in line with the increased interest in this perspective in the selected papers. This perspective scores better than in the first timeframe – an increase that persists into the third timeframe. The exception is the EA benefit area 'evaluation and reuse' which is evaluated quite low. An explanation may be that in practice there often is no time for evaluations because the next challenge is already presenting itself.

4.4 Third Timeframe: From 2014 Until 2021

For the third timeframe, we used the EA benefits that can be found in the publications by Jusuf and Kurnia [28], Niemi and Pekkola [29], Gong and Janssen [3], Kurnia et al. [30] and Saleem and Fakieh [11]. In Table 5 we see that in these papers the agreement about the importance of some areas in the perspective of Financial and Accountability has decreased. The EA benefit areas 'service delivery' and 'technology research' are mentioned for the first time in the literature consulted and the increase in the EA benefit area 'innovation' stands out, which may indicate the contribution EA can make to digital transformation.

The increased interest in digital transformation in these papers is not reflected in the outcomes of the survey that ends this timeframe. Looking at both the high and middle scores the EA benefit area 'innovation' evaluates lower than in the survey of the second timeframe and the evaluation of 'technology research' is also not very high. It seems that the contribution of EA to digital transformation is not yet recognized by the respondents.

In the survey that ends this timeframe [8], almost all EA benefit areas are present, and in many areas we see outcomes that are a bit higher than in the previous timeframe. Striking exceptions with a decrease of 10%pt or more (considering the error margins of Table 2) are found in the EA benefit areas 'governance','product position', 'ecosystem', and 'alignment'.

The increased perceived contribution of EA in the EA benefit areas 'costs and revenues' and 'customer experience' is interesting. In both EA benefit areas, the trend from previous timeframes is continued. A very high evaluation is given to 'compliance', but it is not clear why; maybe regulations have become stricter. Furthermore, in the survey, a new area, not mentioned in the papers selected for this timeframe, is included: 'societal responsibility' – in line with the increased interest in sustainability in society.

5 Analysis of the Results

In the previous section, we have shown that in the selected papers about EA benefits some EA benefit areas are almost always mentioned which is reflected in a '+++' or '++' in Table 5. We will call these the *core EA benefit areas* (Table 6).

Except for the areas 'costs and revenues' and 'agility', as discussed in the previous section, the core EA benefits score high in all three surveys. They also reflect the internal orientation of EA in the early days as discussed above and are comparable to the EA goals identified by Lange and Mendling [31]. The absence of questions about customers and markets in [5] is in line with this internal orientation.

Starting in the second timeframe, we see an extension of the areas where benefits are found, both in the selected papers and in the outcomes of the surveys. On the other hand, there are no areas that disappear; it seems that more is expected from EA. Over time, enterprise architects are becoming more focused on the Customer and partnerships

Table 6. Core EA benefit areas

Financial and accountability	Internal processes	Learning and growth
Costs and revenues	Business processes	Alignment
Compliance	Data management	Agility
Governance	Information management	Communication and
Risk management	General management	knowledge management
	Quality management	

perspective as the starting point for their modeling [32] which is reflected in the perceived importance of the areas where EA benefits are found. As a result, we also see an increase in the scores for 'agility'.

In the third timeframe, we see a further extension of both internal ('competences', 'culture') and external ('technology research', 'innovation', 'service delivery', 'societal responsibility') oriented EA benefit areas. A driving factor behind the extension in the internal areas mentioned may well be the rise of agile implementation methods in organizations [33]. The extension into more externally oriented areas may be driven by digital transformation which asks for a much more flexible and externally oriented approach to EA [34].

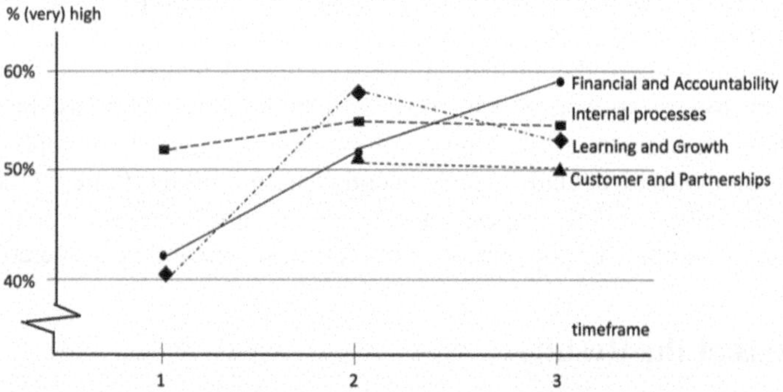

Fig. 1. Evolution of the contribution of EA over time in the Netherlands

In Fig. 1 we have averaged the high scores of the surveys in the four perspectives of the balanced scorecard and plotted these against the timeframes. In the first timeframe, we left out the Customer and Partnerships perspective as almost no questions were asked in the corresponding survey [5]. Overall, we see a clear increase from timeframe 1 to timeframe 2 indicating that the contribution of EA is much more appreciated. From timeframe 2 to timeframe 3 the image is more diffuse, in some perspectives there is a clear increase (Financial and Accountability), but other perspectives stay more or less equal (Customer and Partnerships, Internal processes) or show a small decrease (Learning and Growth). However, these small variations may be due to the error margins (Table 2) in the original surveys. An interesting outcome of the last two surveys is the high score in the Customer and Partnerships perspective – areas from this perspective are not found in the core EA benefit areas (Table 6). This outcome clearly shows the importance of an external orientation of EA.

In the last two timeframes, the high scores averaged by perspective are given by 50% or more respondents and we conclude that starting in timeframe 2, a distinct contribution of EA to organizations is perceived by the respondents.

6 Outlook

From the above outlined evolution of EA benefits, we conclude that the areas where a contribution of EA to the organization is perceived are not static, but are influenced by the role expected of EA. Undoubtedly, this will continue in the future and based on current trends in and around EA [35, 36], we expect the following changes in the benefits expected of EA:

1. In many organizations, software development takes place in agile teams. The proliferation of agile practices in organizations has revived the discussion about the usefulness and value of Enterprise Architecture [37, 38]. The outcome of this discussion may well be that EA has to reinvent itself: from a prescriptive role to a supporting role [33, 39]. This may imply that the core EA benefit areas become less important, while the areas in the Learning and Growth perspective and the Customer and partnerships perspective become more important.
2. Under the influence of the worldwide attention to sustainability, the contribution of EA to 'societal responsibility' will become more important. This area has already been indirectly mentioned by Jusuf and Kurnia [28] and is explicitly incorporated as a trend in Gampfer et al. [40].
3. In the discussion about the consequences of the developments in artificial intelligence, an important topic is its ethical impact [41], which is included in the area 'societal responsibility' (see definition in the Appendix). In our opinion, this should influence the role of EA to explicitly include ethical aspects when new technologies are introduced.
4. In IT, new technologies emerge at an increasing pace and enterprise architects are expected to advise on the usability of new technologies [3] such as cloud, big data, internet of things, and blockchain in the recent past and currently artificial intelligence [42, 43]. We expect that this will make the EA benefit areas 'technology research' and 'innovation' more important as forecasted by Gampfler et al. [40].
5. The trend towards using real-time data to support decision-making [44, 45] may lead to reporting benefits in the EA benefit area 'technology (non-IT)' as these data often originate in the (technical) production process.
6. A major concern for many organizations is their IT security. Cybersecurity is not only an operational challenge but should start on a strategic level [46]. This has led to a sub-domain of EA: Enterprise Information Security Architecture. IT security is in the current set of EA benefit areas included within the area of 'Information management' but with increasing interest, it may become an area in its own right.

7. A final but important development we want to mention is the increased role of EA in digital transformation. This transformation will quite often disrupt the business processes in an organization including their supporting IT/IS. EA can take a leading role in the process [29, 34, 47]. In the current set of EA benefit areas, aspects of digital transformation are spread over various areas, for example, 'business processes', 'information management', 'innovation', and 'agility' and it may be worthwhile to introduce an EA benefit area 'digital transformation' in which these aspects are gathered.

7 Discussion and Conclusion

The comparison presented in this paper has its limitations. First of all, there is the restriction to the Netherlands as the surveys are conducted there. On the other hand, the literature used is international and both the literature and the surveys support each other. Moreover, in international surveys [48, 49] we see the same EA benefit areas, so we tentatively conclude that our conclusions are valid outside the Netherlands as well.

A much more fundamental limitation is how we have constructed Table 5. In the first place, we have interpreted the questions in the various surveys when mapping these into the EA benefit areas. For example: in the first two timeframes no questions are mapped into the area 'logistics', but this topic may be implicitly included in survey questions that are mapped into the area 'business processes'. The same goes for the area 'investments' which may have been implicitly included in survey questions about 'costs and revenues'. Second, in averaging the results of the various questions mapped into one area, we have given them equal weight, which may not have been the intention of the survey constructors. However, by involving some of the original creators of the surveys, we have tried to minimize mapping errors.

Finally, the number of papers selected for the various timeframes is limited, but based on our previous research into the literature about EA value [8, 14, 16], we were able to select a representative range of papers from the literature cited in the papers about three surveys. However, to obtain a more in-depth validation of the results, we plan to discuss the outcomes of this study with a group of experts.The research summarized in this paper shows that the perception of the contribution of EA in the Netherlands has notably increased since 2010. EA nowadays is generally appreciated for its contribution. We also found that there exists a set of 12 core EA benefit areas which are mainly internally oriented. Over time, the focus of EA has become more externally oriented which is most clearly reflected in the Customer and partnerships perspective. We expect that under the influence of agile implementation methods, to maintain the current high appreciation, EA may move from a directive and prescriptive attitude towards a more supportive role.

Appendix

The EA Benefit Areas

In Plessius and van Steenbergen [16] a set of 31 areas is discerned, that together cover all organizational goals where a contribution of EA may be expected. These *EA benefit areas* are validated in a Delphi study by 13 Dutch experts. In Table 7, brief descriptions of these EA benefit areas are given.

Table 7. Brief descriptions of the EA benefit areas

Main goal perspective	EA benefit area	Brief description (Goals related to …)
Financial and Accountability	Costs[a]	… the reduction in expenses made by the organization
	Revenues[a]	… the increase in income that an organization generates from its activities
	Investments	… the commitment of capital to a resource with the expectation of obtaining additional revenues in the future
	Compliance	… how the organization operates in accordance with laws and regulations as well as internal standards
	Governance	… how rules, norms and actions are structured, sustained, regulated and held accountable in the organization
	Risk management	… how risks are identified, minimized, prevented and controlled by the organization
	Societal responsibility	… the moral justifiability to society of the processes, products and services of the organization (includes sustainability)
Customer and Partnerships	(Customer) Experience	… how customers experience their interactions with the organization (at all stages of the customer journey)
	(Customer) Relationships	… how (current and future) interactions with customers are structured by the organization

(*continued*)

Table 7. (*continued*)

Main goal perspective	EA benefit area	Brief description (Goals related to …)
	Product position	… how the products and services of the organization fit in the marketplace and how these are distinguished from the products and services of competitors
	Market strategy	… the long-term plan(s) chosen by the organization to approach markets and customers
	(Business) Ecosystem	… the network of partner organizations that are involved in the delivery of products and services of the organization to customers
Internal processes	Logistics	… managing the storage and flow of products and services into, within and out of the organization (extends from supplier to customer)
	Procurement[b]	… finding and acquiring materials and services from external sources
	Business (Production) processes[c]	… the tasks and activities with which the organization creates its products and services
	Marketing and sales	… the processes responsible for promoting, pricing, selling and delivering the products and services of the organization to customers
	Service delivery	… the supporting activities around the products and services to internal and external stakeholders (customers)

(*continued*)

Table 7. (*continued*)

Main goal perspective	EA benefit area	Brief description (Goals related to …)
	Data management	… the processes and resources used that store, maintain, retrieve and safeguard data important to the organization
	Information management	… the processes and resources used to define, collect, organize, manipulate, store and distribute information by the organization
	Quality management[d]	… ensuring that outputs and the processes by which they are delivered, meet the stated requirements and are fit for purpose
	General management	… deciding on the strategy of the organization and coordinating the efforts of the employees to accomplish the goals of the organization
	Human Resource Management (HRM)	… the recruitment, management, deployment and development of employees in the organization
	Innovation	… the implementation of ideas that result in the introduction of new or improved products, services and processes in the organization
	Technology (non-IT)	… the (non-IT) techniques, skills, methods, resources and processes used in the production of the goods and services of the organization
Learning and Growth	Competences	… developing and utilizing the potential of individuals to perform tasks within the organization

(*continued*)

Table 7. (*continued*)

Main goal perspective	EA benefit area	Brief description (Goals related to …)
	Culture	… the system of shared assumptions, values, and beliefs, governing how people behave in the organization
	Communication and knowledge management (KM)	… how information and knowledge are gathered and shared between individuals and groups
	Alignment	… arranging components of a business to best support the fulfilment of its long-term goals
	Agility	… the ability of the organization to respond to changes in its environment or initiate changes for competitive advantage
	Technology research	… evaluating the possibilities of (new) technology for the organization
	Evaluation and re-use	… the systematic determination of the value of processes and results, using criteria governed by a set of standards and indicating for re-use artifacts that comply with these standards

Notes:
[a]) Because costs and revenues are – from an EA viewpoint - mirror images of each other, they are combined in one EA benefit area: Costs and Revenues
[b]) Often combined with Logistics in one EA benefit area: Logistics and Procurement
[c]) Called Production in the original paper [16]
[d]) Includes project management

References

1. Niemi, E., Pekkola, S.: Enterprise architecture benefit development: review of the models and a case study of a public organization. ACM SIGMIS Database **47**(3), 55–80 (2016)
2. Shanks, G., Gloet, M., Someh, I.A., Frampton, K., Tamm, T.: Achieving benefits with enterprise architecture. J. Strat. Inf. Syst. **27**(2), 139–156 (2018)
3. Gong, Y., Janssen, M.: The value of and myths about enterprise architecture. Int. J. Inf. Manage. **46**, 1–9 (2019)

4. Ahlemann, F., Legner, C., Lux, J.: A resource-based perspective of value generation through enterprise architecture management. Inf. Manage. **58**(1), 1–17 (2021)
5. Foorthuis, R., van Steenbergen, M., Mushkudiani, N., Bruls, W., Brinkkemper, S., Bos, R.: On course, but not there yet: enterprise architecture conformance and benefits in systems development. In: ICIS 2010 Proceedings, pp. 1–19 (2010)
6. Plessius, H., Steenbergen, M. van Slot, R.: Perceived benefits from enterprise architecture. In: Mola, L., Carugati, A., Kokkinaki, A., Pouloudi, N. (eds.). Proceedings of the 8th Mediterranean Conference on Information Systems, Verona, Italy, pp. 1–14 (2014)
7. Plessius, H., van Steenbergen, M., Slot, R.: Towards an enterprise architecture benefits measurement instrument. In: Advanced Information Systems Engineering Workshops: CAiSE 2015 International Workshops, Stockholm, Sweden, June 8–9, 2015, Proceedings 27. Springer International Publishing, pp. 363–374 (2015)
8. Plessius, H., van Steenbergen, M., Ravesteijn, P., Versendaal, J.: Areas where enterprise architecture contributes to organizational goals – a quantitative study in The Netherlands. In: Prince Sales, T. et al. (ed.). Enterprise Design, Operations, and Computing. EDOC 2022 Workshops. Springer, LNBIP, vol. 466, pp. 149–165 (2023)
9. Niemi, E.: Enterprise architecture benefits: perceptions from literature and practice. In: Proceedings of the 7th IBIMA Conference Internet and Information Systems in the Digital Age, 2006. Brescia, Italy, pp. 1–8 (2008)
10. Boucharas, V., van Steenbergen, M., Jansen, S., Brinkkemper, S.: The contribution of enterprise architecture to the achievement of organizational goals: establishing the enterprise architecture benefits framework. Technical report UU-CS-2010–014, Department of Information and Computing Sciences, Utrecht University (2010)
11. Saleem, F., Fakieh, B.: Enterprise architecture and organizational benefits: a case study. Sustainability **12**(19), 8237 (2020)
12. Kaplan, R., Norton, D.: The balanced scorecard - measures that drive performance. Harv. Bus. Rev. **1992**, 71–79 (1992)
13. Lapalme, J.: Three schools of thought on enterprise architecture. IT Prof. **14**(6), 37–43 (2012)
14. Plessius, H., van Steenbergen, M., Slot, R., Versendaal, J.: The enterprise architecture value framework. In: Proceedings of the European Conference on Information Systems (ECIS) 2018, Portsmouth, England, pp. 1–10 (2018)
15. Renkema, T., Berghout, E.: Methodologies for information systems investment evaluation at the proposal stage: a comparative review. Inf. Softw. Technol. **39**(1), 1–13 (1997)
16. Plessius, H., Steenbergen, M.V.: A study into the classification of enterprise architecture benefits. In: Proceedings of the 13th Mediterranean Conference on Information Systems, Naples, Italy, pp. 1–14 (2019)
17. Morganwalp, J., Sage, A.: Enterprise architecture measures of effectiveness. Int. J. Technol. Policy Manage. **1**, 81–94 (2004)
18. Ross, J., Weill, P., Robertson, D.: Enterprise architecture as strategy: Creating a foundation for business execution. Harvard Business Press, Boston, Massachusetts (2006)
19. Kappelman, L., McGinnis, T., Pettite, A., Sidorova, A.: Enterprise architecture: charting the territory for academic research. In: AMCIS 2008 Proceedings, Paper, vol. 162, pp. 1–10 (2008)
20. Slot, R., Dedene, G., Maes, R.: Business value of solution architecture. In: Advances in Enterprise Engineering II: First NAF Academy Working Conference on Practice-Driven Research on Enterprise Transformation, PRET 2009, held at CAiSE 2009, Amsterdam, The Netherlands. Proceedings, vol. 1, pp. 84–108. Springer Berlin Heidelberg (2009)
21. Rohloff, M.: Enterprise architecture-framework and methodology for the design of architectures in the large. In: ECIS 2005 Proceeding, vol. 113, pp. 1659–1672 (2005)

22. Winter, K., Buckl, S., Matthes, F., Schweda. C.M.: Investigating the state-of-the-art in enterprise architecture management methods in literature and practice. (2010). In: Proceedings of the 5th Mediterranean Conference on Information Systems (MCIS) 2010, Tel Aviv, pp. 1–12 (2010)
23. Tamm, T., Seddon, P., Shanks, G., Reynolds, P.: How does enterprise architecture add value to organizations. Commun. Assoc. Inf. Syst. **28**(1), 141–168 (2011)
24. van der Raadt, B.: Enterprise Architecture Coming of Age. Increasing the Performance of an Emerging Discipline. PhD diss., School for Information and Knowledge Systems, Utrecht (2011)
25. Lange, M., Mendling, J., Recker, J.: A comprehensive EA benefit development model - an exploratory study. In: 45th Hawaii International Conference on System Sciences 2020, pp. 4230–4239 (2012)
26. Wan, H., Luo, X., Johansson, B., Chen, H.: Enterprise architecture benefits: the divergence between its desirability and realizability. In: 14th International Conference on Informatics and Semiotics in Organizations (ICISO2013, IFIP WG 8, 1 Working Conference). SciTePress, pp. 62–71 (2013)
27. Rawson, A., Duncan, E., Jones, C.: The truth about customer experience. Harv. Bus. Rev. **91**(9), 90–98 (2013)
28. Jusuf, M., Kurnia, S.: Understanding the benefits and success factors of enterprise architecture. In: Proceedings of the 50th Hawaii International Conference on System Sciences. Hawaii, pp. 4887–4896 (2017)
29. Niemi, E., Pekkola, S.: The benefits of enterprise architecture in organizational transformation. Bus. Inf. Syst. Eng. 1–13 (2019)
30. Kurnia, S., Kotusev, S., Dilnutt, R., Taylor, P., Shanks G., Milton, S.: Artifacts, activities, benefits and blockers: exploring enterprise architecture practice in depth. In: Proceedings of the 53rd Hawaii International Conference on System Sciences, pp. 5584–5592 (2020)
31. Lange, M., Mendling, J.: An experts' perspective on enterprise architecture goals, framework adoption and benefit assessment. In: Enterprise Distributed Object Computing Conference Workshops (EDOCW), 2011. 15th IEEE International, pp. 304–313 (2011)
32. van Steenbergen, M., Plessius, H., Slot, R.: Architectuur in de nieuwe tijd, zijn we er klaar voor? Informatie jaargang **56**(9), 12–17 (2014)
33. Horlach, B., Drechsler, A., Schirmer, I., Drews, P.: Everyone's going to be an architect: design principles for architectural thinking in agile organizations. In: Proceedings of the 53rd Hawaii International Conference on System Sciences (2020) HICSS, pp. 1–10 (2020)
34. Korhonen, J.J., Halén, M.: Enterprise architecture for digital transformation. In: IEEE 19th Conference on Business Informatics (CBI), vol. 1, pp. 349–358 (2017)
35. Management newsletter. 7 Enterprise Architecture Trends to watch in 2024. https://managementevents.com/news/enterprise-architecture-trends-2024/. Accessed 30 June 2024
36. Spratt, C. 12 Enterprise Architecture Trends to watch in 2024. https://www.entasispartners.com/blog/12-enterprise-architecture-trends-to-watch-in-2024#:~:text=In%202024%2C%20the%20integration%20of,and%20effectiveness%20of%20business%20operations. Accessed 30 June 2024
37. Canat, M., Català, N.P., Jourkovski, A., Petrov, S., Wellme, M., Lagerström, R.: Enterprise architecture and agile development: friends or foes? In: 2018 IEEE 22nd International Enterprise Distributed Object Computing Workshop (EDOCW), pp. 176–183 (2018)
38. Hylving, L., Bygstad, B.: Nuanced responses to enterprise architecture management: loyalty, voice, and exit. J. Manag. Inf. Syst. **36**(1), 14–36 (2019)
39. Kotusev, S.: Enterprise architecture: forget systems thinking, improve communication. J. Enterp. Architect. **1**(2020), 12–20 (2020)
40. Gampfer, F., Jürgens, A., Müller, M., Buchkremer, R.: Past, current and future trends in enterprise architecture—a view beyond the horizon. Comput. Ind. **100**, 70–84 (2018)

41. Ashok, M., Madan, R., Joha, A., Sivarajah, U.: Ethical framework for artificial intelligence and digital technologies. Int. J. Inf. Manage. **62**, 102433 (2022)
42. Mühlroth, C., Grottke, M.: Artificial intelligence in innovation: how to spot emerging trends and technologies. IEEE Trans. Eng. Manage. **69**(2), 493–510 (2020)
43. Păvăloaia, V.D., Necula, S.C.: Artificial intelligence as a disruptive technology—a systematic literature review. Electronics **12**(5), 1102 (2023)
44. Helo, P., Shamsuzzoha, A.H.M.: Real-time supply chain—A blockchain architecture for project deliveries. Robot. Comput. Integr. Manuf. **63**, 101909 (2020)
45. Koot, M., Mes, M.R., Iacob, M.E.: A systematic literature review of supply chain decision making supported by the Internet of Things and big data analytics. Comput. Ind. Eng. **154**, 107076 (2021)
46. Ghelani, D.: Cyber security, cyber threats, implications and future perspectives: a review. Am. J. Sci. Eng. Technol. **3**(6), 12–19 (2022)
47. Zimmermann, A., Schmidt, R., Sandkuhl, K., Jugel, D., Bogner, J., Möhring, M.: Evolution of enterprise architecture for digital transformation. In: IEEE 22nd International Enterprise Distributed Object Computing Workshop (EDOCW), pp. 87–96 (2018)
48. Carr, D., Else, S.: State of enterprise architecture survey: results and findings. Enterp. Architect. Prof. J. special edition, 13th May 2018 (2018)
49. Bizzdesign. State of Enterprise Architecture 2023. Publication by Bizzdesign (2023). www.bizzdesign.com

IT and Software Architecture

MVVM Revisited: Exploring Design Variants of the Model-View-ViewModel Pattern

Mario Fuksa(✉), Sandro Speth, and Steffen Becker

Institute of Software Engineering, University of Stuttgart, Universitätsstraße 38, 70569 Stuttgart, Germany
{mario.fuksa,sandro.speth,steffen.becker}@iste.uni-stuttgart.de

Abstract. Many enterprise software systems provide complex Graphical User Interfaces (GUIs) that need robust architectural patterns for well-structured software design. However, popular GUI architectural patterns like Model-View-ViewModel (MVVM) often lack detailed implementation guidance, leading GUI developers to inappropriately use the pattern without a comprehensive overview of design variants and often-mentioned trade-offs. Therefore, this paper presents an extensive review of MVVM design aspects and trade-offs, extending beyond the standard MVVM definition. We conducted a multivocal literature review (MLR), including white and gray literature, to cover essential knowledge from blogs, published papers, and other unpublished formats like books. Using the standard MVVM definition as a baseline, our study identifies (1) 76 additional design constructs grouped into 29 design aspects and (2) 16 additional benefits and 15 additional drawbacks. These insights can guide enterprise application developers in implementing practical MVVM solutions and enable informed design decisions.

Keywords: Model-View-ViewModel · MVVM · Graphical User Interface (GUI) · GUI Architectural Pattern

1 Introduction

Graphical User Interface (GUI) architectural patterns like Model-View-Controller (MVC), Model-View-Presenter (MVP), or Model-View-ViewModel (MVVM) play a central role when building robust and complex GUIs for enterprise applications. Many developers use the MVVM pattern, which promises high testability and helps to decouple the GUI from the business logic. While Microsoft originally introduced the pattern for the Windows Presentation Foundation (WPF) application development, in recent years, the pattern has also gained more prominence for mobile development [16]. For example, ViewModels are part of the suggested architecture for Android apps [14], while it is also popular in iOS development [11]. The origin of the MVVM pattern is often defined in Martin Fowlers *PresentationModel*, which describes the idea of separating the

J. Borbinha et al. (Eds.): EDOC 2024, LNCS 15409, pp. 163–181, 2025.
https://doi.org/10.1007/978-3-031-78338-8_9

presentation state from the View in a dedicated observable data-structure and aims for a Humble View [7,8].

However, while MVVM is prominently used, it is a set of a few guidelines, and standard MVVM definitions leave many design decisions open. For instance, MVVM does not specify how to structure the GUI at the dialog level [6]. Many developers have their interpretation of the pattern and use specific variants in their implementations. This comes with architectural risks: (1) developers select certain MVVM implementations without having an overview of which design alternatives they could consider. (2) MVVM has implicit trade-offs, which developers often do not know in advance.

While significant research exists on MVC and various GUI architectural patterns, no comprehensive literature study explores design variants and additional trade-offs regarding MVVM. Specifically, gray literature and books often contain essential aspects about the usage of MVVM, which has not been covered by white literature so far. The lack of a systematic review that integrates diverse sources leaves a critical void in the literature. Therefore, many developers and researchers might miss a complete overview of MVVM.

To fill this gap, this paper presents a Multivocal Literature Review (MLR), including a qualitative analysis of a broad amount of white and gray literature. The MLR focuses on the conceptual level of the MVVM pattern and does not analyze specific GUI framework implementation details since, in our perspective, GUI frameworks do not implement or even enforce a specific MVVM design variant. Therefore, we guide the MLR by the two research questions:

RQ1: *Which design variants do developers use when implementing MVVM?*

RQ2: *Which trade-offs do developers mention when applying MVVM?*

As a result, we extracted 76 additional *design constructs*, 16 additional *benefits*, and 15 additional *drawbacks*, which go beyond the MVVM standard definition. We synthesized 29 *design aspects* to categorize those design constructs. Therefore, this paper gives an overview of MVVM design variants and trade-offs to help developers make informed decisions when implementing MVVM.

The paper's remainder is structured as follows: Sect. 2 describes the MVVM standard definition and trade-offs. Section 3 outlines the MLR process. Section 4 discusses the results. Section 5 details design variants. Section 6 handles threats to validity. Section 7 covers related work. Section 8 concludes the paper.

2 Standard Definition of Model-View-ViewModel

A central element in our MLR is a *standard definition* about MVVM, which we use as the baseline to identify design deviations, extensions, or additional trade-offs. Our standard definition relies mainly on the definition and trade-offs that John Gossman originally introduced in Microsoft blog posts [16,17]. Additionally, we regard an often cited definition of Josh Smith on a Microsoft blog post and two further official documentation sites of Microsoft about MVVM [25,26,33].

MVVM is a GUI architectural pattern derived from MVC, where the *View-Model* replaces the controller and uses a general data-binding mechanism. It specializes Fowler's *PresentationModel* [7]. Figure 1 shows the three components:

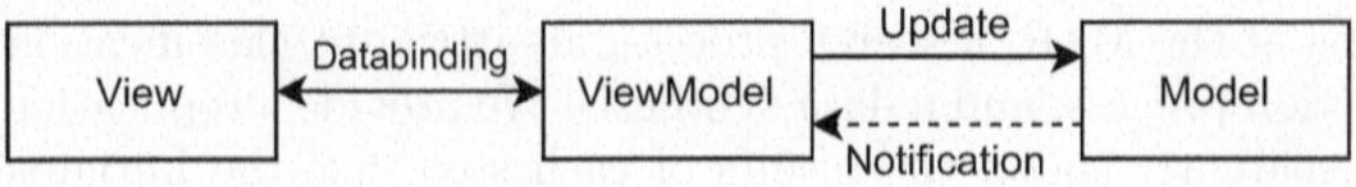

Fig. 1. The Standard Model-View-ViewModel Architectural Pattern.

Model: As in MVC, the *Model* contains the data and business logic completely independent of the GUI. The concrete design of Model classes has almost nothing to do specifically with the MVVM pattern.

View: Also similar to MVC, the *View* consists of visual elements (like buttons, windows, or graphics) and uses one-way[1] or two-way[2] data-binding to View-Model fields to obtain information to visualize. The View can be data-bound directly to Model elements or by further elements defined by the ViewModels.

ViewModel: The ViewModel handles the *presentation logic* like data transformation, acts as the "Model for the View", and provides information by data-binding. It exposes Commands that the View can use to interact with the Model. View-Models might contain (sole or extending) validation logic. Further, the *View-ModelLocator* pattern helps to instantiate and locate ViewModel instances.

Relationships: In MVVM, the View knows the ViewModel, and the ViewModel knows the Model. The Model is unaware of the View and the ViewModel, while the ViewModel is unaware of the View.

Standard benefits of MVVM are that ViewModels provide an abstraction of the View and an easier way to unit-test presentation logic. The components (View, ViewModel, Model) are decoupled from each other, supporting developers to swap, create, or maintain more easily. It can reduce boilerplate code in the View while providing good data-binding performance. Further, a developer-designer workflow helps the development team create robust ViewModels, while a design team can focus on user-friendly View designs. Additionally, it cleanly separates the application's business logic and presentation logic.

Standard drawbacks of MVVM are the complexity for simple GUIs, challenges in designing ViewModels up-front in bigger cases, harder debugging of declarative data bindings, and increased memory consumption by binding overhead.

[1] E.g., updates on a ViewModel's field are automatically reflected to a View's textbox.

[2] E.g., in addition to one-way binding, modifications on the View's textbox are automatically reflected to the ViewModel's field.

3 Methodology

This section describes the applied MLR process in which we conducted a qualitative analysis of MVVM-focused sources. We used the MLR process of Garousi et al. [13] to follow a structured process to review gray and published literature and extract information to answer our research questions. Figure 2 shows an overview of our specific process involving data entities and activities. We separated into the planning of the MLR, a search process, an attribute/classification design, a data extraction process, and a data synthesis. We provide a replication package[3] which transparently shows the results of each step, like the initial search, the attribute scheme with all identified design constructs and trade-offs, or the final data synthesis results. We also included scripts to semi-automate most steps, e.g., to check for duplicate or unrelated search results.

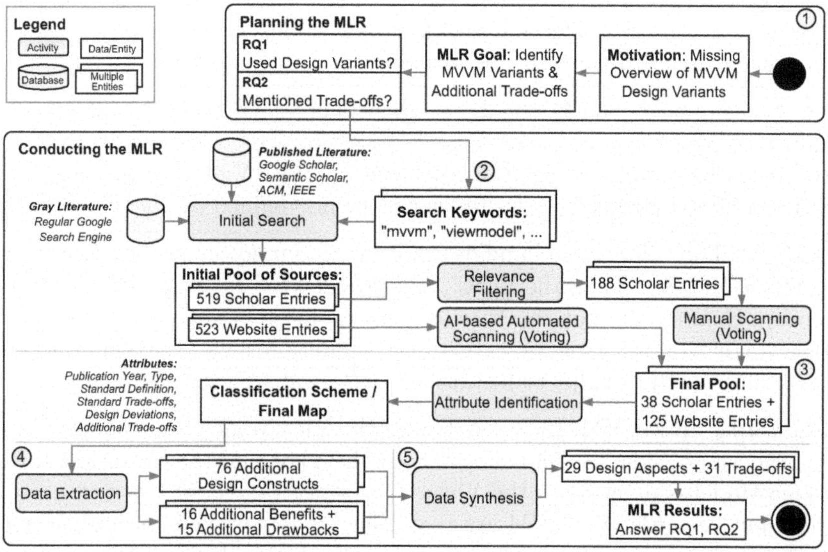

Fig. 2. Overview of the Applied Multivocal Literature Review (based on Garousi [13]).

① *Planning the MLR*: First, we planned the MLR and included our motivation for the missing overview of MVVM design variants that people apply in practice. The goal is to identify essential variants of MVVM, which might cover aspects not mentioned in the standard definition. The outcomes of the planning phase are the two research questions that guide our MLR.

② *Search Process*: The search process covers the initial search for gray and published literature, filtering, and voting. First, we defined relevant keywords:

[3] https://doi.org/10.5281/zenodo.13350488.

"mvvm", "model-view-viewmodel", "viewmodel", and "view model". We varied the combination of keywords depending on the possible search options of the databases. We used the regular Google search engine to find gray literature and multiple databases to find published literature, such as white papers and books. We utilized the tool *Publish or Perish*[4] to search in Google Scholar and Semantic Scholar mainly by title keywords. Further, we did a dedicated search in the ACM and IEEE databases to complement relevant white papers that do not directly contain the keywords' titles. The searches were up-to-date until the beginning of 2024, resulting in 519 scholar entries and 523 website entries.

Table 1. Exclusion Criteria of Scholar Entries.

Criteria	Notes
Not-English	exclude if not written in English
Duplicates	exclude any duplicate entry
Unfocused	exclude if not focusing on MVVM definitions

Next, we filtered and voted on the entries. We first focused on scholar entries and filtered out several entries by exclusion criteria shown in Table 1, which reduced the number of scholar entries to 188. Since scholar entries allowed us to scan efficiently based on titles, abstracts, and their typical scientific structure, we manually voted them for relevance. Here, we also scanned MVVM definitions if they contain no definition, only standard definition constructs, or if they potentially describe significant design constructs or additional trade-offs. For example, we reject papers that only use MVVM as an implementation detail without a clear MVVM definition. This voting resulted in 38 final scholar entries.

We used another voting approach for websites since we cannot easily filter them. Leveraging the capabilities of ChatGPT (using GPT-4), we used AI-based automated voting. The motivation derives from the lack of standardized website structures, which makes it difficult to scan and filter non-relevant entries without reading each website completely. First, we manually read 20 pivot websites and classified them. We then iteratively improved a prompt for ChatGPT, including our criteria, default definition, and trade-offs, until the pivot websites were classified as expected. We finally used chunks of five URLs and let ChatGPT process the voting. As a result, the AI classified the number of websites into the categories "Standard Definition", "Extended Definition", "Extended Trade-offs", or "No Definition". The outcome of this voting is 125 website entries.

In our MLR, we focused on the View/ViewModel-specific aspects of MVVM. We largely filtered out design constructs for the Model layer since they are usually not MVVM-specific, i.e., they also apply to MVC and MVP.

③ *Attribute/Classification Design*: We identified relevant attributes as a classification scheme based on the final pool of 38 scholar entries and 125 websites

[4] https://harzing.com/resources/publish-or-perish.

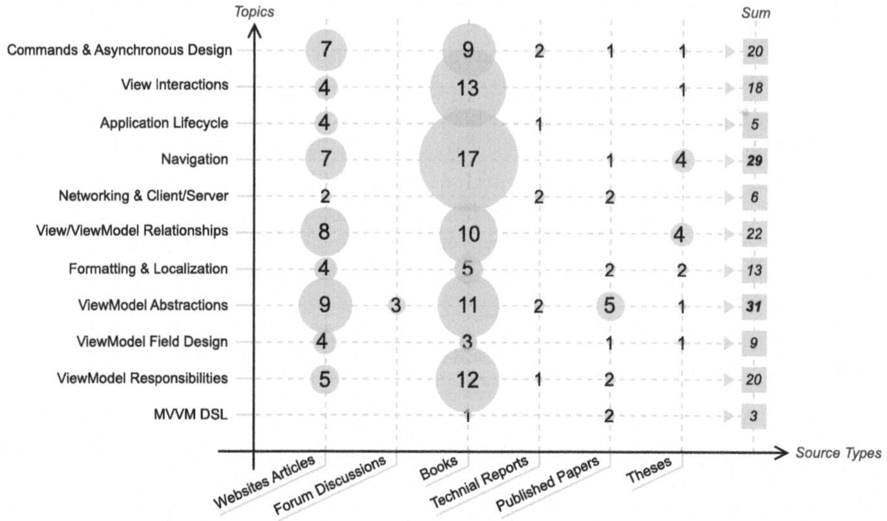

Fig. 3. Distribution of 76 Design Constructs Grouped into Topics.

containing potentially significant data. As meta-data, we are interested in the publication year and type (i.e., personal or professional articles, forum discussions, white papers, technical reports, or books). Qualitatively, we are interested in the attribute if a source aligns with the MVVM standard definition or standard benefits/drawbacks. Besides this, we also classified design extensions and additional trade-offs, which extend the standard constructs. To structure results, we then developed a helper language using JetBrains MPS (see our replication package), which prepares the structure of the classification scheme.

④ *Data Extraction*: In the data extraction phase, we analyzed the sources' data to identify relevant design constructs and trade-offs that align with our classification scheme. This qualitative analysis carefully reviewed each voted entry using the prepared classification scheme. Not every entry contained relevant design constructs; e.g., several websites voted by ChatGPT aligned more or less with the baseline standard definition.

Figure 3 overviews the found design constructs and their occurrences across gray and white literature types. We combine similar *design constructs* into eleven *topics* (e.g., formatting and localization) to consume the figure more easily. The overview shows that most constructs are covered by books, followed by website articles. Further, it highlights that the most referenced topics are navigation (e.g., how one ViewModel navigates to another View/ViewModel) and various ViewModel abstraction constructs (e.g., humble View vs. reusable ViewModels). Therefore, we describe those two topics in Subsects. 5.1 and 5.2 in more detail and briefly examine the further topics in the joint Subsect. 5.3. Finally, we extracted 76 additional design constructs, 16 additional benefits, and 15 additional drawbacks compared to the MVVM standard definition. We discuss a subset of the extracted data in more detail in Sect. 4. The replication package provides the full overview, including details on their occurrences and explanations.

⑤ *Data Synthesis*: We performed a data synthesis from the extracted data to answer RQ1 and RQ2. For RQ1, we classified the 76 design constructs (e.g., *View has Many ViewModels*) into 29 design aspects (e.g., *View/ViewModel Relationships*) and selected aspects of our particular interest to describe in Sect. 5. For RQ2, we processed 16 additional benefits and 15 drawbacks. In the next section, we explicitly answer the two research questions as part of the data synthesis, including a discussion of the results.

4 Discussion and Results

This section discusses the results of the MVVM MLR by addressing the two research questions *RQ1* (used MVVM design variants) and *RQ2* (mentioned MVVM trade-offs). We highlight key findings and practical takeaways for enterprise application developers.

MVVM Design Variants (RQ1). The MLR identified 76 additional design constructs grouped into 29 design aspects, representing variants of the standard MVVM definitions. Due to the breadth of design constructs, we further organize the 29 design aspects into eleven topics, as illustrated in Fig. 4. We focus on the two most referenced: The *ViewModel abstractions* topic includes twelve constructs in five design aspects (*application structure*, *coupling*, *design*, *humble/reusable*, *model wrapper*), mentioned 31 times (see Subsect. 5.1). The *navigation* topic includes eight constructs in three design aspects (*composition*, *responsibility*, *view-based*) mentioned 29 times (see Subsect. 5.2). Further topics include command design, view interactions, lifecycle aspects, networking, View/ViewModel relationships, formatting/localization, ViewModel field design and responsibilities, or using an MVVM Domain Specific Language (DSL) in Subsect. 5.3. We also synthesized relations between design constructs and standard MVVM:

- *Restricting Constructs*: Nine constructs restrict design rules addressed by the MVVM standard definition. For example, while the standard definition does not limit the cardinalities between View and ViewModel, the construct *View has One ViewModel* does.
- *Extending Constructs*: 43 constructs extend the MVVM standard definition by addressing unmentioned aspects. For instance, *Model-View-Presenter-ViewModel* and *MVVM/Controller* handle the modularization of the ViewModel, addressing the often-mentioned drawback of the ViewModel growth due to many responsibilities without proper modularization.
- *Implementing Constructs*: Twelve constructs provide concrete implementations for standard MVVM aspects. For example, standard definitions mention "asynchronous operations" but lack guidance for handling asynchronous data bindings not firing on the *GUI thread.* Constructs like *Asynchronous Results Handling by Mediator* address this using the mediator pattern.

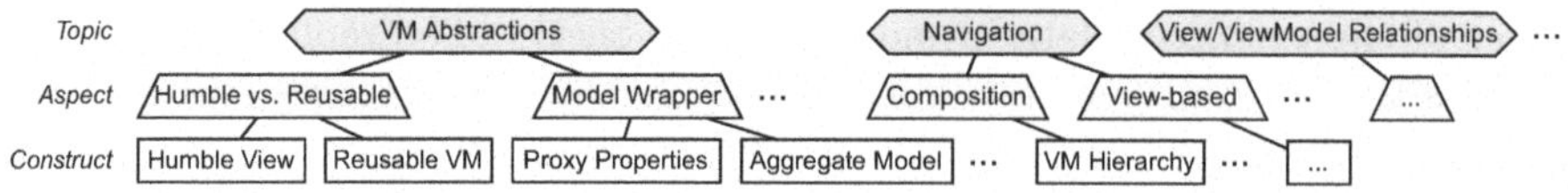

Fig. 4. Design Constructs Hierarchy: Topic ⊃ Aspect ⊃ Construct.

- *Confirming Constructs*: Seven constructs confirm and clarify standard MVVM "tips" or intentions by providing concrete examples. For instance, the *Coloring in ViewModel* construct confirms the responsibility of data conversion in the ViewModel for color formatting.
- *Divergent Constructs*: Four constructs contradict MVVM standard "tips" or intentions. For example, *Coloring in View* contradicts the intention of placing data conversion logic into the ViewModel by describing how the View can implement the responsibility of formatting colors instead.

These design constructs provide a valuable framework for implementing the MVVM pattern, enabling developers to make well-informed design decisions.

RQ1 Key Takeaways:
The MVVM standard definitions stay vague on crucial design aspects, significantly impacting implementations. We identified design constructs that restrict MVVM rules for specialized design variants, address aspects not covered by standard MVVM, provide concrete implementation guidelines, and confirm or diverge from standard MVVM intentions.

MVVM Trade-offs (RQ2). The MLR identified 16 additional MVVM benefits and 15 additional MVVM drawbacks (Table 2), which the standard MVVM definition does not mention. We highlight the three most cited benefits and drawbacks here.

Benefits: First, eight sources mention the benefit that MVVM supports easier reuse of components like the ViewModel [12]. This is especially beneficial if a ViewModel can be reused for multiple Views. Second, it is stated in five sources (including multiple empirical studies) on mobile applications that MVVM can lead to a better application performance [39]. Third, four sources mention that MVVM achieves a higher decoupling of View and ViewModel since the ViewModel usually does not know the View. In the so-called "Pure MVVM", the decoupling is further increased since the View obtains a ViewModel instance without knowing its concrete type, and data binds to its fields dynamically [37].

Drawbacks: Twelve sources state that the ViewModel usually has too many responsibilities. Inexperienced developers, in particular, might place too many responsibilities into the ViewModel without considering modularization. The unclear definition of MVVM could be a possible reason [12]. Second, seven sources discuss the high learning curve, which can hinder developers from applying the MVVM pattern efficiently [1,11,37]. Third, seven sources mention that

MVVM involves substantial boilerplate code, mainly if weak tooling support is used and glue code for data-binding has to be written manually [37].

RQ2 Key Takeaways:
Applying the MVVM pattern yields many benefits and drawbacks that developers might not know explicitly. Understanding additional trade-offs can help evaluate the pattern or its design variants more effectively and support making informed decisions when implementing MVVM.

These results highlight the importance of understanding the various design constructs and trade-offs associated with the MVVM pattern. By leveraging the additional insights from our MLR, enterprise application developers can make informed decisions and tailor their implementations to suit specific project needs better while avoiding common pitfalls.

Table 2. Additional Benefits and Drawbacks of MVVM (with Occurrences Number).

Benefit	No.	Drawback	No.
Easier Reuse of Components	8	Many Responsibilities in ViewModel	12
Better Performance vs. MVC/MVP	5	High Learning Curve	7
Increased Decoupling	4	Lot of Boilerplate	7
Less Boilerplate by Library	3	Difficult Testability	3
UI Requirements Quickly Adapted	3	Developer-Designer Workflow Issues	2
View Easily Replaced/Extended	3	Lack of Pattern Guidance	2
N-Tier: Incr. Security/Performance	2	Async Fetching/Threading	2
Different UI Technologies	2	Poor Reusability	1
Development Speed Increased	2	More Classes/Components	1
Easier to Cache View-state	2	Repeated Code in ViewModels	1
Easier Debugging	1	UI-Framework Features Testability	1
Less Imperative Code	1	Complex User Interactions Impl.	1
Well-organized Design	1	3rd-Party Library Issues	1
Reduced Energy Consumption	1	Command Impl. Overhead	1
Reduced CPU Usage	1	Higher CPU Consumption	1
Easier to Maintain Lifecycle	1		

5 Design Aspects

This section discusses the resulting design aspects of the MLR. We selected design constructs of particular interest, which we discuss in a bit more detail.

5.1 ViewModel Abstractions

This subsection discusses design constructs that focus on designing ViewModel abstractions. The varying ViewModel abstractions significantly impact the implementation of the MVVM. Therefore, we discuss them in more detail.

Reusable ViewModel vs. Humble View. There are two alternatives on how strictly a ViewModel is oriented to a specific View. The first alternative focuses on flexibility and reusability across different Views (i.e., different information formats). The second alternative defines a ViewModel supporting a Humble View to maximize testability and GUI framework exchangeability. Figure 5 illustrates the distinction with a simple example of a `PersonViewModel`: a reusable ViewModel vs. a Humble View design. Both alternatives have different impacts on reusability and testability.

```
class PersonViewModel {
  string FirstName
  string LastName
  int? Age
  Address? Address
}
class Address {
  string Street
  int Number
  string Country
}
```

(a) Reusable-ViewModel / PresentationMapping-View

```
class PersonViewModel {
  string FirstNameText

  string LastNameText

  bool IsAgeVisible
  string AgeText

  bool IsAddressVisible
  string AddressText
}
```

(b) PresentationReady-ViewModel / Humble-View

Fig. 5. Reusable ViewModel vs. Humble View.

Reusable-ViewModel/PresentationMapping-View: The first alternative defines reusable ViewModels, which can be used in multiple Views in a many-to-one relationship (*ViewModel 1:n View*). The ViewModel knows as little as possible about the specific View details and provides abstract data the View can consume. This implies that the presentation mapping of the ViewModel data to certain GUI widget features (e.g., textbox visibility) is the responsibility of each View. Therefore, unit testing reusable ViewModels does not cover presentation mapping logic placed in the View [19]. To fully cover the full presentation logic, the View also needs to be tested. For example, a `PersonViewModel` provides more generic information like age information or an optional Address object, which the View needs to map to boolean or string representations.

PresentationReady-ViewModel/Humble-View: The second alternative defines View-specific ViewModels, designed in a one-to-one relationship with a View (*ViewModel 1:1 View*). Unlike the first alternative, the ViewModel contains the presentation mapping logic, making it *presentation-ready* with a concrete intent on how information maps to GUI widget features. Consequently, the ViewModel provides information primarily as formatted strings or booleans, transforming the View into a *Humble Object* with minimal presentation logic. This supports unit testing of ViewModels covering most of the presentation logic, including mapping logic [19, 37]. For example, the `PersonViewModel` provides presentation-ready fields like a boolean to control the address information visibility. Further, ViewModel fields like `FirstNameText` or `AgeText` have a concrete intent on how they should be mapped to a GUI widget. However, a Humble View limits the ViewModel reusability across Views with different information formats. At the same time, some sources explicitly state that reusing ViewModels should not be a premature goal [3] and almost never happens in practice [34].

Coupling and Model Wrappers. Another particularly interesting aspect from our perspective is the coupling of the ViewModel to GUI frameworks. Suppose developers use GUI framework-specific helper classes like observables, command base classes, or visibility enumerations. In that case, the ViewModels are coupled to the framework and cannot be easily reused for other GUI frameworks in the future. Alternatively, if developers strictly avoid using such utility classes, they might develop them themselves [10, 27]. This makes the ViewModels truly independent of GUI frameworks, and the GUI framework can be migrated without touching them. A further essential aspect of ViewModels is whether it exposes Model objects (e.g., business entities). The reviewed sources state two options:

Aggregate Model: The ViewModel directly exposes Model objects, which implies that the Model objects support observability for data-binding [37].

Model Wrappers: Instead of exposing Model objects, the ViewModel acts as a Model wrapper and provides proxy properties of any Model property [1]. For example, a Model `Person` class with a name is wrapped into a `PersonViewModel` with a dedicated observable name proxy property.

5.2 MVVM with Navigation

Navigation and routing of Views are important responsibilities in many enterprise applications. This subsection discusses three design constructs: MVVM-C, hierarchical ViewModels, and ViewModel navigation events.

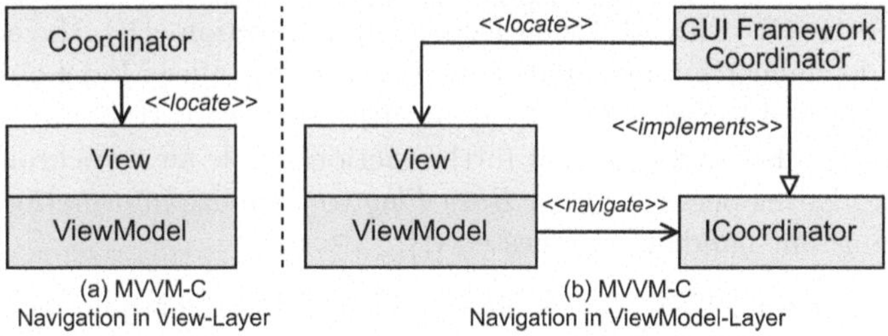

Fig. 6. MVVM-C with Different Navigation Placement.

MVVM-C. In MVVM-Coordinator (MVVM-C), navigation is explicitly included, which extends MVVM by a *Coordinator* component responsible for navigation. We see two options, as illustrated in Fig. 6: The first option places the coordinator into the *View-layer*, solving the navigation using GUI framework-specific tooling. The second option introduces an abstract coordinator or navigation system in the *ViewModel-layer*, providing a GUI framework-independent API for navigating from one ViewModel to another. The abstract coordinator accepts either a type-information about the target ViewModel or it takes a context path (e.g., a URI) to locate the target ViewModel plus context [11].

Hierarchical ViewModels. In projects with hierarchical Views, developers can create dedicated ViewModels for each View. This approach mirrors the View hierarchy in the ViewModel layer. For instance, in a master-detail scenario, a MasterViewModel might contain a DetailViewModel object, supporting direct context navigation to the details [37].

ViewModel Navigation Events. When ViewModels are decoupled and require navigation capabilities, observer or event mechanisms offer an effective solution. The ViewModel triggers navigation events, which the View or an external component listens for handling navigation logic [3].

5.3 Further Design Aspects

This section briefly outlines nine further topics from the MLR results, highlighting a subset of the most relevant design constructs. Our replication package[5] discusses all design constructs in more detail and examples.

Command Design and Handling of Asynchronous Results. WPF introduces first-class framework support for MVVM commands. However, some GUI frameworks do not have such support, and developers must design commands more explicitly. One idea is that the ViewModel provides usual methods, which are called by event handlers (e.g., `OnButtonClicked()`) in the View [1].

Several sources mention asynchronous processing in the ViewModel (e.g., network calls on another thread). The result handling code then has to update the ViewModel, which is usually data-bound to properties of GUI widgets and hence can only be updated from the GUI thread. One idea is to introduce an abstracted dispatcher as a *Mediator*, which provides a GUI framework-independent API to run code on the GUI thread. Using Dependency Injection (DI), the actual GUI framework-dependent implementation is passed to the ViewModel objects, such that it can be used in result handles of asynchronous calls [18].

ViewModels also might prevent further actions while an asynchronous call is still running. Developers can use a *Busy Flag* to visualize information, which is set until the result handler is processed [1].

View Interactions. ViewModels often have to fulfill the requirement to interact with the View, e.g., to let the View show a message box to the user. While

[5] https://doi.org/10.5281/zenodo.13350488.

MVVM, by default, only defines that the View knows the ViewModel instance, the ViewModel cannot directly call the View. We reviewed several design constructs to solve this problem: (1) Introduce a View interface, similar to MVP, which the ViewModel uses for View interaction [27]. (2) Provide events[6] in the ViewModel which the View can subscribe to [37]. (3) Using an interaction service that the ViewModel uses through an interface [37]. (4) Using *Pub/Sub* messaging to publish/subscribe messages. Depending on the programming languages, those options provide a way to solve the interaction problem [37].

Application Lifecycle Aware ViewModels. In mobile apps (e.g., on Android), developers must manage the application lifecycle. For example, if a user pauses an app and resumes it later. Whenever a state is stored in ViewModels, developers should ensure that the state is valid on a resume.

In some MVVM frameworks like Android Jetpack or MvvmCross, explicit support is provided to make ViewModels lifecycle-aware. The idea is that ViewModels know about the application lifecycle's creation, pausing, or resuming events to control a consistent state. A bundle object can store and restore the state, which encapsulates the persistence of data [15,29].

Networking and Client Server. In client/server architectures, MVVM can be essential in structuring the data sent over the network. One design construct defines *Remote ViewModels*, which Singh introduces in a paper as the Remote-Model View Remote-View-Model (RMVRVM) pattern [32]. In RMVRVM, the ViewModel is sent over the network while the server stores the View state to optimize further updates (i.e., send only deltas of an updated ViewModel). Singh also discusses RMVRVM in the context of energy efficiency [32].

View/ViewModel Relationships. In this aspect, we consider any statements about the View/ViewModel cardinalities that are not stated in the standard definition. Reviewed sources mention different combinations, namely that the View has one or many ViewModels [19,20,30] or that the ViewModel has one or many Views (e.g., when developing a wizard) [1,19,20]. Further, some sources explicitly mention a one-to-one relationship, which implies a more strict MVVM version. It implies that the View and ViewModel are a *tandem* developed together [2,3,34].

Formatting and Localization. Some sources mention design constructs on how the ViewModel or View formats data. For example, coloring can be solved in two ways: (1) The ViewModel provides the color of a text box (as a string color code or logical name). (2) The ViewModel provides a logical enumeration state, and the View is responsible for mapping it to a concrete color [2,20].

Another design construct is about how the ViewModel exposes numeric information. The ViewModel can either provide the integer or format it to the presentation-ready string, which the View directly displays to the user [20].

Multiple sources deal with the responsibility of localization. If done in the View, the ViewModel has to provide some logical strings, which the View-layer then localizes using dictionaries. If the ViewModel orchestrates the localization,

[6] For example, the C# language `event` keyword.

the View is free of this responsibility, and the ViewModel uses a dictionary component that it can use to translate strings [38].

ViewModel Field Design. This aspect deals with how developers can design ViewModel fields concretely. One design construct avoids Model types in ViewModels (allowed by the default definition). It allows only using standard types like integer or string, which decouples the View/ViewModel from the Model [24].

Another design construct focuses on visibility information in ViewModel fields. Instead of using GUI framework-specific visibility types, ViewModels use simple boolean types [1].

Further design constructs discuss different orientations when developers design ViewModel fields: (1) View orientation [28]. (2) Explicitly independent of the View [1]. (3) Model orientation by reusing Model types [18].

ViewModel Responsibilities. When designing more complex ViewModels, developers should care about the responsibilities placed in the ViewModel. Sources discuss different ideas, e.g., how bindings are refreshed, how dirty flags indicate state changes, or where validation occurs.

We highlight two further ideas explicitly. First, for list items, filtering, sorting, etc., can be done in View or the ViewModel [1]. Second, modularisation plays a key role in complex scenarios, where input logic could be placed into a separate *Controller* to take this responsibility out of the ViewModel [41].

MVVM Domain-Specific Languages. A team can leverage a DSL to specify ViewModels and to ensure a consistent MVVM implementation. First, developers could use internal DSLs by using fluent API builders, which assist in implementing ViewModel commands or data [12]. Alternatively, external DSLs can help design a ViewModel's API programming language-independent [10].

To test ViewModels, test engineers might also utilize external DSLs, as demonstrated by the *ViMoTest* approach. Especially when using projectional editors, GUI widgets could be pre-rendered in a test case [10].

6 Threats to Validity

In this section, we discuss threats to the validity of our MLR study.

Construct Validity: We used ChatGPT to vote and filter websites automatically. Since ChatGPT's nature is non-deterministic and sometimes unreliable, we might have included false positives and false negatives. In particular, false negatives could negatively affect our results since we might not cover relevant aspects. To mitigate this threat, we confirmed the correctness by checking a random selection of the voting results.

A further threat is about subjective interpretation. The design and application of the classification scheme might involve biases or inconsistencies in categorizing and analyzing data. Further, the manual voting process for scholar entries might introduce selection bias, affecting the relevant sources.

Internal Validity: While we assume that our search did not scan every online resource, our initial Google search yielded over 500 websites, providing a substantial foundation. We have not applied further methods like systematic snowballing since checking every website for references is a considerable effort. Since we reviewed a substantial number of websites, it is unlikely that we missed crucial concepts not covered by the reviewed literature entries.

External Validity: As professionals with specific backgrounds wrote many reviewed sources, our results might be more applicable to specific applications (e.g., enterprise applications) and less to others (e.g., mobile apps or games).

Further, many reviewed sources focus on MVVM inherently integrated into specific technologies like WPF. Therefore, our findings might be limited to the ecosystems where MVVM is commonly used.

Reliability: The reproducibility of our search and selection process based on AI tooling like ChatGPT introduces challenges to reproduction by other researchers, impacting the reliability of the MLR process.

Further, our data synthesizing from extracted design constructs, benefits, and drawbacks into classifications to answer research questions involves subjective judgment, which might vary among researchers.

7 Related Work

This section discusses related work about MVVM or MV* overview studies.

Wongtanuwat et al. created a systematic guideline on detecting the correctness when applying MVVM in Objective-C programs [40]. Weissenberg discusses best practices and lessons learned using the MVVM pattern in an industrial WPF application [38]. While these papers specifically discuss the MVVM pattern, they are context-specific and do not analyze MVVM in a literature review.

Lou compared the MVC, MVP, and MVVM patterns for native Android app architectures regarding testability, modifiability, and performance [22]. Similarly, Sholichin et al. reviewed MVC, MVP, MVVM, and VIPER in the context of iOS architectural patterns [31]. Further, Magics-Verkman et al. compared MVC, MVVM, and MVI for testability and performance in iOS mobile application development [23]. These studies used concrete implementations of MVVM. They quantitatively compared them to other GUI architectural patterns for quality attributes, while our study qualitatively analyses MVVM by a literature review.

Lappalainen and Kobayashi qualitatively compared MVC, MVP, and MVVM by reviewing literature [21]. Syromiatnikov and Weyns selected several GUI architectural patterns like MVVM, reviewed sources describing those patterns, and qualitatively classified them as a landscape of GUI design patterns [35]. While these studies qualitatively review MVVM, they focus on a more extensive landscape of GUI architectural patterns and use no systematic literature survey.

Daoudi et al. empirically studied the occurrence of MVC, MVP, or MVVM in Android apps [5]. Chekhaba et al. introduced the machine learning tool Coach to identify MVC, MVP, or MVVM in Android apps [4]. Unlike our study, they do not qualitatively analyze design variants of MVVM using literature reviews.

Verdecchia et al. performed a systematic mixed-method empirical study on Android app architectures, including semi-structured interviews, gray literature, and white literature [36]. While they review the literature, our paper focuses specifically on MVVM and analyses design aspects and trade-offs more deeply.

8 Conclusion

This paper presented an MLR with a qualitative analysis of white and gray literature about the MVVM pattern. We used the standard definition and standard trade-offs of MVVM from familiar standard sources like Gossman's original blog post, which introduced MVVM. Based on a selection of 519 scholar entries and 523 websites, we filtered out 38 scholar entries and 125 websites, which potentially extend design aspects or trade-offs compared to the standard definition. We then extracted 76 additional design constructs, 16 additional benefits, and 15 additional drawbacks. Finally, we categorized the design constructs into 29 design aspects and further grouped those aspects into eleven topics. We briefly described a subset of design constructs in the paper, while we published a detailed replication package with the results of the planning phase, search and selection process, data extraction, and synthesis.

The synthesized design aspects and trade-offs provide an overview of design variants using the MVVM pattern. Practitioners, such as enterprise application developers, can utilize this overview as a catalog of potential solutions when implementing MVVM and as a checklist to ensure considering common design aspects. Researchers can also benefit from this overview using the selected sources or the results of the replication package when further studying MVVM.

Future work could study the extracted design aspects and trade-offs, systematically analyzing conflicts between design constructs and their associated trade-offs. Such an analysis could lead to an assessment of the design constructs and recommendations on which constructs to adopt and which to avoid. Additionally, there is the potential to create formal pattern descriptions of both the standard MVVM definition and a subset of relevant design variants. Moreover, while we studied literature to identify MVVM design aspects and solutions, scanning public code like GitHub repositories for MVVM implementations could reveal design constructs not covered by literature. Furthermore, we plan to elaborate on the Humble View idea by applying the pattern within our doctoral ViMoTest project, where the ViewModel provides a presentation-ready abstraction by directly aligning with GUI widgets [9,10].

References

1. Anderson, C.: The model-view-viewmodel (MVVM) design Pattern, pp. 461–499. Apress, Berkeley, CA (2012). https://doi.org/10.1007/978-1-4302-3501-9_13
2. Brumfield, B., Cox, G., Hill, D., Noyes, B., Puleio, M., Shifflett, K.: Developer's Guide to Microsoft Prism 4: Building Modular MVVM Applications with Windows Presentation Foundation and Microsoft Silverlight. Microsoft Press (2011). ISBN: 978-0-73565-610-9

3. Burns, K.: Introducing MVVM, pp. 127–140. Apress, Berkeley, CA (2012). https://doi.org/10.1007/978-1-4302-4567-4_9
4. Chekhaba, C., Rebatchi, H., ElBoussaidi, G., Moha, N., Kpodjedo, S.: Coach: classification-based architectural patterns detection in Android apps. In: Proceedings of the 36th Annual ACM Symposium on Applied Computing, pp. 1429–1438. SAC 2021, Association for Computing Machinery, New York (2021). https://doi.org/10.1145/3412841.3442018
5. Daoudi, A., ElBoussaidi, G., Moha, N., Kpodjedo, S.: An exploratory study of MVC-based architectural patterns in Android apps. In: Proceedings of the 34th ACM/SIGAPP Symposium on Applied Computing, pp. 1711–1720. SAC 2019, Association for Computing Machinery, New York (2019). https://doi.org/10.1145/3297280.3297447
6. Engelschall, R.S.: Hierarchical user interface component architecture. BoD–Books on Demand (2018)
7. Fowler, M.: Presentation Model (2004). https://martinfowler.com/eaaDev/PresentationModel.html. Accessed 18 June 2024
8. Fowler, M.: HumbleObject (2020). https://martinfowler.com/bliki/HumbleObject.html. Accessed 18 June 2024
9. Fuksa, M.: ViMoTest: a low code approach to specify viewmodel-based tests with a projectional DSL using jetbrains MPS. In: Proceedings of the 25th International Conference on Model Driven Engineering Languages and Systems: Companion Proceedings, pp. 189–194. MODELS 2022, Association for Computing Machinery, New York (2022). https://doi.org/10.1145/3550356.3558513
10. Fuksa, M., Speth, S., Becker, S.: Applicability of the ViMoTest approach for automated GUI testing: a field study. In: 2023 ACM/IEEE International Conference on Model Driven Engineering Languages and Systems Companion (MODELS-C), pp. 821–830 (2023). https://doi.org/10.1109/MODELS-C59198.2023.00131
11. García, R.F.: MVVM: model–view–viewmodel, pp. 145–224. Apress, Berkeley, CA (2023). https://doi.org/10.1007/978-1-4842-9069-9_4
12. Garofalo, R.: Building Enterprise Applications with Windows Presentation Foundation and the Model View ViewModel Pattern. Microsoft Press (2011). ISBN: 978-0-73565-092-3
13. Garousi, V., Felderer, M., Mäntylä, M.V.: Guidelines for including grey literature and conducting multivocal literature reviews in software engineering. Inf. Softw. Technol. **106**, 101–121 (2019). https://doi.org/10.1016/j.infsof.2018.09.006
14. Google, n.d., O.H.A.: Guide to app architecture (2021). https://developer.android.com/jetpack/guide. Accessed 18 June 2024
15. Google, n.d., O.H.A.: LiveData overview (2024). https://developer.android.com/topic/libraries/architecture/livedata. Accessed 18 June 2024
16. Gossman, J.: Introduction to model/view/viewmodel pattern for building WPF apps (2005). https://docs.microsoft.com/de-de/archive/blogs/johngossman/introduction-to-modelviewviewmodel-pattern-for-building-wpf-apps. Accessed 18 June 2024
17. Gossman, J.: Advantages and disadvantages of M-V-VM (2006). https://docs.microsoft.com/en-us/archive/blogs/johngossman/advantages-and-disadvantages-of-m-v-vm. Accessed 18 June 2024
18. Hall, G.M.: The ViewModel, pp. 81–110. Apress, Berkeley, CA (2010). https://doi.org/10.1007/978-1-4302-3163-9_4
19. Kay, R.M.: How to use model-view-ViewModel on Android like a pro (2020). https://www.freecodecamp.org/news/model-view-viewmodel-android-tutorial. Accessed 18 June 2024

20. Kouraklis, J.: MVVM as Design Pattern, pp. 1–12. Apress, Berkeley, CA (2016). https://doi.org/10.1007/978-1-4842-2214-0_1
21. Lappalainen, S., Kobayashi, T.: A pattern language for MVC derivatives. In: Proceedings of 6th Asian Conference on Pattern Languages of Programs (2017). http://www.washi.cs.waseda.ac.jp/wp-content/uploads/2017/03/Sami-Lappalainen.pdf. Accessed 18 June 2024
22. Lou, T.: A comparison of android native app architecture - MVC, MVP and MVVM. Master's thesis, Aalto University. School of Science (2016). http://urn.fi/URN:NBN:fi:aalto-201610124940
23. Magics-Verkman, H., Zmaranda, D.R., Győrödi, C.A., Győrödi, R.C.: A comparison of architectural patterns for testability and performance quality for iOS mobile applications development. In: 2023 17th International Conference on Engineering of Modern Electric Systems (EMES), pp. 1–4 (2023). https://doi.org/10.1109/EMES58375.2023.10171619
24. Manferdini, M.: MVVM in SwiftUI for a Better Architecture (2023). https://matteomanferdini.com/mvvm-swiftui. Accessed 18 June 2024
25. Microsoft: The MVVM Pattern (2012). https://learn.microsoft.com/en-us/previous-versions/msp-n-p/hh848246(v=pandp.10). Accessed 18 June 2024
26. Microsoft: Model-View-ViewModel (MVVM) (2022). https://learn.microsoft.com/en-us/dotnet/architecture/maui/mvvm. Accessed 18 June 2024
27. Mishra, A.: The MVVM Architectural Pattern, pp. 43–60. Apress, Berkeley, CA (2017). https://doi.org/10.1007/978-1-4842-2689-6_3
28. Moliński, D.: Flutter architecture: implementing the MVVM pattern (2022). https://fivedottwelve.com/blog/flutter-architecture-implementing-the-mvvm-pattern. Accessed 18 June 2024
29. MvvmCross: Introduction to Model/View/ViewModel pattern for building WPF apps (2023). https://www.mvvmcross.com/documentation/fundamentals/viewmodel-lifecycle. Accessed 18 June 2024
30. Rock, V.: Using MVVM for enhanced cross platform development of mobile and desktop application. Master's thesis, Master's Thesis (2015). https://diglib.tugraz.at/using-mvvm-for-enhanced-cross-platform-development-of-mobile-and%2Ddesktop-applications-2015. Accessed 18 June 2024
31. Sholichin, F., Isa, M.A.B., Halim, S.A., Harun, M.F.B.: Review of IOs architectural pattern for testability, modifiability, and performance quality. J. Theor. Appl. Inf. Technol. **97**(15) (2019). https://www.jatit.org/volumes/Vol97No15/3Vol97No15.pdf. Accessed 18 June 2024
32. Singh, L.: RMVRVM - a paradigm for creating energy efficient user applications connected to cloud through REST API. In: 15th Innovations in Software Engineering Conference. ISEC 2022, Association for Computing Machinery, New York, NY, USA (2022). https://doi.org/10.1145/3511430.3511434
33. Smith, J.: Patterns - WPF apps with the model-view-ViewModel design pattern (2009). https://learn.microsoft.com/en-us/archive/msdn-magazine/2009/february/patterns-wpf-apps-with-the-model-view-viewmodel-design-pattern. Accessed 18 June 2024
34. Stein, G.: Introduction to Model/View/ViewModel pattern for building WPF apps (2021). https://www.linkedin.com/pulse/mvvm-fashion-trend-gregory-stein. Accessed 18 June 2024
35. Syromiatnikov, A., Weyns, D.: A journey through the land of model-view-design patterns. In: 2014 IEEE/IFIP Conference on Software Architecture, pp. 21–30 (2014). https://doi.org/10.1109/WICSA.2014.13

36. Verdecchia, R., Malavolta, I., Lago, P.: Guidelines for architecting android apps: a mixed-method empirical study. In: 2019 IEEE International Conference on Software Architecture (ICSA), pp. 141–150 (2019). https://doi.org/10.1109/ICSA.2019.00023
37. Vice, R., Siddiqi, M.S.: MVVM Survival Guide for Enterprise Architectures in Silverlight and WPF. Packt Publishing Ltd (2012). ISBN: 978-1-84968-342-5
38. Weissenberg, C.: Model-View Design Patterns. Tagungsband, p. 102 (2019). ISBN: 978-3-00-064236-4
39. Wisnuadhi, B., Munawar, G., Wahyu, U.: Performance comparison of native android application on MVP and MVVM. In: Proceedings of the International Seminar of Science and Applied Technology (ISSAT 2020), pp. 276–282. Atlantis Press (2020). https://doi.org/10.2991/aer.k.201221.047
40. Wongtanuwat, W., Senivongse, T.: Detection of violation of MVVM design pattern in objective-C programs. In: Proceedings of the 8th International Conference on Computer and Communications Management, pp. 54–58. ICCCM 2020, Association for Computing Machinery, New York (2020). https://doi.org/10.1145/3411174.3411193
41. Zarifis, K., Papakonstantinou, Y.: In-depth Survey of MVVM Web Application Frameworks. Technical reporrt. Technical report of UCSDSE, University of California (2016). https://dbucsd.github.io/paperpdfs/2016_4.pdf. Accessed 18 June 2024

Domain-Driven Design Representation of Monolith Candidate Decompositions

Miguel Levezinho[1(✉)], Stefan Kapferer[2], Olaf Zimmermann[2], and António Rito Silva[1]

[1] INESC-ID, University of Lisbon Instituto Superior Técnico, Lisbon, Portugal
{miguel.levezinho,rito.silva}@tecnico.ulisboa.pt

[2] OST Eastern Switzerland University of Applied Sciences, Rapperswil, Switzerland
{stefan.kapferer,olaf.zimmermann}@ost.ch

Abstract. Microservice architectures have gained popularity as one of the preferred architectural approaches to develop large-scale systems. Similarly, strategic Domain-Driven Design (DDD) gained traction as the preferred architectural design approach for the development of microservices. However, DDD and its strategic patterns are open-ended by design, leading to a gap between the concepts of DDD and the design of microservices. This gap is especially evident in migration tools that identify microservices from monoliths, where candidate decompositions into microservices provide little in terms of DDD refactoring and visualization. This paper proposes a solution to this problem by extending the operational pipeline of a multi-strategy microservice identification tool, called Mono2Micro, with a DDD modeling tool that provides a language, called Context Mapper DSL (CML), for formalizing the most relevant DDD concepts. The results are validated with a case study by comparing the candidate decompositions resulting from a real-world monolith application with and without CML translation.

Keywords: Domain-Driven Design · Microservices · Migration

1 Introduction

Microservice architectures have become one of the architectures of choice for emerging large enterprise applications [6,23]. This adoption results from the advantages of partitioning a large system into several independent services, which provide qualities such as strong boundaries between services; independent development, testing, deployment, and scaling of each service; and service-tailored infrastructures [10,19,27]. On the other hand, topics such as how to distribute the system and the consistency model might stagger the design early on. The use of a monolith architecture, where the business logic of the system is interconnected, has the advantage that it does not require early modularization. The neat identification of modules occurs through refactorings, after initial development, which allows one to explore the application domain first [11].

J. Borbinha et al. (Eds.): EDOC 2024, LNCS 15409, pp. 182–200, 2025.
https://doi.org/10.1007/978-3-031-78338-8_10

Therefore, it is common practice to start with a monolith and, as the system grows in size and complexity, migrate to a more modular architectural approach, such as a modular monolith [12] or a microservice architecture. Since this architectural migration is not trivial [25], recent research has proposed approaches and tools to help the migration process [1,2].

This has led to the development of Mono2Micro, a modular and extensible tool for the identification of microservices in a monolith system [20]. Mono2Micro focuses on identifying transactional contexts to inform its generated candidate decompositions [22]. To this end, it integrates several approaches, such as static code analysis of monolith accesses to domain entities [29], dynamic analysis of monolith execution logs [4], lexical analysis of abstract syntactic trees of monolith methods [8], and analysis of the history of monolith development [21]. Furthermore, Mono2Micro supports a set of measures and graph views to evaluate the quality of the generated candidate decompositions [28].

However, as with most research on the identification of microservices in monolith systems, Mono2Micro does not allow software architects to further model generated candidate decompositions using Domain-Driven Design (DDD) [7], which has shown good results on microservice design [33] and growing interest in the industry [34]. Instead, Mono2Micro representations of candidate decompositions are based on sequences of read and write accesses to the monolith domain entities, which are difficult to work with when trying to redesign the original monolith system and its functionalities for a modular architecture.

This paper addresses this problem by providing a representation of the Mono2Micro candidate decompositions in terms of automatically generated tactical and strategic DDD patterns. In this way, software architects can work on candidate decompositions from the perspective of DDD. This is achieved by extending the operational pipeline of Mono2Micro with a connection to Context Mapper, a DDD-focused modeling tool that provides a Domain-Specific Language, named Context Mapper DSL (CML). CML supports the declarative description of DDD domain models, using DDD concepts as building blocks of the language [16]. With this goal in mind, the following research questions are raised:

- **RQ1**: How can current approaches to the identification of microservices in monolith systems be extended to include DDD?
- **RQ2**: Can the results of a candidate decomposition based on entity accesses be represented in terms of DDD?
- **RQ3**: Can an architect benefit from the use of a tool that integrates DDD when analyzing and working on a candidate decomposition?

To answer these research questions, a real monolith system was used as a case study. The resulting candidate decompositions of this system were generated with and without the new DDD modeling capabilities and then compared.

The remainder of this paper is structured as follows. Section 2 goes over the current literature on DDD application and microservice identification tools. Section 3 gives some background on the Mono2Micro and Context Mapper tools. Section 4 presents the solution to the aforementioned research questions. Section 5 provides the validation of the solution with a case study application, and in Sect. 6 the results and answers to the research questions are discussed. Finally, Sect. 7 concludes the paper.

2 Related Work

The application of DDD in microservice development, although widely practiced, is still poorly formulated [30], the focus being in terms of modeling tools that leverage tactic and strategic DDD patterns [34].

Most research extends existing standards to convey DDD concepts. They use annotated constructs, such as in [26], where a mapping from DDD to UML is presented with the use of annotations inside UML class constructs, or in [18], where an annotation-based DSL was developed to scope objects and attributes within the concepts of DDD. However, they do not support all DDD patterns, especially strategic ones such as *Bounded Context* relationships, which are useful when modeling microservices from candidate decompositions.

Context Mapper is an exception to this, providing a DSL to model tactic and strategic DDD patterns [16], rapid model prototyping by deriving *Domains* and *Bounded Contexts* from use case definitions [17], and integration with other technologies such as Microservice Domain-Specific Language (MDSL) [15].

Other research also explores the extensibility of DDD to better fit other stages of software development. In [13] they define *Domain Views*, which enable different stakeholders to perceive the domain model with their respective knowledge base. The Context Mapper tool also provides *Domain Views* through the definition of types of *Bounded Context* and *Context Maps* [16].

On the other hand, there has been extensive and recent research on tools for the identification of microservices in monolith systems [1]. However, these tools, such as Mono2Micro [20], do not provide output that enables DDD-based editing and modeling, they mostly provide decompositions that are service-oriented and not domain-oriented.

To our knowledge, the only tool that supports the reverse engineering of DDD concepts is the Discovery Library [16], an extension of the Context Mapper tool. It produces domain models from Spring Boot[1] service APIs using discovery strategies. Through code analysis, it finds specific Spring Boot annotations and maps them to the corresponding DDD concepts.

3 Background

To better inform the integration of Context Mapper into the Mono2Micro pipeline, this section gives an overview of the architecture of both tools and compares them.

[1] https://spring.io/projects/spring-boot.

3.1 Mono2Micro

Mono2Micro is a migration tool that provides candidate monolith decompositions composed of clusters of domain classes. This work initially focused on the identification of microservices driven by the identification of transactional contexts [22], but other strategies have been added [4,8,21].

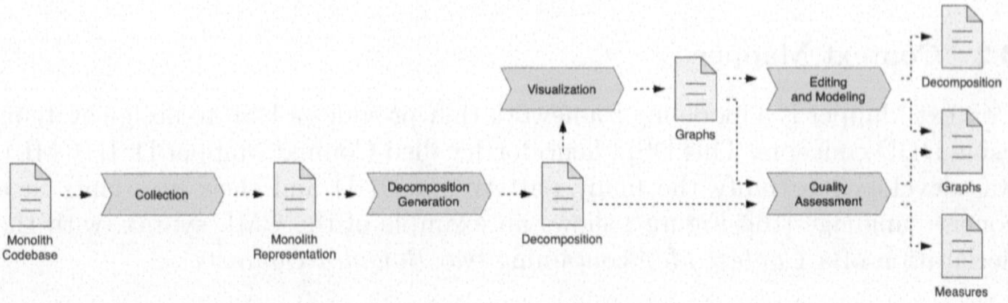

Fig. 1. The five stages of the Mono2Micro operational pipeline [20]. Each stage can use the output of former stages as input.

Mono2Micro is designed as a pipeline, which is represented in Fig. 1. The five stages of the pipeline are:

1. *Collection*: Implements several static and dynamic code collection strategies to represent monoliths, including representations based on accesses to source code domain entities, functionality logs, and commit history and authors.
2. *Decomposition Generation*: Partitions the monolith domain entities into clusters using a set of similarity criteria, with a focus on producing good quality decompositions.
3. *Quality Assessment*: Compares the decompositions and calculates the measures that are used to evaluate the generated decompositions. The measures include coupling, cohesion, size, and complexity.
4. *Visualization*: Depicts decompositions in the form of graphs with multiple levels of detail. Nodes and edges can represent different elements, depending on the chosen collection strategy.
5. *Editing and Modeling*: Provides an interface with operations to modify the automatically generated decompositions so that the architect can refine them. Quality measures are also automatically recalculated, if applicable.

Each stage is composed of one or more modules that output artifacts for the next stage in the pipeline. The underlying model of the tool that makes up these modules and artifacts is also built with several extension points, making it possible to support multiple decomposition strategies.

However, this pipeline does not include any way for an architect to model candidate decompositions using DDD after the *Decomposition Generation* stage.

More concretely, in the *Visualization* stage, graph representations of the decomposition include cluster-based views of the decomposition domain entities, and functionality-based views that represent its sequence of accesses to domain entities ("Graphs" in Fig. 1). There are no DDD-based views that show the model of each candidate microservice. Likewise, the *Editing and Modeling* stage does not contain any operations related to the application of DDD. This is where Context Mapper comes in.

3.2 Context Mapper

Context Mapper is a modeling framework that provides a DSL to design systems using DDD concepts. This DSL, henceforth called Context Mapper DSL (CML), was developed to unify the many patterns of DDD and their invariants in a concise language [16]. Figure 2 shows an example of the CML syntax, with the declaration of a *Context Map* containing two *Bounded Contexts*.

```
1 ContextMap InsuranceContextMap {
2    contains CustomerManagement
3    contains CustomerSelfService
4
5    CustomerManagement [U] -> [D] CustomerSelfService
6 }
7
8 BoundedContext CustomerManagement {
9    Aggregate Customers {
10      Entity Customer {
11         aggregateRoot
12
13         - List<Address> addresses
14         String name
15      }
16
17      Entity Address {
18         String city
19         int postalCode
20      }
21   }
22
23   Application {
24      Service CustomersService {
25         void createCustomer(String name)
26         @Customer getCustomer(String name)
27      }
28   }
29 }
30
31 BoundedContext CustomerSelfService {
32 }
```

Fig. 2. Example syntax of CML, containing the syntax for defining a *Context Map* (1–6); *Bounded Contexts* (8–29, 31–32); *Aggregates* (9–21); *Entities* (10–15,17–20); and *Services* (24–27).

Within *Bounded Contexts*, one can define *Aggregates*, which consist of a group of closely related domain objects that form a unit for the purpose of data consistency. This consistency is enforced inside the *Aggregate* by its root *Entity*, which represents the only entry point. For example, in Fig. 2 the `Customers` aggregate has the `Customer` entity as its root.

Although DDD focuses on the *Domain Layer* of systems, where the business logic is residing, a CML `Bounded Context` can also represent the *Application Layer*, which manages services that call different parts of the system, including processes in other layers. Using the `Application` keyword, *Application Services* can be defined, among other constructs, and contain operations like `createCustomer` and `getCustomer` as represented in Fig. 2.

In addition to the CML language, Context Mapper also contains other utilities to facilitate modeling activities. These include the following:

1. *Discovery Library*: Implements several strategies to reverse engineer source code artifacts and represent them in CML [14].
2. *Architectural Refactoring*: Includes operations to refactor and transform CML code for easier modeling.
3. *Diagram Generators*: Provide translators to visualize CML artifacts in diagram form, such as UML representations of *Bounded Contexts* and BPMN maps of *Aggregate* states.

Each of these features has similarities with the features in Mono2Micro. First, the Discovery Library performs a similar job as the Collectors of Mono2Micro, but more importantly, it provides a way to generate CML from its input. Second, the Architectural Refactoring (AR) module supports the architect on the edition and modeling of CML models, as the Editing and Modeling stage of Mono2Micro. However, AR operations are built on DDD concepts. Finally, the Diagram Generators module can provide ways to view a candidate decomposition from the perspective of DDD, also something missing in Mono2Micro, which presents decompositions as a graph of clustered domain entities. It also includes generation of service contracts in the Microservice Domain Specific Language (MDSL), which is another DSL for specifying microservices, and that can lead to direct code generation for Open API, gRPC, Jolie, GraphQL, and plain Java.

4 Solution Architecture

The proposed extension to the Mono2Micro microservice identification pipeline provides a representation of candidate decompositions in CML, so that DDD can be used for modeling and refactoring activities. Figure 3 shows this extension in terms of modules and their input and output artifacts. The top process bar represents the relevant stages of the Mono2Micro pipeline, and the different colors separate existing modules from new ones. The following sections, each corresponding to one of the research questions, explain each module and artifact in more detail.

4.1 Tool Integration

Mono2Micro and Context Mapper are built with an emphasis on modularity and extensibility. This makes it viable for Context Mapper to integrate into the Mono2Micro pipeline. However, it is still important to respect the models of each tool to avoid compromising their internal cohesion. In practice, this meant pursuing a low-coupling solution when connecting the tools. This solution was achieved by leveraging on the Discovery Library (DL).

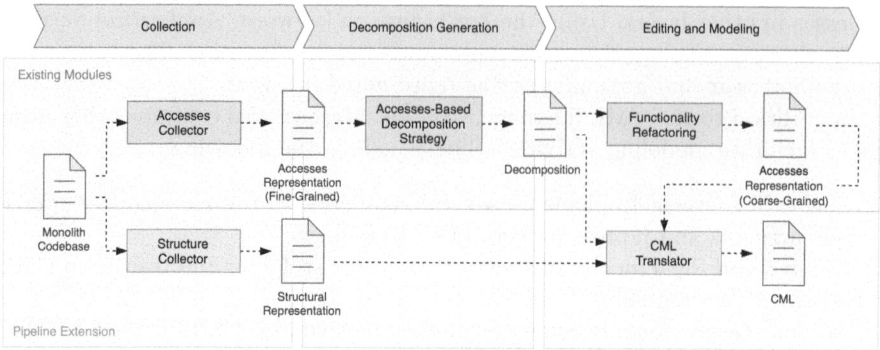

Fig. 3. Mono2Micro pipeline extension to support CML representation of candidate decompositions. In blue, the relevant pipeline steps (top) and modules. In orange, the extension to the pipeline, composed of the addition of new modules. (Color figure online)

As described in Sect. 3, the DL is a standalone tool capable of generating CML code. This is done using discovery strategies that translate input into CML. Since the DL was designed to be highly extensible, it also provides an API for the creation of these discovery strategies. Using this API, the Mono2Micro pipeline was extended with a module that defines new discovery strategies capable of translating candidate decompositions into CML. This module is represented by the *CML Translator* in Fig. 3.

The *CML Translator* has two stages. In the first, the internal representations of a decomposition in the Mono2Micro model are used to create a JSON contract that contains all the information needed to map a candidate decomposition to CML. This contract serves as input for the new discovery strategies and adds a layer of decoupling between the Mono2Micro model and the DL model, ensuring that changes made to the former do not inadvertently propagate to the latter. In the second stage, the new discovery strategies translate the contract to an internal representation of CML in the DL model. This model is, in turn, automatically converted to actual CML code.

4.2 DDD Mapping

For the new discovery strategies to perform the translation to CML, the concepts that form a candidate decomposition must be mapped to the DDD concepts first. Since DDD and its concepts are structural in nature [7], a candidate decomposition was also structurally defined, based on its internal representation in Mono2Micro. A candidate decomposition is composed of three key concepts: **entities**, which represent domain classes in the monolith; **clusters**, which represent a set of entities grouped by similarity criteria through a clustering algorithm; and **functionalities**, which represent sequences of read/write accesses to entities in one or more clusters. Mapping a candidate decomposition to DDD corresponds to mapping these three concepts and understanding what information is needed from Mono2Micro once a DDD concept is chosen. Figure 4 shows a summary of the achieved mappings, which are discussed in the next paragraphs.

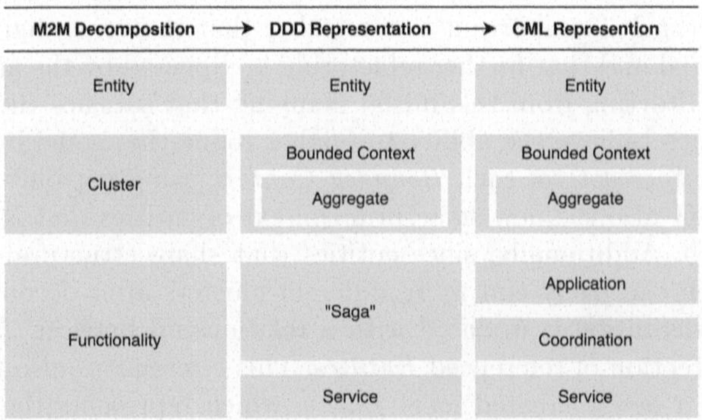

Fig. 4. Mapping strategy of candidate decomposition concepts from Mono2Micro (M2M) to DDD and CML.

Entity Mapping. The entities of a candidate decomposition, by definition, are already based on the concept of *Entity* from DDD, which facilitates this mapping. The main difference is that Mono2Micro does not require the internal structure of entities to generate candidate decompositions, while in DDD and CML the internal state and relationships with other entities are relevant information to model an *Entity*. To guarantee a more complete translation of candidate decomposition entities into CML, a new source code collector module was added to the Mono2Micro Collection stage, aptly named *Structure Collector* as shown in Fig. 3. This module uses the Spoon Framework library [24] to analyze and collect structural information from entities in the monolith domain, including entity names, entity attributes, and relationships between entities, i.e. composition or inheritance.

Cluster Mapping. The main criteria that dictate how entities are clustered in the Mono2Micro Decomposition stage are based on transactional similarity. This means entities commonly accessed together (i.e. read/write) during the same transactions are more likely to belong in the same cluster. Similarly, a DDD *Aggregate* is defined as a group of tightly coupled domain objects that can be seen as a unit for the purpose of data changes during transactions, which makes it a good fit to represent a cluster. However, the concept of cluster also fits the concept of a DDD *Bounded Context.* This is because clusters define physical boundaries between microservices in a candidate decomposition and can be evaluated based on coupling with other clusters in the same decomposition. This dual mapping of the cluster concept could be achieved with different variations in the number of generated *Bounded Contexts* and *Aggregates*, but in the end the chosen mapping was to take each cluster and generate a corresponding *Bounded Context* and single *Aggregate* inside it, which in turn contains all the entities in the cluster. This does not mean that the end product is to have one *Aggregate* per *Bounded Context.* It is important to remember that the generated CML code is by no means final and that further refactoring is expected by the architect doing the modeling. Starting from this initial mapping that satisfies the definition of a cluster, architects have the ability to further refine the model by partitioning the generated *Aggregate* of each *Bounded Context* using not only entity access information, but also the new structural context of entities that is not available in Mono2Micro. Additionally, since entities that share structural relationships in the monolith can likely end up in different clusters after decomposition, the *Context Map* definition is updated with a relationship between *Bounded Contexts* in the direction of referenced *Entities.* This reference is also replaced with a reference to a newly created local *Entity,* which represents the outer *Entity* locally, so that the architect can better visualize which references need to be refactored. This case is shown in Fig. 5.

```
Aggregate Tournaments {

   /* This entity was created to reference the 'Question' entity of the
    * 'Questions' aggregate. */
   Entity Question_Reference

   Entity Topic {
      String name
      - Set<Question_Reference> questions
   }
}
```

Fig. 5. Generated CML example, representing an *Aggregate* that contains 2 *Entities.* Since `Topic` referenced an *Entity* in its fields not present in the *Aggregate*, `Question_Reference` was generated locally to replace this reference.

Functionality Mapping. Functionalities are more challenging to represent in DDD since each functionality is composed of a sequence of read and write accesses to entities, which is a concept very particular to Mono2Micro and without apparent DDD equivalent concept. Additionally, the sequence of accesses that represents a functionality can be quite extensive. The reason for this is the fine-grained nature of the accesses collected from monolith code, due to their object-oriented design. This contrasts with the coarse-grained communication that is expected between microservices to avoid distribution communication costs. Without resolving this granularity issue, it becomes very impractical to represent functionalities compactly. Fortunately, Mono2Micro provides a Functionality Refactoring tool that rewrites the functionalities of a candidate decomposition as Sagas [3,5]. The tool converts several fine-grained microservice invocations into some coarse-grained ones, and is represented in Fig. 3 as part of the pipeline. Refactoring functionalities as Sagas also makes a possible map to DDD more adequate. Although the Saga pattern is not a DDD pattern, in practice it can be used in conjunction with DDD to model distributed transactions [9]. To supply a construct for the representation of Sagas meeting the current requirements, an expansion to the CML syntax was proposed and implemented in Context Mapper, which allows for the definition of distributed workflows without specifying the communication model of the process. For the current functionality mapping use case, this new concept can be used to simply state the steps of the saga, without any implementing technology commitments. This construct is called *Coordination*, and is based on the coordination property of Sagas that specifies whether the steps of a Saga are orchestrated or choreographed [9]. In CML, *Coordinations* can be used to coordinate defined *Service* operations, the same way a Saga coordinates steps. Figure 6 shows an example of the syntax in CML. *Coordinations* are defined within the *Application* layer of a *Bounded Context*. To reference a *Service* operation, a coordination step is divided into three segments, separated by the :: symbol: The name of the Bounded Context where the operation is defined; the name of the application *Service* where the operation is defined; and the name of the operation. Functionalities that do not access other *Bounded Contexts* are simply mapped to a *Service*, also defined in the *Application* layer of the *Bounded Context* where they are defined.

4.3 CML Representation and Interaction

When using Mono2Micro, architects now have the option to convert candidate decompositions to CML using the translation strategy mentioned so far. Like all CML discovery strategies, the initial representation of the candidate decomposition in CML is not final. Further refactoring is expected. However, an effort was made to automatically create a good starting point. The names of entities, clusters, and functionalities from the initial decomposition are maintained and used for naming *Entities*, *Aggregates*, *Bounded Contexts*, and *Coordinations* in CML. The conversion of the format of functionalities to Sagas also creates additional constructs, in the form of *Service* operation calls, which correspond to *Coordination* steps in CML. These operations make up the interface of each *Bounded Context* in CML, but there is no straightforward name that can be used to name each operation. As such, several access-based naming heuristics were implemented in the translation strategy. The architect can further customize the level of detail they want the name to have regarding access information: **Full Access Trace** transcribes the entire ordered entity access sequence that happens within an operation into the name of that operation; **Ignore Access Types** omits the type of access to entities in operation names, i.e. read/write, replacing it with a "ac" prefix; **Ignore Access Order** omits the type and order of access to entities in the operation names. Each heuristic used reduces the number of generated operations, at the cost of entity access details. In its most reduced form, each operation name shows which entities are accessed in that step. Access information is also added to each translated entity in the form of a comment, showing metrics related to the percentage of external and local accesses to the entity in comparison with the total external and local accesses to the *Bounded Context*. In contrast to these heuristics, there is also the option to generate generic names for operations that are not access-based.

```
1 BoundedContext Tournament {
2    Application {
3       Coordination UpdateTournament_Coordination {
4          Tournament :: Tournament_Service :: updateTournament_step0;
5          Quiz :: Quiz_Service :: updateTournament_step1;
6          Tournament :: Tournament_Service :: updateTournament_step2;
7       }
8    } ...
9 } ...
```

Fig. 6. *Coordination* construct in CML. The steps of the *Coordination* (4–6) represent ordered calls to *Service* operations (10,20,11).

5 Case Study

Quizzes-Tutor (QT)[2] is an online quizzes management application developed for educational institutions. It can be used to create, manage, and evaluate quizzes composed of varying types of question formats. Teachers can add questions related to topics of the courses they preside over, while students can answer these questions within quizzes. Other functionalities include the creation of quiz tournaments between students, question proposals from students, and ways to discuss question answers. This real-world monolith, composed of 46 domain entities and 107 functionalities, was used as a case study to validate the Mono2Micro pipeline extension, which provides DDD modeling capabilities.

5.1 Decomposition Generation

To start the validation, a candidate decomposition for the QT application must be generated and chosen. To this end, around 2000 candidate decompositions were generated with different values of similarity criteria and number of clusters. Candidate decompositions were then filtered on the basis of the values of their measures. The heuristic used was to order decompositions based on their coupling value in ascending order, and then based on their cohesion value in descending order, to prioritize decompositions with low coupling and high cohesion. Of the top 100 results, the candidate decomposition with the lowest complexity value was chosen. Figure 7 also shows the clusters view of the decomposition shown in Mono2Micro. Data for this candidate decomposition can be seen in Table 1, with two noteworthy pieces of information.

To start with, the complexity of each cluster is very high. The complexity measure represents the migration cost of the functionalities in a cluster. This

[2] https://quizzes-tutor.tecnico.ulisboa.pt/.

Table 1. Candidate decomposition measures for the QT case study.

Cluster	Entities	Functionalities	Cohesion	Coupling	Complexity
Cluster0	6	7	0.81	0.185	787.571
Cluster1	27	107	0.212	0.657	106.832
Cluster2	4	11	0.727	0.179	431.091
Cluster3	9	35	0.654	0.753	322.486

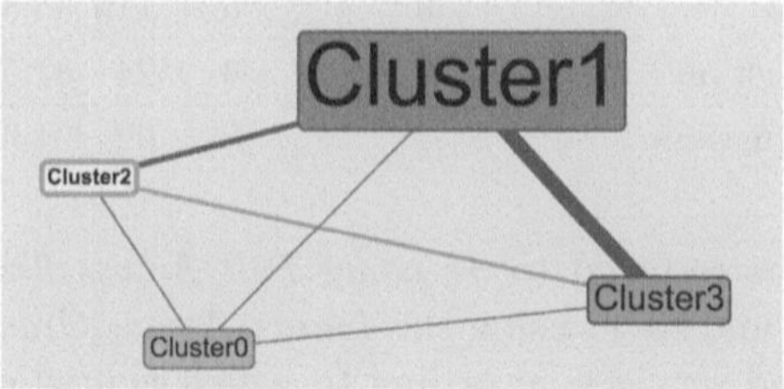

Fig. 7. Mono2Micro decomposition visualization with fine-grained interaction between clusters. Edges represent functionalities shared between clusters.

migration cost is measured as the cost of re-designing from an ACID context to a distributed one. Of the initial 107 functionalities, 31 involve distributed calls composed of several hops between clusters that drive the complexity high. This is because functionalities are still represented by the fine-grained monolith interactions between entities that can now be in different clusters. To reduce this complexity, the *Functionality Refactoring* tool represented in Fig. 3 is used to create coarse-grained interactions between clusters. Table 2 shows the reduction of invocations for some of the QT functionalities. Applying this complexity reduction also makes it viable for functionalities to be represented in a structural language such as CML. Otherwise, any translation strategy would culminate in thousands of operation definitions for just a subset of the functionalities, as the FGI (Fine-Grained Interaction) values show in Table 2. The other noteworthy piece of information is the high number of entities inside Cluster1 compared to the other clusters, which means that the entities inside this cluster are more entangled when it comes to the functionalities that use them, and are more difficult to separate without creating an overly complex decomposition. It is also the reason for the non-optimal levels of cohesion and coupling in this cluster. At this stage, when some manual refactoring of functionalities is needed, modeling using DDD can help.

The candidate decomposition is translated into CML by the discovery strategies, which outputs a `.cml` file with a representation of the candidate decomposition. Figure 8 shows a modified snippet of the generated CML, related to the `ConcludeQuiz` functionality of a decomposition. Without any optimization, the translation generates a total of 121 operations, used by 31 Coordinations that represent the distributed functionalities. With naming heuristics, the number

Table 2. Refactored functionalities for QT case study. CGI stands for Coarse-Grained Interaction, and FGI stands for Fine-Grained Interactions.

Name	#Clusters	CGI	FGI	Reduction%
concludeQuiz	3	4	73	94.52
getQuizByCode	3	4	33	87.88
getQuizAnswers	4	8	84	90.48
exportCourseExecutionInfo	4	9	110	91.82
importAll	3	5	119	95.8
createQuestion	2	3	24	87.5
getQuizAnswers	4	8	92	91.30

of service calls can be reduced to 87 using *Full Access Trace*, to 84 using the *Ignore Access Types*, and to 48 using the *Ignore Access Order*. Table 3 shows the reduction of generated services according to which heuristics are used per cluster. Regarding entity generation, a total of 11 reference entities were generated to signal structural dependencies between entities, also shown in Table 3, and every entity is generated with information on the number of accesses to it, from the total *Bounded Context* accesses (external and local), as shown in Fig. 8. This information can help to refactor the decomposition further.

```
BoundedContext Cluster3 {
   Application {
      Coordination ConcludeQuiz_Coordination {
         Cluster3 :: Cluster3_Service :: acQuestionDetails_acOption;
         Cluster1 :: Cluster1_Service :: acQuiz_acQuizAnswer_acQuestion;
         Cluster0 :: Cluster0_Service :: acAnswerDetails;
         Cluster1 :: Cluster1_Service :: acStudent_acDashboard;
      }
      Service Cluster3_Service {
         void acQuestionDetails_acOption;
      }
   }
   Aggregate Cluster3 {
      /*
       * Metrics:
       * - Percentage of external accesses: 16.46% (13/79)
       * - Percentage of local accesses: 16.41% (21/128) */
      Entity QuestionDetails {
         Integer id
         - Question_Reference question
      }
      /* This entity was created to reference the 'Question' entity of the
       * 'Cluster1' aggregate. */
      Entity Question_Reference
   }
}
BoundedContext Cluster1 {
   Application {
      Service Cluster1_Service {
         void acQuiz_acQuizAnswer_acQuestion;
         void acStudent_acDashboard;
      }
   }
   Aggregate Cluster1 {
      /*
       * Metrics:
       * - Percentage of external accesses: 10.06% (33/328)
       * - Percentage of local accesses: 8.37% (41/490) */
      Entity Question {
         Integer id
         String title
         String content
         - Course course
         - Set<Topic> topics
      }
   }
}
BoundedContext Cluster0 { ... }
```

Fig. 8. Snippet of the generated CML related to the functionality `ConcludeQuiz`. Service operation names were truncated.

Table 3. Generated CML constructs. The number of services is represented by four values: No heuristics used; *Full Access Trace* used; *Ignore Access Types* used; and *Ignore Access Order* used. The number of entities is represented by two values: original entities and reference entities. The most accessed entity is based on external accesses to the *Bounded Context.*

Cluster	#Services	#Entities	Most Accessed Entity
Cluster0	15/7/6/4	6/4	QuizAnswerItem (35.14%)
Cluster1	59/53/52/34	27/3	Quiz (12.2%)
Cluster2	11/5/5/2	4/0	QuestionAnswerItem (30.0%)
Cluster3	36/22/21/8	9/4	QuestionDetails/Image (16.46%)

6 Discussion

This section discusses the findings of applying the DDD-based extension to the operational pipeline of Mono2Micro by analyzing how the implemented solution and the results of its application in the case study answer the research questions raised in the introduction of this paper.

6.1 Results Validation

Starting with the first research question (RQ1), to evaluate whether the Mono2Micro operational pipeline can be extended to integrate DDD, through the use of CML, the first step taken was to measure the level of modularity and extensibility of the solution. First, modularity deals with how divided a system is into logical modules, improving separation of concerns and internal cohesion. The solution is composed of two new modules in Mono2Micro, the *Structure Collector* and *CML Translator*. In terms of cohesion, both modules respect the pipeline architecture of Mono2Micro, and are placed accordingly inside it based on their responsibilities. Second, extensibility deals with how open for extension the features of a system are without putting at risk their core structure, improving the addition of new functionality. The *Structure Collector* was designed from scratch. It provides abstractions for the collection of data from new frameworks and other types of structural data. The *CML Translator* is an extension of the DL API, so it follows that the discovery strategies implemented have the same design and are also open to extension by providing abstractions.

Moving on to the second research question (RQ2), the mappings of the cluster, entity, and functionality concepts demonstrate how a candidate decomposition can be represented with DDD concepts. Mono2Micro entities are already based on the concept of DDD *Entities*, so the mapping is consistent in this regard. In the case of clusters, consistency was maintained by mapping each of them to a *Bounded Context* and an *Aggregate.* For the mapping of functionalities, the sequence of accesses to entities that composed them was first converted into a structured Saga. This significantly reduced the complexity of the sequence in terms of size and hops between clusters, and made it simpler to represent with

DDD. Sagas were mapped to *Coordinations* in CML, which encode an ordered sequence of service calls, just as Sagas encode a sequence of steps.

Finally, in regard to the third research question (RQ3), the case study shows how an architect can benefit from the use of this extension. In the case of entity representation, it is possible to observe the attributes of each entity and also the structural refactorings that must be made in existing entities. In the case of clusters, *Aggregates* can now be defined and used to further partition a cluster and its entities based on access patterns, access percentages, and the structural information provided at generation time. In the case of functionalities, the architect now has the option of editing their Saga representation in CML, by editing the generated *Coordinations*. Mono2Micro only allowed the creation of fine-grained functionality traces, without any way to edit or visualize them in a graphical representation. Using CML, these functionalities can be modeled as *Coordinations* and edited in the language. Furthermore, *Coordinations* can be visualized in BPMN, and the service naming heuristics allow the architect to reduce the number of generated service calls. This does not reduce the number of functionality steps but increases the level of reuse of services.

6.2 Practical Relevance and Adoption

The problem addressed with the presented approach is of high relevance to practitioners, mainly software engineers and architects, who need to modernize existing monolith applications. Such monolith applications without an inner modular structure, a.k.a. *Big Ball of Mud* [32], turned out to be a huge challenge in practice for several reasons, which can also be seen as use cases for our solution presented in this paper:

- **Economic reasons**: Maintaining a *Big Ball of Mud* is often becoming expensive for software companies. Changing such applications, adding new features, or fixing bugs, often takes too much time because of the intertwined code base and dependencies within the system.
- **Scalability and "Cloud readiness"**: Many companies have to decompose their applications to migrate to the cloud. The monolithic architecture approach is not scalable and does not fit the requirements for cloud deployment.
- **Autonomous teams and "DevOps"**: Many companies aim to implement agile development approaches in which teams develop and operate their part of an application autonomously [31]. A team should be able to make its own design and architectural decisions. This requires loosely coupled (micro-)services or at least a system with loosely coupled modules. The structure of the organization (teams) defines the architecture of the software.

As already mentioned, the adoption of DDD for service decomposition is widespread in the software industry. Both our tools, Mono2Micro[3] as well as Context Mapper[4] are open-sourced and, at least individually, have already gained

[3] https://github.com/socialsoftware/mono2micro.
[4] https://github.com/ContextMapper.

some adoption in industry and real-world projects. The proposed approach is therefore foreseen as an important contribution and support for practitioners who want to: use a tool that automatically suggests decompositions for an existing monolith system; and want to express their future architecture and service decomposition in terms of DDD patterns and follow the "domain-driven" approach. Once a CML model is available, practitioners can benefit from all Context Mapper features: iterative and agile modeling, architectural refactorings, model visualization (diagram generators), or even code generation.

6.3 Threats to Validity

With respect to internal validity, the functionalities used in the decomposition and CML mapping process are all linear, meaning code branches, i.e. conditions and loops, are flattened into a single access sequence instead of becoming a tree-like structure. This is due to the existent static entity access collection tool in Mono2Micro, which searches for entity accesses in a depth-first fashion. However, previous research that used the same sequences to develop the Saga representation of functionalities has shown this has little impact on the final results [5], and support for multiple traces per functionality is being developed in the Mono2Micro repository.

In terms of external validity, the current implementation assumes the use of Java and the Spring Boot JPA Framework to collect entity access and structure information, but the process is general enough to be applicable to other programming languages and frameworks. The modules that assume these limitations are also built with abstractions for the implementation of other technologies.

7 Conclusion

This paper proposes a solution pipeline for the lack of DDD in migration tools, composed of the integration of Context Mapper, a modeling framework that provides a DSL to represent DDD patterns, into the Mono2Micro decomposition pipeline, a robust microservice identification tool.

The proposed solution achieves the integration by defining a mapping of concepts between tools, whilst respecting each of the tool models. To support this mapping, the solution includes several new modules and modifications, including a new static collector of entity structural information, a contract for effective communication between the tools, a translation strategy to generate CML from Mono2Micro decompositions, i.e., entities, clusters, and functionalities, an extension to the CML syntax to support concepts from decomposition in the form of *Coordinations*, and new diagram generators from CML based on translated decompositions.

The artifacts developed in the project are publicly[5] available together with the description of the procedures necessary to use them.

[5] https://github.com/socialsoftware/mono2micro/tree/master/tools/cml-converter.

This work was partially supported by Fundação para a Ciência e Tecnologia (FCT) through projects UIDB/50021/2020 (INESC-ID) and PTDC/CCI-COM/2156/2021 (DACOMICO)

References

1. Abdellatif, M., et al.: A taxonomy of service identification approaches for legacy software systems modernization. J. Syst. Softw. **173**, 110868 (2021)
2. Abgaz, Y., et al.: Decomposition of monolith applications into microservices architectures: a systematic review. IEEE Trans. Software Eng. **49**(8), 4213–4242 (2023). https://doi.org/10.1109/TSE.2023.3287297
3. Almeida, J.F., Silva, A.R.: Monolith migration complexity tuning through the application of microservices patterns. In: Jansen, A., Malavolta, I., Muccini, H., Ozkaya, I., Zimmermann, O. (eds.) ECSA 2020. LNCS, vol. 12292, pp. 39–54. Springer, Cham (2020). https://doi.org/10.1007/978-3-030-58923-3_3
4. Andrade, B., Santos, S., Silva, A.R.: A comparison of static and dynamic analysis to identify microservices in monolith systems. In: Tekinerdogan, B., Trubiani, C., Tibermacine, C., Scandurra, P., Cuesta, C.E. (eds.) ECSA 2023. LNCS, pp. 354–361. Springer, Cham (2023). https://doi.org/10.1007/978-3-031-42592-9_25
5. Correia, J., Rito Silva, A.: Identification of monolith functionality refactorings for microservices migration. Softw. Pract. Exp. **52**(12), 2664–2683 (2022). https://doi.org/10.1002/spe.3141
6. Di Francesco, P., Lago, P., Malavolta, I.: Migrating towards microservice architectures: an industrial survey. In: 2018 IEEE International Conference on Software Architecture (ICSA), pp. 29–2909 (2018). https://doi.org/10.1109/ICSA.2018.00012
7. Evans, E.: Domain-Driven Design: Tackling Complexity in the Heart of Software. Addison Wesley, Boston (2003)
8. Faria, V., Silva, A.R.: Code vectorization and sequence of accesses strategies for monolith microservices identification. In: Garrigós, I., Murillo Rodríguez, J.M., Wimmer, M. (eds.) ICWE 2023. LNCS, pp. 19–33. Springer, Cham (2023). https://doi.org/10.1007/978-3-031-34444-2_2
9. Ford, N., Richards, M., Sadalage, P., Dehghani, Z.: Software Architecture: The Hard Parts. O'Reilly Media, Inc. (2021)
10. Fowler, M.: Microservice trade-offs (2015). https://martinfowler.com/articles/microservice-trade-offs.html
11. Fowler, M.: Monolith first (2015). https://martinfowler.com/bliki/MonolithFirst.html
12. Haywood, D.: In defence of the monolith (2017). https://www.infoq.com/minibooks/emag-microservices-monoliths/
13. Hippchen, B., Giessler, P., Steinegger, R., Schneider, M., Abeck, S.: Designing microservice-based applications by using a domain-driven design approach. Int. J. Adv. Softw. **1942–2628**(10), 432–445 (2017)
14. Kapferer, S.: A Modeling Framework for Strategic Domain-driven Design and Service Decomposition. Master's thesis, University of Applied Sciences of Eastern Switzerland (2020). https://doi.org/10.13140/RG.2.2.22950.68167
15. Kapferer, S., Zimmermann, O.: Domain-driven service design. In: Dustdar, S. (ed.) SummerSOC 2020. CCIS, vol. 1310, pp. 189–208. Springer, Cham (2020). https://doi.org/10.1007/978-3-030-64846-6_11

16. Kapferer., S., Zimmermann., O.: Domain-specific language and tools for strategic domain-driven design, context mapping and bounded context modeling. In: Proceedings of the 8th International Conference on Model-Driven Engineering and Software Development - MODELSWARD, pp. 299–306. INSTICC, SciTePress (2020). https://doi.org/10.5220/0008910502990306
17. Kapferer, S., Zimmermann, O.: Domain-driven architecture modeling and rapid prototyping with context mapper. In: Model-Driven Engineering and Software Development, pp. 250–272 (2021). https://doi.org/10.1007/978-3-030-67445-8_11
18. Le, D.M., Dang, D.H., Nguyen, V.H.: On domain driven design using annotation-based domain specific language. Comput. Lang. Syst. Struct. **54**, 199–235 (2018). https://doi.org/10.1016/j.cl.2018.05.001
19. Lewis, J., Fowler, M.: Microservices (2014). http://martinfowler.com/articles/microservices.html
20. Lopes, T., Silva, A.R.: Monolith microservices identification: Towards an extensible multiple strategy tool. In: 2023 IEEE 20th International Conference on Software Architecture Companion (ICSA-C), pp. 111–115 (2023). https://doi.org/10.1109/ICSA-C57050.2023.00034
21. Lourenço, J., Silva, A.R.: Monolith development history for microservices identification: a comparative analysis. In: 2023 IEEE International Conference on Web Services (ICWS), pp. 50–56 (2023). https://doi.org/10.1109/ICWS60048.2023.00019
22. Nunes, L., Santos, N., Rito Silva, A.: From a monolith to a microservices architecture: an approach based on transactional contexts. In: Bures, T., Duchien, L., Inverardi, P. (eds.) ECSA 2019. LNCS, vol. 11681, pp. 37–52. Springer, Cham (2019). https://doi.org/10.1007/978-3-030-29983-5_3
23. O'Hanlon, C.: A conversation with Werner Vogels. Queue **4**(4), 14–22 (2006). https://doi.org/10.1145/1142055.1142065
24. Pawlak, R., Monperrus, M., Petitprez, N., Noguera, C., Seinturier, L.: Spoon: a library for implementing analyses and transformations of java source code. Softw. Pract. Exp. **46**, 1155–1179 (2015). https://doi.org/10.1002/spe.2346
25. Ponce, F., Márquez, G., Astudillo, H.: Migrating from monolithic architecture to microservices: a rapid review. In: 2019 38th International Conference of the Chilean Computer Science Society (SCCC), pp. 1–7 (2019). https://doi.org/10.1109/SCCC49216.2019.8966423
26. Rademacher, F., Sachweh, S., Zündorf, A.: Towards a UML profile for domain-driven design of microservice architectures. In: Cerone, A., Roveri, M. (eds.) SEFM 2017. LNCS, vol. 10729, pp. 230–245. Springer, Cham (2018). https://doi.org/10.1007/978-3-319-74781-1_17
27. Richardson, C.: Developing transactional microservices using aggregates, event sourcing and CQRS. InfoQ (2017). https://www.infoq.com/minibooks/emag-microservices-monoliths/
28. Santos, N., Rito Silva, A.: A complexity metric for microservices architecture migration. In: 2020 IEEE International Conference on Software Architecture (ICSA), pp. 169–178 (2020). https://doi.org/10.1109/ICSA47634.2020.00024
29. Santos, S., Silva, A.R.: Microservices identification in monolith systems: functionality redesign complexity and evaluation of similarity measures. J. Web Eng. **21**(5), 1543–1582 (2022). https://doi.org/10.13052/jwe1540-9589.2158
30. Singjai, A., Zdun, U., Zimmermann, O.: Practitioner views on the interrelation of microservice APIS and domain-driven design: a grey literature study based on grounded theory. In: 2021 IEEE 18th International Conference on Software

Architecture (ICSA), pp. 25–35 (2021). https://doi.org/10.1109/ICSA51549.2021.00011
31. Tune, N., Millett, S.: Designing Autonomous Teams and Services. O'Reilly Media, Incorporated (2017)
32. Vernon, V.: Domain-Driven Design Distilled. Addison-Wesley, Boston (2016)
33. Vural, H., Koyuncu, M.: Does domain-driven design lead to finding the optimal modularity of a microservice? IEEE Access **9**, 32721–32733 (2021). https://doi.org/10.1109/ACCESS.2021.3060895
34. Özkan, O., Önder Babur, van den Brand, M.: Domain-driven design in software development: a systematic literature review on implementation, challenges, and effectiveness (2023). https://doi.org/10.48550/arXiv.2310.01905

Implications of Trust in Cyber-Physical Systems Design: The ASSA Case Study

Pierre Rambert and Irina Rychkova(✉)

University Paris 1, Panthèon-Sorbonne, Paris, France
{pierre.rambert,irina.rychkova}@univ-paris1.fr

Abstract. Cyber-Physical Systems (CPS) refer to integrated computational and physical processes, where computational elements monitor and control physical processes, usually with a feedback loop. Analysis of trust formation within a complex networks of linked social, physical and computational entities has a potential to reveal otherwise implicit trustworthiness requirements and to improve the CPS design and acceptance. We address this challenge with a method for trust analysis that supports the alignment between trust concerns expressed by the prospective CPS users and stakeholders, trustworthiness requirements formulated by the CPS designers and technical elements of the CPS to be developed. We apply this method to a real CPS design project. Our case study shows that the explicit analysis of trust not only improves traceability between user trust concerns and technical features of the CPS, but also allows for identification of new relevant trustworthiness requirements, affecting the system design and acceptance.

Keywords: trust · trustworthiness requirements · CPS

1 Introduction

Cyber-physical systems (CPS) refer to integrated computational capabilities, networking, and physical processes. These systems use embedded computers and networks to monitor and control physical processes, often with feedback loops, where physical actions influence computational decisions and vice versa [12]. Social entities (organizations and individuals) are inherently involved in the CPS lifecycle from development and standardization to implementation and daily use.

Trust is an essential component of the CPS adoption [6]. CPS are characterized by their high degree of complexity, interconnectivity, and the ability to interact with both the physical world and computational elements seamlessly. Compared to social or interpersonal trust [5,13], in a CPS context, there are multiple entities (social, physical, or computational) upon which CPS users need to place their trust. Examining trust formation in such a complex heterogeneous system provides valuable input for CPS designers and developers, improving systems' trustworthiness and positively affecting their acceptance and adoption by the users [6,19,24].

J. Borbinha et al. (Eds.): EDOC 2024, LNCS 15409, pp. 201–218, 2025.
https://doi.org/10.1007/978-3-031-78338-8_11

We address this challenge with a method for iterative analysis and elicitation of trustworthiness requirements elaborated from [16]. The method is grounded on the Six-Variable Model [25] originally defined to support design of control systems. It provides a structured framework for presentation and analysis of the relationships between various CPS elements. The presented method supports traceability and alignment between *trust concerns* expressed by the CPS users and stakeholders, *trust assumptions* made by the CPS designers in order to address these concerns, *trustworthiness requirements*, and technical system *components* that will be developed to meet these requirements. This article presents the details of the method and reports on the case study of the ASSA project where this method was applied. ASSA (Assistance Sécurité Seniors Application) is a startup creating a personal emergency response system for the elderly. ASSA solution uses connected smart devices to monitor user's vital parameters and to trigger an alert in case of emergency. The team of two engineers delivered design documentation for ASSA following a conventional software design process. However, explicit trust analysis and trustworthiness requirements elicitation were not conducted. This led us to consider ASSA an appropriate case for the method application. The goal of our study is to demonstrate that explicit trust analysis offers valuable insights for the CPS design process, enhancing traceability and leading to the identification of new relevant requirements that contribute to the system's trustworthiness.

This article is organized as follows: In Sect. 2, we discuss the background on trust in CPS; In Sect. 3, we provide the details on the method of trustworthiness requirements elicitation; In Sect. 4, we present our research methodology and introduce the ASSA case study; In Sect. 5, we present our case study results; We provide the concluding remarks in Sect. 6.

2 Background

2.1 Trust in CPS Research

Trust is a social construct that emerges from interactions between individuals or groups and can be described by a situation where a subject (trustor) is willing to rely on a chosen actions of an object of trust (trustee) [5,13,20]. Advances in socio-technical systems introduce novel models of social and business interactions, where IT artifacts can take the role of a trustee [22]. Trust in technology reflects trustor's beliefs that a specific technology has the attributes necessary to perform as expected in a given situation where negative consequences are possible [14,15].

CPS applications for assisted living provide individuals with support within their living environments [1,4,23]. Recent technological advances expanded the capabilities of CPS, enabling real-time health monitoring, fall detection, medication management, and personalized assistance. However, multiple issues related to privacy, data security, interoperability, standardization, and integration of CPS systems into larger ecosystems undermine the CPS users' and stakeholders' decision to trust and to be engaged with a CPS [1,6,19]. Trust, defined as the user's willingness to rely on a system in case of an emergency, is a prerequisite for CPS technology adoption and must be explicitly addressed in their design [17,19,24].

While interpersonal or social trust can be defined as a function of trustee's perceived ability, benevolence and integrity [13], physical and computational entities exhibit technical properties and attributes that might predict the user's decision to trust (and by consequence to be involved with) the CPS [14].

Given the complex and interconnected nature of a CPS context, where multiple social, physical and computational entities involved, there may be no obvious central or identifiable trustee upon which to base trust decisions [6]. Moreover, non-technical CPS stakeholders have limited capacity to objectively assess technical properties of a CPS and to reason about its trustworthiness. In [6], the following eight trust constructs in CPS are defined: familiarity and understanding of the CPS by consumers; reliability, predictability and consistency; security; integrity; competence, expertise and functionality required to interact with the CPS; the benevolence and helpfulness of the CPS for consumers; personalizability; faith and belief consumers have in the service delivered. These concepts capture the complex nature of trust relationships in CPS. To accurately address CPS trustworthiness during design, it is essential to conduct a thorough analysis of user trust-related concerns and systematically translate these concerns into trustworthiness requirements [16].

2.2 Trustworthiness Requirements and Trust Assumptions

In systems engineering, trustworthiness of a system means "to be worthy of being trusted" to fulfill some specific requirements [18]. In this work, we elaborate on the method for explicit trustworthiness requirements elicitation proposed in [16]. Trustworthiness requirement (TwR) can be defined as *a statement made by a trustor about the expected trustworthiness of a trustee. This statement must clearly express an operational, functional, design, or other characteristic, which, according to the trustor's beliefs, positively impacts the trustworthiness of this trustee and the interaction between the two.*

Sutcliffe [24] introduces 'soft' requirements as a linguistic concept that encompasses various phenomena related to people, organizations, and society, including trust. Grounded on this work, TwR can be considered as a subclass of soft requirements and can be refined by functional and non-functional requirements. A RE method aiming to systematize the elicitation and analysis of requirements, including trustworthiness requirements, and grounded on the ontological analysis is proposed in [3]. Here, TwR are considered as a special class of quality requirements. The Reference Ontology of Trustworthiness Requirements (ROTwR) [2] proposes decomposition of TwR into reliability requirements, truthful information communication requirements and transparency requirements.

In the context of CPS, TwR define the desired outcomes these systems should achieve to address the trust concerns (TC) of users and stakeholders within the socio-physical environment. However, the CPS controlling software - the main focus of the development project addressed in this study - can only affect the machine domains, not the socio-physical ones. This concept is known as the world-on-machine paradox, as formulated in [26]. Consequently, TCs cannot be directly mapped into functional, non-functional, or quality requirements, nor can they be linked directly to CPS components within the machine domain. Instead, system engineers must interpret these concerns from the social domain to the machine domain [7,21,27]. To do so, they have to make specific design assumptions [9]. Whereas TC are related to user's beliefs and express what user expects or fears in the real world, design assumptions reflect the engineers' understanding of both the real and the machine world. They express something taken as being true or factual about the system, its components or the environment. Design assumptions drive further engineers' decisions about functionalities, features and other properties of the system-to-be.

An ontology of assumptions proposed in [26] defines world assumptions (WA), machine assumptions (MA), world dependence assumptions (WDA), and machine dependence assumptions (MDA). A world assumption is an assumption about world (or social) phenomena, which constraints the machine environment. A machine assumption is an assumption about a machine's internal phenomena. A machine dependence assumption states that an external world phenomenon depends on some machine phenomena. In contrast, a world dependence assumption states that a machine phenomenon depends on some world phenomena. The authors use situation calculus to reason about assumptions and requirements.

Grounded on [8,26], trust assumptions (TA) can be defined as the *assumptions made by the system engineers about the properties of a system-to-be and its various components (including human components), which will positively affect the perceived trustworthiness of the system.*

3 Method for Trustworthiness Requirements Elicitation

The method presented in this work is grounded on [16]. In the original work [17], following the identification of (social) trust concerns in Step 1, the authors define a vector of corresponding (technical) trustworthiness properties the system must possess in Step 2. The trust assumptions are identified and documented in Step 5 of the original method, acknowledging the alignment between the two. However, following the arguments presented above, TW properties are a part of the machine domain and cannot be identified before the trust assumptions are made. In our work, trust assumptions play the pivotal role enabling the mapping between the social domain and the machine domain. In our method, we systematically formulate and refine the TA in order to achieve a certain level of details where TwR can be formulated from the TA (see Fig. 1-b). We omit the TW vector.

For trust analysis, we use the Six-Variable Model [25] originally defined to support design of control systems. This model provides a structured framework for analysis of the relationships between various system elements situated in the socio-physical environment (i.e., users, stakeholders) and in the machine domain (i.e., a control machine, sensors, actuators, other connected systems). It defines

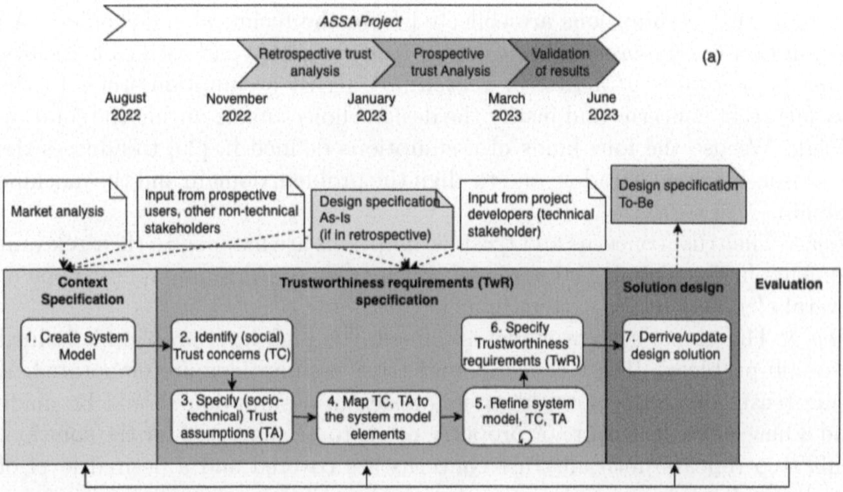

Fig. 1. (a) Overview of the ASSA Case Study: the timeline; (b) Method for Trust Analysis and TwR elicitation integrated into the human-centered design approach [10]

six variables that are depicted as relations between different system elements: referenced variables that focus on the properties that should be observed in the system's environment; monitored variables represent the properties that need to be monitored during the system's operation; input variables represent the external stimuli that affect the system's behavior; output variables refer to the outcomes produced by the system; controlled variables refer to the properties that the system can actively control or actions the system can take to achieve its desired behavior; desired variables refer the properties in the system's environment that should be achieved during the system's operation. Figure 2 illustrates the six-variable model for the ASSA system (our case study).

By analyzing the relationships between monitored, controlled, input, output, referenced, and desired variables, developers can precisely articulate the system requirements - TwR in our case - and their implication of system functionalities and behavior. For trust analysis in CPS, we use the formalism proposed in [8,16] for documenting TC, TA, TwR and traceability between TA, TwR and system elements.

Our method defines seven steps (see Fig. 1-b) as follows:

Step 1: A global system model based on the Six-Variable Model is created. This model focuses on the problem domain and the effects that must be achieved in this domain. It captures the context of use and forms the foundation for the subsequent steps.

Step 2: Trust concerns are collected from the users and project stakeholders. In case of retrospective analysis, trust concerns can be extracted from the existing design documentation;

Step 3: Trust assumptions are collected from the technical stakeholders. An assumption is *something taken as being true or factual and used as a starting point for a course of action or reasoning*[1]. Trust assumptions refer to the (social) trust concerns and justify the design choices made during the solution design. We use the four kinds of assumptions defined in [26] to address the 'world-on-machine paradox' and to align the problem domain and the machine domain.
Step 4: The trust concerns and trust assumptions are mapped to their relevant elements in the global system model. Each trust concern may refer to one or several elements in the system model.
Step 5: The global system model is refined: the high-level problem is refined into sub-problems. Trust concerns and trust assumptions are elaborated. If some trust concern is not addressed - a design assumption should be made and a new element, feature or property needs to be suggested for the solution. This step repeats until all trust concerns are covered and a desired level of detail is achieved;
Step 6: The trustworthiness requirements are derived from the trust assumptions and integrated into system design documentation.
Step 7: The new technical features and/or components are derived, contributing into trustworthiness of the design solution. The design specification is updated.

The method is consistent with the activities of the ISO 9241 human-centered design approach [10]: Specifying the context of use (Step 1); Specifying the user requirements (Step 2–6); Producing the design solutions (Step 7). Based on the evaluation results, a new iteration of trust analysis and TwR elicitation can be triggered. The User-centered evaluation of the design is out of scope for this article and will be addressed in future.

4 The Case Study

To demonstrate our method for eliciting trustworthiness requirements and to evaluate its effectiveness, we conducted a case study on the ASSA software development project.

4.1 ASSA: the Application for Assistance and Security for Elderly

ASSA is an innovative personal emergency response application designed for iOS and Android devices. Potential users of ASSA are elderly people and people living in isolation, both geographically and socially. The application can potentially integrate with compatible smartwatches and other wearable devices to monitor vital parameters (e.g., heart rate, blood pressure, oxygen saturation levels) and detect accidents (e.g. falls). When an irregularity in vital parameters or an accident is detected, the application initiates a series of actions to ensure

[1] https://www.merriam-webster.com/thesaurus/assumption.

quick assistance. First, it triggers a timer, during which the user is prompted to confirm or cancel the emergency. If the emergency is not canceled, ASSA transmits the emergency alert to the designated healthcare providers (e.g., a hospital emergency service) and notifies a designated caregiver (e.g., a person of trust or a family member), providing them with the data related to the situation (e.g., a health report).

The team of two engineers conducted the market analysis, requirements specification and developed initial design documentation for ASSA between August and November 2022 (see Fig. 1-a). Regular monitoring and emergency handling are the main uses-cases of ASSA. Other functionalities have been elaborated later during the project. In particular, systematic generation and management of on-line health reports have been added to ASSA as a result of this study.

According to the latest design specification, the ASSA application ensures user monitoring and alert generation in case of emergency and provides relevant historical data for the medical professionals (for both regular and emergent medical interventions) for more efficient personalized treatment.

4.2 Research Methodology

We adapt the single-project case study research protocol defined by Kitchenham and Pickard in [11].

Planning and Designing of the Case Study. The objectives of the case study is to evaluate the feasibility, efficiency and relevance of our method for the analysis and elicitation of trustworthiness requirements in the ASSA project. While trust was recognized by the ASSA developers as an important factor for adoption, no specific trust analysis has been conducted during the project. This made the project a relevant case for the study. We define the following hypothesis for this case study:

H1: The method is complementary with a design process not focused on trust.
H2: The method application uncovers implicit TwR in the existing system specifications.
H3: The method application leads to identification of the new TwR.
H4: Documentation of trust assumptions enhances traceability and alignment in the designed system.
H5: Method contributes into (re)definition of a valid and relevant design solution.

Conducting the Case Study. The study was conducted between November 2022 and June 2023 (Fig. 1-a). First, we conducted the trust analysis of the system *in retrospective*, applying the method on the data collected in the ASSA project before November 2022 and to the design documentation produced by the ASSA developers. In the second iteration, we conducted the trust analysis of the system *in prospective*, applying the method on the new data. We conducted seven semi-structured interviews with prospective ASSA users and healthcare professionals. Additionally, we organized a series of working sessions with the ASSA developers, concentrating on the themes of trust, trustworthiness, and acceptance of the prospective application. Each interview lasted between 20 and 45 min. After a brief presentation of the assisted living technologies, the interviewees have been introduced to ASSA and invited to discuss their own experience with the assisted living technology and their reasons to adopt (or not) one. Compared to interviews conducted by ASSA developers in the earlier days of the project, this data collection focuses on subjective trust issues and beliefs of the (non-technical) stakeholders. Here are some example questions from the interview guide (translated from French):

- *How would the personal emergency response system improve your work or your personal security?*
- *For what reasons would you take a personal emergency response system?*
- *Do you have any preoccupation when a relative of yours uses a personal emergency response system?*
- *Does a "connected" personal emergency response system changes any preoccupation you have regarding a typical personal emergency response system?* Both retrospective and prospective analysis demonstrated the method feasibility (H1). We addressed the method efficiency (H2, H3) by eliciting the TwR in both iterations. We were able to identify new features contributing to the system trustworthiness and to propose an update for the base line ASSA design solution (As-Is). To evaluate the method relevance (H4, H5), we presented the refined ASSA system model and the updated design specification to the ASSA developers for review and validation. The case study results are presented in the following session.

5 Trustworthiness Requirements Elicitation for ASSA

5.1 The Retrospective Trust Analysis

Step 1: The global system model of ASSA is created based on the market analysis and design documentation produced by the ASSA developers (Fig. 2). Here ASSA mobile application is represented as a control system in a Six-Value-Model [25]. The root requirement is defined by the main use case of ASSA: Provide monitoring and assistance. The problem domain includes the user (an elderly person whose health is monitored), her designated as caregivers and healthcare practitioners. The control machine or the software to-be represents the ASSA mobile application. The connection domain between the machine and the problem domains includes sensors (e.g., smartphone, smart watch) and the external systems with which the control machine interacts by sending alerts, reports, and emergency calls (e.g., health emergency services, messaging service, and online reporting system). Reference variables include "health report" and "help notification"; monitored and input variables include "detection of motion", "vital signs" and "location"; output variables include "call ambulance" linked to the health

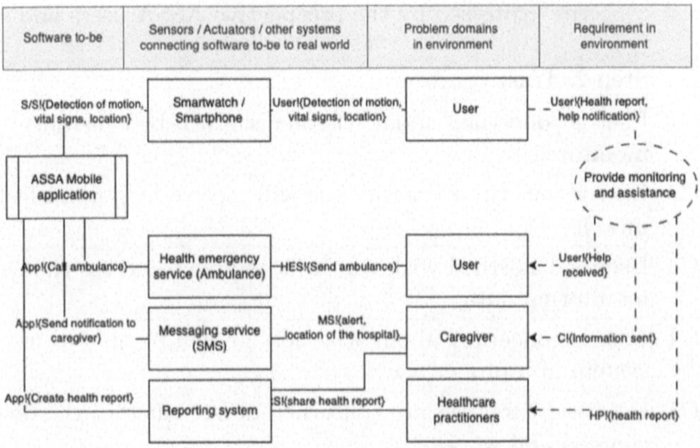

Fig. 2. Step 1: The ASSA global system model

emergency system (e.g., Ambulance), "send notification to caregiver" linked to the messaging service (e.g., SMS), and "create health report" linked to the reporting system. The controlled variables include "send ambulance" linked with the User; "alert", and "location of the hospital" linked to the Caregiver; "share health report" linked to the Healthcare practitioners and Caregiver. The desired variables are composed of "help received", linked to the User; "information sent", linked to the Caregiver; "health report", linked to the Healthcare practitioner.

Step 2: We conducted a semantic analysis of the ASSA design documentation (As-Is) provided by the ASSA developers, including the market reports and interviews with medical professionals, potential users and caregivers. Using various definitions of trust from the literature, we identified seven trust concerns TC1-7 (Table 1).

Step 3: We identified the design decisions related to the TC specified in the previous step from the ASSA design documentation (As-Is). We identify the assumptions made by the ASSA developers about the properties of the ASSA CPS and its various components to justify these decisions. We conducted the interviews with the ASSA developers to validate the TA that have been discovered. We classify them according to the ontology proposed in [26]. Table 2 illustrates the list of TA with their related TC. During the retrospective trust analysis, we extracted 11 trust assumptions TA1.01-TA1.11. We use the assumption ontology from [26], identifying world assumptions (WA), machine assumptions (MA), world dependence assumptions (WDA), and machine dependence assumptions (MDA).

World assumptions are engineers assumptions about the social phenomena. For example, we assume that the healthcare provider sends an ambulance each time the ASSA emergency alert is received (see TA1.10) - this assumption means that our solution cannot be trusted if the healthcare provider ignores the alert or has not enough resources to respond to it. We also assume that the user should

Table 1. Trust concerns expressed by the prospective ASSA users and stakeholders

Iter.		Step 2: Trust concern
1	TC1	User is concerned about whether she will be constantly monitored
1	TC2	User is uncertain whether she will receive help upon feeling unwell
1	TC3	User is concerned with who will be able to access the monitoring data
1	TC4	User is concerned about whether she will be able to use the system in a proper way
1	TC5	User and caregiver are concerned about whether the device is charged and working
1	TC6	Caregiver is concerned about whether the assistance will be timely provided in response to the alert
1	TC7	Healthcare practitioners are concerned about relevance and exactitude of the health report
2	TC8	User is concerned about the system generating false alerts
2	TC9	User is concerned that the monitoring data and the health report will not be used by the healthcare professionals to personalize/improve the treatment
2	TC10	User is concerned that his data will be used for commercial purposes
2	TC11	User is concerned about the health report being shared/used without her consent

find the ASSA interface simple and intuitive (TA1.08). Otherwise the system will not be trusted by the user.

Machine assumptions are engineers assumptions about the internal properties of the application, smart devices or other systems and services that will positively affect the perceived trustworthiness of the system. We assume that the redundant sensors in the system affect reliability of the patient monitoring (TA1.01).

A machine dependence assumption states that an external world phenomenon depends on some machine phenomena. For example, we assume that the user can trust the system if she can check and make sure that the sensor is working and constantly monitoring (see TA1.02).

A world dependence assumption states that a machine phenomenon depends on some world phenomena. For example, we assume that the system detecting an anomaly (and/or raising an alert) means that the user is not well (TA1.03, TA1.03.01).

Step 4: We map the TC (Step 2) and TA (Step 3) to the relevant parts of the ASSA system. We update the system model to show the traceability (Fig. 3). ç Concerns TC1, TC4, TC5 are related to ASSA mobile application and/or

Table 2. Trust assumptions discovered from the retrospective analysis (TA1.xx) and made during the prospective analysis (TA2.xx) linking the trust concerns with system elements

	Trust Assumption:	Kind [26]	TC:	Linked to System elements:
TA1.01	Redundant sensors increase the monitoring reliability	MA	TC1	Smartwatch/Smartphone
TA1.02	User can check the sensor's status and activity	MDA	TC1	ASSA Mobile application; Smartwatch/Smartphone
TA1.03	Irregularities in health metrics are correctly identified from the data	WDA	TC2, TC8	ASSA Mobile application
TA1.03.01	User can trigger an alert manually	WDA	TC2, TC8	ASSA Mobile application
TA1.04	The alert transmission is guaranteed by the system	MDA	TC2	ASSA Mobile application; Network provider
TA1.04.01	WiFi and Mobile communication is reliable	MA	TC2	Network provider
TA1.05	Emergency calls are responded 24/7	WA	TC2	Health Emergency service
TA1.06	Data is encrypted	MA	TC3	ASSA Mobile application; Messaging service; Reporting system
TA1.07	Data can be accessed only by authorized persons with the verified identity	WDA	TC3, TC10-11	Messaging service, Reporting system, Caregiver, Healthcare practitioner
TA1.08	The interface is simple and intuitive	WA	TC4	ASSA Mobile application; Smartwatch/Smartphone
TA1.09	User is informed when the battery of the smartphone or the smartwatch is low	MDA	TC5	ASSA Mobile application
TA1.10	The healthcare provider handles emergency alerts received from the system	WA	TC6, TC9	Health emergency service, Healthcare authorities
TA1.11	Software is certified and recognised by healthcare authorities	WA	TC7, TC9	Healthcare authorities
TA2.01	Redundant sensors prevent from false alerts	MDA	TC8	Smartwatch/Smartphone
TA2.02	Explicit request for the user consent	MDA	TC10-11	ASSA mobile application, Reporting system
TA2.03	GDPR-complience	MDA	TC10-11	ASSA mobile application, Reporting system
TA2.04	Reporting system is highly available	MA	TC9	Reporting system, Healthcare practitioner
TA2.05	Healthcare practitioners recognise and use the health report	WA	TC9	Reporting system, Healthcare practitioner
TA2.06	Healthcare practitioners provide qualified help	WA	TC9	Healthcare practitioner
TA2.07	User training materials are provided	MDA	TC1, TC4-5	ASSA Mobile application; Smartwatch/Smartphone

the smart devices - the User interface. TC2 questions the whole system and its purpose - it is related to the main requirement. TC3, TC7 are related to the ASSA interfaces for data exchange with the external systems. TC6 is related to the interfaces between the system and the control domain. They refer to service-level agreements and operational-level agreements that need to be defined.

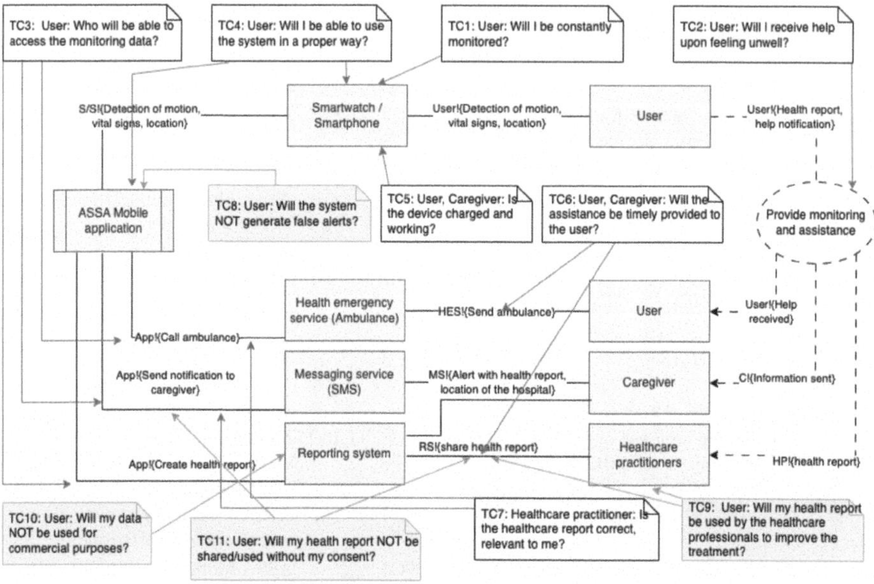

Fig. 3. Global system model of ASSA annotated with trust concerns from the Iteration 1 (TC1-TC7) and Iteration 2 (TC8-11).

Step 5: We refine the global system model by decomposing the main problem 'Provide monitoring and assistance' into the sub-problems corresponding to the use-cases of ASSA defined in coordination with the project developers:

P1: Monitor the User and Detect Emergencies. This sub-problem consists of continuously collecting data about the user's vital parameters from the sensors (e.g., smartwatch, smartphone) and generating user's health metrics. Data are analyzed by the dedicated algorithms (i.e., compared to historical data or some baseline established by a physician). If some irregularities are detected, the alert is triggered.

P2: Send Ambulance to the User if an Emergency is Detected Once the alert is triggered, the system transmits the alert to a healthcare emergency service, which sends an ambulance in response. Healthcare practitioners (e.g., paramedics, physicians) intervene to provide help to the user. User data related to the triggered alert (i.e., the health report) is communicated to healthcare professionals through the reporting system.

P3: Inform the Caregiver About the Emergency. The system notifies the caregiver via a text message (e.g., an SMS), providing her with the data related to the alert and the emergency intervention that followed (e.g., the address of the hospital where the user was transported).

P4: Manage and Share Health Reports. The system records the user's health metrics creating regular health reports and incident health reports in an on-line Reporting system. With the user's authorization, these health reports can be communicated with the caregivers and the healthcare professionals for emergency interventions and regular check-ups.

We illustrate the refined system diagram for the sub-problem P2 in Fig. 4. TA1.01-04, TA1.08, TA1.09 are related to the elements that will be directly manipulated by the user. TA1.05-07, TA1.10 are linked to the external systems in the machine domain (i.e., Health emergency service, Messaging service, Reporting system). These are assumptions about how the ASSA Mobile application should be integrated with these systems and about specific properties or functionalities that these external systems must ensure. TA1.04, TA1.10-11 are related to the entities that are not included in the problem model - Network provider and Healthcare authorities.

Step 6: Using the TA, we formulate 11 trustworthiness requirements (1.01–1.11 in Table 3). We link the TwR with the TC they are addressing. Each TwR reflects one or more TA. For example, the requirement TwR1.05: The system shall be integrated with (recognized by) the health emergency service (e.g., Ambulance) is associated with TA1.05: Emergency calls are responded 24/7 and TA1.10: The healthcare provider handles emergency alerts received from the system (Table 2).

Step 7: The TwR are formulated for ASSA Mobile application, for the external systems and services (e.g., health emergency service, reporting system), and for the entities in the domain environment (e.g., healthcare practitioner, healthcare authorities, mobile network provider). The TwR related to ASSA mobile application can be considered as functional or non-functional requirements. Some of these requirements align with the As-Is design solution (indicated '+' in Table 2), whereas the others lead to new design features. For example, TwR1.01, TwR1.03, TwR1.07 suggest the update in the ASSA mobile interface As-Is. The TwR related to external systems and services can be considered as non-functional, integration requirements, and regulatory and compliance requirements. They also introduce new elements to the design. For example, TwR1.09 focuses on the integration and compliance with the (existing) platforms for sharing medical data. TwR1.05-06, TwR1.08 highlight the importance of service-level agreements with healthcare and mobile network providers.

5.2 The Prospective Trust Analysis

The objective of this analysis is to extend our understanding of the system and its environment, focusing on the trustworthiness and acceptance of the system by its stakeholders. Compared to the retrospective analysis, here we apply the method to the newly collected empirical data for prospective TwR elicitation.

Step 1: We use the global system model of ASSA developed in the Iteration 1 (Fig. 2) and proceed with TC extraction.
Step 2: Through qualitative data analysis we were able to confirm the TC identified in the Iteration 1 and to identify new TC (see Table 1). In particular, the interviews reveal that the prospective users are concerned with a possibility of a false alert and the purposeful use of the collected data (see TC8-11, Table 1).
Step 3: We made the new trust assumptions about the (technical) properties of the system To-Be, which, if implemented, would alleviate the TC expressed by the users (TC8-11) and improve system trustworthiness. Note, that some trust concerns are addressed by the TA formulated in the Iteration 1. For example, TA1.03, 03.01 are already addressing the trust concern about the false alerts (TC8). The new TA are listed in Table 2 (see TA2.01-2.05). For example, we assume that the user can trust the system if she can learn to use the system from the documentation/support materials provided (TA2.07).
Step 4: We associate new TC and TA with the system components. Figure 4 illustrates the traceability between the TA and the system elements for the system model for P2: Send ambulance to the user if an emergency is detected.
Step 5: We update the sub-problems (see the retrospective analysis) and their system models (omitted in this paper).
Step 6: We formulate five TwR (TwR2.01-2.05) and link them with their corresponding TA and TC.
Step 7: While TwR2.01 aligns with the ASSA As-Is design solution, the other four TwR are new. They have been validated by the ASSA developers and led to the design update. TwR2.02, TwR2.05 require the extension of the ASSA application interface whereas TwR2.03-04 need to be addressed by the external Reporting system and by the Healthcare practitioners (integration, regulatory and compliance requirements).

5.3 Discussion

Our study shows that the proposed method is applicable in retrospective (following up on a design process not focused on trust) and in prospective (integrated into a human-centered design), validating H1. We examined the identified TwR with the ASSA developers: five TwR correspond to the ASSA requirements As-Is; six new TwR led to the ASSA specification update (Table 3). This validates our research hypothesis H2, H3 and demonstrates the method efficiency.

We formulated 18 trust assumptions based on the retrospective and prospective trust analysis (Table 2) and created a traceability matrix and system models explicitly linking the (social) trust concerns and the system elements. We conducted feedback sessions with the engineers to ensure a shared understanding and an added value of this traceability, validating H4.

We formulated 11 new TwR with 10 recognized important and validated by the ASSA developers. TwR 1.07: 'The user shall be able to trigger an alert manually' was not validated as it goes against the product vision of ASSA, where

Table 3. Trustworthiness requirements

TwR	Description	Associated with TA	Addressing TC:	Included into ASSA?
TwR1.01	The system shall provide the user with the means to control the sensors status	TA 1.02	TC1	new/val
TwR1.02	The system and the watch shall have a simple and clear interface	TA1.08	TC4	+
TwR1.03	The system shall alert the user when the battery charge is low	TA1.09	TC5	new/val
TwR1.04	The system shall be compatible with certified/reliable sensors/components	TA 1.01/2.01	TC1, TC8	+
TwR1.05	The system shall be integrated with (recognized by) the health emergency service (e.g., Ambulance or SAMU in France)	TA1.10, TA1.05	TC2, TC6, TC9	new/val
TwR1.06	The system shall be certified/approved by the healthcare authority	TA1.11; TA1.03	TC2, TC7, TC8, TC9	new/val
TwR1.07	The user shall be able to trigger an alert manually	TA1.03.01	TC2, TC8	new/ inval
TwR1.08	The system shall use a reliable mobile/internet network provider	TA1.04; TA1.04.01	TC2	new/val
TwR1.09	The system shall use a report format compatible with cloud reporting systems	TA1.06-07 TA2.02-04	TC3, TC9-11	new/val
TwR1.10	The system shall encrypt all data, stored and exchanged	TA1.06	TC3	+
TwR1.11	The system shall be integrated with an on-line Reporting system	TA1.07	TC3, TC10-11	+
TwR2.01	The system has to be GDPR-compliant	TA2.02	TC10-11	+
TwR2.02	The user shall be able to control report sharing	TA2.02; TA1.07	TC3, TC10-11	new/val
TwR2.03	The reporting system must be highly available	TA2.04-05	TC9	new/val
TwR2.04	The healthcare practitioner has to use the received health report while taking the user in charge	TA2.05; TA2.06	TC9	new/val
TwR2.05	The user shall be able to access training materials and guidelines for the ASSA mobile application online (e.g., FAQ, getting started videos etc.)	TA1.02, TA1.03.01, TA1.08-09	TC1-2, TC4-5, TC8	new/val

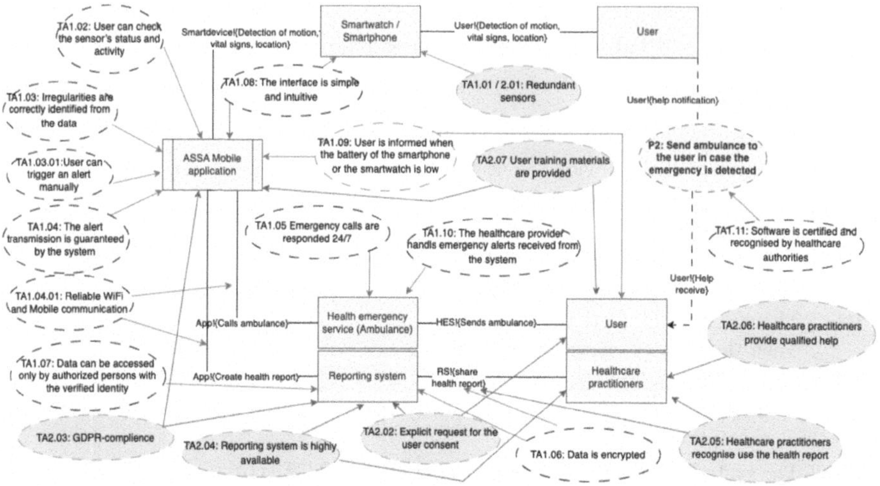

Fig. 4. Refined system diagram for the sub-problem P2: Send ambulance to the user in case the emergency is detected. Trust assumptions from the Iteration 1 (TA1.xx) and from the Iteration 2 (TA2.xx) are linked to the system elements.

the system takes the whole responsibility for the emergency detection. By this, we were able to partly validate H5 and the method relevance.

6 Conclusions

In this work, we applied the method for iterative trustworthiness requirements analysis and elicitation elaborated from [16] to the case study of the ASSA CPS. We formulated trust assumptions that justify technical decisions, supporting alignment between (social) trust concerns and specific properties of the system, and addressing the world-on-machine paradox formulated in [26]. The conducted trust analysis led to updates in the ASSA solution design, with a focus on enhancing system trustworthiness. The ASSA developers acknowledged the significance of this analysis.

In future work, we intend to evaluate the proposed design to assess the impact of TwRs on the perceived trustworthiness of the system. To achieve this, we plan to conduct user-centered evaluations and post-implementation usability testing.

References

1. Abtoy, A., Touhafi, A., Tahiri, A., et al.: Ambient assisted living system's models and architectures: A survey of the state of the art. J. King Saud Univ.-Comput. Inf. Sci. **32**(1), 1–10 (2020)
2. Amaral, G., Guizzardi, R., Guizzardi, G., Mylopoulos, J.: Ontology-based modeling and analysis of trustworthiness requirements: preliminary results. In: International Conference on Conceptual Modeling, pp. 342–352. Springer (2020)

3. Amaral, G., Guizzardi, R., Guizzardi, G., Mylopoulos, J.: Trustworthiness requirements: the pix case study. In: Ghose, A., Horkoff, J., Silva Souza, V.E., Parsons, J., Evermann, J. (eds.) ER 2021. LNCS, vol. 13011, pp. 257–267. Springer, Cham (2021). https://doi.org/10.1007/978-3-030-89022-3_21
4. Caballero, P., Ortiz, G., Medina-Bulo, I.: Systematic literature review of ambient assisted living systems supported by the internet of things. Univ. Access Inf. Soc. 1–26 (2023)
5. Gambetta, D., et al.: Can we trust trust. Trust: Making Breaking Coop. Relat. **13**(2000), 213–237 (2000)
6. Garry, T., Harwood, T.: Trust and its predictors within a cyber-physical system context. J. Serv. Mark. **33**(4), 407–428 (2019)
7. Haley, C.B., Laney, R.C., Moffett, J.D., Nuseibeh, B.: The effect of trust assumptions on the elaboration of security requirements. In: Proceedings. 12th IEEE International Requirements Engineering Conference, 2004, pp. 102–111. IEEE (2004)
8. Haley, C.B., Laney, R.C., Moffett, J.D., Nuseibeh, B.: Picking battles: the impact of trust assumptions on the elaboration of security requirements. In: Trust Management: Second International Conference, iTrust 2004, Oxford, UK, 29 March-1 April 2004, pp. 347–354. Springer (2004)
9. Haley, C.B., Laney, R.C., Moffett, J.D., Nuseibeh, B.: Using trust assumptions with security requirements. Requirements Eng. **11**, 138–151 (2006)
10. ISO/IEC: 9241-210:2019(en) ergonomics of human-system interaction—part 210: Human-centred design for interactive systems. Technical report (2019)
11. Kitchenham, B., Pickard, L., Pfleeger, S.L.: Case studies for method and tool evaluation. IEEE Softw. **12**(4), 52–62 (1995)
12. Lee, E.A.: Cyber physical systems: Design challenges. In: 2008 11th IEEE International Symposium on Object and Component-Oriented Real-time Distributed Computing (ISORC), pp. 363–369. IEEE (2008)
13. Mayer, R.C., Davis, J.H., Schoorman, F.D.: An integrative model of organizational trust. Acad. Manag. Rev. **20**(3), 709–734 (1995)
14. Mcknight, D.H., Carter, M., Thatcher, J.B., Clay, P.F.: Trust in a specific technology: an investigation of its components and measures. ACM Trans. Manag. Inf. Syst. (TMIS) **2**(2), 1–25 (2011)
15. Meeßen, S.M., Thielsch, M.T., Hertel, G.: Trust in management information systems (MIS). Zeitschrift für Arbeits-und Organisationspsychologie A&O (2019)
16. Mohammadi, N.G.: Trustworthy Cyber-Physical Systems: A Systematic Framework Towards Design and Evaluation of Trust and Trustworthiness, 1st edn. Springer Vieweg, Wiesbaden (2019)
17. Mohammadi, N.G., Ulfat-Bunyadi, N., Heisel, M.: Problem-based derivation of trustworthiness requirements from users' trust concerns. In: 2018 16th Annual Conference on Privacy, Security and Trust (PST). IEEE (2018)
18. Neumann, P.G.: Fundamental trustworthiness principles. New Solutions for Cybersecurity (2018)
19. Reichstein, C., Härting, R.C., Häfner, F.: Challenges in the market launch of active assisted living solutions-empirical results from European experts. Procedia Comput. Sci. **176**, 2000–2009 (2020)
20. Rousseau, D.M., Sitkin, S.B., Burt, R.S., Camerer, C.: Not so different after all: a cross-discipline view of trust. Acad. Manag. Rev. **23**(3), 393–404 (1998)
21. Rychkova, I., Ghriba, M.: Trustworthiness requirements in information systems design: lessons learned from the blockchain community. Complex Syst. Inform. Model. Q. **35**, 67–91 (2023)

22. Söllner, M., Hoffmann, A., Hoffmann, H., Wacker, A., Leimeister, J.M.: Understanding the formation of trust in it artifacts (2012)
23. Stokke, R.: The personal emergency response system as a technology innovation in primary health care services: an integrative review. J. Med. Internet Res. **18**(7), e187 (2016)
24. Sutcliffe, A., Sawyer, P., Bencomo, N.: The implications of 'soft' requirements. In: 2022 IEEE 30th International Requirements Engineering Conference (RE), pp. 178–188. IEEE (2022)
25. Ulfat-Bunyadi, N., Meis, R., Heisel, M.: The six-variable model-context modelling enabling systematic reuse of control software. In: International Conference on Software Paradigm Trends, vol. 2, pp. 15–26. SCITEPRESS (2016)
26. Wang, X., Mylopoulos, J., Guizzardi, G., Guarino, N.: How software changes the world: The role of assumptions. In: 2016 IEEE Tenth International Conference on Research Challenges in Information Science (RCIS), pp. 1–12. IEEE (2016)
27. Warwick, L.: Designing trust: the importance of relationships in social contexts. Des. J. **20**(sup1), S3096–S3105 (2017)

Drivers and Metrics for Quantifying IT Landscape Complexity

Eva Stoica(✉), João Moreira, Jean Paul Sebastian Piest, and Faiza Bukhsh

University of Twente, Enschede, The Netherlands
evastoica4@gmail.com,
{j.luizrebelomoreira,j.p.s.piest,f.a.bukhsh}@utwente.nl

Abstract. Mastering complexity is an important topic within the field of Enterprise Architecture (EA), and many companies perceive this as a difficult endeavour due to the growth and perpetual evolution of the Information Technology (IT) landscape. Numerous EA frameworks and methods exist that describe what an IT landscape is. However, there is no consensus regarding the definition of IT landscape complexity, its drivers and how to measure it. To help create a better understanding of what IT landscape complexity entails, this paper reviews established EA literature regarding the common elements of such an IT landscape and investigates prevalent drivers and metrics to quantify complexity. This paper introduces a standard way of describing the IT landscape through a conceptual model, focusing on the elements in the application layer. Furthermore, the prevalent IT complexity drivers and metrics are illustrated. The aim of this research is to support organisations in communication and architecting information systems by considering different kinds of IT elements and their particular characteristics, such as connectivity, adaptation, and complexity. Then, a discussion on how the drivers and metrics of complexity can be used to quantify the complexity of such an IT landscape follows. Our approach is a first step towards better processes for managing complexity. This research supports mastering complexity by allowing organisations to quantify IT landscape complexity when aligning their architectures with the proposed conceptual model.

Keywords: IT Landscape · Complexity · Enterprise Architecture

1 Introduction

The Information Technology (IT) present in a contemporary enterprise is in a continuous transformation and evolution [1]. An overwhelming number of components and elements allow an organisation to perform its day-to-day operations and achieve certain goals and outcomes. The rapid growth and perpetual evolution of elements and their relationships, which create the IT landscape, lead to complexity. From a systems thinking lens, complexity is concerned with a set of parts or components that have vague or difficult-to-understand relationships

J. Borbinha et al. (Eds.): EDOC 2024, LNCS 15409, pp. 219–236, 2025.
https://doi.org/10.1007/978-3-031-78338-8_12

varying across time [2]. The complexity of an IT landscape thus represents the number of components or elements of an architecture, their relationships, and the variation or heterogeneity of these [37].

Given the growth and dynamicity of IT, managing the IT complexity of an organisation can be considered troublesome. Companies must use new technologies on top of their existing stack to match business needs or create temporal measures to address these. Usually, organisations consider that more IT elements can support the delivery of more capabilities. However, these additions can increase the complexity of the landscape and negatively influence agility or increase risks and vulnerabilities [18].

This complexity of IT landscapes is an intangible factor and most organisations experience difficulties in understanding its size or its impact [15,16,42]. Measuring the complexity associated with a change in the IT landscape can be perceived as a very difficult endeavour. This problem is further amplified by the fact that no consensus or well-defined standards are present in either academia or practice to explain what an IT landscape is comprised of, in particular what factors can lead to complexity in such a IT landscape. Without a common understanding of elements of an IT landscape, subjectivity is observed in both modelling the landscape and thinking about what complexity means (e.g., complex landscape as a larger number of IT components versus intricate relationships between components over time). Additionally, the existence of means to quantify complexity is limited and scattered. An acknowledged problem or a "major limitation" [25] is that few companies have suitable methods or tools to systematically assess and evaluate complexity.

To grasp the expected benefits, commonly associated with IT in an organisation, such as lower costs, flexibility, or efficiency [18], complexity needs to be managed and measured. EA methods, tools and techniques can be leveraged for this purpose. With the support of an exploratory and a Systematic Literature Review (SLR), performed according to the extensions proposed by Wolfswinkel et al. [50] to the works of Webster and Watson [46] an answer is provided to the following Main Research Question (MRQ): *Which drivers and metrics can be used in the complexity analysis of an IT landscape?*

This paper introduces a conceptual model which supports a precise definition of the IT landscape, focusing on the elements in the application layer. The model fosters a shared understanding of IT elements which aid with IT modelling processes. Moreover, prevalent complexity drivers and metrics are summarised, enabling stakeholders to define and quantify IT landscape complexity. Based on the conceptual model and the list of drivers and metrics, a blueprint for quantifying IT landscape complexity is developed.

This paper is structured as follows. Section 2 covers the background. Section 3 describes the research methodology for the literature reviews. In Sect. 4 the results of the reviews are analysed. Here, the conceptual model for the IT landscape is introduced, alongside the overview of existing drivers and metrics of complexity. Section 5 discusses the implications of the results. Section 6 concludes this paper and outlines future work.

2 Background

Section 2 offers an overview of the related works that serve as the basis for the literature study. First, it will be acknowledged what an IT landscape is. Then, the overview of what complexity represents in an IT context is introduced.

2.1 IT Landscape Architecture

Architecture. Starting with the term architecture, this represents the philosophy underlying a system which describes its purpose, intent, and structure [22]. Architecture defines the fundamental organisation of a system embodied in its components, their relationships to each other and the environment, as well as the principles guiding its design and evolution [19,23].

Enterprise Architecture. Moving to EA, this represents "a coherent whole of principles, methods, and models that are used in the design and realisation of an enterprise's organisational structure, business processes, information systems, and infrastructure" [23]. Moreover, it is a means to support the business and IT alignment [34] and help bridge the gap between the current and future state of an enterprise [11]. A better alignment leads to "lower cost, higher quality, better time to market and greater customer satisfaction" [11]. For using EA, methodologies, viewpoints and modelling languages are needed. The most used combination that helps deliver EA is using TOGAF [11,17] as a methodology and ArchiMate [12] as a modelling language.

IT Landscape. Next, in literature, the combination of the terms IT and landscape is used interchangeably with concepts such as application architecture, IT infrastructure, technical architecture, or information systems architecture. The IT landscape can represent "A set of hardware, software and facility elements, arranged in a specific configuration, which serves as a fabric to support the business operation of an enterprise" [26]. However, no standard definition of such an IT landscape or its composing elements exists [14,22,33]. Most current IT landscapes are the results of a history of projects that introduced their specialised software, hardware, and infrastructure [22]. Furthermore, over the years, organisations have combined older technologies, e.g., legacy systems, with newer ones [5,49] leading to intricate relationships between components, including artificial intelligence, digital twins, and cloud computing [35]. This fast pace of developments can also influence the prioritisation of short-term or quick fixes which can result in architectural technical debt [21,45].

2.2 IT Landscape Complexity

Definition. IT landscape complexity refers to the number of components or elements of an architecture, their relationships, the variation or heterogeneity of these and the use of different levels of observation and granularity in modelling [31,37].

Classification. For the field of information systems or IT landscape complexity, Schneider [38] unified the existing research by creating a multi-dimensional framework. Four dimensions are included in this framework for classifying complexity: organised vs. disorganised, qualitative vs. quantitative, subjective vs. objective and static vs. dynamic [38]. These dimensions can guide the analysis of EA models.

3 Research Methodology

In Sect. 3, the overarching research question for this paper is introduced. Then, the approach selected to answer it is highlighted.

3.1 Research Questions

The MRQ is stated as: *Which drivers and metrics can be used in the complexity analysis of an IT landscape?*. The answer to this question is presented with the help of an exploratory literature review and SLR. The following two sub-research questions were formulated to further investigate the MRQ:
RQ1. What are the composing elements of an IT landscape?
RQ2. Which factors drive the complexity of an IT landscape?

As no accepted definition of an IT landscape components is present in the literature, RQ1 investigates this by employing an exploratory review. The literature offers various meanings of what an IT landscape represents, hence by employing an exploratory review common elements for an all-encompassing definition have been investigated.

The components and building blocks are pieced together to scope the IT landscape. RQ2 delves into an SLR to gain a better understanding of the drivers of complexity. Once the drivers are identified, existing metrics for their operationalisation have been distinguished via an exploratory literature review.

The motivation for the MRQ is to have a unified view of what an IT landscape means and how complexity can be quantified based on measuring its drivers. The quantification can support organisations in their process of managing the complexity of their IT landscape.

3.2 Literature Review Approach

To structure the research, a mixed-method literature review was performed according to the extensions proposed by Wolfswinkel et al. [50] to the works of Webster and Watson [46]. By combining both an exploratory literature review and a SLR, comprehensive answers can be shaped, alongside a foundation of existing knowledge and a holistic view of the investigated topics.

The scope of the review was to obtain answers to RQ1 and RQ2. By performing an exploratory literature review and a SLR, the questions can progressively become better answerable. The databases used for this research are IEEE Xplore, ACM Digital, Scopus and ISI Web of Science.

Exploratory Literature Execution. To answer RQ1, via an exploratory literature review, the following steps were carried out: the definition of the research question, the scoping of review and data sources, then the database search (based on the keywords from the question such as: "IT architecture elements") preceded by theme and concept identification and lastly the analysis and presentation of the findings. During the theme identification, Wolfswinkel et al.'s advice [50] of prioritising concepts rather than classifying individual articles and creating links between relevant ideas was used. This structure was created by the researcher, as an exploratory literature review does not require one. 6 papers were analysed for the RQ1 out of a pool of 20 selected works.

SLR Execution. Moving to the SLR executed for answering RQ2, the process behind this type of review can be explained according to the five stages[1] proposed by Webster and Watson [46].

In the define phase, the scope of the review is to gather answers to RQ2 by performing searches on the four academic repositories mentioned previously. In this stage, inclusion and exclusion criteria are defined. These aid in increasing the number of adequate results for valuable insights. Furthermore, the number of citations and the peer-review status of articles guided the search. Table 1 showcases the criteria for RQ2.

Table 1. Inclusion and Exclusion Criteria

Inclusion	Based on relevance
	Language - English
	Title, abstract and keywords – Include the term complexity or its derivates
	Thematic relevance – Fall under research areas concerned with information systems, enterprise architecture or computer science
Exclusion	Articles from medicine, social sciences, business management, mathematics natural sciences, education
	Articles discussing IT projects, government, management, supply chain, industry-specific concerns or software design

Next, the search phase is concerned with performing the search on the four above-mentioned repositories. Different queries, as seen in Table 2 were initially created and through episodic searches, they were altered such that sufficient and relevant outcomes could emerge. Wolfswinkel et al. mention that for the sake of transparency, it is important that the search terms, queries, and sources are documented [50].

In the selection phase, the doubles were filtered, the samples were refined based on the abstract and the title, and the full text was considered. Furthermore, forward and backward searching was performed. For RQ2, 417 papers were

[1] For more information the researchers can share additional documentation of the SLR process.

Table 2. Search Queries

Main Search Queries	Scopus	General	(TITLE-ABS-KEY (("IT" OR "IT architecture" OR "IT landscape" OR "Application architecture" OR "Application landscape" OR "Enterprise architecture" OR "Enterprise landscape" OR "Information systems architecture") AND ("complexity" OR "Complexity driver" OR "driver* of complexity" OR "Complexity origin" OR "origin* of complexity" OR "Complexity factor" OR "factor* of complexity" OR "Complexity source" OR "source* of complexity" OR "Complexity cause" OR "cause* of complexity" OR "Complexity root cause" OR "Complexity influence" OR "influence* of complexity")) AND TITLE (complex*) AND KEY (it OR "information system architecture"))
	IEEE Xplore	Title	Complexit*
		Abstract	IT OR IT architecture OR IT landscape OR Application architecture OR Application landscape OR Enterprise architecture OR Enterprise landscape OR Information systems architecture
			Complexity driver OR driver* of complexity OR Complexity origin OR origin* of complexity OR Complexity factor OR factor* of complexity OR Complexity source OR source* of complexity OR Complexity cause OR cause* of complexity OR Complexity root cause OR Complexity influence OR influence* of complexity
	ACM Digital	General	("IT" OR "IT architecture" OR "IT landscape" OR "Application architecture" OR "Application landscape" OR "Enterprise architecture" OR "Enterprise landscape" OR "Information systems architecture") AND ("complexity" OR "Complexity driver" OR "driver* of complexity" OR "Complexity origin" OR "origin* of complexity" OR "Complexity factor" OR "factor* of complexity" OR "Complexity source" OR "source* of complexity" OR "Complexity cause" OR "cause* of complexity" OR "Complexity root cause" OR "Complexity influence" OR "influence* of complexity") AND TITLE (complex*)
	ISI Web of Science	Title	IT OR IT architecture OR IT landscape OR Application architecture OR Application landscape OR Enterprise architecture OR Enterprise landscape OR Information systems architecture
			Complexity driver OR driver* of complexity OR Complexity origin OR origin* of complexity OR Complexity factor OR factor* of complexity OR Complexity source OR source* of complexity OR Complexity cause OR cause* of complexity OR Complexity root cause OR Complexity influence OR influence* of complexity

the result of the aggregated searches from the four repositories, however only 17 of them were chosen for further analysis. The PRISMA flowchart [32] helped in structuring this selection (as seen in Fig. 1). All the academic articles underwent this process of open coding. Axial coding followed next, as relationships between the concepts were discovered and finally, selective coding to integrate and refine the categories. The key concepts were categorised using concept matrices[2], as explained in [50].

The last step is the presentation of the findings from the prevalent works alongside the created relationships between concepts and insights. These are described in Sect. 4.

4 Analysis of Research Results

Sect. 4 details the insights gathered from the mixed-method literature review. First, the concept of IT landscape is addressed, thereby facilitating an understanding of its constituent elements. Subsequently, the drivers of complexity in such a landscape are showcased.

4.1 IT Landscape

Components. To be able to manage a complex environment, it is crucial to observe which elements or components are part of this high-level design space,

[2] These matrices can be shared upon request.

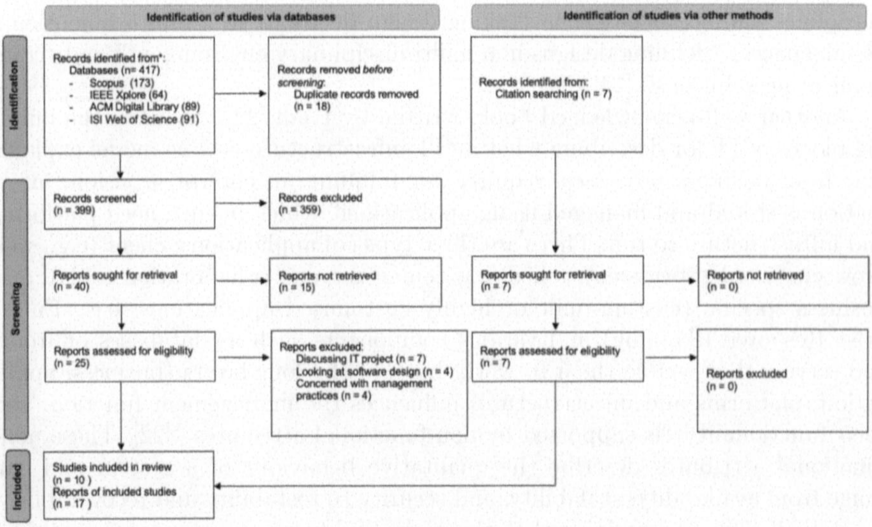

Fig. 1. PRISMA - Literature Review on Complexity Drivers

or the IT landscape. Firstly, a landscape can be represented with a three-dimensional coordinate system showing architectural relationships between chosen domains such as business functions, application components and products [36,44].

The IT landscape is commonly associated with "A set of hardware, software and facility elements, arranged in a specific configuration, which serves as a fabric to support the business operation of an enterprise" [26]. Throughout the years, the term evolved and started being used interchangeably with others such as information systems or technical architecture and nowadays a standard definition of its composing elements is absent [14,22,33]. Several well-acknowledged works mentioning IT landscape components have been analysed and are presented below.

In 1987, Zachman [51], proposed the first framework for IS architecture which described IT landscape components. Nowadays, it represents one of the best-known architectural frameworks. Zachman started by looking at the traditional architecture components to build the basis of the IS architecture. Initially, the scope of the framework focused on data (what something is made of), functions/processes (how something is working) and networks (where something is located) and what those meant to different stakeholders. As the years passed, it expanded to include people, time, and motivation.

Rohloff [34] offers a differentiation between the IT landscape and the IS architecture. As opposed to IS architecture which focuses on a single system, the IT landscape is concerned with the design on a larger scale. To support this larger-scale perspective, one can consider the work of Hammer [14]. He describes IT architecture as a common high-level model or design that supports various disciplines and stakeholders in "taking design decisions in a multi-dimensional design space", "defining designs in a multi-disciplinary environment" and "communicating solutions" [14].

Another well-acknowledged book, written by Laan [22], discusses the building blocks of IT for describing what an IT infrastructure is. The model explains how from business processes, required for fulfilling an enterprise vision, information is stored and managed using applications, which in turn need platforms and infrastructure to run. There are three types of applications: client (e.g., web browsers, word processors), office (e.g., email servers, collaboration tools), and business specific (custom-built or highly customised applications, e.g., Enterprise Resource Planning) and various components such as databases or front-end servers that enable them to work. Each of the four layers (business, application, platforms and infrastructure) influences the management function, and their functionality "is supported by non-functional attributes" [22]. These non-functional attributes describe the qualitative behaviour of a system and can range from availability, scalability, and security to testability and recoverability.

Rohloff [34] also explains that the main IT blueprints, the ones creating a basis for a landscape, are the application landscape (showing how each business process is supported by applications), the data repository (deployment of databases and how they support information clusters), and the service landscape (infrastructure services). These blueprints follow the same division as what Laan [22] described: processes, applications, services, and infrastructure.

From the broad perspective introduced by Zachman [51] and the building blocks of IT discussed by Laan [22], a shift towards more tangible elements of the IT landscape must be in place. Bruckmann [6] mentions that an IT landscape is composed of various IT objects, or artifacts, which can be "hardware platforms, database products, operating systems, application servers, development tools, programming languages [etc.]". In this case, an application uses IT objects. Furthermore, he proposes a conceptual model to illustrate the breakdown of an IT object.

Building upon the proposed conceptual model introduced in [6], the attention can move to Hammer [14] which describes the dimensions of IT architecture. For complex landscapes, alongside components, such as an IT artifact, it is important to consider the behaviour of the system and its interactions. The design space of an IT architecture is composed of "functional and non-functional dimensions" [14]. The functional dimension is concerned with the high-level structure of an architecture, thus, the components, their specifications, interfaces, and restrictions. Moreover, for the functional perspective, behaviour, or dynamic structure, must be analysed. Behavior is touching upon, concurrent activities, interaction sequences or protocols between components. The non-functional dimension must investigate performance (e.g., response time, throughput), dependability (e.g., reliability, availability, security, and robustness) and general aspects (such as desirable future). This dimension is composed of requirements which were also perceived as important by Laan [22], as previously discussed.

Key Takeaways. To combine the perspectives discussed and understand what an IT landscape is comprised of, Fig. 2 is proposed by the researchers. According to the model, an IT landscape refers to the overarching structure, combination and configuration of applications (which can use several IT objects) and their relationships to support the business processes for delivering value to the customer.

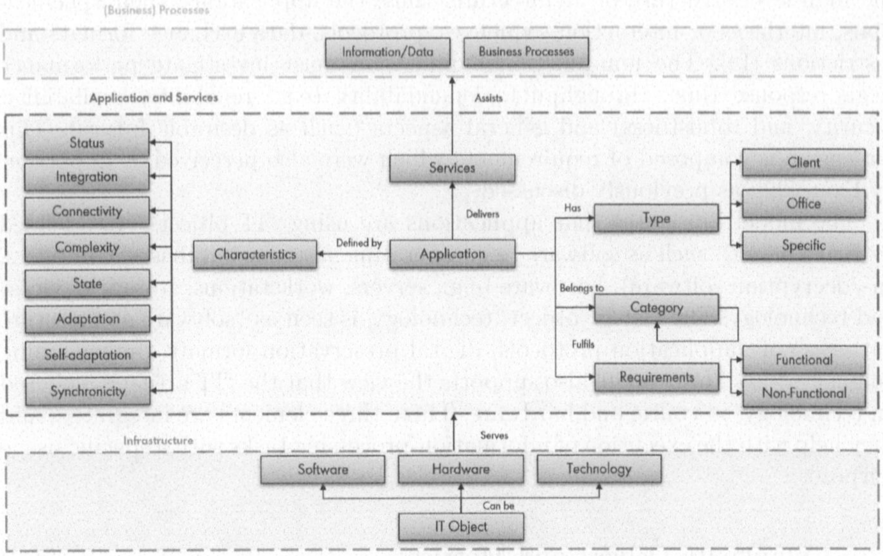

Fig. 2. Conceptual Model of IT Landscape Components

The model is comprised of three layers, similar to the core model of ArchiMate [12]. These are the business processes, applications and services, and the infrastructure layer.

The IT landscape is composed of a myriad of applications that support the business operations of an enterprise. The business has to complete certain processes, created based on information or data entities, that need to be supported by IT. Hence, from the business requirements, applications are selected and used by an organisation. These realise services that assist the business in delivering value to customers.

The applications can be combined and configured in various ways, and each of them has certain characteristics. According to Matook [29], there are seven different characteristics of an application: integration, connectivity, complexity, state, adaptation, self-adaptation, and synchronicity. Furthermore, each application has a status or a lifecycle phase, as mentioned by Bruckmann et al. [6]. For example, an application can be in one of the following phases "proposed, test, productive, standard, and retired" [6].

Next, applications can have a type. For example, Laan [22] distinguished three types of applications: client (e.g., web browsers, word processors), office (e.g., email servers, collaboration tools), and business-specific (custom-built or highly customised applications, e.g., Enterprise Resource Planning). These applications can also belong to a category.

Moreover, the applications in an IT landscape fulfill certain functional or non-functional requirements [14]. The functional dimension is concerned with the high-level structure of architecture, thus, the applications, their specifications, interfaces or interaction sequences, protocols, data exchange formats and restrictions [14]. The non-functional dimension must investigate performance (e.g., response time, throughput), dependability (e.g., reliability, availability, security, and robustness) and general aspects (such as desirable future). This dimension is composed of requirements which were also perceived as important by Laan [22], as previously discussed.

The model illustrates that applications are using "IT objects" (as defined by Bruckmann), such as software (e.g., operating systems, databases, compilers, en-/decryption software), hardware (e.g., servers, workstations, storage devices) and technology. The last IT object, technology, is seen as "software architecture patterns" or "application protocols, digital preservation formats, programming languages" [6]. Matook [29] also supports the view that the "IT artifact" is based on technology, software, and hardware. These three elements are integrated, and they help with the execution of information-processing tasks with a specific usage purpose.

4.2 Complexity Drivers and Metrics

Drivers. The SLR on complexity drivers and metrics leads to numerous insights. The drivers are manifold for an IT landscape and range from well-acknowledged and debated ones such as the number and heterogeneity of applications and their relationships to less researched drivers, such as unnecessary variability [48], lack of knowledge or EA debt [13,28]. A high-level overview of these is introduced next.

Beese et al. [4] suggested five drivers for IT architectural complexity: size, diversity, integration, planning, and dynamics. Schüetz [40] classifies the origin of IT complexity into the following categories: the number and heterogeneity of component and their relationships, the rate of change, and the application to different IT architecture domains (function, data, technology, and interfaces). Similarly to Beese et al. and Schüetz, papers [49] and [39], find the number of applications, heterogeneity, standards or functional scope as causes for IT landscape complexity.

Another aspect that seems to cause complexity is the systems integration, as described by Jain et al. [20] in an eighteen-criteria framework. This includes discussions on interface openness or abstraction of system architecture, that impact the integration complexity. For a more specific origin of complexity that negatively impacts costs, architecture dependability, maintenance, and evolving systems, Wehling's work on unnecessary variability (components supporting the same business process) [47,48] can be analysed.

For large-scale complex IT systems, Sommerville et al. [41] introduce two origins of complexity: trust relationships of components in a system and lack of knowledge about the system (from a human perspective). Mocker [30] also investigates the origins of complexity for application architecture for large-scale IT systems. He discovers that interdependence (interconnectedness), redundancy (supporting the same process), the number of different applications, as well as their age impact cost (e.g., maintenance and operation), agility, and the overall IT complexity. Furthermore, the complexity of the business requirement that an application is helping with can generate overall complexity.

Lentz and Bleizeffer [24] support the above-mentioned points, but they also discuss the impact of unintelligent design as a cause of IT complexity. Frequent application updates and fixes for a faster turnaround are high priorities in larger enterprises, such that everything can operate accordingly. These considerations can lead to architectural technical debt. Quick fixes in one area of the enterprise can mean accepting compromises in other areas, generating a higher complexity, or cost to restore the state of the system in the future [13].

Technical debt describes the delayed technical development activities for getting short-term payoffs or timely release of specific software [52]. Atchison [3] describes how technical debt and complexity go hand in hand and concludes that "Technical debt is the core of IT complexity".

Architectural debt resides under the umbrella of technical debt [28]. Martini [27,28] illustrates possible causes leading to architectural technical debt, for example, business factors, the use of third-party/open-source systems that were not initially part of the architecture, parallel development, non-completed refactoring (e.g., using a new application programming interface, however, the previous one cannot be removed because of backwards compatibility) or the human factor (e.g., differences in knowledge, ignorance, error-prone situations).

As technical and architectural technical debt are both specific to the software domain, Hacks [13,43] coined the term EA Debt to create the link between business and IT. It is defined as "the deviation of the current present state of an enterprise from a hypothetical ideal state" [13]. This can mean elements not optimally implemented, the use of bad interfaces, interoperability issues or different priorities of stakeholders. To understand the taxonomy of EA debt the work of Daoudi et al. [8] serves as a reference point.

Metrics. Upon understanding the potential drivers influencing the IT landscape, it is also important to identify which metrics can quantify them. The most important work addressing this was performed by Iacob et al. [18]. Through a SLR an inventory of complexity metrics was created. This SLR was enhanced with the help of 12 semi-structured interviews with experts from different organisations. Based on the combined results, 42 metrics for quantifying EA complexity were identified. Some of these are counting the number of relations or the number of elements in an architecture, using cyclomatic complexity, conformity, or redundancy.

Beyond these 42 metrics, one recent development in the literature, focusing more on dynamic complexity is introduced by Daoudi [9]. This is called the Adaptive EA, an approach for proactive sensing and responding to change and for managing trade-offs. In moving from as-is to to-be scenarios, the EA Degree of Dynamic Complexity (DDC) is proposed. Furthermore, paper [9] lists existing types of calculation for some complexity metrics, such as an interdependence matrix (for measuring layer interdependency Business-Application-Technology), entropy (for heterogeneity) or a context awareness capability matrix (for subjective complexity). Another important complexity measurement that can be used to choose between EA alternatives is proposed by Rojas [10]. He mentions that complexity metrics at the implementation stage identify elements that can either reduce or increase complexity, for example, a high cohesion between elements, respectively a high coupling between elements. For the design phase, to re-estimate project effort and understand the complexity of EAs, Rojas proposes the Structural Complexity Measure (SCM).

Key Takeaways. To summarise the discussed research streams, Fig. 3 has been created by the researchers. The complexity drivers and potential metrics for their quantification are proposed. The left-hand side column represents the categories of drivers, followed by potential examples of drivers for IT landscape complexity. The right-hand side column depicts possible metrics to quantify these.

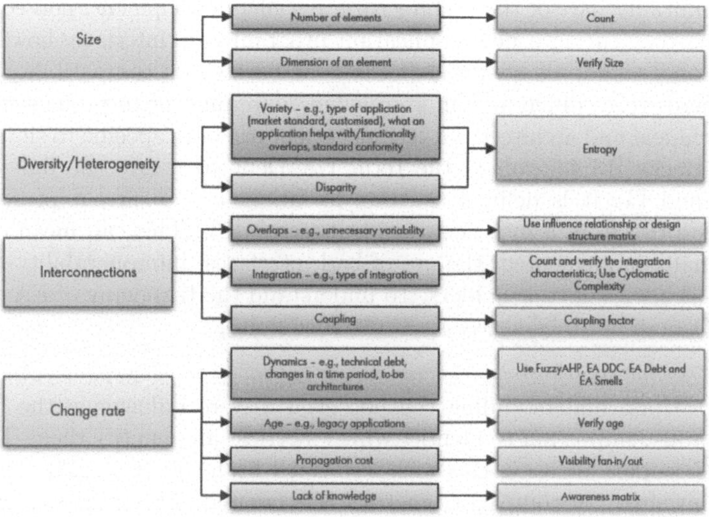

Fig. 3. Drivers and Metrics of IT Landscape Complexity

5 Discussion

This research introduces a conceptual model which unifies different views on what IT landscape components are. This model has been designed to support architects in aligning their views when modeling and communicating about IT landscapes. An important aspect brought forward with the help of the model is the emphasis on the characteristics of applications. Hence, this model can serve as a reference for the elements part of an IT landscape.

Organisations face challenges in managing and measuring the IT landscape complexity. With a defined and aligned view of what constitutes this landscape, as presented in Fig. 2, an understanding of the root causes of complexity can start to form. The research also provides a model of drivers and metrics for IT landscape complexity, in Fig. 3. IT architects can apply these to quantify landscape complexity for architectures aligned with the conceptual model.

By analysing EA designs of IT landscapes, architects can quantify complexity drivers using metrics. For example, in a model depicting applications, services, data, and interfaces, architects can count the number of services realised by an application, check the types of interfaces between the applications or observe the data usage and exchange. It is envisioned that this approach allows the aggregation of these metrics into an overall complexity metric for the IT landscape.

One use case for the approach can be the following: an architect comparing various future options for the current landscape, e.g., different target architectures, and making a choice based on the score of complexity. A certain viewpoint depicted by an architect will be assigned a complexity score. Here, one can observe if a higher level of complexity is linked with certain architectural patterns or changes. A possible way to calculate complexity for this specific use case (comparing as-is and to-be architectures) is shown in Eq. 1, as introduced by Daoudi [9]. Complexity should be seen here as the state changes of the landscape over time.

Considering that adaptation is essential in highly competitive and dynamic business environments, the equation proposed by Daoudi et al. targets proactive sensing and responding to change. In moving from the baseline to the target scenarios, the EA Degree of Dynamic Complexity (DDC) computes the complexity degree of the changes, where i is the indicator of the EA version (i is the current architecture, $i+1$ is a possible target architecture), the first element of the sum is concerned with the values of dynamic factors (changing in time), whereas the second one is related to static factors. N represents the number of factors selected for the analysis.

$$\text{DDC } i, i+1(t) = \sum_{j=1}^{n} \frac{fj(t) + fj}{n}, \text{ where } n \in N \tag{1}$$

Based on the performed work, some further research should be considered as it will bring benefits to both academia and practice. First, the models proposed have to be fully validated in organisations with a high complexity level, e.g., more than 1.000 (preferably integrated) applications in the IT landscape. In such a landscape, one can observe if there are any elements of an IT landscape which are not included in the model. Moreover, drivers of complexity can emerge which might not be discussed in detail in the literature.

One of the researchers is working on creating an aggregated metric for the complexity of an IT landscape, piecing together insights from academia and from a case study. As the metric is being developed, the connection between the IT landscape components and the drivers and metrics influencing complexity needs to be exploited.

6 Conclusion

Starting by creating a conceptual model of the most commonly discussed elements which form the core of the IT landscape and going into more detail on which drivers and metrics could be used for the quantification of complexity, this paper synthesised prevalent related works for supporting architects in managing complexity.

A conceptual model of IT landscape components is proposed based on a mixed-method literature review. The main contribution of this paper is therefore the provision of a standardised description of the IT landscape. Furthermore, the research identifies complexity drivers and metrics and proposes a method for measuring IT landscape complexity. This method's overarching goal is to quantify IT landscape complexity.

This approach establishes a foundation for the management of IT landscape complexity, for both academics and practitioners. A standard terminology for the IT landscape, or a common language, is essential for mastering complexity. Furthermore, by using identified complexity drivers and metrics, enterprises can prioritise and combine these to indicate their respective complexity levels. With such an aggregation, the lack of measurements for complexity can be tackled, as an organisation can find ways in which they can quantify the metrics based on their existing resources. Hence, the model and metrics overview assist enterprises in mastering complexity.

The model and an initial measurement method are under a formal validation with IT experts and the preliminary results show a satisfactory level to address the goal of this research. However, further validation is needed through a set of scenarios within organisations characterised by IT landscape complexity. Each scenario should include a baseline architecture along with potential target architectures that can be inputted into the measurement method, and, preferably, the result of the complexity calculations should be well explained to the IT experts.

As one of the core future avenues of research, improving the semantic expressiveness of the conceptual model can bring additional value to the overall framework. Therefore, making an ontological analysis of this conceptual model based on a foundational ontology might result in such expressiveness gain. In particular, a proposal is made to use existing well-founded ontologies that target system modelling, such as [7], to address this open issue.

References

1. Adomavicius, G., Bockstedt, J.C., Gupta, A., Kauffman, R.J.: Making sense of technology trends in the information technology landscape: a design science approach. MIS Q. **32**, 779–809 (2008). https://api.semanticscholar.org/CorpusID:10592597
2. Arnold, R.D., Wade, J.P.: A definition of systems thinking: a systems approach. Procedia Comput. Sci. **44**, 669–678 (2015). https://doi.org/10.1016/j.procs.2015.03.050, https://linkinghub.elsevier.com/retrieve/pii/S1877050915002860
3. Atchison, L.: Overcoming IT Complexity: Simplify Operations, Enable Innovation, and Cultivate Successful Cloud Outcomes. O'Reilly, Cambridge (2023). oCLC: on1351696495
4. Beese, J., Aier, S., Haki, K., Khosroshahi, P.A.: Drivers and effects of information systems architecture complexity: a mixed-methods study. Res. Pap. (2016). https://aisel.aisnet.org/ecis2016_rp/74
5. Beetz, K., Kolbe, L.: Towards managing IT complexity: an IT governance framework to measure business-IT responsibility sharing and structural IT organization. In: 17th Americas Conference on Information Systems 2011, AMCIS 2011, vol. 1 (2011)
6. Brückmann, M., Schöne, K.M., Junginger, S., Boudinova, D.: Evaluating enterprise architecture management initiatives - how to measure and control the degree of standardization of an IT landscape (2009)
7. Calhau, R.F., et al.: A system core ontology for capability emergence modeling. In: Proper, H.A., Pufahl, L., Karastoyanova, D., Van Sinderen, M., Moreira, J. (eds.) EDOC 2023. LNCS, vol. 14367, pp. 3–20. Springer, Cham (2024). https://doi.org/10.1007/978-3-031-46587-1_1
8. Daoudi, S., Larsson, M., Hacks, S., Jung, J.: Discovering and assessing enterprise architecture debts. Complex Syst. Inform. Model. Q. (35), 1–29 (2023). https://doi.org/10.7250/csimq.2023-35.01, https://csimq-journals.rtu.lv/article/view/csimq.2023-35.01
9. Daoudi, W., Doumi, K., Kjiri, L.: Adaptive enterprise architecture: complexity metrics in a mixed evaluation method. In: Filipe, J., Śmiałek, M., Brodsky, A., Hammoudi, S. (eds.) ICEIS 2021. LNBIP, vol. 455, pp. 505–523. Springer, Cham (2022). https://doi.org/10.1007/978-3-031-08965-7_26
10. González-Rojas, O., López, A., Correal, D.: Multilevel complexity measurement in enterprise architecture models. Int. J. Comput. Integr. Manuf. **30**(12), 1280–1300 (2017). https://doi.org/10.1080/0951192X.2017.1307453, https://www.tandfonline.com/doi/full/10.1080/0951192X.2017.1307453
11. Group, T.O.: TOGAF® Standard. https://pubs.opengroup.org/togaf-standard/adm/chap01.html
12. Group, T.O.: ArchiMate® 3.1 Specification (2019). https://pubs.opengroup.org/architecture/archimate31-doc/toc.html
13. Hacks, S., Hofert, H., Salentin, J., Yeong, Y.C., Lichter, H.: Towards the definition of enterprise architecture debts. In: 2019 IEEE 23rd International Enterprise Distributed Object Computing Workshop (EDOCW), pp. 9–16. IEEE, Paris (2019). https://doi.org/10.1109/EDOCW.2019.00016, https://ieeexplore.ieee.org/document/8907262/
14. Hammer, D.: The many aspects of an IT-architecture. In: Proceedings International Conference and Workshop on Engineering of Computer-Based Systems. pp. 304–311. IEEE Computer. Soc. Press, Monterey, CA, USA (1997). https://doi.org/10.1109/ECBS.1997.581891, http://ieeexplore.ieee.org/document/581891/

15. Hanschke, I.: IT Landscape Management. In: Hanschke, I. (ed.) Strategic IT Management: A Toolkit for Enterprise Architecture Management, pp. 105–217. Springer, Heidelberg (2010). https://doi.org/10.1007/978-3-642-05034-3_4
16. Holub, I.: Methodology for measuring the complexity of enterprise information systems. J. Syst. Integr. **7**, 34–53 (2016). https://doi.org/10.20470/jsi.v7i3.260
17. Iacob, M., Jonkers, H., Quartel, D., Franken, H., van den Berg, H.: Delivering enterprise architecture with TOGAF and ArchiMate. Enschede BiZZdesign 2012 (2012). oCLC: 1073562791
18. Iacob, M.E., Monteban, J., Van Sinderen, M., Hegeman, E., Bitaraf, K.: Measuring enterprise architecture complexity. In: 2018 IEEE 22nd International Enterprise Distributed Object Computing Workshop (EDOCW), pp. 115–124. IEEE, Stockholm (2018). https://doi.org/10.1109/EDOCW.2018.00026, https://ieeexplore.ieee.org/document/8536112/
19. ISO: ISO/IEC/IEEE 42010:2022 (2022). https://www.iso.org/standard/74393.html
20. Jain, R., Chandrasekaran, A., Elias, G., Cloutier, R.: Exploring the impact of systems architecture and systems requirements on systems integration complexity. IEEE Syst. J. **2**(2), 209–223 (2008). https://doi.org/10.1109/JSYST.2008.924130, http://ieeexplore.ieee.org/document/4539770/
21. Kruchten, P., Nord, R.L., Ozkaya, I.: Technical debt: from metaphor to theory and practice. IEEE Softw. **29**(6), 18–21 (2012). https://doi.org/10.1109/MS.2012.167
22. Laan, S.: IT Infrastructure Architecture - Infrastructure Building Blocks and Concepts, 2nd edn. Lulu.com (2013)
23. Lankhorst, M.: Enterprise Architecture at Work. The Enterprise Engineering Series. Springer, Heidelberg (2013). https://doi.org/10.1007/978-3-642-29651-2
24. Lentz, J.L., Bleizeffer, T.M.: IT ecosystems: evolved complexity and unintelligent design. In: Proceedings of the 2007 symposium on Computer human interaction for the management of information technology, p. 6. ACM, Cambridge (2007). https://doi.org/10.1145/1234772.1234780, https://dl.acm.org/doi/10.1145/1234772.1234780
25. Manzur, L., Ulloa, J.M., Sánchez, M., Villalobos, J.: xArchiMate: enterprise architecture simulation, experimentation and analysis. SIMULATION **91**(3), 276–301 (2015). https://doi.org/10.1177/0037549715575188, http://journals.sagepub.com/doi/10.1177/0037549715575188
26. Marshall, A., Winkler, U., Gilani, W.: Business continuity management of business driven IT landscapes (2011). https://api.semanticscholar.org/CorpusID:168205316
27. Martini, A., Bosch, J.: The danger of architectural technical debt: contagious debt and vicious circles. In: 2015 12th Working IEEE/IFIP Conference on Software Architecture, pp. 1–10. IEEE, Montreal (2015). https://doi.org/10.1109/WICSA.2015.31, http://ieeexplore.ieee.org/document/7158498/
28. Martini, A., Bosch, J., Chaudron, M.: Architecture technical debt: understanding causes and a qualitative model. In: 2014 40th EUROMICRO Conference on Software Engineering and Advanced Applications, pp. 85–92. IEEE, Verona (2014). https://doi.org/10.1109/SEAA.2014.65, http://ieeexplore.ieee.org/document/6928795/
29. Matook, S., Brown, S.A.: Characteristics of IT artifacts: a systems thinking-based framework for delineating and theorizing IT artifacts. Inf. Syst. J. **27**(3), 309–346 (2017). https://doi.org/10.1111/isj.12108, https://onlinelibrary.wiley.com/doi/10.1111/isj.12108

30. Mocker, M.: What is complex about 273 applications? Untangling application architecture complexity in a case of European investment banking. In: 2009 42nd Hawaii International Conference on System Sciences, pp. 1–14 (2009). https://doi.org/10.1109/HICSS.2009.506, https://ieeexplore.ieee.org/document/4755701. iSSN 1530-1605
31. Onderdelinden, E., Hooff, B.V.D., Vliet, M.V.: IS architecture complexity dynamics in M&A: does consolidation reduce complexity? In: ECIS 2023 Research Papers (2023). https://aisel.aisnet.org/ecis2023_rp/377
32. Page, M.J., et al.: The PRISMA 2020 statement: an updated guideline for reporting systematic reviews. PLOS Med. **18**(3), e1003583 (2021). https://doi.org/10.1371/journal.pmed.1003583, https://dx.plos.org/10.1371/journal.pmed.1003583
33. Perks, C., Beveridge, T. (eds.): Guide to Enterprise IT Architecture. Springer Professional Computing. Springer, New York (2004). https://doi.org/10.1007/b98880, http://link.springer.com/10.1007/b98880
34. Rohloff, M.: Business oriented development of the IT landscape: architecture design on a large scale. In: Managing Worldwide Operations and Communications with Information Technology (2007)
35. Ross, J., Beath, C., Mocker, M.: Creating digital offerings customers will buy: find the sweet spot between what technologies can deliver and what your customers need (2019)
36. Sanden, W.V.D., Sturm, B.: Informatie-architectuur: de infrastructurele benadering. Panfox, Rosmalen, 2e [herz.] dr. edn. (2000). oCLC: 67354153
37. Schmidt, C.: Business architecture quantified: how to measure business complexity. In: Simon, D., Schmidt, C. (eds.) Business Architecture Management. MP, pp. 243–268. Springer, Cham (2015). https://doi.org/10.1007/978-3-319-14571-6_13
38. Schneider, A., Zec, M., Matthes, F.: Adopting notions of complexity for enterprise architecture management. In: 20th Americas Conference on Information Systems, AMCIS 2014 (2014)
39. Schneider, A.W., Reschenhofer, T., Schutz, A., Matthes, F.: Empirical results for application landscape complexity. In: 2015 48th Hawaii International Conference on System Sciences, pp. 4079–4088. IEEE, HI (2015). https://doi.org/10.1109/HICSS.2015.490, http://ieeexplore.ieee.org/document/7070309/
40. Schuetz, A., Widjaja, T., Gregory, R.: Escape from Winchester Mansion - toward a set of design principles to master complexity in IT architectures. In: International Conference on Information Systems (ICIS 2013): Reshaping Society Through Information Systems Design, vol. 2 (2013)
41. Sommerville, I., et al.: Large-scale complex IT systems. Commun. ACM **55**(7), 71–77 (2012). https://doi.org/10.1145/2209249.2209268, https://dl.acm.org/doi/10.1145/2209249.2209268
42. Storey, V.C., Kaul, M., Woo, C.: A framework for managing complexity in information systems. J. Database Manage. **28**(1), 31–42 (2017). https://doi.org/10.4018/JDM.2017010103
43. Tieu, B., Hacks, S.: Determining enterprise architecture smells from software architecture smells. In: 2021 IEEE 23rd Conference on Business Informatics (CBI), pp. 134–142. IEEE, Bolzano (2021). https://doi.org/10.1109/CBI52690.2021.10064, https://ieeexplore.ieee.org/document/9610644/
44. van der Torre, L., Lankhorst, M.M., ter Doest, H., Campschroer, J.T.P., Arbab, F.: Landscape maps for enterprise architectures. In: Dubois, E., Pohl, K. (eds.) CAiSE 2006. LNCS, vol. 4001, pp. 351–366. Springer, Heidelberg (2006). https://doi.org/10.1007/11767138_24

45. Verdecchia, R., Kruchten, P., Lago, P., Malavolta, I.: Building and evaluating a theory of architectural technical debt in software-intensive systems. J. Syst. Softw. **176**, 110925 (2021). https://doi.org/10.1016/j.jss.2021.110925, https://www.sciencedirect.com/science/article/pii/S0164121221000224
46. Webster, J., Watson, R.T.: Analyzing the past to prepare for the future: writing a literature review. MIS Q. **26**(2), xiii–xxiii (2002). https://www.jstor.org/stable/4132319
47. Wehling, K., Schaefer, I.: Towards an expert system for identifying and reducing unnecessary complexity of IT architectures (2017). https://doi.org/10.18420/IN2017_152, https://dl.gi.de/handle/20.500.12116/3917
48. Wehling, K., Wille, D., Seidl, C., Schaefer, I.: Decision support for reducing unnecessary IT complexity of application architectures. In: 2017 IEEE International Conference on Software Architecture Workshops (ICSAW), pp. 161–168 (2017). https://doi.org/10.1109/ICSAW.2017.47
49. Widjaja, T., Gregory, R.: Monitoring the complexity of IT architectures: design principles and an IT Artifact. J. Assoc. Inf. Syst. **21**(3), 664–694 (2020). https://doi.org/10.17705/1jais.00616, https://aisel.aisnet.org/jais/vol21/iss3/4/
50. Wolfswinkel, J.F., Furtmueller, E., Wilderom, C.P.M.: Using grounded theory as a method for rigorously reviewing literature. Eur. J. Inf. Syst. **22**(1), 45–55 (2013). https://doi.org/10.1057/ejis.2011.51, https://www.tandfonline.com/doi/full/10.1057/ejis.2011.51
51. Zachman, J.A.: A framework for information systems architecture. IBM Syst. J. **26**(3), 276–292 (1987). https://doi.org/10.1147/sj.263.0276, http://ieeexplore.ieee.org/document/5387671/
52. Zazworka, N., Seaman, C., Shull, F.: Prioritizing design debt investment opportunities. In: Proceedings of the 2nd Workshop on Managing Technical Debt, pp. 39–42. ACM, Waikiki (2011). https://doi.org/10.1145/1985362.1985372, https://dl.acm.org/doi/10.1145/1985362.1985372

Modeling Methods, Data and Component

GNN-Based Conceptual Model Modularization: Approach and GA-Based Comparison

Syed Juned Ali[1(✉)], MohammadHadi Dehghani[2], Manuel Wimmer[2], and Dominik Bork[1]

[1] TU Wien, Business Informatics Group, Vienna, Austria
{syed.juned.ali,dominik.bork}@tuwien.ac.at

[2] Johannes Kepler University Linz, CDL-MINT, Linz, Austria
{mohammadhadi.dehghani,manuel.wimmer}@jku.at

Abstract. Due to the crucial role conceptual models play in explicitly representing a subject domain, it is imperative that they are comprehensible and maintainable by humans. Modularization, i.e., decomposing an overarching, monolith model into smaller modules, is an established technique to make the model comprehensible and maintainable. Genetic Algorithms (GA) have been applied to modularize conceptual models by formulating desired structural model characteristics as multiple objectives. Recently, Graph Neural Networks (GNN)-based methods have shown promising performance in graph processing tasks, including graph clustering but outside the conceptual modeling domain. In this paper, we present a novel approach for GNN-based conceptual model modularization and comparatively analyze our approach against an existing multi-objective GA-based one. Furthermore, we provide a comparative analysis of our novel GNN model against two existing GNN-based graph clustering approaches. We investigate the dependence of the quality of the modularized solutions on the model size. We discuss the comparative results of our novel GNN-based approach and the existing GA-based approach to derive future research lines. Furthermore, our results show, that our proposed GNN-based modularization outperforms the existing GNN-based graph clustering approaches and provides a suitable alternative compared to the GA-based modularization.

Keywords: Conceptual modeling · Model Modularization · Graph neural networks · Genetic algorithms · ER · Data modeling

1 Introduction

Conceptual modeling allows to understand complex domains and supports communication among stakeholders, and thus, is essential for enterprise and information systems engineering and beyond [30]. Due to their crucial role, comprehension of conceptual models is a prerequisite for value creation. For instance, Entity Relationship (ER) models are a prominent approach to develop and analyze abstractions as conceptual representation of data models used by humans.

J. Borbinha et al. (Eds.): EDOC 2024, LNCS 15409, pp. 239–258, 2025.
https://doi.org/10.1007/978-3-031-78338-8_13

By this, ER models abstract the technical details of database models and implementations, providing dedicated views of conceptual structures hidden in implementation-oriented data schemas [8].

It has been shown that the usefulness of conceptual models for humans is inversely proportional to the models' sizes [37]. Models having already more than 30 nodes are considered challenging for human comprehension. The more relationships, the less comprehension is given due to the accompanying increase in complexity [37]. Therefore, the increased size and complexity can make models *cognitively intractable* [12]. Clustering or modularizing conceptual models[1] into smaller chunks enables humans to communicate better, validate, and maintain very large models [37].

Existing modularization approaches mostly leverage the topological properties of conceptual models [12], i.e., characteristics that relate to the graph's structure and the arrangement of its elements (vertices and edges) such as degree, connectivity, cyclicity. In the past, Genetic Algorithms (GAs) have been used to transform the modularization of graphs into an optimization problem to partition a model into modules, such that the nodes within each module are closer related to each other than the nodes in the other clusters. These approaches allow exploring a solution space more efficiently than exhaustive search methods. They can be particularly useful when dealing with large and complex graphs where traditional clustering methods might struggle to find optimal or near-optimal solutions. GAs proved valuable for tasks such as community detection in social networks [4], protein function prediction in bioinformatics [35], and modular decomposition in software engineering [8].

Graph Neural Networks (GNN) are a variant of neural networks that can apply deep learning methods on graph-based inputs and train the deep learning model for a specific task. GNN-based solutions learn a vector-based representation, i.e., node embedding that is supposed to reflect the graph structural information captured by a given node in the context of the entire graph. While GNNs have been successfully applied, among many others, in applications such as medical diagnosis and electronic health records modeling [21], drug discovery and chemical compounds synthesis [40], recommender systems [39] and text classification [23], GNNs also showed promising results for unsupervised learning-based graph clustering [10,27,41,42]. Conceptual Model Modularization (CMM) can be transformed into a graph clustering task, however, GNNs have not yet been applied to modularize conceptual models. Therefore, in this paper, we present a novel GNN-based conceptual model modularization approach, a deep conceptual model modularizer (DCMM).

We provide a comparative evaluation with an existing GA-based approach to assess the quality of our GNN-based approach. For this, we extend the GA-based modularization approach ModuleER [8] initially developed for ER models for being able to modularize Ecore-based UML Class Diagrams (CD). We then evaluate the performance of our novel GNN-based approach on CDs and compare it with the extended ModuleER approach using *cohesion* and *coupling* as the

[1] We use clustering, partitioning, and modularization interchangeably in this paper.

modularization quality metrics. Furthermore, we also adapt the existing GNN-based graph clustering approaches Deep Graph Infomax (DGI) [41] and Deep Modularity Network (DMoN) [27] for the CMM task to provide a comparative analysis of the state-of-the-art GNN models with our DCMM GNN model.

The main contributions of this paper comprise: (*i*) DCMM: a novel GNN-based approach for CMM; (*ii*) the adaptation of existing GNN-based graph clustering approaches for CMM; (*iii*) a comparative evaluation of GNN-based approaches with GA-based ones for CMM; (*iv*) a comparative evaluation of several GNN-based graph clustering approaches for CMM; and, finally, (*v*) an analysis of the effect of model size on the different approaches. Note that in this paper we do not use the semantic aspects of conceptual models as graphs and focus on the structural aspects of the conceptual models as graphs.

The remainder of this paper is structured as follows. Section 2 provides background information to the different conceptual and technological aspects of our work. Section 3 presents the details of DCMM. Section 4 comprises the experimental setup for the comparative evaluation of GNN and GA-based modularization and the experimental results. In Sect. 5, we provide insights gained from our results. Section 6 discusses related work before we conclude this paper in Sect. 7 with an outlook to future work.

2 Background

We now introduce the relevant background for this work. In particular, we discuss the existing GA and GNN approaches as well as the metrics to be used for the comparative evaluation.

2.1 Conceptual Model Modularization

Modularization of conceptual models defined in a specific modeling language (e.g., ER, UML) aims to determine a suitable set of elements to form a module. The module elements depend on the intended purpose of modularization while fulfilling the definition of a module. For e.g., if the modularization aims to determine modules optimized to answer individual queries, then the generated modules should be composed of all elements necessary to answer a considered query [20]. Software clustering is a modularization technique for source code elements such as classes or functions. These elements are grouped into sets, so-called modules, in such a way that elements residing in the same module are more similar (to a given definition) to each other than to those in other modules [29].

2.2 Graph-Based Modularization

Graph-based modularization uses the structural aspects of a model for identifying module candidates [29]. It produces modules by interpreting a conceptual model as a graph and applying algorithms to extract related (or sufficiently related) concepts. Graph-based modularization approaches are often intuitive and employ statistical methods to determine similarities of concepts or clusters and require the model to have a graph-based representation (i.e., a set of vertices and edges) [20]. The model is generally represented as an *adjacency matrix* for graph-based clustering tasks. In this matrix, each element captures if an edge between the nodes denoted by the indices of the element exists. Each node can denote an entity of a model, and each edge can represent a dependency between the entities, e.g., the composition relationship.

2.3 Search-Based Modularization

Search techniques, such as Genetic Algorithms (GA), use one or more objective functions to guide the modularization process, i.e., search for the optimal solutions, i.e., the solutions that provide optimal scores using the objective functions [26]. These functions quantify the quality of a candidate solution. In case of CMM, objective functions evaluate the quality of the modules and the modularization achieved for a given set of modules during the process of search the optimal modules. Frequently, the objective functions' intuition is maximizing cohesion within and minimizing coupling across the modules [29]. ModuleER [8,14] uses a GA-based approach for the modularization of ER models. In [2], ModuleER is extended to support graph modularization of multiple different modeling languages using a Generic GA-based Modularization Framework.

2.4 Graph Neural Networks-Based Graph Representation Learning

The nodes of a graph and their structural properties can be represented in dense fixed-sized vectors [36]. Recently, there have been approaches that can learn node representations using the structural aspects of the graphs. Graph Neural Networks (GNNs) are neural models that learn graph representations via *message passing* between graph nodes by information aggregation of a node from its neighborhood [16]. The fundamental paradigm of these node embeddings is, that "similar" nodes have close embeddings. The similarity of nodes is often defined based on their distance in a graph, e.g., based on their co-occurrence probability in a random walk [15,16,42]. It is also argued that two nodes should be similar if they are similar to a graph summary representation [36]. *Node2vec* learns node embeddings by maximizing the likelihood of preserving network neighborhoods of nodes by exploring the network through graph traversal [15]. In recent years, variants of GNNs such as Graph Convolutional Networks (GCN) [17], GraphSage [17], and Graph Attention Networks (GAT) [36] have demonstrated good performance on deep learning tasks such as link prediction, node classification, graph classification, and graph mining [43]. Particularly GraphSage [17] learns a function that generates embeddings by sampling and aggregating features from a node's local neighborhood. This inductive approach enables the model to generalize to unseen nodes or entirely new graphs.

2.5 GNN-Based Modularization

The node embeddings from GNNs can be obtained as a result of optimizing a GNN model to minimize an objective function i.e., the loss function. The loss minimization of a GNN model can be used to steer the GNN toward optimization of graph modularization metrics like cohesion and coupling. Existing approaches i.e., DGI [41] and DMoN [27] use modularity [28] (see Eq. 1) as a modularization metric that approaches graph clustering from a statistical perspective.

$$Q = \frac{1}{2m} \sum_{i,j} \left(A_{ij} - \frac{k_i k_j}{2m} \right) \delta(c_i, c_j) \tag{1}$$

Modularity measures Q as the divergence between the intra-cluster edges from the expected one where m is the total edges, k_i and c_i denotes the degree and cluster of node i and δ function is defined as $\delta(c_i, c_j) = 1$ if nodes i and j are in the same cluster c, and 0 otherwise. Modularity remains one of the most commonly used graph clustering metrics in literature [13].

2.6 Modularization Quality Metrics

Once a modularized solution is available, its cohesion and coupling can be evaluated as given by Eq. 2 and Eq. 3, respectively.

$$cohesion = \frac{1}{c} \sum_{i}^{c} \frac{E_{C_i}}{N_{C_i} * (N_{C_i} - 1) * 0.5} \tag{2}$$

$$coupling = \sum_{C_i, C_j} E_{C_i, C_j} \tag{3}$$

In cohesion, c is the number of cluster, E_{C_i} denotes the number of edges in cluster C_i, and N_{C_i} is the number of nodes in C_i. In coupling, E_{C_i,C_j} denotes the number of edges between the cluster C_i and C_j.

3 Deep Conceptual Model Modularizer

We now describe our end-to-end unsupervised GNN-based conceptual model modularization approach which is applied to UML class diagrams. We sketch the major steps involved in GNN-based CMM in general in Fig. 1b and our node2vec-based structural embedding augmented GNN-based CMM in Fig. 1c and further contrast it with the Genetic Algorithms-based approach ModulER [8] adapted for UML class diagrams in Fig. 1a that we use for a comparative evaluation of our approach. Furthermore, we provide the details about the adaptations of the existing GNN-based graph clustering approaches for our usecase of CMM so as to evaluate the performance of DCMM with existing GNNs.

3.1 Model to Graph Transformation

In order for a UML class diagram (CD) to be modularized by graph-based algorithms, each CD undergoes a model to graph transformation in a preprocessing step. The resulting graph is used as an input to both approaches. We use the

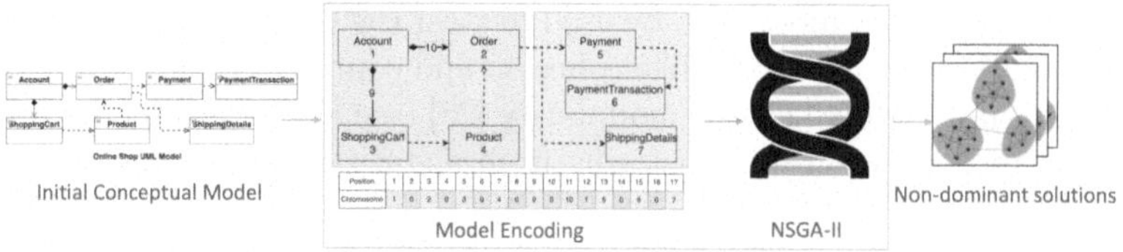

(a) Genetic Algorithms-based CMM [2]

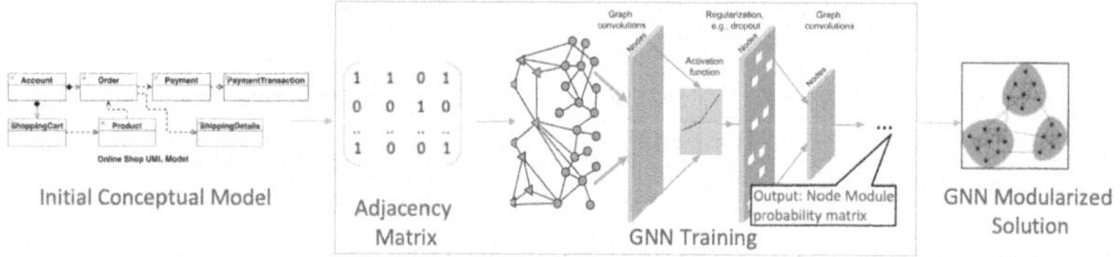

(b) General GNN-based CMM

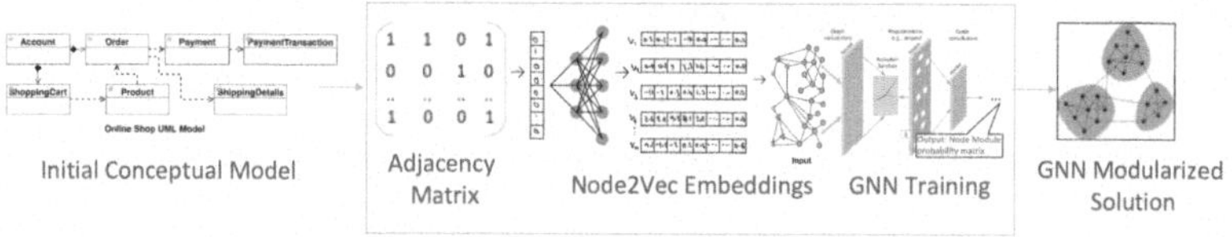

(c) Deep Conceptual Model Modularizer

Fig. 1. Conceptual Model Modularization Approaches

generic conceptual model to knowledge graph transformation methods introduced in [1,32], which transform models into directed graphs. Each class in the class diagram is considered as a node and each reference and an inheritance relation is treated as an edge in the resulting graph.

3.2 Deep Conceptual Model Modularization

Once we have generated the graph, we transform the graph into an *adjacency matrix* A (cf. Sect. 2) as shown in Fig. 1. Next, we generate node embeddings for each node in the graph using A. The embeddings-based representation of the nodes is generated by running the *node2vec* algorithm that captures the structural properties of nodes in a way that preserves their neighborhood relationships. Node2vec transforms each node into a dense fixed-sized vector X in R^{n*d} (see Eq. 4.1) where d is the dimension of the embedding.

$$X = \Phi(A) \quad \text{where} \quad \Phi = \text{node2vec} \quad \text{and} \quad X \in \mathbb{R}^{n \times d} \tag{4.1}$$

$$H^{(0)} = X$$

$$H^{(l)} = \text{ReLU}\left(\sum_{j \in \mathcal{N}(i)} \frac{1}{|\mathcal{N}(i)|} W^{(l)} H_j^{(l-1)}\right) \quad \text{for} \quad l = 1, \ldots, L \tag{4.2}$$

where $\mathcal{N}(i)$ is the set of neighbors of node i

$$Y = \text{softmax}\left(\Omega(X, A)\right) \quad \text{where} \quad \Omega = H^{(L)} \quad \text{and} \quad Y \in \mathbb{R}^{n \times C} \tag{4.3}$$

$$\text{Cohesion} = \sum_{c=1}^{k} \frac{\sum_{i,j} A_{ij} \cdot Y_{ic} \cdot Y_{jc}}{\sum_{i,j} Y_{ic} \cdot Y_{jc}} \tag{4.4}$$

$$\text{Coupling} = \sum_{i,j} A_{ij} \cdot \left(1 - \sum_{c=1}^{k} Y_{ic} \cdot Y_{jc}\right) \tag{4.5}$$

$$\mathcal{L}_{\text{dcmm}} = -\text{Cohesion} + \text{Coupling} \tag{4.6}$$

Next we define DCMM in Eq. 4.2 and 4.3 where DCMM takes the node embeddings X and the adjacency matrix A and maps each node embedding to a particular cluster out of C clusters thereby transforming X in R^{n*d} matrix to Y in R^{n*C} matrix (see. Eq. 4.3). DCMM is built using l layers of the GraphSage GNN model as shown in Eq. 4.2. The GraphSage layers apply ReLU [11] activation which adds the crucial non-linearity required to learn the complex mapping C that provides high modularization scores. Using C, the node is assigned to the module with the highest probability, and the modularization result quality is evaluated using a modularization metric. In general, a GNN model learns to maximize the modularization quality by minimizing the error in the difference between the evaluated modularization and the ground truth values. In unsupervised learning, however, we do not have ground truth values. Therefore, we use metrics that reflect the modularization quality such as cohesion (Eq. 4.4) and coupling (Eq. 4.5). We consider a combination of such metrics as the measure of error during training and aim to minimize such error (see Eq. 4.6).

3.3 Adaptation of Existing GNN-Based Approaches

To compare with existing GNN approaches, we adapt *i)* DMoN, an unsupervised pooling method inspired by the modularity measure of clustering quality [27] and, *ii)* Community Deep Graph Infomax (CommDGI), a GNN designed to handle community detection problems by using a mechanism to capture neighborhood and community information in graphs [41] for CMM. Both DMoN and CommDGI use the modularity metric in their loss function; however, DMoN adds a regularization parameter to prevent trivial solutions to the optimization problem. CommDGI further adds graph and cluster information exchange loss to their loss functions. The modularity loss is given in Eq. 5.

$$\mathcal{L}_{\text{modularity}} = -\frac{1}{2m}\text{Tr}(Y^T(A - \frac{dd^T}{2m}))Y) \tag{5}$$

where Tr is trace of matrix, i.e., sum of the elements in the left diagonal and d is the degree of a node. We provide the code for all the three GNN models, namely DCMM as well as adapted DMoN and DGI for CMM publicly available[2].

4 Comparative Experimental Evaluation

To evaluate our GNN approach, we compare it with the state-of-the-art ModuleER approach introduced in Sect. 2, which uses NSGA-II and existing GNNs—DMoN and DGI. With this evaluation, we aim to systematically answer the following research questions:

Table 1. Model to Graph Transformation Mappings

Size Category	Num. of Models	Min/Max Nodes	Avg±Std Nodes	Min/Max Edges	Avg±Std Edges	Min/Max Combined	Avg±Std Combined
Small	132	30/64	38 ± 7	41/128	80 ± 22	71/163	118 ± 26
Medium	104	31/132	70 ± 19	95/305	178 ± 56	164/420	249 ± 66
Large	27	55/226	130 ± 50	291/1552	591 ± 273	425/1778	722 ± 303
Total	263	30/226	60 ± 34	41/1552	171 ± 177	71/1778	232 ± 206

[RQ1] How do GNNs perform compared to GA for CMM?
- **[RQ1.1]** How do GNNs perform compared to GA on hypervolume, cohesion, and coupling metrics?
- **[RQ1.2]** How do GNNs perform compared to GA for different model sizes?

[RQ2] How does DCMM perform compared to existing GNNs?
- **[RQ2.1]** How does DCMM perform compared to DMoN and DGI on hypervolume, cohesion, and coupling metrics?
- **[RQ2.2]** How do DCMM perform compared to DMoN and DGI for different model sizes?

4.1 Experimental Setup

In the following, we elaborate on the experimental set up the dataset used, the evaluation method and the metrics used for a comparative analysis.

Dataset Used - To evaluate our approach and train the GNN models, we use the Modelset dataset [22] that contains more than 5000 Ecore models. We applied the following exclusion criteria to filter out models of insufficient quality or models which are not appropriate inputs for an modularization approach: *i*) models with less than 30 nodes as this is the limit of cognitive intractability [12]; *ii*) models with edges to nodes ratio of less than 1.2 to reject poorly

[2] https://github.com/junaidiiith/dcmm.

connected models such as models with a large number of nodes with only a few edges; *iii*) duplicate models; and *iv*) models that have very few nodes and edges uncommon. For e.g., given two graphs, one with 126 nodes and 469 edges and another graph with 127 nodes and 475 edges, if both graphs have more than 90% nodes in common, we consider them as duplicates and remove the one with the lower number of nodes. These exclusion criteria left us with 263 models of various sizes. We categorize these models in different sizes as show in Table 1. To compare the size of two models, we consider the combined number of nodes and edges and then chose the first 50 percentile of models as *small models*, *50–90 percentile as medium*, and *above 90 percentile as large models*. The table shows some descriptive statistics of the models in each model size category.

Technical Setup - In case of GNN-based modularization, we use an embedding dimension of 64 for *node2vec*, a learning rate of $1e-3$ and use the Adam optimizer [19] during the training phase. It is common to run the non-deterministic algorithm many times on each input instance and then perform the statistical tests. Therefore, in case of GA, in order to get robust results, we run GA $n = 30$ times and calculate the *score* values for each run. In case of GNN, even though the weights of the GNN model are initialised randomly, however, as a GNN optimizes the loss function and not searches for the best solution like in of GA, we get the same results in terms of modularization quality for each GNN run.

In [8], ModuleER uses five fitness functions: cohesion, coupling, the number of modules, the average number of elements per module, and the standard deviation of module sizes. We have modified the fitness functions to conform to the modularization quality metrics introduced in Sect. 2, i.e., only cohesion and coupling, as we observed that these two can capture the effects of the remaining metrics as well. The GA algorithm is run 30 times for each input model. In this setting, the population size is twice the size of each model's nodes, i.e., it varies between 60 and 452, and the number of iterations is fixed to 2000 because we investigated, that even for the largest models it takes less than 2000 iterations to reach a stable optimum point where no further improvements were observed.

Evaluation Methodology - In the case of GA, we get a set of non-dominating solutions for a multi-objective optimization problem, i.e., a Pareto Set. In case of multiple objectives, ModuleER [8] gives a Pareto Set of solutions for each problem, offering a spectrum of trade-offs between conflicting objectives. However, in case of GNN, we get a single solution. Therefore, in order to compare a single solution from GNN versus a pareto set from GA, we use the hypervolume metric to compare a multi-objective solution with a single solution based on Ishibuchi et al. [18]. NSGA-II runs in a non-deterministic way and it is common to run the non-deterministic algorithm many times on each input instance.

Figure 2 shows a hypervolume metric-based comparison of a pareto set solution from a GA versus a GNN solution. Given a GA solution P_k of a kth UML model with $k \in 1..N$ with P_k having n pareto sets $PS_j \in P_k$ from each run n with $j \in 1..n$ and PS_j having points $p_i \in PS_j$ where each p_i denoted a single modularized result, we define V_p in Eq. 6.1 as the hypervolume of a solution p using cohesion and coupling scores, both of which lie between 0 and 1. Coupling is a minimizing metric, therefore, we inverse coupling by plotting $1 - coupling$. The hypervolume of GNN is V_g where g is the GNN solution. Note, that if V_p of a given point is larger than the other, then the larger V_p solution balances both cohesion and coupling, (see p_3, p_b, g_1 in Fig. 2) whereas a smaller area indicates a preference towards one of the objectives (see p_1, p_4 in Fig. 2). The hypervolume of PS_j is the set union of V_{p_i} for all $p_i's \in PS_j$ (see. Eq. 6.2). We define the score s as given in Eq. 6.3 to calculate the average number of times V_g is higher than the hypervolume of the jth pareto set V_{PS_j} $\forall PS_j$. Then, we define a $HP(.)$ in Eq. 6.4 that determines the better algorithm between GA and GNN, given s. Finally, for a given set of N models, we calculate $PHV(.)$ according to Eq. 6.5 to capture the fraction of models for which one approach outperforms the other. In other words, $P_{GNN} = 0.67$ implies that for a given set of N models, GNN provides better hypervolume score, i.e., $PHV(s) = $ GNN for 67% of the models.

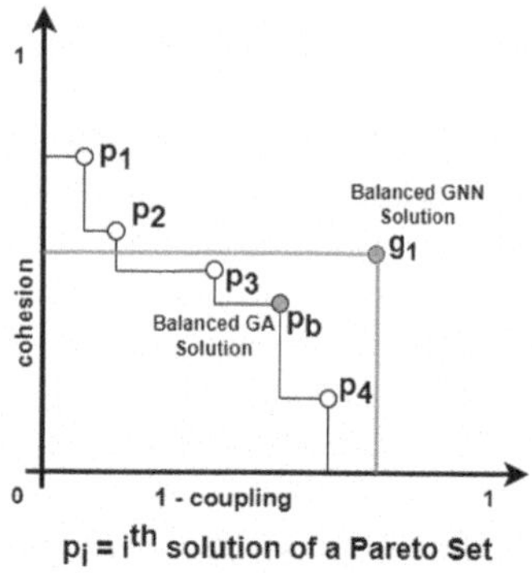

Fig. 2. Hypervolume-based GA and GNN solution comparison

$$V_p = cohesion * (1 - coupling) \quad (6.1)$$

$$V_{PS} = \bigcup_{p=1}^{n} V_p \quad (6.2)$$

$$s = \frac{\sum_{j=1}^{n} \mathbf{1}(V_{p_g} \geq V_{PS_j})}{n} \quad (6.3)$$

$$HP(s) = \begin{cases} \text{GNN} & \text{if } s > 0.5, \\ \text{GA} & \textit{otherwise} \end{cases} \quad (6.4)$$

$$PHV_{\text{x}} = \frac{\sum_{j=1}^{N} \mathbf{1}(HP(s_j) = \text{x})}{N} \quad \text{x} \in \{GNN, GA\} \quad (6.5)$$

$$M(p_b, g, m) = \begin{cases} \text{GNN} & \text{if } m_g > m_{p_b} \\ \text{GA} & \textit{otherwise} \end{cases} \quad (6.6)$$

$$\overline{M}(P, g, m, x) = \frac{\sum_{j=1}^{n} \mathbf{1}(M(p_{b_j}, g, m) = x)}{n} \quad (6.7)$$

$$\sigma(PS, g, m) = \begin{cases} \text{GNN} & \text{if } \overline{M}(PS, g, m, GNN) > 0.5 \\ \text{GA} & \text{if } \overline{M}(PS, g, m, GA) \geq 0.5 \end{cases}, \text{m} \in \{cohesion, 1 - coupling\} \quad (6.8)$$

$$PM_{m,x} = \frac{\sum_{i=1}^{N} \mathbf{1}(\sigma(P_j, g_j, m) = \text{x})}{N} \text{x} \in \{GNN, GA\}, m \in \{cohesion, 1 - coupling\} \quad (6.9)$$

Next, we further compare the cohesion and coupling scores of the solutions of GA and GNN. In case of GA, for a given pareto set of n non-dominating solutions, we select p_b to compare with the GNN solution and p_{b_j} as the trade-off point of each pareto set in j^{th} run. Then, given a GNN solution g and a metric m, we define $M(p_b, g, m)$ which checks if V_g is larger than V_{p_b}. If yes, then we consider GNN as the better trade-off solution over GA on metric m. Next, for a given model with n pareto sets, we take the average $\overline{M}$ that captures the average number of runs for which the approach x is better than the other approach in Eq. 6.7. Then, given the average score, we extract the better approach out of GA and GNN in Eq. 6.8. Finally, we calculate the percentage of models for which a given approach x dominates the other on a metric m in Eq. 6.9.

Finally, to compare the three different GNN solutions, i.e., DCMM(p_{dcmm}), DGI(p_{dgi}), DMoN(p_{dmon}), we consider the V_p, *cohesion* and *coupling* scores (see Eq. 7.1). Then, similar to Eq. 6.4, we get the best performing GNN using Eq. 7.2 and then we calculate the percentage of N models for which a given GNN approach is the best out of the three approaches in Eq. 7.3.

$$GNN_{max}(P, m) = \max(m(p_{\text{dcmm}}), m(p_{\text{dgi}}), m(p_{\text{dmon}})),\ \text{m} \in \{V_p, cohesion, 1 - coupling\} \tag{7.1}$$

$$IGNN(P, m) = \begin{cases} \text{DCMM} & \text{if } p_{\text{dcmm}_m} = GNN_{max}(P, m), \\ \text{DGI} & \text{if } p_{\text{dgi}_m} = GNN_{max}(P, m), \\ \text{DMoN} & \text{if } p_{\text{dmon}_m} = GNN_{max}(P, m). \end{cases} \tag{7.2}$$

$$PGNN_{m,x} = \frac{\sum_{j=1}^{N} \mathbf{1}(IGNN(P_j, m) = \text{x})}{N} \quad \text{x} \in \{\text{DCMM, DGI, DMoN}\} \tag{7.3}$$

4.2 Results

This comparative analysis sheds light on the efficacy of solutions provided by each approach, contributing to a deeper understanding of their strengths and limitations in addressing complex modularization tasks. Therefore, we respond to each RQ in the following. Figure 3 shows the result of CMM using all four of the discussed approaches on an example input class diagram given in the Fig. 3a. The figure shows the hypervolume cohesion, coupling and the number of modules values. The figure shows DCMM with the highest hypervolume for the input class diagram. DGI provides better cohesion but worse coupling compared to DMoN.

Response to RQ1 - GA verus GNN. In this RQ, we provide a comparative analysis of GA approach with GNN. In case of GNN, we take the best performing GNN approach out of the three and compare it with GA. The results for RQ.1 are provided in Table 2 where each value shows the $P_{approach}$ scores across different metrics.

The overall results show that GA outperforms GNN-based approach for hypervolume and cohesion metrics, however GNN outperforms GA for coupling

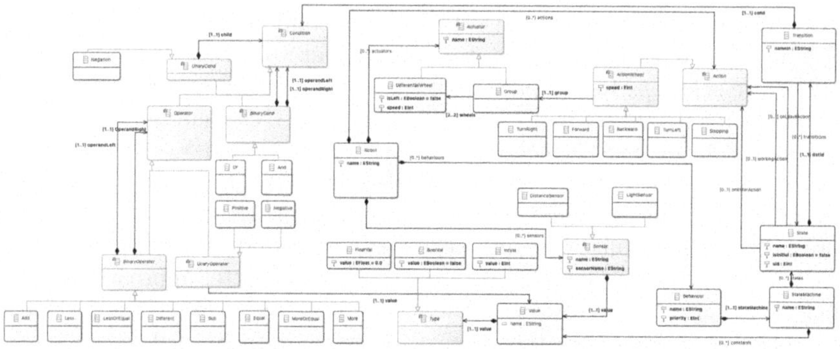

(a) A Robot Behaviour State Machine Class Diagram taken from the ModelSet [22]

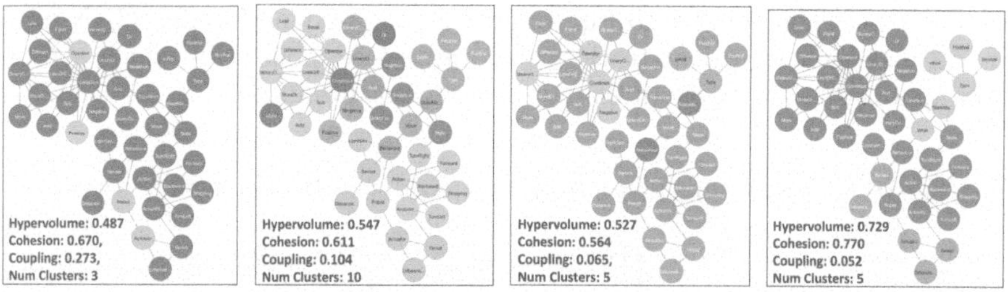

(b) ModuleER (c) DGI (d) DMoN (e) DCMM

Fig. 3. Example modularization results computed by the evaluated approaches

scores. In case of hypervolume, GA outperforms in more than two-third of the models and provides higher cohesion scores in more than 80% of the models. We observe that while GNN approaches outperform GA in almost 60% of the cases for coupling, however, GA still provides a higher hypervolume, a metric which captures the combination of cohesion and coupling, for almost 70% of the cases. An explanation for this can relate to the fact that GA outperforms GNN in cohesion by a larger amount, so the contribution of even better (lower) coupling scores cannot balance out the contribution of higher cohesion to the hypervolume scores. Overall, this indicates that GA is more suitable for optimizing the cohesion scores, whereas GNN is suitable for optimizing coupling.

We further evaluate the effect of different model sizes on the comparative performance of GA and GNN. Interestingly, for hypervolume and cohesion, the performance of GNNs goes down for medium-sized models and then increases again for larger models. Furthermore, we see that the performance of GNNs decreases with larger model sizes for the coupling scores; however, it still provides better coupling scores than GA. Overall, it is interesting to note that GNN does provide better performance than GA in some of the metrics and setups. Moreover, esp. for a large models, we see that GNN produced modularizations of comparable quality or even of better quality with respect to coupling. Thus, we consider GNN-based CMM a promising alternative to GA which can be further investigated for improvements.

Table 2. Overall Performance of GNN over GA

Model Size	PHV		$PM_{cohesion}$		$PM_{coupling}$	
	GA	GNN	GA	GNN	GA	GNN
Small	**63.63%**	36.36%	**68.18%**	31.82%	36.36%	**63.64%**
Medium	**79.80%**	20.20%	**94.23%**	5.77%	44.23%	**55.77%**
Large	**55.55%**	44.44%	**85.18%**	14.82%	48.14%	**51.86%**
Overall	**69.20%**	30.80%	**80.22%**	19.78%	40.68%	**59.32%**

Response to RQ2 - DCMM versus DMoN and DGI. Now, we delve deeper into our DCMM's performance and compare it to the existing GNN models for CMM. We present an overall and a size-based performance comparison in Table 3. Each value in the table shows the percentage of models in a category for which a given GNN model outperforms the other two GNN approaches.

The results in Table 3 show that DCMM performs better than DGI and DMoN in most models for all three metrics. In case of hypervolume, DCMM outperforms DMoN and DGI in over 76% of the cases, outperforming DMoN (14.44%) and DGI (9.12%). This indicates DCMM's consistent superiority across all model sizes. In case of cohesion, DCMM scores highest 66.16%, compared to DMoN's 11.78% and DGI's 22.05%, showing its overall superiority in producing cohesive clusters. Finally, DCMM demonstrates overall dominance for coupling with 62.73%, compared to DMoN's 30.41% and DGI's 6.84%, confirming its consistent performance in reducing coupling.

We further evaluate the size-based comparative performance of the three GNN approaches. We see that in all the three metrics DCMM's performance improves in most cases or remains almost similar with an increase in model size. In case of hypervolume, the performance increases from DCMM being the best GNN model for 66.67% of the small models to DCMM being the best GNN model for 92.59% of the large models. In case of cohesion and coupling as well, DCMM still performs better than the other two GNNs for all the three model size categories. In case of hypervolume and coupling, DCMM performance shows an increase with model size. Overall, with this comparative evaluation we see, that our novel DCMM approach clearly outperforms the state-of-the-art for GNN-based graph clustering for conceptual models.

Based on our results we conclude as follows—*i*) GA-based approach is still a valuable approach for CMM, however, GNN-based approaches also turned out to be very useful alternatives for a large number of models providing better scores than GA for over 30% of the models and particularly for larger models providing better scores than GA for over 44% of the large sized models; *ii*) GNN-based approaches consistently perform better than GA for modularized solutions with

Table 3. Comparative performance of DCMM with existing GNNs for CMM

Model Size	$PGNN_{V_p}$			$PGNN_{cohesion}$			$PGNN_{coupling}$		
	DCMM	DMoN	DGI	DCMM	DMoN	DGI	DCMM	DMoN	DGI
Small	**66.67%**	19.69%	13.63%	**55.30%**	15.90%	28.78%	**50.74%**	41.79%	7.46%
Medium	**84.62%**	10.57%	4.80%	**77.88%**	6.73%	15.38%	**73.52%**	20.58%	5.88%
Large	**92.59%**	3.70%	3.70%	**74.07%**	11.11%	14.81%	**81.48%**	11.11%	7.40%
Overall	**76.42%**	14.44%	9.12%	**66.16%**	11.78%	22.05%	**62.73%**	30.41%	6.84%

lower coupling; and, finally, *iii*) the results underpin our novel DCMM model as a valuable GNN-based CMM approach, outperforming the state-of-the-art graph clustering models. DCMM further proves valuable as an alternative to GA-based approach, especially in case of minimizing coupling between modules.

5 Insights and Threats to Validity

In the following, we present further insights gained through the experiments conducted that yield additional responses to the outlined research questions.

Insights About RQ.1 - We observed that the model size affects the percentage of models for which either of GA and GNN perform better than. GA excels in achieving higher hypervolume and cohesion. This indicates that GA is more effective in maintaining tight, cohesive clusters. This is particularly evident in small and medium models where GA significantly outperforms GNN. However, GNN shows strengths in minimizing coupling, which is crucial for creating distinct, well-separated clusters and is therefore, advantageous for applications where minimizing inter-cluster dependencies is critical whereas GA may be better suited for tasks requiring tight clustering. GNN's performance is more competitive with GA for larger models, indicating its scalability and potential for handling more complex clustering tasks. Overall, our results show a significant potential in applying GNNs for conceptual model modularization; however there is no one size fits all solution and the choice between GA and GNN needs to be guided by the specific requirements of the clustering task concerning a preference over cohesion, coupling, and a combination thereof. Our results do underpin GNN-based approaches as a suitable candidate for CMM, that can be investigated and improved further for a better performance by designing improved GNN architectures and loss functions that even better capture the graph clustering requirements of a conceptual modeler.

Insights About RQ.2 - The results of the comparative performance of DCMM and existing GNN models show, that DCMM consistently outperforms both DMoN and DGI across all model sizes and metrics. The performance of DCMM does not degrade with increasing model size. In fact, the performance gap between DCMM and the other models widens as the model size increases, showcasing its scalability. DCMM's high scores in cohesion and coupling metrics suggest that it effectively balances intra-cluster similarity and inter-cluster dissimilarity, which are crucial for high-quality clustering. This indicates that DCMM is a robust and scalable solution for GNN-based graph clustering in conceptual modeling. Furthermore, to the best of our knowledge, given that DCMM is the first GNN model for graph clustering applied in the domain of conceptual modeling, these results highlight DCMM's tailored effectiveness for this specific domain of conceptual modeling, addressing domain-specific challenges better than the more generic models like DMoN and DGI. The reason for a better DCMM performance can be attributed to the loss function used to train DCMM that directly aims to create solutions with high cohesion and low coupling, compared to the existing GNN solutions that maximize modularity that indirectly optimizes cohesion and coupling scores. This indicates that existing loss functions are not sufficient to produce good solutions and therefore, loss functions specific to CMM need to be developed.

We now elaborate on the threats to validity according to the widely accepted categories introduced by Wohlin et al. [38].

Conclusion Validity regards issues that affect the ability to draw accurate conclusions about relations between the treatments and the outcome of an experiment. The selection of a point from a pareto set to compare with the GNN point falls under this category. There can be several other points in a pareto therefore the selection criteria of selecting the best trade-off point threatens the validity of our results. However, in this work, we focused on selecting the balanced solution and in our future work, we explore other criteria to compare a pareto set of a GA solution with a GNN solution.

Construct Validity regards the ability to generalize the results of an experiment to the theory behind the experiment. We mitigated this threat by using a dataset of 263 UML models for our experiments. These 263 models are the filtered, non duplicated good quality models out of over 5000 models. However, our work still faces the construction validity threat for conceptual models of other modeling languages, which we aim to tackle as part of our future work.

Internal Validity regards the influences that can affect the independent variables with respect to causality. In our work, we set the configuration parameters for all the different approaches using a trial-and-error strategy. It is possible that other parameter settings might yield different results. In fact, parameter tuning of search algorithms is still considered an open research challenge [7]. We mitigated this issue by doing a grid search over the different parameter values possible by trying different possible combinations of the involved configuration parameters.

External Validity regards the extent to which the research elements (subjects, artifacts, etc.) are representative of actual element. We mitigated this threat by using a Modelset dataset [22] of UML models used and peer reviewed in the literature which comprises manually created and not synthetically generated UML models.

6 Related Work

Next, we discuss related work on CMM. We consider works that treat the models as graphs and separate them into *i*) works that focus on the *structural properties* of the model in general, and *ii*) works that utilize some kind of GNN to drive the modularization. We do not cover the works that utilize the *conceptual model semantics* because such works are not within the scope of this research.

Structural Modularization. Bork et al. [8] propose ModuleER, a genetic algorithm-based modularization approach for Entity Relationship (ER) models using the graph structure information. We use ModulER as a baseline for GA-based CMM. Stuckenschmidt and Klein [33] propose a structure-based method clustering models based on the structure of the class hierarchy for real-world ontologies like SUMO and the NCI cancer ontology. In [34], Stuckenschmidt and Schlicht demonstrate that modularization based on structural properties alone produces meaningful modules that intuitively make sense.

Saruladha et al. [31] propose two neighbor-based structural proximity measures, namely TNSP and DNSP, to decompose ontologies into disjoint clusters. They consider concept pairs with common neighbors for clustering. Doran et al. [9] present an approach to ontology module extraction. Furthermore, for software systems, Andritsos et al. [3] present LIMBO which is a hierarchical clustering algorithm based on the minimization of information loss when merging two nodes in a cluster. The authors in [24,25] present a hierarchical clustering-based weighted linkage clustering (WLC) approach. In particular, they merge entities together to form clusters, where two entities are merged together based on their types, relationships and attributes. Hence, the new feature vector correctly reflects relationships between the entities. Pourasghar et al. [29] present a modularization technique named GMA (Graph-based Modularization Algorithm). In their work, they propose several metrics to evaluate the quality of modularization solutions by utilizing structural features of the models.

GNN-Based Modularization. GNNs have been recently used for graph clustering. MinCutPool [6] proposes a graph clustering approach by continuously relaxing the normalized minimum cut problem and training a GNN to compute cluster assignments that minimize this objective. DMoN [27] extends spectral clustering and presents an unsupervised pooling method inspired by the modularity clustering measure. In [41], a GNN-based approach to encode node structural and community-aware representation using mutual information maximization [5] is presented, which captures local and global structural information. In our work, we compared our proposed DCMM with DMoN and DGI.

Synopsis. We summarize, that in case of structural modularization, most approaches related to conceptual model modularization approaches apply search-based techniques such as genetic algorithm techniques for graph structural clustering. We further note that GNN models are used for modularization but are not yet adapted to the specific requirements and applied to conceptual models. In this context, we presented our GNN-based graph modularization i.e., DCMM and provided a comparative evaluation against the existing GA and GNN approaches. We aim to combine the semantics with the graph structural modularization as part of our future work.

7 Conclusion and Future Work

This paper presented a new GNN-based conceptual model modularization approach and evaluated its performance on a dataset of UML class diagrams and compared the results to a GA-based approach and existing GNN-based graph clustering approaches. Our results position our deep conceptual model modularizer approach as a valuable GNN-based CMM approach, outperforming the state-of-the-art GA-based approach in over 30% of the cases overall and in almost 60% of the cases for the objective of minimizing coupling using the balanced trade-off solution from the Pareto set. Our DCMM approach outperformed the existing GNN models for CMM thereby showing DCMM's effectiveness in the specific application to conceptual models, addressing CMM challenges better than the more generic GNN models for graph clustering like DMoN and DGI.

In our current work, we did not include the model's metamodel and natural language label-based semantics and we only focused on UML class diagrams. In the future, we plan to extend our approach to several other modeling languages and utilize further sources of semantics to train GNN models for CMM.

Acknowledgements. Work partially funded by the Austrian Federal Ministry for Digital and Economic Affairs and the National Foundation for Research, Technology and Development (CDG).

References

1. Ali, S.J., Guizzardi, G., Bork, D.: Enabling representation learning in ontology-driven conceptual modeling using graph neural networks. In: Indulska, M., Reinhartz-Berger, I., Cetina, C., Pastor, O. (eds.) CAiSE 2023. LNCS, vol. 13901, pp. 278–294. Springer, Cham (2023). https://doi.org/10.1007/978-3-031-34560-9_17
2. Ali, S.J., Laranjo, J.M., Bork, D.: A generic and customizable genetic algorithms-based conceptual model modularization framework. In: Proper, H.A., Pufahl, L., Karastoyanova, D., van Sinderen, M., Moreira, J. (eds.) EDOC 2023. LNCS, vol. 14367, pp. 39–57. Springer, Cham (2023). https://doi.org/10.1007/978-3-031-46587-1_3
3. Andritsos, P., Tzerpos, V.: Information-theoretic software clustering. IEEE Trans. Software Eng. **31**(2), 150–165 (2005)
4. Behera, R.K., Naik, D., Rath, S.K., Dharavath, R.: Genetic algorithm-based community detection in large-scale social networks. Neural Comput. Appl. **32**, 9649–9665 (2020)
5. Belghazi, M.I., et al.: Mutual information neural estimation. In: International Conference on Machine Learning, pp. 531–540. PMLR (2018)

6. Bianchi, F.M., Grattarola, D., Alippi, C.: Spectral clustering with graph neural networks for graph pooling. In: International Conference on Machine Learning, pp. 874–883. PMLR (2020)
7. Bill, R., Fleck, M., Troya, J., Mayerhofer, T., Wimmer, M.: A local and global tour on MOMoT. Softw. Syst. Model. **18**, 1017–1046 (2019)
8. Bork, D., Garmendia, A., Wimmer, M.: Towards a multi-objective modularization approach for entity-relationship models. In: ER Forum, Demo and Poster 2020, pp. 45–58. CEUR (2020)
9. Doran, P., Tamma, V.A.M., Iannone, L.: Ontology module extraction for ontology reuse: an ontology engineering perspective. In: Proceedings of the Sixteenth ACM Conference on Information and Knowledge Management, CIKM 2007, pp. 61–70. ACM (2007). https://doi.org/10.1145/1321440.1321451
10. Duong, C.T., Nguyen, T.T., Hoang, T.D., Yin, H., Weidlich, M., Nguyen, Q.V.H.: Deep MinCut: learning node embeddings by detecting communities. Pattern Recogn. **134**, 109–126 (2023)
11. Eckle, K., Schmidt-Hieber, J.: A comparison of deep networks with ReLU activation function and linear spline-type methods. Neural Netw. **110**, 232–242 (2019)
12. Figueiredo, G., Duchardt, A., Hedblom, M.M., Guizzardi, G.: Breaking into pieces: an ontological approach to conceptual model complexity management. In: 12th International Conference on Research Challenges in Information Science, RCIS 2018, pp. 1–10. IEEE (2018). https://doi.org/10.1109/RCIS.2018.8406642
13. Fortunato, S., Hric, D.: Community detection in networks: a user guide. Phys. Rep. **659**, 1–44 (2016)
14. Garmendia, A., Bork, D., Eisenberg, M., do Nascimento Ferreira, T., Kessentini, M., Wimmer, M.: Leveraging artificial intelligence for model-based software analysis and design. In: Romero, J.R., Medina-Bulo, I., Chicano, F. (eds.) Optimising the Software Development Process with Artificial Intelligence. Natural Computing Series, pp. 93–117. Springer, Singapore(2023). https://doi.org/10.1007/978-981-19-9948-2_4
15. Grover, A., Leskovec, J.: node2vec: scalable feature learning for networks. In: Proceedings of the 22nd ACM SIGKDD International Conference on Knowledge Discovery and Data Mining, pp. 855–864 (2016)
16. Hamilton, W.L., Ying, R., Leskovec, J.: Representation learning on graphs: methods and applications. IEEE Data Eng. Bull. **40**(3), 52–74 (2017)
17. Hamilton, W.L., Ying, Z., Leskovec, J.: Inductive representation learning on large graphs. In: Advances in Neural Information Processing Systems 30: Neural Information Processing Systems 2017, pp. 1024–1034 (2017)
18. Ishibuchi, H., Nojima, Y., Doi, T.: Comparison between single-objective and multi-objective genetic algorithms: Performance comparison and performance measures. In: 2006 IEEE International Conference on Evolutionary Computation, pp. 1143–1150. IEEE (2006)
19. Kingma, D.P., Ba, J.: Adam: a method for stochastic optimization. In: 3rd International Conference on Learning Representations, ICLR (2015)
20. LeClair, A., Marinache, A., El Ghalayini, H., MacCaull, W., Khedri, R.: A review on ontology modularization techniques-a multi-dimensional perspective. IEEE Trans. Knowl. Data Eng. **35**(5), 4376–4394 (2022)
21. Liu, Z., Li, X., Peng, H., He, L., Philip, S.Y.: Heterogeneous similarity graph neural network on electronic health records. In: 2020 IEEE International Conference on Big Data (Big Data), pp. 1196–1205. IEEE (2020)

22. López, J.A.H., Izquierdo, J.L.C., Cuadrado, J.S.: ModelSet: a dataset for machine learning in model-driven engineering. Softw. Syst. Model. **21**(3), 967–986 (2022). https://doi.org/10.1007/S10270-021-00929-3
23. Malekzadeh, M., Hajibabaee, P., Heidari, M., Zad, S., Uzuner, O., Jones, J.H.: Review of graph neural network in text classification. In: IEEE 12th Annual Ubiquitous Computing, Electronics & Mobile Communication Conference (UEMCON), pp. 84–91. IEEE (2021)
24. Maqbool, O., Babri, H.: Hierarchical clustering for software architecture recovery. IEEE Trans. Software Eng. **33**(11), 759–780 (2007)
25. Maqbool, O., Babri, H.A.: The weighted combined algorithm: a linkage algorithm for software clustering. In: European Conference on Software Maintenance and Reengineering, CSMR 2004, pp. 15–24. IEEE (2004)
26. Mirjalili, S., Mirjalili, S.: Genetic algorithm. In: Evolutionary Algorithms and Neural Networks: Theory and Applications, pp. 43–55 (2019)
27. Müller, E.: Graph clustering with graph neural networks. J. Mach. Learn. Res. **24**, 1–21 (2023)
28. Newman, M.E.: Modularity and community structure in networks. Proc. Natl. Acad. Sci. **103**(23), 8577–8582 (2006)
29. Pourasghar, B., Izadkhah, H., Isazadeh, A., Lotfi, S.: A graph-based clustering algorithm for software systems modularization. Inf. Softw. Technol. **133**, 106469 (2021)
30. Proper, H.A., Guizzardi, G.: Modeling for enterprises; let's go to Rome via rime. In: Clark, T., Zschaler, S., Barn, B., Sandkuhl, K. (eds.) Proceedings of the Forum at Practice of Enterprise Modeling 2022 (PoEM-Forum 2022) co-located with PoEM 2022. CEUR Workshop Proceedings, vol. 3327, pp. 4–15. CEUR-WS.org (2022)
31. Saruladha, K., Aghila, G., Sathiya, B.: Neighbour based structural proximity measures for ontology matching systems. In: Proceedings of the International Conference on Advances in Computing, Communications and Informatics, pp. 1079–1085 (2012)
32. Smajevic, M., Bork, D.: From conceptual models to knowledge graphs: a generic model transformation platform. In: International Conference on Model Driven Engineering Languages and Systems Companion, pp. 610–614. IEEE (2021)
33. Stuckenschmidt, H., Klein, M.: Structure-based partitioning of large concept hierarchies. In: McIlraith, S.A., Plexousakis, D., van Harmelen, F. (eds.) ISWC 2004. LNCS, vol. 3298, pp. 289–303. Springer, Heidelberg (2004). https://doi.org/10.1007/978-3-540-30475-3_21
34. Stuckenschmidt, H., Schlicht, A.: Structure-based partitioning of large ontologies. In: Modular Ontologies: Concepts, Theories and Techniques for Knowledge Modularization, pp. 187–210 (2009)
35. Unger, R.: The genetic algorithm approach to protein structure prediction. Appl. Evol. Comput. Chem. 153–175 (2004)
36. Velickovic, P., Cucurull, G., Casanova, A., Romero, A., Lio, P., Bengio, Y., et al.: Graph attention networks. Stat **1050**(20), 10–48550 (2017)
37. Villegas Niño, A.: A filtering engine for large conceptual schemas. Doctoral thesis (2013)
38. Wohlin, C., Runeson, P., Höst, M., Ohlsson, M.C., Regnell, B., Wesslén, A.: Experimentation in Software Engineering, 2nd edn. Springer, Heidelberg (2024). https://doi.org/10.1007/978-3-662-69306-3
39. Wu, S., Sun, F., Zhang, W., Xie, X., Cui, B.: Graph neural networks in recommender systems: a survey. ACM Comput. Surv. **55**(5), 1–37 (2022)

40. Xiong, J., Xiong, Z., Chen, K., Jiang, H., Zheng, M.: Graph neural networks for automated de novo drug design. Drug Discov. Today **26**(6), 1382–1393 (2021)
41. Zhang, T., Xiong, Y., Zhang, J., Zhang, Y., Jiao, Y., Zhu, Y.: CommDGI: community detection oriented deep graph infomax. In: CIKM 2020: The 29th ACM International Conference on Information and Knowledge Management, pp. 1843–1852. ACM (2020). https://doi.org/10.1145/3340531.3412042
42. Zhao, W., Xu, G., Cui, Z., Luo, S., Long, C., Zhang, T.: Deep graph structural infomax. In: Proceedings of the AAAI Conference on Artificial Intelligence, vol. 37, pp. 4920–4928 (2023)
43. Zhou, J., et al.: Graph neural networks: a review of methods and applications. AI Open **1**, 57–81 (2020)

Automatic Extraction and Formalization of Temporal Requirements from Text: A Survey

Marisol Barrientos[1(✉)], Karolin Winter[2], and Stefanie Rinderle-Ma[1]

[1] Technical University of Munich, Garching, Germany
{marisol.barrientos,stefanie.rinderle-ma}@tum.de
[2] Eindhoven University of Technology, Eindhoven, The Netherlands
k.m.winter@tue.nl

Abstract. Natural Language Processing has opened new paths for business process management and requirements engineering, particularly in automating the extraction and formalization of temporal requirements from diverse documents such as system specifications, legal texts, and business process descriptions. Recently, approaches have been introduced to automate this task, employing various document formats as input and targeting different formal specifications. However, a key challenge persists: effectively comparing these approaches and choosing the most suitable one for a specific task. This paper aims to bridge this research gap by conducting a systematic literature review, including a detailed analysis and comparing existing approaches. This comparison is crucial to determine if the latest Large Language Model-based solutions could surpass existing methods in effectiveness and ease of use. The systematic literature review enables users to select the most suitable method based on their data and end goals. Moreover, this work proposes the NL2MTL (https://github.com/marisol-barrientos/nl2mtl, DLA: 22.04.2024) method to bridge some of the gaps identified in the literature analysis, i.e., establishing a comparable assessment method, under-representation of legal texts, poor output context management, and the necessity to automate the formalization of requirements, considering both quantitative and qualitative aspects of time. Addressing the latter aspect, we select Metric Temporal Logic (MTL) as formalization and provide the associated prompts and an evaluation of the NL2MTL output.

Keywords: requirements formalization · natural language processing (nlp) · temporal logic · legal text · business process

1 Introduction

Natural Language Processing (NLP) has been employed for a range of business process management and requirements engineering challenges [66], e.g., conceptual and goal modeling [13,24], as well as for the formalization of requirements [56]. The recent development of Large Language Models (LLMs) has enhanced particularly challenging tasks. One of those is the extraction, formalization, and

J. Borbinha et al. (Eds.): EDOC 2024, LNCS 15409, pp. 259–278, 2025.
https://doi.org/10.1007/978-3-031-78338-8_14

later verification of temporal requirements from documents such as system specifications [6], legal texts [61], and business process descriptions [4,42]. Automating this task becomes vital due to the steadily increasing amounts of documents and the therein described (legal) requirements that companies have to comply with. The large variety of formalizations, e.g., Linear Temporal Logic (LTL), Signal Temporal Logic (STL), or Metric Temporal Logic (MTL), has led to numerous automated requirements extraction methods. This abundance of automation options often leaves domain experts puzzled about the most suitable approach for their specific problem.

Driven by challenges in accurately converting natural language temporal requirements to formal specifications, this study addresses the adequacy of current methods, particularly in capturing qualitative (event order relations) and quantitative (measurable intervals) time aspects across various domains. Consequently, this research pivots around the following three research questions.

RQ1: What mechanisms exist for the (semi-)automatic translation of temporal requirements into formal specifications?
RQ2: To what extent can temporal requirements be represented by formal specifications in the different application domains?
RQ3: How can temporal requirements, including both quantitative and qualitative aspects, be effectively formalized from textual inputs?

RQ1 is explored in Sect. 2 and 3 through a systematic literature review (SLR), where papers are classified by their goal. Each category analyzes the methodologies used, input formats, and application domain (i.e., domain-specific vs general). For addressing RQ2, in Sect. 4 the findings emerging from the systematic literature review are presented. To address RQ3, in Sect. 5 we introduce the NL2MTL method, utilizing a Large Language Model, i.e., GPT-4, for processing legal texts into MTL formulations. This is evaluated following the four key principles of a *good formalization* [45], i.e., correctness (i.e., detecting all atomic propositions and formalizing them following MTL semantics), transparency (i.e., defining all used elements, and indicating the reasoning behind a formal specification), comprehensibility (i.e., easy to interpret), and support for multiple interpretations. This section is followed by a discussion Sect. 6 and conclusions (c.f., Sect. 7).

2 Systematic Literature Review Methodology

The Systematic Literature Review (SLR) follows [33] and includes five phases. References are provided in the supplementary material[1].

Phase 1 - Strategy Planning. The **selected databases** for the literature search comprise ACM, IEEE, Scopus, and Springer. For each of those, we carried out our initial search by executing our **search string**, which looks as follows:

[1] https://github.com/marisol-barrientos/nl2mtl, DLA: 22.04.2024

```
("natural language" OR "large language model") AND
("temporal logic // requirement" OR "ltl" OR"computational tree logic" OR
"requirement formalization // formalisation // extraction" OR
"formal requirement // specification // verification" OR "automate formalization // formalisation")
```

The search string is created by combining a keyword from the field of natural language processing with another from formal methods, specifically those used for formalizing natural language, e.g., a requirement, into temporal logic. After, we defined the following **inclusion (IC)** and **exclusion criteria (EC)**. The inclusion criteria were defined along with the research questions, but this was not the case for the exclusion criteria. Papers on causality analysis (*EC2*) were excluded, as their focus was quantifying time uncertainty rather than automatically extracting formalizations. In this SLR, we excluded research on automated code extraction (e.g., Python script generation), blockchain, Unified Modeling Language (UML) diagrams, and Attribute-Based Access Control (ABAC) (*EC4*), as our focus was not on these technologies or frameworks, but rather on formal methods or models which support time formalization in a business process (Table 1).

Table 1. Inclusion and Exclusion Criteria for Selecting Research Papers

ID	Definition
IC1	Publicly accessible, in English, peer-reviewed
IC2	Preference for journal versions over conference papers
IC3	Published from January 1, 2018, to April 1, 2024, focusing on recent developments
IC4	Must detail input/output formats, methodology, and evaluations
IC5	Automates formalization and modeling of temporal requirements using AI
IC6	Automates the augmentation of formal specifications using AI
EC1	Previews, abstracts, and theses
EC2	Causality work (e.g., temporal dependency extraction)
EC3	Event log augmentation
EC4	Papers on automatic extraction of code, a blockchain, UML diagrams, and ABAC
EC5	Formal specifications tight to an architecture, e.g., Hanfor [43] or FRETish [18]

Phase 2 and 3 - Initial and Full-Text Screening. Table 2 summarizes the number of selected papers per database and phase. *Phase 1* contains all papers whose title, keywords, or abstract hit the search string. In *Phase 2* papers were filtered by title, while in *Phase 3* are filtered by abstract.

Table 2. Number of Selected Papers per Database and SLR Phase

Database	Phase 1	Phase 2	Phase 3
ACM	65	24	5
IEEE	1042	128	5
Scopus	338	112	12
Springer	886	49	6
Total without duplicates	2.331	313	28

Phase 4 - Back and Forth Snowballing. After completing *Phase 3*, we included 28 papers that satisfied the inclusion and exclusion criteria. We then proceeded to *Phase 4*, where backward and forward snowballing through Google Scholar identified 16 additional relevant publications. This increased the total to 44 papers for further analysis.

Phase 5 - Analysis and Classification. The selected papers are classified and analyzed in Sect. 3 summarizes findings and research gaps in Sect. 4.

3 Classification of Selected Papers

In this section, the 44 papers collected as described in Sect. 2 are analyzed and categorized by goal. This leads to the following categories, *Automatic Generation of Formal Specifications* (cf., Sect. 3.1), *Automatic Generation of Modeling Notations* (cf., Sect. 3.2), and *Automatic Augmentation of Formal Specifications* (cf., Sect. 3.3). All categories can be further divided based on output formats. Tables 3, 4, 5 and 6 contain an overview of the papers by category, including publication year, input and output format, methodology, application, and URL to their project website.

3.1 Automatic Generation of Formal Specifications

Linear Temporal Logic. [49] used the Stanford Parser to extract LTL formulas from system requirements, addressing ambiguity detection limitations but struggled with complex inputs. [57] furthered this by incorporating smart home IoT knowledge to handle ambiguities. [27] also utilized a similar approach, but their focus was within the robotics domain. In this domain, they are interested in automatically generating LTL formulas to verify tasks, including grounding, navigation, and tasks related to surgical procedures. The works of [7] and [57] both emphasize advancements in robotics aimed at interpreting complex inputs from human and robotic perspectives. Future papers will likely concentrate on robots that can understand human speech in particular contexts, adapting to linguistic and environmental shifts.

Still, in the robotics domain, challenges posed by language complexity and the potential to incorporate context are overcome by approaches that leverage LLMs, as discussed in [48], [37], and [50]. Papers that accept as input format unstructured text [19,26] and user input [25] also relied on similar methods. While in the ones which had as input format traffic law [20,36], the formalization of constraints was nearly manual.

Signal Temporal Logic. STL is designed for timing events, suitable for applications like cyber-physical systems and smart cities, enabling requirements such as *the soil moisture at any given sensor must remain above a certain threshold throughout the day.* DeepSTL [31] and NL2TL [14] facilitate STL formula extraction. nl2spec [19] provides a conceptual STL extraction extension. CitySpec [16] employs SaSTL for spatial and aggregation considerations in requirements like

Table 3. Input-Output Mapping - Automatic Generation of Formal Specifications

Ref.	Year	Input Format	Output Format	Methodology	Application	url
[29]	2018	Requirement	Event-B [Ql: yes, Qt: no]	Model federation	Requirements engineering (landing gear system)	yes
[30]	2022	Unstructured Text	FOL, regex, and LTL [Ql: 1/2, Qt: no]	Fine-tune LLM (T5)	General	no
[49]	2019	Natural Language Requirement	Linear Temporal Logic (LTL) [Ql: yes, Qt: no]	Standford Parser, build dependency tree and map it with the LTL dependency tree	Multiple system requirements (focus on consistency checking)	no
[65]	2020	Natural Language Requirement		Grammar based method	Smart home IoT	no
[57]	2020	Robot command		Semantic parser	Robotics (grounding)	no
[20]	2020	Traffic Law / Code		Manual step	Self-driving vehicles	
[36]	2022			First, converted to constraints on Markov Decision Process (manual step)	Self-driving vehicles	no
[25]	2023	User Input		LLM (GPT-based)	Healthcare process	yes
[27]	2020			Grammar-enhanced one-shot learning synthesis	Robotics	yes
[19]	2023	Unstructured Text		LLMs (Boom and Codex)	General	yes
[26]	2023			LLMs (GPT-3x and GPT-4)	General	no
[7]	2023	Procedural natural language		Part-Of-Speech tagging combined with Semantic Role Labeling	Robotics (surgery)	yes
[48]	2023	Robotic Task		Fine-tune LLM (BART)	Robotics	yes
[37]	2023	Ground Temporal Navigational Commands		Leveraging LLMs (GPT-based and T5) and constructing and training a Seq2Seq transformer model	Robotics (navigation)	yes
[50]	2024	Object goal navigation and mobile pick-and-place instructions		Leveraging LLM, using two-stage in context learning strategy	Robotics (grounding, task verification, and motion planning)	yes
[31]	2022	Requirement	Signal Temporal Logic (STL) [Ql: yes, Qt: 1/2]	Grammar-based generation and transformer-based neural translation technique	Safety-critical cyber-physical systems	yes
[16]	2022			Translation models (Seq2Seq, pre-trained Stanford NER Tagger, Bi-LSTM + CRF, and BERT) and online validation (Bayesian CNN-based)	Smart city	no
[14]	2023			Enrich data with LLMs and manual annotations. Fine-tune T5 (compare with Seq2Seq and GPT-3)	Robotics (circuit, navigation, and grounding)	yes
[19]	2023	Unstructured Text		LLMs	General (system verification)	yes
[54]	2023	Natural Language Command		Bi-RNN	General (planning trajectories)	no

the average soil moisture across all sensors in a particular region must remain above a certain threshold for the next 10 days.

Propositional Projection Temporal Logic. In [58], the PPTLGenerator was introduced, leveraging Stanford CoreNLP[2] for analyzing safety system properties and converting them into PPTL formulas. Following up, [35] presented NL2PPTL, utilizing a Seq2Seq[3] model for converting security requirements into PPTL, significantly enhancing automation with modern ML for complexity management, in contrast to the first approach's reliance on traditional NLP.

Table 4. Input-Output Mapping - Automatic Generation of Formal Specifications

Ref	Year	Input Format	Output Format	Methodology	Application	url
[58]	2020	Safety property of self-driving vehicles	Propositional Projection Temporal Logic (PPTL) [Ql: yes, Qt: 1/2]	Stanford CoreNLP, WordNet and JavaCC	Self-driving vehicles (verification of safety properties)	no
[35]	2022	Security Requirement		Neural translation model	Requirements engineering	yes
[63]	2021	Semi-formal Representation Model (RCM)	Metric Temporal Logic (MTL) [Ql: yes, Qt: yes] For [63] also Computational Tree Logic (CTL) [Ql: yes, Qt: no]	Stanford, WordNet, and Prolog	General (system requirements)	yes
[28]	2023	Legal Contract Clauses		Deep learning (3 neural network models)	Legal contract formalization	no
[41]	2023	Legal or planning rules		Semantic Role Labeling and LLMs	Self-driving vehicles (legal or planning rules)	yes
[61]	2024	Traffic Law		Trigger-based hierarchical (manual step)	Self-driving vehicles (monitoring)	yes
[64]	2022	Requirement	Semi-formal Representation Model (RCM) [Ql: yes, Qt: 1/2]	Stanford, WordNet, and Prolog	General (system requirements)	yes
[47]	2023					yes
[6]	2023	Automotive Requirement	Timed Computation Tree Logic (TCTL) [Ql: yes, Qt: yes]	LLM (GPT-J-6B) and OptKATE algorithm	Automotive industry	no

Metric Temporal Logic and Computation Tree Logic. In [62], the Requirement Capture Model (RCM) was introduced to convert system requirements into formal specifications using a blend of formal and semi-formal semantics, enhancing interpretation and conversion to MTL and CTL formulas. Subsequent papers [63,64] utilized Stanford CoreNLP, WordNet[4], and Prolog to assess

[2] https://github.com/stanfordnlp/CoreNLP, DLA: 22.04.2024.
[3] https://google.github.io/Seq2Seq/, DLA: 22.04.2024.
[4] https://wordnet.princeton.edu/, DLA: 22.04.2024.

RCM, identifying challenges with non-prepositional temporal expressions (e.g., *every hour*, *when something happens*, *immediately after*) and clause order. Further research in publication [47] focused on RCM's ability to revert formalized requirements to natural language, addressing ambiguities and aiding in decision-making during requirement formalization.

In [28], they use MTL to formalize legal contracts, addressing the flexibility issues with input text found in previous RCM-based papers. This technique leverages deep learning and intermediate representations for clarity. They included a step to identify functional requirements due to contract complexities. Meanwhile, [41] also explores legal formalization with a focus on autonomous vehicles, utilizing SRL and LLM, suitable for unseen inputs. Conversely, [61] shares the domain of self-driving vehicles but concentrates on MTL's role in monitoring rather than the automatic formalization of laws.

Timed Computation Tree Logic Formalization. In [6], a toolkit was developed for enhancing the clarity and consistency of automotive requirements in natural language, utilizing the GPT-J-6B[5] model to transform them into Structured English before formalizing into Timed Computation Tree Logic (TCTL). The TCTL set is transformed into first-order logic to generate a script, which is verified and tested on data from the former Daimler AG.

3.2 Automatic Generation of Modeling Notations

The analysis of unstructured text, requirements, and robotic tasks previously omitted full process descriptions, overlooking temporal complexities. This has led to a shift towards including process descriptions and policies. Table 5 presents the input-to-output mapping for the *Modeling Notation Generation* category.

Business Process Model. The Annotated Textual Descriptions of Processes (ATDP) language presented in [52] and [53] allows the translation of process descriptions to LTL over finite traces (LTLf). Recognizing the challenge of sparse annotated data, in [5], researchers later used the GPT-3[6] model to refine entity and relationship extraction from business processes with minimal examples. In [44], this effort evolved into enhancing a process extraction tool to better recognize entity identities through a sophisticated neural network, streamlining the extraction of information from texts.

Declarative Process Model. Dynamic Condition Response (DCR) graphs in workflow management represent a visual model evolving beyond traditional declarative approaches like Declare. They allow adaptable task management, extensively used in Danish digital government systems, with further enhancements from tools like the DCR Process Highlighter[7] for model automation and refinement [38,39]. In contrast, DECLARE models and their extensions have been advanced through approaches like Speech2RuM, which converts spoken

[5] https://huggingface.co/EleutherAI/gpt-j-6b, DLA: 22.04.2024.
[6] https://gpt3demo.com.
[7] https://documentation.dcr.design, DLA: 22.04.2024.

Table 5. Input-Output Mapping - Automatic Generation of Modeling Notations

Ref	Year	Input Format	Output Format	Methodology	Application	url
[52]	2019	Process Description	Annotated Textual Description of a Process (ATDP) [Ql: yes, Qt: no]	Machine-readable intermediate language	Compliance, conformance, and model consistency checking	no
[53]	2021					no
[23]	2020	Decision Description	Decision Model [Ql: yes, Qt: 1/2]	NLP pipeline	Decision and dependencies extraction	no
[51]	2021			NLP processing software (FreeLing)	Model extraction	yes
[39]	2021	Textual Artifact	Declarative Process Model	Machine-learning and expert system technique	Business process discovery	yes
[3]	2020	User Input	(DECLARE,	Rules and templates [2]	Support users defining declarative constraints	yes
[1]	2020	Process Description	Dynamic Condition Response (DCR) graph, and Multi-Perspective Declare (MP-Declare)) [Ql: yes, Qt: 1/2]	Extension of the rules and templates from [2]	Support users defining declarative constraints	yes
[38]	2019			NLP module	Support user creation of models	yes
[2]	2019			Rules and templates	Model extraction	yes
[5]	2022	Process Description	Process Element and Relation [Ql: yes, Qt: no]	LLM (GPT-3) and in-context learning	Extraction of process information	yes
[44]	2023			Pretrained end-to-end neural coreference resolution	Extraction of process information and creation of model	yes
[17]	2018	Automobile Requirement	Basic Petri Net [Ql: yes, Qt: no]	NLP and domain-specific ontologies	Requirements engineering (consistency and completeness verification)	no
[4]	2023	Process Description	Temporal Compliance Requirement [Ql: 1/2, Qt: yes]	Extension of a domain-sensitive temporal tagger (Heideltime)	Compliance verification	yes
[42]	2023	Process Description	Resource Compliance Requirement [Ql: 1/2, Qt: no]	LLM (GPT-4) supported by three similarity measures (TF-IDF, BERT, and spaCy)	Compliance verification	yes

input into detailed models, supporting sophisticated constraints as seen in MP-Declare [1,9]. Additionally, the Declo and C-4PM chatbots aid in creating and mining DPM, with the latter utilizing technologies like Rasa[8] and GPT[6] to enhance model support [21,25,26]. These innovations have been particularly impactful in healthcare process management.

[8] https://rasa.com/.

Decision Model and Notation, Petri Nets, and Related. In the study by [23] a limitation was that the extraction of DMN from NL required inputs to be concise, clear, and focused solely on one decision, excluding any irrelevant or repetitive information. In contrast, in [51] does tackle ambiguities, yet it still adheres to a rule-based methodology. In their later work, the authors employed deep learning models to extract decision models. However, the authors noted limitations including difficulties with coreference resolution, handling synonyms, and a limited dataset that only allowed for a maximum of two levels of decision dependency. For Petri Nets extraction, [17] proved to be effective in the automobile sector, although their tool has been tested with a limited number of case studies and remains inaccessible to the public. Lastly, we find [42], and [4] in both cases they did not formalize natural language but extracted a semi-formalization which was later used for compliance verification.

3.3 Automatic Augmentation of Formal Specifications

Table 6 shows the input-to-output mapping for the *Formal Specification Augmentation* category. In [8], the authors stated that converting formal specifications to natural language had limited scope for further advancement. Lately, however, there has been a growing trend in research about converting formal specifications into natural language. Even though these formal specifications are restricted, they can be challenging for a user to interpret when checking the system, leading to potential misunderstandings. This makes users ignore past formal specifications and create new ones.

Table 6. Input-Output Mapping - Automatic Augmentation of Formal Specifications

Ref.	Year	Input Format	Output Format	Methodology	Application	url
[60]	2023	Structural Logic Expression	Natural Language [Ql: 1/2, Qt: no]	Recursive parsing, Tree-LSTM, GCNs, and a decoder	General	no
[32]	2022	Unstructured Text	Requirement [Ql: 1/2, Qt: 1/2]	Fine-tunning the BERT model	Requirements engineering	no
[29]	2018	Formal Specification	Requirement [Ql: 1/2, Qt: 1/2]	Model Federation	Requirements engineering	yes

In [60], the authors analyze methods for translating logic expressions to natural text using end-to-end Seq2Seq[9] models, which sometimes misinterpret dependencies (e.g., *a motorcycle driver in orange dress*). They also highlight issues with pre-trained language models that introduce noise or invert subjects in logical structures (e.g., *a dog is chasing a cat* instead of *a cat is chasing a dog*). They suggest using structured representations like trees to improve translation accuracy. Additionally, [29] discusses *model federation* to enhance the conversion

[9] https://google.github.io/Seq2Seq, DLA: 22.04.2024.

from natural language to formal specifications, improving traceability and inconsistency analysis. A new approach for extracting requirements using BERT[10], compared against fastText[11] and ELMo[12] baselines, is detailed in [32].

4 Systematic Literature Review Findings

In Sect. 3, the different methods employed to extract formal specifications, models, or to augment natural language were presented, as well as, the application domain of these papers. The following details the findings from the classification, input, and output formats, addressing RQ2.

4.1 Summary of Findings from the Classification

Below are the findings from analyzing trends across all categories.

F1 - Difficulties in Establishing Comparable Assessment Methods. Each study has evaluated its results based on the final goal, making it difficult to compare different approaches. Incorporating a universal evaluation framework alongside specific assessments would be advantageous.

F2 - Absence of Collaboration Across Domains. Papers from different categories do not cite each other, suggesting a lack of interdisciplinary engagement (e.g., approaches extracting LTL automatically can be used in those that focus on generating DECLARE models).

F3 - Increased Interest in Human-Robot Interaction. Recent studies have focused on automatically formalizing temporal requirements involving human conversations, posing the challenge of integrating technical text elements, such as centrifuge times, with human speech. For the latter, a particularly challenging case arises when unrelated information is provided which must be distinguished from actual relevant information.

4.2 Findings from the Input Formats

The input formats used in the included papers are categorized into three distinct types as outlined in [31]: ambiguous (containing vague and unclear expressions), indirect (requiring contextual knowledge for interpretation), and clear (directly leading to a formal specification). This is shown in Fig. 1. Black boxes represent input formats from studies in the augmentation category. White boxes are used for studies related to formal specification generation. Gray boxes mean studies focusing on the automatic generation of modeling notations. A process description, for example, is considered to be indirect since interpreting it requires additional contextual knowledge. Below are all the findings from the analysis of the input formats.

[10] huggingface.co/docs/transformers/model_doc/bert, DLA: 22.04.2024.
[11] https://fasttext.cc/, DLA: 22.04.2024.
[12] https://studieswithcode.com/method/elmo, DLA: 22.04.2024.

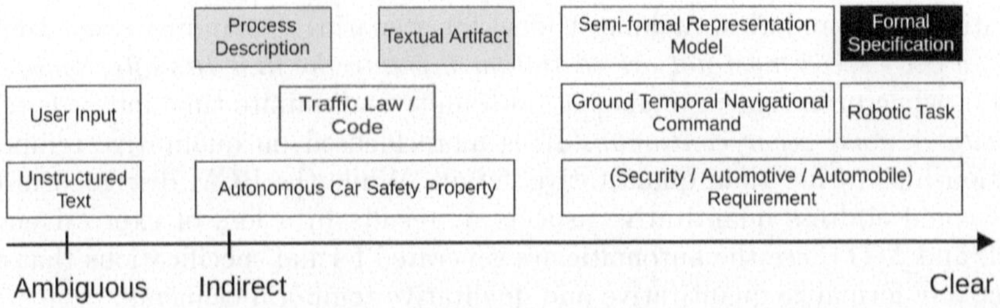

Fig. 1. Input Format Overview

F4 - Inconsistent Terminology. For example, the term *unstructured text* is used variably across studies (e.g., [19,26,30]), applying to both brief instructions and entire documents. Terminology should be more aligned and consistent to avoid confusion and ambiguities in the discussion. Inconsistent terminology mainly hampers comparing findings across different works.

F5 - Insufficient Input Quality. The quality of the input text, e.g., completeness, consistency, relevance, etc., can vary significantly and is not measured. By knowing the input quality, one can optimize further pre-processing tasks, as it is transforming unstructured text into structured requirements.

F6 - Uniform Temporal Information Treatment. In most of the approaches, there was no distinction between functional and non-functional temporal information, a concept introduced in [22]. This can prevent *smells* in temporal specifications, leading to better understanding, easier maintenance, and fewer errors.

F7 - Under-representation of Legal Text. Only five papers specifically considered legal text, indicating a significant gap in integrating legal and regulatory frameworks. Three of them involved manual steps due to higher complexity in compassion to, e.g., robot commands.

4.3 Findings from the Output Formats

This section presents the findings from both how these formats are presented to the user and the various output formats generated by the included papers.

F8 - Poor Context Management. On the one hand, users are asked to provide context, but it is rare to see context included in the output. It would be helpful for users to receive information such as assumptions made by the system, parts that have not been formalized, and any ambiguities found.

F9 - Low Support for Formalizing Quantitative Temporal Information to Formal Specifications. Automatically generated formal specifications like regular expressions, FOL, LTL, and CTL fall short of adequately representing quantitative temporal aspects. In contrast, STL and PPTL offer some capabilities in this area. STL is particularly adept at defining time intervals and quantitative boundaries, making it ideal for scenarios demanding exact timing (e.g., *a car's speed must not exceed 100 km/h within the first 10 s after ignition*). PPTL, while proficient in managing both finite and infinite time intervals (e.g., *activity A must occur continuously*), is more focused on qualitative temporal relationships rather than quantitative details. While the RCM discussed in the SLR could address quantitative aspects, it results in a loss of expressiveness. MTL and TCTL are the automatically generated formal specifications that can effectively formalize quantitative and qualitative temporal elements.

F10 - Low Support for Formalizing Quantitative Temporal Information to Modeling Notations. As shown in Table 5, for the automatic generation of modeling notations, only the MP-Declare models [1] succeed in capturing quantitative temporal aspects. The Petri Nets, decision models, or DECLARE models would need a time extension to achieve this. Furthermore, standard business process models, as detailed in the survey [12], also do not fully capture quantitative aspects. To effectively handle these aspects, they require a time-extended Business Process Model as, e.g., proposed in [46].

5 NL2MTL Approach and Evaluation

This section introduces a prototype to address the most relevant gaps identified in findings F1, F7, F8, F9, and F10. These include the difficulties in establishing a comparable assessment method, under-representation of legal texts (e.g., useful for real-time compliance in self-driving vehicles), poor output context management (improving usability), and the necessity to automate the formalization of requirements, considering both quantitative and qualitative aspects of time. This addresses RQ3. An overview of the NL2MTL approach is depicted in Fig. 2, and all material, including the implementation, dataset, and (reproducible) evaluation, is available at NL2MTL[13].

5.1 NL2MTL Foundations

The choice of MTL as a formal specification is motivated by its widespread use in system verification and its recent application in legal text formalization. Illustrative examples of MTL application in legal contexts include [61], where MTL is utilized to interpret trigger conditions and logical judgments within Chinese traffic regulations; [34] where MTL is applied to formalize marine traffic rules; and [40] where MTL is used to formalize traffic rules for autonomous vehicles on German interstates, based on the German Road Traffic Regulation. Since LLMs have been successfully utilized for extracting and formalizing LTL and STL formulas, we integrate LLMs, i.e., GPT-4, in our NL2MTL prototype.

Preliminary Steps. We explored the possibility of expanding upon an existing open-source tool. The candidates emerged from the SLR and constitute

[13] https://github.com/marisol-barrientos/nl2mtl, DLA: 22.04.2024.

NL2LTL [26], Lang2LTL, nl2tl [15] and nl2spec [19]. Among those NL2LTL [26], and Lang2LTL [37] are excluded because they formalize LTL. Focusing on tools that additionally extract STL, a comparison between nl2tl [15] and nl2spec [19] revealed that nl2spec is easier to extend due to its modular structure and more comprehensive frontend. Consequently, the development of NL2MTL was pursued by extending nl2spec. Nonetheless, despite nl2spec's emphasis on aiding users in resolving ambiguities, it was not intuitive to interpret the output messages. Specifically, nl2spec did not indicate which parts of the input text were formalized and which were not. It could also not process long documents like legal texts or process descriptions. This led to the development of our own prototype.

Approach. Figure 2 depicts the three main parts of the NL2MTL approach, i.e., accepted input formats, prompt content, and output example for a system specification, which is provided in both JSON and HTML format. This facilitates the user interpretation. It was developed in Python 3.9 and integrates other LLMs as needed. We utilized GPT-4 because it was already retrieving stable and correct results for extracting formal specifications (i.e., when testing the nl2spec framework). The tested input (c.f., Sect. 5.2) includes system specifications, legal texts, and business process descriptions. Each temporal requirement is represented in the output as an MTL formula based on **atomic propositions**. Each proposition contains a description of it, together with the **temporal granularity** (e.g., seconds), identified **ambiguities** (i.e., unclear or vague aspects), or those **lacking context** (e.g., the temporal adverb *soon* brings uncertainty), and **assumptions** that are made to come up with the final MTL formula. In addition to this, the output includes a **sequence of dependencies** between MTL formulas (e.g., the temporal adverb *soon* might be considered as *in less than 5 min*). The output also contains the text that was **not formalized** and explanations for its exclusion.

Prompt Design. The structure of the prompt is presented in Fig. 2, and the full version is accessible at NL2MTL (see footnote 12). It was crafted using the reflection and recipe patterns from the prompt engineering pattern catalog presented in [59]. Adhering to the recipe pattern streamlined the reasoning process for better decision-making. This was achieved by breaking tasks into distinct steps and omitting unnecessary information. The steps involve decomposing the input into individual atomic propositions, elucidating temporal relationships within the statement, and extracting MTL formulas. This structured approach ensures a comprehensive and systematic input analysis, leading to more accurate and contextually relevant outcomes. The reflection pattern enhances ambiguity detection and emphasizes a collaborative approach to information sharing, where both the user and the LLM play integral roles in enriching the context. In the prompt, the semantics of MTL are defined, specifying the temporal and boolean operators that should be considered. In the last part of the prompt, it is indicated the exact expected JSON output structure, each field comes together with its explanation (e.g., for the field *reason_for_non_formalization* it comes along *the reason for the inability to formalize*).

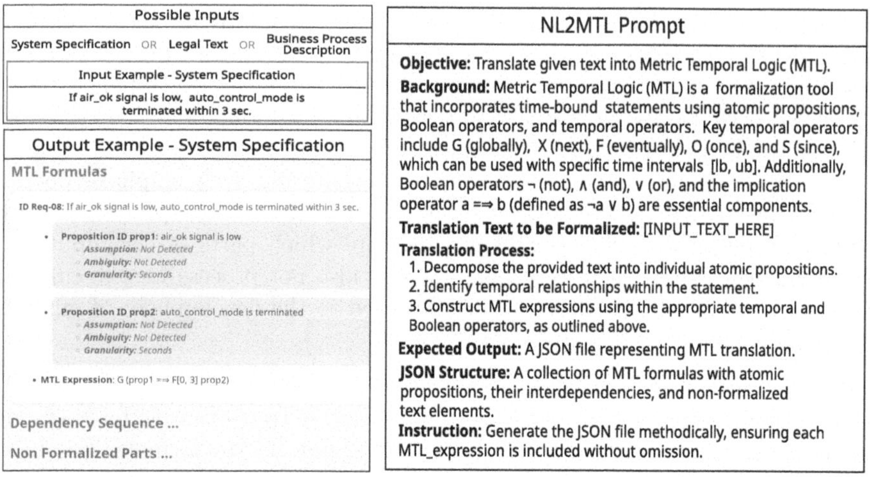

Fig. 2. Overview and Example of NL2MTL Approach

5.2 NL2MTL Evaluation

This section details on the dataset used to evaluate the NL2MTL prototype, the evaluation methodology applied, and the results. The NL2MTL approach extracts a set of MTL expressions from natural language text for each input format, as demonstrated in Fig. 2. To test the stability of the results, this is run five times per input format.

Dataset and Methodology. Table 7 contains an overview of the input files considered to evaluate the NL2MTL prototype, together with the average number per output file of atomic propositions (i.e., *Atom.*), MTL expressions (i.e., *MTL*), assumptions (i.e., *Assu.*), and ambiguities (i.e., *Ambi.*).

Table 7. Dataset Overview and Output Total Averages form Evaluation Run

ID	Description	Atom.	MTL	Assu.	Ambi.
article_78	Article 78 from a Traffic Legal Text [61]	6.75	5.25	4.00	0.50
article_80	Article 80 from a Traffic Legal Text [61]	4.25	2.25	3.00	0.50
syst_req	8 Requirements from CARA Infusion Pump System [47]	12.5	6.25	0.00	0.00
proc_desc	Harvesting Process Description [4]	7.75	6.50	3.25	1.00

The output evaluation is based on the four key principles of *good formalization*, as outlined in the methodologies for legal formalization [45]. These include being **correct** (i.e., detecting all atomic propositions and formalizing them following MTL semantics), **transparent** (i.e., defining all used elements and indicating the reasoning behind a formal specification), **comprehensible** (i.e., easy to interpret), and supportive of **multiple interpretations**.

Results. Table 7 presents the averages of assumptions and ambiguities detected per output file, varying with each round and showcasing NL2MTL's ability to support **multiple interpretations**, all deemed reasonable. This variety raises questions about the practicality and utility of these interpretations for users. All extracted atomic propositions and MTL formulas were **comprehensible** to users. A primary issue noted was in the process descriptions, particularly how time is represented in MTL formulas (e.g., *[0 min,30 min] vs [30 min] vs [0,0.5]*). Symbols and parameters were clearly defined, enhancing **transparency** and preventing hallucination. In cases of unspecified temporal granularity, the system assumes a default setting, which is documented in the assumptions field for user verification. Assessing the **correctness** of the NL2MTL outputs proved challenging. The aim is to confirm that all atomic propositions are correctly represented in the outputs and formalized according to the specified MTL semantics. Errors often arose from parts of the text that were not formalized rather than from ambiguities or assumptions. In 25% of tests, the NL2MTL system stopped translating subsequent atomic propositions after misinterpreting a stop command in the input text.

6 Discussion

Mitigating Threats to Validity. When conducting an SLR, there is always the threat of missing out on important work. We tried to mitigate this in the following ways. In the first phase of the SLR, the search string was broad to expand the scope, and various digital databases were used to ensure that no studies were overlooked due to publication rights. The inclusion and exclusion criteria were clearly defined to align the author's perspectives and ensure reproducibility. Additionally, iterative snowballing was employed to identify relevant papers from slightly different fields where our keywords were not used. In *Phase 1*, we identified five surveys related to ours. These surveys were not included in our paper analysis but were instrumental in proving that existing research had not fully covered our research questions. From them, only three surveys contained a comparison of tools designed to automate the process of formalizing temporal requirements. One paper focused solely on extracting LTL [8], while another included various formal specifications [10]. Similarly, [11] involved converting natural language into LTLf formulas for workflow construction. Neither survey rigorously demonstrated the criteria used to include certain studies over others. Additionally, two other surveys were centered on the analysis of automatic requirement formalization [55,56], which scarcely included methods for formalizing temporal aspects.

Limitations. The NL2MTL approach addressed five elicited findings. In the following, we highlight how the remaining ones could be addressed in future work. For F2, one approach could be to analyze papers excluded by EC4 and EC5, and compare their methodologies with those described in our survey. This could also contribute to addressing F3, as among the cross-domain papers, there is a keen research interest in improving the automatic formalization of natural language for robot-human communication. On the other hand, to adequately cover F4 and F5, concentrating on a specific domain, such as robotics or self-driving vehicles, would be advantageous because these areas have a more specialized vocabulary. Similarly, when working on F6, it would be simpler to first distinguish between functional and non-functional temporal information within a specific domain.

7 Conclusion

This paper features a systematic literature review to address how to effectively compare approaches aiming at extracting and formalizing temporal requirements from text. We classified approaches along their goal and output format. In total, the literature analysis revealed ten findings. To address five of those, we developed NL2MTL which closes a significant gap, i.e., existing approaches mainly focus on qualitative temporal requirements (e.g., LTL). However, quantitative aspects, such as representing exact time units (e.g., STL), are equally important. NL2MTL allows for an automatic translation of system specifications, legal texts, and business process descriptions to MTL utilizing the power of state-of-the-art LLMs. The evaluation of NL2MTL along the key principles of a *good formalization* shows promising results regarding correctness, comprehensiveness, transparency, and interpretation of the results for all input types. Future work can focus on testing the prototype in a real-world scenario and conducting in-depth user studies with domain experts on its usefulness.

Acknowledgements. This work has been funded by the Deutsche Forschungsgemeinschaft (DFG, German Research Foundation) –project number 277991500.

References

1. van der Aa, H., Balder, K.J., Maggi, F.M., Nolte, A.: Say It in your own words: defining declarative process models using speech recognition. In: Fahland, D., Ghidini, C., Becker, J., Dumas, M. (eds.) BPM 2020. LNBIP, vol. 392, pp. 51–67. Springer, Cham (2020). https://doi.org/10.1007/978-3-030-58638-6_4
2. van der Aa, H., Di Ciccio, C., Leopold, H., Reijers, H.A.: Extracting declarative process models from natural language. In: Giorgini, P., Weber, B. (eds.) CAiSE 2019. LNCS, vol. 11483, pp. 365–382. Springer, Cham (2019). https://doi.org/10.1007/978-3-030-21290-2_23
3. Alman, A., Balder, K.J., Maggi, F.M., van der Aa, H.: Declo: a chatbot for user-friendly specification of declarative process models (2020). https://ceur-ws.org/Vol-2673/paperDR12.pdf
4. Barrientos, M., Winter, K., Mangler, J., Rinderle-Ma, S.: Verification of quantitative temporal compliance requirements in process descriptions over event logs. In: Indulska, M., Reinhartz-Berger, I., Cetina, C., Pastor, O. (eds.) CAiSE 2023. LNCS, vol. 13901, pp. 417–433. Springer, Cham (2023). https://doi.org/10.1007/978-3-031-34560-9_25

5. Bellan, P., Dragoni, M., Ghidini, C.: Extracting business process entities and relations from text using pre-trained language models and in-context learning. In: Almeida, J.P.A., Karastoyanova, D., Guizzardi, G., Montali, M., Maggi, F.M., Fonseca, C.M. (eds.) EDOC 2022. LNCS, vol. 13585, pp. 182–199. Springer, Cham (2022). https://doi.org/10.1007/978-3-031-17604-3_11
6. Bertram, V., Kausch, H., Kusmenko, E., Nqiri, H., Rumpe, B., Venhoff, C.: Leveraging natural language processing for a consistency checking toolchain of automotive requirements (2023). https://doi.org/10.1109/RE57278.2023.00029
7. Bombieri, M., Meli, D., Dall'Alba, D., Rospocher, M., Fiorini, P.: Mapping natural language procedures descriptions to linear temporal logic templates: an application in the surgical robotic domain (2023). https://doi.org/10.1007/s10489-023-04882-0
8. Brunello, A., Montanari, A., Reynolds, M.: Synthesis of LTL formulas from natural language texts: state of the art and research directions (2019). https://doi.org/10.4230/LIPIcs.TIME.2019.17
9. Burattin, A., Maggi, F.M., Sperduti, A.: Conformance checking based on multi-perspective declarative process models (2016). https://doi.org/10.1016/J.ESWA.2016.08.040
10. Buzhinsky, I.: Formalization of natural language requirements into temporal logics: a survey (2019). https://doi.org/10.1109/INDIN41052.2019.8972130
11. Chakraborti, T., Rizk, Y., Isahagian, V., Aksar, B., Fuggitti, F.: From natural language to workflows: towards emergent intelligence in robotic process automation. In: Marrella, A., et al. (eds.) BPM 2022. LNBIP, vol. 459, pp. 123–137. Springer, Cham (2022). https://doi.org/10.1007/978-3-031-16168-1_8
12. Cheikhrouhou, S., Kallel, S., Guermouche, N., Jmaiel, M.: The temporal perspective in business process modeling: a survey and research challenges (2015). https://doi.org/10.1007/S11761-014-0170-X
13. Chen, B., et al.: On the use of GPT-4 for creating goal models: an exploratory study (2023). https://doi.org/10.1109/REW57809.2023.00052
14. Chen, Y., Gandhi, R., Zhang, Y., Fan, C.: NL2TL: transforming natural languages to temporal logics using large language models (2023). https://aclanthology.org/2023.emnlp-main.985
15. Chen, Z., et al.: Logic2Text: high-fidelity natural language generation from logical forms (2020). https://doi.org/10.18653/V1/2020.FINDINGS-EMNLP.190
16. Chen, Z., Li, I., Zhang, H., Preum, S.M., Stankovic, J.A., Ma, M.: CitySpec: an intelligent assistant system for requirement specification in smart cities (2022). https://doi.org/10.1109/SMARTCOMP55677.2022.00020
17. Chhabra, A., Sangroya, A., Anantaram, C.: Formalizing and verifying natural language system requirements using petri nets and context based reasoning (2018). https://ceur-ws.org/Vol-2134/paper09.pdf
18. Conrad, E., Titolo, L., Giannakopoulou, D., Pressburger, T., Dutle, A.: A compositional proof framework for FRETish requirements (2022). https://doi.org/10.1145/3497775.3503685
19. Cosler, M., Hahn, C., Mendoza, D., Schmitt, F., Trippel, C.: nl2spec: interactively translating unstructured natural language to temporal logics with large language models. In: Enea, C., Lal, A. (eds.) CAV 2023. LNCS, vol. 13965, pp. 383–396. Springer, Cham (2023). https://doi.org/10.1007/978-3-031-37703-7_18
20. Costescu, D.M.: Building on a traffic code violating monitor for autonomous vehicles: trio overtaking model (2020)

21. Donadello, I., Riva, F., Maggi, F.M., Shikhizada, A.: Declare4Py: a python library for declarative process mining (2022). https://ceur-ws.org/Vol-3216/paper_249.pdf
22. Eder, J., Franceschetti, M., Lubas, J.: Time and processes: Towards engineering temporal requirements (2021). https://doi.org/10.5220/0010625400090016
23. Etikala, V., Van Veldhoven, Z., Vanthienen, J.: Text2Dec: extracting decision dependencies from natural language text for automated DMN decision modelling. In: Del Río Ortega, A., Leopold, H., Santoro, F.M. (eds.) BPM 2020. LNBIP, vol. 397, pp. 367–379. Springer, Cham (2020). https://doi.org/10.1007/978-3-030-66498-5_27
24. Fill, H., Fettke, P., Köpke, J.: Conceptual modeling and large language models: impressions from first experiments with ChatGPT (2023). https://doi.org/10.18417/emisa.18.3
25. Fontenla-Seco, Y., Winkler, S., Gianola, A., Montali, M., Penín, M.L., Diz, A.J.B.: The droid you're looking for: C-4pm, a conversational agent for declarative process mining (2023). https://ceur-ws.org/Vol-3469/paper-20.pdf
26. Fuggitti, F., Chakraborti, T.: NL2LTL - a python package for converting natural language (NL) instructions to linear temporal logic (LTL) formulas (2023). https://doi.org/10.1609/aaai.v37i13.27068
27. Gavran, I., Darulova, E., Majumdar, R.: Interactive synthesis of temporal specifications from examples and natural language (2020). https://doi.org/10.1145/3428269
28. Ge, N., Yang, J., Yu, T., Liu, W.: AutoMTLSpec: learning to Generate MTL Specifications from Natural Language Contracts (2023). https://doi.org/10.1109/ICECCS59891.2023.00018
29. Golra, F.R., Dagnat, F., Souquières, J., Sayar, I., Guerin, S.: Bridging the gap between informal requirements and formal specifications using model federation. In: Johnsen, E.B., Schaefer, I. (eds.) SEFM 2018. LNCS, vol. 10886, pp. 54–69. Springer, Cham (2018). https://doi.org/10.1007/978-3-319-92970-5_4
30. Hahn, C., Schmitt, F., Tillman, J.J., Metzger, N., Siber, J., Finkbeiner, B.: Formal specifications from natural language (2022). https://doi.org/10.48550/ARXIV.2206.01962
31. He, J., Bartocci, E., Nickovic, D., Isakovic, H., Grosu, R.: DeepSTL - from English requirements to signal temporal logic (2022). https://doi.org/10.1145/3510003.3510171
32. Ivanov, V., Sadovykh, A., Naumchev, A., Bagnato, A., Yakovlev, K.: Extracting software requirements from unstructured documents (2022). https://arxiv.org/abs/2202.02135
33. Kitchenham, B.: Procedures for performing systematic reviews (2004)
34. Krasowski, H., Althoff, M.: Temporal logic formalization of marine traffic rules (2021). https://doi.org/10.1109/IV48863.2021.9575685
35. Li, C., Chang, J., Wang, X., Zhao, L., Mao, W.: Formalization of natural language into PPTL specification via neural machine translation. In: Liu, S., Duan, Z., Liu, A. (eds.) SOFL+MSVL 2022. LNCS, vol. 13854, pp. 79–92. Springer, Cham (2022). https://doi.org/10.1007/978-3-031-29476-1_7
36. Lin, J., et al.: Road traffic law adaptive decision-making for self-driving vehicles (2022). https://doi.org/10.1109/ITSC55140.2022.9922208
37. Liu, J.X., Yang, Z., Idrees, I., Liang, S., Schornstein, B., Tellex, S., Shah, A.: Grounding complex natural language commands for temporal tasks in unseen environments (2023)

38. López, H.A., Marquard, M., Muttenthaler, L., Strømsted, R.: Assisted declarative process creation from natural language descriptions (2019). https://doi.org/10.1109/EDOCW.2019.00027
39. López, H.A., Strømsted, R., Niyodusenga, J.-M., Marquard, M.: Declarative process discovery: linking process and textual views. In: Nurcan, S., Korthaus, A. (eds.) CAiSE 2021. LNBIP, vol. 424, pp. 109–117. Springer, Cham (2021). https://doi.org/10.1007/978-3-030-79108-7_13
40. Maierhofer, S., Rettinger, A., Mayer, E.C., Althoff, M.: Formalization of interstate traffic rules in temporal logic (2020). https://doi.org/10.1109/IV47402.2020.9304549
41. Manas, K., Paschke, A.: Semantic role assisted natural language rule formalization for intelligent vehicle. In: Fensel, A., Ozaki, A., Roman, D., Soylu, A. (eds.) RuleML+RR 2023. LNCS, vol. 14244, pp. 175–189. Springer, Cham (2023). https://doi.org/10.1007/978-3-031-45072-3_13
42. Mustroph, H., Barrientos, M., Winter, K., Rinderle-Ma, S.: Verifying resource compliance requirements from natural language text over event logs. In: Di Francescomarino, C., Burattin, A., Janiesch, C., Sadiq, S. (eds.) BPM 2023. LNCS, vol. 14159, pp. 249–265. Springer, Cham (2023). https://doi.org/10.1007/978-3-031-41620-0_15
43. Nayak, A., Timmapathini, H., Murali, V., Ponnalagu, K., Venkoparao, V.G., Post, A.: Req2spec: Transforming software requirements into formal specifications using natural language processing. In: Gervasi, V., Vogelsang, A. (eds.) REFSQ 2022. LNCS, vol. 13216, pp. 87–95. Springer, Cham (2022). https://doi.org/10.1007/978-3-030-98464-9_8
44. Neuberger, J., Ackermann, L., Jablonski, S.: Beyond rule-based named entity recognition and relation extraction for process model generation from natural language text (2023). https://doi.org/10.48550/arXiv.2305.03960
45. Novotná, T., Libal, T.: An evaluation of methodologies for legal formalization. In: Calvaresi, D., Najjar, A., Winikoff, M., Främling, K. (eds.) EXTRAAMAS 2022. LNCS, vol. 13283, pp. 189–203. Springer, Cham (2022). https://doi.org/10.1007/978-3-031-15565-9_12
46. Ocampo-Pineda, M., Posenato, R., Zerbato, F.: TimeAwareBPMN-js: an editor and temporal verification tool for time-aware BPMN processes (2022). https://doi.org/10.1016/J.SOFTX.2021.100939
47. Osama, M., Zaki-Ismail, A., Abdelrazek, M.A., Grundy, J., Ibrahim, A.S.: A comprehensive requirement capturing model enabling the automated formalisation of NL requirements (2023). https://doi.org/10.1007/s42979-022-01449-7
48. Pan, J., Chou, G., Berenson, D.: Data-efficient learning of natural language to linear temporal logic translators for robot task specification (2023). https://doi.org/10.1109/ICRA48891.2023.10161125
49. Pi, X., Shi, J., Huang, Y., Wei, H.: Automated mining and checking of formal properties in natural language requirements. In: Douligeris, C., Karagiannis, D., Apostolou, D. (eds.) KSEM 2019. LNCS (LNAI), vol. 11776, pp. 75–87. Springer, Cham (2019). https://doi.org/10.1007/978-3-030-29563-9_8
50. Quartey, B., Rosen, E., Tellex, S., Konidaris, G.: Verifiably following complex robot instructions with foundation models (2024). https://doi.org/10.48550/ARXIV.2402.11498
51. Quishpi, L., Carmona, J., Padró, L.: Extracting decision models from textual descriptions of processes. In: Polyvyanyy, A., Wynn, M.T., Van Looy, A., Reichert, M. (eds.) BPM 2021. LNCS, vol. 12875, pp. 85–102. Springer, Cham (2021). https://doi.org/10.1007/978-3-030-85469-0_8

52. Sànchez-Ferreres, J., Burattin, A., Carmona, J., Montali, M., Padró, L.: Formal reasoning on natural language descriptions of processes. In: Hildebrandt, T., van Dongen, B.F., Röglinger, M., Mendling, J. (eds.) BPM 2019. LNCS, vol. 11675, pp. 86–101. Springer, Cham (2019). https://doi.org/10.1007/978-3-030-26619-6_8
53. Sànchez-Ferreres, J., Burattin, A., Carmona, J., Montali, M., Padró, L., Quishpi, L.: Unleashing textual descriptions of business processes (2021). https://doi.org/10.1007/s10270-021-00886-x
54. Sharma, S., Brian Lee, K.M., Brown, M., Best, G.: Instructing robots with natural language via bi-RNNs for temporal logic translation (2023). https://www.scopus.com/inward/record.uri?eid=2-s2.0-85184383465&partnerID=40&md5=9a09f07a3d2022b763a0a17f7d14289d
55. Sonbol, R., Rebdawi, G., Ghneim, N.: The use of NLP-based text representation techniques to support requirement engineering tasks: a systematic mapping review (2022). https://doi.org/10.1109/ACCESS.2022.3182372
56. Sudhi, V., Kutty, L., Gröpler, R.: Natural language processing for requirements formalization: how to derive new approaches? (2023). https://doi.org/10.48550/arXiv.2309.13272
57. Wang, C., Ross, C., Kuo, Y.L., Katz, B., Barbu, A.: Learning a natural-language to LTL executable semantic parser for grounded robotics (2020). https://www.scopus.com/inward/record.uri?eid=2-s2.0-85168241969&partnerID=40&md5=6c3e5cd9fe6da29032fae93808c78a09
58. Wang, X., Li, G., Li, C., Zhao, L., Shu, X.: Automatic generation of specification from natural language based on temporal logic. In: Xue, J., Nagoya, F., Liu, S., Duan, Z. (eds.) SOFL+MSVL 2020. LNCS, vol. 12723, pp. 154–171. Springer, Cham (2021). https://doi.org/10.1007/978-3-030-77474-5_11
59. White, J., et al.: A prompt pattern catalog to enhance prompt engineering with chatGPT (2023). https://doi.org/10.48550/ARXIV.2302.11382
60. Wu, X., Cai, Y., Lian, Z., Leung, H., Wang, T.: Generating natural language from logic expressions with structural representation (2023). https://doi.org/10.1109/TASLP.2023.3263784
61. Yu, W., Zhao, C., Wang, H., Liu, J., Ma, X., Yang, Y., Li, J., Wang, W., Hu, X., Zhao, D.: Online Legal Driving Behavior Monitoring for Self-driving Vehicles (2024). https://doi.org/10.6084/m9.figshare.24372535.v1
62. Zaki-Ismail, A., Osama, M., Abdelrazek, M., Grundy, J., Ibrahim, A.S.: RCM: requirement capturing model for automated requirements formalisation (2021). https://doi.org/10.5220/0010270401100121
63. Zaki-Ismail, A., Osama, M., Abdelrazek, M., Grundy, J.C., Ibrahim, A.S.: ARF: automatic requirements formalisation tool (2021). https://doi.org/10.1109/RE51729.2021.00060
64. Zaki-Ismail, A., Osama, M., Abdelrazek, M.A., Grundy, J.C., Ibrahim, A.S.: RCM-extractor: an automated NLP-based approach for extracting a semi formal representation model from natural language requirements (2022). https://doi.org/10.1007/s10515-021-00312-y
65. Zhang, S., Zhai, J., Bu, L., Chen, M., Wang, L., Li, X.: Automated generation of LTL specifications for smart home IoT using natural language (2020)
66. Zhao, L., et al.: Natural language processing for requirements engineering: a systematic mapping study (2022). https://doi.org/10.1145/3444689

Process Mining and Monitoring

Recognizing Relationships: Detecting the 4C Spectrum in $O(P^2 + T^2)$ for Acyclic Sound Process Models

Thomas M. Prinz[1](✉), Torsten Welsch[2], and N. Long Ha[3]

[1] Course Evaluation Service, Friedrich Schiller University Jena, Jena, Germany
Thomas.Prinz@uni-jena.de

[2] Department Information Technologies, HTBLA Grieskirchen, Grieskirchen, Austria
t.welsch@htl-grieskirchen.at

[3] Faculty of Economic Information Systems, University of Economics, Hue University, Hue City, Vietnam
hnlong@hueuni.edu.vn

Abstract. The identification of business process models within large model collections poses a significant challenge. Process querying offers a solution by selecting models that meet specific characteristics, utilizing queries based on behavioral relations. These relations, which include conflict, co-occurrence, causality, and concurrency (collectively known as the 4C Spectrum), describe the potential interactions between tasks within process models during execution. However, existing approaches to compute these behavioral relations are inefficient for models with numerous execution traces, often requiring extensive time. This paper introduces a set of algorithms, termed "Behavioral Relation Computations" (in short BeRelCo), capable of identifying all 4C Spectrum behavioral relations within acyclic sound free-choice workflow nets with quadratic time complexity $O(P^2 + T^2)$. Our experiments demonstrate significant benefits, particularly for process models characterized by many execution traces.

Keywords: Business process models · Behavioral relations · Acyclic · Soundness

1 Introduction

Business process management (BPM) is an interdisciplinary domain that integrates business and computer science principles, focusing on the analysis and improvement of *business process models*. These models act as blueprints, describing task sequences, dependencies, and decision points to achieve business objectives [6]. Established modeling languages, such as the *Business Process Model and Notation* (BPMN), enable organizations to articulate their processes comprehensively. Typically stored in extensive repositories, identifying process models presents a significant challenge when they are to fulfill certain characteristics. For instance, a business analyst searching for a model that concurrently executes payments and deliveries, subsequent to an order, would face the task of manually reviewing each model in the absence of IT support.

Process queries enable businesses to systematically search through their process models in repositories, identifying models that meet specific criteria [14]. The core

J. Borbinha et al. (Eds.): EDOC 2024, LNCS 15409, pp. 281–299, 2025.
https://doi.org/10.1007/978-3-031-78338-8_15

of process queries lies in the exploration of *behavioral relations* [15]. These relations reveal how tasks within a process model interact, indicating whether tasks are mutually exclusive, co-occur, cause one another, or can be executed concurrently. Polyvyanyy et al. [15] introduced a comprehensive set of these behavioral relations, known as the *4C Spectrum*. This spectrum uncovers the fundamental relations of *conflict, co-occurrence, causality*, and *concurrency*, showcasing their various manifestations across different execution traces of process models. The *4C Spectrum* is aligned with other established behavioral relation frameworks in literature, such as the *(causal) behavioral profile* [21, 22], enhancing its validity and application in the field of BPM.

The behavioral relations within the *4C Spectrum* are binary, indicating that the size of each relation scales quadratically with the number of nodes in a process model. Current detection techniques for these relations, however, tend to require exponential time in the worst case. Although it seems acceptable to derive the behavioral relations for a single process model in seconds, indexing and querying process models from huge repositories is difficult to accomplish with such computationally expensive algorithms [10], especially from an ecological perspective. Polyvyanyy et al. [15] laid the computational groundwork for some of these relations, leveraging concepts such as *reachability* and the *covering problem*. Similarly, Wolf [23] linked most behavioral relations back to the reachability problem. Yet, the general reachability problem for Petri nets falls within the `NONELEMENTARY` complexity class [3], posing significant computational challenges. Ha and Prinz [10] explored these relations for acyclic sound workflow graphs, utilizing a *Single-Entry Single-Exit* (SESE) decomposition into fragments [19] (similarly to Weidlich et al. [22]). This approach uses transitive rules but struggles with unstructured process model fragments, known as "rigids"[19], where state-space exploration—a process with exponential time complexity—becomes necessary. *The current gap is the absence of an algorithm capable of efficiently computing all behavioral relations for unstructured fragments in low polynomial (i. e., quadratic to bi-quadratic) time.* Despite these challenges, understanding behavioral relations is also crucial for analyzing process similarity [11] and checking compliance with business rules [13].

This paper introduces a set of algorithms, termed *Behavioral Relation Computations* (in short *BeRelCo*), which are designed for process models that can be represented as *acyclic sound free-choice workflow nets*. Soundness is a minimal quality correctness criterion [5], whereas free-choiceness increases the alignment of workflow nets to industrial process languages [8]. *BeRelCo* is capable of computing all behavioral relations within the *4C Spectrum* with a *quadratic time complexity*, $O(N^2)$, where N represents the number of nodes. Experimental results from two datasets demonstrate the computational advantages of *BeRelCo*, particularly when numerous different execution traces are possible. For both datasets, all pairwise relations were computed in less than 1 s, with some instances experiencing a speed-up factor exceeding 1000. The approach is also effective for models exhibiting inclusive behavior. While the current focus is on acyclic process models, we are convinced that extending the methodology to cyclic models through *loop decomposition* [16]—a method that converts a cyclic model into a set of acyclic models with equivalent behavior—is feasible.

This paper is organized as follows: Sect. 2 introduces basic concepts necessary for understanding the rest of the work. This is followed by a description of the behavioral relations of the *4C Spectrum* in acyclic nets in Sect. 3. We then derive algorithms for these relations, showcasing our methodological contributions in Sect. 4. Section 5 briefly discusses how these algorithms can be extended to inclusive behavior. Related work is investigated in Sect. 6. In Sect. 7, an evaluation of the algorithms demonstrates their effectiveness and computational benefits. The paper concludes in Sect. 8 with a reflection on the implications of our work.

2 Preliminaries

This paper builds upon well-established definitions of Petri and workflow nets.

Definition 1 (Petri net). A *(Petri) net* is a triple (P, T, F) with P and T are finite, disjoint sets of *places* and *transitions* and $F \subseteq (P \times T) \cup (T \times P)$ is the *flow* relation. ⌟

The union $P \cup T$ of a net $N = (P, T, F)$ can be interpreted as *nodes* and F as *edges* between those nodes. For $x \in P \cup T$, $\bullet x = \{p \mid (p, x) \in F\}$ is the *preset* of x (all directly preceding nodes) and $x\bullet = \{s \mid (x, s) \in F\}$ is the *postset* of x (all directly succeeding nodes). Each node in $\bullet x$ is an *input* of x and each node in $x\bullet$ is an *output* of x. The preset and postset of a set of nodes $X \subseteq P \cup T$ is defined as $\bullet X = \bigcup_{x \in X} \bullet x$ and $X\bullet = \bigcup_{x \in X} x\bullet$, respectively. A *path* $(n_1, \ldots, n_m)$ is a sequence of nodes $n_1, \ldots, n_m \in P \cup T$ with $m \geq 1$ and $\forall i \in \{1, \ldots, m-1\}$: $n_i \in \bullet n_{i+1}$. Note that places and transitions alternate on paths. If all nodes of a path are pairwise different, the path is *acyclic*; otherwise, it is *cyclic*. $Paths_N(x, y)$ denotes the set of all paths between nodes x and y in N, where $x, y \in P \cup T$. N is *acyclic* if all its paths are acyclic. Each net in this paper is restricted to be *simple free-choice*: $\forall p \in P, |p\bullet| > 1: \bullet(p\bullet) = \{p\}$ [8]. In the nets shown here, circles represent places, rectangles transitions and directed edges represent flows (see Fig. 1 as an example).

Definition 2 (Workflow and AFW-net). A *workflow net* $WN = (P, T, F, s, f)$ is a net (P, T, F) with $s, f \in P$, $\bullet s = \emptyset$, and $f\bullet = \emptyset$. s is the *source* and f is the *sink* of WN. All nodes are on a path from s to f. If WN is acyclic and free-choice, we call it *AFW-net*. ⌟

Figure 1 visualizes a workflow net. *Markings* of workflow nets describe states, which specify the number of *tokens* at each place:

Definition 3 (Marking). A *marking* of a workflow net $WN = (P, T, F, s, f)$ is a total mapping $M: P \mapsto \mathbb{N}_0$ that assigns a natural number of *tokens* to each place of P. $M(p) = 1$ means that place $p \in P$ carries one token in marking M. ⌟

The *initial* marking M_s is a marking where only the source s has a token. The *terminal* marking M_f is a marking where only the sink f has a token. Transitions whose input places all have tokens are *enabled* in a marking and can be fired, leading to the workflow net's semantics:

Definition 4 (Semantics). Let $WN = (P, T, F, s, f)$ be a workflow net with a marking M. A transition $t \in T$ is *enabled* in M iff every place $p \in \bullet t$ contains at least one token in

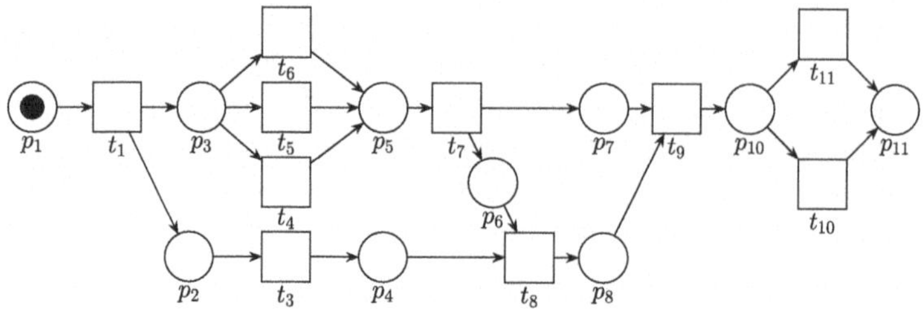

Fig. 1. A graphical example of a Petri net.

M, $\forall p \in \bullet t$: $M(p) \geq 1$. If t is enabled in M, then t can *occur* ("fire"), which leads to a *step* from M to M' via t, denoted as $M \xrightarrow{t} M'$, with

$$M'(p) = M(p) \quad - \begin{cases} 1, & p \in \bullet t \\ 0, & \text{else} \end{cases} \quad + \quad \begin{cases} 1, & p \in t\bullet \\ 0, & \text{else.} \end{cases}$$

┘

I. e., in a step via t, t "consumes" one token from all its input places and "produces" one token for all its output places. Stepwise firings of transitions lead to chains of fired transitions, which describe the behavior of a net as occurrence sequences:

Definition 5 (Occurrence Sequences and Runs). Let $WN = (P, T, F, s, f)$ be a workflow net with a marking M_0. A sequence of transitions $\sigma = \langle t_1, \ldots, t_n \rangle$, $n \in \mathbb{N}_0$, $t_1, \ldots, t_n \in T$, is an *occurrence sequence* of M_0 iff there is a sequence of markings $M_0, M_1, \ldots, M_n$ such that $M_{i-1} \xrightarrow{t_i} M_i$ holds for each $i \in \{1, \ldots, n\}$. It can be said that σ *leads* from M_0 to M_n. A place $p \in P$ occurs in σ, depicted as $p \in \sigma$, iff the steps $M_0 \xrightarrow{t_1} M_1 \xrightarrow{t_2} \ldots \xrightarrow{t_n} M_n$ contain a marking M_i, $i \in \{1, \ldots, n\}$, with $M_i(p) \geq 1$. σ is a *run* iff σ leads from the initial marking M_s to the terminal marking M_f of WN. ┘

A marking M' is *reachable* from a marking M (denoted $M \rightarrow^* M'$) iff there is an occurrence sequence σ of M that leads to M'.

Definition 6 (Soundness). A workflow net $WN = (P, T, F, s, f)$ with its initial marking $M_s = \{s\}$ and its terminal marking $M_f = \{f\}$ is *sound* iff

(1) $\forall M,\ M_s \rightarrow^* M\colon\ M \rightarrow^* M_f$,
(2) $\forall M,\ M_s \rightarrow^* M\colon\ (M(f) \geq 1 \implies M = M_f)$, and
(3) there is no *dead* transition in WN: $\forall t \in T\ \exists M, M'\colon\ M_s \rightarrow^* M \xrightarrow{t} M'$. [1] ┘

This paper focuses on sound AFW-nets.

Definition 7 (Run Net). A net $\pi = (P_R, T_R, F_R)$ is a *run net* of a sound AFW-net $N = (P, T, F, s, f)$ and a run R iff

$$P_R = \{p \in P\colon\ p \in R\} \wedge T_R = \{t \in T : t \in R\} \wedge F_R = \{(x, y) \in F\colon\ x \in (P_R \cup T_R) \wedge y \in (P_R \cup T_R)\}$$

$n \in R$ *occurs* in π, depicted as $n \in \pi$. $\Pi(N)$ depicts the set of all run nets of N. $\Pi(x) = \{\pi \in \Pi(N) : x \in \pi\}$ is the set of all run nets of N, in which the node x occurs. ┘

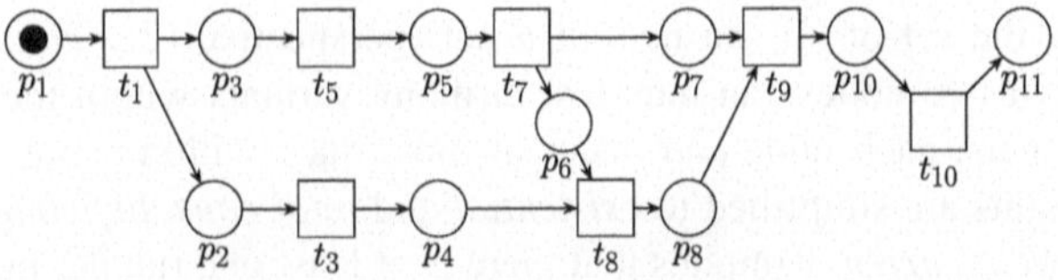

Fig. 2. A run net of the net in Fig. 1.

Figure 2 illustrates one possible run net of the net in Fig. 1. The definition of run nets in this work deviates from that of occurrence nets proposed by Polyvyanyy et al. [15], as it is simplified for the context of sound AFW-nets, wherein each place and transition occurs no more than once. Such run nets are analogous to *instance subgraphs* as defined in the workflow graph theory [18].

3 Behavioral Relations

Investigating the behavior of an AFW-net follows two perspectives: (1) The consideration of a single run net π, or (2) the consideration of all its run nets Π. For (1), it can be examined (a) if a node occurs in π and (b) if two nodes that occur in π are *causal* or *concurrent* to each other. In Fig. 1, t_3 can be *concurrent* to t_4 and t_1 is *causal* for t_8. For (2), the consideration of all run nets contains two sub-perspectives: *Existential* and *total* behavior between two nodes. Examples of *existential* behavior are *can co-occur* (there is a run net, in which two nodes occur) and *can conflict* (there is a run net, in which one node occurs but the other does not). In Fig. 1, t_3 *can conflict* with t_6 as there is a run net, in which t_3 occurs but not t_6. t_1 and t_6 *can co-occur* as there is a run net, in which both occur. Examples of *total* behavior are *total co-occur* (two nodes occur always together) and *total conflict* (two nodes never occur together). In Fig. 1, t_5 and t_6 are in *total conflict*, and t_1 and t_3 are in *total co-occur* relation.

Polyvyanyy et al. [15] introduced the *4C Spectrum* to describe all nuances of *conflict*, *co-occurrence*, *causality*, and *concurrency* within process models. Originally, these behavioral relations were defined solely in terms of transitions. However, analyzing the interactions between places—specifically, whether two places can simultaneously contain tokens in the same marking—is also crucial for understanding the full dynamics of process models. Therefore, this work extends the examination of behavioral relations to include all node pairs, encompassing both places and transitions.

If two nodes occur in a run net, they are either in a *causal* or *concurrency* relation [15]. These basic relations are only defined over a single run net (perspective (1)):

Definition 8 (Concurrency and Causality). Let $N = (P, T, F, s, f)$ be a sound AFW-net with one of its run nets $\pi \in \Pi(N)$.

Two nodes $x, y \in P \cup T$ are *concurrent* in π (depicted as $x \parallel_\pi y$) iff

$$x, y \in \pi \quad \wedge \quad Paths_\pi(x, y) = \emptyset \quad \wedge \quad Paths_\pi(y, x) = \emptyset.$$

x is *causal* for y in π, depicted as $x\ causal_\pi\ y$, iff

$$x, y \in \pi \quad \wedge \quad Paths_\pi(x, y) \neq \emptyset \quad [15].$$

⌟

Considering the set of all run nets of a net (perspective (2)), *causality* and *concurrency* between two nodes can manifest in many variants within the *4C Spectrum*. In sound AFW-nets, each node can occur at most once within a run. Consequently, these many variants are simplified to *existential* and *total causality/concurrency*. *Existential causality/concurrency* implies that there is at least one run net in which the two nodes occur and are in a *causal* or *concurrency* relation, respectively. *Total causality/concurrency* indicates that, in every run net where the two nodes occur, they maintain a *causal* or *concurrency* relation. *Can co-occur* and *can conflict* are defined over the existence of at least one run net. In sound AFW-nets, every pair of two nodes x and y is exactly in one of the following four relations for all run nets [15]: (1) *total conflict*; (2) *total co-occur*; (3) *requires* (each run net that contains x also contains y, however, there are run nets with y but not with x); and (4) *independent* (there are run nets containing either x or y, but also run nets, which contain both). In Fig. 1, t_6 *requires* t_3 and t_6 is *independent* from t_{11}.

Based on *occurrence*, *concurrency* and *causality*, the following definition summarizes all behavioral relations resulting from sound AFW-nets [10]. *Please be aware that existential/total concurrency/causality is only defined for run nets, in which two nodes in relation occur, thus "total" implies "existential"* [15]*:*

Definition 9 (Behavioral Relations). Let $N = (P, T, F, s, f)$ be a sound AFW-net. The behavioral relations between two different nodes $x, y \in P \cup T$ are [10]:

$$
\begin{aligned}
x \; canConflict \; y &\iff \Pi(x) \setminus \Pi(y) \neq \varnothing \\
x \; canCooccur \; y &\iff \Pi(x) \cap \Pi(y) \neq \varnothing \\
x \; totalConflict \; y &\iff x \; canConflict \; y \wedge y \; canConflict \; x \wedge \overline{x \; canCooccur \; y} \\
x \; totalCooccur \; y &\iff \overline{x \; canConflict \; y} \wedge \overline{y \; canConflict \; x} \wedge x \; canCooccur \; y \\
x \; requires \; y &\iff \overline{x \; canConflict \; y} \wedge y \; canConflict \; x \wedge x \; canCooccur \; y \\
x \; independent \; y &\iff x \; canConflict \; y \wedge y \; canConflict \; x \wedge x \; canCooccur \; y \\
x \; concurrent^{\exists} \; y &\iff \exists \pi \in \Pi(x) \cap \Pi(y) : \; x \parallel_{\pi} y \\
x \; concurrent^{\forall} \; y &\iff \forall \pi \in \Pi(x) \cap \Pi(y) : \; x \parallel_{\pi} y \wedge x \; concurrent^{\exists} \; y \\
x \; causal^{\exists} \; y &\iff \exists \pi \in \Pi(x) \cap \Pi(y) : \; x \; causal_{\pi} \; y \\
x \; causal^{\forall} \; y &\iff \forall \pi \in \Pi(x) \cap \Pi(y) : \; x \; causal_{\pi} \; y \wedge x \; causal^{\exists} \; y
\end{aligned}
$$

⌟

4 Structural Computation of the Behavioral Relations

The aim of this paper is to define algorithms that avoid the need for discovery-like computation, which currently exhibits exponential runtime in analyzing AFW-nets. This section examines the structural properties of sound AFW-nets to ultimately compute all behavioral relations between pairs of nodes within a quadratic time complexity.

4.1 Existential Concurrency and Total Concurrency

Prinz et al. [17] have introduced an algorithm with quadratic time complexity for detecting the *concurrency* relation in sound acyclic free-choice workflow nets. Instead of defining concurrency over run nets as in this work, their definition utilizes reachability: Two places are concurrent if there is a reachable marking from the initial marking, in which both places carry tokens. Concurrency between a place and a transition or two transitions is defined similarly. In Theorem 3 on page 140 of [17], they show that concurrency in sound AFW-nets requires the absence of paths between the nodes in relation. As a consequence, two nodes can only be in a concurrency relation if they do not have a path to each other in a run net as well. Therefore, their definition of concurrency aligns with what is termed *existential concurrency* in this work, thereby enabling the relation's determination between all nodes in a quadratic time:

Proposition 1 (Existential Concurrency). Let $N = (P, T, F, s, f)$ be a sound AFW-net. $concurrent^{\exists}$ can be computed in a quadratic time complexity $O(|P|^2 + |T|^2)$ [17]. □

Concurrency in Definition 8 is defined over the absence of paths between two nodes x and y in at least one *run net*. Fortunately, as mentioned before, soundness restricts and simplifies concurrency: If x and y are in an *existential concurrency* relation, then there cannot be a path between x and y and vice versa in the *AFW-net*:

Theorem 1. Let $N = (P, T, F, s, f)$ be a sound AFW-net with two nodes $x, y \in P \cup T, x \neq y$.

$$x\ concurrent^{\exists}\ y \implies Paths_N(x,y) = \varnothing \wedge Paths_N(y,x) = \varnothing \tag{1}$$

$$Paths_N(x,y) \neq \varnothing \vee Paths_N(y,x) \neq \varnothing \implies \overline{x\ concurrent^{\exists}\ y} \tag{2}$$

Proof. See Prinz et al. [17] (Cor. 4 (p. 141) for (1) and Theorem 3 (pp. 140–141) for (2)). □

Please note that Theorem 1 argues over paths in an AFW-net (N) and *not* over paths in a run net (π), as it is done in Definition 8 of *concurrency*. Of course, an AFW-net without paths between two nodes x and y cannot have any paths between x and y in a run net. As a consequence, each run net, in which such x and y occur, cannot have a path between x and y and vice versa. Therefore, x and y are always *concurrent* if they occur (Definition 8). This corresponds to the definition of *total concurrency* in Definition 9. In summary, *existential concurrency* is equal to *total concurrency*:

Theorem 2 (Existential is Total Concurrency). Let $N = (P, T, F, s, f)$ be a sound AFW-net and $x, y \in P \cup T$ two of its nodes.

$$x\ concurrent^{\exists}\ y \iff x\ concurrent^{\forall}\ y$$

┘

Proof. Of course, $x\ concurrent^{\forall}\ y \implies x\ concurrent^{\exists}\ y$ directly follows from Definition 9. For this reason, this proof focuses on $x\ concurrent^{\exists}\ y \implies x\ concurrent^{\forall}\ y$.

The preconditions by Theorem 2 are a sound AFW-net $N = (P, T, F, s, f)$ and two nodes $x, y \in P \cup T$. The theorem demands for the validity of $x\ concurrent^{\exists}\ y$. By

x *concurrent*$^{\exists}$ y and Theorem 1, there is no path between x and y as well as between y and x in the AFW-net N:

$$Paths_N(x,y) = \varnothing \quad \wedge \quad Paths_N(y,x) = \varnothing$$

From this, it follows:

$$\forall \pi \in \Pi(x) \cap \Pi(y): \; Paths_\pi(x,y) = \varnothing \wedge Paths_\pi(y,x) = \varnothing \wedge x \; concurrent^{\exists} \; y$$
$$\overset{\text{Def. 8}}{\iff} \quad \forall \pi \in \Pi(x) \cap \Pi(y): \; x \parallel_\pi y \wedge x \; concurrent^{\exists} \; y$$

Following this and Definition 9: $x \; concurrent^{\forall} \; y$ ✓ □

4.2 Existential Causality and Total Causality

Existential causality requires a path in the AFW-net between two nodes in relation, as Definition 8 needs a path in the run net [9, 10]. Since the AFW-nets considered here are sound and free-choice, the existence of a path between x and y implies the existence of a run net, in which x has a path to y, i. e., x and y are in an *existential causality* relation:

Theorem 3 (Existential Causality). Let $N = (P, T, F, s, f)$ be a sound AFW-net and $x, y \in P \cup T$ two of its nodes.

$$x \; causal^{\exists} \; y \quad \iff \quad Paths_N(x,y) \neq \varnothing$$

⌟

Proof. See the contraposition of Lemma 4.2 in Ha and Prinz [10]. □

A node in an acyclic graph has (1) a path to itself and (2) only paths to nodes to which some outputs has a path too. A reverse topological order ensures that a node is only processed after all its output nodes have been addressed (the reverse topological order of the net in Fig. 1 is $(p_{11}, t_{11}, t_{10}, p_{10}, t_9, p_8, p_7, t_8, p_4, t_3, p_2, p_6, t_7, p_5, t_4, t_5, t_6, p_3, t_1, p_1)$). For this reason, a check for all nodes, if there is a path between them in an ASW-net, can be performed in $O(|P| + |T| + |F|)$ [2]. In the worst case, $|F|$ can be quadratic to $|P| + |T|$ according to Definition 1. Thus, finding all pairs in *existential causality* relation can be achieved in a quadratic time complexity of $O((|P| + |T| + (|P| + |T|)^2) = O(|P|^2 + |T|^2)$.

If a node x is *existential causal* to a node y, then there is a path between x and y in the AFW-net by Theorem 3. Following Theorem 1 of *existential concurrency*, x and y can *never* be in a *concurrency* relation as there is a path between x and y in the AFW-net. As a consequence, if x and y are *existential causal*, then x and y are not *existential concurrent*. Polyvyanyy et al. [15] state that if two nodes occur in a run net, they are either in a *concurrency* or *causality* relation. Therefore, x and y must be in a *causality* relation for all run nets, in which both occur. This fits the definition of *total causality* in Definition 9. In summary, *existential causality* implies *total causality*:

Theorem 4 (Existential is Total Causality). Let $N = (P, T, F, s, f)$ be a sound AFW-net and $x, y \in P \cup T$ two of its nodes.

$$x\ causal^{\exists}\ y \iff x\ causal^{\forall}\ y$$

Proof. Of course, $x\ causal^{\forall}\ y \implies x\ causal^{\exists}\ y$ directly follows from Definition 9. For this reason, this proof focuses on $x\ causal^{\exists}\ y \implies x\ causal^{\forall}\ y$.

By Theorem 4, we have a sound AFW-net $N = (P, T, F, s, f)$ with two nodes $x, y \in P \cup T$. The theorem requires $x\ causal^{\exists}\ y$. Following from $x\ causal^{\exists}\ y$ and Theorem 3, there is a path between x and y in the AFW-net N:

$$Paths_N(x, y) \neq \varnothing \tag{3}$$

Thus, x and y cannot be in an *existential concurrency* relation according to Theorem 1:

$$\begin{aligned}\overline{x\ concurrent^{\exists}\ y} &\overset{\text{Def. 9}}{\iff} \forall \pi \in \Pi(x) \cap \Pi(y):\ x \nparallel_{\pi} y \\ &\overset{\text{Def. 8}}{\iff} \forall \pi \in \Pi(x) \cap \Pi(y):\ Paths_{\pi}(x, y) \neq \varnothing \vee Paths_{\pi}(y, x) \neq \varnothing\end{aligned}$$

As N is acyclic and given (3), there cannot be a path between y and x in N. Thus, $Paths_{\pi}(y, x) = \varnothing$ must hold, resulting in $Paths_{\pi}(y, x) \neq \varnothing$ to be invalid. Finally, this leads to $\forall \pi \in \Pi(x) \cap \Pi(y):\ Paths_{\pi}(x, y) \neq \varnothing$ and $x\ causal^{\exists}\ y$. So for all run nets π, in which x and y occur, $x\ causal_{\pi}\ y$ by Definition 8 and $x\ causal^{\exists}\ y$. This meets Definition 9 of $x\ causal^{\forall}\ y$. ✓ □

4.3 Can Co-Occur and Can Conflict

In a sound AFW-net, if two nodes occur in a run net, then always in a *causal* or *concurrency* relation [15], i. e., if two nodes are neither *causal* nor *concurrent*, they *can never occur* together in a run net. This leads to *can co-occur*:

Proposition 2 (Can Co-occur). Let $N = (P, T, F, s, f)$ be a sound AFW-net and two nodes $x, y \in P \cup T$. Following Polyvyanyy et al. [15], it holds:

$$x\ canCooccur\ y \iff x\ causal^{\exists}\ y \vee y\ causal^{\exists}\ x \vee x\ concurrent^{\exists}\ y. \quad \square$$

The derivation of the *can conflict* relation is not obvious. Instead of deriving it directly, its negation is derived: $\overline{canConflict}$. By Definition 9, $\overline{x\ canConflict\ y}$ is defined as $\Pi(x) \setminus \Pi(y) = \varnothing$ for a sound AFW-net N, which is equal to $\Pi(x) \subseteq \Pi(y)$. Therefore, if there is a run net π with $x \in \pi$, then $y \in \pi$; i. e., x occurs always with y. Soundness of N restricts $\overline{x\ canConflict\ y}$ because there is always a run net, which contains x:

Proposition 3. Let $N = (P, T, F, s, f)$ be an AFW-net.

$$N \text{ sound} \overset{\text{Def. 6}}{\implies} \forall x \in P \cup T:\ \Pi(x) \neq \varnothing \quad \square$$

Resulting from Proposition 3, $\overline{x\ canConflict\ y}$ implies $x\ canCooccur\ y$:

Proposition 4. Let $N = (P, T, F, s, f)$ be a sound AFW-net and $x, y \in P \cup T$ are two of its nodes. It follows from Proposition 3 :

$$\overline{x \; canConflict \; y} \quad \Longrightarrow \quad x \; canCooccur \; y$$

□

From Proposition 3, it holds that $\Pi(x) \neq \emptyset$ and $\Pi(y) \neq \emptyset$ and $\overline{x \; canConflict \; y}$ is equal to $\Pi(x) \subseteq \Pi(y)$. For this reason, a node x can only be in $\overline{canConflict}$ relation with nodes, which occur together with x in at least one run net. In Fig. 1, p_7 *cannot conflict with* t_8 but not with t_6.

Again, if a node x *cannot conflict* with a node y, then in each run net, in which x occurs, y occurs as well. y may appear before, after, without or concurrent to x. As a first step of the derivation, a special case of *cannot conflict* is considered: All run nets, in which x and y occur *and* x is causal to y, i. e., $\overline{x \; canConflict \; y}$ and $x \; causal^{\exists} \; y$. This special case is called the *trigger* relation:

Definition 10 (Trigger). Let $N = (P, T, F, s, f)$ be a sound AFW-net and two nodes $x, y \in P \cup T$. x *triggers* y iff $x = y \lor (\overline{x \; canConflict \; y} \land x \; causal^{\exists} \; y)$. ⌟

In Fig. 1, t_7 *triggers* t_9 but not t_3. By $x = y$, the *trigger* relation is reflexive. From *causality* and Theorem 3 follows that between two nodes x and y in *trigger* relation, there is a path from x to y in the AFW-net. Furthermore, in each run net where x occurs, there must be a path from x to y. However, it is not necessary for this to be the same path across different run nets. Whether there is always a path between two nodes x and y in every run net in which they occur can be derived by three transitive rules for a sound AFW-net $N = (P, T, F, s, f)$:

(1) $x = y$: Follows directly from Definition 10.
(2) $x \in T$: If one of x's outputs o *triggers* y, then in each π, where o occurs, y occurs as well and there is a path from o to y in π. If x occurs in a π, then $o \in \pi$ (since $x \in T$) and there is the path (x, o) in π. Thus, if x occurs in a π, then $y \in \pi$ with a path from x via o to y in π. In summary, if x *triggers* y, then there must be at least one output o of x, which *triggers* y.
(3) $x \in P$: Since the net is free-choice, x represents the sink ($|x\bullet| = 0$), a simple sequence ($|x\bullet| = 1$) or a decision ($|x\bullet| \geq 2$). The sink is not of interest, as it can only *trigger* itself. Thus, we consider the case $|x\bullet| \geq 1$. If there would be a transition $o \in x\bullet$, which does not *trigger* y, there would be a run net with o but not with y or without a path from o to y. If x occurs in a π and o is fired, then π must not contain y or there is no path from x to y in π, i. e., x does not *trigger* y. Therefore, only if each $o \in x\bullet$ *triggers* y, x *triggers* y as well.

The next equation summarizes the transitive rules:

$$x \; triggers \; y \quad \Longleftrightarrow \quad \begin{aligned} & x = y \;\; \lor \\ & x \in T \land \exists o \in x\bullet\!: \; o \; triggers \; y \;\; \lor \\ & x \in P \land \forall o \in x\bullet\!: \; o \; triggers \; y \end{aligned} \tag{4}$$

These three transitive rules are utilized to formulate Algorithm 1, which is designed for detecting the *trigger* relation. The algorithm organizes this relation into an adjacency

Algorithm 1. Determination of the *triggers* relation as an adjacency list R for all nodes of a sound AFW-net $N = (P, T, F, s, f)$.

1: **function** COMPUTETRIGGER($N = (P, T, F, s, f)$)
2:     *// Initialize R and a list L of nodes to compute.*
3:     $R \leftarrow \varnothing$
4:     $L \leftarrow P \cup T$ in reverse topological order starting from f
5:     **for all** $x \in L$ **do**
6:         *// All nodes in x's postset were processed.*
7:         **if** $x \in T$ **then**
8:             $R(x) \leftarrow \{x\} \cup \bigcup_{o \in x\bullet} R(o)$ *// R(x) represents all nodes triggered by x*
9:         **else**
10:             $R(x) \leftarrow \{x\} \cup \bigcap_{o \in x\bullet} R(o)$
11:     **return** R

list R and iteratively processes the net in reverse topological order, beginning with the net's sink (line 4). This sequential processing in reverse order ensures that a node is only processed after all its output nodes have been addressed. If a node x is processed, either it is handled as a transition (line 8) or place (line 10). In both cases, x is added to $R(x)$ following the transitive rule $x = x$. If $x \in T$, x *triggers* all nodes that are *triggered* from x's output places, following the transitive rule $x \in T \wedge \exists o \in x\bullet:\ o\ triggers\ y$. Otherwise, if $x \in P$, x *triggers* all nodes that are *triggered* from all x's output transitions, following the transitive rule $x \in P \wedge \forall o \in x\bullet:\ o\ triggers\ y$.

Time complexity: The topological ordering can be achieved in $O(|P| + |T| + |F|)$ [2]. Given that each node, along with all its postset nodes, is considered exactly once, the algorithm is guaranteed to terminate. According to Definition 1, the worst-case scenario for the number of flows is quadratic regarding the number of nodes. Consequently, this establishes that the algorithm operates with a quadratic time complexity of $O(|P|^2 + |T|^2)$.

As mentioned before, the *trigger* relation is a special case of $\overline{canConflict}$, in which the nodes in relation require *existential/total causality*. This special case helps to derive the general case of $\overline{canConflict}$, i. e., in which the nodes in relation do not require *causality*: If a node x *cannot conflict* with a node y in general, there is not the necessity for a path from x to y. However, if x and y occur in a run net, then always with a path from the source s of the AFW-net N to x and y, respectively.

For an imaginative visualization, consider the following metaphor: Imagine a mountain summit representing a node x. From your starting point, the source s, several paths W lead to this summit. If, on each of these paths, there is a trigger z capable of causing an avalanche in the valley (a node y), then reaching the summit (x) invariably results in an avalanche in the valley (y). Conversely, if at least one path exists without such a trigger, it is possible to reach the summit without causing an avalanche in the valley (y). The following theorem uses a similar approach to derive $\overline{canConflict}$:

Theorem 5 (Cannot Conflict). Let $N = (P, T, F, s, f)$ be a sound AFW-net with two nodes $x, y \in P \cup T$, $x \neq y$.

$$x\ \overline{canConflict}\ y \iff \forall W \in Paths(s, x)\ \exists z \in W:\ z\ triggers\ y$$

⌟

Proof (Theorem 5). The theorem requires a sound AWF-net $N = (P, T, F, s, f)$ with two nodes $x, y \in P \cup T$, $x \neq y$. The proof considers both directions:

$\forall W \in Paths(s,x)\ \exists z \in W:\ z\ triggers\ y \implies \overline{x\ canConflict\ y}$. By Proposition 3, $\Pi(x) \neq \varnothing$. Let $\pi \in \Pi(x)$ be such a run net. Since $x \in \pi$, there is a path $W \in Paths_{\pi}(s,x)$ from the source s to x in π. Furthermore, for all such paths W, there exists a $z \in W$, $z\ triggers\ y$. As a consequence, $y \in \pi$ by Definition 10. For this reason:

$$\Pi(x) \subseteq \Pi(y) \iff \overline{x\ canConflict\ y}\ \checkmark$$

$\overline{x\ canConflict\ y} \implies \forall W \in Paths(s,x)\ \exists z \in W:\ z\ triggers\ y$. Proof by contradiction:

$$\overline{x\ canConflict\ y} \quad \wedge \quad \exists W \in Paths(s,x)\ \forall z \in W:\ \overline{z\ triggers\ y} \tag{5}$$

Let W be such a path from the source s to x, on which no node triggers y. Therefore, $\overline{x\ triggers\ y}$ and $y \notin W$. Since $\overline{x\ triggers\ y}$, there is a path $W' \in Paths(s,f)$ from s to the sink f with $\forall z \in W':\ \overline{z\ triggers\ y}$. We construct a run net π that is based on the path W'. If further places and transitions must be added to construct π, which are *not* on path W', we add only places $p \in P$ with $\overline{p\ triggers\ y}$ following the transitive rules (4) of *triggers*. Since no node is added to π, which *triggers* y, $y \notin \pi$. Since $x \in W'$, $x \in \pi$. It holds by Definition 9:

$$\Pi(x) \setminus \Pi(y) \neq \varnothing \iff x\ canConflict\ y$$

This contradicts with (5). ↯ Therefore, the original statement must hold. ✓ □

Following the last Theorem 5, $\overline{canConflict}$ can be derived from the *trigger* relation. Algorithm 2 accounts for all paths from the source to each node indirectly. The nodes are processed in topological order (line 4), ensuring that a node is not addressed until all its inputs have been processed. This method guarantees that all paths leading from the source to these inputs are considered before the node itself is processed (the topological order of the nodes in Fig. 1 is (p_1, t_1, p_3, t_4, t_5, t_6, p_5, t_7, p_7, p_6, p_2, t_3, p_4, t_8, p_8, t_9, p_{10}, t_{10}, t_{11}, p_{11})). A node x *cannot conflict* with all nodes that are *triggered* by x (except itself) and with all nodes that are *triggered* on all paths to x's preset nodes (line 7). Since $\overline{canConflict}$ is irreflexive, x is removed from $R(x)$ (lines 8–9).

Time complexity: Algorithm 2 can compute $\overline{canConflict}$ in $O(2|P| + 2|T| + |F|)$, using a linear topological ordering algorithm [2]. Since $|F|$ is quadratic regarding the number of nodes in the worst case by Definition 1, $\overline{canConflict}$ can be computed in $O(|P|^2 + |T|^2)$. Note that the negation of $\overline{canConflict}$ leads to the *can conflict* relation. Therefore, *can conflict* can also be computed in $O(|P|^2 + |T|^2)$:

Proposition 5 (Can Conflict). Let $N = (P, T, F, s, f)$ be a sound AFW-net. *canConflict* can be computed in $O(|P|^2 + |T|^2)$. ⌟

Proof. The proposition requires a sound AFW-net $N = (P, T, F, s, f)$. $\overline{canConflict}$ can be computed in $O(|P|^2 + |T|^2)$ for each pair of nodes with Algorithm 2. For this reason, *canConflict* can also be computed in $O(|P|^2 + |T|^2)$ after pairwise checking the $\overline{canConflict}$ relation for all nodes. □

Algorithm 2. Determination of the $\overline{canConflict}$ relation as an adjacency list R for all nodes of a sound AFW-net $N = (P, T, F, s, f)$.

function COMPUTECANNOTCONFLICT($N = (P, T, F, s, f)$)
    $R_{trigger} \leftarrow$ COMPUTETRIGGER(N) // $R_{trigger}$ *is an adjacency list*
    // Initialize R and a list L of nodes to compute.
    $R \leftarrow \varnothing$
    $L \leftarrow P \cup T$ in a topological order starting from s
    for all $x \in L$ **do**
        // All nodes in x's preset were already processed.
        $R(x) \leftarrow R_{trigger}(x) \cup \bigcap_{z \in \bullet x} R(z)$
    for all $x \in L$ **do**
        $R(x) \leftarrow R(x) \setminus \{x\}$
    return R

4.4 Total Co-occur, Total Conflict, Requirement, and Independence

Proposition 6 (Total Co-Occur, Total Conflict, Requires, and Independent). Let $N = (P, T, F, s, f)$ be a sound AFW-net. Since *canCooccur* can be computed in $O(|P|^2 + |T|^2)$ by Proposition 1 and Proposition 2, and *canConflict* can be computed in $O(|P|^2 + |T|^2)$ by Proposition 5, *totalCooccur*, *totalConflict*, *requires*, and *independent* can be computed in a quadratic time complexity $O(|P|^2 + |T|^2)$ by applying Definition 9 on each pair of nodes. □

In summary, *it is possible to derive the complete 4C Spectrum for sound AFW-nets in a quadratic time complexity,* $O(|P|^2 + |T|^2)$. We have named the set of derivation algorithms *Behavioral Relation Computations*, or *BeRelCo* for short.

5 Inclusive Behavior in Process Models

Inclusive behavior, a concept in BPM, serves as a middle ground between exclusive behavior—achievable through places with at least two output transitions—and concurrent behavior—characterized by transitions with at least two output places. Nodes exhibiting this inclusive behavior are typically referred to as *OR* nodes. On one hand, an OR node produces tokens for a non-empty subset of its output places. On the other hand, not all inputs of an OR node need to carry a token for the OR to be activated. It is a widely accepted principle that OR nodes, especially those with multiple inputs, "wait for all possible tokens" that might arrive, particularly in acyclic process models [20].

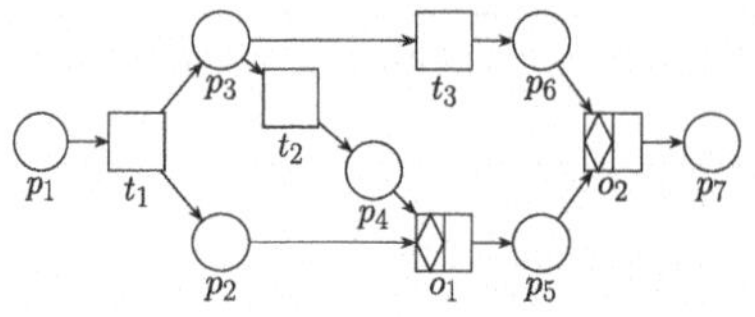

Fig. 3. An example of a net with ORs. Definition 8 of concurrency by Polyvyanyy et al. [15] is counter-intuitive in terms of time as ...

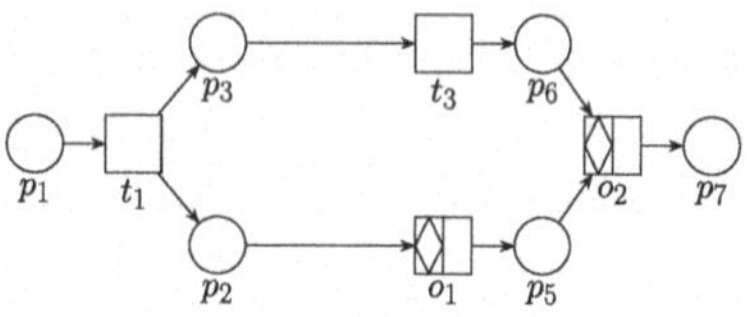

Fig. 4. ...one of its run nets has no path between p_3 and p_5 but p_3 loses its token always before p_5 gets one.

OR nodes can significantly increase the number of potential run nets [10], making the management of ORs crucial in the detection of behavioral relations. Despite their frequent occurrence in process models, OR nodes are not directly representable in Petri nets. One approach to accommodate ORs, as done in this paper, is to extend the Petri net concept: Nets get a further set for inclusive nodes (represented as rectangles with diamonds in figures in the following). We took the accepted semantics of Völzer [20] for acyclic nets (OR-joins "wait for all possible tokens"). Alternatively, ORs can be translated into a Petri net by substituting them with combinations of transitions and places. However, these substitutions can result in a *non*-free-choice net or expand the net to a free-choice variant where the number of nodes exponentially increases compared to the original model [8]. In essence, translating ORs can lead to either a non-free-choice or an exponentially larger net, both posing significant computational challenges due to a combinatorial increase in run nets.

Another challenge arises from the definition of concurrency (as per Definition 8, based on the work of Polyvyanyy et al. [15]), which defines concurrency on the absence of a direct path between two nodes in at least one run net. With the introduction of OR constructs, situations may arise where two nodes appear to be concurrent under Definition 8 but cannot actually be enabled simultaneously or share tokens in the same marking. This discrepancy makes the standard definition of concurrency (e.g., [15,21]) counter-intuitive in scenarios involving ORs, where parallelism does not align with the expected behavior. For instance, consider nodes p_3 and p_5 in Fig. 3, where transitions marked with diamonds signify ORs. Here, p_3 invariably loses a token *before* p_5 receives one, avoiding premature firing of o_1. Despite this sequential token transfer, these nodes are deemed concurrent by Definition 8 in the run net depicted in Fig. 4.

To address this imprecision in acyclic AFW-nets, soundness offers a solution. We recommend to refine the concurrency definition regarding the results of this paper: *Two nodes x and y are concurrent iff there is no path between x and y in the AFW-net (instead of a run net) and x and y co-occur.*

The *BeRelCo* algorithms are effectively designed to accommodate OR constructs within Petri nets, employing this refined definition of concurrency (as per Definition 8) to seamlessly integrate these elements: (1) The concurrency detection by [17] starts with transitions, as transitions with multiple outputs cause concurrency. Instead of only starting with transitions, the algorithm can simply be extended so that it also starts with ORs, as, in the "worst case", the ORs also cause concurrency for each pair of outputs.

(2) Algorithm 1 determines the *trigger* relation and distinguishes between places and transitions as the only other algorithm of *BeRelCo*. Line 7 checks whether the current node x is a transition, or not. If x is an OR, then it can represent a simple decision like a place with multiple outputs. Therefore, ORs should be treated as place-like in line 10.

6 Related Work

In the following, we analyze the related work concerning computational complexity and the limitations associated with the behavioral relations defined in Definition 9.

The (causal) behavioral profile defined by Weidlich et al. [21,22] has been extensively studied in research. This profile comprises four relations: *strict order*, *exclusiveness*, *interleaving order*, and *co-occurrence*. The challenge lies in aligning these relations with those defined in Definition 9. The *strict order* and *exclusiveness* relations are equal to $causal^{\forall}$ and *totalConflict*, respectively. The *co-occurrence relation* is similar to *requires*, as it is *not* defined as a symmetric relation [22]. The *interleaving order* relation is a mix of $concurrent^{\exists}$ and *independent*. For sound free-choice workflow nets that can be decomposed into structured SESE fragments [19], the computational complexity of determining these four relations is linear for a single pair of nodes, resulting in cubic complexity for all pairs. However, in the more general case involving unstructured SESE fragments, this complexity increases to $O(|P|^5 + |T|^5)$.

Polyvyanyy et al. [15] and Wolf [23] mapped most of the 4C Spectrum relations to the reachability problem. For acyclic sound free-choice workflow nets, the reachability problem has polynomial computational complexity [24], however, the specific polynomial is not known. Ha and Prinz [10] have investigated the set of behavioral relations of Definition 9 for acyclic sound *workflow graphs*. Their approach has a complexity of $O(|F|^3)$ for a single pair of nodes and, therefore, $O(|F|^3 \cdot (|P|^2 + |T|^2))$ for all pairs.

In summary, the computational complexity for acyclic sound free-choice nets is $O(|P|^5 + |T|^5)$ for $causal^{\forall}$, *totalConflict*, and *requires*, and $O(|F|^3 \cdot (|P|^2 + |T|^2))$ for the other relations. Furthermore, except for the algorithm in [10], the other approaches are only applicable to workflow nets *without* inclusive behavior. *To the best of the authors' knowledge, the approach presented in this paper offers the lowest computational worst-case complexity for computing the behavioral relations defined in Definition* 9 *and is the only approach capable of computing these relations for inclusive behavior with polynomial complexity.*

7 Evaluation

The *BeRelCo* algorithms, detailed in Sect. 4, have been implemented using a simple script-based approach in PHP for evaluation purposes. This implementation is open-source and accessible on GitHub[1]. Our experiments were conducted on a machine outfitted with an Intel® Core™ i7 CPU, featuring 14 cores and 64 GB of main memory, running Microsoft Windows 11 Professional. PHP version 8 was utilized for the execution of the scripts. To guarantee the reliability of our results, each runtime measurement

[1] https://github.com/guybrushPrince/berelco.

was performed ten times. We excluded the fastest and slowest runs from this set and calculated the mean values from the remaining measurements. We then compared the performance of the BeRelCo algorithms against a brute-force approach for deriving all run nets according to Definition 7, hereinafter referred to as 'RunNets'. The brute-force approach was chosen since all approaches in the literature finally depends on a similar strategy for inherently unstructured fragments (e.g., for [22] and [10]).

The evaluation of the algorithms was conducted using two well-known datasets: the IBM Websphere Business Modeler dataset [7, 12], henceforth referred to as the *IBM* dataset, which includes 1,386 files, and the SAP Reference Models dataset [4], hereafter referred to as the *SAP* dataset, containing 604 files. The data sets were selected because they represent real process models for which numerous analyses can already be found in the literature. Given the algorithms' prerequisites for analyzing sound AFW-nets, a subset of the datasets was selected for investigation—specifically, 604 nets from the IBM collection and 414 from the SAP collection are sound acyclic free-choice workflow nets (all nets of IBM are free-choice, 178 nets are cyclic, and, from the remaining 1208 acyclic nets, 604 are unsound; all nets of SAP are free-choice, 31 nets are cyclic, and, from the remaining 569 acyclic nets, 152 are unsound). The nets within the IBM dataset were provided in PNML format, facilitating direct analysis. Conversely, the SAP dataset's nets, present in a simplified JSON format that describes BPMN-like models with AND, XOR, and OR nodes, required conversion into Petri nets for compatibility. This conversion was guided by the extended Petri net concept discussed in Sect. 5.

Subsequently, runtime measurements of both datasets are presented in the form $x_I \mid y_S$ with measures x_I for *IBM* and y_S for *SAP*. The size of the nets under investigation varies, with 75% of the nets having $57_I \mid 36_S$ nodes or fewer. The largest nets contain a maximum of $546_I \mid 133_S$ nodes. Places are more frequent than transitions ($61\%\pm4\%_I \mid 56\%\pm6\%_S$ of all nodes are places). The SAP nets contain $7\%\pm7\%$ OR nodes.

Upon application to *IBM* and *SAP*, both algorithms successfully identified the same node relations across all eligible nets. The main objective was to establish the *BeRelCo* algorithm as a more efficient alternative to *RunNets* or similar exploratory algorithms. Consequently, we assessed the computational time required by both algorithms to derive all relations within a net. The findings indicate that the *BeRelCo* algorithms outperform *RunNets* in processing speed across both datasets: It needs just $0.655_I \mid 0.328_S$ [s] to compute $>6.3\text{M}_I \mid >1.2\text{M}_S$ pairs of nodes being in relation. In contrast, the *RunNets* algorithm requires $4.038_I \mid 435.066_S$ [s] for doing the same job, i. e., the *BeRelCo* algorithm is approx. $6_I \mid 1326_S$ times faster. Notably, *RunNets* was unable to process 2 nets from *SAP* because the number of run nets exceeded 500k. We introduced this limit artificially after conducting several experiments, as it would otherwise result in a memory allocation issue, causing an uncatchable error in PHP. Figure 5 illustrates the computation times of some of the nets in relation to their size (number of nodes). It shows the computation times for three sets: (1) For nets requiring more than 0.01 [s] for *RunNets* (illustrated as red dots); (2) for nets requiring more than 0.01 [s] for *BeRelCo* (illustrated with green triangles) and (3) for intractable nets with *RunNets*. In summary, the *BeRelCo* algorithm demonstrates superior efficiency, processing all nets that took more than 0.01 [s] with *RunNets* in less than 0.01 [s]. Furthermore, any net that required more than 0.01 [s] with *BeRelCo* was processed in a similar or longer duration by *RunNets*.

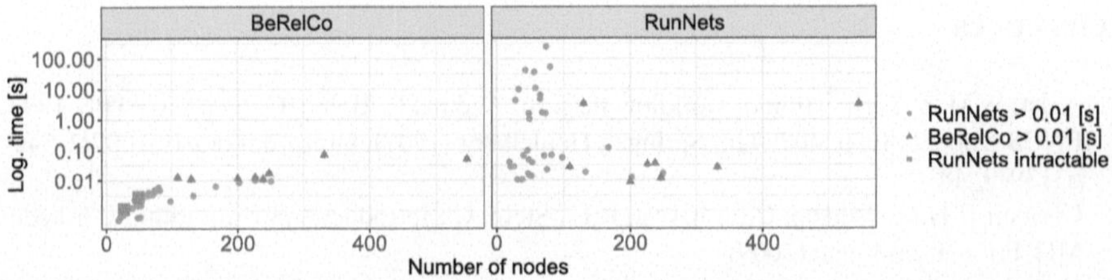

Fig. 5. Comparison between the number of nodes and the logarithmic time to compute all behavioral relations for three different subsets of all nets regarding their computation times.

Notably, intractable nets with *RunNets* were processed by *BeRelCo* in under 0.01 [s]. *BeRelCo* consistently achieves tractable processing times for each net, with a maximum duration of up to 0.1 [s], showcasing a significant improvement.

8 Conclusion

Systematically identifying business process models within extensive collections poses a considerable challenge. Process queries facilitate the identification of models that meet specific characteristics, relying on behavioral relations, to illustrate how tasks in a process model interact during execution. The *4C Spectrum*—comprising *conflict*, *co-occurrence*, *causality*, and *concurrency*—provides a comprehensive framework for these behavioral relations. However, current computational methods for analyzing these relations can be time-consuming for various process models. This paper introduces a suite of algorithms, named *Behavioral Relation Computations* (*BeRelCo*), designed to efficiently detect all behavioral relations within the *4C Spectrum* in quadratic time complexity, $O(|P|^2 + |T|^2)$, for models that can be represented as acyclic sound free-choice workflow nets. Our experiments validate the *BeRelCo* algorithms' effectiveness, notably in models with numerous execution traces.

Industrial process modeling languages, often aligned with workflow graphs, can be depicted as free-choice workflow nets [8]. *Soundness* was identified as a critical requirement [5]. Therefore, the algorithms we have introduced hold substantial value for the BPM community, not only facilitating process queries but also underpinning process similarity analysis, compliance checking, and other key BPM activities.

Currently, our approach is limited to acyclic nets. Future efforts will focus on extending these algorithms to handle cyclic nets through loop decomposition [16] by devising combinatorial rules for behavioral relations for the resulting acyclic nets. Moreover, we aim to adapt our algorithms for models that feature duplicated labels, where tasks may occur multiple times, broadening their applicability and utility in complex process model analyses.

References

1. Aalst, W.M.P.: Verification of workflow nets. In: Azéma, P., Balbo, G. (eds.) ICATPN 1997. LNCS, vol. 1248, pp. 407–426. Springer, Heidelberg (1997). https://doi.org/10.1007/3-540-63139-9_48
2. Cormen, T.H., Leiserson, C.E., Rivest, R.L., Stein, C.: Introduction to Algorithms, 3rd edn. MIT Press, Cambridge (2009)
3. Czerwinski, W., Lasota, S., Lazic, R., Leroux, J., Mazowiecki, F.: The reachability problem for Petri nets is not elementary. J. ACM **68**(1), 7:1–7:28 (2021)
4. van Dongen, B.F., Jansen-Vullers, M.H., Verbeek, H.M.W., van der Aalst, W.M.P.: Verification of the SAP reference models using EPC reduction, state-space analysis, and invariants. Comput. Ind. **58**(6), 578–601 (2007)
5. van Dongen, B.F., Mendling, J., van der Aalst, W.M.P.: Structural patterns for soundness of business process models. In: Tenth IEEE International Enterprise Distributed Object Computing Conference (EDOC 2006), 16–20 October 2006, Hong Kong, China, pp. 116–128. IEEE Computer Society (2006). https://doi.org/10.1109/EDOC.2006.56
6. Dumas, M., Rosa, M.L., Mendling, J., Reijers, H.A.: Fundamentals of Business Process Management, 2nd edn. Springer, Heidelberg (2018)
7. Fahland, D., Favre, C., Koehler, J., Lohmann, N., Völzer, H., Wolf, K.: Analysis on demand: instantaneous soundness checking of industrial business process models. Data Knowl. Eng. **70**(5), 448–466 (2011). https://web.archive.org/web/20131208132841/http://service-technology.org/publications/fahlandfjklvw_2009_bpm. Accessed March 2024
8. Favre, C., Fahland, D., Völzer, H.: The relationship between workflow graphs and free-choice workflow nets. Inf. Syst. **47**, 197–219 (2015)
9. García-Bañuelos, L., van Beest, N., Dumas, M., Rosa, M.L., Mertens, W.: Complete and interpretable conformance checking of business processes. IEEE Trans. Software Eng. **44**(3), 262–290 (2018). https://doi.org/10.1109/TSE.2017.2668418
10. Ha, N.L., Prinz, T.M.: Partitioning behavioral retrieval: an efficient computational approach with transitive rules. IEEE Access **9**, 112043–112056 (2021)
11. Kunze, M., Weidlich, M., Weske, M.: Behavioral similarity - a proper metric. In: Rinderle-Ma, S., Toumani, F., Wolf, K. (eds.) BPM 2011. LNCS, vol. 6896, pp. 166–181. Springer, Cham (2011). https://doi.org/10.1007/978-3-642-23059-2_15
12. Mendling, J., Verbeek, H.M.W., van Dongen, B.F., van der Aalst, W.M.P., Neumann, G.: Detection and prediction of errors in EPCs of the SAP reference model. Data Knowl. Eng. **64**(1), 312–329 (2008). https://doi.org/10.1016/j.datak.2007.06.019
13. Polyvyanyy, A., Pika, A., ter Hofstede, A.H.M.: Scenario-based process querying for compliance, reuse, and standardization. Inf. Syst. **93**, 101563 (2020)
14. Polyvyanyy, A., ter Hofstede, A.H., La Rosa, M., Ouyang, C., Pika, A.: Process query language: design, implementation, and evaluation. Inf. Syst. **122**, 102337 (2024)
15. Polyvyanyy, A., Weidlich, M., Conforti, R., La Rosa, M., ter Hofstede, A.H.M.: The 4C spectrum of fundamental behavioral relations for concurrent systems. In: Ciardo, G., Kindler, E. (eds.) PETRI NETS 2014. LNCS, vol. 8489, pp. 210–232. Springer, Cham (2014). https://doi.org/10.1007/978-3-319-07734-5_12
16. Prinz, T.M., Choi, Y., Ha, N.L.: Understanding and decomposing control-flow loops in business process models. In: Ciccio, C.D., Dijkman, R.M., del-Río-Ortega, A., Rinderle-Ma, S. (eds.) BPM 2022. LNCS, vol. 13420, pp. 307–323. Springer, Cham (2022). https://doi.org/10.1007/978-3-031-16103-2_21
17. Prinz, T.M., Klaus, J., van Beest, N.R.T.P.: Pushing the limits: concurrency detection in acyclic sound free-choice workflow nets in $O(P^2 + T^2)$. In: Köhler-Bussmeier, M., Moldt, D.,

Rölke, H. (eds.) Proceedings of the International Workshop on Petri Nets and Software Engineering 2024 co-located with the 45th International Conference on Application and Theory of Petri Nets and Concurrency (PETRI NETS 2024), 24–25 June 2024, Geneva, Switzerland. CEUR Workshop Proceedings, vol. 3730, pp. 132–154. CEUR-WS.org (2024). https://ceur-ws.org/Vol-3730/paper08.pdf
18. Sadiq, W., Orlowska, M.E.: Analyzing process models using graph reduction techniques. Inf. Syst. **25**(2), 117–134 (2000). https://doi.org/10.1016/S0306-4379(00)00012-0
19. Vanhatalo, J., Völzer, H., Koehler, J.: The refined process structure tree. Data Knowl. Eng. **68**(9), 793–818 (2009). https://doi.org/10.1016/j.datak.2009.02.015
20. Völzer, H.: A new semantics for the inclusive converging gateway in safe processes. In: Hull, R., Mendling, J., Tai, S. (eds.) BPM 2010. LNCS, vol. 6336, pp. 294–309. Springer, Heidelberg (2010). https://doi.org/10.1007/978-3-642-15618-2_21
21. Weidlich, M., Mendling, J., Weske, M.: Efficient consistency measurement based on behavioral profiles of process models. IEEE Trans. Software Eng. **37**(3), 410–429 (2011)
22. Weidlich, M., Polyvyanyy, A., Mendling, J., Weske, M.: Causal behavioural profiles - efficient computation, applications, and evaluation. Fundam. Inform. **113**(3–4), 399–435 (2011). https://doi.org/10.3233/FI-2011-614
23. Wolf, K.: Interleaving based model checking of concurrency and causality. Fundam. Inform. **161**(4), 423–445 (2018). https://doi.org/10.3233/FI-2018-1709
24. Yamaguchi, S.: Polynomial time verification of reachability in sound extended free-choice workflow nets. IEICE Trans. Fundam. Electron. Commun. Comput. Sci. **97-A**(2), 468–475 (2014). https://doi.org/10.1587/TRANSFUN.E97.A.468

Process Tree Alignments

Christopher T. Schwanen[1(✉)], Wied Pakusa[2], and Wil M. P. van der Aalst[1]

[1] Chair of Process and Data Science (PADS), RWTH Aachen University, Aachen, Germany
{schwanen,wvdaalst}@pads.rwth-aachen.de
[2] Federal University of Applied Administrative Sciences, Brühl, Germany
Wied.Pakusa@hsbund.de

Abstract. The state-of-the-art approach for computing alignments is to apply an exhaustive state-space search with a well-tailored A*-heuristic function. If the heuristic fails to provide good estimates, the alignment computation quickly becomes infeasible even for small event logs given the exponential search space. Since intractability is unavoidable for general process models, we here consider the restricted class of process trees which provides a good balance between expressiveness and algorithmic feasibility. As our main result, we prove that alignments on process trees can be expressed as solutions of Mixed Integer Linear Programs (MILP). Our novel approach does not only position the problem inside the class of NP, but also paves the way for applying a host of new optimization techniques from the field of mathematical programming to alignments on process trees. We further show that for process trees without parallel executions, our MILP formulation becomes a Linear Program (LP) which can be solved efficiently. This result gives fresh insights into the structure of the alignment problem and the role of concurrency as a key factor for intractability. Finally, we implement our new algorithmic approach in PM4Py and evaluate the performance against the standard algorithms.

Keywords: Process Mining · Conformance Checking · Alignments · Process Trees · Mixed Integer Linear Programming

1 Introduction

Constructing optimal alignments between a trace and a process model is a key task in conformance checking. The standard approach is to formulate the alignment computation as a reachability problem on the product of the model and the trace. In general, this product is of exponential size which leads to high computational costs and hinders scalability of alignment computations. This, in turn, poses a major obstacle for practical applications where massive event logs and business models have to be analyzed.

Unfortunately, computing alignments on sound workflow nets (the standard modeling notation in process mining) is a PSPACE-complete problem. While

J. Borbinha et al. (Eds.): EDOC 2024, LNCS 15409, pp. 300–317, 2025.
https://doi.org/10.1007/978-3-031-78338-8_16

this might seem discouraging, we rather see it as a call for a more intensive root-cause analysis of the algorithmic complexity of alignments. In fact, we are going to show that one can derive much better bounds if certain syntactic restrictions are imposed on the process models. This goes in line with the observation that, in practice, process models often provide such extra structure that we can exploit to speed up alignment computations.

In this paper, we focus on the important example of *process trees*, a class of models that can be decomposed into subprocesses which are interconnected in a tree-like fashion. Process trees are highly relevant in practice and form the basis for one of the most popular family of mining algorithms, the so-called *Inductive Miner* [14]. Our key observation is that process trees have optimal alignments of *linear* length (linear in the size of the trace plus the size of the process tree). This allows us to solve the alignment problem on process trees in NP (rather than PSPACE). As our central contribution, we give the first *Mixed Integer Linear Programming* (MILP) formulation of the alignment problem on process trees.

More specifically, we encode the alignment problem as a minimum-cost network flow problem. This network flow construction can then, in a second step, be readily expressed as a MILP instance. For the former translation, the difficult part is to express the *parallel operator* in a process tree as a flow gateway in a network graph. The parallel operator models independent concurrent computations and is the root cause for the exponential state explosion that we get from a translation of process trees to standard transition systems (aka. finite automata). It should be noted that the parallel operator can be expressed succinctly using Petri nets, but it is unclear, how we could get an efficient MILP formulation from this presentation. Intuitively, we model the parallel operator by splitting up a flow into equal parts and send the subflows through different parts of the network. When all subflows have completed their subcomputations, we merge the subflows again, and get back the original flow. It turns out that for this synchronized split and merge we need to use *integer variables*. In fact, this is the only part where discrete variables are required. As a consequence, for process trees without the parallel operator, our MILP instance becomes a *Linear Program* (LP) which can be solved in polynomial time.

To complement our MILP encoding, we provide a proof-of-concept implementation based on the *PM4Py* ecosystem [3] and the *Gurobi Optimizer* [13]. We further evaluate the performance of our MILP approach on a set of synthetic and real-life benchmark logs in comparison with the state-of-the-art alignment algorithms based on A* and the reachability approach. Our experiments show that the MILP-based approach is extremely promising and outperforms the two other alignment algorithms for process trees which are available in PM4Py.

2 Related Work

Alignments were introduced by [1] and are now the state-of-the-art technique for conformance checking [8,9]. In particular, they have surpassed token-based replay [18] in terms of accuracy and flexibility. Due to the high computational costs of the textbook algorithm based on A^*, several techniques have been studied to improve scalability, see, e.g., [4,5]. This also includes techniques from mathematical optimization. Most notably, [12] uses Linear Programming (LP) to improve A^*-heuristics and to reduce the runtime significantly. Furthermore, approximative algorithms have been proposed, see, e.g., [20] for a scheme based on Mixed Integer Linear Programming (MILP). However, until today, no full MILP encoding of the alignment problem has been studied. The only work that somewhat goes into this direction is [5,6]. There, the authors showed that computing alignments is in NP if the length of optimal alignments is polynomially bounded. Since it can be shown that this holds for process trees and since NP problems can be encoded into MILPs, this result implies the existence of a MILP encoding. However, the authors did neither provide a MILP formulation nor any concrete example of an interesting model class with this property.

The notion of process trees is inspired by the observation that many real-life process models can be decomposed into distinct blocks that are interconnected in a tree-like fashion. This allows divide-and-conquer strategies for solving algorithmic problems. Process trees were first applied by [7,21] in the context of genetic process discovery. Since then, process trees have proven to be a modeling language with a great balance between expressiveness and algorithmic simplicity. In particular, they form the basis of one of the most popular process discovery algorithms, the so-called *Inductive Miner* [14]. Thus, it comes at no surprise that also optimized algorithms for alignment computations on process trees have been studied. Most notably, [19] proposed an approximation algorithm which performs well on many process trees, but which does not guarantee to compute optimal alignments in all cases. This is in stark contrast with our MILP encoding approach which always yields optimal solutions.

Finally, we like to mention work on the *error correction problem* for regular languages. Here, the goal is to compute edit distances between an input string and a regular expression. This is very intimately related to computing optimal alignments. In essence, process trees correspond to regular expressions extended by the shuffle operator and for those languages it was shown a long time ago that deciding membership (i.e., edit distance 0) is NP-complete, see, e.g., [17]. Since the membership problem is a special case of the alignment problem (where the costs of an optimal alignment are 0), our MILP encoding in this work can also be used as an error-correction algorithm for regular expressions with shuffle.

3 Preliminaries

Let $\mathbb{N}$ be the set of natural numbers excluding 0. For any tuple a, $\pi_i(a)$ denotes the *projection* on its ith element, i.e., $\pi_i \colon A_1 \times \cdots \times A_n \to A_i, (a_1, \ldots, a_n) \mapsto a_i$. For any node v in a graph, let $\delta^-(v)$ ($\delta^+(v)$) denote the set of incoming (outgoing) arcs at node v.

Definition 1 (Alphabet). An *alphabet* Σ is a finite, non-empty set of *labels* (also referred to as *activities*).

Definition 2 (Sequence). *Sequences* with index set I over a set A are denoted by $\sigma = \langle a_i \rangle_{i \in I} \in A^I$. The *length* of a sequence σ is written as $|\sigma|$ and the set of all finite sequences over A is denoted by A^*. For a sequence $\sigma = \langle a_i \rangle_{i \in I} \in A^I$, $\sum \sigma$ is a shorthand for $\sum_{i \in I} a_i$. The restriction of a sequence $\sigma \in A^*$ to a set $B \subseteq A$ is the subsequence $\sigma|_B$ of σ consisting of all elements in B. A function $f\colon A \to B$ can be applied to a sequence $\sigma \in A^*$ given the recursive definition $f(\langle\rangle) := \langle\rangle$ and $f(\langle a \rangle \cdot \sigma) := \langle f(a) \rangle \cdot f(\sigma)$. For a sequence of tuples $\sigma \in (A^n)^*$, $\pi_i^*(\sigma)$ denotes the sequence of every ith element of its tuples, i.e., $\pi_i^*(\langle\rangle) := \langle\rangle$ and $\pi_i^*(\langle(a_1, \ldots, a_n)\rangle \cdot \sigma) := \langle \pi_i(a_1, \ldots, a_n) \rangle \cdot \pi_i^*(\sigma) = \langle a_i \rangle \cdot \pi_i^*(\sigma)$.

Definition 3 (Shuffle $\sqcup\!\sqcup$). For two sequences $x, y \in \Sigma^*$, the *shuffle* $x \sqcup\!\sqcup y$ of x and y is defined as

$$x \sqcup\!\sqcup y := \{v_1 w_1 \cdots v_k w_k \mid x = v_1 \cdots v_k, y = w_1 \cdots w_k, v_i, w_i \in \Sigma^*, 1 \leq i \leq k\}.$$

Let $\mathcal{L}_1, \mathcal{L}_2 \subseteq \Sigma^*$ be two languages. Then the shuffle of the two languages is defined as

$$\mathcal{L}_1 \sqcup\!\sqcup \mathcal{L}_2 := \bigcup \{w_1 \sqcup\!\sqcup w_2 \mid w_1 \in \mathcal{L}_1, w_2 \in \mathcal{L}_2\}.$$

Definition 4 (Transition System). A *transition system* TS is a tuple $TS = (S, \Sigma, T, s_{init}, s_{final})$ where S is the set of *states*, Σ is the set of *activities*, $T \subseteq S \times \Sigma \times S$ is the set of *transitions*, and $s_{init}, s_{final} \in S$ are two distinguished states, namely the *initial state* s_{init} and the *final state* s_{final}.

Definition 5 (Process Tree). Let Σ be an alphabet of activities and let $\tau \notin \Sigma$ be the silent activity. A *process tree* is defined recursively where

- each activity $a \in \Sigma$ and the silent activity τ is a process tree,
- $\rightarrow(PT_1, \ldots, PT_n)$, $\times(PT_1, \ldots, PT_n)$, $\circlearrowleft(PT_1, PT_2)$, and $\wedge(PT_1, \ldots, PT_n)$ are process trees with $PT_1, \ldots, PT_n$, $n \in \mathbb{N}$ being process trees as well.

The symbols $\rightarrow$ (sequence), $\times$ (exclusive choice), $\circlearrowleft$ (loop), and $\wedge$ (parallel) are *process tree operators*. The *language* of a process tree PT is denoted by $\mathcal{L}(PT)$ and is also recursively defined where

- $\mathcal{L}(\tau) = \{\langle\rangle\}$ and $\mathcal{L}(a) = \{\langle a \rangle\}$,
- $\mathcal{L}(\rightarrow(PT_1, \ldots, PT_n)) = \mathcal{L}(PT_1) \cdot \ldots \cdot \mathcal{L}(PT_n)$,
- $\mathcal{L}(\times(PT_1, \ldots, PT_n)) = \mathcal{L}(PT_1) \cup \cdots \cup \mathcal{L}(PT_n)$,
- $\mathcal{L}(\circlearrowleft(PT_1, PT_2)) = \mathcal{L}(PT_1) \cdot (\mathcal{L}(PT_2) \cdot \mathcal{L}(PT_1))^*$, and
- $\mathcal{L}(\wedge(PT_1, \ldots, PT_n)) = \mathcal{L}(PT_1) \sqcup\!\sqcup \cdots \sqcup\!\sqcup \mathcal{L}(PT_n)$.

The τ-language $\mathcal{L}^\tau(PT)$ of a process tree PT preserves silent activities and is defined accordingly, but with $\mathcal{L}^\tau \tau = \{\langle\tau\rangle\}$ instead. A sequence $x \in \mathcal{L}^\tau PT$ is also referred to as an *execution* of the process tree PT.

4 Computing Alignments on Process Trees

Alignments [1] juxtapose observed and modeled behavior. Thereby, activities in the observed trace are compared in pairs with activities from an execution of the process tree. These pairs are called moves and they are considered legal if the observed activity matches the activity from the process tree execution or the pair consists of just one activity, either from the observation or the model, while its counterpart is considered to have not yet proceeded, indicated by a special "no move" symbol $\gg$.

$$\gamma_1 = \frac{b \quad a \quad c \quad \gg}{\gg \quad a \quad c \quad b} \qquad\qquad \gamma_2 = \frac{\gg \quad b \quad a \quad c}{\tau \quad b \quad \gg \quad c}$$

Let γ_1 and γ_2 be two exemplary alignments between an observed trace $\langle b, a, c \rangle$ and a process tree $\rightarrow(\times(a, \tau), \wedge(b, c))$. The top row indicates the progress in the trace, while the bottom row contains the labels executed in the process tree. In γ_1, the second and third move show that the observed activities could be synchronized with the execution of the process tree; hence, they are called *synchronous moves*. While the first move $(b, \gg)$ indicates that the observed activity b was not performed in the model, the fourth move $(\gg, b)$ indicates the reverse, namely that activity b executed by the process tree could not be matched with an activity in the trace. A move only proceeding on the trace is called *log move* and a move only proceeding on the model is called *model move*. The model move $(\gg, \tau)$ in γ_2 is special as the silent activity τ cannot be observed. Such moves are therefore not considered as deviations and also called *silent moves*.

Definition 6 (Legal Move, Alignment)**.** Let Σ be an alphabet of activities, let $\tau \notin \Sigma$ be the silent activity, let $\sigma \in \Sigma^*$ be a trace, let PT be a process tree, and let $\gg \notin \Sigma$ be a distinguished "no move" symbol. Without loss of generality, we assume the trace σ and the process tree PT being defined over the same alphabet Σ. A *move* is an ordered pair $(a, t) \in (\Sigma \cup \{\gg\}) \times (\Sigma \cup \{\tau, \gg\})$ and we distinguish three types of *legal moves*: The move (a, t) is a

- *synchronous move* if $a, t \in \Sigma$ and $a = t$,
- *log move* if $a \in \Sigma$ and $t = \gg$,
- *model move* if $a = \gg$ and $t \in \Sigma \cup \{\tau\}$.

A model move $(\gg, \tau)$ is also called *silent move*. All other moves are considered to be illegal. The set LM denotes all legal moves between alphabet Σ and process tree PT, i.e., $LM := \{(a, a) \mid a \in \Sigma\} \cup (\Sigma \times \{\gg\}) \cup (\{\gg\} \times (\Sigma \cup \{\tau\}))$. A sequence of legal moves $\gamma \in LM^*$ is an *alignment* between trace σ and process tree PT if and only if $\sigma = \pi_1^*(\gamma)|_\Sigma$ and $\pi_2^*(\gamma)|_{\Sigma \cup \{\tau\}} \in \mathcal{L}^\tau PT$. The set Γ_σ denotes all alignments between a trace $\sigma \in \Sigma^*$ and process tree PT.

Looking at the two alignments γ_1 and γ_2 from above, we see that there are multiple ways to align observed and modeled behavior. In general, we are interested in an *optimal* alignment, i.e., an alignment that fits a trace to the closest execution of the process model and only consists of inevitable deviations. Therefore, deviations are associated with costs so that minimizing the costs leads to an alignment where the synchronization between trace and model is maximal. Formally, this is achieved via a cost function that assigns costs to moves and then finding an alignment with minimal costs.

Definition 7 (Optimal Alignment). Let LM be the set of all legal moves and Γ_σ be the set of all alignments between a trace $\sigma \in \Sigma^*$ and a process tree PT and let $c\colon LM \to \mathbb{Q}_{\geq 0}$ be a cost function. An alignment $\gamma_{opt} \in \Gamma_\sigma$ is *optimal* if and only if no other alignment between σ and PT has lower costs, i.e., $\sum c(\gamma_{opt}) = \min_{\gamma \in \Gamma_\sigma}\{\sum c(\gamma)\}$.

Note that, in principle, for the approach presented in this paper, any function $c\colon LM \to \mathbb{Q}_{\geq 0}$ can be chosen as a cost function. For better comprehensibility, however, the *standard cost function* is assumed in the following where synchronous or silent moves have no costs and log or non-silent model moves are associated with costs of 1.

4.1 Alignments Based on Transition Systems

The standard approach to find optimal alignments is to solve a shortest path problem in the *synchronous product* between the trace and the model. We now give a translation of process trees into equivalent transition systems (where *equivalent* means, that the traces generated by the process tree and the transition system are the same). Our approach is a relatively straightforward textbook translation of a process tree into a finite automaton except for the *parallel* operator (note that process trees without concurrency correspond to regular expressions). Unfortunately, a transition system has no means to express concurrency. Typically, this problem is circumvented by first using Petri nets and, in a second step, by transforming the resulting Petri nets into equivalent transition systems. In this paper, we skip the detour through Petri nets and directly translate process trees into equivalent transitions systems.

Definition 8 (Transition System of a Process Tree). Let PT be a process tree. The *transition system* of PT is denoted by $\mathcal{TS}(PT) := (S, \Sigma \cup \{\tau\}, T, s_{init}, s_{final})$ and can be constructed recursively by starting with the initial and final state $s_{init}, s_{final} \in S$ and

- if $PT = \tau$, adding a transition $(s_{init}, \tau, s_{final})$,
- for each activity $a \in \Sigma$, if $PT = a$, adding a transition (s_{init}, a, s_{final}),
- for process trees $PT_1, \ldots, PT_n$ (with pairwise disjoint state spaces), $n \in \mathbb{N}$,
  - if $PT = \rightarrow(PT_1, \ldots, PT_n)$, adding new states $s_1, \ldots, s_{n-1}$ and inserting $\mathcal{TS}PT_i$ with initial state s_{i-1} and final state s_i for $1 \leq i \leq n$ where $s_0 = s_{init}$ and $s_n = s_{final}$,
  - if $PT = \times(PT_1, \ldots, PT_n)$, we take all $\mathcal{TS}PT_i$, for $1 \leq i \leq n$, as independent subsystems and then merge all initial states to the initial state s_{init} and all final states to the final state s_{final},
  - if $PT = \circlearrowleft(PT_1, PT_2)$, adding new states s_1 and s_2, transitions (s_{init}, τ, s_1) and (s_2, τ, s_{final}), and inserting $\mathcal{TS}PT_1$ with initial state s_1 and final state s_2 and inserting $\mathcal{TS}PT_2$ with initial state s_2 and final state s_1,
  - if $PT = \wedge(PT_1, \ldots, PT_n)$, we take $\mathcal{TS}PT$ to be the direct product of the transition systems $\mathcal{TS}PT_i$, $1 \leq i \leq n$, where we declare the state $(s_1, \ldots, s_n)$, where s_i is the initial state of $\mathcal{TS}PT_i$, to be the initial state s_{init} of $\mathcal{TS}PT$ and, analogously, $(s'_1, \ldots, s'_n)$, where s'_i is the final state of $\mathcal{TS}PT_i$, to be the final state s_{final} of $\mathcal{TS}PT$.

Table 1. Comparison between the construction of a transition system $\mathcal{TS}(PT)$ and a process tree network $\mathcal{N}(PT)$ based on a process tree PT.

Process Tree PT	Construction of $\mathcal{TS}(PT)$	Construction of $\mathcal{N}(PT)$
a	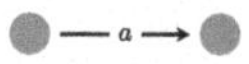	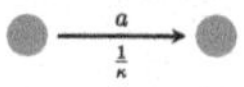
τ	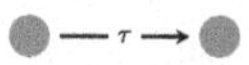	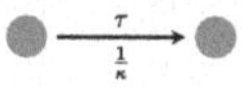
$\rightarrow(PT_1, \dots, PT_n)$		
$\times(PT_1, \dots, PT_n)$		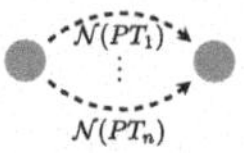
$\circlearrowleft(PT_1, PT_2)$	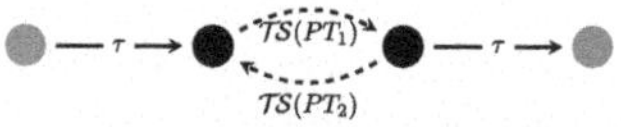	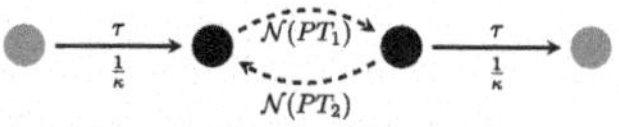
$\wedge(PT_1, \dots, PT_n)$	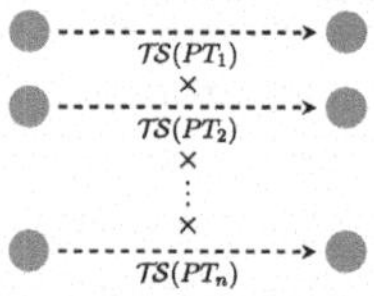	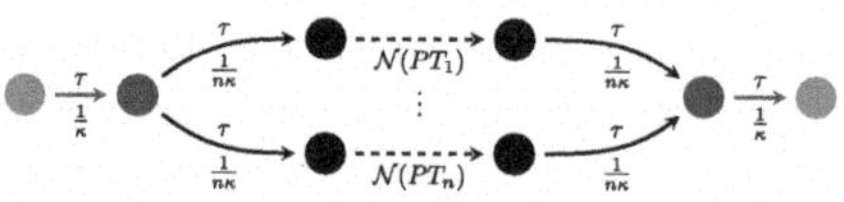

The construction of a transition system from a process tree is also illustrated in Table 1. For any process tree PT it can be easily verified that $\mathcal{L}(PT) = \mathcal{L}(\mathcal{TS}PT)$. Here, the language $\mathcal{L}(TS)$ of a transition system TS consists of all label sequences of paths from the initial to the final state. Figure 1a shows the transition system of the exemplary process tree $\rightarrow(\times(a, \tau), \wedge(b, c))$. For better recognizability, the initial state is marked in green and the final state in red. A trace $\sigma \in \Sigma^*$ is expressed by a directed path TS_σ, which consists of $|\sigma| + 1$ states and where each event in the trace is associated with a transition, i.e., $TS_\sigma = (\{s_i \mid 0 \leq i \leq |\sigma|\}, \Sigma, \{(s_{i-1}, \pi_i(\sigma), s_i) \mid 1 \leq i \leq |\sigma|\}, s_0, s_{|\sigma|})$.

Now, to obtain an optimal alignment between a trace and a process tree, we construct the synchronous product of their transition systems [cf. 1]. We start off from a standard direct product of two transition systems, i.e., we take as state space all pairs consisting of states of the trace and states of the model (the trace can easily be encoded as a labeled directed path). We then extend both components by a new *idle* transition $\gg$ which is always active and does not alter the current state (i.e., a self-loop on every state with label $\gg$). For the product, we allow transition pairs where either both (original) transitions have the same activity label or where precisely one of them is the idle transition. Note that the resulting transitions in the synchronous product are the *legal moves* which we defined above (for details see [1,22]).

Definition 9 (Synchronous Product). Let TS_1 and TS_2 be two transition systems. Their *synchronous product* is denoted by $TS_1 \otimes TS_2$ and defined according to [22, Definition 8.6] where we restrict the resulting transitions to those where either both original transitions have the same activity or one of them is idle (denoted by $\gg$). The initial and final state of the synchronous product are the states that are compositions of the original initial or final states, respectively.

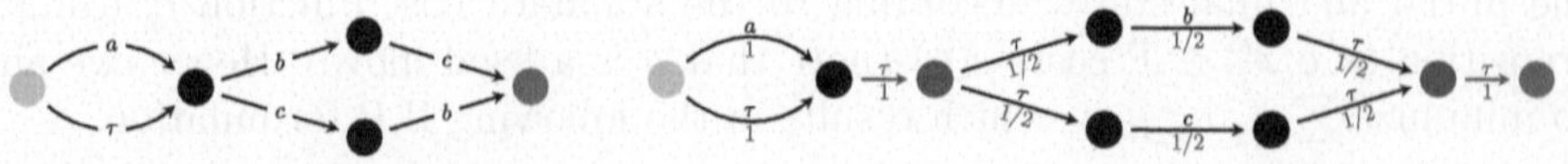

(a) Transition system $\mathcal{TS}(PT)$). (b) Process tree network $\mathcal{N}(PT)$.

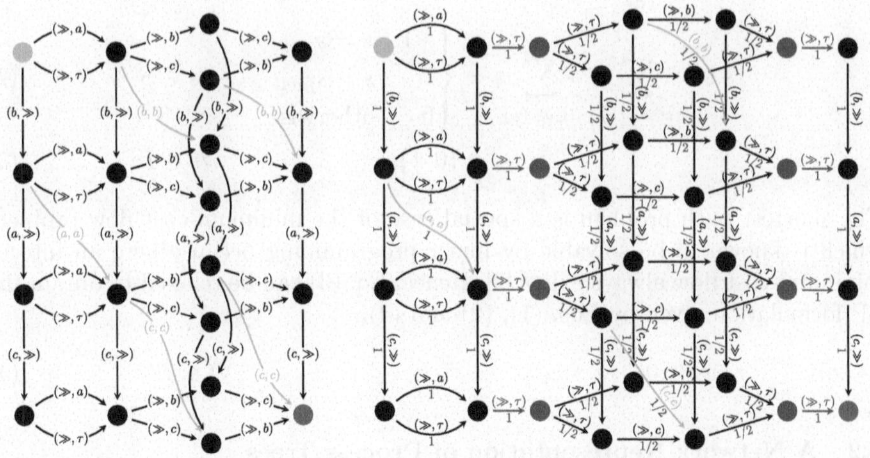

(c) Synchronous product of transition systems TS_σ and $\mathcal{TS}(PT)$. (d) Synchronous network $\mathcal{N}(\sigma, PT)$.

Fig. 1. Comparison between the transition system and the process tree network of $PT = \to(\times(a,\tau), \wedge(b,c))$ and between the transition system of the synchronous product with trace $\sigma = \langle b, a, c\rangle$ and the corresponding synchronous network. Transitions representing synchronous moves and synchronous arcs, respectively, are highlighted in green, synchronization nodes and arcs in blue.

Figure 1c shows the synchronous product of the transition system of the trace $\langle b, a, c\rangle$ and that of the process tree $\to(\times(a,\tau), \wedge(b,c))$. It can be seen that the activities of the resulting transitions correspond to legal moves where synchronous moves are highlighted in green. Thus, each path from the initial to the final state of the synchronous product corresponds to an alignment. If each arc is weighted with the cost function according to the move it represents, an optimal alignment is found via a shortest path. Alignment γ_2 from above represents the shortest path in the synchronous product and is therefore optimal.

We can also solve an optimization problem to find a shortest path from the initial state to the final state. Let $x_t \in \{0, 1\}$ be a binary decision variable indicating whether a transition $t \in T$ is part of the shortest path ($x_t = 1$) or not ($x_t = 0$). To obtain a valid path from the initial state to the final state, we do not only have to ensure that it originates in the initial state and terminates in the final state, but also that it is not interrupted in any other state. This can be achieved by requiring the number of incoming transitions $\delta^-(s)$ and outgoing transitions $\delta^+(s)$ used in the path to be equal in any state $s \in S$ except for the initial and final state. According to the standard cost function c, using a transition $(s, a, s') \in T$ costs $c(a)$ (note that a is a legal move). Hence, we aim to minimize $\sum_{t\in T} c_{\pi_2(t)} x_t$ which results in the following ILP formulation.

$$\min \quad \sum_{t\in T} c_{\pi_2(t)} x_t \tag{1}$$

$$\text{s.t.} \quad \sum_{t\in\delta^-(s)} x_t - \sum_{t\in\delta^+(s)} x_t = \begin{cases} -1 & s = s_{init} \\ 1 & s = s_{final} \\ 0 & \text{otherwise} \end{cases} \qquad \forall s \in S \tag{2}$$

$$x_t \in \{0, 1\} \qquad \forall t \in T \tag{3}$$

The shortest path problem is a special case of the minimum-cost flow problem which is known to be solvable by linear programming because here an integer minimum-cost flow always exists [2]. Hence, Eq. (3) can be relaxed to obtain the LP formulation given by Eqs. (1), (2) and (4).

$$x_t \geq 0 \qquad \forall t \in T \tag{4}$$

4.2 A Network Representation of Process Trees

When we transform process trees into equivalent transition systems, we see that concurrency causes the state space to grow exponentially. Of course, when we solve the shortest path problem on the resulting systems via an (I)LP as above, the exponential number of states results in an exponential number of variables and constraints. In the synchronous product, however, this state explosion problem in essence confines itself to transitions representing model moves while the ordering of both, log moves and synchronous moves is already widely determined by the sequence of activities defined in the trace.

Formally, we introduce a network representation of a process tree which we use as a basis for the alignment problem. This *process tree network* is largely similar to the transition system of a process tree except for the representation of the parallel operator. Apart from that, the most important change is the introduction of arc capacities, which allow us to split the flow for parallel subtrees. The idea is for the resulting subflows to capture (independent) computation sequences in the parallel subprocesses. Intuitively, the reader might think of the subflows as tokens that move through a Petri net.

Definition 10 (Process Tree Network)**.** Let PT be a process tree. Its *process tree network* $\mathcal{N}PT = (V, \Sigma \cup \{\tau\}, A, V', A', u, v_{init}, v_{final})$ is a tuple where V is the set of nodes, $A \subseteq V \times (\Sigma \cup \{\tau\}) \times V$ is the set of arcs, $V' \subset V$ and $A' \subset A$ are the sets of synchronization nodes and arcs, respectively, $u\colon A \to [0,1]$ is a capacity function, $v_{init} \in V$ is the source node, and $v_{final} \in V$ is the target node. It is constructed recursively by starting with the source and target node $v_{init}, v_{final} \in V$ and a constant $\kappa = 1$ as follows:

- if $PT = \tau$, adding an arc $(v_{init}, \tau, v_{final})$ with capacity $1/\kappa$,
- for each activity $a \in \Sigma$, if $PT = a$, adding an arc (v_{init}, a, v_{final}) with capacity $1/\kappa$,
- for process trees $PT_1, \ldots, PT_n$ (with pairwise disjoint state spaces), $n \in \mathbb{N}$,
  - if $PT = \rightarrow (PT_1, \ldots, PT_n)$, adding new nodes $v_1, \ldots, v_{n-1}$ and inserting $\mathcal{N}PT_i$ with constant κ, source node v_{i-1}, and target node v_i for $1 \leq i \leq n$ where $v_0 = v_{init}$ and $v_n = v_{final}$,
  - if $PT = \times(PT_1, \ldots, PT_n)$, we take all $\mathcal{N}PT_i$ with constant κ, for $1 \leq i \leq n$, as independent subsystems and then merge all source nodes to source node v_{init} and all target nodes to target node v_{final},
  - if $PT = \circlearrowleft (PT_1, PT_2)$, adding new nodes v_1 and v_2, arcs (v_{init}, τ, v_1) and (v_2, τ, v_{final}) with capacity $1/\kappa$, and inserting $\mathcal{N}PT_1$ with constant κ, source node v_1, and target node v_2 and $\mathcal{N}PT_2$ with constant κ, source node v_2, and target node v_1, and
  - if $PT = \wedge(PT_1, \ldots, PT_n)$, adding new synchronization nodes v_S and v'_S, synchronization arcs (v_{init}, τ, v_S) and (v'_S, τ, v_{final}) with capacity $1/\kappa$, taking all $\mathcal{N}PT_i$ with constant $n\kappa$, for $1 \leq i \leq n$, as independent subsystems and then adding arcs (v_S, τ, v_i) and (v'_i, τ, v'_S) with capacity $1/(n\kappa)$ where v_i is the source and v'_i the target node of $\mathcal{N}PT_i$.

Let us give some intuition on the construction of a process tree network, also illustrated in Table 1. Given the process tree $\rightarrow (\times(a, \tau), \wedge(b, c))$ of our running example, the resulting process tree network shown in Fig. 1b is constructed recursively and in a similar fashion as a transition system, except for the arc capacities and the modeling of the parallel operator. The inverse of κ, i.e., $1/\kappa$, represents the intended intensity of the flow propagating through the particular network (from v_{init} to v_{final}). Initially, κ is set to 1 and therefore, all arc capacities outside the parallel construct are 1. We now take a closer look at the subtree $\wedge(b, c)$. Every parallel construct begins and ends with a synchronization arc and node (highlighted in blue) which connect the parallel subprocesses to the outer network construct. First, κ is set to 2 because there are two parallel subtrees b and c. Then, each subtree is constructed with $\kappa = 2$. Finally, every parallel subtree is connected with τ-arcs of capacity $1/\kappa = 1/2$ (so that the network flow is split) to the synchronization nodes leading to the final result.

A trace $\sigma \in \Sigma^*$ can also be expressed by a process tree network N_σ, which consists of $|\sigma| + 1$ nodes and where each event in the trace is associated with an arc of unit capacity, i.e., $N_\sigma = (\{v_i \,|\, 0 \leq i \leq |\sigma|\}, \Sigma, \{(v_{i-1}, \pi_i(\sigma), v_i) \,|\, 1 \leq i \leq |\sigma|\}, \emptyset, \emptyset, 1, v_0, v_{|\sigma|})$. Analogously to transition systems, we can now form a *synchronous network* following the same idea, but based on process tree networks, to provide the basic structure for the MILP formulation.

Definition 11 (Synchronous Network). Let $\sigma \in \Sigma^*$ be a trace and let PT be a process tree. Given the trace network $N_\sigma = (\{v_i \mid 0 \leq i \leq |\sigma|\}, \Sigma, \{(v_{i-1}, \pi_i(\sigma), v_i) \mid 1 \leq i \leq |\sigma|\}, \emptyset, \emptyset, 1, v_0, v_{|\sigma|})$ and the network of the process tree $\mathcal{N}(PT) := (V_{PT}, \Sigma \cup \{\tau\}, A_{PT}, V'_{PT}, A'_{PT}, u_{PT}, v_{PT}, v'_{PT})$, their *synchronous product* $N_\sigma \otimes \mathcal{N}(PT) := (V, LM, A, V', A', u, v_{init}, v_{final})$, also denoted as *synchronous network* $\mathcal{N}(\sigma, PT)$, can be constructed iteratively where

- $V := V_\sigma \times V_{PT}$ and $V' := V_\sigma \times V'_{PT}$,
- $A := A^M \cup A^L \cup A^S \cup A' \subseteq V \times LM \times V$ where
  - $A^M := \bigcup_{0 \leq i \leq |\sigma|} A_i^M$ and $A^\tau := \bigcup_{0 \leq i \leq |\sigma|} A_i^\tau$ are model arcs with $A_i^M := \{((v_i, \pi_1(a)), (\gg, \pi_2(a)), (v_i, \pi_3(a))) \mid a \in A_{PT} \setminus A'_{PT} \wedge \pi_2(a) \neq \tau\}$ and $A_i^\tau := \{((v_i, \pi_1(a)), (\gg, \tau), (v_i, \pi_3(a))) \mid a \in A_{PT} \setminus A'_{PT} \wedge \pi_2(a) = \tau\}$,
  - $A^L := \bigcup_{1 \leq i \leq |\sigma|} A_i^L$ are log arcs with $A_i^L := \{((v_{i-1}, v), (\pi_i(\sigma), \gg), (v_i, v)) \mid v \in V_{PT} \setminus V'_{PT}\}$,
  - $A^S := \bigcup_{1 \leq i \leq |\sigma|} A_i^S$ are synchronous arcs with $A_i^S := \{((v_{i-1}, \pi_1(a)), (\pi_i(\sigma), \pi_2(a)), (v_i, \pi_3(a))) \mid a \in A_{PT} \setminus A'_{PT} \wedge \pi_2(a) = \pi_i(\sigma)\}$,
  - $A' := \bigcup_{0 \leq i \leq |\sigma|} A'_i$ are synchronization arcs with $A'_i := \{((v_i, \pi_1(a)), (\gg, \pi_2(a)), (v_i, \pi_3(a))) \mid a \in A'_{PT}\}$,
- $\forall a \in A$: $u(a) := \min(\{1\} \cup \{u_{PT}(a') \mid a' \in A_{PT} \wedge \pi_3(a') = \pi_2(\pi_1(a))\}) \in [0, 1]$,
- $v_{init} := (v_0, v_{PT}) \in V$ and $v_{final} := (v_{|\sigma|}, v'_{PT}) \in V$.

Figure 1d shows the resulting synchronous network of the trace $\langle b, a, c\rangle$ and the process tree $\rightarrow(\times(a, \tau), \wedge(b, c))$. There are no loops in the example, but note that their arc capacity is bounded like all other arcs. Due to the capacity constraint, running through a loop repeatedly is not possible (when we assume flows with maximal intensity). However, this is not a contradiction, as it ultimately represents model moves and only the shortest firing sequence between two states is sought. Moreover, it should be emphasized that synchronization nodes are only incident with synchronization and model arcs.

In terms of the ILP formulation in Eqs. (1) to (3), we have to adapt to the new network structure with arc capacities and adjust the cost function accordingly. The binary decision variable $x_a \in \{0, 1\}$ still indicates whether an arc $a \in A$ is part of the shortest path ($x_a = 1$) or not ($x_a = 0$).

$$\min \sum_{a \in A^M} x_a + \sum_{a \in A^L} u_a x_a - \sum_{a \in A^S} (1 - u_a) x_a \tag{5}$$

$$\text{s.t.} \quad \sum_{a \in \delta^-(v)} u_a x_a - \sum_{a \in \delta^+(v)} u_a x_a = \begin{cases} -1 & v = v_{init} \\ 1 & v = v_{final} \\ 0 & \text{otherwise} \end{cases} \quad \forall v \in V \tag{6}$$

$$\sum_{a \in A_i^S} x_a \leq 1 \quad \forall 1 \leq i \leq |\sigma| \colon |A_i^S| > 1 \tag{7}$$

$$x_a \in \{0, 1\} \quad \forall a \in A \tag{8}$$

Obviously, we now have to account for the arc capacities u_a in the flow conservation constraint for each node in Eq. (6). Further, we have to adjust the objective such that the costs of moves accord with the standard cost function. Based on the network structure, we see that using a model arc $a \in A^M \cup A^\tau$ always corresponds to a model move; therefore, their cost remain the same. This does not necessarily apply to log moves because in case of a log move within a parallel construct, a log arc $a \in A^L$ must be used for each flow in parallel subtrees; therefore, their cost are weighted with the arc capacity u_a. For the same reason, the costs for using a synchronous arc $a \in A^S$ must also be adjusted as the other partial flows within a parallel construct must switch to log arcs, whose additional costs must be compensated for here; therefore, their cost are reduced based on the difference to their arc capacity. Note that due to the network structure, neither log nor synchronous moves can be part of a cycle. Thus, the solution space remains bounded even with negative costs for synchronous arcs. In case of duplicate labels in the process tree, the network might allow to use more than one synchronous move on the same trace activity; however, the newly introduced constraint in Eq. (7) ensures that at most one of the synchronous arcs is used per activity in the trace.

4.3 Relaxed MILP Formulation

Due to the construction of the network, each synchronization node $v' \in V'$ is incident with exactly one synchronization arc $a' \in A'$. Hence, let $\delta' \colon V' \to A'$ be the bijection which assigns that particular arc $a' \in A'$ to each node $v' \in V'$. The binary decision variable $y_{v'} \in \{0,1\}$ therefore implicitly indicates whether the corresponding synchronization arc $\delta'(v') \in A'$ is used ($y_{v'} = 1$) or not ($y_{v'} = 0$). For better readability, we also introduce the function ρ^+ (ρ^-) which adapts the function δ^+ (δ^-) in such a way that synchronization arcs are resolved.

$$\rho^\pm \colon V \to \mathcal{P}(A \setminus A'), v \mapsto \rho^\pm(v) := (\delta^\pm(v) \setminus A') \cup \bigcup_{a' \in \delta^\pm(v) \cap A'} \rho^\pm(\pi_{2\pm1}(a'))$$

This way, we are able to isolate the synchronization arcs and relax the decision variable for all remaining arcs to represent the flow on that arc. That is, the continuous variable $x_a \in [0, u_a]$ denotes the flow on arc $a \in A \setminus A'$. As a result, capacities no longer have to be taken into account separately.

The isolation of the synchronization arcs also permits that they can be ignored in the flow conservation constraint in Eq. (10) at any node $v \in V \setminus V'$ as the corresponding arcs before or after the synchronization arc are now considered here instead. For each synchronization node $v' \in V'$, Eq. (11) ensures flow conservation where the flow on a synchronization arc is still determined via its capacity. Due to the network structure, the synchronization arc at a node $v' \in V'$ is always oriented contrary to all remaining arcs; thus, we simply use $\delta(v') := \delta^+(v') \cup \delta^-(v')$ here. Finally, the objective is adjusted by factoring in the flow via the arc capacities.

$$\min \quad \sum_{a\in A^M} \frac{1}{u_a} x_a + \sum_{a\in A^L} x_a - \sum_{a\in A^S} \left(\frac{1}{u_a} - 1\right) x_a \tag{9}$$

$$\text{s.t.} \quad \sum_{a\in\rho^-(v)} x_a - \sum_{a\in\rho^+(v)} x_a = \begin{cases} -1 & v = v_{init} \\ 1 & v = v_{final} \\ 0 & \text{otherwise} \end{cases} \qquad \forall v \in V \setminus V' \tag{10}$$

$$\sum_{a\in\delta(v')\setminus A'} x_a = u_{\delta'(v')} y_{v'} \qquad \forall v' \in V' \tag{11}$$

$$\sum_{a\in A_i^S} \frac{1}{u_a} x_a \leq 1 \qquad \forall 1 \leq i \leq |\sigma| : |A_i^S| > 1 \tag{12}$$

$$x_a \leq u_a \qquad \forall a \in A \setminus A' \tag{13}$$

$$x_a \geq 0 \qquad \forall a \in A \setminus A' \tag{14}$$

$$y_{v'} \in \{0, 1\} \qquad \forall v' \in V' \tag{15}$$

It remains to show that the relaxation leads to the same optimal solution as the ILP formulation in Eqs. (5) to (8). The network structure outside of parallel constructs is identical to that of the transition system and the individual subtree representations within a parallel construct are structurally independent. Although the arc capacities are not necessarily integer, they are constant for each subcomponent and Eqs. (11) ensures that the flow within a subcomponent is exactly this constant. Therefore, there exists a common factor such that all arc capacities are integer and because of the structural independence of subcomponents an integer minimum-cost flow would always exist [2].

5 Evaluation

To analyze the performance of our MILP approach, we developed a proof-of-concept implementation and evaluation[1] in the *PM4Py* ecosystem [3] using the *Gurobi Optimizer* [13]. We compared the performance of our implementation (*MILP*) with the general PM4Py implementation based on the A* approach (*Standard*) and an optimized approximation algorithm for alignments on process trees (*Approximation*). For each algorithm and trace variant, we took the best out of 10 repetitions (meaning the minimum required time for computing the costs of an optimal alignment). To visualize the results, we computed the *performance factors* for each trace variant, that is, we took the best runtime and divided the runtime of all three algorithms by this optimal runtime (trace-variant-wise). For instance, a performance factor of 2 indicates, that the algorithm took twice as long as the best algorithm.

Not all algorithms finished computation in a reasonable amount of time, so we set a timeout of 65 s (incl. 5 s to compensate for overhead and give each algorithm

[1] https://github.com/christopher-schwanen/process-tree-alignments.

the safe chance to finish within one minute). Algorithms that hit this timeout in any run were considered to have failed (on this variant), and performance factors are not computed. In the charts below, we plotted the empirical CDF of the performance factors per algorithm. In cases where the frequencies do not sum up to 1, the algorithm ran into timeouts on a certain fraction of instances.

Real-world event logs: We used the well-known *Sepsis Cases event log* [16] and the *Inductive Miner* [14] to discover process trees with different noise thresholds (0 %, 10 %, 25 %, and 50 %) against which we aligned the log. The Inductive Miner produces process trees with *unique labels*. Since the alignment problem for such trees is much simpler (solvable in polynomial time), we further renamed duplicate labels in traces (adding a suffix, up to 5 repetitions) so that we could later (after discovery) merge the labels again (by removing the suffix). The results are depicted in Fig. 2. It can be seen that our MILP approach outperforms both other algorithms clearly on the Sepsis Cases event log. The picture is even clearer for lower noise thresholds. We obtain a similar picture on the BPI Challenge 2012 and 2017 event logs [10,11]. While on process trees with unique labels, the MILP and the approximation algorithm are usually close (and clearly superior to the standard algorithm), as soon as we drop the unique label property, our MILP approach dramatically outperforms the other two algorithms. Table 2 provides some benchmark results for these event logs and the process trees created using our duplicate label strategy (cf. above) with respect to the different noise thresholds (0 %, 10 %, 25 %, and 50 %). Here, we depict the median computation times of the three algorithms for the different runs together with the percentage of instances solved, i.e., the fraction of variants where the algorithm did not run into a timeout. To give one example, for the BPI Challenge 2017 (with configuration 0 % noise threshold and duplicate labels) the approximation algorithm could align *none* of the 1000 randomly chosen variants within the time bound, while the standard algorithm could only align about 9 % of the variants. At the same time, our MILP approach was successful on 99.8 % of all variants with a median computation time of about 14 s (time bound 65 s).

Artificial Event Log: Concurrency is the main driver for the complexity of the alignment problem, so we also took artificial examples which put concurrency into focus. For $m = 10$ and $n = 10$ we considered traces $w_m = \langle a\rangle^m \cdot \langle b\rangle \cdot \langle a\rangle^m$ with two activities a and b of which we grouped n copies together to get a process tree $\mathcal{L}(PT[m,n]) = w_m \sqcup\!\sqcup\, w_m \sqcup\!\sqcup \cdots \sqcup\!\sqcup\, w_m$. We then sampled several traces of the form $\langle a, \ldots, a, b, a, \ldots, a\rangle^n$ and aligned them against the tree $PT[m,n]$. Our MILP approach could always find a solution (within the time bound of 65 s). The Approximation algorithm was only able to solve 8.0 % of instances. After extending the time bound to 330 s (incl. 30 s to compensate for overhead and give each algorithm the safe chance to finish within five minutes), it could find a solution in most cases, but was far beyond the performance of our MILP approach. The Standard algorithm uniformly failed to solve these instances, so we excluded it from the analysis. Figure 3 demonstrates that in more than 70 % of instances it took more than twice as long.

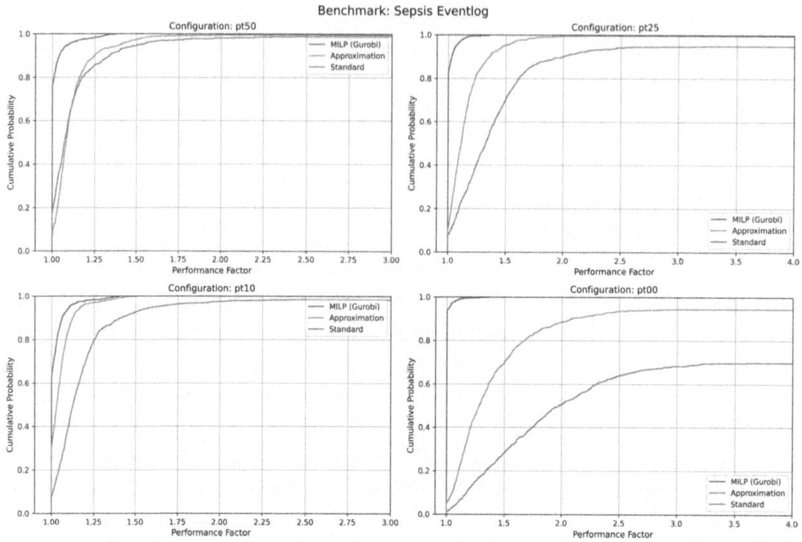

Fig. 2. Performance factors of our MILP approach, the Approximation approach, and the Standard approach on the runtimes when computing alignments for the *Sepsis Cases* event log [16].

Table 2. Comparison of median computation times ($\tilde{t}_{comp}$, in seconds) and percentages of instances solved with respect to the time bound of 65 s (% solved) for different event logs and process trees.

	MILP		Approximation		Standard	
	$\tilde{t}_{comp}$	% solved	$\tilde{t}_{comp}$	% solved	$\tilde{t}_{comp}$	% solved
Sepsis Cases [16]					(846 trace variants)	
50 %	**7.35**	**100.00**	7.54	**100.00**	7.55	99.76
25 %	**7.09**	**100.00**	8.11	94.68	8.16	98.23
10 %	**7.34**	**100.00**	7.41	**100.00**	7.49	99.88
0 %	**7.31**	**100.00**	8.30	98.70	19.48	98.58
BPI Challenge 2012 [10] (1000 randomly chosen trace variants)						
50 %	**13.48**	99.20	15.97	**99.80**	50.80	52.60
25 %	**18.93**	**93.40**	—	45.40	—	16.40
10 %	**8.34**	**100.00**	11.13	99.90	11.61	90.70
0 %	**9.62**	**100.00**	30.34	85.10	—	12.70
BPI Challenge 2017 [11] (1000 randomly chosen trace variants)						
50 %	**11.10**	**100.00**	17.10	85.20	—	27.50
25 %	**14.31**	**99.60**	40.11	59.10	—	28.90
10 %	**12.78**	**100.00**	21.84	60.40	—	5.20
0 %	**16.45**	**99.80**	—	0.00	—	8.30

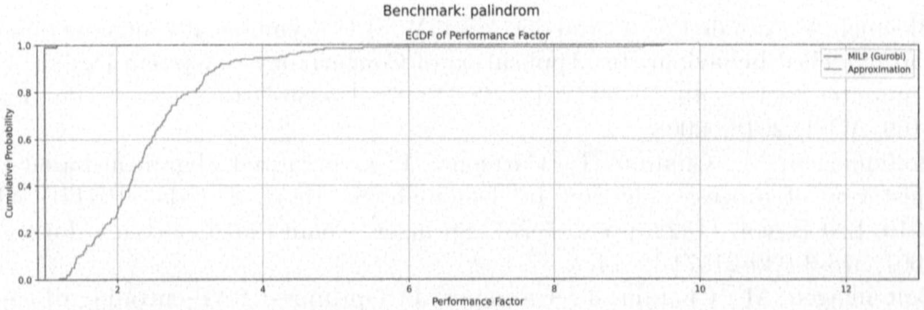

Fig. 3. Performance factors of our MILP approach and the Approximation approach on the runtimes when computing alignments for the artificial *Palindrome* event log.

6 Conclusion

We gave the first MILP formulation for alignments on process trees together with a proof-of-concept implementation and evaluation. Our experiments show that our new approach outperforms the existing algorithms in PM4Py. This sheds new light on the alignment problem which is known to be inherently difficult to solve in practice. In particular, our work demonstrates that the study of restricted model classes can lead to new algorithmic approaches and to specialized algorithms which perform more efficiently due to the utilization of additional structure. It is clear that our techniques generalize to larger classes of process models. It remains a key question for future research to see how far our MILP approach can be pushed. At the same time, there are many angles for deeper investigations of MILP encodings on process trees. For instance, are there other encodings for which common solvers perform even better or can we further improve the encoding given in this paper? Also, we can now access the huge toolbox of mathematical optimization and study questions such as how accurate LP relaxations of the alignment computation become. Specifically, it would be interesting to investigate the accuracy loss when we relax the MILP to become an efficiently solvable LP.

Acknowledgement. The research of the first author is funded by the IGF project 22485 N by the Federal Ministry for Economic Affairs and Climate Action (BMWK) on the basis of a decision of the German Bundestag. The first and third author thank the Alexander von Humboldt (AvH) Stiftung for supporting their research.

References

1. Adriansyah, A.: Aligning observed and modeled behavior, Ph.D. dissertation, Technische Universiteit Eindhoven (2014). ISBN: 978-90-386-3574-3. https://doi.org/10.6100/IR770080
2. Ahuja, R.K., Magnanti, T.L., Orlin, J.B.: Network Flows, Theory, Algorithms, and Applications. Englewood Cliffs, Prentice Hall, NJ (1993). ISBN: 0-13-617549-X
3. Berti, A., van Zelst, S.J., Schuster, D.: PM4Py: a process mining library for Python. Softw. Impacts **17**, 100–556 (2023). https://doi.org/10.1016/j.simpa.2023.100556

4. Bloemen, V., van de Pol, J., van der Aalst, W.M.P.: Symbolically aligning observed and modelled behaviour. In: Application of Concurrency to System Design, IEEE Computer Society, pp. 50–59 (2018). ISBN: 978-1-5386-7013-2, https://doi.org/10.1109/ACSD.2018.00008
5. Boltenhagen, M., Chatain, T., Carmona, J.: Generalized alignment-based trace clustering of process behavior. In: Donatelli, S., Haar, S. (eds.) PETRI NETS 2019. LNCS, vol. 11522, pp. 237–257. Springer, Cham (2019). https://doi.org/10.1007/978-3-030-21571-2_14
6. Boltenhagen, M., Chatain, T., Carmona, J.: Optimized SAT encoding of conformance checking artefacts. Computing **103**(1), 29–50 (2020). https://doi.org/10.1007/s00607-020-00831-8
7. Buijs, J. C.A.M., van Dongen, B.F., van der Aalst, W.M.P.: A genetic algorithm for discovering process trees. In: 2012 IEEE Congress on Evolutionary Computation, pp. 1–8 (2012). https://doi.org/10.1109/CEC.2012.6256458
8. Carmona, J., van Dongen, B.F., Solti, A., Weidlich, M.: conformance checking, relating processes and models. Springer, Cham (2018). 978-3-319-99413-0. https://doi.org/10.1007/978-3-319-99414-7
9. Carmona, J., van Dongen, B.F., Weidlich, M.: Conformance checking: foundations, milestones and challenges. In: van der Aalst, W.M.P., Carmona, J. (eds.) Process Mining Handbook, LNBIP, vol. 448. Springer, Cham (2022). https://doi.org/10.1007/978-3-031-08848-3_5
10. van Dongen, B.F.: BPI challenge 2012. Eindhoven University of Technology (2012). https://doi.org/10.4121/uuid:3926db30-f712-4394-aebc-75976070e91f
11. van Dongen, B.F.: BPI challenge 2017. Eindhoven University of Technology (2017). https://doi.org/10.4121/uuid:5f3067df-f10b-45da-b98b-86ae4c7a310b
12. van Dongen, B.F.: Efficiently computing alignments. In: Weske, M., Montali, M., Weber, I., vom Brocke, J. (eds.) BPM 2018. LNCS, vol. 11080, pp. 197–214. Springer, Cham (2018). https://doi.org/10.1007/978-3-319-98648-7_12
13. Gurobi Optimization, LLC, Gurobi Optimizer Reference Manual (2023). https://www.gurobi.com
14. Leemans, S.J.J., Fahland, D., van der Aalst, W.M.P.: Discovering block-structured process models from incomplete event logs. In: Ciardo, G., Kindler, E. (eds.) PETRI NETS 2014. LNCS, vol. 8489, pp. 91–110. Springer, Cham (2014). https://doi.org/10.1007/978-3-319-07734-5_6
15. de Leoni, M., Marrella, A.: Aligning real process executions and prescriptive process models through automated planning. Expert Syst. Appl. **82**, 162–183 (2017). https://doi.org/10.1016/j.eswa.2017.03.047
16. Mannhardt, F.: Sepsis cases - event log. Eindhoven University of Technology (2016). https://doi.org/10.4121/uuid:915d2bfb-7e84-49ad-a286-dc35f063a460
17. Mayer, A.J., Stockmeyer, L.J.: The complexity of word problems - this time with interleaving. Inf. Comput. **115**(2), 293–311 (1994). https://doi.org/10.1006/inco.1994.1098
18. Rozinat, A., van der Aalst, W.M.P.: Conformance checking of processes based on monitoring real behavior. Inf. Syst. **33**(1), 64–95 (2008). https://doi.org/10.1016/j.is.2007.07.001
19. Schuster, D., van Zelst, S.J., van der Aalst, W.M.P.: Alignment approximation for process trees. In: Leemans, S., Leopold, H. (eds.) ICPM 2020. LNBIP, vol. 406, pp. 247–259. Springer, Cham (2021). https://doi.org/10.1007/978-3-030-72693-5_19
20. Taymouri, F., Carmona, J.: A recursive paradigm for aligning observed behavior of large structured process models. In: La Rosa, M., Loos, P., Pastor, O. (eds.) BPM

2016. LNCS, vol. 9850, pp. 197–214. Springer, Cham (2016). https://doi.org/10.1007/978-3-319-45348-4_12
21. van der Aalst, W.M.P., Buijs, J., van Dongen, B.F.: Towards improving the representational bias of process mining. In: Aberer, K., Damiani, E., Dillon, T. (eds.) SIMPDA 2011. LNBIP, vol. 116, pp. 39–54. Springer, Heidelberg (2012). https://doi.org/10.1007/978-3-642-34044-4_3
22. Winskel, G.: Synchronization trees. Theoret. Comput. Sci. **34**(1–2), 33–82 (1984). https://doi.org/10.1016/0304-3975(84)90112-9

DigiEMine: Towards Leveraging Decision Mining and Context Data for Quality Control

Beate Wais[1,2](✉) and Stefanie Rinderle-Ma[3]

[1] Faculty of Computer Science, Research Group Workflow Systems and Technology, University of Vienna, Vienna, Austria
beate.wais@univie.ac.at
[2] UniVie Doctoral School Computer Science DoCS, University of Vienna, Vienna, Austria
[3] TUM School of Computation, Information and Technology, Technical University of Munich, Garching, Germany
stefanie.rinderle-ma@tum.de

Abstract. Quality control processes in manufacturing often still rely on manual tasks. Applying decision mining can support users by providing valuable insight into the process. This paper discusses the potential of integrating contextual information into decision mining to achieve accurate and meaningful decision rules in the context of a case study stemming from the manufacturing domain. To explore this, a new approach, DigiEMine, is presented, which addresses the gap between information extraction and practical decision mining applications by integrating information extracted from engineering drawings with time sequence data in the form of diameter measurements of workpieces. The discovery of relational decision rules is enabled, allowing for contextualization of the decision rules. The output of this approach is presented in both textual decision rules and visually on engineering drawings, empowering users to make informed quality control decisions. The case study includes three datasets originating from cylindrical workpiece production. Results demonstrate the feasibility of the approach and the ability to generate meaningful decision rules across the tested datasets. Its potential applicability extends beyond the presented case study, with conceivable scenarios in multiple domains, such as healthcare or logistics, where integrating context information, such as regulatory data, with time sequence data is required to provide additional context for decisions.

Keywords: Decision Mining · Context Data · Manufacturing · Quality Control

1 Introduction

Process mining, including process discovery, conformance checking, and process enhancement [1], plays an essential role in driving automation and digitalization

J. Borbinha et al. (Eds.): EDOC 2024, LNCS 15409, pp. 318–335, 2025.
https://doi.org/10.1007/978-3-031-78338-8_17

and can be applied in multiple ways, delivering valuable insights into operations and enabling the identification of bottlenecks, inefficiencies, and deviations from the intended process flow. This information can be used to optimize production processes, reduce waste, and improve overall productivity [20]. An essential aspect of process mining involves decision mining, i.e., discovering decision points and the underlying decision rules in processes [15]. The need for improving knowledge about and around decisions is increasing as *"[e]ffective decision making – that is connected, contextual and continuous – results in a host of business benefits, including greater transparency, accuracy, scalability and speed"*[1]. Decision mining enables increased transparency in processes by capturing the underlying logic of decisions, allowing users to understand the decisions in a process. Decision mining typically employs classification techniques and aims to provide decision rules that are in human-readable form. This, in turn, can lead to faster detection of deviations and allows for evaluation whether these detected deviations are intentional or due to errors, decreasing the time until errors are detected and thereby minimizing the impact of errors on the overall outcome.

Typically, the input data for decision mining comprises process event log data for determining decision points in the process and process data such as patient age or the loan amount to determine the decision rules at the decision points based on classification techniques, mostly decision trees [15]. In domains where IoT data provides context to process event data, e.g., manufacturing, logistics, and healthcare, sensor data might also influence decisions and should hence be part of potentially more complex decision rules, i.e., turning from, e.g., "temperature > 30" to "temperature exceeds 30 for three times in a row" [2,9, 23].

Input data for decision mining might comprise additional structured or unstructured context data. Context data defined as being *"additional process-related information"* [5] might be crucial for decisions in a process. An example of context data in manufacturing are *engineering drawings (EDs)*. EDs are the source of information on how a product is going to be produced and also serve as input for quality checks after production [21] and, therefore, provide important process-related information.

Including context data explicitly in decision mining can lead to more accurate and meaningful results with decision rules that are set in the appropriate context. This means that the resulting decision model and the mined decision rule are more meaningful to employees using and interpreting the decision rules. However, integrating data, specifically less structured data such as images, is not trivial and might lead to features that are not easy to interpret for humans. Including context data explicitly, therefore, requires the use of features that can transport as much information as possible to the users. This can be done by building relational features, where two features are connected, e.g., "$age\_customer <= maximum\_age$". Multiple decision mining approaches exist in the literature; see [15], including approaches that enable the extraction of relational decision rules [3,14,22]. So far, to the best of our knowledge, no approach exists that enables

---

1 www.gartner.com/smarterwithgartner/how-to-make-better-business-decisions.

the integration of time sequence data and unstructured context data. However, combinations of time sequence data and additional context data occur in multiple domains, for example in manufacturing where sensor data is set in relation to specifications. This paper, therefore, explores the integration of context data in decision mining embedded in a case study from the manufacturing domain to answer the following research question RQ:

RQ: How can context data, such as dimensioning information, and time sequence data be combined and integrated into decision mining algorithms?

We employ a case study methodology [19] to gain an in-depth understanding of the challenges and complexities of a specific use case and the corresponding implementation, providing valuable insights into its functionality and potential challenges. The main contribution of this paper is the introduction of the DigiEMine approach. This novel approach integrates unstructured context data with time sequence data for decision mining, allowing the construction of relational decision rules that provide explicit reference to the input data. Thereby, the traceability and reconfigurability of the resulting decision rules are increased. Traceability refers to understanding why a specific value is essential in a decision rule. In contrast, reconfigurability refers to decision rules being easily adapted if the underlying decision logic changes. The presented approach bridges the gap between information extraction from engineering drawings and its practical application in decision mining, contributing to a more seamless and effective automated quality control process.

The rest of the paper is organized as follows: a case study exploring the research challenges in depth is presented in Sect. 2. The DigiEMine approach is described in Sect. 3 and the results of applying the approach to the cases are presented in Sect. 4. The results are then discussed in Sect. 5 and related work is presented in Sect. 6. A conclusion is given in Sect. 7.

2 Case Study

The case study stems from the manufacturing domain, particularly the production of cylindrical workpieces, such as valve lifters. These workpieces are produced in small batches using a turning machine. The dimensions stem from a CAD (Computer Aided Design) model, which is nowadays mainly used in production. In addition, an engineering drawing is generated from the CAD model, where additional information, such as applicable regulatory guidelines and default tolerances, is noted. After producing the workpiece, its quality is assessed by measuring different attributes and comparing the measurements to the requirements specified in the corresponding ED. The best-case scenario would involve all specifications being part of the CAD model, including tolerances, which can be automatically extracted for quality control. However, engineering drawings are still frequently applied as a contractual basis and as a reference for quality control as the necessary information is often missing in the CAD models [12].

As shown in Fig. 1, the quality control process involves taking two measurements for efficiency and quality reasons. Firstly, a silhouette measuring machine (Keyence) checks the workpiece diameter. This step takes a few seconds but can be inaccurate as not all essential quality factors can be measured this way. Therefore, the workpieces are transferred to a second measuring machine (MicroVu) to measure more attributes, e.g., surface quality and flatness, resulting in more precise results. This step takes a couple of minutes. Hence, an optimization of the quality control would be to classify instances as "ok" or "not ok" after Keyence and let only workpieces with a high probability of being "ok" continue to MicroVu. This optimization can be expressed by a decision point (DP1), highlighted by a red circle in Fig. 1; at this point, the Keyence measurements should be compared to the dimensions and tolerances stated in the ED.

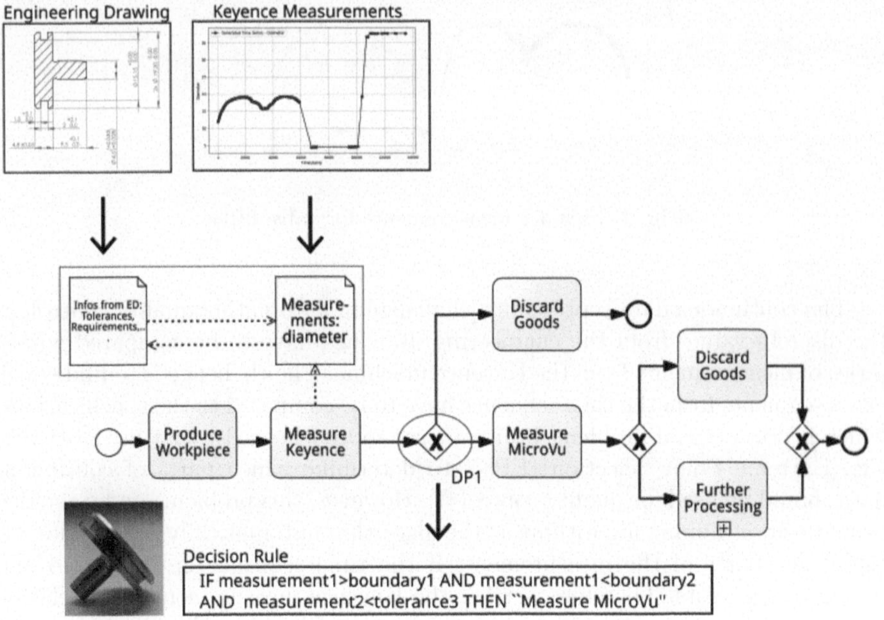

Fig. 1. Valve lifter production process, engineering drawings, measurement values, and resulting decision rule.

The Keyence measuring machine[2] works by illuminating the workpieces with a green LED and a telecentric lens. When the workpiece is put through the machine, it breaks the beam, creating a shadow on the sensor. Different features,

[2] https://www.keyence.eu/ss/products/measure/measurement_library/type/optical, accessed: 12/04/2024.

such as size and angle, can be calculated by measuring this shadow. As the valve lifter is a cylindrical workpiece, the main feature is the diameter of the workpiece. The resulting measurements correspond to the outline of the workpiece (cf. close-up in Fig. 2). The data points up to timestamp *10000* (measured in milliseconds) correspond to the actual silhouette of the workpiece. For the remaining time, the measured values, including the steep increase, are artifacts produced by the robot arm holding the workpiece in place while it is being measured. It can be seen that the measurements do not explicitly correspond to discrete values measuring each dimension but are continuous measurements, i.e., time sequence measurements, as the workpiece is pulled through the laser beam.

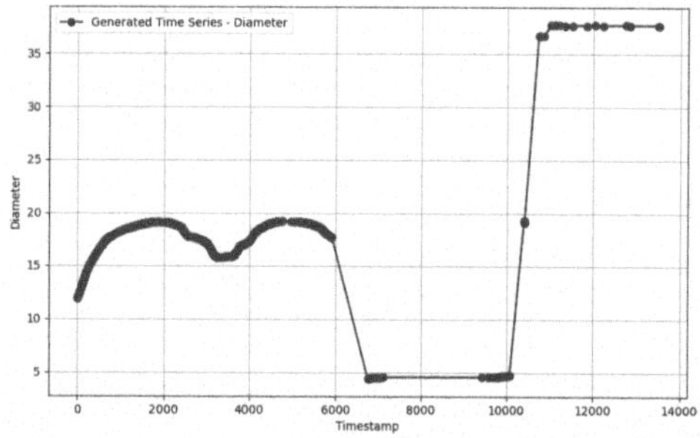

Fig. 2. Keyence measurements for valve lifter.

The continuous data represents a challenge in automating quality control, as the discrete values from the engineering drawings have to be compared with a series of measurements from the Keyence machine. The challenge is to find which exact segments from the time sequence have to be compared to the specifications, which is not a trivial problem. In literature, approaches exist that use statistics, e.g., Extreme Point Selection (EPS), to determine which parts of continuous data should be used for quality control [7]. However, this problem can be avoided using decision mining algorithms as the algorithm automatically determines the significant parts of the measurements if the time sequence is discretized and split into segments. Therefore, setting the Keyence measurements into relation to the requirements and tolerances specified in the ED can enable the mining of a meaningful decision rule for DP1 and thereby support quality control by enabling tracking of which decision logic is actually used to make quality decisions as well as provide a basis for automated quality control.

A decision rule can consist of multiple conditions, which are usually of the form $v(ariable)$ $op(erator)$ $c(onstant)$, for example "measurement1 > 18.5", which are concatenated to form a decision rule. However, in scenarios like the one described above, including the tolerance values in the conditions to embed the measurements in the context of the required dimensions can provide benefits. The corresponding condition is of the form $v(ariable)$ $op(erator)$ $v(ariable)$, for example “measurement1 > tolerance1”. These relational conditions capture the relationships between two variables. An example of a relational condition in a loan application scenario is: “IF *amount* < *amount_treshold*”, where *amount_threshold* is referring to contextual data, e.g., compliance regulations, instead of the classic decision rule: “IF *amount* < 100.000”. Similarly, an example from the healthcare domain could be: “IF *heart_rate* > *max_threshold* OR *blood_pressure* < *min_threshold*” In these examples, the relational conditions compare a variable to another variable that is derived from contextual data, such as regulatory documents or guidelines. This allows the rules to be more flexible and adaptable to changing circumstances. In addition, it provides context information to the user as it is not a constant value but specifies what it relates to; thereby, potential deviations from the intended process can be detected more easily. In the case study, a potential insight could be whether the workpiece quality is assessed based on the required dimensions or on arbitrary values. In addition, constant values might not be exactly the same as the specifications set in the drawing due to learning of the algorithm; e.g., 2.00 was approximated as a threshold instead of the true maximum value of 1.98, which could potentially sum up to account for bigger errors. Therefore, using relational conditions enables more transparent and informative decision rules. An exemplary decision rule for DP1 using relational conditions can be seen in Fig. 1.

Applying decision mining to support quality control in the case study involves several challenges. Firstly, the dimensioning information must be extracted from the engineering drawing in a form that allows for further automated processing. Secondly, the measurements are in the form of time sequence data, which has to be integrated with the dimensioning information in a meaningful way to classify the workpieces accurately. Thirdly, the classification rules have to be communicated to the domain experts transparently [25], i.e., the user has to know according to which rules the workpieces are classified to evaluate if the rules relate to the actual specifications or if unwanted deviations occurred in the quality control process. This process and the related challenges are similar for various workpieces produced using a turning machine, i.e., cylindrical workpieces.

Previous work [21] shows how dimensioning information can be extracted from technical drawings. However, how this information can be implemented as part of the process was not further investigated. Decision mining approaches found in the literature can extract decision rules from event log data [15]. Still, so far, these approaches are not able to relate time sequence data to other data, i.e. embedding the measurements in the context of the required dimensions.

Therefore, integrating information from EDs with time sequence data for decision mining in a meaningful way to automate and optimize the quality assurance process remains to be done. Thus, the primary object of this paper is to bridge the gap between information extraction from EDs and its practical application in decision mining to contribute to seamless and effective automated quality control. This integration is achieved by the DigiEMine approach, which enables the classification of workpieces according to their quality and the extraction of decision rules set in the specifications' context.

Methodology: This paper follows a case study methodology [19]. A case study approach was chosen due to its suitability for in-depth exploration of the real-world complexities involved in implementing and testing the system within this unique use case. The case study and the research questions are introduced as part of this section. Data collection involves implementing and applying the DigiEMine approach on three datasets from the presented scenario. Results are analyzed with regard to their performance as well as their ability to include context information, allowing us to understand the strengths, challenges, and overall effectiveness of the implementation for this use case.

3 The DigiEMine Approach

The DigiEMine approach is defined through Algorithm 1 and consists of three phases. An overview of the approach can be seen in Fig. 3. The gray highlighted lines mark lines that use existing algorithms. As input, the engineering drawing as well as the event log of the production process, are needed.

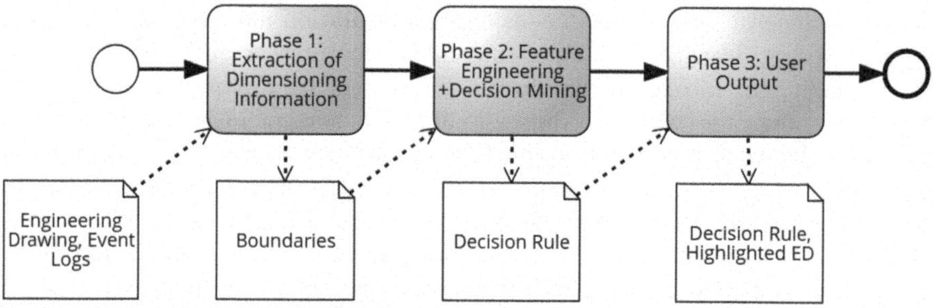

Fig. 3. Overview of the DigiEMine approach (modeled using Signavio©).

In the first phase, dimensioning information, including nominal values and tolerances, is extracted from an engineering drawing using the approach presented in [21]. The nominal values are combined with the tolerances to get upper and lower boundaries, which are used for feature engineering in the next phase.

In the second phase, time sequence data, in this case, the measurement data of the individual workpieces, is extracted from the event logs. New features representing the underlying pattern are extracted from the measurements. These features are combined with the information extracted in Phase 1 to form relational features, which enable the mining of relational conditions. Subsequently, a decision mining algorithm uses the generated features to mine decision rules.

In the third phase, the mined rules are displayed to the user textually. In addition, all tolerances that are part of the resulting decision rule are highlighted in the ED. Therefore, the algorithm's output consists of the decision rule and the highlighted drawing.

Phase 1 Extraction of Dimensions - Algorithm 1 Lines 1–3
The algorithm starts by calling a function provided by [21], using an ED as input, returning dimensioning requirements (D) and coordinates of the bounding box (C) of those requirements on the drawing. The requirements are in JSON format, where the nominal value and the upper and lower tolerances are given, e.g. 4.8, +0.2, –0.2. The next step includes using regular expressions to get from the requirements in the above-described form to requirements of the form "lower acceptable value" and "upper acceptable value", e.g., 4.6 and 5 for the example given above. These values are referred to as boundaries. A data frame (DF)[3] is created, and the lower and upper boundaries (B) are saved as features that stay constant for all instances. The algorithm can be adapted to extract the information from the ED only once and reuse this information every time a new batch of workpieces is produced.

Phase 2 Feature Engineering + Decision Mining - Algorithm 1 Lines 4–16
The next step is to get the measurements ($TSvalues$) and status information ($Status$) for all workpieces (W) from event log files. For the investigated use cases, the log files are in yaml format. For each instance, the measurement values of the Keyence measuring process and the result of the MicroVu measuring process, i.e., the status that indicates whether the workpieces are "ok" or "not ok", are extracted from the event log and stored in the data frame. As the decision mining technique used in this approach is a decision tree, a supervised learning technique, a ground truth must be available, here in the form of MicroVu status. The measurement values, i.e., the time sequence values extracted from the log file and the status, are then stored in the data frame for each instance.

Next, the time sequence values are used to create new features(TSF) that reflect the characteristics of the time sequence by applying the feature engineering part of the *EDT-TS* approach [23]. *EDT-TS* is an approach to discover decision rules that depend on time series data and works by applying different feature engineering methods reflecting different time sequence characteristics. Three types of features are produced: 1) global features that summarize the entire time series, 2) interval-based features that calculate features for subsequences of the time series, and 3) pattern-based features that look at the distribution of values in a time series, e.g., a value has to appear more than five times. The algorithm works by pre-processing event log data to detect time sequence values. Subsequently, different time sequence features are calculated for each instance. Examples of global features generated by EDT-TS are the maximum value, e.g., *diameter_maximum*, the slope of a time series, or more complex values such as a Fourier transform. The time series is divided into intervals for interval-based features, and features are calculated for each interval. The time series can be split

[3] Using pandas, https://pandas.pydata.org/pandas-docs/stable/reference/api/pandas.DataFrame.html.

Algorithm 1. DigiEMine Approach

```
Input: ED, Workpiece Event Logs WL
Output: Textual Decision Rules, Highlighted ED
D, C ← dimensions and coordinates from ED                          ▷ Using [21]
DF ← new data frame
DF[B] ← upper and lower boundaries from D using regex
for W ∈ WL do
    DF[W][TSvalues] ← measurement values for W
    DF[W][Status] ← final status of W
end for
TSF ← generate time sequence features                              ▷ Using [23]
for tsf ∈ TSF do
    if abs(correlation(tsf, Status)) > 0.1 then
        DF[RelevantTSF] ← tsf
    end if
end for
DF[RelationalF] ← generate relational features(DF, B)              ▷ Using [22]
DM ← build decision tree using DF
DR ← generate decision rules using DM
for Condition C ∈ DR do
    RelevantBoundary ← use regex to find which boundary included in C
    if RelevantBoundary = ∅ then
        for b_lower, b_upper ∈ B do
            if b_lower < C_value < b_upper then
                RelevantBoundary ← B
            end if
        end for
    end if
    if RelevantBoundary = ∅ then
        for b ∈ B do
            if min_difference(C_value, b) then
                RelevantBoundary ← B
            end if
        end for
        output warning to user
    end if
    CB ← coordinates for RelevantBoundary using C
    draw rectangle around CB on ED
end for
return textual decision rules and highlighted ED
```

by measurement points or time spans. Examples include the mean, maximum, and percentage change of each interval, e.g., *diameter_segment2_percentchange*, referring to the percent change of values in the second interval. Per default the time series is split into three, five and ten intervals, however this can be manually adapted to fit the specific use case. In this case, the default intervals were used. Pattern-based features consider the distribution of values in the time series. The algorithm identifies values that occur more often in one class than in another. These values are then used as thresholds to create binary features. For example, if the value 26 occurs more than four times in the temperature time series, the feature $temperature\_list.count(26.0) >= 4.0$ would be set to $True$. As all potential features are calculated for each instance, the number of features increases exponentially, leading to increased computational complexity. To avoid working with potentially irrelevant features, the correlation between the engineered features and the resulting outcome, i.e., the status (OK/NOK), is computed. This is done using the Phi Coefficient for two outcome classes and the Pearson correlation coefficient for more than two outcome classes. Only features with an absolute correlation coefficient of at least 0.1 are considered potentially relevant ($RelevantF$) and used for the next steps. The threshold of 0.1 worked well for the tested cases but can be adapted.

In the next step, relational features are created to enable extracting relational conditions instead of conditions using constant values. The relevant features ($RelevantF$) are combined with the boundaries B to create relational features ($RelationalF$), i.e., features of the form $measurement1 <= boundary1$, to set the measurements in relation to the boundaries. After all potential combinations of measurements and boundaries are created, they are calculated (true/false) for each instance, leading to features such as "$measurement1 <= boundary1 ==$ TRUE". The last step in phase 2 consists of mining decision rules. Decision rule mining is usually done using classification algorithms; see [15]. Decision trees are especially useful as these produce white-box decision models and allow for the generation of textual decision rules. Therefore, decision trees are also used in this use case[4] The created features ($RelationalF$ and $RelevantF$) are used as input to the decision tree implementation. Decision trees recursively split the feature space into distinct regions based on the values of input features. Each internal node within the tree represents a decision condition based on a specific feature, with different branches from nodes corresponding to different possible feature values [4]. This partitioning process continues until a stopping criterion is reached, typically when the data points within the leaf node are predominantly of a single class. The resulting decision model (DM) contains a tree structure, enabling the classification of new instances by traversing the tree from the root node to a leaf node based on the feature values of the instance. As a result, textual decision rules containing one or more conditions are generated(DR).

Phase 3 User Output - Algorithm 1 Lines 17–37

In the last phase, the mined decision rule has to be communicated to the domain expert. In production, not all specifications in the ED are relevant to the result. The further use of the workpiece is often decisive in determining which features are essential and which are less critical. However, the production process can also influence which dimensions are most critical, e.g., chips might form on one specific part of a workpiece. Therefore, knowing which parts of the workpiece are most relevant to the outcome enables additional insight. To enable a visual understanding of which dimensions contribute to the classification of an instance,

[4] Here, the Scikit-learn implementation of CART is used, see [18].

all boundaries that are part of the decision rule are mapped to the corresponding dimension and highlighted in the original ED. Therefore, regular expressions are used to extract the boundaries (*RelevantBoundary*) used for each condition (C). The condition's specific value (C_{value}) is analyzed if the conditions do not contain relational features. The value is mapped to a dimension if it lies between the upper and lower boundary (b_{lower}, b_{upper}). If neither approach can map conditions to dimensions, a textual warning is given to the user as dimensions and rules do not overlap, and conformance issues could be involved. In addition, the nearest boundary for each value, b_{lower} or b_{upper}, is analyzed, with "near" being defined as the minimum absolute difference, as this might be the appropriate boundary. This mapping is speculative, and therefore, the warning is displayed. Lastly, for all dimensions that are part of a condition, the coordinates of the bounding boxes (CB)are retrieved to highlight the dimensions on the ED, which is shown to the user and stored.

4 Case Study Findings

Algorithm 1 was implemented using Python and tested on three datasets stemming from the production of cylindrical workpieces. The implementation is available online[5], including all used datasets and the full results.

As this is, to the best of our knowledge, the first approach that enables integration of time sequence data and relational features, the evaluation focuses on feasibility and applicability. The feasibility of the approach was shown by implementing it. The approach is tested on three datasets to evaluate its applicability. The resulting conditions are compared to EDT-TS results, which allows for the integration of time sequence data but not the generation of relational features. Accuracy is calculated for EDT-TS and DigiEMine to analyze if the application of DigiEMine leads to changes in performance.

The datasets used for the case study should stem from a cylindrical workpiece production process. In addition, the engineering drawing of the workpiece or at least the tolerance values should be available. Furthermore, the dataset should contain measurements of the workpieces and information about whether the workpieces are "ok" or "not ok", i.e., some ground truth has to be known to learn the decision tree as well as to evaluate performance of the mined decision. As it is challenging to find appropriate datasets, we used three datasets based on the case study described in Sect. 2: one real-life dataset ("Valve Lifter") corresponding to the case presented in Sect. 2, a second dataset taken from the same scenario but involving a different workpiece, called "Turm" and a third, synthetically created, dataset. The third dataset ("Synthetic") is similar to the "Turm" dataset but includes generated time sequence values.

Results: Table 1 shows the accuracy values achieved by the DigiEMine approach and *EDT-TS* approach for the three datasets and an excerpt from the mined decision rules.

[5] https://github.com/bscheibel/digiemine.

Table 1. Evaluation results for the datasets Valve Lifter, Turm and Synthetic.

DataSet / Approach		DigiEMine		EDT-TS	
	N	Accuracy	Example Condition	Accuracy	Example Condition
Valve Lifter	37	1	boundary10>=segment8_min is TRUE	0.75	segment5_min <= 15.79
Turm	33	0.75	boundary2>segment6_max is FALSE	0.75	segment1_max <= 77.73
Synthetic	70	1	boundary4<segment8_max is TRUE	0.86	segment5_max <= 22.17

The table shows that the accuracy values are medium to high for all datasets and approaches. However, the values achieved by DigiEMine are at least as high and, in some instances, even considerably higher than the results achieved by *EDT-TS*. The conditions look similar in each approach. The *EDT-TS* conditions involve minimum or maximum segment values which are set in comparison to a threshold value instead of a boundary. In the case of the valve lifter, EDT-TS extracted dimensions that are not precisely accurate, i.e., the exact specification would be 15.2 as the maximum value compared to the extracted value of 15.79; similarly, for the synthetic dataset, the specified maximum value is 22.1, whereas 22.17 was mined as maximum in EDT-TS. These are minor differences but can accumulate and may account for the differences in accuracy. In addition, even minor differences might be impactful in production when exact measurements are needed for specific workpieces. For the "Turm" dataset, the decision rule discovered by EDT-TS involves only one condition. However, this condition does not include a value related to the dimensions but is an artifact created by measuring. Therefore, despite high-performance values, the discovered conditions include no valid classification rule. The DigiEMine conditions involve comparing a segment's minimum or maximum to a boundary and specifying if those conditions should be *True* or *False*. The full decision rules contain concatenations of three or more of those conditions, each comparing segments and boundaries. Therefore, users working with these decision rules can assess which segments have to be compared to which specifications set by the engineering drawing. In

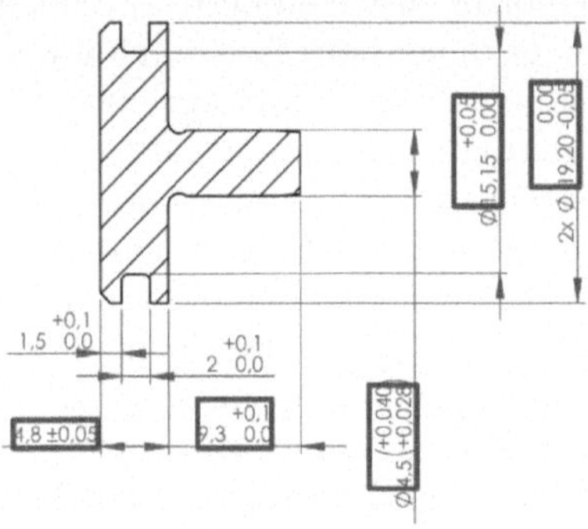

Fig. 4. Valve lifter engineering drawing with highlighted dimensions.

addition, Fig. 4 shows the visual output for the described use case: the dimensions used as part of the decision rule are highlighted in the original ED.

5 Discussion

The application of the DigiEMine approach in the case study shows that the approach is feasible and able to discover decision rules, including time sequence and contextual data, and to set them in relation to each other, thereby providing an answer to the **RQ** stated in Sect. 1. The results indicate that the performance is at least as high or even higher than without the inclusion of dimensioning requirements. The high accuracy values for DigiEMine can be due to the ability to use the exact specifications instead of having to approximate them using the available instances. This is also a benefit for classifying new instances, as these might include values not seen during testing.

In the results, excerpts of the mined decision rules are given, showing that the measurements are always set in relationship to a boundary, i.e., a dimension from the ED. A visual output, in the form of an engineering drawing with highlighted dimensions, is also provided. This can further support the employees supervising the process as well as improve the understanding of which dimensions are decisive for the outcome of the process. If measurements cannot be linked to the dimensions found in the ED, this could indicate that the measuring process cannot detect quality-relevant attributes; for example, only the diameter is measured, which is irrelevant to the process outcome as only surface attributes like flatness are decisive for the result. Alternatively, it could also indicate that the classification of workpieces is not based on the requirements specified in the ED. If this is the case, a potential conformance issue could be involved. On the other hand, not all dimensions found in the ED can be linked to measurements, as not all requirements can be measured using one measuring machine.

The integration of dimensions and tolerances through the use of an algorithm can also lead to the introduction of errors. Therefore, ideally, the dimensions are integrated into the CAD model and can be read automatically. However, as mentioned in Sect. 2 this is not industry standard. Extracting the dimensions manually from a file is labor-intensive and error-prone, as an engineering drawing can include hundreds of dimensions for complex workpieces. Therefore, the automatic extraction can be used as a starting point and combined with a manual check to ensure the extracted dimensions are valid. This application might be particularly interesting for runtime application, as changes in the contractual basis can be detected. If the measured dimensions do not change accordingly, compliance issues can be registered, and employees notified accordingly.

The approach can be used in addition to manual checking or for fully automated pre-checking, thereby providing a smoother and more efficient manufacturing process, reducing quality assurance time, and providing the best quality workpieces to customers. The application of the DigiEMine approach can provide benefits to manufacturing companies that are on their way to digitalization but still use some form of legacy data. Specifically companies that produce smaller batches can benefit from this approach, as smaller batches mean less training data. Relating the measurements to the boundaries might lead to faster learning with less training data, as the boundaries do not have to be estimated using many instances but can be learned from the information in the provided engineering drawing. If this approach leads to faster learning will be evaluated in future work. In addition, this approach also allows for automated updating if customer requirements, i.e., the engineering drawing, change.

The approach can be generalized to a scenario where time sequence data (e.g., sensor data) and additional context data (e.g. data extracted from regulatory documents or guidelines) should be combined to form meaningful decision rules, which is conceivable in many scenarios, such as healthcare or logistics. An example in healthcare would be monitoring cardiac conditions where blood pressure or heart rate measurements are compared to clinical guidelines, e.g., the European Society of Cardiology (ESC) guidelines to diagnose specific illnesses. An example from the logistics domain could be the combination of customer requirements regarding transport conditions (e.g., temperature) extracted from emails with the temperature measurement values. This paper provides an approach for a specific use case from manufacturing. However, the fundamental approach is similar, regardless of which data should be integrated. It consists of the following steps: First, a **Data Collection** step, where contextual data and process data are gathered. After that, **Feature Engineering** has to be performed, where features are engineered from unstructured data, and subsequently, relational features are generated. If the decision points are already known, **Decision Mining** can be performed in the next step. Depending on the use case, different decision mining algorithms can be applied. If the decision points are not known, process mining and decision point discovery have to be performed beforehand. Quality metrics, see for example [25] and user feedback can be used to assess and validate the resulting decision rules and potentially initiate a remining of the decision rules, leading to an iterative process. Lastly, in the **Output** step, textual decision rules are displayed to the user; in addition, visualizations can be generated to help the user gain insights into the process.

Limitations and threats to validity: The most significant limitation is the generalizability, as the implementation and evaluation of the approach are set in the context of the case study. In addition, only silhouette measuring was used; thereby, not all quality-relevant criteria can be evaluated. More testing must be done to assess the generalizability of this approach to other kinds of workpieces and in other settings. Furthermore, we currently assume that each dimension is unique. If multiple dimensions with the same values exist, we cannot accurately map the conditions to the dimensions in the drawing. As the classification technique is a supervised learning technique, a ground truth is necessary to learn the decision rules, either by having a second measurement as in the proposed scenario or by including manual measurements. As mentioned above, an analogous usage of this approach in scenarios with time sequence data and additional contextual information is conceivable. However, the approach must be adapted and tested in other scenarios in future work.

6 Related Work

An extensive research domain investigates the **extraction of information** from EDs in CAD formats (DXF, DWG, STEP or IGES) [28,30,31] or from scanned images using vectorization and OCR [17]. DigiEMine uses the approach described in [21] as this is the only approach extracting information from PDF format, which brings together the ability to obtain textual information and to be more accurate than by using OCR. Other kinds of contextual information are investigated, such as extracting information from regulatory documents [6,27] or using news sentiment analysis for additional context [29].

Time series and time sequence data as context data, e.g., additional sensor data or constraints, has been used in multiple scenarios to improve process mining or process monitoring techniques [10,24]. Similarly, existing work integrates time sequence data in process and decision mining by using feature engineering methods [2,9,23]. However, these approaches did not analyze how time sequence data can be connected with additional context data.

Decision Mining includes algorithms for mining decision points from processes and classification techniques to mine the corresponding decision rules. A variety of decision mining approaches exist, focusing on different aspects, such as finding overlapping rules [16], aligning control and data flow to discover decision rules [13], integrating time sequence data [9,23] or mining rules that involve relationships between features, i.e. relational decision rules, [3,14,22]. An overview can be found in [15]. This work integrates existing decision mining approaches to work with time sequence-based and relational features.

A multitude of works investigate data mining for **quality control in manufacturing** [8,11,26]. These overviews include scenarios where techniques classify instances according to their outcome. Often used techniques include neural networks, support vector machines, k-means, and decision trees. Decision trees are specifically used to generate flowcharts to classify outcomes based on different features. Some works use time sequence data and different discretization methods to generate higher-level features.

To the best of our knowledge, DigiEMine is the first approach that combines the information contained in EDs with time sequence measurements, thereby bridging multiple fields. DigiEMine is flexible in that the techniques used can be replaced by other appropriate techniques, e.g., the generation of time sequence features can also be done using other discretization methods.

7 Conclusion

The case study presented in this paper shows how the DigiMine approach can support quality control processes in manufacturing. DigiEMine enables the integration of context information, specifically dimensioning information from EDs with time sequence data, i.e., workpiece measurements, to enable the mining of relational decision rules, providing more transparency in quality control processes. The evaluation showed that the approach is feasible and produces results setting time sequence data in relation to context data, achieving accuracy values between 0.75 and 1 for the tested datasets. Further testing and generalization of DigiEMine for different scenarios is planned for future work. Moreover, we aim to use the approach in runtime decision mining scenarios to test the hypothesis that this approach allows for faster mining of accurate decision rules. Furthermore, a user study can evaluate different presentations of the textual rules (e.g., in the form of trees or tables) as well as the visualizations in the drawing.

Acknowledgments. This work has been partly supported and funded by the Austrian Research Promotion Agency (FFG) via the Austrian Competence Center for Digital Production (CDP) under the contract number 881843.

References

1. Aalst, W.: Data Science in Action. In: Process Mining, pp. 3–23. Springer, Heidelberg (2016). https://doi.org/10.1007/978-3-662-49851-4_1
2. Banham, A., Leemans, S.J.J., Wynn, M.T., Andrews, R., Laupland, K.B., Shinners, L.: xPM: enhancing exogenous data visibility. Artif. Intell. Med. 102409 (2022). https://doi.org/10.1016/j.artmed.2022.102409
3. Bazhenova, E., Buelow, S., Weske, M.: Discovering decision models from event logs. In: Abramowicz, W., Alt, R., Franczyk, B. (eds.) BIS 2016. LNBIP, vol. 255, pp. 237–251. Springer, Cham (2016). https://doi.org/10.1007/978-3-319-39426-8_19
4. Breiman, L., Friedman, J., Olshen, R.A., Stone, C.J.: Classification and Regression Trees. Chapman and Hall/CRC, New York, October 2017. https://doi.org/10.1201/9781315139470
5. Brunk, J.: Structuring Business Process Context Information for Process Monitoring and Prediction. In: Conference on Business Informatics, vol. 1, pp. 39–48, June 2020. https://doi.org/10.1109/CBI49978.2020.00012
6. Chen, Q., Winter, K., Rinderle-Ma, S.: Predicting unseen process behavior based on context information from compliance constraints. In: Di Francescomarino, C., Burattin, A., Janiesch, C., Sadiq, S. (eds.) Business Process Management Forum, BPM 2023, LNBIP, vol. 490. Springer, Cham (2023). https://doi.org/10.1007/978-3-031-41623-1_8
7. Colosimo, B.M., Moya, E.G., Moroni, G., Petrò, S.: Statistical sampling strategies for geometric tolerance inspection by CMM. Econ. Qual. Control **23**(1) (2008). https://doi.org/10.1515/EQC.2008.109
8. Dogan, A., Birant, D.: Machine learning and data mining in manufacturing. Expert Syst. Appl. **166**, 114060 (2021). https://doi.org/10.1016/j.eswa.2020.114060
9. Dunkl, R., Rinderle-Ma, S., Grossmann, W., Anton Fröschl, K.: A method for analyzing time series data in process mining: application and extension of decision point analysis. In: Nurcan, S., Pimenidis, E. (eds.) CAiSE 2014. LNBIP, vol. 204, pp. 68–84. Springer, Cham (2015). https://doi.org/10.1007/978-3-319-19270-3_5
10. Ehrendorfer, M., Mangler, J., Rinderle-Ma, S.: Assessing the impact of context data on process outcomes during runtime. In: Hacid, H., Kao, O., Mecella, M., Moha, N., Paik, H. (eds.) ICSOC 2021. LNCS, vol. 13121, pp. 3–18. Springer, Cham (2021). https://doi.org/10.1007/978-3-030-91431-8_1
11. Koeksal, G., Batmaz, I., Testik, M.C.: A review of data mining applications for quality improvement in manufacturing industry. Expert Syst. Appl. **38**(10), 13448–13467 (2011). https://doi.org/10.1016/j.eswa.2011.04.063

12. Labisch, S., Weber, C.: Technisches Zeichnen Selbstständig lernen und effektiv üben. Viewegs Fachbücher der Technik, 3 edn. (2008)
13. de Leoni, M., van der Aalst, W.M.P.: Data-aware process mining: discovering decisions in processes using alignments. In: Applied Computing, p. 1454. ACM Press, Coimbra, Portugal (2013). https://doi.org/10.1145/2480362.2480633
14. de Leoni, M., Dumas, M., García-Bañuelos, L.: Discovering branching conditions from business process execution logs. In: Cortellessa, V., Varró, D. (eds.) FASE 2013. LNCS, vol. 7793, pp. 114–129. Springer, Heidelberg (2013). https://doi.org/10.1007/978-3-642-37057-1_9
15. de Leoni, M., Mannhardt, F.: Decision Discovery in Business Processes. In: Encyclopedia of Big Data Technologies, pp. 1–12. Springer, Cham (2018). https://doi.org/10.1007/978-3-319-63962-8_96-1
16. Mannhardt, F., Leoni, M.d., Reijers, H.A., van der Aalst, W.M.P.: Decision mining revisited - discovering overlapping rules. In: Advanced Information Systems Engineering, pp. 377–392. Springer, Cham, June 2016. https://doi.org/10.1007/978-3-319-39696-5_23
17. Moreno-García, C.F., Elyan, E., Jayne, C.: New trends on digitisation of complex engineering drawings. Neural Comput. Appl. **31**(6), 1695–1712 (2018). https://doi.org/10.1007/s00521-018-3583-1
18. Pedregosa, F., et al.: Scikit-learn: machine learning in Python. J. Mach. Learn. Res. **12**, 1–6 (2011)
19. Recker, J.: Scientific Research in Information Systems. Springer, Berlin (2013). https://doi.org/10.1007/978-3-642-30048-6
20. Reinkemeyer, L. (ed.): Process mining in action: principles, use cases and outlook. Springer, Cham (2020). https://doi.org/10.1007/978-3-030-40172-6
21. Scheibel, B., Mangler, J., Rinderle-Ma, S.: Extraction of dimension requirements from engineering drawings for supporting quality control in production processes. Comput. Ind. **129**, 103442 (2021). https://doi.org/10.1016/j.compind.2021.103442
22. Scheibel, B., Rinderle-Ma, S.: Comparing decision mining approaches with regard to the meaningfulness of their results. arXiv:2109.07335 [cs], September 2021
23. Scheibel, B., Rinderle-Ma, S.: Decision mining with time series data based on automatic feature generation. In: Franch, X., Poels, G., Gailly, F., Snoeck, M. (eds.) Advanced Information Systems Engineering, CAiSE 2022, LNCS, vol. 13295. Springer, Cham (2022). https://doi.org/10.1007/978-3-031-07472-1_1
24. Stertz, F., Rinderle-Ma, S., Mangler, J.: Analyzing process concept drifts based on sensor event streams during runtime. In: Fahland, D., Ghidini, C., Becker, J., Dumas, M. (eds.) BPM 2020. LNCS, vol. 12168, pp. 202–219. Springer, Cham (2020). https://doi.org/10.1007/978-3-030-58666-9_12
25. Wais, B., Rinderle-Ma, S.: Towards a comprehensive evaluation of decision rules and decision mining algorithms beyond accuracy. In: Guizzardi, G., Santoro, F., Mouratidis, H., Soffer, P. (eds.) Advanced Information Systems Engineering, CAiSE 2024, LNCS, vol. 14663. Springer, Cham (2024). https://doi.org/10.1007/978-3-031-61057-8_24
26. Wang, K.: Applying data mining to manufacturing: the nature and implications. J. Intell. Manuf. **18**(4), 487–495 (2007). https://doi.org/10.1007/s10845-007-0053-5
27. Winter, K., Rinderle-Ma, S.: Detecting constraints and their relations from regulatory documents using NLP techniques. In: Panetto, H., Debruyne, C., Proper, H.A., Ardagna, C.A., Roman, D., Meersman, R. (eds.) OTM 2018. LNCS, vol. 11229, pp. 261–278. Springer, Cham (2018). https://doi.org/10.1007/978-3-030-02610-3_15

28. Ye, B., Liu, J., Wu, B., Wu, C.: New method of feature recognition from engineering drawings based on multi-granularity information acquisition. Int. Conf. Fuzzy Syst. Knowl. Disc. **5**, 129–133 (2009). https://doi.org/10.1109/FSKD.2009.802
29. Yeshchenko, A., Durier, F., Revoredo, K., Mendling, J., Santoro, F.: Context-aware predictive process monitoring: the impact of news sentiment. In: Panetto, H., Debruyne, C., Proper, H.A., Ardagna, C.A., Roman, D., Meersman, R. (eds.) OTM 2018. LNCS, vol. 11229, pp. 586–603. Springer, Cham (2018). https://doi.org/10.1007/978-3-030-02610-3_33
30. Zhang, H., Li, X.: Data extraction from DXF File and visual display. In: HCI International 2014, vol. 434, pp. 286–291 (2014). https://doi.org/10.1007/978-3-319-07857-1_51
31. Zhang, J., Zhao, L., Hao, Y.: Multi-level block information extraction in engineering drawings based on depth-first algorithm. Adv. Mater. Res. **468–471**, 2100–2103 (2012). https://doi.org/10.4028/www.scientific.net/AMR.468-471.2100

Sustainability and Resilience

Unlocking Sustainability Compliance: Characterizing the EU Taxonomy for Business Process Management

Finn Klessascheck[1,3](✉), Stephan A. Fahrenkrog-Petersen[2,3], Jan Mendling[2,3], and Luise Pufahl[1,3]

[1] School of CIT, Technical University of Munich, Heilbronn, Germany
{finn.klessascheck,luise.pufahl}@tum.de
[2] Humboldt-Universität zu Berlin, Berlin, Germany
{stephan.fahrenkrog-petersen,jan.mendling}@hu-berlin.de
[3] Weizenbaum Institute, Berlin, Germany

Abstract. To promote sustainable business practices, and to achieve climate neutrality by 2050, the EU has developed the *taxonomy of sustainable activities*, which describes when exactly business practices can be considered sustainable. While the taxonomy has only been recently established, progressively more companies will have to report how much of their revenue was created via sustainably executed business processes. To help companies prepare to assess whether their business processes comply with the constraints outlined in the taxonomy, we investigate in how far these criteria can be used for *conformance checking*, that is, assessing in a data-driven manner, whether business process executions adhere to regulatory constraints. For this, we develop a few-shot learning pipeline to characterize the constraints of the taxonomy with the help of an LLM as to the *process dimensions* they relate to. We find that many constraints of the taxonomy are useable for conformance checking, particularly in the sectors of energy, manufacturing, and transport. This will aid companies in preparing to monitor regulatory compliance with the taxonomy automatically, by characterizing what kind of information they need to extract, and by providing a better understanding of sectors where such an assessment is feasible and where it is not.

Keywords: Sustainability · Conformance Checking · EU Taxonomy · Business Processes

1 Introduction

In light of the issue of climate change and unsustainable human activity [43], it is important to promote *sustainable* business practices, i.e., conducting business in a way that can meet the needs of the present generations without endangering those of the future [6]. This need has also been identified by governing bodies, such as the *European Union* (EU). As a consequence, the EU has defined the *taxonomy for sustainable activities* [10,13], subsequently referred to by us as *taxonomy*. The taxonomy aims to create clear indicators of when business activities are contributing towards sustainability and when not, and to create financial incentives

J. Borbinha et al. (Eds.): EDOC 2024, LNCS 15409, pp. 339–359, 2025.
https://doi.org/10.1007/978-3-031-78338-8_18

for proven sustainable business practices and investments into them [29,41]. For various *business practices*,[1] the taxonomy defines criteria along which a *substantial contribution* towards *sustainability goals* can be verified, and criteria which must not be violated. Increasingly, companies *will* face having to assess their business processes for compliance with the taxonomy [29]. However, assessing whether a business practice does or does not meet relevant criteria is, so far, a manual process: Some companies offer manual or semi-automatic questionnaire-based assessments; a *taxonomy calculator* provided by the EU relies exclusively on manual input in the form of an Excel sheet.[2]

To overcome the challenges of manually assessing whether a business activity meets the criteria of the taxonomy, it appears feasible to *check in a data-driven manner* whether the execution of a business practice complies with relevant taxonomy criteria or not. Since the definition of business practice [11] is closely related to that of business processes [44], we interpret business practices as "categories" of business processes, which allows us to investigate the taxonomy and its criteria from a *business process management* (BPM) standpoint.

Conformance checking, which is a technique of the *process mining* and BPM fields, aims to compare recorded business process executions in the form of an event log with a formal representation of the to-be process behavior, so that either, the process execution can be improved to more closely resemble the formal representation, or vice versa [7]. Automatic compliance monitoring can use conformance checking techniques with the goal of assessing whether a business process complies with regulatory constraints—such as those described in the taxonomy—during its execution, based on recorded event data [16,21]. An overview of this is provided in Fig. 1. For applying conformance checking with the aim of monitoring compliance to the regulatory constraints described in the taxonomy, this taxonomy first needs to be *operationalized*, that is, translated into the form of a *prescriptive model*. Further, the prescriptive model and the event data used for conformance checking need to align w.r.t. what information they contain. For this, companies need to be aware of what data they need to capture during the execution of their business processes. Therefore, we see a need

Fig. 1. Conceptual overview of compliance monitoring with conformance checking [7, 21]

[1] Referred to as *economic activities* in the taxonomy; to avoid confusion with the notion of business process activities we use the term *business practice*.

[2] See https://viridad.eu, https://www.briink.com/solutions/esg-questionnaire-assistant and https://ec.europa.eu/sustainable-finance-taxonomy/wizard [Accessed: 23/05/2024].

to better understand what data-capturing requirements the taxonomy imposes on business processes, and in how far the constraints contained therein are even applicable for conformance checking.

Related work has focussed on extracting constraints from text directly into process models (e.g., [1,30,47]) and on characterizing textual constraints based on i.a. their relation to other constraints, process models, or their relevance to a given business process (e.g., [39,45,46]). Our investigation, however, aims at an earlier stage of conformance checking that does not require operationalization into a concrete prescriptive model or a concrete business process against which conformance is to be checked. Rather, we aim to understand what kind of requirements the taxonomy imposes on event log data so that it can be captured and prepared for regulatory compliance checking with conformance checking w.r.t. the taxonomy. For this, we first need to understand what kinds of constraints the taxonomy embodies (i.e., which characteristics a prescriptive model would to make prescriptions towards, such as certain activities that need to be executed in a specific order, certain thresholds that activities must not exceed, etc.), and whether all of them can be related to a process view, since so far, it is unclear to what extent the taxonomy can even be operationalized for conformance checking. Therefore, this work aims to address the following *research questions* (RQ):

RQ1: How can the EU taxonomy be operationalized with regard to business processes?

RQ2: Which constraints of the EU taxonomy can be used for automatically assessing whether a business process fulfills its respective sustainability criteria with conformance checking techniques?

Since the taxonomy contains constraints for around 80 types of business practices [28,41] – which makes a manual characterization of the entire taxonomy infeasible – this work uses a *few-shot machine learning approach* to gain insights into what constraints the taxonomy consists of, and how they might be operationalized in practice. In doing so, we also explore the potential of novel approaches based on *large language models* (LLMs) for operationalizing regulations in the area of conformance checking.

The remainder of the article is organized as follows: Sect. 2 provides background on the taxonomy, regulatory compliance monitoring with conformance checking, and few-shot learning approaches. Section 3 provides related work on approaches for extracting rules from text for compliance monitoring. In Sect. 4, we present the research approach of this paper. Section 5 provides the results thereof, characterizing the constraints of the taxonomy and its potential for conformance checking uses. We further discuss their implications for practice in Sect. 6. Finally, Sect. 7 provides future work and concludes the article.

2 Background

Next, we will outline the general idea of the EU taxonomy, and we will give an overview of automatic compliance monitoring approaches within the business process literature.

2.1 EU Taxonomy for Sustainable Activities

In order to create incentives for investments in sustainable technologies and to provide a transparent classification system for when business practices are sustainable, the EU has established the *taxonomy for sustainable activities* [2, 10, 41]. The ultimate objective behind the taxonomy is to support the EU in transiting to climate neutrality by 2050 [29, 41].

In essence, the taxonomy defines six *environmental objectives* with which sustainable business practices are identified: 1) mitigating climate change; 2) adapting to climate change; 3) sustainably using and protecting water and marine resources; 4) transitioning to a circular economy; 5) preventing and controlling pollution; and 6) protecting and restoring biodiversity and the ecosystem [8, 28]. Not all possible business practices of all industries are covered by the taxonomy, but only those which are deemed to be able to make a *substantial contribution* towards climate neutrality, or are needed for other sectors to make a substantial contribution [41]. If a business practice is part of the taxonomy, it is called taxonomy-*enabled*, and can *potentially* make a contribution to one of the six environmental objectives. If a taxonomy-enabled business practice: 1) indeed contributes to one of the environmental objectives; 2) causes no *significant harm* (DNSH) to any of the six objectives; 3) meets *minimum safeguards* (such as the UN Guiding Principles on Business and Human Rights); 4) adheres to *technical screening criteria*, it is, in fact, *sustainable* according to the taxonomy [2, 8, 28]. Business practices that meet all of these criteria are also called *taxonomy-aligned*. In short, to be taxonomy-aligned, a taxonomy-enabled business practice *must* contribute to at least one of the six environmental objectives, *must not* cause significant harm to any of the others, and *must* meet minimum safeguards [2, 8, 28]. Notably, the minimum safeguards are not directly defined *in* the taxonomy, but rather, are references to taxonomy-external guidelines and regulations. Concretely, organizations need to ensure that they follow the *OECD Guidelines for Multinational Enterprises*, *UN Guiding Principles on Business and Human Rights*, the *Declaration of the International Labour Organisation on Fundamental Principles and Rights at Work* as well as the *International Bill of Human Rights* [13, Article 18]. Since the focus of our work is on compliance of business processes and not of organizations or supply chains, and minimum safeguards are often not assessed on the level of business processes [29], we forgo including these external constraints in our investigation. Figure 2 provides a schematic overview of the taxonomy and its concepts.

For assessing the taxonomy alignment of a taxonomy-enabled business practice, the taxonomy describes *technical screening criteria*, which describe under which circumstances an activity either makes a contribution or causes significant harm to an environmental objective [28, 41]. It should be noted that a business practice is not necessarily able to make substantial contributions to more than one economic objective, and hence may have only one set of technical screening criteria for one substantial contribution.

For an illustration of how the taxonomy documents technical screening criteria for environmental objectives, we refer to the EU's *taxonomy compass* and

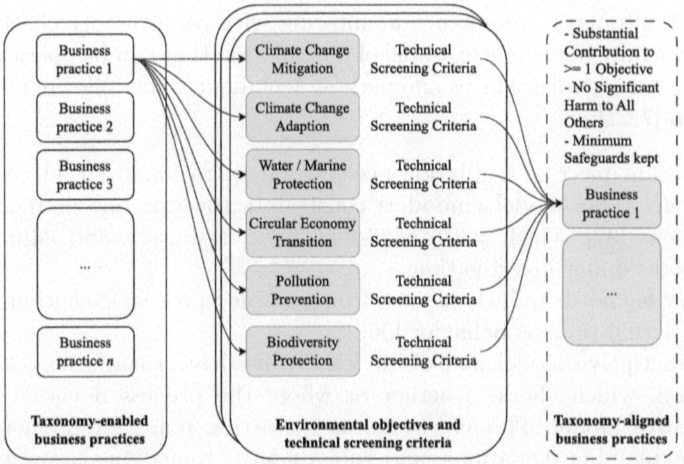

Fig. 2. Schematic overview of the EU taxonomy for sustainable activities and its concepts, derived from [10,12]

the corresponding Excel file.[3] Generally, for each business practice, a set of possible environmental objectives to which a substantial contribution can be made is provided—for each objective, criteria for a substantial contribution, as well as DNSH, are documented.

By determining how many of their business processes align with the taxonomy, companies can report how much of their business output is generated via sustainable business practices [12,29]. For this, companies need to know exactly which of their business practices are not just taxonomy-enabled, but also taxonomy-aligned—and in the future, these taxonomy disclosures will be subject to mandatory audits [29]. Notably, from 2025 onwards, companies that meet certain characteristics (i.e., more than 250 employees, more than EUR 25M balance sheet total, or more than EUR 50M net turnover) will be obligated to do so, with the threshold for having to report decreasing in subsequent years [29]. Small and medium-size enterprises will also be subject to a disclosure obligation [29]. Therefore, it appears prudent to investigate how automatic business process compliance monitoring can help companies in assessing the taxonomy-alignment of their business processes.

2.2 Automatic Business Process Compliance Monitoring

The automatic monitoring of business process compliance [27] allows organizations to ensure their business practices comply with regulations [18]. Through an analysis of process execution data, it is possible to check at runtime if a business process complies with specified rules [16,21]. Figure 1 provides a conceptual

[3] See https://ec.europa.eu/sustainable-finance-taxonomy/taxonomy-compass/the-compass and https://ec.europa.eu/sustainable-finance-taxonomy/assets/documents/taxonomy.xlsx [Accessed: 18/06/2024].

overview of automatic compliance monitoring with conformance checking, with the EU taxonomy being one example of a regulation that can be operationalized. In order for an organization to adopt these techniques, the following steps need to be taken [7,21]:

1. The relevant piece of regulation needs to be operationalized into a *prescriptive model.* This model embodies constraints towards one or more *process dimensions* [37], which are *control-flow*, *time*, *resources*, and *data* [7,21], of the process under investigation.
2. An *event log* needs to be extracted from recorded process executions, describing the actual process behavior [36].
3. The prescriptive model and event log are used by a conformance checking *algorithm*, which checks whether or where the process deviated from the prescriptive model. This can serve as a starting point for further diagnosing or explaining deviations, and subsequently, remedying unwanted deviations [7,21,35].

It should be noted, however, that the prescriptive model and event log need to align in their respective process dimensions: If, for example, the prescriptive model imposes constraint on the data dimension of the investigated process, but the event log does not contain this information, the conformance check *cannot* yield the desired insights [7]. Hence, organizations need to know, potentially in advance, which process dimensions are, in fact, *relevant* for the conformance check. Based on this, they can appropriately capture the relevant execution data and extract it into the subsequent event log.

3 Related Work

In this paper, we investigate the properties of the EU taxonomy for sustainable business practices and its potential for being used for compliance monitoring with conformance checking, by extracting insights from the taxonomy's regulatory texts and the compliance constraints described therein. In that respect, our work relates to other contributions that also deal with rule extraction for conformance checking/process mining purposes, and contributions that use machine learning techniques to do so.

Constraint Extraction from Text. For extracting compliance constraints from regulatory documents, Dragoni et al. [9] propose a pipeline that combines multiple *natural language processing* (NLP) approaches. With their proposed pipeline, rules (in this case in the form of *obligations*, *permissions*, and *prohibitions*, see Hashmi et al. [19]) can be extracted into formal representations for a given regulatory text. Using semantic annotations, a process model can then be checked for whether it complies with the formal representations – this check is further described by Governatori et al. [15]. Moreover, Winter and Rinderle-Ma [47] describe an approach to generate process model fragments from regulatory documents by extracting constraints and their relation. Similarly, van der Aa et al. [1] describe an automatic approach for extracting declarative process models from natural language text that describes a process. Barrientos et al. [3] design an approach for extracting temporal constraints from natural language texts and determining violations thereof in an event log. Focussing on resource compliance, Mustroph et al. [30] extract compliance requirements from natural language with GPT-4, which are then matched to and verified against an event log. Further, Mustroph et al. [31] describe how generative AI, or more specifically, GPT-4, can be used to pre-process resource-related regulations into social network graphs. Based on these, they are able to detect compliance violations of process executions.

Characterization of Constraints. In terms of characterizing constraints present in regulatory documents, Winter et al. [48] provide a technique for characterizing regulations based on text mining and clustering algorithms that can derive significant sentences for a regulatory document, which can be manually translated into e.g. process models. Similarly, Winter and Rinderle-Ma [46] design an approach to group constraints from textual documents and detect relations between them, e.g. based on similarity. Moreover, Winter et al. [45] provides a method for matching parts of regulatory documents with process models, which then allows a compliance assessment of the matched regulatory constraints and the process model. Aiming to facilitate a better understanding of regulatory documents, Sai et al. [38] propose an approach to parse legal definitions and relations between terms from regulatory documents into a knowledge graph, so that regulatory documents can be better understood and analyzed. Further, in order to compare regulatory documents with their translation into company-internal requirements, Sai et al. [40] provide an NLP-based which can detect deviations between the two documents, and helps to detect root causes of textual deviations. Finally, Sai et al. [39] investigate an automated approach for identifying passages of regulatory texts that are relevant for a business process based on the processes textual description. They find that expert judgement cannot be replaced by generative AI, but see the potential of AI uses for taking into account vaster amounts of context, which the authors deem to be advantageous in more complex settings.
In contrast to these contributions, which primarily focus on extracting constraints directly or characterizing them w.r.t a process model, event log or other texts, we exclusively focus on characterizing the constraints for the process dimensions they constrain. This would facilitate data extraction of recorded process execution and translation of the taxonomy into concrete constraints for subsequent analyses. However, with our categorization as a starting point, relevant extraction and matching approaches can be chosen, and the relevant data can be stored during process execution.

Notably, there is currently no automated approach that helps companies to understand the requirements posed on business process executions by regulatory texts w.r.t. the process dimensions so that the log and the subsequent prescriptive model pertain to the relevant perspectives and contain relevant information for compliance monitoring with conformance checking. In particular, the taxonomy has not yet been considered in this light—however, concepts from existing approaches can inform the design of new mechanisms, such as ours.

4 Mapping Sustainability Regulation to Conformance Constraints

In order to operationalize the taxonomy for business processes, we need to identify process constraints within the taxonomy. This allows us to transform the abstract rules for business practices into specific problems that can be addressed using automatic conformance monitoring.

We assume that it would be best to use an industry expert with conformance checking knowledge to classify each rule of the taxonomy. However, since such experts are rare and the taxonomy covers many varying industries, an alternative solution becomes necessary. Because of this, we decide to use LLMs, since they are trained on a wide variety of texts from different domains. Furthermore, our task can be framed as a text classification problem, and it was shown that LLMs can be used as *Few-Shot-Classifiers* [5]. Meaning that an LLM, which is trained for one task such as next text token prediction, can be with sufficient instructions utilized to perform another machine learning task, in our case text classification of the taxonomy. In particular, previous work has shown that LLMs can be successfully be used for process analysis tasks [17].

In order to characterize the taxonomy, which consists of several regulatory texts for each business practice and environmental objective it considers, we need to apply an LLM to each regulatory text and extract relevant information about the constraints. For this, we developed a pipeline, which we outline in the subsequent Sect. 4.1, drawing on the capability of LLMs to be applied in this manner.

4.1 Overview

The overall approach for characterizing the constraints, or technical screening criteria, of the taxonomy for the process dimensions they pertain to, is illustrated in Fig. 3. The pipeline we describe consists of three stages: First, the taxonomy is *preprocessed* (see Sect. 4.2). Second, for each set of technical screening criteria of each business practice and environmental objective, an LLM is *prompted* to identify the types of constraints contained therein (see Sect. 4.3). Third, the LLM's output is *parsed*, and the numbers and types of constraint per business practice and environmental objective is extracted (see Sect. 4.4). Finally, the resulting data is collected and can be *analyzed*.

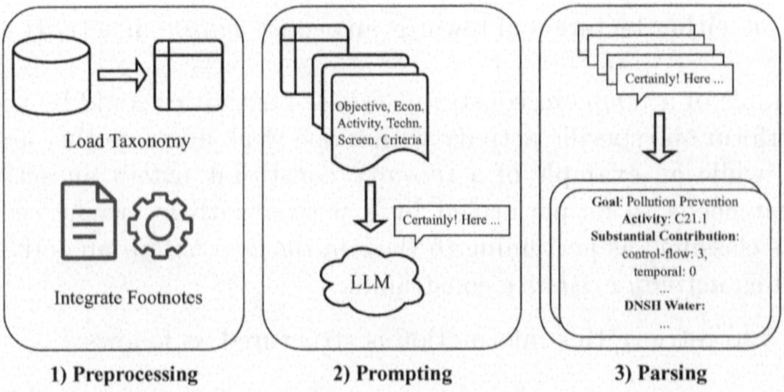

Fig. 3. Schematic overview of the taxonomy constraint characterization pipeline

4.2 Preprocessing

For the preprocessing step, we begin to read the entire taxonomy, which is available in the form of an Excel file.[4] For each environmental objective, the taxonomy file contains a sheet, in which each environmental activity as well as 1) the corresponding technical screening criteria for a substantial contribution to the objective, and 2) the technical screening criteria for DNSH to all other objectives are listed. Further, footnotes pertaining to each activity are contained in a column in each sheet. In order to make all relevant information available to the subsequent prompting step, the footnotes are appended to each technical screening criteria block of an activity if they are referenced therein.

4.3 Prompting

Subsequently, the approach iterates through the taxonomy in the following manner: For each of the six climate objectives, and for each business practice that can make a substantial contribution to that objective, the taxonomy contains: 1) a text that describes the technical screening criteria with which a substantial contribution can be determined, and 2) up to five texts that describes the technical screening criteria with which significant harm to the other objectives can be determined. For each of these texts, the approach prepares a prompt to an LLM, with which the types of constraints and numbers thereof present in the respective technical screening criteria can be determined. The prompt includes a small task description and a brief explanation of the process constraint types, as well as the text passage that is currently being characterized.

We differentiate the process constraints along two aspects: (i) We classify what **process dimension** [7,37] is targeted by a constraint. We categorize constraints into one of the following dimensions: *control-flow*, *temporal*, *resource*, and *data*. Alternatively, a constraint can be *irrelevant* from a process perspective; (ii) Furthermore, we distinguish the **granularity** of a constraint: meaning a

[4] https://ec.europa.eu/sustainable-finance-taxonomy/assets/documents/taxonomy.xlsx [Accessed: 18/06/2024].

constraint can either be targeted towards an aspect *within* an activity or *between* activities.

An example of a *temporal* constraint *between* activities could be the requirement to perform one specific activity within one week after another activity was performed, while an example of a *resource* constraint *within* an activity is an activity that needs to be performed by a person with a specific certification. Constraints classified as pertaining to the *control-flow within* an activity can be understood as *activity existence* constraints.

The prompt to retrieve this information is structured as follows:

- Briefly, the overall objective is described;
- The different types of process constraints are described, as well as the difference in granularity;
- Examples consisting of excerpts of the taxonomy and their potential classification are provided;
- The exact task of characterizing a section of the taxonomy is described;
- Requirements regarding the output are described;
- A placeholder is provided where, during pipeline execution, a description of the business practice can be inserted; and
- A placeholder for the text passage of the taxonomy for which the characterization needs to be done is provided, which will be filled during pipeline execution.

The entire prompt template is available online.[5] As a result, we receive the following information as a response from the LLM, giving us insights into the process constraints covered by a particular set of criteria:

- # of **activity existence** constraints of process activities
- # of **control-flow constraints** *between* process activities
- # of **temporal constraints** *within* process activities
- # of **temporal constraints** *between* process activities
- # of **resource constraints** *within* process activities
- # of **resource constraints** *between* process activities
- # of **data constraints** *within* process activities
- # of **data constraints** *between* process activities
- # of **process-irrelevant** constraints

4.4 Parsing

Each response of the LLM to a prompt of one text (that describes a set of technical screening criteria) is parsed individually. The prompt instructs the LLM to return the results in a particular *JSON*-like notation. This is depicted in Listing 1.1.

---

[5] https://github.com/fyndalf/unlocking-sustainability-compliance-replication-package.

Listing 1.1. Excerpt of the prompt template, describing the required response structure

```
{'control-flow': {
    'within_activities': [no. of activity existence constraints],
    'between_activities': [no. of control-flow constraints between
        activities]},
 'temporal': {
    'within_activities': [no.  of temporal constraints within activities
        ],
    'between_activities': [no. of temporal constraints between activities
        ]},
 'resource': {
    'within_activities': [no. of resource constraints within activities],
    'between_activities': [no. of resource constraints between activities
        ]},
 'data':{
    'within_activities': [no. of data constraints within activities],
    'between_activities': [no. of data constraints between activities]},
 'irrelevant': [no. of process-irrelevant constraints]}
```

In addition to some further processing steps (such as replacing comment-like symbols), this structure and the number of the respective constraints are extracted from the response. Additionally, we store the entire response text, as it often contains the LLMs "explanation" for the constraints that were identified. As a result, we know the number of constraints and types of one set of technical screening criteria for one business practice and one environmental goal. The parsing step is repeated for all further sets of technical screening criteria and prompt responses of each activity. Ultimately, we end up with six datasets, one for each environmental objective. Each dataset contains information on the number of constraints imposed on each business practice by the substantial contribution and DNSH criteria, which, once collated, subsequently allows further analyses.

5 Experimental Validation

In this section, we use our approach to validate the extraction of conformance constraints from the EU taxonomy. First, we outline our experimental setup in Sect. 5.1. Next, we apply our approach to the EU taxonomy and report the results in Sect. 5.2. Finally, we show the validity of our approach in Sect. 5.3.

5.1 Experimental Setup

We implemented the pipeline using Python 3 and Pandas in a Jupyter Notebook. The entire implementation, as well as all data we used and generated, is made available online for reproducibility purposes.[6] Additionally, the LLM we used in this study was Meta's Llama3,[7] which is openly available. More precisely, we used *llama-3-8b-instruct*, which is a version of Llama3 with 8 billion parameters that is fine-tuned for following instructions. Our prompting followed the official

[6] https://github.com/fyndalf/unlocking-sustainability-compliance-replication-package.

[7] https://llama.meta.com/llama3/ [Accessed: 18/06/2024].

Llama3 documentation. For guaranteeing a quasi-deterministic output, we followed guidance on model-specific settings (such as *temperature*, *seed*). Instead of self-hosting Llama3, we opted for using a web-based service (https://groq.com), which at the time of writing offered free API access to a hosted instance of Llama3. However, our implementation can easily be adapted to access other hosts or LLMs.

5.2 Results

Constraint Types. When analyzing the process constraints extracted with our pipeline, we observe the following distribution of constraint types: Out of a total of 1636 constraints we identified, we see a large focus on control-flow constraints (activity existence: 624; between: 8). For example, in order to make a substantial contribution to climate mitigation, market research and development business practices in the area of emission reduction technologies are required to have obtained a permit for operating a demonstration site, which can be interpreted as an activity existence constraint. Further, to contribute to the climate mitigation objective, business practices concerned with the construction, extension and operation of waste water collection and treatment must under some circumstances conduct an assessment of greenhouse gas emissions and subsequently disclose the result to investors (which can be understood as a control-flow constraint). This is followed by process-irrelevant constraints (323). For example, the substantial contribution criteria to climate mitigation of operating and providing personal mobility devices logistics requires that the vehicles are allowed to operate on the same infrastructure as bicycles and pedestrians, which is related rather to the environment in which the business practice is conducted, and not the business practice itself. The third-most present constraint type is the one of data constraints, both within process activities (284) and between them (255). For example, the substantial contribution criteria for climate mitigation of the manufacturing of iron and steel describes greenhouse gas emission threshold for individual steps of the manufacturing process. As another example, the DNSH to pollution criteria for the biodiversity objective of conservation and environmental protection requires the use of fertilizers across the entire business practice to be minimized, which can be understood as a data constraint between activities. Less common are resource constraints (within: 96; between: 2) such as the substantial contribution criteria for the circular economy objective of the business practice of preparing end-of-life products and components for re-use, which makes requirements towards the tools and equipment being used. Finally, temporal constraints (within: 8; between: 36) are the least common: For example, the business practice of providing solutions for flood and drought risk prevention and protection is required to review the implemented solution periodically, in order to make a substantial contribution to the water protection objective.

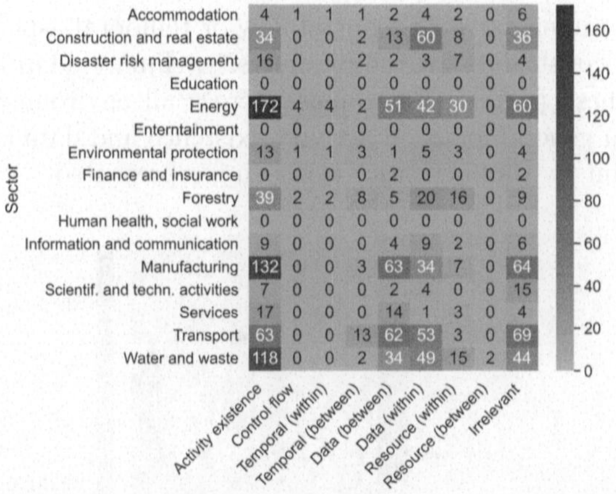

Fig. 4. Constraint types per industry sector across all environmental objectives and screening criteria

Industry Sectors. Looking at the individual industry sectors, we can further observe several patterns in the constraint types. Figure 4 depicts the sectors and constraints identified across all environmental objectives and screening criteria. First, we observe that energy, manufacturing, water, and transport are the industries most often constrained as to their contribution towards one or more climate goals. Noticeably, we see that activity existence criteria (such as permits that need to be obtained, assessments that need to be conducted) and data constraints (such as greenhouse gas limits, energy usage limits, etc.) play a vital role in assessing the taxonomy alignment in these sectors. Second, we see that resource constraints between activities, as well as control flow and temporal constraints play less of a role across all sectors. In the finance and insurance sector, we only identified two process-relevant constraints and two irrelevant ones. Finally, we see that three sectors, namely education, entertainment and human health/social work, have no identified constraints at all. A manual investigation into the taxonomy reveals that for both sectors, the taxonomy only provides substantial contribution criteria to the climate adaption goal, and no DNSH criteria. The substantial contribution criteria are provided in a very abstract manner, and we were unable to manually identify fine-grained process constraints.

Environmental Objectives. Next, we analyze the constraint types belonging to the screening criteria of different environmental goals (meaning, the respective substantial contribution criteria of one goal and the associated DNSH criteria for all other goals). Figure 5 illustrates the number of constraints of each type per environmental objective. Here, we see that climate adaption and climate mitigation—which are the two environmental objectives with the highest number of business practices for which they govern taxonomy alignment—also contain the highest number of constraints across all types. Interestingly, we see that constraints related to the goals of pollution prevention and water protection are not at all characterized w.r.t. control-flow or temporal aspects within activities, while some constraints for the biodiversity, climate adaption, and climate mitigation use these process dimensions. Across all environmental objectives, however, we see a general focus on activity existence and data constraints, with resource constraints within activities also being represented.

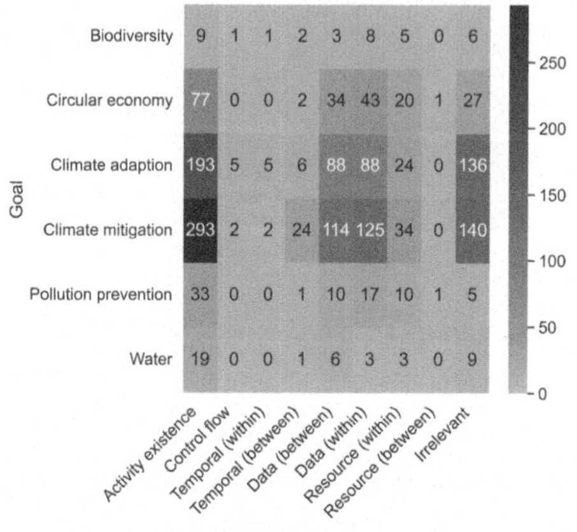

Fig. 5. Number of constraints per type and environmental objective

5.3 Validation

For validating our approach and the resulting insights, a research assistant with a background in environmental and resource management and one of the authors with a background in computer science and BPM manually assessed a sample of the taxonomy and constraint characterization (i.e., all 357 characterizations for the environmental objectives of water protection, circular economy, pollution prevention, biodiversity protection). We compared each characterization and the underlying response of the LLM with the taxonomy's original text and assessed whether the result was *entirely plausible* (we deem that all constraints have been found and classified accurately), *largely plausible* (we deem that all constraints have been found, with a slight deviation in the constraint types; such as when a constraint that can be read as an activity existence constraint requiring an activity to be executed has instead been read as a resource constraint requiring the activity to be executed by a specific role or resource), *somewhat plausible* (we deem that most relevant constraints have been found, but their classification is debatable), or *implausible* (we deem that central constraints have not been found, or constraints have been clearly mischaracterized). Conflicts regarding the plausibility assessment were resolved in discussions. This mode of validation allows us to assess the results of our approach without creating a "gold standard" result (as other studies do, see e.g., [39]), since we lack the regulatory expertise which would be necessary for creating such a standard.

Table 1 shows the share of constraints we assessed regarding their plausibility. We see that 340 of 357 characterizations are *at least* assessed as somewhat plausible. Distributing the plausibility on a four-step scale (three being entirely plausible, zero being implausible), we see an **average plausibility of 2.74**, i.e., more than largely plausible. This means that, in general, we expect a characterization to be at least largely plausible. While we observed implausible characterizations, they seem to largely stem from references to taxonomy-external regulatory texts and standards which have not been considered and ambiguous terminologies (such as "times" as a frequency instead of referring to a temporal aspect). Overall, we infer that the classification approach can serve as a starting point for creating prescriptive models, and that it provides largely plausible constraint characterizations, which may need to be supplemented with a manual investigation. This is particularly the case when external regulations are involved.

Table 1. Plausibility assessment of 357 constraint characterizations

Assessment	Entirely Plausible	Largely Plausible	Somewhat Plausible	Implausible
Characterizations	308	24	8	17

6 Discussion

After presenting and validating our results, we now discuss them further. As we have seen, business practices in the industry sectors of energy, manufacturing, transport, and water and waste constitute a large part of the process-relevant constraints we identified and thus appear well-suited to be investigated for their taxonomy alignment with conformance checking. In some sectors, particularly finance, education, entertainment, human health and social work, we were unable to identify a high number of constraints that would have been operationalizable for conformance checking. Therefore, we conclude, that these sectors appear less promising for applications of compliance monitoring with conformance checking.

In general, we can apply conformance checking to around 80% (i.e., 1313 of 1636) of the constraints which we identified in the taxonomy. For all other constraints, and in particular, in sectors where we had difficulties automatically identifying constraints, conducting manual compliance monitoring and taking further expert knowledge into account appears indispensable. Hence, we have answered RQ2.

Further, as we have shown, the approach we have designed can aid in the creation of prescriptive models for compliance monitoring with conformance checking by helping end users to better understand: 1) what types of constraints are likely to be present in a single relevant piece of regulation (since it can be difficult to determine the concrete constraint type, or whether constraint is actually operationalizable), and 2) what types of constraints comprise a larger set of regulations (as it helps in choosing and implementing correct techniques). As a subsequent step, end users then need to operationalize the constraints into a prescriptive model for automatic compliance monitoring with conformance checking, drawing on existing approaches for this, in relation to actual business processes. This allows the taxonomy to be operationalized for business processes. Therefore, we have addressed RQ1.

Taking a broader look at relevant BPM techniques, we believe that a particular focus on greenhouse gas emissions as data constraints, especially in the sectors of manufacturing, transport and energy, gives new importance to BPM approaches focussed on assessing emissions of business processes on process and activity levels (see, e.g., [22,33,34]). Broader still, the taxonomy itself has been the subject of various criticisms. On the one hand, the taxonomy's underlying notion of sustainable development [2] has been criticized as ambiguous and an *oxymoron* [20], and counterproductive to *actual* sustainability [32]. On the other hand, the taxonomy has also been described as *too* restrictive and as a bureaucratic burden that would be unable to benefit the overall economy [25]. Hence, the role played by the taxonomy in promoting sustainability is still subject to scholarly debate.

Nonetheless, this is one of the first papers to bring an understanding of the taxonomy to the business process management and enterprise computing communities. We have striven to provide conceptual clarity and impulses for future research on the taxonomy and its potential for sustainable business practices. Further, we believe that the pipeline we developed can potentially be applied to other regulatory frameworks as well.

Threats to Validity. There are several threats to the validity of our study. First, we have not validated the constraint characterization in its entirety, and have rather focussed on plausibility instead of completeness. However, our experimental validation showed that the characterization is generally plausible, and can serve as a *starting point* for further manual investigation. Second, for compliance monitoring with conformance checking, the prescriptive process model into which regulations are operationalized needs to be shown to be regulatory compliant as well (see [16]). This is a concern explicitly not addressed in our approach, as we have investigated in how far a prescriptive process model can be created at all. Moreover, technical limitations of LLMs, such as "confabulations", "hallucinations" and inherent biases (see, e.g., [4,26,42]), apply to our study as well. However, our application is concerned with a very technical lens and is less of a generative application scenario. By following existing knowledge on prompt engineering in the BPM discipline, we sought to curb the impact of these limitations. Further, while our approach may produce results with some inaccuracies, the classification can still serve as a starting point for investigating individual constraints in depth. Finally, other techniques in the compliance checking space exist that may allow further kinds of constraints to be extracted from regulations against which processes can be checked. However, as our investigation has been concerned only with conformance checking applications—which are limited to the four process dimensions of control-flow, time, resources, and data—we did not consider them further.

7 Conclusion and Future Work

To conclude, in this paper we have investigated if the EU taxonomy for sustainable activities can be operationalized for automatic compliance monitoring. For this, we have developed a pipeline that uses few-shot learning with an LLM, to identify and characterize the types of constraints applicable for conformance checking. We saw that many constraints of various industries can, in fact, be operationalized for this, which will allow companies to automatically monitor compliance with regard to the taxonomy. We have demonstrated that operationalizing the EU taxonomy into constraints for conformance checking may be partially automated; in this paper, we provide a starting point for such an automation. Besides this technical contribution, we have also introduced the taxonomy to the business process management and enterprise computing communities. The characterization pipeline may provide beneficial for assessing the capability of other complex regulatory frameworks as well.

Future work includes translating our classification approach into real-world application scenarios—further investigating how stakeholders can be supported in creating prescriptive models in line with the EU taxonomy, and how event log capturing and extraction benefits from our constraint classification would be a valuable contribution. We also aim to conduct more in-depth empirical evaluations of our mapping approach by comparing automatically generated results with results generated by taxonomy experts. Moreover, since we focus exclusively on business process compliance and have abstracted away from constraints regarding their broader context, we have explicitly excluded the analysis of minimum safeguards. However, approaches that enable compliance monitoring of constraints across organizations exist (such as [14,23,24]), and fruitful future work might lie in operationalizing the regulations and guidelines relevant to the taxonomy's minimum safeguard criterion for these approaches. Finally, we believe that providing concrete guidance to end users in the form of a "handbook" or constraint patterns based on our preliminary findings reported herein would be a relevant addition.

Acknowledgments. This study was supported by the Deutsche Forschungsgemeinschaft (DFG, German Research Foundation) under grants no. 465904964, 496119880 and 531115272, by the German Federal Ministry of Education and Research (BMBF) under grant no. 16DII133 (Weizenbaum Institute), and by the Einstein Foundation Berlin under grant no. EPP-2019-524. Further, the authors would like to thank Man Tuen Chan for his support in validating the approach presented in this paper.

Disclosure of Interests. The authors have no competing interests to declare that are relevant to the content of this article.

References

1. van der Aa, H., Di Ciccio, C., Leopold, H., Reijers, H.A.: Extracting declarative process models from natural language. In: Giorgini, P., Weber, B. (eds.) CAiSE 2019. LNCS, vol. 11483, pp. 365–382. Springer, Cham (2019). https://doi.org/10.1007/978-3-030-21290-2_23
2. Alessi, L., Battiston, S., Melo, A.S., Roncoroni, A.: The EU sustainability taxonomy: a financial impact assessment (KJ-NA-29970-EN-N (online)) (2019). https://doi.org/10.2760/347810
3. Barrientos, M., Winter, K., Mangler, J., Rinderle-Ma, S.: Verification of quantitative temporal compliance requirements in process descriptions over event logs. In: Indulska, M., Reinhartz-Berger, I., Cetina, C., Pastor, O. (eds.) Advanced Information Systems Engineering, vol. 13901, pp. 417–433. Springer, Cham (2023). https://doi.org/10.1007/978-3-031-34560-9_25
4. Bender, E.M., Gebru, T., McMillan-Major, A., Shmitchell, S.: On the dangers of stochastic parrots: can language models be too big? In: Proceedings of the 2021 ACM Conference on Fairness, Accountability, and Transparency, pp. 610–623. ACM, Virtual Event Canada, March 2021. https://doi.org/10.1145/3442188.3445922
5. Brown, T., et al.: Language models are few-shot learners. Adv. Neural. Inf. Process. Syst. **33**, 1877–1901 (2020)
6. Brundtland, G.H.: Our common future-call for action. Environ. Conserv. **14**(4), 291–294 (1987). https://doi.org/10.1017/S0376892900016805
7. Carmona, J., Van Dongen, B., Solti, A., Weidlich, M.: Conformance Checking: Relating Processes and Models. Springer, Cham (2018). https://doi.org/10.1007/978-3-319-99414-7
8. Conea, A.M.: EU taxonomy: qualifying as green. LESIJ-Lex ET Sci. Int. J. **29**(2), 26–39 (2022)
9. Dragoni, M., Villata, S., Rizzi, W., Governatori, G.: Combining natural language processing approaches for rule extraction from legal documents. In: Pagallo, U., Palmirani, M., Casanovas, P., Sartor, G., Villata, S. (eds.) AICOL 2015-2017. LNCS (LNAI), vol. 10791, pp. 287–300. Springer, Cham (2018). https://doi.org/10.1007/978-3-030-00178-0_19
10. European Comission: EU taxonomy for sustainable activities - European Commission, https://finance.ec.europa.eu/sustainable-finance/tools-and-standards/eu-taxonomy-sustainable-activities_en
11. European Comission: NACE Rev. 2. Office for Official Publications of the European Communities, Luxembourg, revision 2, English edition edn. (2008)
12. European Comission: A User Guide to Navigate The EU Taxonomy for Sustainble Activities (2023). https://ec.europa.eu/sustainable-finance-taxonomy/assets/documents/Taxonomy%20User%20Guide.pdf
13. European Commission: Regulation (EU) 2020/852 of the european parliament and of the council of 18 June 2020 on the establishment of a framework to facilitate sustainable investment, and amending regulation (EU) 2019/2088 (2020). https://eur-lex.europa.eu/eli/reg/2020/852/oj
14. Fdhila, W., Rinderle-Ma, S., Knuplesch, D., Reichert, M.: Decomposition-based verification of global compliance in process choreographies. In: 2020 IEEE 24th International Enterprise Distributed Object Computing Conference (EDOC), pp. 77–86 (2020). https://doi.org/10.1109/EDOC49727.2020.00019

15. Governatori, G., Hashmi, M., Lam, H.-P., Villata, S., Palmirani, M.: Semantic business process regulatory compliance checking using LegalRuleML. In: Blomqvist, E., Ciancarini, P., Poggi, F., Vitali, F. (eds.) EKAW 2016. LNCS (LNAI), vol. 10024, pp. 746–761. Springer, Cham (2016). https://doi.org/10.1007/978-3-319-49004-5_48
16. Groefsema, H., van Beest, N.R.T.P., Governatori, G.: On the use of the conformance and compliance keywords during verification of business processes. In: Di Ciccio, C., Dijkman, R., Del Río Ortega, A., Rinderle-Ma, S. (eds.) Business Process Management Forum, vol. 458, pp. 21–37. Springer, Cham (2022). https://doi.org/10.1007/978-3-031-16171-1_2
17. Grohs, M., Abb, L., Elsayed, N., Rehse, J.R.: Large language models can accomplish business process management tasks. In: De Weerdt, J., Pufahl, L. (eds.) Business Process Management Workshops, vol. 492, pp. 453–465. Springer, Cham (2024). https://doi.org/10.1007/978-3-031-50974-2_34
18. Hashmi, M., Governatori, G., Lam, H.-P., Wynn, M.T.: Are we done with business process compliance: state of the art and challenges ahead. Knowl. Inf. Syst. **57**(1), 79–133 (2018). https://doi.org/10.1007/s10115-017-1142-1
19. Hashmi, M., Governatori, G., Wynn, M.T.: Normative requirements for regulatory compliance: an abstract formal framework. Inf. Syst. Front. **18**(3), 429–455 (2015). https://doi.org/10.1007/s10796-015-9558-1
20. Johnston, P., Everard, M., Santillo, D., Robèrt, K.H.: Reclaiming the definition of sustainability. Environ. Sci. Pollut. Res. Int. **14**(1), 60–6 (2007). https://doi.org/10.1065/espr2007.01.375
21. Klessascheck, F., Knoche, T., Pufahl, L.: Reviewing conformance checking uses for run-time regulatory compliance. In: van der Aa, H., Bork, D., Schmidt, R., Sturm, A. (eds.) Enterprise, Business-Process and Information Systems Modeling, pp. 100–113. Springer Nature Switzerland, Cham (2024)
22. Klessascheck, F., Weber, I., Pufahl, L.: SOPA: a framework for sustainability-oriented process analysis and re-design in business process management (2024). http://arxiv.org/abs/2405.01176
23. Knuplesch, D., Fdhila, W., Reichert, M., Rinderle-Ma, S.: Detecting the effects of changes on the compliance of cross-organizational business processes. In: Johannesson, P., Lee, M.L., Liddle, S.W., Opdahl, A.L., Pastor López, Ó. (eds.) Conceptual Modeling, pp. 94–107. Springer International Publishing, Cham (2015)
24. Knuplesch, D., Reichert, M., Kumar, A.: A framework for visually monitoring business process compliance. Inf. Syst. **64**, 381–409 (2017)
25. Kooths, S.: EU taxonomy: mission impossible. Econ. Voice **19**(2), 243–249 (2023). https://doi.org/10.1515/ev-2022-0028
26. Ladkin, P.B.: Involving LLMs in legal processes is risky: an invited paper. Digital Evidence and Electronic Signature Law Review, pp. 40–46, June 2023. https://doi.org/10.14296/deeslr.v20i.5610
27. López, H.A., Debois, S., Slaats, T., Hildebrandt, T.T.: Business process compliance using reference models of law. In: FASE 2020. LNCS, vol. 12076, pp. 378–399. Springer, Cham (2020). https://doi.org/10.1007/978-3-030-45234-6_19
28. Malecki, C.: The EU taxonomy regulation: giving a good name to sustainable investment. Env Liability **26**(4), 149–156 (2021). https://ssrn.com/abstract=4235527
29. McClellan, A., Gehrke, N., Picard, N., Schellhas, C.: EU Taxonomy reporting 2023. Technical Report (2023). https://www.pwc.de/de/content/20e6bff9-ea5a-4d03-b375-a6a58f7b8b46/pwc-eu-taxonomy-reporting-2023.pdf

30. Mustroph, H., Barrientos, M., Winter, K., Rinderle-Ma, S.: Verifying resource compliance requirements from natural language text over event logs. In: Di Francescomarino, C., Burattin, A., Janiesch, C., Sadiq, S. (eds.) Business Process Management, vol. 14159, pp. 249–265. Springer, Cham (2023).https://doi.org/10.1007/978-3-031-41620-0_15
31. Mustroph, H., Winter, K., Rinderle-Ma, S.: social network mining from natural language text and event logs for compliance deviation detection. In: Sellami, M., Vidal, M.E., Van Dongen, B., Gaaloul, W., Panetto, H. (eds.) Cooperative Information Systems, vol. 14353, pp. 347–365. Springer, Cham (2024). https://doi.org/10.1007/978-3-031-46846-9_19
32. Purvis, B., Mao, Y., Robinson, D.: Three pillars of sustainability: in search of conceptual origins. Sustain. Sci. **14**(3), 681–695 (2018). https://doi.org/10.1007/s11625-018-0627-5
33. Recker, J., Rosemann, M., Gohar, E.R.: Measuring the carbon footprint of business processes. In: zur Muehlen, M., Su, J. (eds.) BPM 2010. LNBIP, vol. 66, pp. 511–520. Springer, Heidelberg (2011). https://doi.org/10.1007/978-3-642-20511-8_47
34. Recker, J., Rosemann, M., Hjalmarsson, A., Lind, M.: Modeling and analyzing the carbon footprint of business processes. In: vom Brocke, J., Seidel, S., Recker, J. (eds.) Green Business Process Management, pp. 93–109. Springer, Berlin (2012). https://doi.org/10.1007/978-3-642-27488-6_6
35. Rehse, J., Pufahl, L., Grohs, M., Klein, L.: Process mining meets visual analytics: the case of conformance checking. In: Bui, T. (ed.) Proceedings of the 56th Annual Hawaii International Conference on System Sciences, HICSS 2023, pp. 5452–5461. Proceedings of the Annual Hawaii International Conference on System Sciences, IEEE Computer Society (2023)
36. Remy, S., Pufahl, L., Sachs, J.P., Böttinger, E., Weske, M.: Event log generation in a health system: a case study. In: Fahland, D., Ghidini, C., Becker, J., Dumas, M. (eds.) BPM 2020. LNCS, vol. 12168, pp. 505–522. Springer, Cham (2020). https://doi.org/10.1007/978-3-030-58666-9_29
37. Russell, N., van der Aalst, W., Ter Hofstede, A.: Workflow Patterns: The Definitive Guide. MIT Press, Cambridge, MA (2015)
38. Sai, C., Damaratskaya, A., Winter, K., Rinderle-Ma, S.: Identification and visualization of legal definitions and legal term relations. In: Sales, T.P., Araújo, J., Borbinha, J., Guizzardi, G. (eds.) Advances in Conceptual Modeling, vol. 14319, pp. 151–161. Springer, Cham (2023). https://doi.org/10.1007/978-3-031-47112-4_14
39. Sai, C., Sadiq, S., Han, L., Demartini, G., Rinderle-Ma, S.: Which legal requirements are relevant to a business process? comparing AI-driven methods as expert aid. In: Araújo, J., De La Vara, J.L., Santos, M.Y., Assar, S. (eds.) Research Challenges in Information Science, vol. 513, pp. 166–182. Springer, Cham (2024). https://doi.org/10.1007/978-3-031-59465-6_11
40. Sai, C., Winter, K., Fernanda, E., Rinderle-Ma, S.: Detecting deviations between external and internal regulatory requirements for improved process compliance assessment. In: Indulska, M., Reinhartz-Berger, I., Cetina, C., Pastor, O. (eds.) Advanced Information Systems Engineering, vol. 13901, pp. 401–416. Springer, Cham (2023). https://doi.org/10.1007/978-3-031-34560-9_24
41. Schütze, F., Stede, J.: The EU sustainable finance taxonomy and its contribution to climate neutrality. J. Sustain. Finan. Invest. **14**(1), 128–160 (2024). https://doi.org/10.1080/20430795.2021.2006129
42. Sui, P., Duede, E., Wu, S., So, R.J.: Confabulation: the surprising value of large language model hallucinations (2024). https://doi.org/10.48550/ARXIV.2406.04175

43. UN Environment (ed.): Global Environment Outlook – GEO-6: Summary for Policymakers. Cambridge University Press, Cambridge (2019). https://doi.org/10.1017/9781108639217
44. Business Process Management. Lecture Notes in Computer Science, Springer, Heidelberg (2012). https://doi.org/10.1007/978-3-642-28616-2
45. Winter, K., van der Aa, H., Rinderle-Ma, S., Weidlich, M.: Assessing the compliance of business process models with regulatory documents. In: Dobbie, G., Frank, U., Kappel, G., Liddle, S.W., Mayr, H.C. (eds.) ER 2020. LNCS, vol. 12400, pp. 189–203. Springer, Cham (2020). https://doi.org/10.1007/978-3-030-62522-1_14
46. Winter, K., Rinderle-Ma, S.: Detecting constraints and their relations from regulatory documents using NLP techniques. In: Panetto, H., Debruyne, C., Proper, H.A., Ardagna, C.A., Roman, D., Meersman, R. (eds.) OTM 2018. LNCS, vol. 11229, pp. 261–278. Springer, Cham (2018). https://doi.org/10.1007/978-3-030-02610-3_15
47. Winter, K., Rinderle-Ma, S.: Deriving and combining mixed graphs from regulatory documents based on constraint relations. In: Giorgini, P., Weber, B. (eds.) CAiSE 2019. LNCS, vol. 11483, pp. 430–445. Springer, Cham (2019). https://doi.org/10.1007/978-3-030-21290-2_27
48. Winter, K., Rinderle-Ma, S., Grossmann, W., Feinerer, I., Ma, Z.: Characterizing regulatory documents and guidelines based on text mining. In: Panetto, H., et al. (eds.) OTM 2017. LNCS, vol. 10573, pp. 3–20. Springer, Cham (2017). https://doi.org/10.1007/978-3-319-69462-7_1

Author Index

J. Borbinha et al. (Eds.): EDOC 2024, LNCS 15409, p. 361, 2025.
https://doi.org/10.1007/978-3-031-78338-8

The manufacturer's authorised representative in the EU is Springer Nature Customer Service Centre GmbH, Europaplatz 3, 69115 Heidelberg, Germany. If you have any concerns regarding our products, please contact ProductSafety@springernature.com

Printed and bound by CPI Group (UK) Ltd, Croydon, CR0 4YY
30/09/2026
02225597-0015